Automatic Flight Control Systems

Prentice Hall International
Series in Systems and Control Engineering

M. J. Grimble, Series Editor

BANKS, S. P., *Control Systems Engineering: Modelling and Simulation, Control Theory and Microprocessor Implementation*
BANKS, S. P., *Mathematical Theories of Nonlinear Systems*
BENNETT, S., *Real-time Computer Control: An Introduction*
CEGRELL, T., *Power Systems Control*
COOK, P. A., *Nonlinear Dynamical Systems*
LUNZE, J., *Robust Multivariable Feedback Control*
PATTON, R., CLARK, R. N., FRANK, P. M. (editors), *Fault Diagnosis in Dynamic Systems*
SÖDERSTRÖM, T., and STOICA, P., *System Identification*
WARWICK, K., *Control Systems: An Introduction*

Automatic Flight Control Systems

Donald McLean

Westland Professor of Aeronautics
University of Southampton, UK

PRENTICE HALL

New York · London · Toronto · Sydney · Tokyo · Singapore

First published 1990 by
Prentice Hall International (UK) Ltd
66 Wood Lane End, Hemel Hempstead
Hertfordshire HP2 4RG
A division of
Simon & Schuster International Group

Typeset in 10/12 pt Times
by Columns of Reading
Printed and bound in Great Britain at the
University Press, Cambridge

Library of Congress Cataloging-in-Publication Data

McLean, Donald. 1936–
Automatic flight control systems / by Donald McLean.
p. cm.
Bibliography: p.
Includes index.
ISBN 0–13–054008–0: $60.00
1. Flight control. I. Title.
TL589.4.M45 1990
629.132'6 – – dc20 89–22857
CIP

British Library Cataloguing in Publication Data

McLean, D. (Donald, 1936–)
Automatic flight control systems.
1. Aircraft. Automatic flight control systems
I. Title
629.135'2
ISBN 0–13–054008–0

1 2 3 4 5 94 93 92 91 90

Contents

Preface

This is an introductory textbook on automatic flight control systems (AFCSs) for undergraduate aeronautical engineers. It is hoped that the material and the manner of its presentation will increase the student's understanding of the basic problems of controlling an aircraft's flight, and enhance his ability to assess the solutions to the problems which are generally proposed. Not every method or theory of control which can be used for designing a flight controller is dealt with in this book; however, if a reader should find that some favourite technique or approach has been omitted, the fault lies entirely with the author upon whose judgement the selection depended. The method is not being impugned by its omission.

Before understanding how an aircraft may be controlled automatically in flight it is essential to know how any aircraft will respond dynamically to a deliberate movement of its control surfaces, or to an encounter with unexpected and random disturbances of the air through which it is flying. A sound knowledge of an aircraft's dynamic response is necessary for the succesful design of any AFCS, but that knowledge is not sufficient. A knowledge of the quality of aircraft response, which can result in the aircraft's being considered by a pilot as satisfactory to fly, is also important. In this book the first six chapters are wholly concerned with material relevant to such important matters.

There are now so many methods of designing control systems that it would require another book to deal with them alone. Instead, Chapters 7 and 8 have been included to provide a reasonably self-contained account of the most significant methods of designing linear control systems which find universal use in AFCSs. Emphasis has been placed upon what are spoken of as modern methods of control (to distinguish them from the classical methods): it is most unlikely that today's students would not consider the use of a computer in arriving at the required solution. Being firmly based upon time-domain methods, modern control theory, particularly the use of state equations, is a natural and effective technique for use with computer aided engineering and harmonizes with the mathematical description of the aircraft dynamics which are most completely, and conveniently, expressed in terms of a state and an output equation. The form involved leads naturally to the use of eigenvalues and eigenvectors which make consideration of the stability properties of the aircraft simple and straightforward. Since computers are to be used, the need for normalizing the dynamic equations can be dispensed with and the differential equations can be solved to find the aircraft's motion in real time. The slight cost to be borne for this convenience is that the stability derivatives of the aircraft which are used in the analysis are dimensional;

however, since the aircraft dynamics are in real time, the dynamics of the flight controller, the control surface actuators, and the motion sensors can also be dealt with in real time, thereby avoiding the need for cumbersome and unnecessary transformations. Since dimensional stability derivatives were to be used, the American system of notation for the aircraft equations of motions was adopted: most papers and most data throughout the world now use this system.

Chapters 9 to 11 relate to particular modes of an AFCS, being concerned with stability augmentation systems, attitude and path control systems. A particular AFCS may have some, or all, of these modes involved in its operation, some being active at all times in the flight, and others being switched in by the pilot only when required for a particular phase of flight. Although helicopter flight control systems do not differ in principle from those used with fixed wing aircraft, they are fitted for different purposes. Furthermore, both the dynamics and the means of controlling a helicopter's flight are radically different from fixed wing aircraft. Consequently, helicopter AFCSs are dealt with wholly in Chapter 13 to emphasize the distinctive stability and handling problems that their use is intended to overcome.

Active control systems are dealt with in Chapter 12 and only a brief treatment is given to indicate how structural motion can be controlled simultaneously, for example, with controlling the aircraft's rigid body motion. Ride control and fuselage pointing are flight control modes dealt with in this chapter.

In the thousands of commercial airliners, the tens of thousands of military aircraft, and the hundreds of thousands of general aviation aircraft which are flying throughout the world today, examples of the types of AFCS discussed in this book can easily be found. But most modern AFCSs are digital, and to account for this trend Chapter 14 has been added to deal solely with digital control methods. The consequences for the dynamic response of the closed-loop system of implementing a continuous control law in a digital fashion is emphasized. Results complementary to those in Chapters 9 to 11, obtained using wholly digital system analysis, are also shown.

The final chapter deals briefly with the subject of adaptive flight control systems, and three appendices provide a summary of information relating to actuators, sensors, aircraft stability data, and human operators.

In writing a textbook, ideas and techniques which have been used effectively and easily by the author over the years are discussed and presented, but the original source is often forgotten. If others find their work used here but unacknowledged, please be assured that it was unintentional and has occurred mostly as a result of a middle-aged memory rather than malice, for I am conscious of having had many masters in this subject. At the risk of offending many mentors, I wish to acknowledge here only the special help of three people, for the list of acknowledgements would be impossibly long otherwise. Two are American scholars: Professors Jack d'Azzo and Dino Houpis, of the United States Air Force Institute of Technology, in Dayton, Ohio. They are nonpareil as teachers of control and taught me in a too-short association the importance of the student and his needs. The other is my secretary, Liz Tedder, who now knows, to her lasting regret, more about automatic flight control systems than she ever wished to know.

D. McLEAN
Southampton

1

Aircraft Flight Control

1.1 INTRODUCTION

Whatever form a vehicle may take, its value to its user depends on how effectively it can be made to proceed in the time allowed on a precisely controllable path between its point of departure and its intended destination. That is why, for instance, kites and balloons find only limited application in modern warfare. When the motion of any type of vehicle is being studied it is possible to generalize so that the vehicle can be regarded as being fully characterized by its velocity vector. The time integral of that vector is the path of the vehicle through space (McRuer *et al.*, 1973). The velocity vector, which may be denoted as $\dot{\mathbf{x}}$, is affected by the position, $\mathbf{x}$, of the vehicle in space by whatever kind of control, $\mathbf{u}$, can be used, by any disturbance, $\boldsymbol{\xi}$, and by time, t. Thus, the motion of the vehicle can be represented in the most general way by the vector differential equation:

$$\dot{\mathbf{x}} = \mathbf{f}(\mathbf{x}, \mathbf{u}, \boldsymbol{\xi}, t) \tag{1.1}$$

where $\mathbf{f}$ is some vector function. The means by which the path of any vehicle can be controlled vary widely, depending chiefly on the physical constraints which obtain. For example, everyone knows that a locomotive moves along the rails of the permanent way. It can be controlled only in its velocity; it cannot be steered, because its lateral direction is constrained by the contact of its wheel rims on the rails. Automobiles move over the surface of the earth, but with both speed and direction being controlled. Aircraft differ from locomotives and automobiles because they have six degrees of freedom: three associated with angular motion about the aircraft's centre of gravity and three associated with the translation of the centre of gravity.[1] Because of this greater freedom of motion, aircraft control problems are usually more complicated than those of other vehicles.

Those qualities of an aircraft which tend to make it resist any change of its velocity vector, either in its direction or its magnitude, or in both, are what constitutes its *stability*. The ease with which the velocity vector may be changed is related to the aircraft's quality of *control*. It is *stability* which makes possible the maintenance of a steady, unaccelerated flight path; aircraft manoeuvres are effected by *control*.

Of itself, the path of any aircraft is never stable; aircraft have only neutral stability in heading. Without control, aircraft tend to fly in a constant turn. In order to fly a straight and level course continuously-controlling corrections must be made, either through the agency of a human pilot, or by means of an *automatic flight control system* (AFCS). In aircraft, such AFCSs employ feedback control to achieve the following benefits:

1. The speed of response is better than from the aircraft without closed loop control.
2. The accuracy in following commands is better.
3. The system is capable of suppressing, to some degree, unwanted effects which have arisen as a result of disturbances affecting the aircraft's flight.

However, under certain conditions such feedback control systems have a tendency to oscillate; the AFCS then has poor stability. Although the use of high values of gain in the feedback loops can assist in the achievement of fast and accurate dynamic response, their use is invariably inimical to good stability. Hence, designers of AFCSs are obliged to strike an acceptable, but delicate, balance between the requirements for stability and for control.

The early aeronautical experimenters hoped to make flying easier by providing 'inherent' stability in their flying machines. What they tried to provide was a basic, self-restoring property of the airframe without the active use of any feedback. A number of them, such as Cayley, Langley and Lilienthal, discovered how to achieve longitudinal static stability with respect to the relative wind, e.g. by setting the incidence of the tailplane at some appropriate value. Those experimenters also discovered how to use wing dihedral to achieve lateral static stability. However, as aviation has developed, it has become increasingly evident that the motion of an aircraft designed to be inherently very stable, is particularly susceptible to being affected by atmospheric turbulence. This characteristic is less acceptable to pilots than poor static stability.

It was the great achievement of the Wright brothers that they ignored the attainment of inherent stability in their aircraft, but concentrated instead on making it controllable in moderate weather conditions with average flying skill. So far in this introduction, the terms dynamic and static stability have been used without definition, their imprecise sense being left to the reader to determine from the text. There is, however, only one dynamic property – stability – which can be established by any of the theories of stability appropriate to the differential equations being considered. However, in aeronautical engineering, the two terms are still commonly used; they are given separate specifications for the flying qualities to be attained by any particular aircraft. When the term static stability is used, what is meant is that if a disturbance to an aircraft causes the resulting forces and moments acting on the aircraft to tend initially to return the aircraft to the kind of flight path for which its controls are set, the aircraft can be said to be statically stable. Some modern aircraft are not capable of stable equilibrium – they are statically unstable. Essentially, the function of static stability is to recover the original speed of equilibrium flight. This does not mean that the initial flight path is resumed, nor is the new direction of motion necessarily the same as the old. If, as a result of a disturbance, the resulting forces and moments do not tend initially to restore the aircraft to its former equilibrium flight path, but leave it in its disturbed state, the aircraft is neutrally stable. If it tends initially to deviate further from its equilibrium flight path, it is statically unstable. When an aircraft is put in a state of equilibrium by the action of the pilot adjusting the controls, it is said to be trimmed. If, as a result of a disturbance, the aircraft tends to return eventually to its equilibrium flight path, and remains at that position, for some time, the aircraft is said to be dynamically stable. Thus, dynamic stability governs how an aircraft recovers its equilibrium after a disturbance. It will be seen later how some aircraft may be statically stable, but are dynamically unstable, although aircraft which are statically unstable will be dynamically unstable.

1.2 CONTROL SURFACES

Every aeronautical student knows that if a body is to be changed from its present state of motion then external forces, or moments, or both, must be applied to the body, and the resulting acceleration vector can be determined by applying Newton's Second Law of Motion. Every aircraft has control surfaces or other means which are used to generate the forces and moments required to produce the accelerations which cause the aircraft to be steered along its three-dimensional flight path to its specified destination.

A conventional aircraft is represented in Figure 1.1. It is shown with the usual control surfaces, namely elevator, ailerons, and rudder. Such conventional aircraft have a fourth control, the change in thrust, which can be obtained from the engines. Many modern aircraft, particularly combat aircraft, have considerably more control surfaces, which produce additional control forces or moments. Some of these additional surfaces and motivators include horizontal and vertical canards, spoilers, variable cambered wings, reaction jets, differentially operating horizontal tails and movable fins. One characteristic of flight control is that the required motion often needs a number of control surfaces to be used simultaneously. It is shown later in this book that the use of a single control surface always produces other motion as well as the intended motion. When more than one control surface is deployed simultaneously, there often results

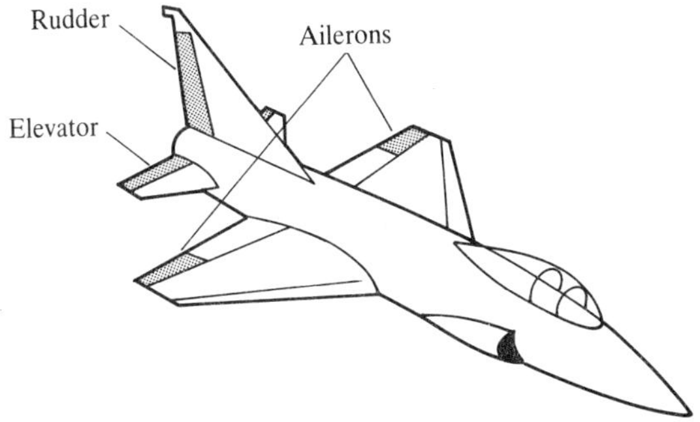

Figure 1.1 Conventional aircraft.

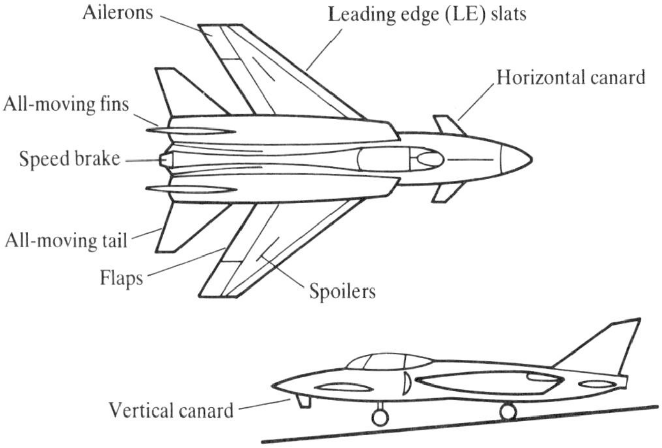

Figure 1.2 A proposed control configured vehicle.

considerable coupling and interaction between motion variables. It is this physical situation which makes AFCS design both fascinating and difficult. When these extra surfaces are added to the aircraft configuration to achieve particular flight control functions, the aircraft is described as a 'control configured vehicle' (CCV). A sketch of a proposed CCV is illustrated in Figure 1.2 in which there are shown a number of extra and unconventional control surfaces. When such extra controls are provided it is not to be supposed that the pilot in the cockpit will have an equal number of extra levers, wheels, pedals, or whatever, to provide the appropriate commands. In a CCV such commands are obtained directly from an AFCS and the pilot has no direct control over the deployment of each individual surface. The AFCS involved in this activity are said to be *active control technology* systems. The surfaces are moved by actuators which are signalled electrically (fly-by-wire) or by means of fibre optic paths (fly-by-light). But, in a conventional aircraft, the pilot has direct mechanical links to the surfaces, and how he commands the deflections, or changes, he requires from the controls is by means of what are called the *primary flying controls*.

1.3 PRIMARY FLYING CONTROLS

In the UK, it is considered that what constitutes a flight control system is an arrangment of all those control elements which enable controlling forces and moments to be applied to the aircraft. These elements are considered to belong to three groups: pilot input elements, system output elements and intervening linkages and elements.

The primary flying controls are part of the flight control system and are defined as the input elements moved directly by a human pilot to cause an operation of the control surfaces. The main primary flying controls are pitch control, roll control and yaw control. The use of these flight controls affects motion principally about the transverse, the longitudinal, and the normal axes respectively, although each may affect motion about the other axes. The use of thrust control via the throttle levers is also effective, but its use is primarily governed by considerations of engine management. Figure 1.3 represents the cockpit layout of a typical, twin engined, general aviation aircraft. The yoke is the primary flying control used for pitch and roll control. When the yoke is pulled towards, or pushed away from, the pilot the elevator is moved correspondingly. When the yoke is rotated to the left or the right, the ailerons of the aircraft are moved. Yaw control is effected by means of the pedals, which a pilot pushes left or right with his feet to move the rudder. In the kind of aircraft with the kind of cockpit illustrated here, the link between these primary flying controls and the control surfaces is by means of cables and pulleys. This means that the aerodynamic forces acting on the control surfaces have to be countered directly by the pilot. To maintain a control surface at a fixed position for any period of time means that the pilot must maintain the required counterforce, which can be very difficult and fatiguing to sustain. Consequently, all aircraft have trim wheels (see Figure 1.3) which the pilot adjusts until the command, which he has set initially on his primary flying control, is set on the control surface and the pilot is then relieved of the need to sustain the force. There are trim wheels for pitch, roll and yaw (which is sometimes referred to as 'nose trim').

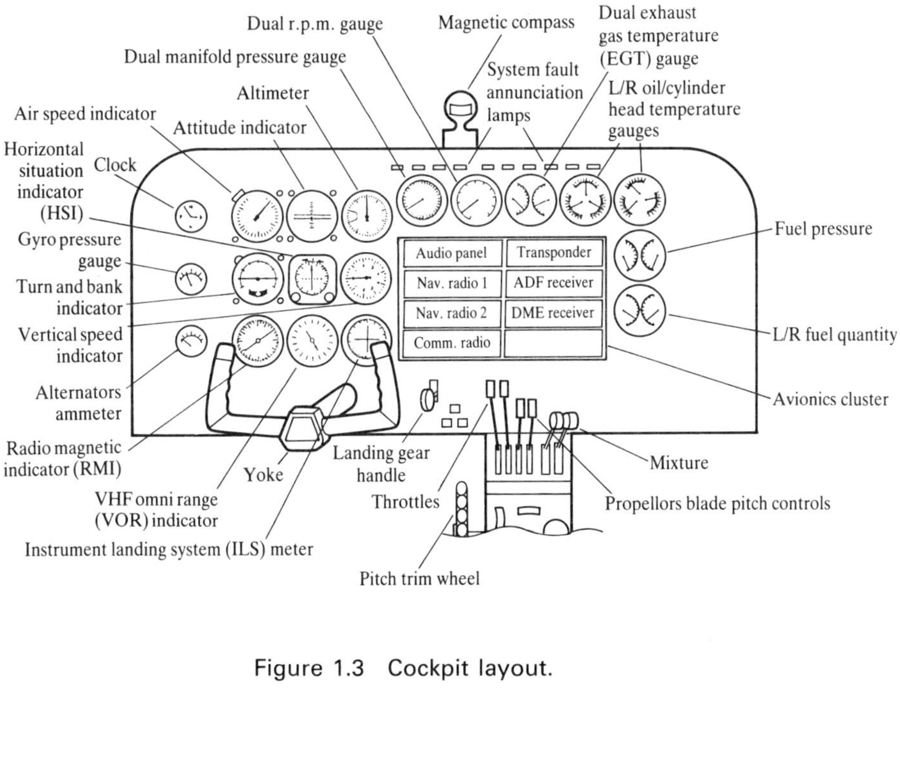

Figure 1.3 Cockpit layout.

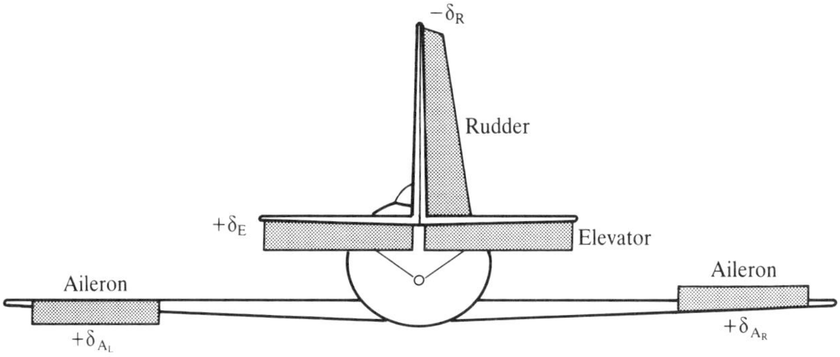

$+\delta_A = \frac{1}{2}(\delta_{A_L} + \delta_{A_R})$

Figure 1.4 Control surface deflection conventions.

In large transport aircraft, or fast military aircraft, the aerodynamic forces acting on the control surfaces are so large that it is impossible for any human pilot to supply or sustain the force required. Powered flying controls are then used. Usually the control surfaces are moved by means of mechanical linkages driven by electrohydraulic actuators. A number of aircraft use electrical actuators, but there are not many such types. The command signals to these electrohydraulic actuators are electrical voltages supplied from the controller of an AFCS, or directly from a suitable transducer on the primary flying control itself. By providing the pilot with power assistance, so that the only force he needs to produce is a tiny force, sufficient to move the transducer, it has been found necessary to provide artificial feel so that some force, representing what the aircraft is doing, is produced on the primary flying control. Such forces are cues to a pilot and are essential to his flying the aircraft successfully. The conventions adopted for the control surface deflections are shown in Figure 1.4.

In the event of an electrical or hydraulic failure such a powered flying control system ceases to function, which would mean that the control surface could not be moved: the aircraft would therefore be out of control. To prevent this occurring, most civilian and military aircraft retain a direct, but parallel, mechanical connection from the primary flying control to the control surface which can be used in an emergency. When this is done the control system is said to have 'manual reversion'. Fly-by-wire (and fly-by-light) aircraft have essentially the same kind of flight control system, but are distinguished from conventional aircraft by having no manual reversion. To meet the emergency situation, when failures occur in the system, fly-by-wire (FBW) aircraft have flight control systems which are triplicated, sometimes quadruplicated, to meet this stringent reliability requirement.

With FBW aircraft and CCVs it has been realized that there is no longer a direct relationship between the pilot's command and the deflection, or even the use, of a particular control surface. What the pilot of such aircraft is commanding from the AFCS is a particular manoeuvre. When this was understood, and when

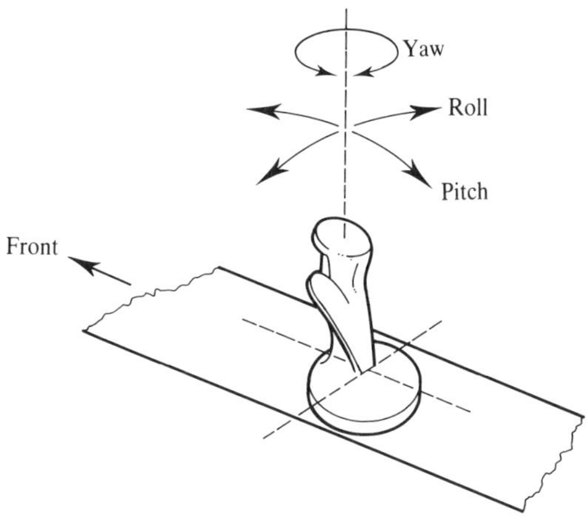

Figure 1.5 Side arm controller.

the increased complexity of flying was taken into account, it was found that the provision of a yoke or a stick to introduce commands was unnecessary and inconvenient. Modern aircraft are being provided with side arm controllers (see Figure 1.5) which provide signals corresponding to the forces applied by the pilot. Generally, these controllers do not move a great deal, but respond to applied force. By using such controllers a great deal of cockpit area is made available for the growing number of avionics displays which modern aircraft require.

1.4 FLIGHT CONTROL SYSTEMS

In addition to the control surfaces which are used for steering, every aircraft contains motion sensors which provide measures of changes in motion variables which occur as the aircraft responds to the pilot's commands or as it encounters some disturbance. The signals from these sensors can be used to provide the pilot with a visual display, or they can be used as feedback signals for the AFCS. Thus, the general structure of an AFCS can be represented as the block schematic of Figure 1.6. The purpose of the controller is to compare the commanded motion with the measured motion and, if any discrepancy exists, to generate, in accordance with the required control law, the command signals to the actuator to produce the control surface deflections which will result in the correct control force or moment being applied. This, in turn, causes the aircraft to respond appropriately so that the measured motion and commanded motion are finally in correspondence. How the required control law can be determined is one of the principal topics of this book.

Whenever either the physical or abstract attributes of an aircraft, and its motion sensing and controlling elements, are considered in detail, their effects are so interrelated as almost to preclude discussion of any single aspect of the system,

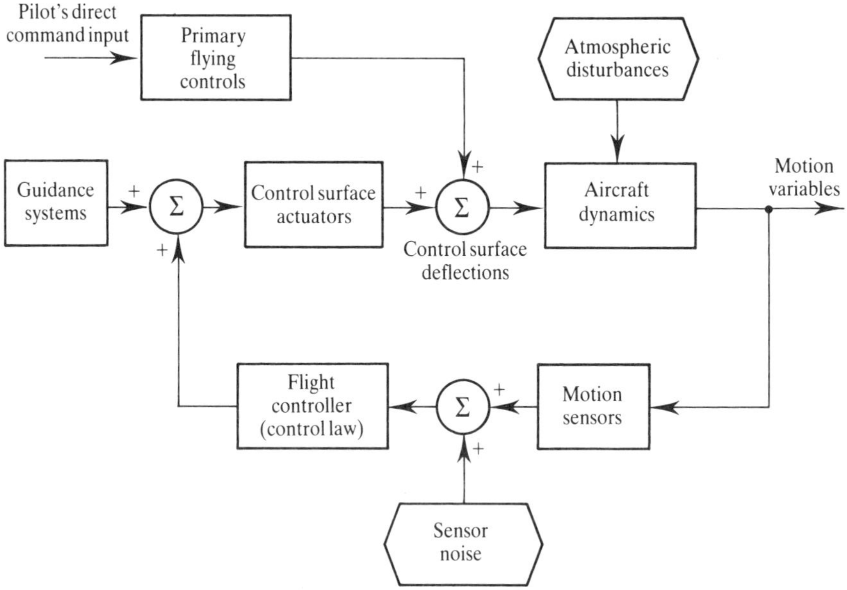

Figure 1.6 General structure of an AFCS.

without having to treat most of the other aspects at the same time. It is helpful, therefore, to define here, albeit somewhat broadly, the area of study upon which this book will concentrate.

1. The development of forces and moments for the purpose of establishing an equilibrium state of motion (operating point) for an aircraft, and for the purpose of restoring a disturbed aircraft to its equilibrium state, and regulating within specific limits the departure of the aircraft's response from the operating point, are regarded here as constituting *flight control.*
2. Regulating the aircraft's response is frequently referred to as *stabilization.*
3. Guidance is taken to mean the action of determining the course and speed to be followed by the aircraft, relative to some reference system. Flight control systems act as interfaces between the guidance systems and the aircraft being guided in that the flight control system receives, as inputs from the guidance systems, correction commands, and provides, as outputs, appropriate deflections of the necessary control surfaces to cause the required change in the motion of the aircraft (Draper, 1981). For this control action to be effective, the flight control system must ensure that the whole system has adequate stability.

   If an aircraft is to execute commands properly, in relation to earth coordinates, it must be provided with information about the aircraft's orientation so that right turn, left turn, up, down, roll left, roll right, for example, are related to the airborne geometrical reference. For about sixty years, it has been common practice to provide aircraft with reference coordinates for control and stabilization by means of gyroscopic instruments. The bank and climb indicator, for example, effectively provides a horizontal reference plane, with an accuracy of a few degrees, and is as satisfactory today for the purposes of control as when it was first introduced. Similarly, the turn indicator, which shows the aircraft's turning left or right, to about the same accuracy, is also a gyroscopic instrument and the use of signals from both these devices, as feedback signals for an AFCS, is still effective and valid. However, the use of conventional gyroscopic instruments in aircraft has fundamental limitations which lie in the inherent accuracy of indication, which is to within a few degrees only, and also in the inherent drift rates, of about ten degrees per hour. Such instruments are unsuitable for present-day navigation, which requires that the accumulated error in distance for each hour of operation, after an inertial fix, be not greater than 1.5 km. An angle of one degree between local gravitational directions corresponds to a distance on the earth's surface of approximately 95 km. Consequently, special motion sensors, such as ring laser gyros, NMR gyros, strap-down, force-balance accelerometers, must be used in modern flight control systems.

Because this book is concerned with control, rather than guidance, it is more convenient to represent the motion of aircraft in a system of coordinates which is fixed in the aircraft and moves with it. By doing this, the coordinate transformations generally required to obtain the aircraft's motion in some other coordinate system, such as a system fixed in the earth, can be avoided. When the origin of such a body-fixed system of coordinates is fixed at the centre of gravity of the aircraft, which is in an equilibrium (or trimmed) state of motion along a nominal flight path, then, when only small perturbations of the aircraft's motion about this equilibrium state are considered, the corresponding equations of motion can be linearized. Since many flight control problems are of very short duration (5–20 seconds), the coefficients of these equations of motion can be regarded as constant, so that transfer functions can sometimes be conveniently used to describe the dynamics of the aircraft. However, it must be remembered that a notable feature of an aircraft's dynamic response is how it changes markedly with forward speed, height, and the aircraft's mass. Some of the most difficult problems of flight control occurred with the introduction of jet propulsion, the consequent expansion of the flight envelope of such aircraft, and the resulting changes in configuration, most notable of which were the use of swept wings, of very short span and greatly increased wing loading, and the concentrated mass of the aircraft being distributed in a long and slender fuselage. In aircraft of about 1956 these changes led to marked deficiences in the damping of the classical modes of aircraft motion, namely the short period mode of the aircraft's longitudinal motion, and the Dutch roll mode of its lateral motion. Other unknown, coupled modes also appeared, such as fuel sloshing and roll instability; the use of thinner wings and more slender fuselages meant greater flexibility of the aircraft structure, and the modes associated with this structural flexibility coupled with the rigid-body modes of the aircraft's motion, caused further problems.

One of the first solutions to these problems was the use of a *stability augmentation system* (SAS), which is simply a feedback control system designed to increase the relative damping of a particular mode of the motion of the aircraft. Such an increase in damping is achieved by augmenting one or more of the coefficients of the equations of motion by imposing on the aircraft appropriate forces or moments as a result of actuating the control surfaces in response to feedback signals derived from appropriate motion variables. After SAS, the following AFCS modes were developed: *sideslip suppression SAS*, *pitch attitude hold*, *autothrottle (speed control system)*, *mach hold*, *height hold*, and *turn coordination systems*.

An integrated flight control system is a collection of such AFCS modes in a single comprehensive system, with particular modes being selected by the pilot to suit the task required for any particular phase of flight. In the past such functions were loosely referred to as an *autopilot*, but that name was a trademark registered by the German company Siemens in 1928. Today, AFCS not only augment the stability of an aircraft, but they can follow path and manoeuvre commands, thereby providing the means of automatic tracking and navigation; they can perform automatic take-off and landing; they can provide structural mode control, gust load alleviation, and active ride control.

1.5 BRIEF HISTORY OF FLIGHT CONTROL SYSTEMS

The heavier-than-air machine designed and built by Hiram Maxim in 1891 was colossal for its time: it was 34 m long and weighed 3 600 kg. Even now, the largest propeller to be seen in the aviation collection of the Science Museum in London is one of the pair used by Maxim. It was obvious to Maxim, if to no-one else at the time, that when his aircraft flew, its longitudinal stability would be inadequate, for he installed in the machine a flight control system which used an actuator to deflect the elevator and employed a gyroscope to provide a feedback signal. It was identical, except in inconsequential detail, to a present-day pitch attitude control system. Two of the minor details were the system's weight, over 130 kg, and its power source, steam. The concept remains unique.

Between 1910 and 1912 the American father-and-son team, the Sperrys, developed a two-axis stabilizer system in which the actuators were powered by compressed air and the gyroscopes were also air-driven. The system could maintain both pitch and bank angles simultaneously and, from a photographic record of a celebrated demonstration flight, in which Sperry Snr is seen in the open cockpit, with his arms stretched up above his head, and a mechanic is standing on the upper surface of the upper wing at the starboard wing tip, maintaining level flight automatically was easily within its capacity.

During World War I, aircraft design improved sufficiently to provide, by the sound choice of size, shape and location of the aerodynamic control surfaces, adequate stability for pilots' needs. Many aircraft were still unstable, but not dangerously so, or, to express that properly, the degree of damage was acceptable in terms of the loss rates of pilots and machines.

In the 1920s, however, it was found that, although the early commercial airliners were quite easy to fly, it was difficult to hold heading in poor visibility. Frequently, in such conditions, a pilot and his co-pilot had to divide the flying task between them. The pilot held the course by monitoring both the compass and the turn indicator and by using the rudder; the co-pilot held the speed and the attitude constant by monitoring both the airspeed and the pitch attitude indicator and by controlling the airspeed via the engine throttles and the pitch attitude by using the elevator. From the need to alleviate this workload grew the need to control aircraft automatically.

The most extensive period of development of early flight control systems took place between 1922 and 1937: in Great Britain, at the Royal Aircraft Establishment (RAE) at Farnborough; in Germany, in the industrial firms of Askania and Siemens; and in the USA, in Sperrys and at NACA (National Advisory Committee for Aeronautics – now NASA). Like all other flight control systems up to 1922, the RAE's Mk I system was two-axis, controlling pitch attitude and heading. It was a pneumatic system, but its superior performance over its predecessors and competitors was due to the fact that it had been designed scientifically by applying the methods of dynamic stability analysis which had been developed in Great Britain by some very distinguished applied mathematicians and aerodynamicists (see McRuer *et al.*, 1973; Draper, 1981; Hopkin and Dunn, 1947; McRuer and Graham, 1981; Oppelt, 1976). Such comprehensive theoretical analysis, in association with extensive experimental flight tests and trials carried out by the RAF, led to a clear understanding of which particular motion variables were most effective for use as feedback signals in flight control systems.

In 1927, in Germany, the firm of Askania developed a pneumatic system which controlled heading by means of the aircraft's rudder. It used an air-driven gyroscope, designed and manufactured by Sperrys of the USA. The first unit was flight tested on the Graf Zeppelin-LZ127; the system merits mention only because of its registered trade name, Autopilot. However, the Germans soon decided that as a drive medium, air, which is very compressible, gave inferior performance compared to oil, which was considered to be very nearly incompressible. Thus, in its two-axis 'autopilot' of 1935, the Siemens company successfully used hydraulic actuators and thereby established the trend, still followed today, of using hydraulic oil in preference to air, which in turn was used in preference to Maxim's steam. In 1950, the Bristol Aeroplane Company built a four-engined, turbo-prop transport aircraft which used electric actuators, but it was not copied by other manufacturers. At present, NASA and the USAF are actively pursuing a programme of reasearch designed to lead to 'an all-electric airplane' by 1990.

The reader should not infer from earlier statements that the RAE solved every flight control problem on the basis of having adequate theories. In 1934, the Mk IV system, which was a three-axis pneumatic system, was designed for installation in the Hawker Hart, a biplane in service with the RAF. In flight, a considerable number of stability problems were experienced and these were never solved. However, when the same system was subsequently fitted to the heavy bombers then entering RAF service (the Hampdens, Whitleys and Wellingtons) all the stability problems vanished and no satisfactory reasons for this improvement were ever adduced. (McRuer and Graham (1981) suggest that the increased inertia and the consequently slower response of the heavier aircraft were the major improving factors.)

In 1940, the RAE had developed a new AFCS, the Mk VII, which was again two-axis and pneumatic, but, in the longitudinal axis, used both airspeed and its rate of change as feedback signals, and, in the lateral axis, moved the ailerons in response to a combination of roll and yaw angles. At cruising speed in calm weather the system was adjudged by pilots to give the best automatic control yet devised. But, in some aircraft at low speeds, and in all aircraft in turbulence, the elevator motion caused such violent changes in the pitch attitude that the resultant vertical acceleration so affected the fuel supply that the engines stopped. It was only in 1943 that the problem was eventually solved by Neumark (see Neumark, 1943) who conducted an analysis of the problem entirely by time-domain methods. He used a formulation of the aircraft dynamics that control engineers now refer to as the state equation.

German work did not keep pace with British efforts, since, until very late in World War II, they concentrated on directional and lateral motion AFCSs, only providing a three-axis AFCS in 1944. The American developments had been essentially derived from the Sperry Automatic Pilot used in the Curtiss 'Condors' operated by Eastern Airlines in 1931. Subsequently, electric, three-axis autopilots were developed in the USA by firms such as Bendix, Honeywell and Sperry. The Minneapolis Honeywell C1 was developed from the Norden Stabilized Bomb-sight and was much used in World War II by both the American Air Forces and the Royal Air Force.

The development of automatic landing was due principally to the Blind Landing Experimental Unit of RAE, although in 1943 at the Flight Development Establishment at Rechlin in Germany, at least one aircraft had been landed automatically. The German efforts on flight control at this time were devoted to the systems required for the V1 and V2 missiles. On 23 September 1947 an American Douglas C-54 flew across the Atlantic completely under automatic control, from take-off at Stephenville, in Newfoundland, Canada, to landing at Brize Norton, in England. A considerable effort has been given to developing AFCSs since that time to become the ultra-reliable integrated flight control systems which form the subject of this book. The interested reader is referred to

Hopkin and Dunn (1947), McRuer and Graham (1981), Oppelt (1976) and Howard (1973) for further discussions of the history of flight control systems.

1.6 OUTLINE OF THE BOOK

Chapters 2 and 3 deal with the dynamic nature and characteristics of aircraft and, in so doing, it is hoped to establish the significance and appropriateness of the axis systems commonly used, and to derive mathematical models upon which it is convenient subsequently to base the designs of the AFCS.

Chapters 4 and 5 have been included to provide the reader with a clear knowledge of those significant dynamic effects which greatly affect the nature of an aircraft's flight, but over which a designer had no control. The complexity, which inevitably arises in providing a consistent account of the structural flexibility effects in aircraft dynamics, has to be understood if the important development of active control technology is to make sense. The principal objective of Chapter 4 is to provide a reasonable and consistent development of the additional dynamical equations representing the structural flexibility effects, to show how to incorporate them into the mathematical model of the aircraft, and to provide the reader with an account of their physical significance. One of the chief reasons why aircraft require flight control systems is to achieve smooth flight in turbulent atmospheric conditions. An explanation of the important forms of atmospheric turbulence is given in Chapter 5. How they can be represented mathematically, and how their effects can be properly introduced into the aircraft equations, are also covered there. Chapter 6 deals with the important subject of flying and handling qualities which are expressed mostly in terms of desirable dynamic properties which have been shown, from extensive flight and simulation experiments, to be most suited to pilots' skills and passengers' comfort. These qualities are the chief source of the performance criteria by which AFCS designs are assessed.

In a subject as extensive as AFCSs many methods of control system design are tried, used and reported in the technical reports and journals. It is necessary for any student to be competent in some of these methods, and reasonably familiar with the general nature of them all. Although it is not intended to provide a text book in control theory, Chapters 7 and 8 have been included to provide students with a self-contained summary of the most commonly applied methods, together with some indication of the relative advantages and disadvantages of each from the viewpoint of a designer of AFCSs for aircraft.

It is the objective of Chapters 9 to 11 to introduce students to the basic flight control modes which form the integrated flight control systems found in most modern aircraft. The nature of the dynamic response and the effects upon the performance of each subsystem of its inclusion as an inner loop in a larger system are both dealt with.

Chapter 12 provides students with a clear account of the type of AFCS which is now finding use in aircraft under current development, the so-called control configured vehicle. The flight control modes involved are specialist (except relaxed static stability, which can be handled by the methods outlined in Chapter 8) and, since the assessment of the performance of these active control technology (ACT) systems is not based upon the criteria dealt with in Chapter 6, they have been gathered together and dealt with separately in this chapter.

Rotary wing aircraft have quite distinctive methods of control and also have special dynamical problems. Although in forward flight, at all but the lowest speeds, they can be treated in the same manner as fixed-wing aircraft, the control problems are, in general, so distinctive that they are dealt with separately in Chapter 13, although the AFCSs employed in helicopters still involve stability augmentation and attitude and path control.

Chapter 14 demonstrates how the control laws developed earlier can be treated by digital control methods, so that digital AFCSs, which are commonly fitted to modern aircraft, can be considered and also to provide an outline of the effects upon the AFCS's performance in terms of the particular features of the digital method used.

Modern fighter and interdiction aircraft have flight envelopes which are so extensive that those changes which arise in the characteristic equation of the aircraft are too great to be handled by control laws devised on the basis of the control methods dealt with earlier. For such situations, the use of adaptive control is advocated. Chapter 15 presents some information about the theories which are used to develop such systems. Since the dynamic equations of these systems are non-linear, special stability considerations apply and these are also dealt with.

1.7 CONCLUSIONS

In considering the design of an AFCS an engineer will succeed only if he is able both to establish an adequate model representing the appropriate dynamical behaviour of the aircraft to be controlled and to recognize how an effective control system design can be realized.

Consequently, the control engineer working with AFCSs must completely understand the equations of the aircraft's motion, be familiar with their methods of solution, understand the characteristic responses associated with them, know what influence they have on the aircraft's flying qualities, appreciate how atmospheric disturbances can be characterized and know how such disturbances affect performance. Additionally, it is important to understand how primary flying controls can be improved, or their worst effects reduced, so that the match between a human pilot and the aircraft is optimized.

In addition, the theory of control, with its attendant design techniques, must be thoroughly mastered so that it, and they, can be used to produce an AFCS based upon control surface actuators and motion sensors which are available, and whose dynamic behaviour is thoroughly known.

The alternative methods of carrying out the required computation to produce the appropriate control laws have also to be completely understood, and the engineer is expected to be sound in his appreciation of the limitations of whatever particular method was chosen to perform the control design.

Detailed engineering considerations of installing and testing such AFCSs, particularly in regard to certification procedures for airworthiness requirements, and the special reliability considerations of the effect of subsystem failure upon the integrity of the overall system, are special studies beyond this book. The influence of these topics on the final form of the AFCS is profound and represents one of the most difficult aspects of flight control work. Any flight control engineer will be obliged to master both subjects early in his professional career.

1.8 NOTE

1. Sometimes 'centre of mass' and 'centre of gravity' are used interchangeably. For any group of particles in a uniform gravitational field these centres coincide. For spacecraft, their separation is distinctive and this separation results in an appreciable moment due to gravity being exerted on the spacecraft. For aircraft flying in the atmosphere the centres are identically located.

1.9 REFERENCES

DRAPER, C.S. 1981. Control, navigation and guidance. *IEEE Control Systems Magazine.* 1(4): 4–17.

HOPKIN, H.R. and R.W. DUNN. 1947. Theory and development of automatic pilots 1937–1947. RAE report. IAP 1459. August.

HOWARD, R.W. 1973. Automatic flight controls in fixed wing aircraft – the first hundred years. *Aero. J.* 77(11): 553–62.

McRUER, D.T., I.L. ASHKENAS and D.C. GRAHAM. 1973. *Aircraft Dynamics and Automatic Control.* Princeton University Press.

McRUER, D.T. and D.C. GRAHAM. 1981. Eighty years of flight control: triumphs and pitfalls of the systems approach. *J. Guid. and Cont.* 4(4): 353–62.

NEUMARK, S. 1943. The disturbed longitudinal motion of an uncontrolled aeroplane and of an aeroplane with automatic control. ARC R&M 2078. January.

OPPELT, W. 1976. An historical review of Autopilot development, research and theory in Germany. *J. Dyn. Sys., Meas. and Cont.* 98(3): 215–23.

2

The Equations of Motion of an Aircraft

2.1 INTRODUCTION

If the problems associated with designing an AFCS were solely concerned with large area navigation then an appropriate frame of reference, in which to express the equations of motion of an aircraft, would be inertial, with its centre in the fixed stars. But problems involving AFCSs are generally related to events which do not persist: the dynamic situation being considered rarely lasts for more than a few minutes. Consequently, a more convenient inertial reference frame is a tropocentric coordinate system, i.e. one whose origin is regarded as being fixed at the centre of the Earth: the Earth axis system. It is used primarily as a reference system to express gravitational effects, altitude, horizontal distance, and the orientation of the aircraft. A set of axes commonly used with the Earth axis system is shown in Figure 2.1; the axis, X_E, is chosen to point north, the axis, Y_E, then pointing east with the orthogonal triad being completed when the axis, Z_E, points down. If the Earth axis system is used as a basic frame of reference, to which any other axis frames employed in the study are referred, the aircraft itself

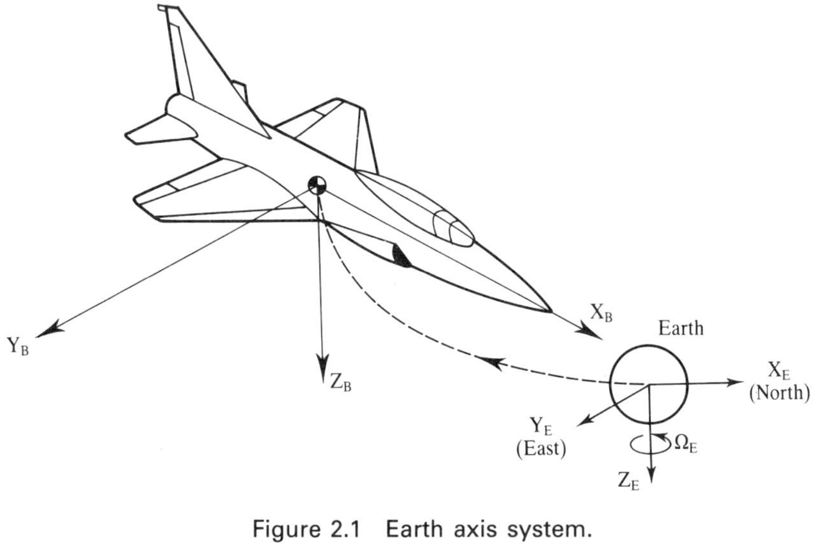

Figure 2.1 Earth axis system.

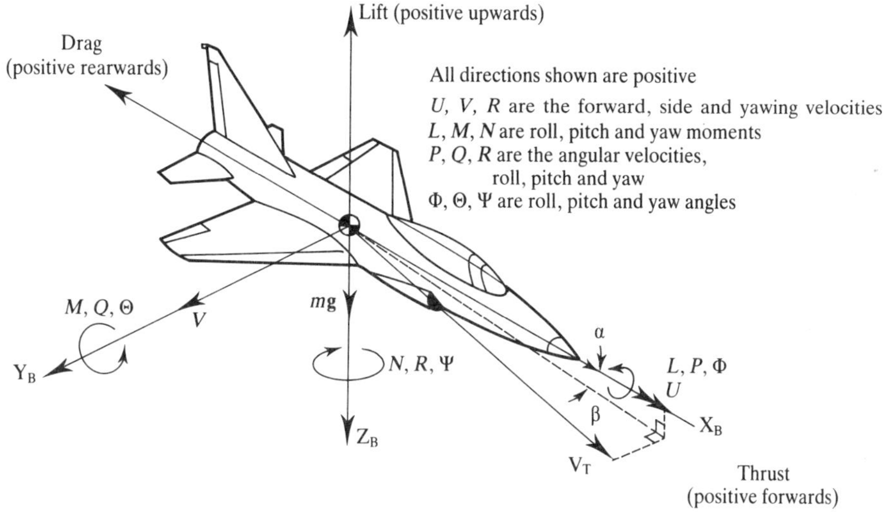

Figure 2.2 Body axis system.

must then have a suitable axis system. Several are available which all find use, to a greater or lesser extent, in AFCS work. The choice of axis system governs the form taken by the equations of motion. However, only body-fixed axis systems, i.e. only systems whose origins are located identically at an aircraft's centre of gravity, are considered in this book. For such a system, the axis, X_B, points forward out of the nose of the aircraft; the axis, Y_B, points out through the starboard (right) wing, and the axis, Z_B, points down (see Figure 2.2). Axes X_B, Y_B and Z_B emphasize that it is a body-fixed axis system which is being used. Forces, moments and velocities are also defined. By using a system of axes fixed in the aircraft the inertia terms, which appear in the equations of motion, may be considered to be constant. Furthermore, the aerodynamic forces and moments depend only upon the angles, α and β, which orient the total velocity vector, $\mathbf{V}_T$, in relation to the axis, X_B. The angular orientation of the body axis system with respect to the Earth axis system depends strictly upon the orientation sequence. This sequence of rotations is customarily taken as follows (see Thelander, 1965):

1. Rotate the Earth axes, X_E, Y_E, and Z_E, through some azimuthal angle, Ψ, about the axis, X_E, to reach some intermediate axes X_1, Y_1 and Z_1.
2. Next, rotate these axes X_1, Y_1 and Z_1 through some angle of elevation, Θ, about the axis Y_1 to reach a second, intermediate set of axes, X_2, Y_2, and Z_2.
3. Finally, the axes X_2, Y_2 and Z_2 are rotated through an angle of bank, Φ, about the axis, X_2, to reach the body axes X_B, Y_B and Z_B.

Three other special axis systems are considered here, because they can be found to have been used sufficiently often in AFCS studies. They are: the stability axis system; the principal axis system; and the wind axis system. In AFCS work, the most commonly used system is the stability axis system.

2.2 AXIS (COORDINATE) SYSTEMS

2.2.1 The Stability Axis System

The axis X_s is chosen to coincide with the velocity vector, $\mathbf{V}_T$, at the start of the motion. Therefore, between the X-axis of the stability axis system and the X-axis of the body axis system, there is a trimmed angle of attack, α_o. The equations of motion derived by using this axis system are a special subset of the set derived by using the body axis system.

2.2.2 The Principal Axis System

This set of body axes is specially chosen to coincide with the principal axes of the aircraft. The convenience of this system resides in the fact that in the equations of motion, all the product of inertia terms are zero, which greatly simplifies the equations.

2.2.3 The Wind Axis System

Because this system is oriented with respect to the aircraft's flight path, time-varying terms which correspond to the moments and cross-products of inertia appear in the equations of motion. Such terms considerably complicate the analysis of aircraft motion and, consequently, wind axes are not used in this text. They have appeared frequently, however, in American papers on the subject.

2.2.4 Sensor Signals

Because an AFCS uses feedback signals from motion sensors, it is important to remember that such signals are relative to the axis system of the sensor and not to the body-fixed axis system of the aircraft. This simple fact can sometimes cause the performance obtained from an AFCS to be modified and, in certain flight tasks, may have to be taken into account. However, in straight and level flight at cruise it is insignificant.

2.3 THE EQUATIONS OF MOTION OF A RIGID BODY AIRCRAFT

2.3.1 Introduction

The treatment given here closely follows that of McRuer *et al.* (1953).

It is assumed, first, that the aircraft is rigid-body; the distance between any points on the aircraft do not change in flight. Special methods to take into account the flexible motion of the airframe are treated in Chapter 4. When the aircraft can be assumed to be a rigid body moving in space, its motion can be considered to have six degrees of freedom. By applying Newton's Second Law to that rigid body the equations of motion can be established in terms of the translational and angular accelerations which occur as a consequence of some forces and moments being applied to the aircraft.

In the introduction to this chapter it was stated that the form of the equations of motion depends upon the choice of axis system, and a few of the advantages of using a body-fixed axis system were indicated there. In the development which follows, a body axis system is used with the change to the stability axis system being made at an appropriate point later in the text. In order to be specific about the atmosphere in which the aircraft is moving, it is also assumed that the inertial frame of reference does not itself accelerate, in other words, the Earth is taken to be fixed in space.

2.3.2 Translational Motion

From Newton's Second Law it can be deduced that:

$$\mathbf{F} = \frac{\mathrm{d}}{\mathrm{d}t}\{m\mathbf{V}_{\mathrm{T}}\} \tag{2.1}$$

$$\mathbf{M} = \frac{\mathrm{d}}{\mathrm{d}t}\{\mathbf{H}\} \tag{2.2}$$

where **F** represents the sum of all externally applied forces, **M** represents the sum of all applied torques, and **H** is the angular momentum.

The sum of the external forces has three components: aerodynamic, gravitational and propulsive. In every aircraft some part of the propulsive (thrust) force is produced by expending some of the vehicle's mass. But it can easily be shown[1] that if the mass, m, of an aircraft is assumed to be constant, the thrust, which is a force equal to the relative velocity between the exhausted mass and the aircraft and the change of the aircraft's mass/unit time, can be treated as an external force without impairing the accuracy of the equations of motion. If it is assumed, for the present, that there will be no change in the propulsive force, changes in the aircraft's state of motion from its equilibrium state can occur if and only if there are changes in either the aerodynamic or gravitational forces (or both). If it becomes necessary in a problem to include the changes of thrust (as it will be when dealing with airspeed control systems, for example) only a small extension of the method being outlined here is required. Details in relation to the stability axis system are given in section 2.2. For the present, however, the thrust force can be considered to be contained in the general applied force, **F**.

When carrying out an analysis of an AFCS it is convenient to regard the sums of applied torque and force as consisting of an equilibrium and a perturbational component, namely:

$$\mathbf{F} = \mathbf{F}_0 + \Delta\mathbf{F} = m \frac{\mathrm{d}}{\mathrm{d}t}\{\mathbf{V}_\mathrm{T}\} \tag{2.3}$$

[2]

$$\mathbf{M} = \mathbf{M}_0 + \Delta\mathbf{M} = \frac{\mathrm{d}}{\mathrm{d}t}\{\mathbf{H}\} \tag{2.4}$$

The subscript 0 denotes the equilibrium component, Δ the component of perturbation. Since the axis system being used as an inertial reference system is the Earth axis system, eqs (2.3) and (2.4) can be re-expressed as:

$$\Delta\mathbf{F} = m \frac{\mathrm{d}}{\mathrm{d}t}\{\mathbf{V}_\mathrm{T}\}_\mathrm{E} \tag{2.5}$$

$$\Delta\mathbf{M} = \frac{\mathrm{d}}{\mathrm{d}t}\{\mathbf{H}\}_\mathrm{E} \tag{2.6}$$

By definition, equilibrium flight must be unaccelerated flight along a straight path; during this flight the linear velocity vector relative to fixed space is invariant, and the angular velocity is zero. Thus, both $\mathbf{F}_0$ and $\mathbf{M}_0$ are zero.

The rate of change of $\mathbf{V}_\mathrm{T}$ relative to the Earth axis system is given by:

$$\frac{\mathrm{d}}{\mathrm{d}t}\{\mathbf{V}_\mathrm{T}\}_\mathrm{E} = \frac{\mathrm{d}}{\mathrm{d}t}\mathbf{V}_\mathrm{T}\Big|_\mathrm{B} + \omega \times \mathbf{V}_\mathrm{T} \tag{2.7}$$

where ω is the angular velocity of the aircraft with respect to the fixed axis system. Wnen the vectors are expressed in coordinates in relation to the body-fixed axis system, both velocities may be written as the sum of their corresponding components, with respect to X_B, Y_B and Z_B, as follows:

$$\mathbf{V}_\mathrm{T} = \mathbf{i}U + \mathbf{j}V + \mathbf{k}W \tag{2.8}$$

$$\omega = \mathbf{i}P + \mathbf{j}Q + \mathbf{k}R \tag{2.9}$$

$$\therefore \quad \frac{\mathrm{d}}{\mathrm{d}t}\mathbf{V}_\mathrm{T}\Big|_\mathrm{B} = \mathbf{i}\dot{U} + \mathbf{j}\dot{V} + \mathbf{k}\dot{W} \tag{2.10}$$

and the cross-product, $\omega \times \mathbf{V}_\mathrm{T}$, is given by:

$$\omega \times \mathbf{V}_\mathrm{T} = \begin{bmatrix} \mathbf{i} & \mathbf{j} & \mathbf{k} \\ P & Q & R \\ U & V & W \end{bmatrix}$$

$$= \mathbf{i}(QW - VR) + \mathbf{j}(UR - PW) + \mathbf{k}(PV - UQ) \tag{2.11}$$

In a similar fashion, the components of the perturbation force can be expressed as

$$\Delta\mathbf{F} = \mathbf{i}\Delta F_x + \mathbf{j}\Delta F_y + \mathbf{k}\Delta F_z \tag{2.12}$$

Hence,

$$\begin{aligned}\Delta\mathbf{F} = m\{&\mathbf{i}(\dot{U} + QW - VR) + \mathbf{j}(\dot{V} + UR - PW) \\ &+ \mathbf{k}(\dot{W} + PV - UQ)\}\end{aligned} \tag{2.13}$$

From which it can be inferred that:

$$\Delta F_x = m(\dot{U} + QW - VR) \tag{2.14}$$

$$\Delta F_y = m(\dot{V} + UR + PW) \tag{2.15}$$

$$\Delta F_z = m(\dot{W} + VP - UQ) \tag{2.16}$$

Rather than continue the development using the cumbersome notation, ΔF_i, to denote the ith component of the perturbational force, it is proposed to follow the American custom and use the following notation:

$$\Delta X \triangleq \Delta F_x \qquad \Delta Y \triangleq \Delta F_y \qquad \Delta Z \triangleq \Delta F_z \tag{2.17}$$

It must be remembered that now X, Y and Z denote *forces*. With these substitutions in eqs (2.14)–(2.16), the equations of translational motion can be expressed as:

$$\Delta X = m(\dot{U} + QW - VR) \tag{2.18}$$

$$\Delta Y = m(\dot{V} + UR - PW) \tag{2.19}$$

$$\Delta Z = m(\dot{W} + VP - UQ) \tag{2.20}$$

2.3.3 Rotational Motion

For a rigid body, angular momentum may be defined as:

$$\mathbf{H} = I\boldsymbol{\omega} \tag{2.21}$$

The inertia matrix, I, is defined as:

$$I = \begin{bmatrix} I_{xx} & -I_{xy} & -I_{xz} \\ -I_{xy} & I_{yy} & -I_{yz} \\ -I_{xz} & -I_{yz} & I_{zz} \end{bmatrix} \tag{2.22}$$

where I_{ii} denotes a moment of inertia, and I_{ij} a product of inertia $j \neq i$.

$$\mathbf{M} = \frac{\mathrm{d}}{\mathrm{d}t}\mathbf{H} + \boldsymbol{\omega} \times \mathbf{H} \tag{2.23}$$

Transforming from body axes to the Earth axis system (see Gaines and Hoffman, 1972) allows eq. (2.23) to be re-expressed as:

$$\mathbf{M} = I\left\{\frac{\mathrm{d}}{\mathrm{d}t}\,\boldsymbol{\omega} + \boldsymbol{\omega} \times \boldsymbol{\omega}\right\} + \boldsymbol{\omega} \times \mathbf{H} \tag{2.24}$$

However,

$$\boldsymbol{\omega} \times \boldsymbol{\omega} \triangleq 0 \tag{2.25}$$

$$\frac{\mathrm{d}}{\mathrm{d}t}\,\boldsymbol{\omega} = \mathbf{i}\dot{P} + \mathbf{j}\dot{Q} + \mathbf{k}\dot{R} \tag{2.26}$$

and

$$\boldsymbol{\omega} \times \mathbf{H} = \begin{bmatrix} \mathbf{i} & \mathbf{j} & \mathbf{k} \\ P & Q & R \\ h_x & h_y & h_z \end{bmatrix} \tag{2.27}$$

where h_x, h_y and h_z are the components of $\mathbf{H}$ obtained from expanding eq. (2.21) thus:

$$h_x = I_{xx}P - I_{xy}Q - I_{xz}R \tag{2.28}$$

$$h_y = -\,I_{yx}P + I_{yy}Q - I_{yz}R \tag{2.29}$$

$$h_z = -\,I_{zx}P - I_{zy}Q + I_{zz}R \tag{2.30}$$

In general, aircraft are symmetrical about the plane XZ, and consequently it is generally the case that:

$$I_{xy} = I_{yz} = 0 \tag{2.31}$$

Therefore:

$$h_x = I_{xx}P - I_{xz}R \tag{2.32}$$

$$h_y = I_{yy}Q \tag{2.33}$$

$$h_z = -\,I_{zx}P + I_{zz}R \tag{2.34}$$

and

$$\Delta M_x = I_{xx}\dot{P} - I_{xz}(\dot{R} + PQ) + QR(\mathrm{I}_{zz} - \mathrm{I}_{yy}) \tag{2.35}$$

$$\Delta M_y = I_{yy}\dot{Q} + I_{xz}(P^2 - R^2) + PR(I_{xx} - I_{zz}) \tag{2.36}$$

$$\Delta M_z = I_{zz}\dot{R} - I_{xz}\dot{P} + PQ(I_{yy} - I_{xx}) + I_{zz}QR \tag{2.37}$$

Again, following American usage:

$$\Delta M_x = \Delta L \qquad \Delta M_y = \Delta M \qquad \Delta M_z = \Delta N \tag{2.38}$$

where L, M and N are moments about the rolling, pitching and yawing axes respectively.

$$\Delta L = I_{xx}\dot{P} - I_{xz}(\dot{R} + PQ) + (I_{zz} - I_{yy})QR \tag{2.39}$$

$$\Delta M = I_{yy}\dot{Q} + I_{xz}(P^2 - R^2) + (I_{xx} - I_{zz})PR \tag{2.40}$$

$$\Delta N = I_{zz}\dot{R} - I_{xz}\dot{P} + PQ(I_{yy} - I_{xx}) + I_{xz}QR \tag{2.41}$$

2.3.4 Some Points Arising from the Derivation of the Equations

It is worth emphasizing here that the form of equations arrived at, having used a body axis system, is not entirely convenient for flight simulation work (Fogarty and Howe, 1969). For example, suppose a fighter aircraft has a maximum velocity of 600 m s^{-1} and a maximum angular velocity Q_{B} of 2.0 rad s^{-1}. The term, UQ, in eq. (2.20) can have a value as large as 1 200 m s^{-2}, i.e. 120 g, whereas the term, ΔZ, the normal acceleration due to the external forces (primarily aerodynamic and gravitational) may have a maximum value in the range 10.0 to 20.0 m s^{-2} (i.e. 1–2 g). It can be seen, therefore, how a (dynamic) acceleration of very large value, perhaps fifty times greater than the physical accelerations, can occur in the equations merely as a result of the high rate of rotation experienced by the body axis system. Furthermore, it can be seen from inspection of eqs (2.18)–(2.20) how angular motion has been coupled into translational motion. Moreover, on the right-hand side of eqs (2.39)–(2.41) the third term is a non-linear, inertial coupling term. For large aircraft, such as transports, which cannot generate large angular rates, these terms are frequently neglected so that the moment equations become:

$$\Delta L = I_{xx}\dot{P} - I_{xz}(\dot{R} + PQ) \tag{2.42}$$

$$\Delta M = I_{yy}\dot{Q} + I_{xz}(P^2 - R^2) \tag{2.43}$$

$$\Delta N = I_{zz}\dot{R} - I_{xz}(\dot{P} - QR) \tag{2.44}$$

A number of other assumptions are frequently invoked in relation to these equations:

1. Sometimes, for a particular aircraft, the product of inertia, I_{xz}, is sufficiently small to allow of its being neglected. This often happens when the body axes, X_{B}, Y_{B}, and Z_{B} have been chosen to almost coincide with the principal axes.
2. For aircraft whose maximum values of angular velocity are low, the terms PQ, QR, and $P^2 - R^2$ can be neglected.
3. Since R^2 is frequently very much smaller than P^2, it is often neglected.

It is emphasized, however, that the neglect of such terms can only be practised after very careful consideration of both the aircraft's characteristics and the AFCS problem being considered. Modern fighter aircraft, for example, may lose control as a result of roll/pitch inertial coupling. In such aircraft, pitch-up is sensed when a roll manoeuvre is being carried out. When an AFCS is fitted, such a sensor signal would cause an elevator deflection to be commanded to provide a nose-down attitude until the elevator can be deflected no further and the aircraft cannot be controlled. Such a situation can happen whenever the term $(I_{xx} - I_{zz})PR$ is large enough to cause an uncontrollable pitching movement.

2.3.5 Contributions to the Equations of Motion of the Forces Due to Gravity

The forces due to gravity are always present in an aircraft; however, by neglecting any consideration of gradients in the gravity field, which are important only in extra-atmospheric flight if all other external forces are essentially non-existent, it can be properly assumed that gravity acts at the centre of gravity (c.g.) of the aircraft. Hence, since the centres of mass and gravity coincide in an aircraft, there is no external moment produced by gravity about the c.g. Hence, for the body axis system, gravity contributes only to the external force vector, **F**.

The gravitational force acting upon an aircraft is most obviously expressed in terms of the Earth axes. With respect to these axes the gravity vector, $m\mathbf{g}$, is directed along the Z_E axis. Figure 2.3 shows the alignment of the gravity vector with respect to the body-fixed axes. In Figure 2.3 Θ represents the angle between the gravity vector and the Y_BZ_B plane; the angle is positive when the nose of the aircraft goes up. Φ represents the bank angle between the axis Z_B and the projection of the gravity vector on the Y_BZ_B plane; the angle is positive when the right wing is down. Direct resolution of the vector $m\mathbf{g}$, into X, Y and Z components produces:

$$\begin{aligned}
\delta X &= m\mathbf{g}\sin[-\Theta] = -m\mathbf{g}\sin\Theta \\
\delta Y &= m\mathbf{g}\cos[-\Theta]\sin\Phi = m\mathbf{g}\cos\Theta\sin\Phi \\
\delta Z &= m\mathbf{g}\cos[-\Theta]\cos\Phi = m\mathbf{g}\cos\Theta\cos\Phi
\end{aligned} \tag{2.45}$$

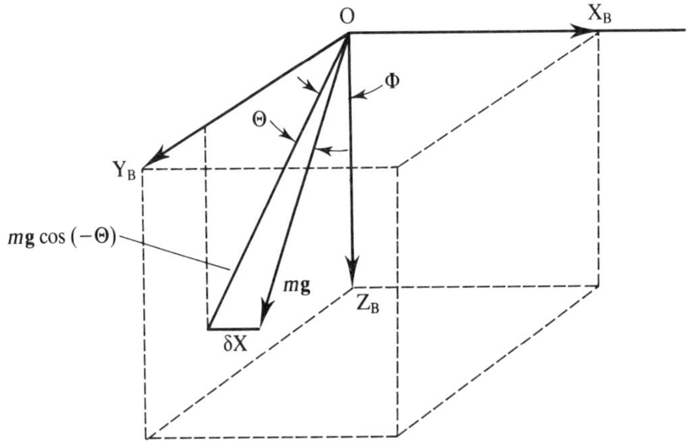

Figure 2.3 Orientation of gravity vector with body axis systems.

In general, the angles Θ and Φ are not simply the integrals of the angular velocity P and Q; in effect, two new motion variables have been introduced and it is necessary to relate them and their derivatives to the angular velocities, P, Q and R. How this is done depends upon whether the gravitational vertical seen from the aircraft is fixed or whether it rotates relative to inertial space. Aircraft speeds being very low compared to orbital velocities, the vertical may be regarded as fixed. In very high speed flight the vertical will be seen as rotating and the treatment which is being presented here will then require some minor amendments.

The manner in which the angular orientation and velocity of the body axis system with respect to the gravity vector is expressed depends upon the angular velocity of the body axes about the vector $m\mathbf{g}$. This angular velocity is the azimuth rate, $\dot{\Psi}$; it is not normal to either $\dot{\Phi}$ or $\dot{\Theta}$, but its projection in the Y_BZ_B plane is normal to both (see Figure 2.4). By resolution, it is seen that:

$$\begin{aligned} P &= \dot{\Phi} - \dot{\Psi}\sin\Theta \\ Q &= \dot{\Theta}\cos\Phi + \dot{\Psi}\cos\Theta\sin\Phi \\ R &= -\dot{\Theta}\sin\Phi + \dot{\Psi}\cos\Theta\cos\Phi \end{aligned} \tag{2.46}$$

Also,

$$\begin{aligned} \dot{\Phi} &= P + \dot{\Psi}\sin\Theta \\ \dot{\Theta} &= Q\cos\Phi - R\sin\Phi \\ \dot{\Psi} &= \frac{R\cos\Phi}{\cos\Theta} + \frac{Q\sin\Phi}{\cos\Theta} \end{aligned} \tag{2.47}$$

Using substitution, it is easy to show that:

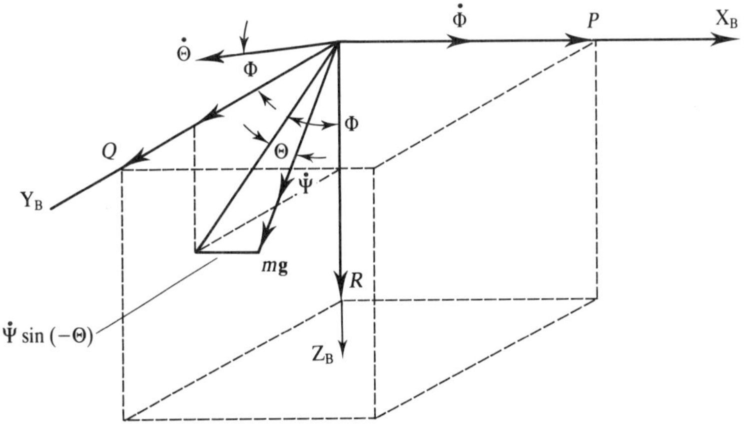

Figure 2.4 Angular orientation and velocities of gravity vector, **g**, relative to body axis.

$$\dot{\Phi} = P + R \tan\Theta \cos\Phi + Q \tan\Theta \sin\Phi \tag{2.48}$$

Φ, Θ and Ψ are referred to as the Euler angles.

2.3.6 Axis Transformations

The physical relationships established so far depend upon two frames of reference: the Earth axis system and the body axis system. To orient these systems one to another requires the use of axis transformations. Any set of axes can be obtained from any other set by a sequence of three rotations. For each rotation a transformation matrix is applied to the variables. The total transformation array is obtained simply by taking the product of the three matrices, multiplied in the order of the rotations. In aircraft dynamics, the most common set of transformations is that between the Earth axis system which incorporates the gravity vector, **g**, as one axis, and the body-fixed axes, X_B, Y_B and Z_B. The rotations follow the usual order: azimuth Ψ, pitch Θ, and roll Φ. The corresponding matrices are:

$$T_\Psi = \begin{bmatrix} \cos\Psi & \sin\Psi & 0 \\ -\sin\Psi & \cos\Psi & 0 \\ 0 & 0 & 1 \end{bmatrix} \tag{2.49}$$

$$T_\Theta = \begin{bmatrix} \cos\Theta & 0 & -\sin\Theta \\ 0 & 1 & 0 \\ \sin\Theta & 0 & \cos\Theta \end{bmatrix} \tag{2.50}$$

$$T_\Phi = \begin{bmatrix} 1 & 0 & 0 \\ 0 & \cos\Phi & \sin\Phi \\ 0 & -\sin\Phi & \cos\Phi \end{bmatrix} \tag{2.51}$$

The complete transformation matrix T is called the direction cosine array and is defined as:

$$T = [T_\Psi][T_\Theta][T_\Phi] \tag{2.52}$$

Before expressing the matrix T in full, a notational shorthand is proposed whereby a term such as $\cos\xi$ is written as $c\xi$ and a term such as $\sin\xi$ is written as $s\xi$. Thus:

$$T = \begin{bmatrix} c\Psi c\Theta & s\Psi s\Theta & -s\Theta \\ (c\Psi s\Theta s\Phi - s\Psi c\Phi) & (s\Psi s\Theta s\Phi + c\Psi c\Phi) & c\Theta s\Phi \\ (c\Psi s\Theta c\Phi + s\Psi s\Phi) & (s\Psi s\Theta c\Phi - c\Psi s\Phi) & c\Theta c\Phi \end{bmatrix} \tag{2.53}$$

It is worth noting that the order of rotation $\Psi-\Theta-\Phi$ is that which results in the least complicated resolution of the gravity vector **g** into the body axis system. It can easily be shown that:

$$\mathbf{g} = g\{- s\Theta\mathbf{i} + c\Theta s\Phi\mathbf{j} + c\Theta c\Phi\mathbf{k}\} \tag{2.54}$$

Another practical advantage is that the angles are those which are measured by a typically oriented vertical gyroscope. A two degree of freedom, gravity erected, vertical gyroscope, oriented such that the bearing axis of its outer gimbal lies along OX_B, measures on its inner and outer gimbals the Euler angles Θ and Φ, respectively.

2.3.7 Linearization of the Inertial and Gravitational Terms

Equations (2.14)–(2.16) and (2.39)–(2.41) represent the inertial forces acting on the aircraft. Equation (2.45) represents the contribution of the forces due to gravity to those equations. All these forces are proportional to the mass of the aircraft. Consequently, these terms may be conveniently combined into components to represent the accelerations which would be measured by sensors located on the aircraft in such a manner that the input axes of the sensors would be coincident with the body axes X_B, Y_B and Z_B. The external forces acting on the aircraft can be re-expressed as:

$$\begin{aligned} X &= \Delta X + \delta X \\ Y &= \Delta Y + \delta Y \\ Z &= \Delta Z + \delta Z \end{aligned} \tag{2.55}$$

where δX, δY and δZ are the gravitational terms and ΔX, ΔY and ΔZ represent the aerodynamic and thrust forces. For notational convenience, ΔL, ΔM and ΔN are now denoted by L, M and N. Thus the equations of motion of the rigid body, for its six degrees of freedom, may be expressed as:

$$\begin{aligned} X \triangleq ma_{x_{cg}} &= m[\dot{U} + QW - RV + g\sin\Theta] \\ Y \triangleq ma_{y_{cg}} &= m[\dot{V} + RU - PW - g\cos\Theta\sin\Phi] \\ Z \triangleq ma_{z_{cg}} &= m[\dot{W} + PV - QU - g\cos\Theta\cos\Phi] \\ L &= \dot{P}I_{xx} - I_{xz}(\dot{R} + PQ) + (I_{zz} - I_{yy})QR \\ M &= \dot{Q}I_{yy} + I_{xz}(P^2 - R^2) + (I_{xx} - I_{zz})PR \\ N &= \dot{R}I_{zz} - I_{xz}\dot{P} + PQ(I_{yy} - I_{xx}) + I_{xz}QR \end{aligned} \tag{2.56}$$

The auxiliary equations of eq. (2.46) must also be used since they relate Ψ, Θ and Φ to R, Q and P.

The equations which constitute eq. (2.56) are non-linear since they contain terms which comprise the product of dependent variables, the squares of dependent variables, and some of the terms are transcendental. Solutions of such equations cannot be obtained analytically and would require the use of a computer. Some simplification is possible, however, by considering the aircraft to comprise two components: a mean motion which represents the equilibrium, or trim, conditions, and a dynamic motion which accounts for the perturbations about the mean motion. In this form of analysis it is customary to assume that the perturbations are small. Thus, every motion variable is considered to have two components. For example:

$$\begin{aligned} U &\triangleq U_0 + u \qquad & R &\triangleq R_0 + r \\ Q &\triangleq Q_0 + \mathrm{q} \qquad & M &\triangleq M_0 + m_l \quad \text{etc.} \end{aligned} \tag{2.57}$$

The trim, or equilibrium, values are denoted by a subscript 0 and the small perturbation values of a variable are denoted by the lower case letter.[3]

In trim there can be no translational or rotational acceleration. Hence, the equations which represent the trim conditions can be expressed as:

$$\begin{aligned} X_0 &= m[Q_0W_0 - R_0V_0 + g\sin\Theta_0] \\ Y_0 &= m[U_0R_0 - P_0W_0 - g\cos\Theta_0\sin\Phi_0] \\ Z_0 &= m[P_0V_0 - Q_0U_0 - g\cos\Theta_0\cos\Phi_0] \\ L_0 &= Q_0R_0(I_{zz} - I_{yy}) - P_0Q_0I_{xz} \\ M_0 &= (P_0^2 - R_0^2)I_{xz} + (I_{xx} - I_{zz})P_0R_0 \\ N_0 &= I_{xz}Q_0R_0 + (I_{yy} - I_{xx})P_0Q_0 \end{aligned} \tag{2.58}$$

Steady rolling, pitching and yawing motion can occur in the trim condition; the equations which define P_0, Q_0 and R_0 are given by eq. (2.46) but with Φ, Θ and Ψ being subscripted by 0.

The perturbed motion can be found either by substituting eq. (2.57) into (2.56), expanding the terms and then subtracting eq. (2.58) from the result, or by differentiating both sides of eq. (2.56). When perturbations from the mean conditions are small, the sines and cosines can be approximated to the angles themselves and the value unity, respectively. Moreover, the products and squares of the perturbed quantities are negligible. Thus, the perturbed equations of motion for an aircraft can be written as:

$$\begin{aligned} \mathrm{d}X &= m[\dot{u} + W_0q + Q_0w - V_0r - R_0v + g\cos\Theta_0\theta] \\ \mathrm{d}Y &= m[\dot{v} + U_0r + R_0u - W_0p - P_0w - (g\cos\Theta_0\cos\Phi_0)\phi \\ &\qquad + (g\sin\Theta_0\sin\Phi_0)\theta] \\ \mathrm{d}Z &= m[\dot{w} + V_0p + P_0v - U_0q - Q_0u + (g\cos\Theta_0\sin\Phi_0)\phi \\ &\qquad + (g\sin\Theta_0\cos\Phi_0)\theta] \end{aligned} \tag{2.59}$$

$$\mathrm{d}L = I_{xx}\dot{p} - I_{xz}\dot{r} + (I_{zz} - I_{yy})(Q_0 r + R_0 q) - I_{xz}(P_0 q + Q_0 p)$$
$$\mathrm{d}M = I_{yy}\dot{q} + (I_{xx} - I_{zz})(P_0 r + R_0 p) - (2R_0 r - 2P_0 p)I_{xz}$$
$$dN = I_{zz}\dot{r} - I_{xz}\dot{p} + (I_{yy} - I_{xx})(P_0 q + Q_0 p) + I_{xz}(Q_0 r + R_0 q)$$

where Ψ_0, Θ_0 and Φ_0 have been used to represent steady orientations, and Ψ, θ and ϕ the perturbations in the Euler angles. Equations (2.59) are now linear. Obviously, perturbation equations are required for the auxiliary set of equations given as eq. (2.46), because the gravitional forces must be perturbed by any small change in the orientation of the body axis system with respect to the Earth axis system. However, the full set of perturbed, auxiliary equations is rarely used since it is complicated. But the components of angular velocity which represent the rotation of the body-fixed axes X_B, Y_B and Z_B relative to the Earth axes X_E, Y_E and Z_E are sometimes required. These are:

$$\begin{aligned}
p &= \dot{\phi} - \dot{\Psi} \sin \Theta_0 - \theta(\dot{\Psi}_0 \cos \Theta_0) \\
q &= \dot{\phi} \cos \Phi_0 - \theta(\dot{\Psi}_0 \sin \Phi \sin \Theta_0) + \dot{\Psi} \sin \Psi_0 \cos \Theta \\
&\quad + \phi(\dot{\Psi}_0 \cos \Theta_0 \cos \Phi_0 - \dot{\Theta}_0 \sin \Phi_0) \\
r &= \dot{\Psi} \cos \Theta_0 \cos \Phi_0 - \phi(\dot{\Psi}_0 \cos \Theta_0 \sin \Phi_0 + \dot{\Psi}_0 \cos \Phi_0) \\
&\quad - \dot{\theta} \sin \Phi_0 - \theta(\dot{\Psi}_0 \sin \Theta_0 \cos \Phi_0)
\end{aligned} \tag{2.60}$$

Although these equations are linear, they are still too cumbersome for general use owing to the completely general trim conditions which have been allowed. What is commonly done in AFCS studies is to consider flight cases with simpler trim conditions, a case of great interest being, for example, when an aircraft has been trimmed to fly straight in steady, symmetric flight, with its wings level. Steady flight is motion with the rates of change of the components of linear and angular velocity being zero. Possible steady flight conditions include level turns, steady sideslip and helical turns. Steady pitching flight must be regarded as merely a 'quasi-steady' condition because $\dot{U}$ and $\dot{W}$ cannot both be zero for any appreciable time if Q is not zero. Straight flight is motion with the components of angular velocity being zero. Steady sideslips and dives and climbs without longitudinal acceleration are straight flight conditions. Symmetric flight is motion in which the plane of symmetry of the aircraft remains fixed in space throughout the manoeuvre taking place. Dives and climbs with wings level, and pull-ups without sideslipping, are examples of symmetric flight. Sideslip, rolls and turns are typical asymmetric flight conditions. The significance of the specified trim conditions may be judged when the following implications are understood:

1. That straight flight implies $\dot{\Psi}_0 = \Theta_0 = 0$.
2. That symmetric flight implies $\Psi_0 = V_0 = 0$.
3. That flying with wings level implies $\Phi_0 = 0$.

For this particular trimmed flight state, the aircraft will have particular values of

U_0, W_0 and Θ_0. These may be zero, but for conventional aircraft the steady forward speed, U_0, must be greater than the stall speed if flight is to be sustained. However, certain rotary wing and V/STOL aircraft can achieve a flying state in which U_0, W_0 and Θ_0 may be zero; when U_0 and W_0 are simultaneously zero the aircraft is said to be hovering.

Hence, for straight, symmetric flight with wings level, the equations which represent translational motion in eq. (2.59) become:

$$\begin{aligned} x &= m[\dot{u} + W_0 q + Q_0 w - R_0 v + g\cos\Theta_0\theta] \\ y &= m[\dot{v} + U_0 r + R_0 u - W_0 p - P_0 w - g\cos\Theta_0\phi] \\ z &= m[\dot{w} + P_0 v - U_0 q - Q_0 u + g\sin\Theta_0\theta] \end{aligned} \tag{2.61}$$

The equations (2.59) which represent rotational motion are unaffected. Equation (2.60), however, becomes:

$$\begin{aligned} p &= \dot{\phi} - \dot{\Psi}\sin\Theta_0 \\ q &= \dot{\theta} \\ r &= \Psi\cos\Theta_0 \end{aligned} \tag{2.62}$$

From the same expression, for this trimmed flight state, it may be assumed that:

$$Q_0 = P_0 = R_0 = 0 \tag{2.63}$$

Therefore, it is possible to write eqs (2.59) and (2.61) in the new form:

$$\begin{aligned} x &= m[\dot{u} + W_0 q - g\cos\Theta_0\theta] \\ y &= m[\dot{v} + U_0 r - W_0 p - g\cos\Theta_0\phi] \\ z &= m[\dot{w} - U_0 q + q\sin\Theta_0\theta] \\ l &= I_{xx}\dot{p} - I_{xz}\dot{r} \\ m_1 &= I_{yy}\dot{q} \\ n &= I_{zz}\dot{r} - I_{xz}\dot{p} \end{aligned} \tag{2.64}$$

Consideration of eq. (2.64) indicates not only that the equations have been simplified, but that the set can be separated into two distinct groups which are given below:

$$\begin{aligned} x &= m[\dot{u} + W_0 q - g\cos\Theta_0\theta] \\ z &= m[\dot{w} - U_0 q + g\sin\Theta_0\theta] \\ m_1 &= I_{yy}\dot{q} \end{aligned} \tag{2.65}$$

and

$$\begin{aligned} y &= m[\dot{v} + U_0 r - W_0 p - g\cos\Theta_0\phi] \\ l &= I_{xx}\dot{p} - I_{xz}\dot{r} \end{aligned} \tag{2.66}$$

$$n = I_{zz}\dot{r} - I_{xz}\dot{p}$$

In eq. (2.65) the dependent variables are u, w, q and θ and these are confined to the plane $X_B Z_B$. The set of equations is said to represent the longitudinal motion. The lateral/directional motion, consisting of sideslip, rolling and yawing motion is represented in eq. (2.66). Although it appears from this equation that the sideslip is not coupled to the rolling and yawing accelerations, the motion is, however, coupled (at least implicitly). In practice, a considerable amount of coupling can exist as a result of aerodynamic forces which are contained within the terms on the left-hand side of the equations.

It is noteworthy that this separation of lateral and longitudinal equations is merely a separation of gravitational and inertial forces: this separation is possible only because of the assumed trim conditions. But 'in flight', the six degrees of freedom model may be coupled strongly by those forces and moments which are associated with propulsion or with the aerodynamics.

2.4 COMPLETE LINEARIZED EQUATIONS OF MOTION

2.4.1 Expansion of Aerodynamic Force and Moment Terms

To expand the left-hand side of the equations of motion, a Taylor series is used about the trimmed flight condition. Thus, for example,

$$z = \frac{\partial Z}{\partial u} u + \frac{\partial Z}{\partial \dot{u}} \dot{u} + \frac{\partial Z}{\partial w} w + \frac{\partial Z}{\partial \dot{w}} \dot{w} + \frac{\partial Z}{\partial q} q + \frac{\partial Z}{\partial \dot{q}} \dot{q} + \frac{\partial Z}{\partial \delta_E} \delta_E + \frac{\partial Z}{d\dot{\delta}_E} \dot{\delta}_E + \ldots \tag{2.67}$$

Equation (2.67) supposes that the perturbed force z has a contribution from only one control surface, the elevator. However, if any other control surface on the aircraft being considered were involved, additional terms, accounting for their contribution to z, would be used. For example, if changes of thrust (T), and the deflection of flaps (F) and symmetrical spoilers (sp) were also used as controls for longitudinal motion, additional terms, such as

$$\frac{\partial Z}{\partial \delta_T} \delta_T, \quad \frac{\partial Z}{\partial \delta_F} \delta_F \text{ and } \frac{\partial Z}{\partial \delta_{sp}} \delta_{sp}$$

would be added to eq. (2.67). Furthermore, some terms depending on other motion variables, such as θ, are omitted because they are generally insignificant.

For the moment only longitudinal motion is treated, and, for simplicity, it is assumed that only elevator deflection is involved in the control of the aircraft's longitudinal motion. Thus, it is now possible to write eq. (2.65) as:

$$\frac{\partial X}{\partial u}u + \frac{\partial X}{\partial \dot{u}}\dot{u} + \frac{\partial X}{\partial w}w + \frac{\partial X}{\partial \dot{w}}\dot{w} + \frac{\partial x}{\partial q}q + \frac{\partial X}{\partial \dot{q}}\dot{q} + \frac{\partial X}{\partial \delta_E}\delta_E + \frac{\partial X}{d\dot{\delta}_E}\dot{\delta}_E = m[\dot{u} + W_0 q - g\cos\Theta_0\theta]$$

$$\frac{\partial Z}{\partial u}u + \frac{\partial Z}{\partial \dot{u}}\dot{u} + \frac{\partial Z}{\partial w}w + \frac{\partial Z}{\partial \dot{w}}\dot{w} + \frac{\partial Z}{\partial q}q + \frac{\partial Z}{\partial \dot{q}}\dot{q} + \frac{\partial Z}{\partial \delta_E}\delta_E + \frac{\partial Z}{d\dot{\delta}_E}\dot{\delta}_E = m[\dot{w} - U_0 q + g\sin\Theta_0\theta] \quad (2.68)$$

$$\frac{\partial M}{\partial u}u + \frac{\partial M}{\partial \dot{u}}\dot{u} + \frac{\partial M}{\partial w}w + \frac{\partial M}{\partial \dot{w}}\dot{w} + \frac{\partial M}{\partial q}q + \frac{\partial M}{\partial \dot{q}}\dot{q} + \frac{\partial M}{\partial \delta_E}\delta_E + \frac{\partial M}{d\dot{\delta}_E}\dot{\delta}_E = I_{yy}\dot{q}$$

To simplify the notation it is customary to make the following substitutions:

$$X_x = \frac{1}{m}\frac{\partial X}{\partial x}$$

$$Z_x = \frac{1}{m}\frac{\partial Z}{\partial x} \quad (2.69)$$

$$M_x = \frac{1}{I_{yy}}\frac{\partial M}{\partial x}$$

When this substitution is made the coefficients, such as M_x, Z_x, and X_x, are referred to as the stability derivatives.

2.4.2 Equations of Longitudinal Motion

Equation (2.68) may now be rewritten in the following form:

$$\dot{u} = X_u u + X_{\dot{u}}\dot{u} + X_w w + X_{\dot{w}}\dot{w} + X_q q + X_{\dot{q}}\dot{q} - W_0 q - g\cos\Theta_0\theta + X_{\delta_E}\delta_E + X_{\dot{\delta}_E}\dot{\delta}_E$$

$$\dot{w} = Z_u u + Z_{\dot{u}}\dot{u} + Z_w w + Z_{\dot{w}}\dot{w} + Z_q q + Z_{\dot{q}}\dot{q} + U_0 q - g\sin\Theta_0\theta + Z_{\delta_E}\delta_E + Z_{\dot{\delta}_E}\dot{\delta}_E \quad (2.70)$$

$$\dot{q} = M_u u + M_{\dot{u}}\dot{u} + M_w w + M_{\dot{w}}\dot{w} + M_q q + M_{\dot{q}}\dot{q} + M_{\delta_E}\delta_E + M_{\dot{\delta}_E}\dot{\delta}_E$$

For completeness, the second equation of (2.62) is usually added to eq. (2.70), i.e.

$$\dot{\theta} = q \quad (2.70a)$$

From studying the aerodynamic data of a large number of aircraft it becomes evident that not every stability derivative is significant and, frequently, a number can be neglected. However, it is essential to remember that such stability derivatives depend both upon the aircraft being considered and the flight condition which applies. Thus, before ignoring stability derivatives, it is important to check the appropriate aerodynamic data. Without loss of generality it can be assumed that the following stability derivatives are often insignificant, and may be ignored:

$$X_{\dot{u}}, X_q, X_{\dot{w}}, X_{\delta_E}, Z_{\dot{u}}, Z_{\dot{w}}, M_{\dot{u}}, Z_{\dot{\delta}_E} \text{ and } M_{\dot{\delta}_E}.$$

The stability derivative Z_q is usually quite large but often ignored if the trimmed forward speed, U_0, is large. If the case being studied is hovering motion, then Z_q ought not to be ignored. With these assumptions, the equations of perturbed longitudinal motion, for straight, symmetric flight, with wings level, can be expressed as:

$$\begin{aligned} \dot{u} &= X_u u + X_w w + W_0 q - g\cos\Theta_0\theta \\ \dot{w} &= Z_u u + Z_w w + U_0 q - g\sin\Theta_0\theta + Z_{\delta_E}\delta_E \\ \dot{q} &= M_u u + M_w w + M_{\dot{w}}\dot{w} + M_q q + M_{\delta_E}\delta_E \\ \dot{\theta} &= q \end{aligned} \tag{2.71}$$

Notice that each term in the first three equations of (2.71) is an acceleration term, but since the motion and control variables, u, w, q, θ and δ_E, have such units as m s^{-1}, and s^{-1} the stability derivatives appearing in these equations are dimensional. It is possible to write similar equations using non-dimensional stability derivatives, and this is frequently done in American literature and is always done in the British system; but when it is done, the resulting equations must be written in terms of 'dimensionless' time. The responses obtained from those equations are then expressed in units of time which differ from real time. If the reader requires details of the use of non-dimensional stability derivatives, Babister (1961) should be consulted. It has been decided in this book to use the form of equations given in (2.71) where dimensional stability derivatives must be used (these are the stability derivatives which are usually quoted in American works) but where time is real. Such a decision makes the design of AFCSs much easier and more direct for it allows direct simulation, and also makes the interpretation of the aircraft responses in terms of flying qualities more straightforward.

2.4.3 Equations of Lateral Motion

From eqs (2.64) and (2.62) the following set of equations applies to lateral motion:

$$\begin{aligned} y &= m[\dot{v} + U_0 r - W_0 p - g\cos\Theta_0\phi] \\ l &= I_{xx}\dot{p} - I_{xz}\dot{r} \\ n &= I_{zz}\dot{r} - I_{xz}\dot{p} \end{aligned} \tag{2.72}$$

$$\dot{p} = \dot{\phi} - \dot{\Psi} \sin \Theta_0$$
$$\dot{r} = \dot{\Psi} \cos \Theta_0$$

Expanding the left-hand side of the first three equations results in the following (subscripts A and R indicate aileron and rudder, respectively):

$$\begin{aligned}
&\frac{\partial Y}{\partial v} v + \frac{\partial Y}{\partial \dot{v}} \dot{v} + \frac{\partial Y}{\partial r} r + \frac{\partial Y}{\partial \dot{r}} \dot{r} + \frac{\partial Y}{\partial p} p + \frac{\partial Y}{\partial \dot{p}} p + \frac{\partial Y}{\partial \delta_A} \delta_A + \frac{\partial Y}{\partial \delta_R} \delta_R \\
&\qquad = m[\dot{v} + U_0 r - W_0 p - g \cos \Theta_0 \phi] \\
&\frac{\partial L}{\partial v} v + \frac{\partial L}{\partial \dot{v}} \dot{v} + \frac{\partial L}{\partial r} r + \frac{\partial L}{\partial \dot{r}} \dot{r} + \frac{\partial L}{\partial p} p + \frac{\partial L}{\partial \dot{p}} p + \frac{\partial L}{\partial \delta_A} \delta_A + \frac{\partial L}{\partial \delta_R} \delta_R \\
&\qquad = I_{xx}\dot{p} - I_{xz}\dot{r} \qquad (2.73) \\
&\frac{\partial N}{\partial v} v + \frac{\partial N}{\partial \dot{v}} \dot{v} + \frac{\partial N}{\partial r} r + \frac{\partial N}{\partial \dot{r}} \dot{r} + \frac{\partial N}{\partial p} p + \frac{\partial N}{\partial \dot{p}} p + \frac{\partial N}{\partial \delta_A} \delta_A + \frac{\partial N}{\partial \delta_R} \delta_R \\
&\qquad = I_{zz}\dot{r} - I_{xz}\dot{p}
\end{aligned}$$

Adopting the more convenient notation, namely:

$$Y_j \triangleq \frac{1}{m} \frac{\partial Y}{\partial j} \qquad L_j \triangleq \frac{1}{I_{xx}} \frac{\partial L}{\partial j} \qquad N_j \triangleq \frac{1}{I_{zz}} \frac{\partial N}{\partial j} \qquad (2.74)$$

allows the eqs (2.73) to be written more simply as:

$$\begin{aligned}
\dot{v} &= Y_v v + Y_{\dot{v}} \dot{v} + Y_r r + Y_p p + Y_{\dot{r}} \dot{r} + Y_{\dot{p}} \dot{p} + Y_{\delta_A} \delta_A + Y_{\delta_R} \delta_R + U_0 r \\
&\quad - W_0 p - g \cos \Theta_0 \phi \\
\dot{p} &= \frac{I_{xz}}{I_{xx}} \dot{r} + L_v v + L_{\dot{v}} \dot{v} + L_r r + L_{\dot{r}} \dot{r} + L_p p + L_{\dot{p}} \dot{p} + L_{\delta_A} \delta_A + L_{\delta_R} \delta_R \\
&\qquad (2.75) \\
\dot{r} &= \frac{I_{xz}}{I_{zz}} \dot{p} + N_v v + N_{\dot{v}} \dot{v} + N_r r + N_{\dot{r}} \dot{r} + N_p p + N_{\dot{p}} \dot{p} + N_{\delta_A} \delta_A + N_{\delta_R} \delta_R
\end{aligned}$$

For conventional aircraft, it can usually be assumed that the following stability derivatives are insignificant:

$$Y_{\dot{v}},\ Y_{\mathrm{p}},\ Y_{\dot{p}},\ Y_r,\ Y_{\dot{r}},\ Y_{\delta_A},\ L_{\dot{v}},\ L_{\dot{r}},\ N_{\dot{v}},\ N_{\dot{r}}\ .$$

Note, however, that Y_r may be significant if U_0 is small. When this assumption is made the equations governing perturbed lateral/directional motion of the aircraft are given by:

$$\begin{aligned}
\dot{v} &= Y_v v + U_0 r - W_0 p - g \cos \Theta_0 \phi + Y_{\delta_R} \delta_R \\
\dot{p} &= \frac{I_{xz}}{I_{xx}} \dot{r} + L_v v + L_p p + L_r r + L_{\delta_A} \delta_A + L_{\delta_R} \delta_R \\
\dot{r} &= \frac{I_{xz}}{I_{zz}} \dot{p} + N_v v + N_p p + N_r r + N_{\delta_A} \delta_A + N_{\delta_R} \delta_R \qquad (2.76)
\end{aligned}$$

$$\dot{p} = \dot{\phi} - \dot{\Psi} \sin \Theta_0$$
$$\dot{r} = \dot{\Psi} \cos \Theta_0$$

2.5 EQUATIONS OF MOTION IN STABILITY AXIS SYSTEM

The aerodynamic forces which contribute to the x, y and z terms in eq. (2.65) are the components of lift and drag resolved into the body-fixed axes. The angles which orient the forces of lift and drag relative to the body-fixed axes are: the angle of attack, α, and the angle of sideslip, β. The angles are defined in Figure 2.5 where the subscript 'α' has been used to indicate that the velocity and its components are relative in the sense of airframe to air mass. If the velocity of the air mass is constant relative to inertial space, then the subscript 'α' can be dropped. The velocity components along the body axes are:

$$\begin{aligned} U_\alpha &= V_{T_\alpha} \cos\beta \cos\alpha \\ V_\alpha &= V_{T_\alpha} \sin\beta \\ W_\alpha &= V_{T_\alpha} \cos\beta \sin\alpha \end{aligned} \tag{2.77}$$

Earlier it was shown that if symmetric flight was assumed, V_0 would be zero. Therefore, if the axis system is oriented such that W_0 is zero, then both α_0 and β_0 are zero. This orientation results in the X_B axis, in the steady state, pointing into the relative wind and the X_B axis and the velocity vector being aligned such that:

$$U_0 = V_T \tag{2.78}$$

Such an orientation results in a stability axis system which, initially, is inclined to the horizon at some flight path angle, γ_0, since:

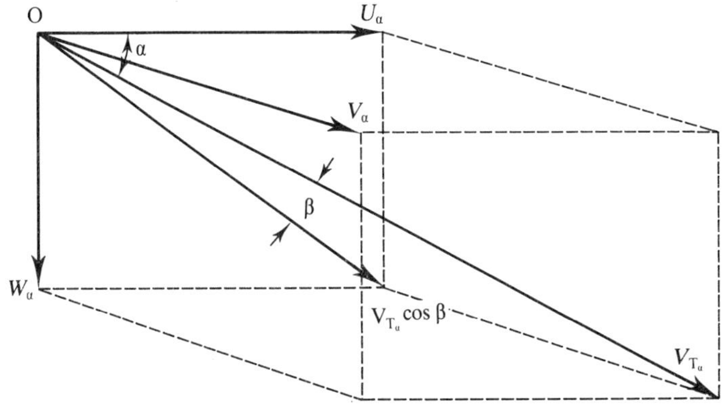

Figure 2.5 Orientation of relative wind with body axis system.

$$\Theta_0 \triangleq \gamma_0 + \alpha_0 \tag{2.79}$$

and α_0 is zero.

This initial alignment does not affect the body-fixed character of the axis system: all the motion due to perturbations is still measured in a body-fixed frame of reference. However, the alignment of the stability axis system with respect to the body axis system changes as a function of the trim conditions. When an aircraft is disturbed from its trim condition, the stability axes rotate with the airframe and, consequently, the perturbed X_s axis may or may not be parallel to the relative wind while the aircraft motion is being disturbed. The situation is illustrated in Figure 2.6.

Using the stability axis system, in which $W_0 = 0$ and $\Theta_0 = \gamma_0$, eq. (2.71) may be expressed as:

$$\begin{aligned}
\dot{u} &= X_u u + X_w w - g \cos \gamma_0 \theta \\
\dot{w} &= Z_u u + Z_w w + U_0 q - g \sin \gamma_0 \theta + Z_{\delta_E} \delta_E \\
\dot{q} &= M_u u + M_w w + M_{\dot{w}} \dot{w} + \mathrm{M}_q q + M_{\delta_E} \delta_E \\
\dot{\theta} &= q
\end{aligned} \tag{2.80}$$

whereas eq. (2.76) may now be written as:

$$\dot{v} = Y_v v + U_0 r - g \cos \gamma_0 \phi + Y_{\delta_R} \delta_R$$

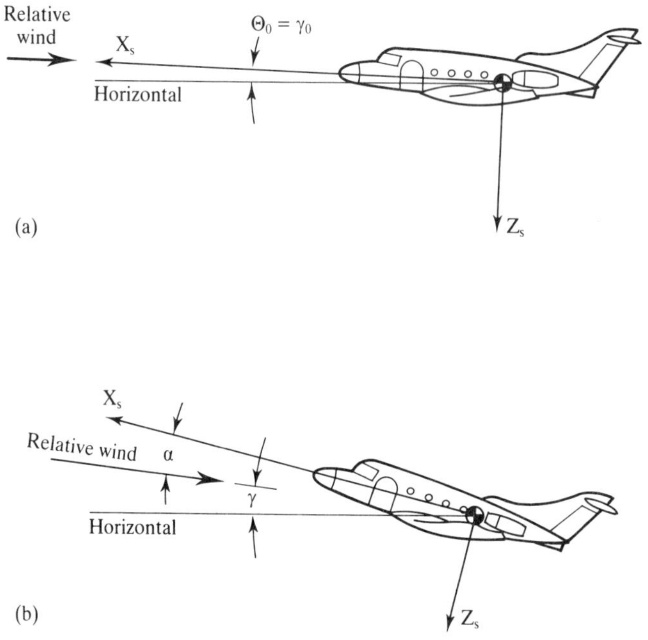

Figure 2.6 Direction of stability axes with respect to the relative wind. (a) Steady flight. (b) Perturbed flight.

$$
\begin{aligned}
\dot{p} &= \frac{I_{xz}}{I_{xx}}\dot{r} + L_v v + L_p p + L_r r + L_{\delta_A}\delta_A + L_{\delta_R}\delta_R \\
\dot{r} &= \frac{I_{xz}}{I_{zz}}\dot{p} + N_v v + N_p p + N_r r + N_{\delta_A}\delta_A + N_{\delta_R}\delta_R \\
\dot{\phi} &= p + r\tan\gamma_0 \\
\psi &= r/\cos\gamma_0
\end{aligned}
\tag{2.81}
$$

The cross-product inertia terms which appear in eq. (2.81) can be eliminated by a simple mathematical procedure: the use of primed stability derivatives. By ignoring second order effects, the cross-product of inertia terms are taken into account in the following primed stability derivatives:

$$
\begin{aligned}
L'_\beta &= L_\beta + I_B N_\beta & N'_\beta &= N_\beta + I_A L_\beta \\
L'_p &= L_p + I_B N_p & N'_p &= N_p + I_A L_p \\
L'_r &= L_r + I_B N_r & N'_r &= N_r + I_A L_r \\
L'_{\delta_A} &= L_{\delta_A} + I_B N_{\delta_A} & N_{\delta_A} &= N_{\delta_A} + I_A L_{\delta_A} \\
L'_{\delta_R} &= L_{\delta_R} + I_B N_{\delta_R} & N'_{\delta_R} &= N_{\delta_R} + I_A L_{\delta_R}
\end{aligned}
\tag{2.82}
$$

in which

$$I_A \triangleq I_{xz}/I_{xx} \tag{2.83}$$

$$I_B \triangleq I_{xz}/I_{zz} \tag{2.84}$$

Then eq. (2.18) becomes

$$
\begin{aligned}
\dot{v} &= Y_v v + U_0 r - g\cos\gamma_0\phi + Y_{\delta_R}\delta_R \\
\dot{p} &= L'_v v + L'_p p + L'_r r + L'_{\delta_A}\delta_A + L'_{\delta_R}\delta_R \\
\dot{r} &= N'_v v + N'_p p + N'_r r + N'_{\delta_A}\delta_A + N'_{\delta_R}\delta_R \\
\dot{\phi} &= p + r\tan\gamma_0 \\
\dot{\psi} &= r\sec\gamma_0
\end{aligned}
\tag{2.85}
$$

2.6 EQUATIONS OF MOTION FOR STEADY MANOEUVRING FLIGHT CONDITIONS

Steady flight conditions provide the reference values for many studies of aircraft motion. Once the relationships for steady flight are known, they are used subsequently to eliminate initial forces and moments from the equations of motion. How these steady relationships are determined is covered in the next sections.

2.6.1 Steady, Straight Flight

This is the simplest case of steady flight. All time derivatives are zero and there is no angular velocity about the centre of gravity. Therefore, setting to zero all time derivatives, the angular velocities P, Q, R, and the time derivatives of angular position (attitude) reduces eq. (2.56) to:

$$\begin{aligned} X_0 &= mg \sin \Theta \\ Y_0 &= -\, mg \cos \Theta \sin \Phi \\ Z_0 &= -\, mg \cos \Theta \cos \Phi \\ L_0 &= M_0 = N_0 = 0 \end{aligned} \tag{2.86}$$

These equations can be applied to a steady sideslip manoeuvre, for the velocity components V, W, and the bank angle, Φ, are not necessarily zero. However, if the motion is restricted to symmetric flight, the bank angle is zero. For this case, the equations become:

$$\begin{aligned} X_0 &= mg \sin \Theta \\ Y_0 &= 0 \\ Z_0 &= -\, mg \cos \Theta \end{aligned} \tag{2.87}$$

Again, all the moments are zero.

2.6.2 Steady Turns

In this case, the time derivatives are all zero again and the rates of change of the Euler angles, Φ and Θ, are also zero; the rate of turn, $\dot{\Psi}$, is constant. Generally, such steady, turning manoeuvres are carried out for very small pitching angles, or for shallow climbing or diving turns. Hence, for small θ, the following relationships hold (see eq. (2.46)):

$$\begin{aligned} P &= -\, \dot{\Psi}\, sin\, \Theta \simeq -\, \dot{\Psi}\theta \\ Q &= \dot{\Psi} \cos \Theta \sin \Phi \simeq \dot{\Psi} \sin \Phi \\ R &= \dot{\Psi} \cos \Theta \cos \Phi \simeq \dot{\Psi} \cos \Phi \end{aligned} \tag{2.88}$$

For most manoeuvres of this type, $\dot{\Psi}$, although constant, is small so that the products of P, Q and R may be neglected. Furthermore, for co-ordinated shallow turns, the side force Y is zero (by definition) and the velocity components V and W are small. Therefore, for a steady, co-ordinated, shallow turn, the equations become:

$$\begin{aligned} X &= mg\Theta \\ Z &= -\, m(\dot{\Psi} U \sin \Phi + g \cos \Phi) \end{aligned} \tag{2.89}$$

$$\dot{\Psi} = \frac{g}{U_0} \tan \Phi$$

Again, all the moments are zero.

2.6.3 Steady Pitching Flight

Symmetric flight of an aircraft along a curved flight path, with constant pitching velocity Q, results in a quasi-steady flight condition. In this case, U and W do vary with time but V, P, R, Φ and Ψ are all zero. Therefore, the equations of motion for a rigid body aircraft reduce to:

$$\begin{aligned} X &= m(\dot{U} + QW) + mg \sin \Theta \\ Z &= m(\dot{W} - QU) - mg \cos \Theta \qquad (2.90) \\ L &= M = N = Y = 0 \end{aligned}$$

Equation (2.90) can be used to evaluate the initial conditions which are used in the small perturbation analysis. For reasonable values of pitch rate, the linear accelerations $\dot{u}$ and $\dot{w}$ are negligibly small; consequently, eq. (2.90) becomes the initial conditions:

$$\begin{aligned} X_0 &= m(Q_0 W_0 + g \sin \Theta_0) \\ Z_0 &= -m(Q_0 U_0 + g \cos \Theta_0) \end{aligned} \qquad (2.91)$$

If the second equation is solved, a relationship is obtained between the initial pitch rate Q_0 and the initial load factor n_{z_0}, along the Z_B axis:

$$\begin{aligned} Q_0 &= \frac{g}{U_0}\left(-\frac{Z_0}{mg} - \cos \Theta_0\right) \\ &= \frac{g}{U_0}(n_{z_0} - \cos \Theta_0) \end{aligned} \qquad (2.92)$$

where

$$n_{z_0} = -Z_0/mg \qquad (2.93)$$

2.6.4 Steady Rolling (Spinning) Flight

The equations of motion for steady rolling (spinning) flight cannot be simplified without improperly describing the physical situation so that the results obtained are unrepresentative of the actual motion. Special methods of treatment are required and, consequently, no such simplified equations are developed here. See, for example, Thelander (1965) for such methods.

2.7 ADDITIONAL MOTION VARIABLES

Even for the straightforward case of straight, steady, wings level, symmetric flight, the designer of AFCSs may be interested in motion variables other than the primary ones of change in forward speed u, in vertical velocity w, in pitch rate q, in pitch attitude θ, in sideslip velocity v, in roll rate p, in yaw rate r, in bank angle ϕ, and in yaw angle ψ. Other commonly used motion variables are treated here, with particular regard to the development of their relationship to the primary motion variables. Such additional motion variables are usually those which can be measured by the sensors commonly available on aircraft.

2.7.1 Longitudinal Motion

Normal acceleration, for perturbed motion, and measured at the c.g. of the aircraft, is defined as:

$$a_{z_{cg}} = (\dot{w} - U_0 q) \tag{2.94}$$

For small angles of attack, α,

$$\begin{aligned} w &\simeq U_0\alpha \\ \therefore \quad a_{z_{cg}} &= U_0(\dot{\alpha} - q) \end{aligned} \tag{2.95}$$

In aircraft applications, acceleration is often measured in units of g, in which case

$$n_{z_{cg}} = \frac{a_{z_{cg}}}{g} \tag{2.96}$$

When an aircraft changes its attitude, the steady, normal acceleration due to gravity, g, also changes. In that case:

$$a_{z_{cg}} = \dot{w} - U_0 q - g \tag{2.97}$$

If it is required to know the acceleration at some point, x distant from the c.g. by l_x, but still on the fuselage centre line, that acceleration is given by:

$$a_{z_x} = \dot{w} - U_0 q - l_x \dot{q} \tag{2.98}$$

The distance l_x from the c.g. is measured positive forwards. By definition:

$$\ddot{h}_{cg} = -\, a_{z_{cg}} \tag{2.99}$$

where h is the height of the aircraft's c.g. above the ground. Consequently:

$$\dot{h}_{cg} = -\, w + U_0\theta \tag{2.100}$$

$$\begin{aligned} h_{cg} &= U_0\int\theta dt - \int w dt \\ &= U_0\int\gamma dt \end{aligned} \tag{2.101}$$

$$\therefore \quad n_{z_{cg}} = -U_0\dot{\gamma}/g \tag{2.102}$$

The variation of load factor with the angle of attack of an aircraft, n_{z_α}, is an important aircraft parameter known as the acceleration sensitivity. It will be shown in Chapter 3 how n_{z_α} can be determined from the stability derivatives and the equations of motion; the result obtained there is quoted here for convenience:

$$\begin{aligned} n_{z_\alpha} &= \frac{U_0}{g} \frac{(Z_{\delta_E} M_w - M_{\delta_E} Z_w)}{\left(M_{\delta_E} - Z_{\delta_E} \frac{M_q}{U_0} \right)} \\ &\simeq \frac{U_0}{g M_{\delta_E}} (Z_{\delta_E} M_w - M_{\delta_E} Z_w) \end{aligned} \tag{2.103}$$

Usually, for conventional aircraft, $M_{\delta_E} Z_w \gg Z_{\delta_E} M_w$; consequently:

$$n_{z_\alpha} = -\, Z_w U_0 / g \tag{2.104}$$

For straight and level flight, at 1 g,

$$n_{z_\alpha} = -\, Z_w U_0 = C_{L_\alpha} / C_L \tag{2.105}$$

where C_{L_α} is the lift curve slope and C_L is the coefficient of lift.

2.7.2 Lateral Motion

In lateral motion, the perturbed acceleration at the c.g. of the aircraft is defined by:

$$a_{y_{cg}} \triangleq \dot{v} - g\phi + U_0 r \tag{2.106}$$

If it is required to know the lateral acceleration at some point, x_{lat}, on the OX axis, distant from the c.g. by $l_{x_{lat}}$, and displaced a distance, l_z, on the OZ axis, the appropriate equation is:

$$a_{y_{x_{lat}}} = a_{y_{cg}} + l_{x_{lat}} \dot{r} - l_z \dot{p} \tag{2.107}$$

$l_{x_{lat}}$ is measured positive forwards of the c.g. and l_z is measured positive downwards. Heading angle, λ, is defined as the sum of sideslip, β, and yaw angle, Ψ.

2.8 THE STATE AND OUTPUT EQUATIONS

2.8.1 The State Equation

A state equation is a first order, vector differential equation. It is a natural form in which to represent the equation of motion of an aircraft. Its most general expression is:

$$\dot{\mathbf{x}} = A\mathbf{x} + B\mathbf{u} \qquad (2.108)^4$$

where $\mathbf{x} \in R^n$ is the state vector, $\mathbf{u} \in R^m$ is the control vector.

The elements of the vector $\mathbf{x}$ are termed the state variables and the elements of the vector $\mathbf{u}$ the control input variables. A is the state coefficient matrix and B the driving matrix; they are of order $(n \times n)$ and $(n \times m)$, respectively.

From an inspection of eq. (2.108) it should be observed that the l.h.s. terms involve only first derivatives of the state variables with respect to time; the r.h.s. depends solely upon the state vector $\mathbf{x}$ and the control vector $\mathbf{u}$. Thus, the state equation is an attractive mathematical form for aircraft control and stability studies since its solution for known inputs can easily be obtained by means of integration. Furthermore, this same form of equation lends itself to simulation. In Chapter 1 it was stated that the flight of an aircraft can be affected as much by disturbances such as atmospheric turbulence as by deliberate control inputs, $\mathbf{u}$. Such disturbances can be taken into account by adding a term to the r.h.s. of eq. (2.108), i.e.:

$$\dot{\mathbf{x}} = A\mathbf{x} + B\mathbf{u} + E\mathbf{d} \qquad (2.109)$$

where $\mathbf{d}$ is a vector of dimension l which represents the l sources of disturbance. The associated matrix, E, is of order $(n \times l)$. If the disturbances are random, special methods are used to introduce the disturbances into the aircraft's state equation which is generally considered to be deterministic. These methods are dealt with separately in Chapter 5, and, consequently, for the remainder of this chapter $\mathbf{d}$ will be regarded as a null vector.

Any set of first order, linear, constant coefficient, ordinary differential equations can be combined into the form of eq. (2.108).

2.8.2 The Output Equation

If the concern is with motion variables other than those chosen as state variables, then an output equation is wanted. The output equation is merely an algebraic equation which depends solely upon the state vector, and, occasionally, upon the control vector also. Its customary form of expression is:

$$\mathbf{y} = C\mathbf{x} + D\mathbf{u} \qquad (2.110)^5$$

The output vector is $\mathbf{y} \in R^P$ and its elements are referred to as the output variables. The matrices C and D, the output and direct matrix respectively, are generally rectangular and are of order $(p \times n)$ and $(p \times m)$, respectively.

For AFCS work the sensors used to measure motion variables, for use as feedback signals, are often subject to measurement noise. To incorporate these noise effects into an output equation requires the addition of another term to eq. (2.110):

$$\mathbf{y} = C\mathbf{x} + D\mathbf{u} + F\boldsymbol{\xi} \qquad (2.111)^6$$

The characterization of sensor noise and how it is modelled dynamically are dealt with in Chapter 5. For the rest of this present chapter $\boldsymbol{\xi}$ is assumed to be null.

2.8.3 Aircraft Equations of Longitudinal Motion

If the state vector is defined as, say:

$$\mathbf{x} = \begin{bmatrix} u \\ w \\ q \\ \theta \end{bmatrix} \tag{2.112}$$

and if an aircraft is being controlled only by means of elevator deflection, δ_E, such that its control vector is defined as:

$$\mathbf{u} \triangleq \delta_E \tag{2.113}$$

then, from eq. (2.80):

$$A \triangleq \begin{bmatrix} X_u & X_w & 0 & -g\cos\gamma_0 \\ Z_u & Z_w & U_0 & -g\sin\gamma_0 \\ \tilde{M}_u & \tilde{M}_w & \tilde{M}_q & \tilde{M}_\theta \\ 0 & 0 & 1 & 0 \end{bmatrix} \tag{2.114}$$

$$B \triangleq \begin{bmatrix} X_{\delta_E} \\ Z_{\delta_E} \\ \tilde{M}_{\delta_E} \\ 0 \end{bmatrix} \tag{2.115}$$

The significance of the tilde in row 3 of eq. (2.114) is easily explained. In eq. (2.80) the equation for $\dot{q}$ was written as:

$$\dot{q} = M_u u + M_w w + M_{\dot{w}}\dot{w} + M_q q + M_{\delta_E}\delta_E \tag{2.116}$$

It is obvious that a term in $\dot{w}$ exists on the r.h.s. of the equation. The state equation, though, does not admit on its r.h.s. terms involving the first (or even higher) derivatives of any of the state or control variables. Fortunately, $\dot{w}$, itself, depends only upon $\mathbf{x}$ and $\mathbf{u}$ and, therefore, an easy substitution is possible. In eq. (2.80) the equation for $\dot{w}$ is given as:

$$\dot{w} = Z_u u + Z_w w + U_0 q - g\sin\gamma_0\theta + M_{\delta_E}\delta_E \tag{2.117}$$

Substituting for w in the equation for q yields:

$$\dot{q} = (M_u + M_{\dot{w}}Z_u)u + (M_w + M_{\dot{w}}Z_w)w$$

$$+ (M_q + M_{\dot{w}}U_0)q - gM_{\dot{w}} \sin \gamma_0\theta + (M_{\delta_E} + M_{\dot{w}}Z_{\delta_E})\delta_E$$

i.e.

$$\dot{q} = \tilde{M}_u u + \tilde{M}_w w + \tilde{M}_q q + \tilde{M}_\theta \theta + \tilde{M}_{\delta_E}\delta_E \tag{2.118}$$

where

$$\begin{aligned}
\tilde{M}_u &= (M_u + M_{\dot{w}}Z_u) \\
\tilde{M}_w &= (M_w + M_{\dot{w}}Z_w) \\
\tilde{M}_q &= (M_q + U_0 M_{\dot{w}}) \\
\tilde{M}_\theta &= (-\, gM_w \sin \gamma_0) \\
\tilde{M}_{\delta_E} &= (M_{\delta_E} + M_{\dot{w}}Z_{\delta_E})
\end{aligned} \tag{2.119}$$

If there were some other control inputs on the aircraft being considered, say, for example, a change of thrust, δ_{th}, and a deflection of symmetrical spoilers, δ_{sp}, then the order of the driving matrix, B, becomes (4×3) and the elements of the matrix become:

$$B = \begin{bmatrix} X_{\delta_E} & X_{\delta_{th}} & X_{\delta_{sp}} \\ Z_{\delta_E} & Z_{\delta_{th}} & Z_{\delta_{sp}} \\ \tilde{M}_{\delta_E} & \tilde{M}_{\delta_{th}} & \tilde{M}_{\delta_{sp}} \\ 0 & 0 & 0 \end{bmatrix} \tag{2.120}$$

It must be understood that the state equation is not an unique description of the aircraft dynamics. For example, if the state vector had been chosen to be

$$\mathbf{x} \triangleq \begin{bmatrix} \theta \\ q \\ u \\ w \end{bmatrix} \tag{2.121}$$

rather than the choice of eq. (2.11), A and B must be changed to:

$$A = \begin{bmatrix} 0 & 0 & 1 & 0 \\ \tilde{M}_u & \tilde{M}_w & \tilde{M}_q & \tilde{M}_\theta \\ X_u & X_w & 0 & -\, g \cos \gamma_0 \\ Z_u & Z_w & U_0 & -\, g \sin \gamma_0 \end{bmatrix} \tag{2.122}$$

$$B = \begin{bmatrix} 0 \\ \tilde{M}_{\delta_E} \\ X_{\delta_E} \\ Z_{\delta_E} \end{bmatrix} \tag{2.123}$$

When the state equation is solved, with either set of A and B, the responses obtained for the same control input, δ_E, will be identical.

In American work it is common to use as a primary motion variable the angle of attack, α, rather than the heave velocity, w. Since, for small angles:

$$\alpha = w/U_0 \tag{2.124}$$

then:

$$\dot{\alpha} = \dot{w}/U_0 \tag{2.125}$$

$$d\alpha U_0 = dw \tag{2.126}$$

$$\therefore \quad \dot{\alpha} = \frac{Z_u}{U_0}u + Z_w\frac{w}{U_0} + q + \frac{Z_{\delta_E}}{U_0}\delta_E \tag{2.127}$$

$$= Z_u^* u + Z_w\alpha + q + Z_{\delta_E}^*\delta_E \quad (2.127)$$

where

$$Z_u^* = Z_u/U_0 \text{ and } Z_{\delta_E}^* = Z_{\delta_E}/U_0 .$$

Frequently, again in American papers, a stability derivative Z_α is quoted, and eq. (2.127) is written as:

$$\dot{\alpha} = Z_u^* u + Z_\alpha\alpha + q + Z_{\delta_E}^*\delta_E \tag{2.128}$$

The reader is warned, however, that confusion can occur with this form. In eq. (2.128) Z_α is identical to Z_w in eq. (2.127), but, for consistency of notation, Z_α ought to be defined as:

$$Z_\alpha \triangleq \partial Z/\partial\alpha = Z_w U_0 \tag{2.129}$$

Z_α is sometimes quoted as a value which turns out to be identical to Z_w, and sometimes as equal to $Z_w U_0$. The student is advised *always* to use the form of equation given in (2.117) and from the state equation obtain the heave velocity w. If the angle of attack is required, then determine α from eq. (2.124). In this way, ambiguity and confusion can be avoided.

If the output variable of interest was, say, a_{z_x}, then eq. (2.98) can easily be shown (by substitution for w and q) to be given by:

$$a_{z_x} = (Z_u - l_x\tilde{M}_u)u + (Z_w - l_x\tilde{M}_w)w - l_x\tilde{M}_q q + (Z_{\delta_E} - l_x\tilde{M}_{\delta_E})\delta_E \tag{2.130}$$

Hence:

$$y \triangleq a_{z_x} = [(Z_u - l_x\tilde{M}_u)(Z_w - l_x\tilde{M}_w) - l_x\tilde{M}_q \;\; 0]\mathbf{x} + [(Z_{\delta_E} - l_x\tilde{M}_{\delta_E})]\mathbf{u} \tag{2.131}$$

which is the same form as eq. (2.110), where

$$C = [(Z_u - l_x\tilde{M}_u)(Z_w - l_x\tilde{M}_w) - l_x\tilde{M}_q \quad 0] \tag{2.132}$$

$$D = (Z_{\delta_E} - l_x\tilde{M}_{\delta_E}) \tag{2.133}$$

If the concern is with the height of an aircraft at its c.g., then:

$$\ddot{h}_{cg} = -a_{z_{cg}} \tag{2.99}$$

$$a_{z_{cg}} = Z_u u + Z_w w + Z_{\delta_E}\delta_E \tag{2.134}$$

i.e.

$$\ddot{h} = -Z_u u - Z_w w - Z_{\delta_E}\delta_E$$

To express this in terms of state variables let:

$$x_6 = h \tag{2.135}$$

and let:

$$x_5 = \dot{x}_6 = \dot{h} \tag{2.136}$$

$$\therefore \quad \dot{x}_5 = -Z_u u - Z_w w - Z_{\delta_E}\delta_E \tag{2.137}$$

Hence:

$$\mathbf{x} \triangleq \begin{bmatrix} u \\ w \\ q \\ \theta \\ h \\ \dot{h} \end{bmatrix} \text{ and } \mathbf{u} = [\delta_E] \tag{2.138}$$

Then the state equation (2.108) is obtained once more, i.e.:

$$\dot{\mathbf{x}} = A\mathbf{x} + B\mathbf{u} \tag{2.108}$$

but now:

$$A = \begin{bmatrix} X_u & X_w & 0 & -g\cos\gamma_0 & 0 & 0 \\ Z_u & Z_w & U_0 & -g\sin\gamma_0 & 0 & 0 \\ \tilde{M}_u & \tilde{M}_w & \tilde{M}_q & \tilde{M}_\delta & 0 & 0 \\ 0 & 0 & 1 & 0 & 0 & 0 \\ -Z_u & -Z_w & 0 & 0 & 0 & 0 \\ 0 & 0 & 0 & 0 & 1 & 0 \end{bmatrix} \tag{2.139}$$

$$B = \begin{bmatrix} X_{\delta_E} \\ Z_{\delta_E} \\ \tilde{M}_{\delta_E} \\ 0 \\ -Z_{\delta_E} \\ 0 \end{bmatrix} \tag{2.140}$$

If the motion variable being considered is the flight path angle γ then it can be inferred from eq. (2.79) that:

$$\gamma = \theta - \alpha = \theta - (w/U_0) \tag{2.141}$$

Consequently, if $\mathbf{y} \triangleq \gamma$, then

$$\mathbf{y} = \begin{bmatrix} 0 & -\frac{1}{U_0} & 0 & 1 \end{bmatrix} \mathbf{x} = C\mathbf{x} \tag{2.142}$$

where $\mathbf{x}$ is defined as in eq. (2.112).

2.8.4 Aircraft Equations of Lateral Motion

For lateral motion, the control vector may be defined as:

$$\mathbf{u} \triangleq \begin{bmatrix} \delta_A \\ \delta_R \end{bmatrix} \tag{2.143}$$

If the state vector, $\mathbf{x}$, is defined as:

$$\mathbf{x} \triangleq \begin{bmatrix} v \\ p \\ r \\ \phi \\ \psi \end{bmatrix} \tag{2.144}$$

then the state equation is given by:

$$\dot{\mathbf{x}} = A\mathbf{x} + B\mathbf{u} \tag{2.108}$$

where:

$$A = \begin{bmatrix} Y_v & 0 & U_0 & -g\cos\gamma_0 & 0 \\ L'_v & L'_p & L'_r & 0 & 0 \\ N'_v & N'_p & N'_p & 0 & 0 \\ 0 & 1 & \tan\gamma_0 & 0 & 0 \\ 0 & 0 & \sec\gamma_0 & 0 & 0 \end{bmatrix} \tag{2.145}$$

$$B = \begin{bmatrix} 0 & Y_{\delta_R} \\ L'_{\delta_A} & L'_{\delta_R} \\ N'_{\delta_A} & N'_{\delta_R} \\ 0 & 0 \\ 0 & 0 \end{bmatrix} \tag{2.146}$$

The sideslip angle, β, is often used as a state variable, rather than the sideslip velocity, v. From eq. (2.77), for small angles:

$$v = U_0\beta \tag{2.147}$$

and consequently:

$$\dot{\beta} = Y_v\beta - r + \frac{g}{U_0}\cos\gamma\phi + \frac{Y_{\delta_R}}{U_0}\delta_R \tag{2.148}$$

which may be written as:

$$\dot{\beta} = Y_v\beta - r + \frac{g}{U_0}\cos\gamma_0\phi + Y^*_{\delta_R}\delta_R \tag{2.149}$$

where:

$$Y^*_{\delta_R} = Y_{\delta_R}/U_0 \tag{2.150}$$

If, now, the state vector is defined as:

$$\mathbf{x} = \begin{bmatrix} \beta \\ p \\ r \\ \phi \\ \psi \end{bmatrix} \tag{2.151}$$

then eq. (2.108) obtains, but the coefficient matrix has become:

$$A = \begin{bmatrix} Y_v & 0 & -1 & \frac{g}{U_0}\cos\gamma_0 & 0 \\ L'_\beta & L'_p & L'_r & 0 & 0 \\ N'_\beta & N'_p & N'_r & 0 & 0 \\ 0 & 1 & \tan\gamma_0 & 0 & 0 \\ 0 & 0 & \sec\gamma_0 & 0 & 0 \end{bmatrix} \tag{2.152}$$

The driving matrix has become:

$$B = \begin{bmatrix} 0 & Y^*_{\delta_R} \\ L'_{\delta_A} & L'_{\delta_R} \\ N'_{\delta_A} & N'_{\delta_R} \\ 0 & 0 \\ 0 & 0 \end{bmatrix} \tag{2.153}$$

The fifth column of A in both eqs (2.145) and (2.152) is composed entirely of zeros. The physical significance of this is explained in Chapter 3, but the presence of such a column of zeros can often be avoided by redefining the state vector, as in eq. (2.154) which has now dimension 4; i.e. let:

$$\mathbf{x} = \begin{bmatrix} \beta \\ p \\ r \\ \phi \end{bmatrix} \tag{2.154}$$

then A becomes:

$$A = \begin{bmatrix} Y_v & 0 & -1 & g/U_0 \\ L'_\beta & L'_p & L'_r & 0 \\ N'_\beta & N'_p & N'_r & 0 \\ 0 & 1 & \tan\gamma_0 & 0 \end{bmatrix} \tag{2.155}$$

and B becomes:

$$B = \begin{bmatrix} 0 & Y^*_{\delta_R} \\ L'_{\delta_A} & L'_{\delta_R} \\ N'_{\delta_A} & N'_{\delta_R} \\ 0 & 0 \end{bmatrix} \tag{2.156}$$

It must be emphasized that in straight and level flight (i.e. non-climbing or diving) γ_0 is zero. Consequently, for this flight condition, those elements which appear in the various forms of A, and which depend upon γ_0, will take a value of zero if the element has the form $\sin\gamma_0$ or $\tan\gamma_0$, or will take the value unity if the element involves $\cos\gamma_0$ or $\sec\gamma_0$. Sometimes there is interest in the lateral acceleration of an aircraft at some point x, which is a distance l_x from the c.g. (l_x is positive forwards) and a distance l_z off the axis OX (l_z is positive when down from the c.g.). Hence:

$$a_{y_x} = a_{y_{cg}} + l_x\dot{r} - l_z\dot{p} \tag{2.107}$$

which can easily be shown to be:

$$\begin{aligned} a_{y_x} = {} & (Y_v + l_xN'_v - l_zL'_v)v + (l_xN'_p - l'_zL'_p)p \\ & + (l_xN'_r - l_zL'_r)r + (l_xN'_{\delta_A} - l_zL'_{\delta_A})\delta_A \\ & + (Y^*_{\delta_R} + l_xN'_{\delta_R} - l_zL'_{\delta_R})\delta_R \end{aligned} \tag{2.157}$$

If the output variable $\mathbf{y}$ is taken as the lateral acceleration, then eq. (2.157) can be expressed as:

$$\mathbf{y} = [(Y_v + l_xN'_v - l_zL'_v)(l_xN'_p - l_zL'_p)(l_xN'_r - l_zL'_r) \quad 0]\mathbf{x}$$

$$+ [(l_x N'_{\delta_A} - l_z L'_{\delta_A})(Y^*_{\delta_R} + l_x N'_{\delta_R} - l_z L'_{\delta_R})]\mathbf{u}$$
$$= C\mathbf{x} + D\mathbf{u} \qquad (2.158)$$

2.9 OBTAINING A TRANSFER FUNCTION FROM STATE AND OUTPUT EQUATIONS

Whenever the variables of a linear system are expressed in the complex frequency domain, i.e. as functions of the Laplace variable s, then, whenever the initial conditions can be assumed to be zero, the ratio of the output variable to some particular input variable (all other input variables being considered identically zero) is the transfer function of the system.

Given that the small perturbation dynamics of an aircraft can be represented by a state equation of the form of eq. (2.108) and an output equation of the form of eq. (2.110), namely $\dot{\mathbf{x}} = A\mathbf{x} + B\mathbf{u}$ and $\mathbf{y} = C\mathbf{x} + D\mathbf{u}$ respectively, then, provided that $\mathbf{y}$ is scalar and that only those columns of matrices B and D are used which correspond to the particular control input u_j being considered, then a transfer function relating $\mathbf{y}$ and u_j can be found. If $\mathbf{y}$ is a vector and it is required to find the transfer function corresponding to some particular element, y, as a result of some control input, u_j, the rows of the matrices C and D which correspond to y_i are used in the calculation. To illustrate the procedure consider that $\mathbf{y}$ and $\mathbf{u}$ are scalars. Taking Laplace transforms, and assuming initial conditions are zero, results in eqs (2.108) and (2.110) being expressed as:

$$s\mathbf{X}(s) - A\mathbf{X}(s) = BU(s) \qquad (2.159)$$

$$y(s) = C\mathbf{X}(s) + DU(s) \qquad (2.160)$$

$$\therefore \quad \mathbf{X}(s) = (sI - A)^{-1} BU(s)$$
$$\therefore \quad y(s) = [C(sI - A)^{-1} B + D]U(s) \qquad (2.161)^7$$

$$\therefore \quad y(s)/U(s) \triangleq G(s) = C[sI - A]^{-1} B + D \qquad (2.162)$$

In general, if:

$$G(s) = y_i(s)/u_j(s) \qquad (2.163)$$

then:

$$G(s) = C_i[sI - A]^{-1} B_j + D_{ij} \qquad (2.164)$$

where B_j represents the column of matrix B which corresponds to u_j, and D_{ij} is the ith row of the matrix D corresponding to y_i and the jth column corresponding to u_j. C_i is the ith row of matrix C corresponding to y_i.

It is evident that transfer function relationships can be found for output motion caused by sensor noise or by atmospheric disturbances rather than manoeuvre commands acting through the control inputs, but these are not treated until Chapter 5.

2.10 IMPORTANT STABILITY DERIVATIVES

All stability derivatives are important but some are more important for flight control than others. This section treats only the latter type.

A number of parameters appear frequently in the equations defining stability derivatives. They are listed here for convenience (note that all the stability derivatives presented are dimensional): S is the surface area of the wing, $\bar{c}$ is the mean aerodynamic chord, ρ is the density, and b is the wing span.

2.10.1 Longitudinal Motion

Motion-related

$$M_u \triangleq \frac{\rho S U_0 \bar{c}}{I_{yy}} (C_{m_u} + C_m) \qquad (2.165)^8$$

The non-dimensional pitching moment coefficient C_m is usually zero in trimmed flight, except in cases of thrust asymmetry. M_u represents the change in pitching moment caused by a change in forward speed. Its magnitude can vary considerably and its sign can change with changes in Mach number and in dynamic pressure and also as a result of aeroelastic effects. In modern aircraft, the Mach number effects and the effects of aeroelasticity have become increasingly important. ■

$$Z_w = \frac{\rho S U_0}{2m} (C_{L_\alpha} + C_D) \qquad (2.166)$$

The change in lift coefficient with a change in angle of attack, C_{L_α}, is often referred to as the lift curve slope. It is always positive for values of angle of attack below the stall value. The lift curve slope for the total airframe comprises components due to the wing, the fuselage and the tail. For most conventional aircraft it has been found to be generally true that the wing contributes 85–90 per cent to the value of C_{L_α}. Consequently, any aeroelastic distortion of the wing can appreciably alter C_{L_α} and, hence, Z_w. ■

$$M_w = \frac{\rho S U_0 \bar{c}}{2 I_{yy}} C_{m_\alpha} \qquad (2.167)$$

The non-dimensional stability derivative, C_{m_α}, is the change in the pitching moment coefficient with angle of attack. It is referred to as the 'longitudinal static stability derivative'. C_{m_α} is very much affected by any aeroelastic distortions of the wing, the tail and the fuselage. However, both sign and magnitude of C_{m_α} are principally affected by the location of the c.g. of the aircraft. C_{m_α} is proportional to the distance, x_{AC}, between the c.g. and the aerodynamic centre (a.c.) of the whole aircraft. x_{AC} is measured positive forwards. If x_{AC} is zero, C_{m_α} is zero. If $x_{AC} < 0$, C_{m_α} is negative and the aircraft is statically stable. If the c.g. is aft of the a.c., $x_{AC} < 0$ and C_{m_α} is positive, with the consequence that the aircraft is statically unstable. In going from subsonic to supersonic flight the a.c. generally moves aft, and, therefore, if the c.g. remains fixed, C_{m_α} will tend to increase for a statically stable aircraft. $M_w(M_\alpha)$ is closely related to the aircraft's static margin. The significance of stability, static margin and M_w, is discussed in section 3.3 of Chapter 3, but it can be stated simply here that M_w (or M_α) is the most important longitudinal derivative. ■

$$M_{\dot{w}} = \frac{\rho S \bar{c}^2}{4I_{yy}} C_{m_{\dot{\alpha}}} \tag{2.168}$$

Although $C_{m_{\dot{\alpha}}}$ does not have a powerful effect upon an aircraft's motion, particularly the short period motion, it does have a significant effect. Usually $M_{\dot{w}} < 0$; it increases the damping of the short period motion. ■

$$M_q = \frac{\rho S U_0 \bar{c}^2}{4I_{yy}} C_{m_q} \tag{2.169}$$

For conventional aircraft, M_q contributes a substantial part of the damping of the short period motion. This damping comes mostly from changes in the angle of attack of the tail and it is also proportional to the tail length, l_T. But l_T is the lever arm through which the lift force on the horizontal tail is converted into a moment, i.e.:

$$M_q \alpha l_T^2 \tag{2.170}$$

M_q is a very significant stability derivative which has a primary effect on the handling qualities of the aircraft (see Chapter 6). ■

Control-related

$$Z_{\delta_E} = \frac{-\rho U_0^2 S}{2m} C_{L_{\delta_E}} \tag{2.171}$$

Since $C_{L_{\delta_E}}$ is usually very small, Z_{δ_E} is normally unimportant except when an AFCS involving feedback of normal acceleration is used. Also, if a tailless aircraft is being considered, the effective lever arm for the elevator (or ailerons) is small, hence $C_{L_{\delta_E}}$ may be relatively large compared to $C_{m_{\delta_E}}$. In these cases, Z_{δ_E} cannot safely be neglected in any analysis. ■

$$M_{\delta_E} = \frac{\rho U_0^2 S \bar{c}}{2I_{yy}} C_{m_{\delta_E}} \tag{2.172}$$

$C_{m_{\delta_E}}$ is termed the 'elevator control effectiveness'; it is very important in aircraft design and for AFCS work. When the elevator is located aft of the c.g.,[9] the normal location, $C_{m_{\delta_E}}$ is negative. Its value is determined chiefly by the maximum lift of the wing and also the range of c.g. travel which can occur during a flight. ■

2.10.2 Lateral Motion

Motion-related

$$Y_v = \frac{\rho U_0 S}{2m} C_{y_\beta} \tag{2.173}$$

The sideforce which results from any sideslip motion is usually obtained from the fin of the aircraft, and usually opposes the sideslip motion, i.e. $C_{y_\beta} < 0$. But for aircraft with a slender fuselage, at large values of the angles of attack the forces can be in an aiding direction. For certain (rare) configurations having a wing of low aspect ratio but required to operate at a large value of angle of attack, this force on the fuselage can counter the resisting force of the fin which results in the stability derivative C_{y_β} being positive. Such positive values, even if very small, are undesirable because the reversed (or small) side force makes it difficult for a pilot to detect sideslip motion and consequently makes a co-ordinated turn difficult to achieve. Such values of C_{y_β} also reduce the damping ratio of the dutch roll mode, whereas C_{y_β} normally makes a large contribution to this damping. In the normal case C_{y_β} is not a derivative which causes great difficulty to AFCS designers. ■

$$L_\beta = U_0 L_v = \frac{\rho U_0^2 S b}{2 I_{xx}} C_{l_\beta} \tag{2.174}$$

Note that:

$$L'_\beta = \frac{L_\beta + (I_{xz}/I_{xx}) N_\beta}{1 - (I_{xz}^2/I_{xx} I_{zz})} \tag{2.175}$$

The change in the value of the rolling moment coefficient with sideslip angle C_{l_β} is called the 'effective dihedral'. This derivative is very important in studies concerned with lateral stability and control. It features in the damping of both the dutch roll and the spiral modes. It also affects the manoeuvring capability of an aircraft, particularly when lateral control is being exercised near stall by rudder action only. Usually small negative values of C_{l_β} are wanted, as such values improve the damping of both the dutch roll and the spiral modes, but such values are rarely obtained without considerable aerodynamic difficulty. ■

$$N_\beta = \frac{\rho U_0^2}{2} \frac{S b}{I_{yy}} C_{n_\beta} \tag{2.176}$$

The change in the yawing moment coefficient with change in sideslip angle C_{n_β} is referred to as the 'static directional' or 'weathercock' stability coefficient. It depends upon the area of the fin and the lever arm. The aerodynamic contribution to C_{n_β} from the fin is positive, but the contribution from the aircraft body is negative. A positive value of C_{n_β} is regarded as static directional stability; a negative value signifies static directional instability (see Chapter 3). C_{n_β} primarily establishes the natural frequency of the dutch roll mode and is an important factor in establishing the characteristics of the spiral mode stability. For good handling qualities C_{n_β} should be large, although such values magnify the disturbance effects from side gusts. At supersonic speeds C_{n_β} is adversely affected because the lift curve slope of the fin decreases. ■

$$L_p = \frac{\rho U_0 S b^2}{4 I_{xx}} C_{l_p} \tag{2.177}$$

The change in rolling moment coefficient with change in rolling velocity, C_{l_p} is referred to as the roll damping derivative. Its value is determined almost entirely by the geometry of the wing. In conjunction with $C_{l_{\delta_A}}$ (q.v.), C_{l_p} establishes the maximum rolling velocity which can be obtained from the aircraft: an important flying quality. C_{l_p} is always negative, although it may become positive when the wing (or parts of it) are stalled. ■

$$N_p = \frac{\rho U_0 S b^2}{4 I_{xz}} C_{n_p} \tag{2.178}$$

The change in rolling moment coefficient with a change in rolling velocity, C_{n_p}, is usually negative, although a positive value is desirable. The more negative is C_{n_p} the smaller is the damping ratio of the dutch roll mode and the greater is the sideslip motion which accompanies entry to, or exit from, a turn. ■

$$L_r = \frac{\rho U_0 \mathrm{Sb}^2}{4 I_{xx}} C_{l_r} \tag{2.179}$$

The change in rolling moment coefficient with a change in yawing velocity, C_{l_r}, has a considerable effect on the spiral mode, but does not much affect the dutch roll mode. For good spiral stability, C_{l_r} should be positive but as small as possible. A major contributing factor to C_{l_r} is the lift force from the wing, but if the fin is located either above or below the axis OX it also makes a substantial contribution to C_{l_r}, being positive or negative dependent upon the fin's geometry. ■

$$N_r = \frac{\rho U_0 \mathrm{Sb}^2}{4 I_{zz}} C_{n_r} \tag{2.180}$$

The change in yawing moment coefficient with a change in yawing velocity, C_{n_r}, is referred to as the 'yaw damping derivative'. It is proportional to l_{T}^2. Usually C_{n_r} is negative and is the main contributor to the damping of the dutch roll mode. It also contributes to the stability of the spiral mode. ■

Control-related

$$Y_\delta = \frac{\rho U_0^2 S}{2m} C_{y_\delta} \tag{2.181}$$

The change in side force coefficient with rudder deflection, $C_{y_{\delta_R}}$, is unimportant *except* when considering an AFCS using lateral acceleration as feedback. $C_{y_{\delta_A}}$ is nearly always negligible. Because positive rudder deflection produces a positive side force, $C_{y_{\delta_R}} < 0$. ■

$$L_\delta = \frac{\rho U_0^2 Sb}{2I_{xx}} C_{l_\delta} \tag{2.182}$$

$C_{l_{\delta_R}}$ is the change in rolling moment coefficient which results from rudder deflection. It is usually negligible. Because the rudder is usually located above the axis OX, positive rudder deflection produces positive rolling motion, i.e. $C_{l_{\delta_R}} > 0$.

The change in rolling moment coefficient with a deflection of the ailerons, $C_{l_{\delta_A}}$, is referred to as the *aileron effectiveness*. In lateral dynamics it is the most important control-related stability derivative. It is particularly important for low speed flight where adequate lateral control is needed to counter asymmetric gusts which tend to roll the aircraft. ■

$$N_\delta = \frac{\rho U_0^2 Sb}{2I_{zz}} C_{n_\delta} \tag{2.183}$$

The change in yawing moment coefficient which results from a rudder deflection, $C_{n_{\delta_R}}$, is referred to as the *rudder effectiveness*. When the rudder is deflected to the left (i.e. $\delta_R > 0$) a negative yawing moment is created on the aircraft, i.e. $C_{n_{\delta_R}} < 0$.

The change in yawing moment coefficient which results from an aileron deflection, $C_{n_{\delta_A}}$, results in *adverse yaw* if $C_{n_{\delta_A}} < 0$, for when a pilot deflects the ailerons to produce a turn, the aircraft will yaw initially in a direction opposite to that expected. When $C_{n_{\delta_A}} > 0$ the yaw which results is favourable to that turning manoeuvre, and this is referred to as *proverse yaw*. Whatever sign $C_{n_{\delta_A}}$ takes, its value ought to be small for good lateral control. ■

2.11 THE INCLUSION OF THE EQUATIONS OF MOTION OF THRUST EFFECTS

1. Many of the stability derivatives which are used in the equations of motion are the result not only of aerodynamic forces but of forces arising from flows induced by the propulsion system. Such flows profoundly modify the derivatives but the effects are usually difficult to predict,

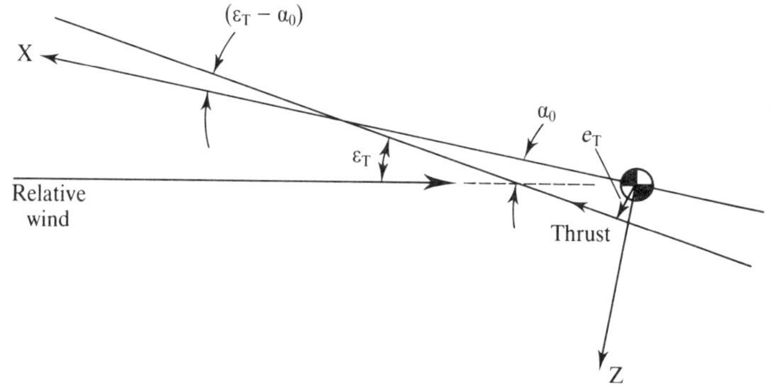

Figure 2.7 Thrust alignment geometry.

requiring special wind tunnel tests for their resolution. But where slipstream interference is minimal, such being the case when a subsonic jet has a central exhaust aft of the tail, the forces and moments associated with direct thrust make considerable contributions to various derivatives. The number of forces associated with the propulsion system include:

(a) The forces acting on the inlet which result when the air mass entering the engine changes direction.
(b) The moments caused by the angular velocity of a tube containing a mass of moving air.
(c) The forces and moments resulting from the thrust itself.

2. The angle which the thrust line makes with the relative wind is ε_T (see Figure 2.7) and is fixed by both the geometry of the aircraft and its trim condition. The angle of the thrust line with respect to the X-axis is fixed at $(\varepsilon_T - \alpha_0)$. Hence:

$$X_T = T \cos(\varepsilon_T - \alpha_0) \tag{2.184}$$

$$Z_T = -T \sin(\varepsilon_T - \alpha_o) \tag{2.185}$$

$$M_T = e_T T \tag{2.186}$$

where the thrust offset e_T is positive downwards.

3. Of course, thrust is a function of density, throttle setting, and the relative speed of the aircraft (on rare occasions it is a function of α_0). Hence:

$$\mathrm{d}X_T = \cos(\varepsilon_T - \alpha_0)\left\{\frac{\partial T}{\partial V}\left(\frac{\partial V}{\partial U}u + \frac{\partial V}{\partial W}w\right) + \frac{\partial T}{\partial \delta_{th}}\delta_{th}\right\} \tag{2.187}$$

$$\mathrm{d}Z_T = \sin(\varepsilon_T - \alpha_0)\left\{\frac{\partial T}{\partial V}\left(\frac{\partial V}{\partial U}u + \frac{\partial V}{\partial W}w\right) + \frac{\partial T}{\partial \delta_{th}}\delta_{th}\right\} \tag{2.188}$$

However:

$$\frac{\partial X_T}{\partial U} = \frac{\partial T}{\partial V}(\cos\varepsilon_T \cos^2\alpha_0 + \sin\varepsilon_T \sin\alpha_0 \cos\alpha_0) \tag{2.189}$$

$$\frac{\partial X_{\rm T}}{\partial W} = \frac{\partial T}{\partial V}(\cos \varepsilon_{\rm T} \sin \alpha_0 \cos \alpha_0 + \sin \varepsilon_{\rm T} \sin^2 \alpha_0) \tag{2.190}$$

$$\frac{\partial X_{\rm T}}{\partial \delta_{\rm th}} = \frac{\partial T}{\partial \delta_{\rm th}}(\cos \varepsilon_{\rm T} \cos \alpha_0 + \sin \varepsilon_{\rm T} \sin \alpha_0) \tag{2.191}$$

$$\frac{\partial Z}{\partial U} = \frac{-\partial T}{\partial V}(\sin \varepsilon_{\rm T} \cos^2 \alpha_0 - \cos \varepsilon_{\rm T} \sin \alpha_0 \cos \alpha_0) \tag{2.192}$$

$$\frac{\partial Z_{\rm T}}{\partial W} = \frac{-\partial T}{\partial V}(\sin \varepsilon_{\rm T} \sin \alpha_0 \cos \alpha_0 - \cos \varepsilon_{\rm T} \sin^2 \alpha_0) \tag{2.193}$$

$$\frac{\partial Z_{\rm T}}{\partial \delta_{\rm th}} = \frac{-\partial T}{\partial \delta_{\rm th}}(\sin \varepsilon_{\rm T} \cos \alpha_0 - \cos \varepsilon_{\rm T} \sin \alpha_0) \tag{2.194}$$

At the trim condition, however, the total moment must be zero, i.e. the thrust moment must be balanced by an equal and opposite aerodynamic moment. Thus:

$$M_0 = T_0 e_{\rm T} + \frac{\rho U_0^2}{2} S\bar{c}C_m = 0 \tag{2.195}$$

$$\begin{aligned} {\rm d}M = e_{\rm T}\left\{\frac{\partial T}{\partial V}\left(\frac{\partial V}{\partial U}u + \frac{\partial V}{\partial W}w\right) + \frac{\partial T}{\partial \delta_{\rm th}}\delta_{\rm th}\right\} \\ + \rho U_0 S\bar{c}C_m\left(\frac{\partial V}{\partial U}u + \frac{\partial V}{\partial W}w\right) \end{aligned} \tag{2.196}$$

From eq. (2.195), however:

$$T_0 e_{\rm T} = \frac{-\rho U_0^2 S\bar{c}}{2} C_m \tag{2.197}$$

i.e.

$$\rho U_0 S\bar{c}C_m = \frac{-2T_0 e_{\rm T}}{U_0} \tag{2.198}$$

$$\therefore \quad {\rm d}M = e_{\rm T}\left\{\left(\frac{\partial T}{\partial V} - \frac{2T_0}{U_0}\right)(u \cos \alpha_0 + w \sin \alpha_0) + \frac{\partial T}{\partial \delta_{\rm th}}\delta_{\rm th}\right\} \tag{2.199}$$

It is evident that the perturbations in moment due to thrust are influenced by the trim condition term, T_0/U_0.

4. Thrust can be written as:

$$T = \frac{\rho U_0^2}{2} SC_{\rm th} \tag{2.200}$$

However, $C_{\rm th}$ is *not* an aerodynamic coefficient so that eq. (2.200) is misleading. The thrust contribution manifests itself chiefly in X_u and is expressed in the form:

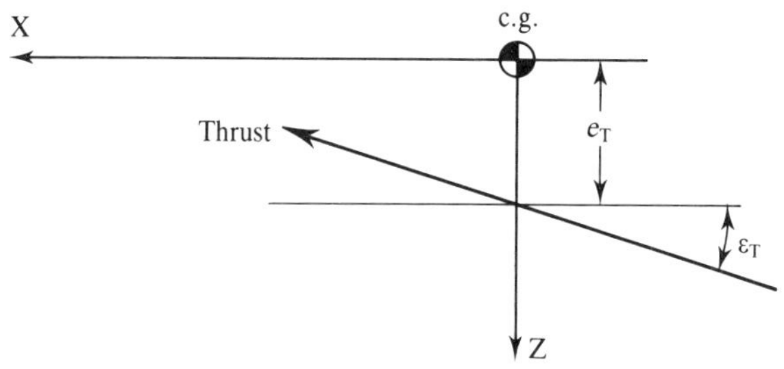

Figure 2.8 Resolution of thrust into forces and moments.

$$X_u = \frac{-\rho S U_0}{m}\left(\frac{U_0}{2}\frac{\partial C_D}{\partial U} + C_D\right) + \frac{1}{m}\frac{\partial T_x}{\partial U} \tag{2.201}$$

where T_x is the component of thrust along the axis OX. The partial derivative $\partial T_x/\partial U$ is found from data on the power plant. The direct contribution of thrust to other stability derivatives is usually negligible.

5. When the throttle setting, δ_{th}, is increased there is a corresponding increase in thrust. Figure 2.8 shows how thrust is resolved into forces and moments.

   From Figure 2.8:

$$X_{\delta_{th}} = \frac{1}{m}\left(\frac{\partial T}{\partial \delta_{th}}\right)\cos \varepsilon_T \tag{2.202}$$

$$Z_{\delta_{th}} = -\frac{1}{m}\left(\frac{\partial T}{\partial \delta_{th}}\right)\sin \varepsilon_T \tag{2.203}$$

$$M_{\delta_{th}} = -\left(\frac{e_T}{I_{yy}}\right)\left(\frac{\partial T}{\partial \delta_{th}}\right)\cos \varepsilon_T \tag{2.204}$$

2.12 CONCLUSIONS

The form of the equations of motion of an aircraft depends upon the axis system which has been chosen. Once a particular axis system is adopted, it is helpful to expand the aerodynamic force and moment terms, and to linearize the inertial and gravitational terms so that when small perturbations are considered the resulting equations will be linear and can be separated into longitudinal and lateral motion. Using the stability axis system is the most convenient for AFCS work. Sometimes, small motion is not of concern, however, and it is essential instead to consider steady manoeuvring flight such as pitching or turning. Not every motion variable of interest appears in the resulting equations of motion; such important variables as flight path angle, height, heading, and normal and lateral accelerations, are related, however, to these equations and this chapter shows how these variables can be obtained from a knowledge of the equations of motion. The form of the equation lends itself to representing the longitudinal and lateral dynamics of the aircraft directly as state equations, with the other variables being obtained from associated output equations. Once the state and output equations are known it is possible to determine any transfer function relating a particular output variable to a particular control input.

Not every stability derivative is significant in terms of its influence on the dynamics of the aircraft and only the most important need to be studied for their likely effects on the subsequent performance of an AFCS. Thrust changes do affect the motion of an aircraft, of course, but the thrust line does not always act through the c.g. of the aircraft, the origin of the stability axis system upon which the equations of motion are based. Consequently, special techniques are needed to introduced threse thrust effects into the equations of motion.

2.13 EXERCISES

2.1 Write down the state equation representing the small perturbation longitudinal motion of the aircraft CHARLIE-3.

2.2 Derive the transfer function relating the vertical velocity, w, in m s^{-1}, to the elevator deflection, δ_E, in radians, for the aircraft CHARLIE-4.

2.3 Using the stability derivatives of aircraft BRAVO-4 calculate the state and output equations, if the output variable is defined as the normal acceleration of the aircraft at its c.g.

2.4 The stability derivatives for VTOL aircraft in hovering flight are given below. Any stability derivative not listed should be taken as zero.

$$X_u = -0.2 \qquad g = 9.81 \text{ m s}^{-2} \qquad M_u = 0.01$$
$$Z_w = -0.1 \qquad M_q = -0.1$$
$$Z_{\delta_E} = 2.6 \qquad M_{\delta_E} = 0.75$$

(a) Calculate the transfer function relating normal acceleration, $a_{z_{cg}}$, to elevator deflection, δ_E.
(b) Sketch the response of $a_{z_{cg}}$ to a step deflection of the elevator of 0.03846 radian.
(c) If the aircraft is hovering at a height of 100 m, calculate the sinking speed at, and the time of, ground contact after the application of a step deflection of the elevator. State any assumptions made.
(d) In your opinion is the sinking speed obtained in part (c) excessive? Give a reason for your answer.

2.5 The lateral motion of the aircraft FOXTROT-2 is to be considered. Its rudder is not used at high Mach numbers. Derive the corresponding state and output equations, if the output variables of interest are heading angle, λ, and change in roll angle, ϕ.

2.6 For exercise 2.5 derive the corresponding transfer function relating, $a_{y_{cg}}$, to aileron deflection, δ_A.

2.7 An experimental VTOL aircraft in hovering motion has the following stability derivatives:

$$Y_v = -0.14 \qquad N'_\beta = 0.001$$

$$Y_{\delta_A} = 0.0 \qquad N'_p = 0.002$$

$$Y_{\delta_R} = 1.02 \qquad N'_p = -0.66$$

$$L'_\beta = -0.012 \qquad N'_{\delta_A} = -0.05$$

$$L'_p = -0.273 \qquad N'_{\delta_R} = -0.53$$

$$L'_r = 0.083 \qquad U_0 = 0.3 \text{ m s}^{-1}$$

$$L'_{\delta_A} = 0.7$$

$$L'_{\delta_R} = -0.12$$

p, r, β, and ϕ have their usual meanings of roll rate, yaw rate, sideslip angle and roll attitude, respectively. δ_A denotes the aileron deflection and δ_R denotes the rudder deflection.

(a) Calculate the transfer function relating the yaw rate to the rudder deflection.
(b) If the rudder deflection is an impulse function of 0.022 s, calculate by how much the heading of the aircraft will have changed some 10 s after the control deflection is applied.

2.8 A fighter aircraft, flying at 200 m s^{-1} and at a height of 10^4 m has the following short period equations of motion:

$$\dot{\alpha} = -6\alpha + q$$

$$\dot{q} = -5.0\alpha - 0.6q - 12.0\delta_E$$

(a) Derive the transfer function relating the pitch rate to the elevator deflection.
(b) If the aircraft's static stability is reduced to zero determine the pitch rate response of the modified aircraft to a step deflection of the elevator of $-1.0°$.
(c) Calculate the resulting steady state normal acceleration which the aircraft would sense at its c.g. as a result of the manoeuvre of part (b).
(d) Evaluate the response ratio (the acceleration sensitivity) of the aircraft. If the angle of attack is changed by 5.73°, calculate by how much the load factor would change.

2.9 The linearized equations of perturbed longitudinal motion are given (in SI units) by:

$$\dot{q} = -0.65q - 0.2\dot{\alpha} - \alpha - 1.2\delta_E$$

$$\dot{u} = 225.0\delta_{th} + 0.035\alpha - 9.81\theta - 0.18u$$

$$\dot{\alpha} = q - 0.2u - 0.6\alpha - 0.035\delta_E$$

$$\dot{\theta} = q$$

(a) Determine the equilibrium flight speed of the aircraft.
(b) Calculate the transfer function relating changes in forward speed to changes in thrust.

2.10 For the aircraft CHARLIE-1:

(a) Derive the state and output equations so that a change in flight path angle, γ, as a result of a deflection, δ_E, of the elevator can be evaluated.

(b) Find a transfer function relating change in γ to a change in pitch attitude using the equations found in part (a).

(c) Comment on the validity of the transfer function found in part (b).

(d) Find the value of elevator deflection needed to produce a steady state value (if any) of $-1.0°$ of pitch attitude. Find the corresponding value (if any) of the flight path angle.

2.11 A large jet cargo aircraft, DELTA, is powered by four engines, each having a thrust of 182 kN. The mass of the aircraft is 264 000 kg. The flight condition is F/C#2.

(a) Determine an appropriate state equation for the aircraft's motion.

(b) Thence find the transfer function relating changes in forward speed, u, to a change in thrust, δ_{th}.

(c) The pilot is located 25.0 m forward of the aircraft's c.g. and 2.5 m above it. Calculate the steady normal acceleration experienced by the pilot if the angle of attack of the aircraft is changed suddenly by 2.85°.

2.12 A high performance fighter is on approach at 165 knots. The linearized equations of perturbed lateral motion are given by:

$$\dot{\beta} = -0.16\,\beta + 0.174\,p - r + 0.114\,\phi - 0.0016\,\delta_A + 0.033\,\delta_R - 0.103\,\delta_{dht}$$

$$\dot{p} = -12.7\,\beta - 2.13\,p + 2.19\,r + 4.38\,\delta_A + 1.1\,\delta_R + 4.09\,\delta_{dht}$$

$$\dot{r} = 1.44\,\beta + 0.065\,p - 0.56\,r - 0.21\,\delta_A - 1.2\,\delta R + 0.22\,\delta_{dht}$$

$$\dot{\phi} = p + 0.176\,r$$

where δ_{dht} denotes differential deflection of the horizontal tail.

(a) Is it possible to find a combination of control surface deflections which will result in there being no lateral acceleration in the steady state, even though some of the state variables have finite values?

(b) If your answer to part (a) was in the affirmative, determine the corresponding values of the steady surface deflections required.

(c) Determine the transfer functions relating the lateral acceleration at the c.g. to each control surface independently, i.e. find:

$$\frac{a_{y_{cg}}(s)}{\delta_A(s)}, \quad \frac{a_{y_{cg}}(s)}{\delta_R(s)} \text{ and } \frac{a_{y_{cg}}(s)}{\delta_{dht}(s)}$$

Can you decide from these transfer functions which control surface is the most important for manoeuvring the aircraft on approach?

2.14 NOTES

1. For example, see chapter 4 of McRuer *et al.* (1973).
2. This depends upon the assumption of constant aircraft mass.

3. m_1 has been used to denote the perturbation in the pitching moment, M, to avoid confusion with the aircraft's mass, m.
4. This form applies to linear, time-invariant systems only; when the system is non-linear, the appropriate form is $\dot{\mathbf{x}} = \mathbf{f}(\mathbf{x}, \mathbf{u}, t)$.
5. For linear, time invariant systems only; when the output relationship is non-linear the appropriate form is $\mathbf{y} = \mathbf{g}(\mathbf{x}, \mathbf{u}, t)$.
6. If the output equation is non-linear, the presence of measurement noise modifies $\mathbf{y}$ to become: $\mathbf{y} = \mathbf{g}(\mathbf{x}, \mathbf{u}, \boldsymbol{\xi}, t)$.
7. This assumes that the matrix $(sI - A)$ is non-singular, which can be proved by recalling that $\mathcal{L}^{-1}\{[sI - A]^{-1}\} = e^{At}$.
8. Although U_0 is used in these equations, the correct value to be used is the true airspeed. For small perturbations, the errors are insignificant if U_0 is used instead of V_T.
9. If the elevator is located forward of the c.g. it is renamed *canard*. This description is increasingly common, although canard referred originally to an aircraft configuration which flew 'tail first', the forward tail surface being called a foreplane. It is this foreplane which is now considered to be a canard.

2.15 REFERENCES

BABISTER, A.W. 1961. *Aircraft Stability and Control.* Oxford: Pergamon Press.

FOGARTY, L.E. and R.M. HOWE. 1969. Computer mechanization of six-degree-of-freedom flight equations. NASA CR-1344, May.

GAINES, T.G. and S. HOFFMAN. 1972. Summary of transformation equations and equations of motion. NASA Sp-3070.

McRUER, D.T., I.L. ASHKENAS and D.C. GRAHAM. 1973. *Aircraft Dynamics and Automatic Control.* Princeton University Press.

McRUER, D.T., C.L. BATES and I.L. ASHKENAS. 1953. Dynamics of the airframe. Bur. Aero. Rpt. AE-61-4 (Vol. II) USA.

THELANDER, J.A. 1965. Aircraft motion analysis. FDL-TDR-67-70, WPAFB, Ohio, USA. March.

3

Aircraft Stability and Dynamics

3.1 INTRODUCTION

The equations of motion have been derived in some detail in Chapter 2. Only under a large number of assumptions about how an aircraft is being flown is it possible to arrive at a set of linear differential equations which can adequately represent the motion that results from the deflection of a control surface or from the aircraft's encountering atmospheric turbulence during its flight. This resulting motion is composed of small perturbations about the equilibrium (trim) values. To achieve such equilibrium values requires the use of certain steady deflections of the appropriate control surfaces. Consequently, the entire range of the angle of deflection of any particular control surface will not necessarily be available for the purposes of automatic control, since much of that range is required to trim the aircraft. What is meant, then, by small perturbation is that any angle be sufficiently small to guarantee that the assumptions concerning any trigonometrical functions involved remain valid. For practical purposes, a change of angle of 15° or more should be regarded as large, and the designer should then consider the likely effects of continuing to use the small perturbation theory whenever such angular values can occur. Similarly, translational velocity should always be small in relation to the steady speeds; when the steady speed, such as V_0 or W_0, is zero then changes of velocity of 5 m s^{-1} should be regarded as being the limit of validity. However, it must be strongly emphasized that these are not firm rules but depend upon the type of aircraft being considered, its flight condition, and the manoeuvres in which it is involved.

For the remainder of this chapter it is considered that all the assumptions of Chapter 2 hold, that any aircraft being considered is fixed wing and flying straight and level in a trimmed condition, and that its motion is properly characterized by eqs (2.109) and (2.110). For example, for longitudinal motion, eq. (2.112) is taken as the definition of the state vector **x**, i.e.:

$$\mathbf{x} \triangleq \begin{bmatrix} u \\ w \\ q \\ \theta \end{bmatrix} \tag{2.112}$$

and the control vector **u** is defined as:

$$\mathbf{u} \triangleq [\delta_E] \tag{2.113}$$

The state coefficient matrix A is then given by:

$$A = \begin{bmatrix} X_u & X_w & 0 & -g \\ Z_u & Z_w & U_0 & 0 \\ \tilde{M}_u & \tilde{M}_w & \tilde{M}_q & 0 \\ 0 & 0 & 1 & 0 \end{bmatrix} \tag{3.1}$$

and the driving matrix B by:

$$B = \begin{bmatrix} X_{\delta_E} \\ Z_{\delta_E} \\ \tilde{M}_{\delta_E} \\ 0 \end{bmatrix} \tag{3.2}$$

For lateral motion, the appropriate equations are (2.143) and (2.154), respectively where the coefficient matrix is:

$$A = \begin{bmatrix} Y_v & 0 & -1 & g/U_0 \\ L'_\beta & L'_p & L'_r & 0 \\ N'_\beta & N'_p & N'_r & 0 \\ 0 & 1 & 0 & 0 \end{bmatrix} \tag{3.3}$$

and the driving matrix is:

$$B = \begin{bmatrix} Y^*_{\delta_A} & Y^*_{\delta_R} \\ L'_{\delta_A} & L'_{\delta_R} \\ N'_{\delta_A} & N'_{\delta_R} \\ 0 & 0 \end{bmatrix} \tag{3.4}$$

3.2 LONGITUDINAL STABILITY

3.2.1 Short Period and Phugoid Modes

The dynamic stability of perturbed longitudinal motion is most effectively established from a knowledge of the eigenvalues of the coefficient matrix A. They can be found by solving the linear equation:

$$|\lambda I - A| = 0 \tag{3.5}$$

I is a 4×4 identity matrix. By expanding the determinant, the longitudinal stability quartic, a fourth degree polynomial in λ, can be expressed as:

$$\lambda^4 + a_1\lambda^3 + a_2\lambda^2 + a_3\lambda + a_4 = 0 \tag{3.6}$$

An aircraft may be said to be dynamically stable if all its eigenvalues, λ_i, being real, have negative values, or, if they be complex, have negative real parts. Zero, or positive, values of the real part of any complex eigenvalue means that the aircraft will be dynamically unstable.[1] Rather than solving the polynomial by numerical methods it is more effective to use a numerical routine to compute the four eigenvalues of A.

It has been observed that for the majority of aircraft types, the quartic of eq. (3.6) invariably factorizes into two quadratic factors in the following manner:

$$(\lambda^2 + 2\zeta_{ph}\omega_{ph}\lambda + \omega_{ph}^2)(\lambda^2 + 2\zeta_{sp}\omega_{sp}\lambda + \omega_{sp}^2) \tag{3.7}$$

The first factor corresponds to a mode of motion which is characterized by an oscillation of long period. The damping of this mode is usually very low, and is sometimes negative, so that the mode is unstable and the oscillation grows with time. The low frequency associated with the long period motion is defined as the natural frequency, ω_{ph}; the damping ratio has been denoted as ζ_{ph}. The mode is referred to as the *phugoid* mode, a name improperly given to it by the English aerodynamicist, Lanchester, who coined it from the Greek word which he believed meant 'flight-like'. Unfortunately, φυγη implies flight as demonstrated by a fugitive, not a bird (Sutton, 1949). The second factor corresponds to a rapid, relatively well-damped motion associated with the short period mode whose frequency is ω_{sp} and damping ration is ζ_{sp}.

As an example, consider the passenger transport aircraft, referred to as aircraft DELTA in Appendix B. If flight condition 4 is considered, the aircraft is flying straight and level in its cruise phase, at Mach 0.8 and at a height of 13 000 m. From the values of the stability derivatives quoted in the appendix, A is found to be:

$$A = \begin{bmatrix} -0.033 & 0.0001 & 0 & -9.81 \\ 0.168 & -0.387 & 260.0 & 0 \\ 55\times 10^{-4} & -0.0064 & -0.551 & 0 \\ 0 & 0 & 1 & 0 \end{bmatrix} \tag{3.8}$$

The eigenvalues corresponding to this matrix are found to be:

$$\lambda_1, \lambda_2 = +0.0033 \pm j0.0672 \tag{3.9}$$ [2]

$$\lambda_3, \lambda_4 = -0.373 \pm j0.889 \tag{3.10}$$ [2]

The eigenvalues of eq. (3.9) are seen to be those associated with the phugoid mode since the damping ratio, although positive, is very small (0.0489) and the frequency is very low (0.067 rad s^{-1}), hence the period is long. Such an inference can be drawn because the solution of any quadratic equation of the form:

$$x^2 + 2\zeta\omega x + \omega^2 = 0 \tag{3.11}$$

is given by:

$$\begin{aligned} x_1 &= -\zeta\omega + j\omega\sqrt{(1-\zeta^2)} \\ x_2 &= -\zeta\omega - j\omega\sqrt{(1-\zeta^2)} \end{aligned} \tag{3.12}$$

whenever $\zeta < 1.0$. Complex roots occur only when the damping ratio has a positive value less than unity.

From eq. (3.10) the eigenvalues can be deduced to be those associated with the short period mode, for which the frequency is 0.964 rad s^{-1} and the damping ratio is 0.387.

3.2.2 Tuck Mode

Supersonic aircraft, or aircraft which fly at speeds close to Mach 1.0, occasionally have a value of the stability derivative, M_u, such that M_u takes a large value which is sufficiently negative to result in the term ω_{ph}^2 in the phugoid quadratic becoming negative too (see Section 3.6). When this happens, the roots of the quadratic equation are both real, with one being negative and the other positive. Hence the phugoid mode is no longer oscillatory but has become composed of two real modes; one being convergent, which corresponds to the negative real root, and the other being divergent, which corresponds to the positive real root. The unstable mode is referred to as the 'tuck mode' because the corresponding motion results in the nose of the aircraft dropping (tucking under) as airspeed increases. Aircraft DELTA in Appendix B will exhibit a divergent tuck mode in flight condition 3.

3.2.3 A Third Oscillatory Mode

The c.g. of a modern combat aircraft is often designed to lie aft of the neutral point (n.p.) (see Section 3.3). When this is the case the stability derivative, M_w, can take a value which will result in every root of the longitudinal stability quartic being real. As the c.g. is then moved further aft of the n.p., the value of M_w changes so that one of the real roots of the short period mode, and one of the real roots of the phugoid mode, migrate in the complex plane to a point where they form a new complex pair, corresponding to the third oscillatory mode. When this has occurred, that mode is the main influence upon the dynamic response of any AFCS which is used. The phugoid mode has now become a very slow aperiodic mode, and there also exists another extremely rapid real mode. Too positive a value of M_w can result in dynamic instability, for one of these real eigenvalues can become positive (see Section 3.5.2).

3.2.4 s-plane Diagram

The location of eigenvalues in the complex frequency domain is often represented by means of an s-plane diagram (which is simply a special Argand diagram). In Figure 3.1 are shown the locations (denoted by ×) of eigenvalues for a typical conventional aircraft. For an aircraft which exhibits a tuck mode the locations are denoted by ○ and for an aircraft with a third oscillatory mode they are denoted by △.

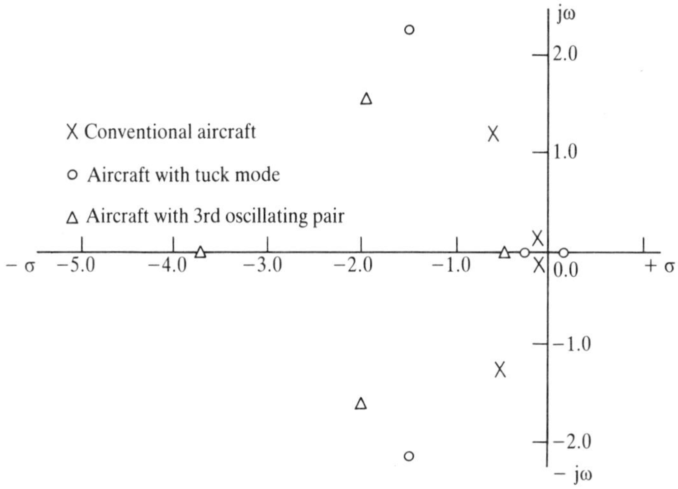

Figure 3.1 s-plane diagram.

A popular method of investigating how sensitive is an aircraft's stability to values of some particular stability derivative (and, consequently, some aerodynamic, inertial, or geometric parameter) is to illustrate how the eigenvalues travel around the s-plane as the values of the stability derivative are changed. This is a form of root locus diagram. Another effective way of determining to which stability derivative the aircraft's dynamic response is most sensitive is to carry out a sensitivity analysis on coefficient matrix, A (Barnett and Storey, 1966). It is important to remember that when the aircraft dynamics can be assumed to be linear those stability derivatives associated with the control surfaces play no part in governing the stability properties of the aircraft. Their importance for achieving effective automatic flight control, including stability augmentation, is paramount nevertheless.

3.3 STATIC STABILITY

3.3.1 Trim Condition

In Chapter 2 where the derivation of the equations of motion for an aircraft was shown, a point was reached (in Section 2.6) where the set of equations governing the small perturbation motion about some equilibrium flight condition was considered. To achieve that equilibrium required a number of forces and moments to be balanced. The balance equations, for straight and level flight, were shown to be:

$$\begin{aligned} X_0 - mg \sin\Theta &= 0 \\ Z_0 + mg \cos\Theta &= 0 \\ Y_0 = L_0 = M_0 = N_0 &= 0 \end{aligned} \qquad (2.87)^3$$

For the linearized equations, the control required to achieve trim is:

$$\mathbf{u} = [B]^{\dagger} A\mathbf{x} \qquad (3.13)$$

where $[B]^{\dagger}$ is the generalized inverse of matrix B.

When reference is made to the stability of these static components what is meant is the inherent tendency of an aircraft to develop forces or moments (or both) which directly oppose any deviation of this motion from equilibrium flight. The only forces which can change significantly as a result of disturbances are sideforce, lift and drag, the values of which depend upon the orientation of the aircraft relative to the oncoming airstream. Obviously, each motion variable can be considered from a stability viewpoint. Only the most significant criteria of aircraft stability are considered here.

3.3.2 Forward Speed Stability

An aircraft is considered to be statically stable for any disturbance, u, in its forward speed if the value of the stability derivative, X_u, is negative. It is particularly important in the approach phase of flight that X_u should not be positive. This requirement may be understood from considering Figure 3.2. Suppose the aircraft in the figure is in a steady, trimmed flight condition corresponding to point A, i.e. the throttle setting is fixed and constant thrust is being produced which results in the aircraft's flying at some speed, V_A. If, for any reason, the aircraft speed increases to, say, $V_A + u$, a drag force is generated which opposes the increase in speed, i.e.:

$$\partial F_x / \partial u \triangleq X_u < 0 \qquad (3.14)$$

Another way of interpreting Figure 3.2 is to see that, at point A, if it is wished to increase the speed of the aircraft, the thrust has to be increased; to reduce its speed requires a reduction in thrust. Point B represents a lower speed (at which

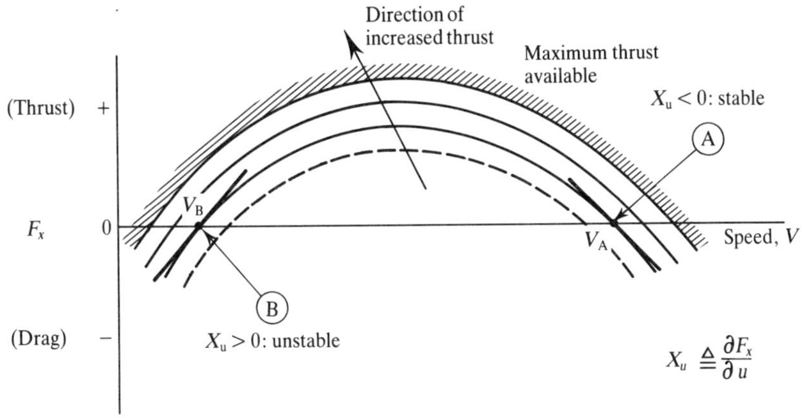

Figure 3.2 Speed stability diagram.

many aircraft would typically fly on approach). There it is seen that any decrease in speed leads to an increase in the drag force which will result in a further reduction in speed. At point B, $X_u > 0$ and the situation is regarded as unstable. If the difference between the thrust available from the engines and what is required to sustain flight in a particular manoeuvre is small (sometimes this is expressed by saying that the thrust margin is small), or if the change in thrust from the engines, as a result of a change in throttle setting, is slow, then it is possible for an aircraft operating at point B to be in a position where recovery of the required airspeed is possible only by diving the aircraft. During the approach phase of flight, if this was not regarded as undesirable, it would certainly be regarded as unseemly. At speeds lower than V_B the aircraft will tend to stall. If the unstable portion of the curve corresponding to maximum thrust intersects the line for which F_x is zero at a value of speed higher than V_{stall}, the aircraft's speed will diverge, which will result in a stall, unless the pilot is able and willing to dive the aircraft. It is principally delta wing aircraft, such as the F-106, B-58 and Concorde, which tend to have positive values of X_u on approach.

3.3.3 Vertical Speed Stability

An aircraft will be statically stable for any disturbance in the vertical speed, w, if the value of the stability derivative, Z_w, is negative. This means that if, somehow, there is generated a positive velocity increment along the axis OZ, a force is generated which tends to oppose the initial disturbance in w. For this to be true, the lift curve slope of the wing must be positive for all values of angle of attack, an aerodynamic condition which is always satisfied. However, for wings of high aspect ratio (when span^2/surface area is large) and which are highly swept, aeroelastic effects generally cause the wing to distort so that the lift curve slope, and hence Z_w, is reduced. On delta wings, aeroelastic effects often increase Z_w.

3.3.4 Sideslip Stability

Generally, the static stability requirement that the value of Y_β be negative is unimportant. However, although $Y_\beta < 0$ is the usual condition, it is of advantage to the pilot. Sideslip angle β is not easily detected by pilots when $Y_\beta < 0$ because the condition causes symmetrical aircraft (which most are) to bank in steady sideslip manoeuvres. Also, if a pilot is turning at very low height, and there is a restriction on the bank angle which can be commanded, because of the proximity of the terrain, a negative value of Y_β will allow a skidding turn to be performed. It can assist the side-step manoeuvre, which is sometimes performed when an aircraft on its final approach is not correctly aligned with the runway centre line.

3.3.5 Static Directional Stability

An aircraft is said to have static directional stability if the value of the stability derivative, N'_β, is positive. This means that the yawing moment N will increase as a result of a positive (sideslip) velocity v and the aircraft aligns itself with the relative airflow. The non-dimensional stability derivative C_{n_β} is referred to as the 'weathercock stability'. A large part of C_{n_β} is contributed by the volume of the vertical tail.[4] For supersonic transport aircraft, such as Concorde, the high Mach numbers and high values of the angle of attack, which commonly occur in operational flight, can cause considerable deterioration in the value of N'_β.

3.3.6 Lateral Static Stability

If there is a positive change in the sideslip angle then the aircraft's right wing drops and the aircraft slides to the right. L'_β must be negative for stability; the 'dihedral effect' results in the right wing being pitched up to negate the sideslip. When L'_β is negative, the spiral mode (see Section 3.4) will be convergent.

3.3.7 Longitudinal Static Stability

It is explained in Chapter 1 that in the XZ plane, an intentional change of the aircraft's orientation can be achieved by deflecting the elevator, or flaps. Deflection of either surface produces a small, unbalanced force which, because of the distance of the point through which it acts from the aircraft's c.g., can result in a large pitching moment. Such a moment causes an aircraft to rotate about its c.g. until the steady moments adjust themselves to come into balance. How fast an aircraft will rotate, i.e. its angular acceleration, depends upon the size of the moment and the value of the moment of inertia about the axis OY, namely I_{yy}.

Since the centre of pressure moves with changes in the angle of attack, any change in lift causes a change in the moment produced by the lift force

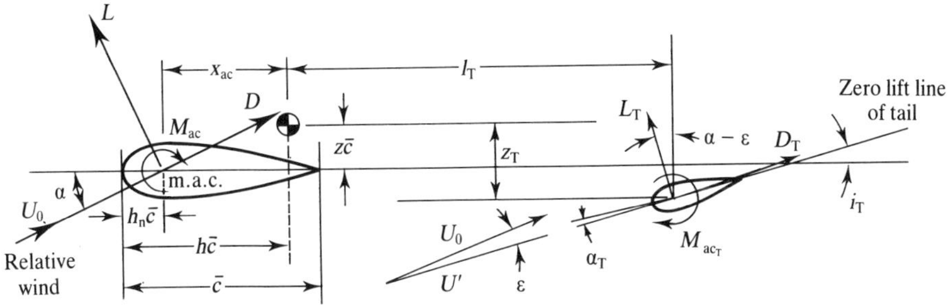

Figure 3.3 Geometry of wing/tail.

about the c.g. Thus, an aircraft rotates to a new orientation when disturbed and, as a result, the moments due to drag, to the lift from the wing and from the tail, etc. must all change. If they change in a way that increases the extent of the rotation, this is an unstable condition. As a result, it is customary to take as a criterion of longitudinal static stability the sign of the stability derivative M_w, for when $M_w < 0$ any increase in the angle of attack, α, will cause an increase in the nosedown pitching moment, thereby tending to reduce the angle of attack.

Once the configuration of an aircraft has been fixed, then, for any particular flight condition, the stability derivative M_w depends principally upon the normalized distance $x_{ac}/\bar{c}$ from the mean aerodynamic centre of the wing to the aircraft's c.g. where x_{ac} is the distance from the a.c. of the aircraft and its c.g. and $\bar{c}$ is the chord length (the chord measured along the zero lift line of the wing – see Figure 3.3). If the mean a.c. and the c.g. are coincident, that is, if the lift force acts through the c.g., then the stability derivative M_w takes the value zero. This condition is known as *neutral* static stability. The c.g. location, which corresponds to this condition, is called the stick-fixed neutral point (n.p.).

If the c.g. is located aft of the n.p., then M_w has a positive value and the aircraft is statically unstable. If the c.g. is then located even further aft of the n.p., a condition is reached where an 'infinite' normal acceleration, $a_{z_{cg}}$ is produced with no force being applied to the control stick. This particular location of the c.g. is called the stick fixed manoeuvre point (m.p.).

By varying the location of the c.g. the manoeuvre stability can be made zero, positive, or negative. The m.p. corresponds to neutral manoeuvring stability. The distance between the c.g. and the m.p. is called the manoeuvre margin. The distance of the c.g. from the n.p. is referred to as the static margin. To be statically stable the c.g. of an aircraft must be located forward of its n.p. Its m.p. for this condition must be aft of the c.g., but for conventional aircraft to be as manoeuvrable as possible, i.e. to produce as much acceleration as possible in response to a given control surface deflection, the c.g. should be only just forward of the n.p. In modern fighter aircraft this static stability is relaxed and the c.g. is often deliberately located aft of the n.p., thereby reducing the manoeuvre margin but, as a result, increasing the manoeuvrability of the aircraft, which is the desired result. In this case, however, it turns out that, for pilots to fly the aircraft successfully, dynamic stability is required, which has to be provided by a stability augmentation system specially fitted for the purpose.

It is a relatively simple matter to show that the static margin can be expressed by

$$\frac{C_m}{C_L} = \frac{C_{m_\alpha}}{C_{L_\alpha}} \triangleq (h - h_n) = \frac{x_{ac}}{\bar{c}} \tag{3.15}$$

where C_m is the coefficient of the pitching moment and C_L is the lift coefficient. h, h_n, x_{ac} and $\bar{c}$ are defined in Figure 3.3. C_{m_α} and C_{L_α} denote $\partial C_m/\partial\alpha$ and $\partial C_L/\partial\alpha$ respectively. The stability derivative $\overset{\circ}{M}_w$ represents the change in pitching moment which occurs as a result of a change in the vertical velocity, w. If moments are taken about the c.g. of the aircraft (nose-up moments being defined as positive), L, D and M_{ac}, which is the moment about the aerodynamic centre, all contribute to the moment about the c.g., i.e.:

$$\begin{aligned} M_{cg} = M_{ac} &+ L \cos\alpha\,(h\bar{c} - h_n\bar{c}) + D \sin\alpha\,(h\bar{c} - h_n\bar{c}) \\ &+ L \sin\alpha\; z\bar{c} - D \cos\alpha\; z\bar{c} \end{aligned} \tag{3.16}$$

but for small angles of attack:

$$\cos\alpha \simeq 1.0 \qquad \sin\alpha \simeq \alpha \tag{3.17}$$

Consequently,

$$M_{cg} = M_{ac} + (L + D\alpha)(h - h_n)\bar{c} + (L\alpha - D)z\bar{c} \tag{3.18}$$

Dividing both sides of eq. (3.18) by $\bar{q}S\bar{c}$ results in:

$$C_{m_{cg}} = C_{m_{ac}} + (C_L + C_D\alpha)(h - h_n) + (C_L\alpha - C_D)z \tag{3.19}$$

When the c.g. is closely located near the zero lift line, z is negligible. Moreover, α is usually a small radian quantity and $C_D < C_L$, consequently $C_D\alpha$ may be neglected. Hence eq. (3.19) can be written as:

$$C_{m_{cg}} = C_{m_{ac}} + C_{L_\alpha}\alpha(h - h_n) \tag{3.20}$$

where

$$C_L \simeq C_{L_\alpha}\alpha \tag{3.21}$$

and C_{L_α} is the slope of the lift curve of the aircraft.

$$\therefore \quad \partial C_{m_{cg}}/\partial\alpha \triangleq C_{m_\alpha} = C_{L_\alpha}(h - h_n) = \frac{-x_{ac}}{\bar{c}} C_{L_\alpha} \tag{3.15}$$

because:

$$-x_{ac} = (h - h_n)\bar{c} \tag{3.22}$$

If the static margin is positive, the aircraft is stable, i.e. C_{m_α} is negative.

3.4 TRANSFER FUNCTIONS RELATED TO LONGITUDINAL MOTION

3.4.1 Relationship Between Transfer Function and State Equation

The theory relating to deriving transfer functions from the linearized equations of motion is given in Section 2.9 of Chapter 2. In this present section, some of the more commonly used transfer functions for longitudinal motion will be derived, but the reader should be aware that a number of computer programs are available (see for example, Systems Control Technology, Inc., 1986; Larimer, 1978) for the automatic determination of appropriate transfer functions from a knowledge of the stability derivatives. These programs are usually based on the Leverrier algorithm (Faddeeva, 1959).

The purpose of deriving analytically a number of transfer functions in this present section is to arrive at their final forms, to see which parameters and terms are significant, and to note possible simplifications which can lead to useful approximations.

It has been shown in Chapter 2 that if only a single control, δ_E, is considered, the linearized, small perturbation equations of longitudinal motion are given by:

$$\dot{\mathbf{x}} = A\mathbf{x} + B\mathbf{u} \tag{3.23}$$

where:

$$\mathbf{x} \triangleq \begin{bmatrix} u \\ w \\ q \\ \theta \end{bmatrix} \tag{3.24}$$

$$\mathbf{u} \triangleq [\delta_E] \tag{3.25}$$

The coefficient matrix, A, and the driving matrix, B, are given by:

$$A = \begin{bmatrix} X_u & X_w & 0 & -g \\ Z_u & Z_w & U_0 & 0 \\ \tilde{M}_u & \tilde{M}_w & \tilde{M}_q & 0 \\ 0 & 0 & 1 & 0 \end{bmatrix} \tag{3.26}$$

$$B = \begin{bmatrix} X_{\delta_E} \\ Z_{\delta_E} \\ \tilde{M}_{\delta_E} \\ 0 \end{bmatrix} \tag{3.27}$$

From eq. (2.164), the transfer function relating output variable, y_i, to control input, u_i, is given by:

$$G(s) = C_i[sI - A]^{-1} B_j + D_{ij} \tag{2.164}$$

Thus, every transfer function depends upon the variable chosen as the output and the control surface deflection used to change the motion variable. But it must always be remembered that when the control deflection is used to change some particular motion variable that same control deflection changes other motion variables simultaneously. It is this simple fact which sometimes causes great difficulty for the designers of AFCSs, and it is this fact which results in so many systems, designed by means of the conventional theory of control for single input, single output, linear systems, producing aircraft performance which is unacceptable to pilots. Although transfer functions are useful, their use is limited, particularly for AFCS design for modern aircraft where many control surfaces are employed simultaneously. However, from eq. (2.164) it is evident that every transfer function relating to the motion of the aircraft must depend on the inherent characteristics of the aircraft through the resolvent matrix, $[sI - A]^{-1}$.

3.4.2 Use of Output Matrix, C, to Select a Particular Motion Variable

For the present, normal acceleration, and those motion variables such as h which are directly related to it, are not being considered. Thus:

$$\mathbf{y} = C\mathbf{x} \tag{3.28}$$

and, for further simplicity, since transfer functions are being considered, only a single output variable will be dealt with at a time. Consequently, eq. (3.28) now becomes:

$$y = C\mathbf{x} \tag{3.29}$$

where C is a 1×4 rectangular matrix. C contains only one non-zero element and that element has the value unity. The column in which this value is to be found depends upon which state variable is being taken as the output variable of concern. For example, if the output variable is chosen to be u, then:

$$y \triangleq [1 \ 0 \ 0 \ 0]\mathbf{x} \tag{3.30}$$

The other three relationships are:

$$y \triangleq w = [0 \ 1 \ 0 \ 0]\mathbf{x} \tag{3.31}$$

$$y \triangleq q = [0 \ 0 \ 1 \ 0]\mathbf{x} \tag{3.32}$$

$$y \triangleq \theta = [0 \ 0 \ 0 \ 1]\mathbf{x} \tag{3.33}$$

Thus, the unit element can be looked upon as a kind of pointer indicating which state variable has been chosen as the output variable.

Quite often, the output matrix C is used to achieve conversion of physical units. For example, if the state variable q is defined in rad s^{-1} but is required to work with pitch rate in degree s^{-1}, then defining q in degree s^{-1} as an output variable results in $y = [0 \ 0 \ 57.3 \ 0]\mathbf{x}$.

3.4.3 Transfer Function Notation

It will be plain to the reader now that four transfer functions can be determined, namely:

$$u(s)/\delta_E(s),\ w(s)/\delta_E(s),\ q(s)/\delta_E(s) \text{ and } \theta(s)/\delta_E(s)$$

The form of these transfer functions is identical:

$$G(s) = N(s)/D(s) \tag{3.34}$$

The denominator polynomial is the characteristic polynomial of the aircraft, namely $\det[\lambda I - A]$ which was dealt with in Section 3.2. When the roots of the polynomial are known, i.e. those values of s are known which result in:

$$\Delta_{\text{long}}(s) = \det[sI - A] = 0 \tag{3.35}$$

it will be seen that they are identical to the eigenvalues of A. The polynomial $\det[sI - A]$ is often called the stability quartic. Every transfer function for longitudinal motion has the same denominator, because every transfer function must represent the characteristic motion of the same aircraft. Therefore, the only way in which the transfer functions can differ for a particular motion, longitudinal or lateral, of an aircraft, is in their numerator polynomials. These numerator polynomials are direct functions of the output variable and the control input, and to emphasize this fact, they are often denoted, in American reports especially, as $N_{uj}^{yi}(s)$. The superscript yi denotes the particular output variable, and uj denotes the control input. Thus, for the four transfer functions considered up to this point, the corresponding denotations would be: $N_{\delta_E}^{u}(s)$, $N_{\delta_E}^{w}(s)$, $N_{\delta_E}^{q}(s)$, and $N_{\delta_E}^{\theta}(s)$.

For longitudinal motion the matrix $[sI - A]^{-1}$ can be shown to be:

$$[sI - A]^{-1} \triangleq \frac{\text{adj}[sI - A]}{\det[sI - a]} = \frac{\begin{bmatrix} n_{11}(s) & n_{12}(s) & n_{13}(s) & n_{14}(s) \\ n_{21}(s) & n_{22}(s) & n_{23}(s) & n_{24}(s) \\ n_{31}(s) & n_{32}(s) & n_{33}(s) & n_{34}(s) \\ n_{41}(s) & n_{42}(s) & n_{43}(s) & n_{44}(s) \end{bmatrix}}{(s^4 + a_1 s^3 + a_2 s^2 + a_3 s + a_4)} \tag{3.36}$$

The elements, n_{11}, of the numerator matrix are given as follows:

$$n_{11}(s) = s\{s^2 - [M_q + M_{\dot{w}}U_0 + Z_w]s + [Z_w M_q - M_w U_0]\} \tag{3.37}$$

$$n_{12}(s) = X_w s^2 - X_w[M_q + M_{\dot{w}}U_0]s - g[M_w + M_{\dot{w}}Z_w] \tag{3.38}$$

$$n_{13}(s) = s(U_0 X_w - g) + gZ_w \tag{3.39}$$

$$n_{21}(s) = Z_u s^2 - [Z_u M_q - M_u U_0]s = s[Z_u s - (Z_u M_q - M_u U_0)] \tag{3.40}$$

$$n_{22}(s) = s^3 - [X_u + M_q + M_{\dot{w}}U_0]s^2 + X_u[M_q + M_{\dot{w}}U_0]s + g[M_u + M_{\dot{w}}Z_u] \tag{3.41}$$

$$n_{23}(s) = U_0 s^2 - X_u U_0 s - gZ_u \tag{3.42}$$

$$n_{31}(s) = s\{s[M_u + M_{\dot{w}}Z_u] + [Z_uM_{\dot{w}} - Z_wM_u]\} \tag{3.43}$$

$$n_{32}(s) = s^2[M_w + M_{\dot{w}}Z_w] - s[X_uM_w - X_wM_u + M_{\dot{w}}[Z_wX_u - Z_uX_w)] \tag{3.44}$$

$$n_{33}(s) = s\{s^2 - [X_u + Z_w]s + [X_uZ_w - Z_uX_w]\} \tag{3.45}$$

$$n_{41}(s) = s[M_u + M_{\dot{w}}Z_u] + [Z_uM_w - M_uZ_w] \tag{3.46}$$

$$n_{42}(s) = s[M_w + M_{\dot{w}}Z_w] + Z_wM_u - X_uM_w + M_{\dot{w}}[Z_uX_w - X_uZ_w] \tag{3.47}$$

$$n_{43}(s) = s^2 - [X_u + Z_w]s + [X_uZ_w - Z_uX_w] \tag{3.48}$$

The elemental functions, $n_{14}(s)$, $n_{24}(s)$, $n_{34}(s)$ and $n_{44}(s)$ are all identically zero (because the fourth element in the driving matrix, B, is zero, i.e. $b_{41} = 0$). The coefficients, a_i, of the characteristic polynomial can be determined by evaluating $\det[sI - A]$. They are:

$$a_1 = -\ (X_u + M_q + Z_w + M_{\dot{w}}U_0) \tag{3.49}$$

$$a_2 = (M_qZ_w - M_wU_0 + X_uZ_w - Z_uX_w + X_uM_q + X_uU_0M_{\dot{w}}) \tag{3.50}$$

$$a_3 = -\ (X_uZ_wM_q + X_uM_wU_0 - M_qZ_uX_w + M_uX_wU_0 - gM_u - gM_{\dot{w}}Z_u) \tag{3.51}$$

$$a_4 = g(Z_uM_w - Z_wM_u) \tag{3.52}$$

Thus, firstly:

$$\frac{u(s)}{\delta_E(s)} = \frac{n_{11}(s)b_{11} + n_{12}(s)b_{21} + n_{13}(s)b_{31}}{\Delta_{\text{long}}(s)}$$

$$\therefore\quad \frac{u(s)}{\delta_E(s)} = \frac{N^u_{\delta_E}(s)}{\Delta_{\text{long}}(s)} = \frac{b_3s^3 + b_2s^2 + b_1s + b_0}{s^4 + a_1s^3 + a_2s^2 + a_3s + a_4} \tag{3.54}$$

where:

$$b_3 = X_{\delta_E} \tag{3.55}$$

$$b_2 = -X_{\delta_E}[Z_w + M_q + M_{\dot{w}}U_0] + Z_{\delta_E}X_w \tag{3.56}$$

$$b_1 = X_{\delta_E}[Z_wM_q - M_wU_0] - Z_{\delta_E}[X_wM_q + gM_{\dot{w}}] + M_{\delta_E}[X_wU_0 - g] \tag{3.57}$$

$$b_0 = g[M_{\delta_E}Z_w - Z_{\delta_E}M_w] \tag{3.58}$$

The a_i are defined in eqs (3.49)–(3.52).

Secondly:

$$\frac{w(s)}{\delta_E(s)} = \frac{N^w_{\delta_E}(s)}{\Delta_{\text{long}}(s)} = \frac{\hat{b}_3s^3 + \hat{b}_2s^2 + \hat{b}_1s + \hat{b}_0}{\Delta_{\text{long}}(s)} \tag{3.59}$$

where:

$$\hat{b}_3 = Z_{\delta_E} \tag{3.60}$$

$$\hat{b}_2 = X_{\delta_E}Z_u - Z_{\delta_E}[X_u + M_q] + M_{\delta_E}U_0 \tag{3.61}$$

$$\hat{b}_1 = X_{\delta_E}[U_0M_u - Z_uM_q] - X_u[Z_{\delta_E}M_q + U_0M_{\delta_E}] \tag{3.62}$$

$$\acute{b}_0 = g[Z_{\delta_E}M_u - M_{\delta_E}Z_u] \tag{3.63}$$

Thirdly:

$$\frac{q(s)}{\delta_E(s)} = \frac{N^q_{\delta_E}(s)}{\Delta_{\text{long}}(s)} = \frac{s\{b_2's^2 + b_1's + b_0'\}}{\Delta_{\text{long}}(s)} \tag{3.64}$$

where

$$b_2' = [M_{\delta_E} + M_{\dot{w}}Z_{\delta_E}] \tag{3.65}$$

$$b_1' = X_{\delta_E}[M_u + M_{\dot{w}}Z_u] + Z_{\delta_E}[M_w - M_{\dot{w}}X_u] - M_{\delta_E}[X_u + Z_w] \tag{3.66}$$

$$\begin{aligned} b_0' = {} & X_{\delta_E}[Z_uM_w - Z_wM_u] + Z_{\delta_E}[X_wM_u - X_uM_w] \\ & + M_{\delta_E}[X_uZ_w - Z_uX_w] \end{aligned} \tag{3.67}$$

Note that knowing eq. (3.64) means that $\theta(s)/\delta_E(s)$ is known:

$$\theta(s)/\delta_E(s) = (b_2's^2 + b_1's + b_0')/\Delta_{\text{long}}(s) \tag{3.68}$$

3.4.4 Transfer Functions Involving Motion Variables Other Than State Variables

It has been shown how the four primary transfer functions relating to longitudinal motion can be evaluated. Other longitudinal transfer functions can be as easily found. For example, since it is known that:

$$\alpha = w/U_0 \tag{3.69}$$

then:

$$\frac{\alpha(s)}{\delta_E(s)} = \frac{1}{U_0}\frac{w(s)}{\delta_E(s)} = \frac{\acute{b}_3s^3 + \acute{b}_2s^2 + \acute{b}_1s + \acute{b}_0}{U_0[\Delta_{\text{long}}(s)]}$$

$h(s)/\delta_E(s)$ can be evaluated by making use of eq. (2.94):

$$a_{z_{cg}} = \dot{w} - U_0q = -\ddot{h} \tag{2.94}$$

$$\therefore \quad -\frac{s^2h(s)}{\delta_E(s)} = \frac{sw(s)}{\delta_E(s)} - U_0\frac{q(s)}{\delta_E(s)} \tag{3.71}$$

$$\therefore \quad -\frac{sh(s)}{\delta_E(s)} = \frac{w(s)}{\delta_E(s)} - U_0\frac{\theta(s)}{\delta_E(s)} \tag{3.72}$$

$$\begin{aligned} \therefore \quad -\frac{sh(s)}{\delta_E(s)} &= \frac{\acute{b}_3s^3 + \acute{b}_2s^2 + \acute{b}_1s + \acute{b}_0}{\Delta_{\text{long}}(s)} - \frac{U_0(b_1's^2 + b_1's + b_0')}{\Delta_{\text{long}}(s)} \\ &= \frac{\bar{b}_3s^3 + \bar{b}_2s^2 + \bar{b}_1s + \bar{b}_0}{\Delta_{\text{long}}(s)} \end{aligned} \tag{3.73}$$

where:

$$\acute{b}_3 = \bar{b}_3 = Z_{\delta_E} \tag{3.74}$$

$$\acute{b}_2 = (\hat{b}_2 - U_0 b_2') = X_{\delta_E} Z_u - Z_{\delta_E}(X_u + M_q + M_{\dot{w}} U_0) \tag{3.75}$$

$$\begin{aligned}\acute{b}_1 = (\hat{b}_1 - U_0 b_1') = & - X_{\delta_E} Z_u [M_q + M_{\dot{w}} Z_u] \\ & - Z_{\delta_E}[X_u M_q + U_0 M_w - U_0 M_{\dot{w}} X_u] + M_{\delta_E} U_0 Z_w\end{aligned} \tag{3.76}$$

$$\begin{aligned}\acute{b}_0 = (\hat{b}_0 - U_0 b_0') = & X_{\delta_E}(U_0 Z_w M_u - U_0 M_w Z_u] - Z_{\delta_E}[M_u(U_0 X_w - g) \\ & - M_w U_0 X_u] - M_{\delta_E}[U_0 Z_w X_u + Z_u(g - X_w Z_u U_0)]\end{aligned} \tag{3.77}$$

3.4.5 Numerical Example

Using the numerical data presented in Appendix B for aircraft BRAVO at flight condition 1, it is easy to determine that the characteristic equation is given by:

$$\Delta_{\text{long}}(s) = (s^4 + 2.92\,s^3 + 2.178\,s^2 + 0.015\,s + 0.01) = 0 \tag{3.78}$$

which can be factorized as:

$$\Delta_{\text{long}}(s) = (s^2 + 0.00068\,s + 0.0046)(s^2 + 2.9136\,s + 2.17) = 0 \tag{3.79}$$

Then:

$$\frac{u(s)}{\delta_E(s)} = \frac{-0.003\,s^2 + 0.435\,s + 0.48}{(s^4 + 2.92\,s^3 + 2.178\,s^2 + 0.015\,s + 0.01)} \tag{3.80}$$

$$\frac{w(s)}{\delta_E(s)} = \frac{-95.166(s^3 + 85.426\,s^2 + 1.9717\,s + 80.86)}{(s^4 + 2.92\,s^3 + 2.178\,s^2 + 0.015\,s + 0.01)} \tag{3.81}$$

$$\frac{q(s)}{\delta_E(s)} = \frac{-13.04(s^2 + 0.707\,s + 0.01)}{(s^4 + 2.92\,s^3 + 2.178\,s^2 + 0.015\,s + 0.01)} \tag{3.82}$$

Equation (3.79) shows that, at this flight condition, the characteristic motion of aircraft BRAVO is composed of phugoid mode, with damping ratio, ζ_{ph}, of 0.073 and frequency, ω_{ph}, of 0.0682 rad s^{-1}, and a short period mode with damping ratio, ζ_{sp}, of 0.557 and frequency, ω_{sp}, of 1.774 rad s^{-1}.

3.5 TRANSFER FUNCTIONS OBTAINED FROM SHORT PERIOD APPROXIMATION

3.5.1 Pitch Rate and Angle-of-attack Transfer Functions

The short period approximation consists of assuming that any variations, u, which arise in airspeed as a result of control surface deflection, atmospheric turbulence, or just aircraft motion, are so small that any terms in the equations of motion involving u are negligible. In other words, the approximation assumes that short period transients are of sufficiently short duration that U_0 remain essentially constant, i.e. $u = 0$. Thus, the equations of longitudinal motion may now be written as:

$$\dot{w} = Z_w w + U_0 q + Z_{\delta_E}\delta_E \tag{3.83}$$

$$\begin{aligned}\dot{q} &= M_w w + M_{\dot{w}}\dot{w} + M_q q + M_{\delta_E}\delta_E = (M_w + M_{\dot{w}}Z_w)w \\ &\quad + (M_q + U_0 M_w)q + (M_{\delta_E} + Z_{\delta_E}M_{\dot{w}})\delta_E\end{aligned} \tag{3.84}$$

If the state vector for short period motion is now defined as:

$$\mathbf{x} \triangleq \begin{bmatrix} w \\ q \end{bmatrix} \tag{3.85}$$

and the control vector, u, is taken as the elevator deflection, δ_E, then eqs (3.83) and (3.84) may be written as a state equation:

$$\dot{\mathbf{x}} = A\mathbf{x} + B\mathbf{u} \tag{3.86}$$

where:

$$A = \begin{bmatrix} Z_w & U_0 \\ (M_w + M_{\dot{w}}Z_w) & (M_q + U_0 \mathrm{M}_{\dot{w}}) \end{bmatrix} \tag{3.87}$$

$$B = \begin{bmatrix} Z_{\delta_E} \\ (M_{\delta_E} + Z_{\delta_E}M_{\dot{w}}) \end{bmatrix} \tag{3.88}$$

$$\therefore \quad [sI - A] = \begin{bmatrix} (s - Z_w) & -U_0 \\ -(M_w + M_{\dot{w}}Z_w) & (s - [M_q + U_0 M_{\dot{w}}]) \end{bmatrix} \tag{3.89}$$

$$\begin{aligned}\Delta_{sp}(s) = \det[sI - A] &= s^2 - [Z_w + M_q + M_{\dot{w}}U_0]s + [Z_w M_q - U_0 M_w] \\ &= s^2 + 2\zeta_{sp}\omega_{sp}s + \omega_{sp}^2\end{aligned} \tag{3.90}$$

where:

$$2\zeta_{sp}\omega_{sp} = -(Z_w + M_q + M_{\dot{w}}U_0) \tag{3.91}$$

$$\omega_{sp} = (Z_w M_q - U_0 M_w)^{1/2} \tag{3.92}$$

It is easy to show that:

$$\frac{w(s)}{\delta_E(s)} = \frac{(U_0 M_{\delta_E} - M_q Z_{\delta_E})\left\{1 + \dfrac{Z_{\delta_E}}{(U_0 M_{\delta_E} - M_q Z_{\delta_E})}s\right\}}{\Delta_{sp}(s)} = \frac{K_w(1 + sT_1)}{\Delta_{sp}(s)} \tag{3.93}$$

where:

$$K_w = (U_0 M_{\delta_E} - M_q Z_{\delta_E}) \tag{3.94}$$

$$T_1 = Z_{\delta_E}/K_w \tag{3.95}$$

Also:

$$\frac{q(s)}{\delta_E(s)} = \frac{(Z_{\delta_E}M_w - M_{\delta_E}Z_w)\left\{1 + \dfrac{M_{\delta_E} + Z_{\delta_E}M_{\dot{w}}}{(Z_{\delta_E}M_w - M_{\delta_E}Z_w)}s\right\}}{\Delta_{sp}(s)} = \frac{K_q(1 + sT_2)}{\Delta_{sp}(s)} \tag{3.96}$$

where:

$$K_q = (Z_{\delta_E}M_w - M_{\delta_E}Z_w) \tag{3.97}$$

$$T_2 = (M_{\delta_E} + Z_{\delta_E}M_{\dot{w}})/K_q \tag{3.98}$$

3.5.2 The Effect of Changes in Static Stability on Short Period Dynamics

When the steady forward speed is fixed, it is possible to increase the value of the short period damping ratio, ζ_{sp}, by augmenting (increasing) any or all of the stability derivatives: Z_w, $M_{\dot{w}}$ and M_q.

If $M_{\dot{w}}$ is augmented, T_2 is increased; the value of the short period frequency, ω_{sp}, is unchanged. If the value of M_{δ_E} is arranged to be equal to $Z_{\delta_E}M_{\dot{w}}$ it is possible for T_2 to be zero.

Augmenting the value of M_q causes an increase in the value of the damping ratio of the short period motion. The frequency of the short period mode is also increased by this change in the value of M_q. The value of T_1 is reduced, although the value of T_2 remains unchanged.

The damping ratio, ζ_{sp}, is also a direct function of M_w, the stability derivative whose value is related to the static stability. When the value of M_w approaches zero, the damping ratio of the short period increases, since the value of the natural frequency is reduced. If the aircraft is statically unstable, M_w is positive and if $U_0M_w > M_qZ_w$ the aircraft will become dynamically unstable (see Section 3.2.3).

3.5.3 The Aircraft Time Constant

If the inequality (3.99) holds, i.e.:

$$Z_{\delta_E}M_w \ll M_{\delta_E}Z_w \tag{3.99}$$

and if:

$$Z_{\delta_E}M_{\dot{w}} \rightarrow 0 \tag{3.100}$$

then:

$$T_2 = M_{\delta_E}/M_{\delta_E}Z_w = -1/Z_w = T_A \tag{3.101}$$

T_2 is usually referred to as the aircraft time constant. How good the approximation is may be judged from Table 3.1 in which are quoted, for a wide

Table 3.1 Aircraft time constants

Parameter	*Aircraft type*						
	A-4D	*F-4C*	*Jaguar*	*Jetstar*	*DC-8*	*B-747*	*C-5a*
Z_w	− 0.307	− 0.452	− 0.6	− 1.01	− 0.63	− 0.512	− 0.634
T_A^{-1}	0.31	0.39	0.57	0.95	0.56	0.49	0.595

variety of aircraft operating at about the same flight condition, the values of Z_w and of the inverse of T_2 (determined from the full equations).

3.5.4 Flight Path Angle

There is a useful kinematic relationship which can be found by means of the short period approximation: to change the flight path angle, γ, of an aircraft it is customary to command a change in the pitch attitude, θ, of the aircraft. Since

$$\gamma = \theta - \alpha \tag{3.102}$$

$$\frac{\gamma(s)}{\theta(s)} = 1 - \frac{\alpha(s)}{\delta_E(s)} \cdot \frac{\delta_E(s)}{\theta(s)} \tag{3.103}$$

By means of eqs (3.93) and (3.96), and remembering that:

$$\alpha = w/U_0 \tag{3.104}$$

and

$$\dot{\theta} = q \tag{3.105}$$

it can be shown that:

$$\begin{aligned}\frac{\gamma(s)}{\theta(s)} = &\frac{-Z_{\delta_E}s^2 + [U_0(M_{\delta_E} + Z_{\delta_E}M_{\dot{w}}) - (M_{\delta_E}U_0 - M_qZ_{\delta_E})s]}{U_0(M_{\delta_E} + Z_{\delta_E}M_{\dot{w}})s + U_0(M_wZ_{\delta_E} - Z_wM_{\delta_E})} \\ &+ \frac{U_0(M_wZ_{\delta_E} - Z_wM_{\delta_E})}{U_0(M_{\delta_E} + Z_{\delta_E}M_{\dot{w}})s + U_0(M_wZ_{\delta_E} - Z_wM_{\delta_E})}\end{aligned} \tag{3.106}$$

Generally Z_{δ_E} is negligible. Then:

$$\frac{\gamma(s)}{\theta(s)} \rightarrow \frac{-Z_wM_{\delta_E}U_0}{U_0(M_{\delta_E}s - Z_wM_{\delta_E})} = \frac{-Z_w}{(s - Z_w)} = \frac{1}{1 + sT_A}$$

where:

$$T_A = -Z_w^{-1} \tag{3.107}$$

as before. From eq. (3.107) it is easy to derive that:

$$\dot{\gamma} = \alpha/T_A \tag{3.108}$$

3.6 TRANSFER FUNCTIONS OBTAINED FROM PHUGOID APPROXIMATION

Lanchester (Sutton, 1949) studied the slow period motion of aircraft and noted that the phugoid motion consists of large oscillatory changes in speed u, height h, and pitch attitude θ. In that classic treatment, Lanchester took the value of the stability derivative M_u, i.e. the change in pitching moment due to changes in airspeed, to be negligible for all aircraft, i.e.:

$$M_u = 0 \tag{3.109}$$

However, for modern aircraft M_u is seldom zero and the total static stability moment of the aircraft becomes:

$$M_u u + M_w w = 0 \tag{3.110}$$

Since short period changes in q, for example, are not of interest the equations of motion can be written as:

$$\begin{aligned} \dot{u} &= X_u u + X_w w - g\theta + X_\delta \delta \\ \dot{w} &= Z_u u + Z_w w + U_0 q + Z_\delta \delta \\ 0 &= M_u u + M_w + M_\delta \delta \end{aligned} \qquad (3.111)^5$$

Hence, taking Laplace transforms:

$$\begin{aligned} su(s) - X_u u(s) - X_w w(s) + g\theta(s) &= X_\delta \delta(s) \\ sw(s) - Z_u u(s) - Z_w w(s) - U_0 s\theta(s) &= Z_\delta \delta(s) \\ - M_u u(s) - M_w w(s) &= M_\delta \delta(s) \end{aligned} \tag{3.112}$$

i.e.:

$$\begin{bmatrix} (s - X_u) & -X_w & g \\ -Z_u & (s - Z_w) & -U_0 s \\ -M_u & -M_w & 0 \end{bmatrix} \begin{bmatrix} u(s) \\ w(s) \\ \theta(s) \end{bmatrix} = \begin{bmatrix} X_\delta \\ Z_\delta \\ M_\delta \end{bmatrix} \delta(s) \tag{3.113}$$

i.e.:

$$Q(s)x(s) = P(s)\delta(s) \tag{3.114}$$

hence:

$$x(s) = Q^{-1}(s)P(s)\delta(s) \tag{3.115}$$

$$\therefore \quad \frac{u(s)}{\delta(s)} = \frac{s[X_w U_0 M_\delta - gM_\delta - U_0 M_w X_\delta] + g[M_\delta Z_w - M_w Z_\delta]}{\Delta_{ph}(s)} \tag{3.116}$$

$$\frac{\theta(s)}{\delta(s)} = \frac{s^2 M_\delta + [M_u X_\delta + M_w Z_\delta - (X_u + Z_w)M_\delta]s}{\Delta_{ph}(s)} \tag{3.117}$$

$$-\frac{[(Z_uM_w - M_uZ_w)X_\delta - (M_uX_w - M_wX_u)Z_\delta]}{\Delta_{ph}(s)}$$

where:

$$\Delta_{ph}(s) = -U_0M_w\left\{s^2 - \left[x_u + \frac{M_u(U_0X_w - g)}{U_0M_w}\right]s - \frac{g}{U_0}\left[Z_u - \frac{M_uZ_w}{M_w}\right]\right\} \quad (3.118)$$

From eq. (3.118):

$$\omega_{ph}^2 = \frac{-g}{U_0}\left[Z_u - \frac{M_uZ_w}{M_w}\right] \quad (3.119)$$

$$2\zeta_{ph}\omega_{ph} = -\left[X_u + \frac{M_u(U_0X_w - g)}{U_0M_w}\right] \quad (3.120)$$

If M_u is sufficiently negative the result is that ω_{ph}^2 becomes negative: that unstable mode is called the divergent tuck mode (see Section 3.2.2).

If Lanchester's classical approximation is invoked, i.e. $M_u = 0$, then:

$$2\zeta_{ph}\omega_{ph} = -X_u \quad (3.121)$$

and

$$\omega_{ph}^2 = -gZ_u/U_0 \quad (3.122)$$

The stability derivative, Z_u, can be shown to be:

$$Z_u \simeq \frac{-\rho SU_0}{m}C_L \quad (3.123)$$

but the lift coefficient, C_L, can be shown to be (in steady, straight and level flight):

$$C_L = \frac{\text{weight}}{\bar{q}S} = \frac{2mg}{\rho U_0^2 S} \quad (3.124)$$

$$\therefore \quad Z_u = -2g/U_0 \quad (3.125)$$

$$\therefore \quad \omega_{ph} \simeq \sqrt{2}\frac{g}{U_0} \quad (3.126)$$

Based on the assumption that the stability derivative, M_u, had a value of zero, the resulting approximation, the classical phugoid approximation, was called the two degrees of freedom phugoid approximation, i.e.:

$$\begin{aligned}(s - X_u)\,u(s) + g\theta(s) &= 0\\ -Z_uu(s) - U_0s\,\theta(s) &= Z_\delta\delta(s)\end{aligned} \quad (3.127)$$

Therefore the characteristic equation is

Table 3.2 Comparison of phugoid parameters

Aircraft type	U_0 *(m s^{-1})*	Z_u		ω_{ph}		$\omega_{ph} = -Z_u/\sqrt{2}$	M_u
		Actual	*Calculated* eq. (3.125)	*Actual*	*Calculated* eq. (3.126)		
DC-3	45	− 0.476	− 0.474	0.301	0.33	0.337	0.0
F-89	210	− 0.0955	− 0.0976	0.063	0.069	0.0678	0.0
DC-8	285	− 0.0735	− 0.076	(− 0.0016)	0.053	0.0527	− 0.00254

$$s^2 - X_u s - (gZ_u/U_0) = 0 \tag{3.128}$$

For modern aircraft, the three degrees of freedom approximation represented by eq. (3.114) is preferred. Table 3.2 illustrates the character of the approximations.

It can be seen from the table that the classical, and even the three degrees of freedom, approximation is unacceptable in the case of the DC-8 where a divergent tuck mode exists.

In the classical approximation, the assumption that the value of M_u is zero corresponds to an assumption that the coefficient of drag due to changes in forward speed, C_{D_u}, is also zero.

Now,

$$\zeta_{ph} = -\frac{X_u}{2\omega_{ph}} = -\frac{X_u U_0}{2\sqrt{(2g)}} \tag{3.129}$$

However,

$$X_u = \frac{\bar{q}S}{mU_0}(C_{D_u} + 2C_D) \simeq \frac{2\bar{q}S}{mU_0} C_D \tag{3.130}$$

From eq. (3.124):

$$C_L = \frac{2mg}{\rho U_0^2 S} \tag{3.124}$$

$$\therefore \quad X_u = \frac{2g}{U_0}\frac{C_D}{C_L} \tag{3.131}$$

Hence,

$$\zeta_{ph} = -\left(\frac{2g}{U_0}\right)\left(\frac{C_D}{C_L}\right)\frac{U_0}{2\sqrt{(2g)}} = \frac{1}{\sqrt{2}}\frac{C_D}{C_L} = \frac{1}{\sqrt{2}(L/D)} \tag{3.132}$$

where L/D is the lift/drag ratio of the aircraft. For example, at $U_0 = 210\ \text{m s}^{-1}$ the F-89 has a lift/drag ratio of 12.0, therefore:

$$\zeta_{ph} = 1/\sqrt{2} \times 12 \simeq 0.06$$

$$\omega_{ph} = \sqrt{2} \times 9.81/210 \simeq 0.0661\ \text{rad s}^{-1}$$

3.7 LATERAL STABILITY

The characteristic polynomial of lateral motion, $\det[\lambda I - A]$, is of fifth degree, i.e. it is a quintic of the form: $\lambda^5 + d_1\lambda^4 + d_2\lambda^3 + d_3\lambda^2 + d_4\lambda$. This 'stability quintic' can usually be factorized into the following form: $\lambda(\lambda + e)(\lambda + f)(\lambda^2 + 2\zeta_D\omega_D\lambda + \omega_D^2)$. The simple term in λ corresponds to the heading (directional) mode. Because $\lambda = 0$ is a root of the characteristic equation, once an aircraft's heading has been changed, by whatever agency, there is no natural tendency for the aircraft to be restored to its equilibrium heading. An aircraft has neutral heading stability and it will remain at its perturbed heading until some corrective control action is taken. The term $(\lambda + e)$ corresponds to the spiral convergence/divergence mode, which is usually a very slow motion corresponding to a long term tendency either to maintain the wings level or to 'roll off' in a divergent spiral. The term $(\lambda + f)$ corresponds to the rolling subsidence mode; the quadratic term represents the 'dutch roll' motion for which the value of damping ratio, ζ_D, is usually small, so that 'dutch' rolling motion is oscillatory.

When the dihedral on the wing is great, and roll damping (L'_p) is low, the roll and spiral modes can couple and become a single roll/spiral oscillation (often referred to as the 'lateral phugoid' mode). If such aircraft have also a very lightly damped 'dutch roll' mode, then these aircraft have poor handling qualities and are difficult to fly.

3.8 TRANSFER FUNCTIONS RELATED TO LATERAL MOTION

3.8.1 State and Output Equations

By following the method used in Section 3.4 a number of important transfer functions relating to lateral motion can be found. However, in this case there are, even for conventional aircraft, two control surfaces, the aileron and the rudder, which are used simultaneously in certain phases of flight, such as final approach. When two inputs act simultaneously, then the use of transfer functions is less exact, since they are strictly single-input, single-output functions.

If the state vector for straight and level lateral motion is taken as that defined in eq. (2.151), namely:

$$\mathbf{x} = \begin{bmatrix} \beta \\ p \\ r \\ \phi \\ \psi \end{bmatrix} \tag{2.151}$$

and the control vector is defined as

$$\mathbf{u} = \begin{bmatrix} \delta_A \\ \delta_R \end{bmatrix} \tag{2.143}$$

the corresponding coefficient and driving matrices are given in eqs (2.152) and (2.153) as:

$$A = \begin{bmatrix} Y_v & 0 & -1 & \frac{g}{U_0} & 0 \\ L'_\beta & L'_p & L'_r & 0 & 0 \\ N'_\beta & N'_p & N'_r & 0 & 0 \\ 0 & 1 & 0 & 0 & 0 \\ 0 & 0 & 1 & 0 & 0 \end{bmatrix} \tag{2.152}$$

$$B = \begin{bmatrix} 0 & Y^*_{\delta_R} \\ L'_{\delta_A} & L'_{\delta_R} \\ N'_{\delta_A} & N'_{\delta_R} \\ 0 & 0 \end{bmatrix} \tag{2.153}$$

Assuming that no acceleration term, such as $a_{y_{cg}}$, is defined as an output variable and that the output will be taken as a single state variable, then:

$$y = C\mathbf{x} \tag{3.133}$$

If:

$$y \triangleq \beta \tag{3.134}$$

then:

$$C_\beta = [1 \ 0 \ 0 \ 0 \ 0] \tag{3.135a}$$

Similarly, the following output matrices can be defined:

$$\begin{aligned} C_p &= [0 \ 1 \ 0 \ 0 \ 0] \qquad C_\phi = [0 \ 0 \ 0 \ 1 \ 0] \\ C_r &= [0 \ 0 \ 1 \ 0 \ 0] \qquad C_\Psi = [0 \ 0 \ 0 \ 0 \ 1] \end{aligned} \tag{3.135b}$$

If the transfer function being evaluated depends upon the aileron deflection, δ_A, the first column of the driving matrix, B, is used; the second column of B is used when the control input is the rudder deflection δ_R. Consequently, the development will proceed using δ as a control input; the appropriate subscript A or R should be added when the input is particular, and the corresponding values of the control stability derivatives Y^*_δ, L'_δ, and N'_δ should be used.

3.8.2 Transfer Functions in Terms of Stability Derivatives

From eq. (2.152) it is evident that the characteristic polynomial will be a quintic (i.e. of fifth degree) since:

$$\begin{aligned}\det[sI - A] &= s^5 - (L'_p + N'_r + Y_v)s^4 \\ &\quad + (L'_pN'_r - L'_rN'_p + Y_vL'_p + Y_vN'_r + N'_\beta)s^3 \\ &\quad + \left(L'_pN'_p - L'_pN'_\beta - \frac{g}{U_0}L'_p - Y_vL'_pN'_r + Y_vL'_pN'_p\right)s^2 \\ &\quad + \left(\frac{g}{U_0}[N'_rL'_\beta - L'_rN'_\beta]\right)s \\ &= s\Delta_{\text{lat}}(s) \end{aligned} \tag{3.136}$$

where

$$\Delta_{\text{lat}}(s) = s^4 + d_1s^3 + d_2s^2 + d_3s + d_4 \tag{3.137}$$

$$d_1 = -(L'_p + N'_r + Y_v) \tag{3.138}$$

$$d_2 = (L'_pN'_r - L'_rN'_p + Y_vL'_p + Y_vN'_r + N'_\beta) \tag{3.139}$$

$$d_3 = \left(L'_\beta N'_p - L'_pN'_\beta - \frac{g}{U_0}L'_\beta - Y_vL'_pN'_r + Y_vL'_rN'_p\right) \tag{3.140}$$

$$d_4 = \frac{g}{U_0}[N'_rL'_\beta - L'_rN'_\beta] \tag{3.141}$$

The adjoint of $[sI - A]$ takes the form:

$$\operatorname{adj}[sI - A] \triangleq \begin{bmatrix} n_{11}(s) & n_{12}(s) & n_{13}(s) & n_{14}(s) & n_{15}(s) \\ n_{21}(s) & n_{22}(s) & n_{23}(s) & n_{24}(s) & n_{25}(s) \\ n_{31}(s) & n_{32}(s) & n_{33}(s) & n_{34}(s) & n_{35}(s) \\ n_{41}(s) & n_{42}(s) & n_{43}(s) & n_{44}(s) & n_{45}(s) \\ n_{51}(s) & n_{52}(s) & n_{53}(s) & n_{54}(s) & n_{55}(s) \end{bmatrix} \tag{3.142}$$

where $n_{ij}(s)$ is a cofactor of $[sI - A]$. The cofactors are:

$$n_{11}(s) = s^2\{s^2 - [L'_p + N'_r]s + [N'_rL'_p - L'_rN'_p]\} \tag{3.143}$$

$$n_{12}(s) = -s\left\{\left(N'_p - \frac{g}{U_0}\right]s + \frac{N'_rg}{U_0}\right\} \tag{3.144}$$

$$n_{13}(s) = -s\left\{s^2 - L'_ps - \frac{L'_r}{U_0}\right\} \tag{3.145}$$

$$n_{21}(s) = s^2\{sL'_\beta + [N'_\beta L'_r - L'_\beta N'_r]\} \tag{3.146}$$

$$n_{22}(s) = s^2\{s^2 - [Y_v + N'_r]s + [Y_vN'_r + N'_\beta]\} \tag{3.147}$$

$$n_{23}(s) = s^2\{sL'_r - [Y_vL'_r + L'_\beta]\} \tag{3.148}$$

$$n_{31}(s) = s^2\{sN'_\beta + [L'_\beta N'_p - L'_pN'_\beta]\} \tag{3.149}$$

$$n_{32}(s) = s\left\{s^2N'_p - Y_vN'_ps + \frac{N'_\beta g}{U_0}\right\} \tag{3.150}$$

$$n_{33}(s) = s\left\{s^3 - [Y_v + L'_p]s^2 + Y_vL'_ps - \frac{g}{U_0}L'_p\right\} \tag{3.151}$$

$$n_{41}(s) = s\{sL'_\beta + [N'_\beta L'_r - L'_\beta N'_r]\} \tag{3.152}$$

$$n_{42}(s) = s\{s^2 - [Y_v + N'_r]s + [Y_vN'_r + N'_\beta]\} \tag{3.153}$$

$$n_{43}(s) = s\{sL'_r - [Y_vL'_r + L'_\beta]\} \tag{3.154}$$

$$n_{51}(s) = s^3\{sN'_\beta + [L'_\beta N'_p - N'_\beta L'_p]\} \tag{3.155}$$

$$n_{52}(s) = s^2\left\{s^2N'_p - Y_vN'_ps + \frac{N'_\beta g}{U_0}\right\} \tag{3.156}$$

$$n_{53}(s) = s^2\left\{s^3 - [Y_v + L'_p]s^2 + Y_vL'_ps - \frac{g}{U_0}L'_\beta\right\} \tag{3.157}$$

Those cofactors not listed above are zero. Obviously,

$$\frac{\beta(s)}{\delta(s)} = C_\beta[sI - A]^{-1}B = \frac{[n_{11}(s)\ n_{12}(s)\ n_{13}(s)\ n_{14}(s)\ n_{15}(s)]}{s\Delta_{\text{lat}}(s)}B$$

$$= \frac{n_{11}(s)\,Y^*_\delta + n_{12}(s)\,L'_\delta + n_{13}(s)\,N'_\delta}{s\Delta_{\text{lat}}(s)} \tag{3.158}$$

$$\therefore\quad \frac{\beta(s)}{\delta(s)} = \frac{Y^*_\delta s^3 - [(L'_p + N'_r)Y^*_\delta + N'_\delta]s^2}{\Delta_{\text{lat}}(s)} + \frac{\left[(N'_rL'_p - L'_rN'_p)Y^*_\delta + (L'_pN'_\delta - N'_pL'_\delta) + \dfrac{gL'_\delta}{U_0}\right]s}{\Delta_{\text{lat}}(s)} + \frac{\dfrac{g}{U_0}(N'_\delta L'_r - N'_rL'_\delta)}{\Delta_{\text{lat}}(s)} \tag{3.159}$$

$$\frac{p(s)}{\delta(s)} = s\left\{\frac{s^2L'_\delta + [(L'_\beta Y^*_\delta - L'_\delta(N'_r + Y_v) + N'_\delta L'_r]s}{\Delta_{\text{lat}}(s)} + \frac{Y^*_\delta(L'_rN'_\beta - N'_rL'_\delta + L'_\delta(Y_vN'_r + N'_\beta) - N'_\delta(L'_\beta + Y_vL'_r)}{\Delta_{\text{lat}}(s)}\right\}$$

$$\therefore\quad \frac{s\phi(s)}{\delta(s)} \triangleq \frac{N^p_\delta(s)}{\Delta_{\text{lat}}(s)} \tag{3.160}$$

$$
\begin{aligned}
\frac{r(s)}{\delta(s)} &= \frac{s\psi(s)}{\delta(s)} \\
&= \frac{N'_{\delta}s^3 + [Y^*_{\delta}N'_{\beta} + L'_{\delta}N'_p - N'_{\delta}(Y_v + L'_p)]s^2}{\Delta_{\text{lat}}(s)} \\
&\quad + \frac{[Y^*_{\delta}(L'_{\beta}N'_p - N'_{\beta}L'_p) - \mathrm{L}'_{\delta}Y_vN'_p + N'_{\delta}Y_vL'_p]s}{\Delta_{\text{lat}}(s)} \\
&\quad + \frac{\frac{g}{U_0}[L'_{\delta}N'_{\beta} - N'_{\delta}L'_{\beta})}{\Delta_{\text{lat}}(s)}
\end{aligned}
\tag{3.161}
$$

3.8.3 Lateral Acceleration as an Output Variable

If the transfer function relating the lateral acceleration at the aircraft's c.g. to some control input δ is required, it may be obtained by noting that, from eq. (2.158),

$$a_{y_{\text{cg}}} = C_{a_y}\mathbf{x} + D\mathbf{u} \triangleq y \tag{3.162}$$

$$C_{a_y} = [Y_v \;\; 0 \;\; 0 \;\; 0 \;\; 0] \tag{3.163}$$

$$D = [0 \;\; Y^*_{\delta_{\text{R}}}] \tag{3.164}$$

3.8.4 Some Representative Transfer Functions

Taking the large passenger jet aircraft CHARLIE in Appendix B, for flight condition 4, the following transfer functions can be evaluated:

$$\frac{\beta(s)}{\delta_{\text{R}}(s)} = \frac{0.012(s - 0.027)(s + 0.52)(s + 40.1)}{(s - 0.012)(s + 0.562)(s + 0.091s + 0.656)} \tag{3.165}$$

$$\frac{r(s)}{\delta_{\text{R}}(s)} = \frac{-0.48(s + 0.587)(s^2 - 0.066s + 0.059)}{(s - 0.012)(s + 0.562)(s^2 + 0.091s + 0.656)} \tag{3.166}$$

$$\frac{p(s)}{\delta_{\text{A}}(s)} = \frac{0.14(s^2 - 0.2s + 0.668)}{(s - 0.012)(s + 0.562)(s^2 + 0.091s + 0.656)} \tag{3.167}$$

$$\frac{a_{y_{\text{cg}}}(s)}{\delta_{\text{R}}(s)} = \frac{0.012(s - 0.027)(s - 31.6)(s + 17.744)(s + 0.52)}{(s - 0.012)(s + 0.562)(s^2 + 0.091s + 0.656)} \tag{3.168}$$

3.8.5 Some Transfer Function Approximations

In every transfer function, except eq. (3.167), the dutch roll mode is a major component of the weighting function of the aircraft, i.e. its response to an

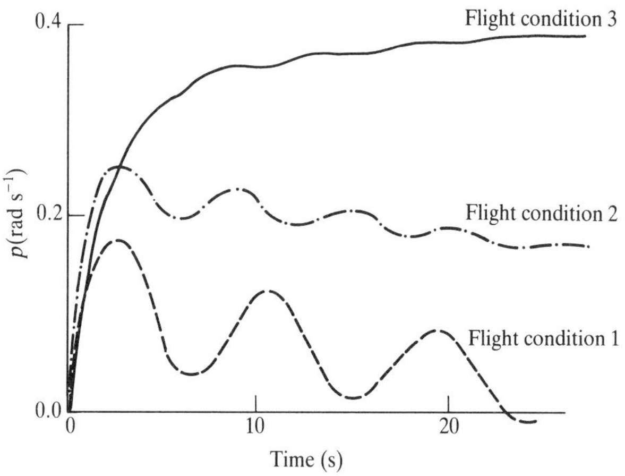

Figure 3.4 Roll rate response for CHARLIE.

impulse. For the transfer function, $p(s)/\delta_A(s)$, the quadratic numerator term very nearly cancels the quadratic term in the denominator. If that cancellation were exact, no dutch roll motion would be evident in the rolling motion of the aircraft; however, there is usually a small amount evident (see Figure 3.4). In every transfer function above, except the rolling motion transfer function eq. (3.167), a first order numerator term almost exactly cancels the term $(s + 0.56)$ in the denominator; this term corresponds to the rolling subsidence mode. The transfer function relating the lateral acceleration at the c.g. to a rudder deflection $a_{y_{cg}}(s)/\delta_R(s)$ approximates very closely to a constant value of -33.0, because all the numerator terms very nearly cancel the corresponding denominator terms. Inspection of the transfer function eq. (3.165) shows that a much simpler, approximate form might be used, namely:

$$\frac{\beta(s)}{\delta_R(s)} = \frac{0.012(s + 40.1)}{(s^2 + 0.091s + 0.656)} = \frac{0.481(1 + 0.025s)}{(s^2 + 0.091s + 0.656)} \qquad (3.169)$$

The time constant of the numerator term, $0.025s$, is very short and can be ignored, so that the approximation may be taken as:

$$\frac{\beta(s)}{\delta_R(s)} = \frac{0.48}{(s^2 + 0.091s + 0.656)} \qquad (3.170)$$

The primary response to aileron deflection is in roll rate and the evidence of any dutch roll motion excited by an aileron deflection is principally found in sideslip β and yaw rate r. In the spiral motion of an aircraft, rolling and yawing motion are predominant and, although the mode is usually unstable, the motion is very nearly co-ordinated. Sideslip is almost non-existent in the spiral mode, and the motion which occurs is a co-ordinated bank turn defined by:

$$a_{y_{cg}} = \ddot{y} = U_0(\dot{\beta} + r) = U_0(v + r) = 0 \tag{3.171}$$

$$\dot{y} = U_0(\beta + \psi) = 0 \tag{3.172}$$

where y denotes lateral displacement.

3.9 THREE DEGREES OF FREEDOM APPROXIMATIONS

3.9.1 Dutch Roll Approximation

From a consideration of the appropriate cancellation of terms in transfer functions, it appears likely that there are some useful approximations which can lead to simpler transfer functions of acceptable accuracy, which still represent the functional relationship between the motion variable of the aircraft and the control deflection which caused it. The first of these approximations is the three degrees of freedom approximation which is arrived at by taking the equations of motion for straight and level flight given by eq. (2.85), and neglecting a few insignificant terms. Thus, the following terms are small for small perturbation motion and flight at moderate and higher speeds, and are assumed to be zero: the term due to gravity, $g\phi/U_0$; rolling acceleration as a result of yaw rate, $L'_r r$; yawing acceleration as a result of roll rate, $N'_p p$. Therefore, the equations of motion may now be written as:

$$\begin{aligned}\dot{\beta} &= Y_v\beta - r + Y^*_{\delta}\delta \\ \dot{p} &= L'_{\beta}\beta + N'_p p + L^*_{\delta}\delta \\ \dot{r} &= N'_{\beta}\beta + N'_p p + N^*_{\delta}\delta\end{aligned} \tag{3.173}$$

i.e.

$$\begin{bmatrix} \dot{\beta} \\ \dot{p} \\ \dot{r} \end{bmatrix} = \begin{bmatrix} Y_v & 0 & -1 \\ L'_{\beta} & L'_p & 0 \\ N'_{\beta} & 0 & N'_p \end{bmatrix} \begin{bmatrix} \beta \\ p \\ r \end{bmatrix} + \begin{bmatrix} Y^*_{\beta} \\ L'_{\delta} \\ N'_{\delta} \end{bmatrix} \delta \tag{3.174}$$

This is referred to as the dutch roll approximation.

From eq. (3.174) it is easy to show that:

$$\Delta_{lat}(s) = s^3 - [Y_v + L'_p + N'_r]s^2 + [Y_vL'_p + Y_vN'_p + L'_pN'_r + N'_{\beta}]s - L'_p[N'_{\beta} + N'_rY_v] \tag{3.175}$$

and that, for example,

$$\frac{\beta(s)}{\delta_R(s)} = \frac{Y^*_{\delta}s^2 - [(L'_p + N'_p)Y^*_{\delta} + N'_{\delta}]s + [L'_pN'_rY^*_{\delta} + L'_pN'_{\delta}]}{\Delta_{lat}(s)} \tag{3.176}$$

$$\frac{p(s)}{\delta_A(s)} = \frac{L'_\delta s^2 + [Y^*_\delta L'_\beta - Y_v L'_\delta - N'_r L'_\delta]s}{\Delta_{lat}(s)} + \frac{[Y_v N'_r L'_\delta + N'_\beta L'_s - L'_\beta N'_\delta - Y^*_\delta L'_\beta N'_r]}{\Delta_{lat}(s)} \tag{3.177}$$

3.9.2 An Example of Dutch Roll Approximation

For aircraft CHARLIE at flight condition 4,

$$\frac{p(s)}{\delta_A(s)} = \frac{0.14(s^2 + 0.193s + 0.673)}{(s + 0.506)(s^2 + 0.135s + 0.63)} \tag{3.178}$$

By cancelling the quadratic terms of the numerator and denominator the resulting transfer function becomes:

$$\frac{p(s)}{\delta_A(s)} = \frac{0.14}{(s + 0.506)} \tag{3.179}$$

Inspection of eq. (3.167), with appropriate cancellations, will indicate how closely the results correspond. The transfer function for the same aircraft and flight condition is easily determined:

$$\frac{\beta(s)}{\delta_R(s)} = \frac{0.012(s + 0.48)(s + 40.1406)}{(s + 0.506)(s^2 + 0.135s + 0.68)} \simeq \frac{0.481(1 + 0.025s)}{(s^2 + 0.135s + 0.68)} \tag{3.180}$$

Since the time constant of the numerator term is negligibly small, the approximate transfer function is given by:

$$\frac{\beta(s)}{\delta_R(s)} = \frac{0.48}{(s^2 + 0.14s + 0.68)} \tag{3.181}$$

which should be compared with eq. (3.170): note how close the transfer functions are.

3.9.3 Spiral and Roll Subsidence Approximations

The approximations are founded on the observation that, for both spiral and roll modes, the corresponding sideslip motion is small and that, for the spiral mode, the term $\dot{\beta}$ is negligible with respect to the remaining terms in the equation for side force. Consequently, eq. (2.85) can be rewritten as:

$$0 = \frac{g}{U_0}\phi - r + Y^*_\delta \delta + Y_v \beta$$

$$\dot{p} = L'_\beta \beta + L'_p p + L'_r r + L'_\delta \delta \tag{3.182}$$

$$\dot{r} = N'_{\beta}\beta + N'_{p}p + N'_{r}r + N'_{\delta}\delta$$
$$\dot{\phi} = p$$

Thus, when $\beta = 0$, the equations of motion reduce to the following set:

$$\begin{aligned}\dot{p} &= L'_{p}p + L'_{r}r + L'_{\delta_R}\delta_R \\ \dot{r} &= N'_{p}p + N'_{r}r + N'_{\delta_R}\delta_R \\ \dot{\phi} &= p\end{aligned} \qquad (3.183)$$

i.e. if:

$$\mathbf{x} \triangleq \begin{bmatrix} p \\ r \\ \phi \end{bmatrix} \qquad (3.184a)$$

$$u \triangleq \delta_R \qquad (3.184b)$$

then:

$$\dot{\mathbf{x}} = A\mathbf{x} + B\mathbf{u} \qquad (3.184c)$$

when:

$$A \triangleq \begin{bmatrix} L'_p & L'_r & 0 \\ N'_p & N'_r & 0 \\ 1 & 0 & 0 \end{bmatrix} \qquad (3.185a)$$

$$B \triangleq \begin{bmatrix} L'_{\delta_R} \\ N'_{\delta_R} \\ 0 \end{bmatrix} \qquad (3.185b)$$

To find the sideslip angle, β, which results from a rudder deflection, it is necessary to define β as an output variable, y, i.e.

$$\begin{aligned} y \triangleq \beta &= \frac{1}{Y_v} r - \frac{g}{U_0 Y_v}\phi - \frac{Y^*_{\delta_R}}{Y_v}\delta_R \\ &= \left[0 \;\; \frac{1}{Y_v} \;\; -\frac{g}{U_0 Y_v}\right]\mathbf{x} + \left[-\frac{Y^*_{\delta_R}}{Y_v}\right]u \\ &= C_{\beta}\mathbf{x} + D_{\beta}\alpha \end{aligned} \qquad (3.186)$$

For CHARLIE-4

$$A = \begin{bmatrix} -0.47 & 0.39 & 0.0 \\ -0.032 & -0.115 & 0.0 \\ 1.0 & 0.0 & 0.0 \end{bmatrix}$$

$$B = \begin{bmatrix} 0.15 \\ -0.48 \\ 0.0 \end{bmatrix}$$

$$C_{\beta} = [0.0 \ -17.857 \ 0.7]$$

$$D_{\beta} = [0.2143]$$

It can easily be shown that the following transfer functions are obtained using this three degree of freedom approximation, namely:

$$\frac{\beta(s)}{\delta_R(s)} = \frac{0.2143(s-0.026)(s+0.52)(s+40.1)}{s(s+0.155)(s+0.43)} \simeq \frac{0.2143(s+40.1)}{(s+0.155)} \quad (3.187)$$

$$\frac{p(s)}{\delta_R(s)} = \frac{0.15(s-1.133)}{(s+0.155)(s+0.43)} \quad (3.188)$$

$$\frac{r(s)}{\delta_R(s)} = \frac{-0.48(s+0.48)}{(s+0.43)(s+0.155)} \simeq \frac{-0.48}{(s+0.155)} \quad (3.189)$$

It is evident from these transfer functions that the dutch roll mode is absent from this characterization, which is really unacceptable. Consequently, the approximation is rarely used.

3.10 TWO DEGREES OF FREEDOM APPROXIMATION

If it is assumed that the bank angle motion is negligible then the sum of the rolling moments is zero at all times; consequently, the roll equation is eliminated along with the bank angle perturbations. Thus:

$$\dot{\beta} = Y_v\beta - r + Y_{\delta}^{*}\delta \qquad \dot{r} = N'_{\beta}\beta + N'_r r + N'_{\delta}\delta \quad (3.190)$$

$$\begin{bmatrix} \dot{\beta} \\ \dot{r} \end{bmatrix} = \begin{bmatrix} Y_v & -1 \\ N'_{\beta} & N'_r \end{bmatrix} \begin{bmatrix} \beta \\ r \end{bmatrix} + \begin{bmatrix} Y_{\delta}^{*} \\ N'_{\delta} \end{bmatrix} \delta \quad (3.191)$$

$$\therefore \quad \Delta_{lat}(s) = s^2 - (Y_v + N'_r)s + (N'_{\beta} + Y_v N'_r) \quad (3.192)$$

and

$$\frac{\beta(s)}{\delta_R(s)} = \frac{(s - N'_r)Y_{\delta}^{*} - N'_{\delta}}{\Delta_{lat}(s)} \quad (3.193)$$

$$\frac{r(s)}{\delta_R(s)} = \frac{(s - Y_v)N'_{\delta} + Y_{\delta}^{*}N'_{\beta}}{\Delta_{lat}(s)} \quad (3.194)$$

For aircraft CHARLIE, at flight condition 4:

$$\frac{\beta(s)}{\delta_R(s)} = \frac{0.012(s + 40.115)}{(s^2 + 0.173s + 0.61)} \tag{3.195}$$

$$\frac{r(s)}{\delta_R(s)} = \frac{-0.48(s + 0.4)}{(s^2 + 0.173s + 0.061)} \tag{3.196}$$

The approximation (3.195) is reasonably close to that obtained as eq. (3.169), although the damping ratio is about twice the proper value. Nevertheless this approximation (3.193) is used frequently in AFCS work.

3.11 SINGLE DEGREE OF FREEDOM APPROXIMATION

In this approximation only rolling motion is assumed to occur as a result of an aileron deflection, i.e.

$$\dot{p} = L'_p p + L'_{\delta_A}\delta_A \tag{3.197}$$

i.e.:

$$(s - L'_p)p(s) = L'_{\delta_A}\delta_A(s) \tag{3.198}$$

$$\therefore \quad \frac{p(s)}{\delta_A(s)} = \frac{L'_{\delta_A}}{(s - L'_p)} \tag{3.199}$$

For aircraft CHARLIE, at flight condition 4:

$$\frac{p(s)}{\delta_A(s)} = \frac{0.14}{(s + 0.47)} \tag{3.200}$$

If the corresponding numerator and denominator terms in eq. (3.167) are cancelled, the result is:

$$\frac{p(s)}{\delta_A(s)} = \frac{0.14}{(s + 0.56)} \tag{3.201}$$

which is very close to eq. (3.200). For bank angle control systems, the single degree of freedom approximation is frequently used as a first approximation.

3.12 STATE EQUATION FORMULATION TO EMPHASIZE LATERAL/DIRECTIONAL EFFECTS

If the state vector for lateral motion is defined thus:

$$\mathbf{x} = \begin{bmatrix} r \\ \beta \\ p \\ \phi \end{bmatrix} \tag{3.202}$$

and the control vector, **u**, is defined as:

$$\mathbf{u} = \begin{bmatrix} \delta_R \\ \\ \delta_A \end{bmatrix} \tag{3.203}$$

then:

$$A = \begin{bmatrix} N'_r & N'_\beta & N'_p & 0 \\ -1 & Y_v & 0 & \frac{g}{U_0} \\ L'_r & L'_\beta & L'_p & 0 \\ 0 & 0 & 1 & 0 \end{bmatrix} \tag{3.204}$$

$$B = \begin{bmatrix} N'_{\delta_R} & N'_{\delta_A} \\ Y^*_{\delta_R} & Y^*_{\delta_A} \\ L'_{\delta_R} & L'_{\delta_A} \\ 0 & 0 \end{bmatrix} \tag{3.205}$$

By choosing the state and control vectors in this fashion, A can be partitioned as follows:

$$\left[\begin{array}{c|c} \textit{Directional effects} & \textit{Lateral/directional coupling} \\ \hline \textit{Directional/lateral coupling} & \textit{Lateral effects} \end{array}\right] \tag{3.206}$$

or, more compactly:

$$A = \left[\begin{array}{c|c} A_D & A_D^L \\ \hline A_L^D & A_L \end{array}\right] \tag{3.207}$$

In a similar way:

$$B = \left[\begin{array}{c|c} B_D & B_D^L \\ \hline B_L^D & B_L \end{array}\right] \tag{3.208}$$

The strength of the lateral/directional coupling depends upon the relative magnitude of the 'off-diagonal' blocks.

In A, the coupling effects are 'stability' effects, while the coupling effects in B represent control effects. They are quite separate phenomena. But coupling effects in A almost always lead to coupled control response whether or not there are any explicit coupling effects in B. Control coupling can affect stability only when there is external feedback as a result of a pilot's action or of the AFCS.

If the off-diagonal blocks are negligible then dutch roll motion is approximated by the directional equation:

$$\begin{bmatrix} \dot{r} \\ \dot{\beta} \end{bmatrix} = \begin{bmatrix} N'_r & N'_\beta \\ -1 & Y_v \end{bmatrix} \begin{bmatrix} r \\ \beta \end{bmatrix} + \begin{bmatrix} N'_{\delta_R} & N'_{\delta_A} \\ Y^*_{\beta_R} & Y^*_{\delta_A} \end{bmatrix} \begin{bmatrix} \delta_R \\ \delta_A \end{bmatrix} \tag{3.209}$$

The lateral equation is given by:

$$\begin{bmatrix} \dot{p} \\ \dot{\phi} \end{bmatrix} = \begin{bmatrix} L'_p & 0 \\ 1 & 0 \end{bmatrix} \begin{bmatrix} p \\ \phi \end{bmatrix} + \begin{bmatrix} L'_{\delta_A} \\ 0 \end{bmatrix} \delta_A \tag{3.120}$$

As always, the stability of the respective motions is governed by the roots of the characteristic equations. For the dutch roll motion it is easy to show that:

$$\omega_D = (N'_\beta + N'_r Y_v)^{1/2} \tag{3.211}$$

$$\zeta_D = -\frac{(N'_r + Y_v)}{2\omega_D} \tag{3.212}$$

For the lateral motion the characteristic equation is given by:

$$s(s - L'_p) = 0 \tag{3.213}$$

The time constant of the roll mode (which is described by the single degree of freedom approximation) is $-(L'_p)^{-1}$. The other mode – the spiral mode – is neutrally stable since the remaining eigenvalue associated with eq. (3.213) is 0.0. Effectively, this approximation assumes that $L'_\beta \rightarrow 0$ (i.e. the dihedral effect of the wing is small) and U_0 is large. For further discussion, the reader should refer to Stengel (1980).

3.13 CONCLUSIONS

There are many ways of representing the dynamics of an aircraft. Which form to choose depends principally upon the task being considered. Where only a single control input or a single source of disturbance is being considered, it is natural to use the transfer function approach: the relationship between the output and the input is unique. The state equation is not a unique representation of the aircraft dynamics, but depends upon the definition of the state and control and disturbance vectors. Nevertheless, even for cases where the designer can be certain that only a single forcing function applies, there is great merit in using state space methods since they afford information about the response of all the state variables to that single input, and not just about response of a single output.

More and more, modern AFCS problems are multivariable in their nature; state space methods are now the natural tools for design and analysis of such dynamic systems.

3.14 EXERCISES

3.1 Calculate the damping ratio of the short period mode of the aircraft CHARLIE-3.

3.2 Using the classical phugoid approximation calculate the period of the phugoid mode for GOLF-1. How does this value compare with that obtained from the full set of equations?

3.3 A supersonic fighter is known to have the following dimensional stability derivatives: $Z_w = -2.11$, $Z_{\delta_E} = -8 \times 10^{-4}$, $M_{\delta_E} = -60.0$. Its equilibrium speed is 375 m s^{-1} and its characteristic roots are shown on the complex plane of Figure 3.5.

(a) Calculate the undamped natural frequency and also the damping ratio of the aircraft's short period mode.
(b) Calculate the corresponding stability derivatives M_q and M_w.

3.4 A VTOL aircraft has the following stability derivatives when it is hovering:

$$X_u = -0.06 \qquad M_u = 0.002$$
$$Z_w = -0.02 \qquad M_q = -0.08$$
$$Z_{\delta_{th}} = -36.0 \qquad M_{\delta_{th}} = 0.25$$

(a) Determine the transfer function relating the change in vertical velocity w to a change in the control input δ_{th}.

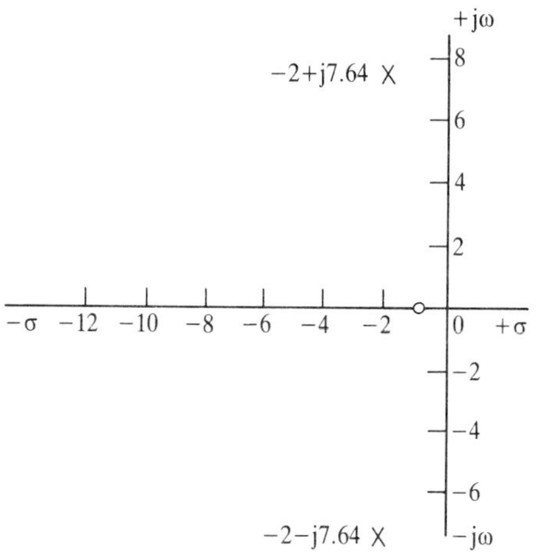

Figure 3.5 s-plane diagram for Exercise 3.3.

(b) Show that changes in forward speed u, and pitch attitude θ, to any disturbance are unstable.

3.5 The rolling motion of an aircraft may be expressed, using the single degree of freedom approximation, by a first order differential equation, namely:

$$\frac{\bar{q}b^2S}{2U_0} C_{L_p}p + \bar{q}bSC_{L_{\delta_A}}\delta_A = I_{xx}\dot{p}$$

where p denotes roll rate, S the surface area of the wing, b its span, $\bar{q}$ the dynamic pressure and I_{xx} the rolling moment of inertia, δ_A the aileron deflection, and U_0 the equilibrium flight speed.

C_{L_x} represents the non-dimensional stability derivative corresonding to a variable, x. For a business jet aircraft the following data apply:

$$S = 21.55\ \text{m}^2 \qquad b = 10.424\ \text{m}$$

$$C_{L_p} = -0.385 \qquad C_{L_{\delta_A}} = 0.15$$

$$\rho = 1.225\ \text{kg m}^{-3} \qquad U_0 = 112\ \text{knots}$$

$$I_{xx} = 14\,500\ \text{kg m}^2\ \text{(wing tip fuel tanks empty)}$$
$$= 40\,670\ \text{kg m}^2\ \text{(wing tip fuel tanks full)}$$

(a) If the maximum deflection of the ailerons is $\pm 28.65°$, calculate the maximum roll rate which can be achieved when the wing tip fuel tanks are (i) empty, (ii) full.

(b) Determine the aileron deflection required to achieve a steady roll rate of $+ 40°\ \text{s}^{-1}$ when the wing tip tanks are full.

(c) Calculate the response in roll rate to a step deflection of the ailerons of $- 10°$ for the case of empty wing tip tanks.

3.6 (a) Using the stability derivatives for the aircraft DELTA-2 and the two degrees of freedom dutch roll approximation, evaluate the following transfer functions: (i) $\beta(s)/\delta_R(s)$, (ii) $r(s)/\delta_R(s)$.

(b) Assume that the aircraft flies at the same height, but increases its speed to $253\ \text{m s}^{-1}$ (i.e. DELTA-3). What effect does this change of speed have upon the frequency of the dutch roll oscillation?

(c) If an impulse deflection of 2° of rudder is applied, calculate the steady change in heading angle, λ, for the first flight condition.

3.7 A high speed reconnaissance aircraft has the following linearized equations of lateral motion:

$$\dot{\beta} = -0.5\beta - r + 0.02\phi - 0.02\delta_A + 0.05\delta_R$$

$$\dot{p} = -150.0\beta - 7.0p - 0.15r + 56.0\delta_A + 45.0\delta_R$$

$$\dot{r} = 30.0\beta + 0.1p - r + \delta_A - 20.0\delta_R$$

$$\dot{\phi} = p$$

(a) Using the full set of equations, derive the transfer function $p(s)/\delta_A(s)$.

(b) Derive the same transfer function using the single degree of freedom approximation.

(c) Determine the roll rate response to a unit step deflection of ailerons for each model. From studying these responses can it be deduced that the single degree of freedom approximation is valid for this aircraft?

3.8 (a) For the aircraft FOXTROT-4 write down the state equation if the state vector is defined as $\mathbf{x}' = [r\ \beta\ p\ \phi]$, and the control vector as $\mathbf{u}' = [\delta_R\ \delta_A]$.
(b) Determine the submatrices which represent the lateral/directional and the directional/lateral coupling effects.
(c) If these submatrices are negligible, calculate the approximate frequency and damping ratio of the dutch roll mode.

3.9 For the general aviation aircraft, GOLF, for all four flight conditions, determine the steady state response of the aircraft's longitudinal motion for the following steady deflections of the control surfaces:

(a) $\delta_F = +1.0°$ $\quad\delta_E = 0.0°$

(b) $\delta_F = 0.0°$ $\quad\delta_E = -1.0°$

(c) $\delta_F = -1.0°$ $\quad\delta_E = +1.0°$

3.10 A large, jet transport aircraft with a horizontal tail has the following properties and parameters:

area of wing	280 m^2	distance between	
m.a.c., $\bar{c}$	7 m	a.c. of tail and	
tail area	55 m^2	c.g. of aircraft	22 m
wing span	46 m	η_H	0.9
tail span	15 m	a_0	0.104 deg^{-1}

The aircraft is *just stable* about the point $0.25\bar{c}$

$$dC_m/dC_L = -0.015 \qquad \partial\varepsilon/d\alpha = 0.5$$

where ε is the downwash angle. Both the wing and the tail have elliptical lift, i.e.

$$\frac{\partial C_L}{d\alpha} = \frac{a_0}{1 + (57.3\,\alpha_0 AR/\pi)}\ /\text{degree}$$

where α_0 is the trimmed angle of attack and AR the aspect ratio. When the c.g. is located at a distance of $0.1\bar{c}$ ahead of the neutral point $dC_m/dC_L = -0.1$. Determine the aftmost location of the c.g. for which dC_m/dC_L will be at leat -0.1.

3.11 A fighter aircraft, flying straight and level at a height of 10 000 m and a steady speed of 190 m s^{-1} has the stability derivatives given below:

$$Z_w = -0.73 \qquad M_w = -3.0$$

$$Z_q = -0.01 \qquad M_q = -0.6$$

$$Z_{\delta_E} = 0.0 \qquad M_{\delta_E} = -12.0$$

All other stability derivatives may be assumed to be neglibible.
(a) Determine the transfer function relating the flight path angle γ to the pitch attitude θ.
(b) Show that the rate of change of height is proportional to the change in flight path angle γ.

(c) If the pitch attitude changes by $-1°$, by how much does the flight path angle change?

(d) If the angle of attack of the aircraft is changed by $11.5°$, what is the corresponding change in the load factor measured at the c.g. of the aircraft?

3.15 NOTES

1. A zero real part corresponds to a mode having simple harmonic motion, which, for practical flight situations, is considered to be unstable.
2. By computer, using NAG library routines (from NAG, Mayfield House, Oxford, England), or the routine available in the EISPACK package (Garbow *et al.*, 1977) or the EIG function in CTRL-C (Systems Control Technology, Inc., 1986).
3. It is assumed here, again, that any forces, which may arise owing to the thrust lines not coinciding with the aircraft axes, are negligible and may be ignored.
4. In aeronautics, volume is the product of the area of a flying surface and the distance of that surface from the c.g. of the aircraft measured to $0.25\,\bar{c}$ of the surface.
5. δ is used here to indicate any control surface deflection. To be specific an appropriate subscript is used.

3.16 REFERENCES

BARNETT, S. and C. STOREY. 1966. Insensitivity of optimal linear control systems to persistent changes in parameters. *Int. J. Control.*, 4(2): 179–84.

FADDEEVA, V.N. 1959. Computational Methods of Linear Algebra. New York: Dover Press.

GARBOW, B.S., J.M. BOYLE, J.J. DONGARRA and C.B. MOLER. 1977. *Matrix Eigensystem Routines – EISPACK Guide Extensions.* Springer-Verlag Lecture Notes in Computer Science, Vol 6.

LARIMER, S.J. 1978. TOTAL. MSc thesis, AFIT/ENE, WPAFB, Dayton, Ohio.

STENGEL, R.F. 1980. Some effects of parameter variations on the lateral–directional stability of aircraft. *J. Guid. and Cont.* 3(2): 124–31.

SUTTON, O.G. 1949. *The Science of Flight.* Harmondsworth: Penguin.

Systems Control Technology, Inc., 1986. *Ctrl-C Users Guide: Version 4.0.* SCT, Inc., Palo Alto, California.

4

The Dynamic Effects of Structural Flexibility Upon the Motion of an Aircraft

4.1 INTRODUCTION

The current design and mission requirements for military and commercial transport aircraft are such that the resulting configurations of such vehicles have required the use of thin lifting surfaces, long and slender fuselages, low mass fraction structures, high stress design levels, and low dynamic load factors. In turn, those features have resulted in aircraft which are structurally light and flexible. Such aircraft can develop large values of displacement and acceleration as a result of structural deflection, in addition to those components of displacement and acceleration which arise owing to the rigid body motion of the aircraft. Such structural deflections may occur as a result of aircraft manoeuvres which have been commanded by a pilot, or as a result of the aircraft's passage through turbulent air. Aircraft motion of this kind can result in a reduction of the structural life of the airframe because of the large dynamic loads and the consequent high levels of stress. The amplitude of the aircraft's response, caused by gust-induced structural flexibility, depends upon either the amount of energy transferred from the gust disturbance to the structural bending modes or, if any energy is absorbed from the gust, the dissipation of that energy by some form of damping. When the amplitude of the response of the elastic motion is such that it compares with that of the rigid body motion, there can be an interchange between the rigid body energy and the elastic energy to the detriment of the flying qualities of the aircraft.

This chapter deals with such effects of structural flexibility, with how they may be described in mathematical terms, and how these terms can be incorporated into the equations of motion of an aircraft. The resulting equations must be used in studies of active control technology and in any studies connected with those special control systems which permit control configured vehicles to produce the performance expected by their designers.

4.2 BENDING MOTION OF THE WING

A wing's lift force, L, is defined by:

$$L = 1/2\,\rho V^2 S C_{L_\alpha}\alpha \tag{4.1}$$

where ρ is the density of the atmosphere, α the angle of attack, S the wing surface area, C_{L_α} the lift curve slope of the wing, and V the speed of the airstream. The dynamic pressure is defined as:

$$\bar{q} = 1/2\,\rho V^2 \tag{4.2}$$

Hence

$$L = \bar{q} S C_{L_\alpha}\alpha = K_w\alpha \tag{4.3}$$

where:

$$K_w = \bar{q} S C_{L_\alpha} \tag{4.4}$$

Equation (4.3) can be represented by Figure 4.1 for all values of α below the stall value, i.e. for all values of angle of attack for which the relationship between lift and angle of attack remains linear.

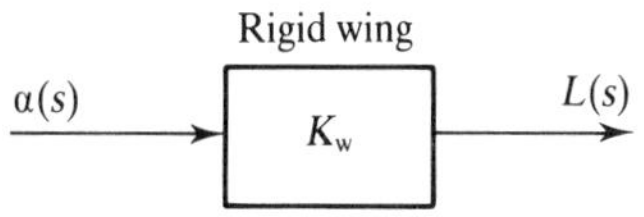

Figure 4.1 Block diagram representation of an ideal wing.

If a rigid, non-swept, rectangular wing of chord c and semi-span $b/2$ is hinged at its root, as represented in Figure 4.2, the wing has freedom of motion only in bending. The bending angle, λ, is taken as positive when the wing tip is down. The spring has stiffness, K_s, which represents the bending stiffness of the wing in its fundamental mode. The wing also possesses a moment of inertia, I, given by:

$$I = \int_{\text{wing}} \delta m\, y^2 \tag{4.5}$$

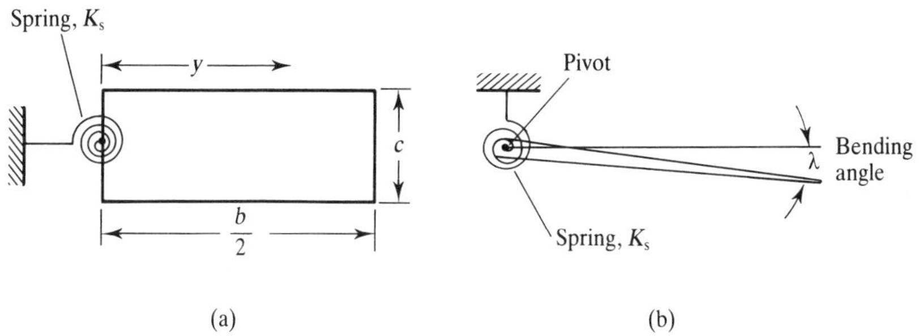

Figure 4.2 Hinged wing.

where δm represents an element of mass. It can be deduced from Figure 4.2(b) that

$$I\ddot{\lambda} + K_s\lambda = 0 \tag{4.6}$$[1]

where K_s is the bending moment stiffness. This is true only in still air and when structural damping is absent. Equation (4.6) may be re-expressed as:

$$\ddot{\lambda} + \omega^2\lambda = 0 \tag{4.7}$$

where the natural frequency of the bending motion is given by:

$$\omega = (K_s/I)^{1/2} \tag{4.8}$$

When the wing is in a stream of air with relative velocity V, then it can be shown (for example, from quasi-steady aerodynamic strip theory – see Bisplinighoff *et al.*, 1955) that:

$$\begin{aligned} I\ddot{\lambda} + K_s\lambda &= -\,1/2\,\rho V^2 \int_0^{b/2} \bar{c} y \, \mathrm{d}y \, C_{L_\alpha}\left(\frac{y}{V}\dot{\lambda}\right) \\ &= -\,\bar{q}\,\frac{\bar{c}C_{L_\alpha}}{V}\,\dot{\lambda}\int_0^{b/2} y^2\,\mathrm{d}y \\ &= -\,\bar{q}\,\frac{\bar{c}C_{L_\alpha}}{V}\,\dot{\lambda}\left[b^3/_{24}\right] \end{aligned} \tag{4.9}$$

Now:

$$S \triangleq b\bar{c}/2 \tag{4.10}$$

$$\therefore I\ddot{\lambda} + K_s\lambda = -\,\frac{K_w b^2}{12V}\,\dot{\lambda} \tag{4.11}$$

i.e.

$$\ddot{\lambda} + \frac{K_w b^2}{12VI}\,\dot{\lambda} + \frac{K_s}{I}\,\lambda = 0 \tag{4.12}$$

or

$$\ddot{\lambda} + 2\,\zeta\omega\dot{\lambda} + \omega^2\lambda = 0 \tag{4.13}$$

where

$$\zeta = \frac{K_w b^2}{24\,V\,\surd(K_s I)} \tag{4.14}$$

Thus, wing bending motion is characterized by a linear, second order, differential equation in which the damping is provided by aerodynamic forces.

Further discussion of wing flexure can be found in Hancock *et al.* (1985).

4.3 TORSION OF THE WING

Imagine the same rectangular, non-swept wing now hinged about an axis which allows a single degree of freedom in torsion (see Figure 4.3).

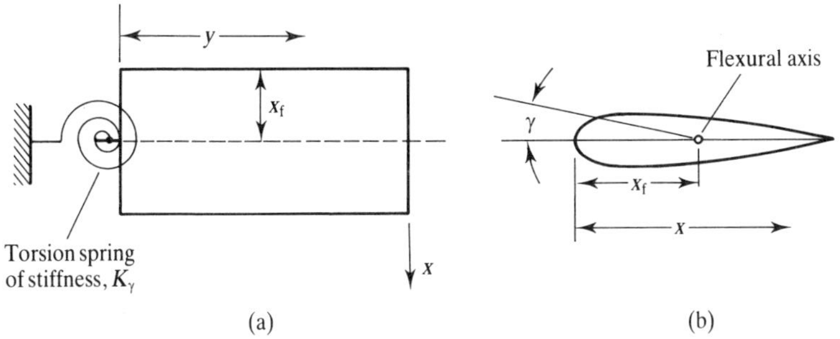

Figure 4.3 Wing with torsion.

In still air, and with structural damping absent, the equation of torsional motion is:

$$I_\gamma \ddot{\gamma} + K_\gamma \gamma = 0 \tag{4.15}$$

where:

$$I_\lambda = \int_{\text{wing}} (x - x_f)^2 \delta m \tag{4.16}$$

γ, x and x_f are defined in Figure 4.3; δm is the mass element.

The natural frequency is given by:

$$\omega_\gamma^2 = K_\gamma / I_\gamma \tag{4.17}$$

Whenever the wing encounters an airstream of relative velocity V, an aerodynamic lift force acts at the wing's a.c. This centre is located at some distance $h\bar{c}$ ahead of the flexural axis (see Figure 4.4). When the aerofoil is symmetrical there can be no steady moment about the a.c. The equation of motion then becomes (referring to Figure 4.4):

$$I_\gamma \ddot{\gamma} + K_\gamma \gamma = \int_0^{b/2} 1/2\, \rho V^2 \bar{c}\, dy\, C_{L_\alpha} \gamma h\bar{c} = \bar{q} C_{L_\alpha} h\bar{c}^2 \gamma \int_0^{b/2} dy$$

$$= \bar{q} C_{L_\alpha} S\bar{c} \gamma h = \bar{c} h K_w \gamma \tag{4.18}$$

$$\therefore \quad I_\gamma \ddot{\gamma} + (K_\gamma - \bar{c} h K_w)\gamma = 0 \tag{4.19}$$

There is no aerodynamic damping; the aerodynamic loads, however, contribute to the effective stiffness. It can be inferred from eq. (4.19) that the twisting of the wing is oscillatory, i.e. it is twisting in a simple harmonic motion, at a frequency given by:

$$\omega^2 = (K_\gamma - \bar{c} h K_w)/I_\gamma \tag{4.20}$$

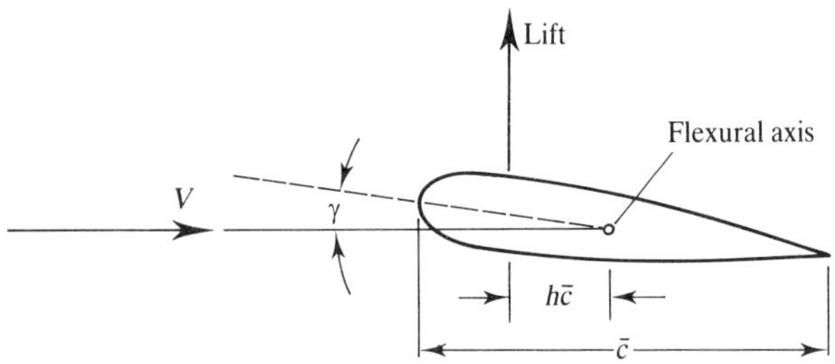

Figure 4.4 Location of aerodynamics centre.

When h is positive, this frequency reduces with dynamic pressure, $\bar{q}$. The torsional motion can be become unstable when:

$$\bar{c}hK_{\mathrm{w}} > K_{\gamma} \tag{4.21}$$

The speed at which $\bar{c}h\ K_{\mathrm{w}} = K_{\gamma}$ is known as the *wing divergence speed*, V_{D}, given by:

$$V_{\mathrm{D}} = \sqrt{\left(\frac{2K_{\gamma}}{\rho SC_{L_{\alpha}}\bar{c}h}\right)} \tag{4.22}$$

In practice, unsteady aerodynamic effects are present and these introduce some aerodynamic damping. A picture of how the unstable condition just described can occur may be obtained from the simple block diagram of Figure 4.5 from which the following transfer function is easily obtained. The twisting moment, M, is proportional to lift and causes a deflection, γ. The relationship between moment and lift is defined by K_1, and between deflection and moment by K_2.

$$\frac{L(s)}{\alpha(s)} = \frac{K_{\mathrm{w}}}{1 - K_1K_2K_{\mathrm{w}}} = \frac{\bar{q}SC_{L_{\alpha}}}{1 - K_1K_2\bar{q}SC_{L_{\alpha}}} \tag{4.23}$$

The system becomes unstable, i.e. lift grows without limit, when:

$$\bar{q} = \frac{1}{K_1K_2SC_{\mathrm{L}_{\alpha}}} \tag{4.24}$$

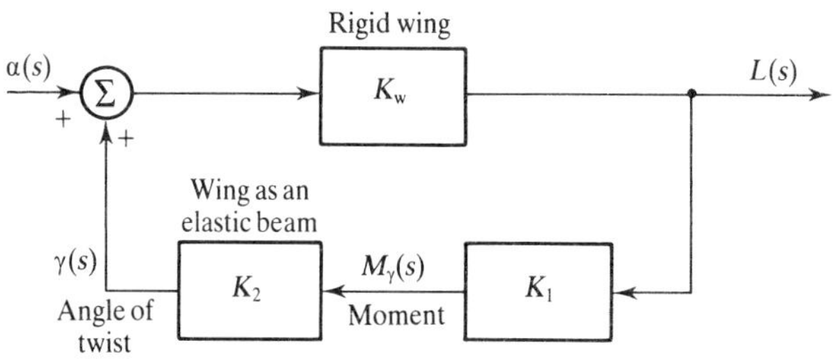

Figure 4.5 Block diagram of wing with torsion.

or

$$V_D = \sqrt{\left(\frac{2}{K_1 K_2 \rho S C_{L_\alpha}}\right)} \qquad (4.25)$$

Equations (4.22) and (4.25) are identical when:

$$K_1 = \bar{c}h \qquad (4.26)$$

and

$$K_2 = 1/K_\gamma \qquad (4.27)$$

4.4 COUPLED MOTIONS

Suppose the non-swept, rectangular wing now has two degrees of freedom, i.e. it may now bend and twist. In still air, the coupled equations of motion are given by:

$$I\ddot{\lambda} + I_{\lambda\gamma}\ddot{\gamma} + K_s\lambda = 0 \qquad (4.28)$$

$$I_\gamma\ddot{\gamma} + I_{\lambda\gamma}\ddot{\lambda} + K_\gamma\gamma = 0 \qquad (4.29)$$

The product of inertia, $I_{\lambda\gamma}$, is given by:

$$I_{\lambda\gamma} = \int_{\text{wing}} (x - x_f)y\,\delta m = m(x_{cm} - x_f)y_{cm} \qquad (4.30)$$

where x_{cm}, y_{cm} are the coordinates of the wing centre of mass. The coupled natural frequencies are found from:

$$(-I\omega^2 + K_s)(-I_\gamma\omega^2 + K_\gamma) - I_{\lambda\gamma}^2\omega^4 = 0 \qquad (4.31)$$

One frequency has a value just a little larger than the natural frequency of the torsional motion; the other natural coupled frequency has a value a little smaller than the natural frequency of the bending motion. The mode associated with the first coupled natural frequency is composed of motion which is primarily torsion, but with some bending motion cross-coupled by virtue of the product of inertia. The motion associated with the other mode is essentially bending, but with torsion cross-coupled via the product of inertia.

When the wing is an airstream of relative velocity V, eqs (4.28) and (4.29) become:

$$I\ddot{\lambda} + I_{\lambda\gamma}\ddot{\gamma} + K_s\lambda = -\bar{q}\frac{Sb}{2}C_{L_\alpha}\left(\frac{b}{6V}\dot{\lambda} + \frac{\gamma}{2}\right) = -K_w\frac{b}{4}\left(\frac{b}{3V}\dot{\lambda} + \gamma\right)$$

$$I_\gamma\ddot{\gamma} + I_{\lambda\gamma}\ddot{\lambda} + K_\gamma\gamma = -K_w\bar{c}\left\{h\left(\frac{b}{4V}\dot{\lambda} + \gamma\right) + \frac{M_{\dot{\gamma}}\dot{\gamma}\bar{c}}{C_{L_\alpha}V}\right\}$$

The damping term $M_{\dot{\gamma}}\dot{\gamma}\bar{c}$ arises as a consequence of unsteady, aerodynamic effects. Each mode of motion is now damped, but there is a condition when the damping in one of the modes can be zero: this is the critical condition known as flutter. It occurs at a critical speed, referred to as the flutter speed, V_F. The corresponding frequency is ω_F. Hence, for the critical flutter condition, the effective damping for each separate motion must be zero. When that occurs, the frequencies associated with bending and torsional motion are identical.

4.5 THE DYNAMICS OF A FLEXIBLE AIRCRAFT

When aeroelastic effects have to be taken into account, it becomes necessary to augment the aircraft's rigid body equations by adding to the state variables a set of generalized coordinates associated with the normal bending modes and which have been calculated by assuming, first, that the structural behaviour is linear and, next, that any structural displacement is small compared to the overall dimensions of the aircraft.[2] These bending modes are the normal modes of vibration, *in vacuo*. With these assumptions, each mode is characterized by a distinct natural frequency ω_i, and by a mode shape vector, υ. If the ith bending mode, say, is now considered to be damped, it can be represented using generalized coordinates by the following second order equation:

$$A_i\ddot{q}_i + B_i\dot{q}_i + C_iq_i = Q_i \tag{4.33}$$

where Q_i is a generalized force. A_i, B_i, and C_i are coefficients of the ith generalized coordinates, q_i, and of its associated rates.

Let:

$$\begin{aligned} x_1 &\triangleq q_i \\ x_2 &\triangleq \dot{q}_i = \dot{x}_1 \end{aligned} \tag{4.34}$$

From eqs (4.33) and (4.34) it is then easy to show that:

$$\dot{x}_1 = x_2 \tag{4.35}$$

$$\dot{x}_2 = \frac{-B_i}{A_i}x_2 - \frac{C_i}{A_i}x_1 + \frac{1}{A_i}Q_i \tag{4.35}$$

The ith bending mode has been represented by two first order, linear, differential equations, eq. (4.35) (Schwanz, 1972). In such a fashion is it possible to augment the rigid body dynamics with pairs of first order differential equations which correspond to each bending mode being considered. Usually, only enough generalized coordinates, q_i, to adequately represent the aeroelastic effects, are included. If, for example, a number of bending modes are considered to be significant and are to be included in the mathematical model, it is conventional for mode 1 to be regarded as the mode with the lowest bending frequency. The mode number goes in ascending order as the frequency associated with each mode increases.

In some applications it can happen that the shortest period associated with the overall motion is long compared with the longest vibration period, $2\pi/\omega_1$. When that occurs, then all the inertia ($\ddot{q}_i$) and damping ($\dot{q}_i$) terms may be negligible. For example, if the ratio of the periods being considered is 5 : 1, the terms $A_i\ddot{q}_i$ *and* $B_i\dot{q}_i$ will not generally exceed in value 5 per cent of the value of C_iq_i; it is then possible, in theory, to solve for the stiffness terms (q_i) in terms of the rigid body variables, which eliminates from the aerodynamic terms in the rigid body equations every q_i term, and results in a set of rigid body equations which have been 'corrected' for the aeroelastic effects. By employing such 'structural influence coefficients' the steady-state aeroelastic effects are accounted for, without having to increase the order of the equations of motion (Bisplinighoff *et al.*, 1955). With modern aircraft, however, it is a trend that the shortest period is not usually long compared with the largest period of vibration. As a result, the inertia terms must be included. For AFCS designers, the question then arises of how many structural bending modes need to be considered to adequately represent the effective aeroelastic effect. The following are the methods most commonly used:

1. *Quasi-static*, in which the motions of the structure are assumed to be in-phase with the rigid body motion. The acceleration associated with elastic motion is regarded as being instantaneous. This is the method outlined earlier and finds use in AFCS design only when the designer can be sure that there is a wide separation between the natural frequencies of the rigid body and those of the elastic motions.

2. *Exact*, in which the motion of the structure is determined from an eigenvector solution of the equations of motion representing the deformable aircraft. In general, there is considerable difficulty in obtaining a numerical solution since the resulting eigenvectors are complex.

3. *Modal substitution*, in which the motions of the structure are assumed to be *in vacuo* and governed by orthogonal eigenvectors, which contain only real numbers.

4. *Residual stiffness*, in which the eigenvectors representing the elastic motion in the modal substitution formulation are separated into 'retained' and 'deleted' modes. In the deleted modes, the inertia and damping terms are neglected. The resulting algebraic equations then contain only stiffness terms which are used to modify the retained equations by way of the coupling terms. The retained modes customarily have the lowest frequencies, since it is found that most of the elastic energy is contained in these low frequency modes.

5. *Residual flexibility*, which is similar to the residual stiffness method except that the aerodynamic correction factor is related to the retained, not the deleted, modes.

6. *Model truncation*, in which the deleted modes of the residual stiffness

modes are not represented by any correction factor. This formulation is by far the most commonly used method in AFCS design, often in association with the quasi-static method. It is important for designers, however, to verify these formulations at critical design points for the AFCS since it may be inappropriate to represent the bending motion by *in vacuo* normal modes, particularly when considerable aerodynamic damping might arise (see equation (4.9) for example).

Further discussion of dynamics can be found in McLean (1978) and Schwanz (1972).

4.6 MATHEMATICAL REPRESENTATION OF THE DYNAMICS OF A FLEXIBLE AIRCRAFT

Provided that there is no cross-coupling between its longitudinal and lateral motion, the motion of an aircraft about its straight and level equilibrium path, assuming small perturbations, can be represented, using the stability axis system, by two independent sets of equations, namely:

Longitudinal motion

$$\dot{u} = X_u u + X_w w - g\theta + \sum_{i=1}^{m} X_{\delta_i}\delta_i$$

$$\dot{w} = Z_u u + Z_w w + (U_0 + Z_q)q + \sum_{i=1}^{m} Z_{\delta_i}\delta_i \tag{4.36}$$

$$\dot{q} = M_u u + M_{\dot{w}}\dot{w} + M_w w + M_q q + \sum_{i=1}^{m} M_{\delta_i}\delta_i$$

$$\dot{\theta} = q$$

Lateral motion

$$\dot{\beta} = Y_v\beta - r + \frac{g}{U_0}\phi + \sum_{i=1}^{s} Y^*_{\delta_i}\delta_i$$

$$\dot{p} = L'_\beta\beta + L'_p p + L'_r r + \sum_{i=1}^{s} L'_{\delta_i}\delta_i$$

$$\dot{r} = N'_\beta\beta + N'_p p + N'_r + \sum_{i=1}^{s} N'_{\delta_i}\delta_i \tag{4.37}$$

$$\dot{\phi} = p$$

$$\dot{\psi} = r$$

It has been assumed in eq. (4.36) that there are m control inputs; on any conventional aircraft m is usually equal to two, and the controls involved are elevator deflection, δ_E, and the change in thrust, δ_{th}. On a control configured vehicle (CCV) there may be a number of additional control surfaces, such that $m > 2$. Similarly, for lateral motion, it has been assumed that there are s inputs; on any conventional aircraft s is usually equal to two, and the controls involved are aileron deflection, δ_A, and rudder deflection, δ_R. On a CCV, s may be greater than two.

Suppose that the flexibility effects of an aircraft are considered to be adequately represented, by using modal truncation, in longitudinal motion by five bending modes (1, 5, 7, 8, and 12) and in lateral motion by lateral bending modes (1, 2, 3, 9, 10).[3] For longitudinal motion, the state vector may be defined as:

$$\mathbf{x}' = [\alpha q \lambda_1 \dot{\lambda}_1 \lambda_5 \dot{\lambda}_5 \lambda_7 \dot{\lambda}_7 \lambda_8 \dot{\lambda}_8 \lambda_{12} \dot{\lambda}_{12}] \qquad (4.38)$$

For lateral motion, the corresponding state vector may be defined as:

$$\mathbf{x}' = [\beta p r \phi \psi \gamma_1 \dot{\gamma}_1 \gamma_2 \dot{\gamma}_2 \gamma_3 \dot{\gamma}_3 \gamma_9 \dot{\gamma}_9 \gamma_{10} \dot{\gamma}_{10}] \qquad (4.39)$$

The meaning of the symbols is explained in Table 4.1. The corresponding equations of longitudinal motion are presented in eq. (4.40) and lateral motion in eq. (4.41). Note that there is coupling in the longitudinal motion between bending modes 7 and 8; there is also coupling in the lateral motion between modes 2 and 3, and between modes 9 and 10.

$$\dot{\alpha} = Z_\alpha \alpha + q + \sum_{j=1}^{m} Z_{\delta_j} \delta_j + Z_{\lambda_1} \lambda_1 + Z_{\dot{\lambda}_1} \dot{\lambda}_1$$

$$\dot{q} = M_\alpha \alpha + M_{\dot{\alpha}} \dot{\alpha} + M_q q + \sum_{j=1}^{m} M_{\delta_j} \delta_j + M_{\lambda_1} \lambda_1 + M_{\dot{\lambda}_1} \dot{\lambda}_1$$

$$\ddot{\lambda}_1 = -(2\zeta_1 \omega_1 + \eta_{1_{\dot{\lambda}_1}}) \dot{\lambda}_1 + (-\omega_1^2 + \eta_{1_{\lambda_1}}) \lambda_1 + \eta_{1_\alpha} \alpha + \eta_{1_q} q + \sum_{j=1}^{m} \eta_{1_{\delta_j}} \delta_j$$

Table 4.1 Symbols used in a mathematical model of a flexible aircraft

α = angle of attack	β = sideslip angle
q = pitch rate	p = roll rate
λ_j = displacement of jth symmetrical bending mode	r = yaw rate
δ_E = deflection of the elevator	ϕ = roll angle
δ_{th} = change in thrust	ψ = yaw angle
U_0 = equilibrium airspeed	δ_A = aileron deflection
g = acceleration due to gravity	δ_R = rudder deflection
V_{BM_x} = vertical bending moment at body station x	γ_l = displacement of lth asymmetrical bending mode
a_{z_x} = vertical acceleration at body station x	l_x = distance from c.g. to body station x, positive forwards
a_{y_x} = lateral acceleration at body station x	S_{BM_x} = lateral bending moment at body station x

$$\ddot{\lambda}_5 = -(2\zeta_5\omega_5 + \eta_{5_{\dot{\lambda}_5}})\dot{\lambda}_5 + (-\omega_5^2 + \eta_{5_{\lambda_5}})\lambda_5 + \eta_{5_\alpha}\alpha + \eta_{5_q}q + \sum_{j=1}^{m}\eta_{5_{\delta_j}}\delta_j \quad (4.40)$$

$$\ddot{\lambda}_7 = -(2\zeta_7\omega_7 + \eta_{7_{\dot{\lambda}_7}})\dot{\lambda}_7 + (-\omega_7^2 + \eta_{7_{\lambda_7}})\lambda_7 + \eta_{7_{\dot{\lambda}_8}}\dot{\lambda}_8 + \eta_{7_{\lambda_8}}\lambda_8 + \eta_{7_\alpha}\alpha + \eta_{7_q}q + \sum_{j=1}^{m}\eta_{7_{\delta_j}}\delta_j$$

$$\ddot{\lambda}_8 = -(2\zeta_8\omega_8 + \eta_{8_{\dot{\lambda}_8}})\dot{\lambda}_8 + (-\omega_8^2 + \eta_{8_{\lambda_8}})\lambda_8 + \eta_{8_{\dot{\lambda}_7}}\dot{\lambda}_7 + \eta_{8_{\lambda_7}}\lambda_7 + \eta_{8_\alpha}\alpha + \eta_{8_q}q + \sum_{j=1}^{m}\eta_{8_{\delta_j}}\delta_j$$

$$\lambda_{12} = -(2\zeta_{12}\omega_{12})\dot{\lambda}_{12} - \omega_{12}^2\lambda_{12} + \eta_{12_\alpha}\alpha + \eta_{12_q}q + \sum_{j=1}^{m}\eta_{12_{\delta_j}}\delta_j$$

$$\dot{\beta} = Y_v\beta + Y_p^*p - r + \frac{g}{U_0}\phi + \sum_{i=1}^{s}Y_{\delta_i}^*\delta_i + Y_{\gamma_9}\gamma_9 + Y_{\dot{\gamma}_9}\dot{\gamma}_9$$

$$\dot{p} = L'_\beta\beta + L'_p p + L'_r r + \sum_{i=1}^{s}L'_{\delta_i}\delta_i + L'_{\gamma_9}\gamma_9 + L'_{\dot{\gamma}_9}\dot{\gamma}_9\ ; \quad \dot{\phi} = p$$

$$\dot{r} = N'_\beta\beta + N'_p p + N'_r r + \sum_{i=1}^{s}N'_{\delta_i}\delta_i + N'_{\dot{\gamma}_9}\dot{\gamma}_9 + N'_{\gamma_9}\gamma_9\ ; \quad \dot{\psi} = r$$

$$\ddot{\gamma}_1 = -2\zeta_A\omega_A\dot{\gamma}_1 - \omega_A^2\gamma_1 + \mu_{1_\beta}\beta + \mu_{1_p}p + \mu_{1_r}r + \sum_{i=1}^{s}\mu_{\delta_i}\delta_i$$

$$\ddot{\gamma}_2 = -2\zeta_B\omega_B\dot{\gamma}_2 - \omega_B^2\gamma_2 + \mu_{2_{\dot{\gamma}_3}}\dot{\gamma}_3 + \mu_{2_{\gamma_3}}\gamma_3 + \mu_{2_\beta}\beta + \mu_{2_p}p + \mu_{2_r}r + \sum_{i=1}^{s}\mu_{2_{\delta_i}}\delta_i \quad (4.41)$$

$$\ddot{\gamma}_3 = -2\zeta_C\omega_C\dot{\gamma}_3 - \omega_C^2\gamma_3 + \mu_{3_{\dot{\gamma}_2}}\dot{\gamma}_2 + \mu_{3_{\gamma_2}}\gamma_2 + \mu_{3_\beta}\beta + \mu_{3_p}p + \mu_{3_r}r + \sum_{i=1}^{s}\mu_{3_{\delta_i}}\delta_i$$

$$\ddot{\gamma}_9 = -2\zeta_D\omega_D\dot{\gamma}_9 - \omega_D^2\gamma_9 + \mu_{9_{\dot{\gamma}_{10}}}\dot{\gamma}_{10} + \mu_{9_{\gamma_{10}}}\gamma_{10} + \mu_{9_\beta}\beta + \mu_{9_p}p + \mu_{9_r}r + \sum_{i=1}^{s}\mu_{9_{\delta_i}}\delta_i$$

$$\ddot{\gamma}_{10} = -2\zeta_E\omega_E\dot{\gamma}_{10} - \omega_E^2\gamma_{10} + \mu_{10_{\dot{\gamma}_9}}\dot{\gamma}_9 + \mu_{10_{\gamma_9}}\gamma_9 + \mu_{10_\beta}\beta + \mu_{10_p}p + \mu_{10_r}r + \sum_{i=1}^{s}\mu_{10_{\delta_i}}\delta_i$$

If the state vectors are taken as those already defined in eqs (4.38) and (4.39), and if the corresponding control vectors are defined as:

$$\mathbf{u}_{\text{long}} = \begin{bmatrix} \delta_E \\ \delta_{th} \end{bmatrix} \quad (4.42)$$

$$\mathbf{u}_{lat} = \begin{bmatrix} \delta_A \\ \delta_R \end{bmatrix} \qquad (4.43)$$

the corresponding coefficient matrices for the example aircraft at the particular flight condition are given in eqs (4.44) and (4.46) respectively; the driving matrices are given in eqs (4.45) and (4.47).

$$B_{long} = \begin{bmatrix} -0.07 & -0.006 \\ 3.74 & -0.276 \\ 0 & 0 \\ 22.52 & 0.765 \\ 0 & 0 \\ -18.3 & -2.14 \\ 0 & 0 \\ -22.93 & -2.1 \\ 0 & 0 \\ -4.41 & -1.37 \\ 0 & 0 \\ 36.57 & 3.993 \end{bmatrix} \qquad (4.45)$$

$$B_{lat} = \begin{bmatrix} 15.78 & -274.47 \\ -0.794 & -0.312 \\ 0.052 & -4.32 \\ 0 & 0 \\ 0 & 0 \\ 0 & 0 \\ 2.14 & -25.68 \\ 0 & 0 \\ 0.4 & -4.32 \\ 0 & 0 \\ 4.716 & 7.132 \\ 0 & 0 \\ -0.411 & 6.46 \\ 0 & 0 \\ 0.712 & -24.28 \end{bmatrix} \qquad (4.47)$$

$$A_{\text{long}} = \begin{bmatrix} -1.6 & +1 & -0.03 & -0.003 & 0 & 0 & 0 & 0 & 0 & 0 & 0 & 0 \\ 6.9 & -2.24 & -0.039 & +0.03 & 0 & 0 & 0 & 0 & 0 & 0 & 0 & 0 \\ 0 & 0 & 0 & 1 & 0 & 0 & 0 & 0 & 0 & 0 & 0 & 0 \\ -283.3 & -17.52 & -56.81 & -5.53 & 0 & 0 & 0 & 0 & 0 & 0 & 0 & 0 \\ 0 & 0 & 0 & 0 & 0 & 1 & 0 & 0 & 0 & 0 & 0 & 0 \\ -53.1 & 9.71 & 0 & 0 & -231.39 & 0.09 & 0 & 0 & 0 & 0 & 0 & 0 \\ 0 & 0 & 0 & 0 & 0 & 0 & 0 & 1 & 0 & 0 & 0 & 0 \\ -82.4 & 9.52 & 0 & 0 & 0 & 0 & -348.87 & -2.68 & -10.71 & -0.52 & 0 & 0 \\ 0 & 0 & 0 & 0 & 0 & 0 & 0 & 0 & 0 & 1 & 0 & 0 \\ 12.1 & 2.2 & 0 & 0 & 0 & 0 & 1.24 & -0.176 & -390.1 & -0.474 & 0 & 0 \\ 0 & 0 & 0 & 0 & 0 & 0 & 0 & 0 & 0 & 0 & 0 & 1 \\ -147.1 & 5.24 & 0 & 0 & 0 & 0 & 0 & 0 & 0 & 0 & -1\,466.1 & -1.75 \end{bmatrix} \quad (4.44)$$

$$
A_{\text{lat}} = \begin{bmatrix}
-0.18 & 4.9 & 6724.0 & 385 & 0 & 0 & 0 & 0 & 0 & 0 & 0 & -103.6 & 5.5 & 0 & 0 \\
-0.0004 & -2.26 & -0.343 & 0 & 0 & 0 & 0 & 0 & 0 & 0 & 0 & 0.864 & 0.046 & 0 & 0 \\
-0.00037 & 0.06 & 0.413 & 0 & 0 & 0 & 0 & 0 & 0 & 0 & 0 & -0.437 & 0.001 & 0 & 0 \\
0 & 1 & 0 & 0 & 0 & 0 & 0 & 0 & 0 & 0 & 0 & 0 & 0 & 0 & 0 \\
0 & 0 & 1 & 0 & 0 & 0 & 0 & 0 & 0 & 0 & 0 & 0 & 0 & 0 & 0 \\
0 & 0 & 0 & 0 & 0 & 0 & 1 & 0 & 0 & 0 & 0 & 0 & 0 & 0 & 0 \\
-0.01 & -7.98 & -10.63 & 0 & 0 & -97.67 & -1.89 & 0 & 0 & 0 & 0 & 0 & 0 & 0 & 0 \\
0 & 0 & 0 & 0 & 0 & 0 & 0 & 0 & 1 & 0 & 0 & 0 & 0 & 0 & 0 \\
-0.003 & -32.27 & -1.61 & 0 & 0 & 0 & 0 & -151.0 & -3.57 & 150.1 & 3.73 & 0 & 0 & 0 & 0 \\
0 & 0 & 0 & 0 & 0 & 0 & 0 & 0 & 0 & 0 & 1 & 0 & 0 & 0 & 0 \\
0.0043 & 6.73 & 2.35 & 0 & 0 & 0 & 0 & 8.72 & 0.6 & -160 & 1.54 & 0 & 0 & 0 & 0 \\
0 & 0 & 0 & 0 & 0 & 0 & 0 & 0 & 0 & 0 & 0 & 0 & 1 & 0 & 0 \\
-0.0027 & -4.35 & -4.5 & 0 & 0 & 0 & 0 & 0 & 0 & 0 & 0 & -532.64 & -1.72 & 3.25 & -0.36 \\
0 & 0 & 0 & 0 & 0 & 0 & 0 & 0 & 0 & 0 & 0 & 0 & 0 & 0 & 1 \\
-0.018 & -2.27 & -14.29 & 0 & 0 & 0 & 0 & 0 & 0 & 0 & 0 & 1.54 & 0.92 & -930.3 & -2.3
\end{bmatrix} \quad (4.46)
$$

The form of the coefficient matrix in the state equation for either longitudinal or lateral motion is given as:

Rigid body terms	*Aeroelastic coupling terms*
Rigid body coupling terms	*Structural flexibility terms*

This form can be inferred from the coefficient matrices shown as eqs (4.42) and (4.44). The eigenvalues associated with longitudinal and lateral motion are given in Table 4.2.

Table 4.2 Eigenvalues of flexible aircraft

Longitudinal	*Lateral*
	0.0
− 0.703 + j2.68	− 0.0024
− 0.703 − j2.68	− 2.264
− 2.982 + j6.994	− 0.356 + j1.577
− 2.982 − j6.994	− 0.356 − j1.577
− 0.046 + j15.21	− 0.094 + j9.838
− 0.046 − j15.21	− 0.094 − j9.838
− 1.348 + j18.65	− 0.479 + j10.952
− 1.348 − j18.65	− 0.479 − j10.952
− 0.23 + j19.73	− 2.076 + j13.626
− 0.23 − j19.73	− 2.076 − j13.626
− 0.89 + j38.28	− 0.856 + j23.068
− 0.89 − j38.28	− 0.856 − j23.068
	− 1.156 + j30.466
	− 1.156 − j30.466

If it is required to sense the acceleration of rigid body motion, an accelerometer should be placed at the aircraft's c.g. In practice, it is unlikely that any sensor could be located precisely at the c.g. but it can be located at some distance, say l_x, from the c.g. The distance l_x is taken to be positive when the sensor is located forward of the aircraft's c.g. It is shown in Chapter 2, eq. (2.98), that the normal acceleration measured by a sensor is:

$$a_{z_x} = a_{z_{cg}} - l_x\dot{q} \tag{4.48}$$

When bending effects are included in the aircraft dynamics, however, the acceleration, occurring as a result of the structural motion, has to be added, so that the normal acceleration becomes:

$$a_{z_x} = U_0(\dot{\alpha} - q) - l_x\dot{q} + \Phi_{x,1}\ddot{\lambda}_1 + \Phi_{x,5}\ddot{\lambda}_5 + \Phi_{x,7}\ddot{\lambda}_7 + \Phi_{x,8}\ddot{\lambda}_8 + \Phi_{x,12}\ddot{\lambda}_{12} \tag{4.49}$$

If:

$$y \triangleq a_{z_x} \tag{4.50}$$

then:

$$y = C\mathbf{x} + D\mathbf{u} \tag{4.51}$$

where:

$$C = [C_{11}C_{12}C_{13}C_{14}C_{15}C_{16}C_{17}C_{18}C_{19}C_{110}C_{111}C_{112}] \tag{4.52}$$

in which

$$C_{11} = \{U_0Z_\alpha - l_x(M_\alpha + M_{\dot{\alpha}}Z_\alpha) + \Phi_{x,1}\eta_{1_\alpha} + \Phi_{x,5}\eta_{5_\alpha} + \Phi_{x,7}\eta_{7_\alpha} + \Phi_{x,8}\eta_{8_\alpha} + \Phi_{x,12}\eta_{12_\alpha}\} \tag{4.53}$$

$$C_{12} = \{-l_x(M_q + M_{\dot{\alpha}}) + \Phi_{x,1}\eta_{1_q} + \Phi_{x,5}\eta_{5_q} + \Phi_{x,7}\eta_{7_q} + \Phi_{x,8}\eta_{8_q} + \Phi_{x,12}\eta_{12_q}\} \tag{4.54}$$

$$C_{13} = \Phi_{x,1}(\eta_{1_{\dot{\lambda}_1}} - 2\zeta_1\omega_1) \tag{4.55}$$

$$C_{14} = \Phi_{x,1}(\eta_{1_{\lambda_1}} - \omega_1^2) \tag{4.56}$$

$$C_{15} = \Phi_{x,5}(\eta_{5_{\dot{\lambda}_5}} - 2\zeta_5\omega_5) \tag{4.57}$$

$$C_{16} = \Phi_{x,5}(\eta_{5_{\lambda_5}} - \omega_5^2) \tag{4.58}$$

$$C_{17} = \Phi_{x,7}(\eta_{7_{\dot{\lambda}_7}} - 2\zeta_7\omega_7) + \Phi_{x,8}\eta_{8_{\dot{\lambda}_7}} \tag{4.59}$$

$$C_{18} = \Phi_{x,7}(\eta_{7_{\lambda_7}} - \omega_7^2) + \Phi_{x,8}\eta_{8_{\lambda_7}} \tag{4.60}$$

$$C_{19} = \Phi_{x,8}(\eta_{8_{\dot{\lambda}_8}} - 2\zeta_8\omega_8) + \Phi_{x,7}\eta_{7_{\dot{\lambda}_8}} \tag{4.61}$$

$$C_{110} = \Phi_{x,8}(\eta_{8_{\dot{\lambda}_8}} - \omega_8^2) + \Phi_{x,7}\eta_{7_{\dot{\lambda}_8}} \tag{4.62}$$

$$C_{111} = -\Phi_{x,12}2\zeta_{12}\omega_{12} \tag{4.63}$$

$$C_{112} = -\Phi_{x,12}\omega_{12}^2 \tag{4.64}$$

and

$$D = [(U_0 - l_xM_{\dot{\alpha}})Z_{\delta_E} - l_xM_{\delta_E} + \Phi_{x,1}\eta_{1\delta_E} + \Phi_{x,5}\eta_{5\delta_E} + \Phi_{x,7}\eta_{7\delta_E} + \Phi_{x,8}\eta_{8\delta_E} + \Phi_{x,12}\eta_{12\delta_E}] \tag{4.65}$$

Similarly, when lateral bending effects are included, the lateral acceleration at a location l_x ahead of the c.g. and l_z (measured positive down) above the c.g. is (for the elastic aircraft being considered) given by:

$$a_{y_x} = \dot{v} - g\phi + U_0r + l_x\dot{r} - l_z\dot{p} + \Phi_{y,1}\ddot{\gamma}_1 + \Phi_{y,2}\ddot{\gamma}_2 + \Phi_{y,3}\ddot{\gamma}_3 + \Phi y_{,9}\ddot{\gamma}_g + \Phi_{y,10}\ddot{\gamma}_{10} \tag{4.66}$$

The coefficients, $\Phi_{x,i}$ and $\Phi_{y,i}$ are the bending mode displacement coefficients which must be obtained from graphs of bending mode deflection versus body station provided by the aircraft's manufacturer. If they are unavailable, values can only be obtained from experiment.

In a similar fashion, the signals produced from rate gyros used as sensors are also affected by bending motion. If a vertical gyroscope is used to measure the local inclination of either the fuselage or the wing, at some point A, it means that, for longitudinal motion:

$$\theta_A = \theta + \sum_j \Phi_{A,j}\lambda_j \tag{4.67}$$

and, for lateral motion:

$$\Psi_A = \Psi + \sum_k \Phi_{A,k}\gamma_k \tag{4.68}$$

Rate gyroscopes, located at the same point A, measure q_A and r_A, respectively, where:

$$q_A = q + \sum_j \Phi_{A,j}\dot{\lambda}_j \tag{4.69}$$

$$r_A = r + \sum_k \Phi_{A,k}\dot{\lambda}_k \tag{4.70}$$

4.7 LIFT GROWTH EFFECTS

Owing to non-stationary aerodynamic effects, lift is not generated instantaneously. Such lift growth effects are accounted for by using approximations such as the Wagner and Küssner functions. The Wagner function, usually denoted by $w(t)$ (not to be confused with the heave velocity, w, of the aircraft motion) defines the variation of the lift of an airfoil with time for any unit step change of the angle of attack, α.

The Küssner function, denoted by $k(t)$, defines the variation of the lift of an airfoil with time for any unit step change in a gust input. Usually the functions are approximated, and one of the usual approximations for the Wagner function is:

$$w(t) = 0.5 + 0.165(1 - e^{-at}) + 0.335(1 - e^{-bt}) \tag{4.71}$$

where $a = 0.0455(2U_0/\bar{c})$ and $b = 0.3(2U_0/\bar{c})$. U_0 has its usual meaning of the equilibrium forward speed of the aircraft and $\bar{c}$ is the mean chord. Figure 4.6 shows how the Wagner function is incorporated in the aircraft dymamics.

One of the most effective approximations to the Küssner function is the Jones' lift growth function (Jones, 1940) which is defined by:

$$k(t) = 1 - 0.236e^{-0.058\sigma t} - 0.513e^{-0.364\sigma t} - 0.171e^{-2.42\sigma t} \tag{4.72}$$

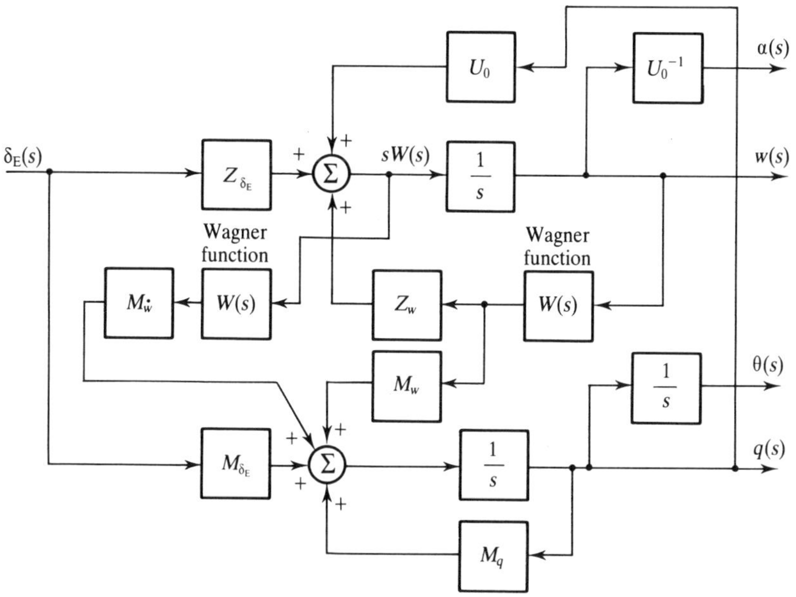

Figure 4.6 Block diagram of aircraft dynamics.

where

$$\sigma = U_0/2\bar{c}.$$

For $U_0 = 195\ \mathrm{m\ s^{-1}}$ and $\bar{c} = 6.88$ m:

$$k(t) = 1 - 0.236\mathrm{e}^{-0.8t} - 0.513\mathrm{e}^{-10t} - 0.171\mathrm{e}^{-33.3t}$$

Since the Laplace transform of eq. (4.72) is:

$$K(s) = \frac{1}{s} - \frac{0.236}{(s + 0.8)} - \frac{0.513}{(s + 10)} - \frac{0.171}{(s + 33.3)} \tag{4.73}$$

the Jones' function, $k(t)$, can be obtained by applying a unit step function to a transfer function, $J(s)$, given by:

$$J(s) = \frac{0.189}{(s + 0.8)} + \frac{5.139}{(s + 10)} + \frac{5.665}{(s + 33.3)} \tag{4.74}$$

A block diagram representation of how such a Küssner function may be generated is shown in Figure 4.7.

4.8 BENDING MOMENTS

If the aircraft is regarded as a simple beam, a bending moment of the fuselage can be defined by:

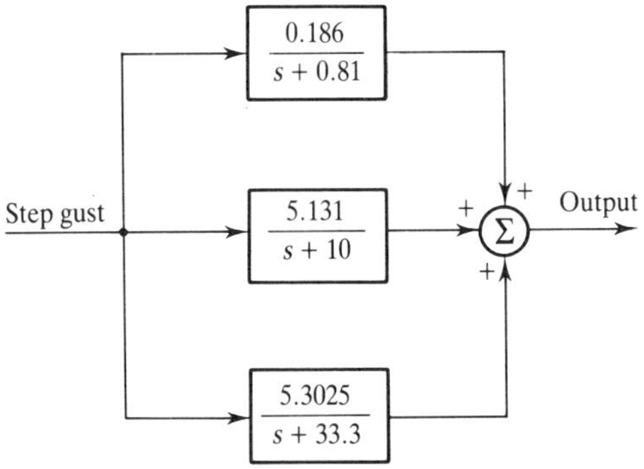

Figure 4.7 Block diagram of Jones' function.

$$V_{\mathrm{bm}_i} = \left\{ EI\left(\frac{-\,\mathrm{d}^2\xi}{\mathrm{d}y^2}\; i \right) \right\} \Bigg|_{y\,=\,0} \tag{4.75}$$

where, according to normal mode theory, the deflection at point i on the fuselage can be expressed as:

$$-\,\xi_i = \Phi_i h + \Phi_{12}\theta + \sum_{k\,>\,2} \Phi_{ik}\lambda_{k\,-\,2} \tag{4.76}$$

h can be obtained from:

$$\dot{h} = U_0\theta - w \tag{4.77}$$

It can be shown that:

$$\frac{-\,\mathrm{d}^2\xi_i}{\mathrm{d}y^2} = \frac{\mathrm{d}^2\Phi_{i1}}{\mathrm{d}y^2}\,h + \frac{\mathrm{d}^2\Phi_{i2}}{\mathrm{d}y^2}\,\theta + \frac{\mathrm{d}^2\Phi_{i3}}{\mathrm{d}y^2}\,\lambda_1 + \frac{\mathrm{d}^2\Phi_{i4}}{\mathrm{d}y^2}\,\lambda_2 + \ldots \tag{4.78}$$

For rigid body modes:

$$\frac{\mathrm{d}^2\Phi_{i1}}{\mathrm{d}y^2} = \frac{\mathrm{d}^2\Phi_{i2}}{\mathrm{d}y^2} = 0 \tag{4.79}$$

Hence,

$$V_{\mathrm{bm}_i} = \left\{ EI\left[\frac{\mathrm{d}^2\Phi_{i3}}{\mathrm{d}y^2}\,\lambda_1 + \frac{\mathrm{d}^2\Phi_{i4}}{\mathrm{d}y^2}\,\lambda_2 + \ldots \right] \right\} \tag{4.80}$$

V_{bm_i} can be expressed as:

$$V_{\mathrm{bm}_i} = M_{i1}\lambda_1 + M_{i2}\lambda_2 + \ldots \tag{4.81}$$

Thus, if a bending moment at some particular wing or fuselage station, j, is considered to be an output variable say, y, then,

$$y = C\mathbf{x} \tag{4.82}$$

where:

$$C \triangleq [0\ 0\ M_{i1}\ M_{i1}\ .\ .\ .] \quad (4.83)$$

if:

$$\mathbf{x}' = [w\ q\ \lambda_1\lambda_2\ .\ .\ .\ \lambda_n] \quad (4.84)$$

4.9 BLADE FLAPPING MOTION

A blade of the rotor of an helicopter is a rotating wing. Being of high aspect ratio it is flexible and is characterized by flapping motion. The forces and moments which act on a rotating blade of length R are illustrated in Figure 4.8 which represents the simplest kind of rotor blade: rigid, articulated and without flap hinge offset or spring restraint [Johnson (1981)]. The out-of-plane deflection is denoted by z, the moment arm by r, the flapping angle by β and the angular velocity of the rotor by Ω. It is assumed that the value of β is never large; hence:

$$z = \beta r \quad (4.85)$$

A number of forces are acting on the mass element $m\,dr$ where m is the mass/unit length, namely:

1. An inertial force which opposes the flapping motion. This force has a moment arm, r, about the flap hinge. From Figure 4.8 it can be seen that:

$$\hat{m}\ddot{z} = \hat{m}r\ddot{\beta} \quad (4.86)$$

2. A centrifugal force acting radially outwards. This force is $\hat{m}\Omega^2 r$; its moment arm is z.

3. An aerodynamic force normal to the blade. For small values of the flap angle, this force is the lift L. Its moment arm is r.

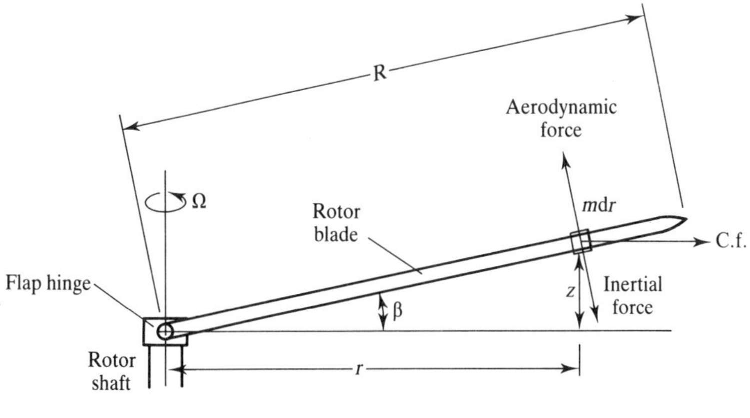

Figure 4.8 Rigid rotor articulated blade.

The equation of flapping motion can be written as the sum of the moments:

$$\int_0^R \hat{m} r \ddot{\beta} r \,\mathrm{d}r + \int_0^R \hat{m} \Omega^2 r (r\beta) \mathrm{d}r - \int_0^R F_z r \,\mathrm{d}r = 0 \tag{4.87}$$

or

$$\int_0^R \hat{m} r^2 \mathrm{d}r (\ddot{\beta} + \Omega^2 \beta) = \int_0^R F_z r \,\mathrm{d}r \tag{4.88}$$

If the moment of inertia of the rotor blade, about the flap hinge, is taken as:

$$J_\mathrm{B} = \int_0^R \hat{m} r^2 \mathrm{d}r \tag{4.89}$$

then:

$$(\ddot{\beta} + \Omega^2 \beta) = \frac{1}{J_\mathrm{B}} \int_0^R F_z r \,\mathrm{d}r \tag{4.90}$$

By using dimensionless time, such that:

$$\Psi = \Omega t \tag{4.91}$$

and the Lock number, γ, where:

$$\gamma = \rho a c R^4 / J_\mathrm{B} \tag{4.92}$$

the flapping equation becomes:

$$\ddot{\beta} + \beta = \gamma M_\mathrm{F} \tag{4.93}$$

In eq. (4.92) ρ denotes the density of the air, c the chord of the rotor blade, and a the blade section two-dimensional lift curve slope.

The l.h.s. of eq. (4.93) represents an undamped, second order, linear system with a natural frequency of 1/rev. If the aerodynamic forces involved have the same natural frequency of once per revolution, resonance will occur in the blade flapping motion. The flap moment, M_F, which arises owing to the aerodynamic forces, can be shown to be:

$$M_\mathrm{F} = M_\theta \theta_\mathrm{C} + M_{\theta_\mathrm{T}} \theta_\mathrm{T} + M_\lambda \lambda + M_{\dot{\beta}} \dot{\beta} + M_\beta \beta \tag{4.94}$$

where θ_C represents the cyclic control, θ_T the twist angle of the flexible rotor blade, $\dot{\beta}$ the flapping velocity, β the displacement of the flapping motion, and λ the inflow. Therefore, assuming $\gamma = 1$:

$$\ddot{\beta} - M_{\dot{\beta}} \dot{\beta} + (1 - M_\beta)\beta = M_\theta \theta_C + M_\lambda \lambda + M_{\theta_\mathrm{T}} \theta_\mathrm{T} \tag{4.95}$$

In hovering motion the net periodic flap moments, as a result of inertial forces, inflow or blade twist, are zero, i.e.:

$$M_\mathrm{F} = M_\theta \theta_\mathrm{C} + M_{\dot{\beta}} \dot{\beta} + M_\beta \beta \tag{4.96}$$

$$\therefore \quad \ddot{\beta} - M_{\dot{\beta}} \dot{\beta} + (1 - M_\beta)\beta = M_\theta \theta_\mathrm{C} \tag{4.97}$$

Taking Laplace transforms allows eq. (4.98) to be expressed as:

$$(s^2 + 2\zeta\omega_n s + \omega_n^2)\beta(s) = \alpha\omega_n^2\theta_C(s) \qquad (4.98)$$

A block diagram representation is shown in Figure 4.9. Representation of eq. (4.97) in state variable form to allow the effects of the blade flapping motion to be easily incorporated into the state equation representing an helicopter's motion, is easily achieved. Let:

$$x_1 = \beta \qquad (4.99)$$

$$x_2 = \dot{\beta} = \dot{x}_1 \qquad (4.100)$$

$$\therefore \quad \dot{x}_2 = \ddot{\beta} = + M_{\dot{\beta}}x_2 + (M_\beta - 1)x_1 + M_\theta\theta_C \qquad (4.101)$$

i.e.:

$$\begin{aligned} \dot{x}_1 &= x_2 \\ \dot{x}_2 &= M_{\dot{\beta}}x_2 + (M_\beta - 1)x_1 + M_\theta\theta_C \end{aligned} \qquad (4.102)$$

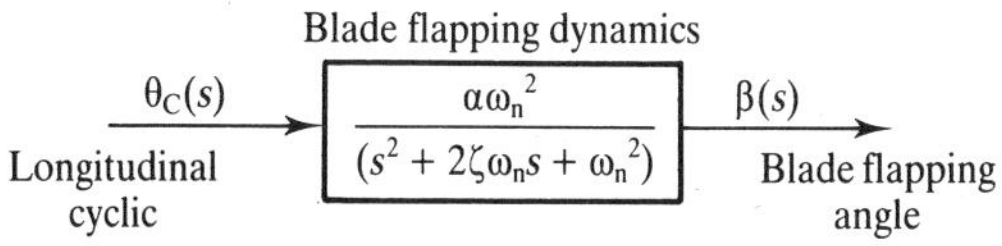

Figure 4.9 Block diagram of blade flapping motion.

4.10 CONCLUSION

This chapter deals with how structural flexibility and unsteady aerodynamic effects can be adequately approximated by suitable mathematical models. These models allow these aeroelastic effects to be incorporated easily into the state and output equations which represent the dynamics of an aircraft.

4.11 EXERCISES

4.1 An aircraft has a rectangular wing of semi-span 8 m and chord 3 m. Its effective stiffness is 350 kN m^{-1} and its inertia is 1 000 kg m^2. If the aircraft flies at sea level at a speed of 136 m s^{-1} its wing lift curve slope is 0.94.

(a) Calculate the frequency and damping ratio of the first bending mode.

(b) If the wing is subjected to a vertical impulse of unit amplitude, what is the peak deflection?

4.2 The same wing of exercise 4.1 is hinged about an axis which allows a single degree of freedom in torsion. The corresponding inertia is 852 kg m^2, and the torsional stiffness is 440 kN-m rad^{-1}. The aerodynamic centre is located 0.6 m ahead of the flexural axis.

(a) Calculate the divergence speed of the wing.
(b) At what frequency does the wing oscillate in torsion?
(c) At what frequency will the wing oscillate if the aircraft is flying at V_D?

4.3 If the wing of exercise 4.1 is considered once more, and it is known that $I_{\lambda\gamma}$ is 147 kg m^2, determine, for still air, the coupled natural frequencies. Show that one value is just greater than the frequency found in exercise 4.2(b), and the other value is just lower than that found in exercise 4.1(a).

(b) Suppose that the damping in the bending and torsional modes is zero, but the wing is moving in an airstream of relative velocity, V_F. Calculate the flutter speed.

4.4 A mathematical model of the aircraft DELTA, which includes actuator dynamics and three significant fuselage bending modes, is:

$$A = \begin{bmatrix} -0.88 & 4.03 & -0.1 & -0.06 & -0.1 & -1.0 & -5.26 & -5.9 & -317.9 & 333.02 \\ -0.46 & -1.25 & -0.06 & 1.15 & -0.54 & -0.38 & 17.11 & -12.92 & -700 & -3\,117.2 \\ -1.55 & -0.14 & -1.87 & -1.26 & -0.77 & -32.2 & -66.1 & -44 & -385.5 & 135.7 \\ 0.56 & 0.42 & -0.04 & -1.28 & 0.07 & 0.59 & -375.1 & 6.2 & -286.3 & 1\,166 \\ 0.73 & -0.34 & 0.12 & 0.1 & -0.01 & 2.38 & 16.39 & -211.5 & -1531 & -1\,614 \\ 0 & 0 & 1 & 0 & 0 & 0 & 0 & 0 & 0 & 0 \\ 0 & 0 & 0 & 1 & 0 & 0 & 0 & 0 & 0 & 0 \\ 0 & 0 & 0 & 0 & 1 & 0 & 0 & 0 & 0 & 0 \\ 0 & 0 & 0 & 0 & 0 & 0 & 0 & 0 & -6.0 & 0 \\ 0 & 0 & 0 & 0 & 0 & 0 & 0 & 0 & 0 & -6.0 \end{bmatrix}$$

$$B' = \begin{bmatrix} 0 & 0 & 0 & 0 & 0 & 0 & 0 & 0 & 6.0 & 0 \\ 0 & 0 & 0 & 0 & 0 & 0 & 0 & 0 & 0 & 6.0 \end{bmatrix}$$

$\mathbf{x}' = [x_1\ x_2\ x_3\ x_4\ x_5\ x_6\ x_7\ x_8\ x_9\ x_{10}]$

$\mathbf{u} = [\delta_{A_C}\ \delta_{E_C}]$

where x_1 = vertical velocity of rigid body (in s^{-1})
x_2 = normalized pitch rate of rigid body (in s^{-1})
x_3 = first bending moment rate (in s^{-1})
x_4 = sixth bending moment rate (in s^{-1})
x_5 = third bending moment rate (in s^{-1})
x_6 = first bending moment deflection
x_7 = sixth bending moment deflection
x_8 = third bending moment deflection
x_9 = symmetrical aileron deflection angle (rad)
x_{10} = inboard elevator deflection angle (rad)

(a) Obtain a new set of equations if it is required that the displacement and velocities are expressed in SI units.

(b) If only the first and third bending modes are now considered to be significant, and only the inboard elevator is used to control the motion, obtain a new set of equations to represent the aircraft's motion.

4.5 A sketch of a flexible structure consisting of a rotating hub, a flexible beam, and a tip mass is shown in Figure 4.10.

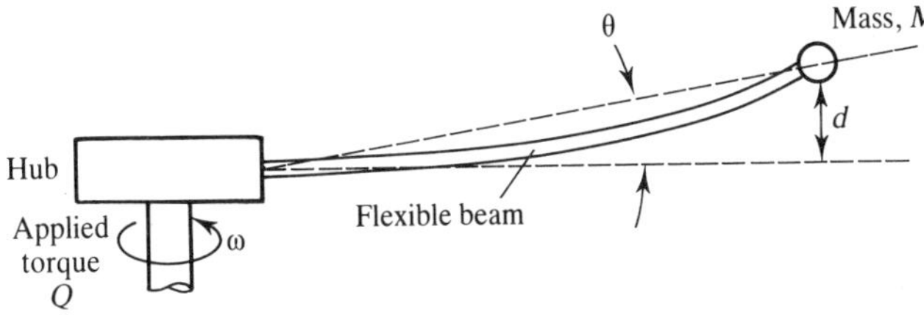

Figure 4.10 Blade system for Exercise 4.5.

It has two outputs: the angle of the blade and the deflection of the tip mass; and a single input, the control torque Q.

(a) If the damping coefficient, F, has a value 10^{-3}, and if $\mathbf{\Omega}$ is a diagonal matrix
containing the natural frequencies of the system, show that the equations of motion of the system can be represented by the state and output equations shown.

$$\dot{\tilde{\mathbf{x}}} = A\tilde{\mathbf{x}} + B\mathbf{u}$$

$$\mathbf{y} = C\tilde{\mathbf{x}}$$

where:

$$A = \begin{bmatrix} 0 & I_4 \\ -\mathbf{\Omega}^2 & -F\mathbf{\Omega} \end{bmatrix}$$

$$B' = [0 \;\; B_0]$$

$$C = \begin{bmatrix} C_0 & 0 \\ B_0' & 0 \end{bmatrix}$$

$$\tilde{\mathbf{x}}' = [x_1 \; x_2 \; x_3 \; x_4 \; \dot{x}_1 \; \dot{x}_2 \; \dot{x}_3 \; \dot{x}_4]$$

(b) The diagonal matrix, $\mathbf{\Omega}$, containing the natural frequencies of the model is given below. The first element is zero since it corresponds to the rigid body mode. The driving and output matrices, B_0 and C_0 corresponding to system of Figure 4.10 are also given.

$$B_0' = [0.0078 \;\; -0.0366 \;\; -0.0576 \;\; -0.0521]$$

$$C_0 = [0 \;\; 4.4025 \;\; 6.1228 \;\; 5.8639]$$

$$\mathbf{\Omega} = \text{diag}[0 \;\; -20 \;\; -25.93 \;\; -30.984]$$

Determine the eigenvalues and hence the eigenvectors of the system. Sketch the mode shape of the second bending mode.

4.12 NOTES

1. λ is assumed to be the chord of a small circle. Only small perturbations are being considered.
2. The equations describe the aircraft's motion relative to a mean-axes coordinate system: with small displacements, the stability axes can be assumed to coincide with the mean axes.
3. The example used here is the B-52, an eight-engined strategic bomber in service with the USAF.

4.13 REFERENCES

BISPLINIGHOFF, R.L., H. ASHLEY and R. HALFMAN. 1955. *Aeroelasticity*. Reading, Mass.: Addison Wesley.

HANCOCK, G.J., J.R. WRIGHT and A. SIMPSON. 1985. On the teaching of the principles of wing flexure – torsion flutter. *Aero Journal, RAeS*. Oct., 285–305.

JOHNSON, W. 1981. *Helicopter Theory*. Princeton Univ. Press.

JONES, R.T. 1940. The unsteady lift of a wing of finite aspect ratio. NACA Rpt 681.

McLEAN, D. 1978. Gust alleviation control systems for aircraft. *Proc. IEE*. 125 (7): 675–85.

SCHWANZ, R.C. 1972. Formulations of the equations of motion of an aeroelastic aircraft for stability and control and flight control applications. AFFDL/FGC-TM-72-14. August.

5

Disturbances Affecting Aircraft Motion

5.1 INTRODUCTION

When an aircraft is controlled automatically its motion may be affected by: manoeuvre commands, atmospheric effects, and noise from the system and its sensors.

Manoeuvre commands are applied either by a human pilot or are provided by a guidance, a navigation or a weapons system. Such commands are deliberate inputs to the AFCS, and are intended to change the aircraft's path. The other effects are unwanted disturbances to the aircraft's motion. It is one of the principal functions of an AFCS to suppress as much as possible the unwanted effects of such disturbances. In this chapter only disturbances caused either by atmospheric effects or by sensor noise are considered.

5.2 ATMOSPHERIC DISTURBANCES

The air through which an aircraft flies is never still. As a consequence, whenever an aircraft flies, its motion is erratic. The nature of those disturbances to the air is influenced by many factors, but it is customary to consider turbulence, which occurs above that region where the atmosphere behaves as a boundary layer, as belonging to either of these classes:

1. Convective turbulence, which occurs in and around clouds. This includes thunderstorms particularly.
2. Clear air turbulence (CAT). Below the cloudbase, direct convection heats the air and causes motion which, together with the many small eddies arising as a result of surface heating, are often regarded as mild CAT. Above a cluster of cumulus clouds a regular, short broken motion can persist, particularly when the change in velocity with height is large. More virulent CAT is usually to be found near mountains, and, depending upon the meteorological conditions, flights near the tropopause can often be turbulent. The most virulent turbulence of all, however, is caused by thunderstorms and squall lines, especially when the same area is simultaneously being subjected to rain, hail, sleet or snow.

Another violent atmospheric phenomenon which can be encountered in flight is the microburst, a severe downburst of air. Microbursts are associated with considerable changes in the direction and/or velocity of the wind as the height changes. They exist for only very brief periods. Such severe changes in the nature of the wind over resticted ranges of height are caused by convection and they are often referred to as 'wind shears'. Rising, or falling, columns of air, ringed by toroids of extreme vorticity, are produced by the convection and it is this phenomenon which is called the microburst. A fuller account is presented in Section 5.11.

Because the mechanisms of turbulence are so varied and involved, it has been found that the only effective methods of analysing dynamic problems in which turbulence is involved are statistical methods. However, large gusts, which are reasonably well defined by a particular deterministic function, do occur, but at random times. To assess the effect on the structure of an aircraft encountering such gusts, it is common practice to employ a discrete gust as a load testing function. Even though its time of occurrence may be random, a wind shear can be regarded, once it has occurred, to be effectively a deterministic phenomenon. Thus, in this chapter, there will be presented mathematical models of three types of atmospheric turbulence. The models are not entirely descriptive of the phenomena, but they do represent the significant characteristics sufficiently well to permit an analysis to be carried out with adequate accuracy for engineering purposes. Another method of analysis, which uses an analogue signal in a transient fashion to represent continuous turbulence, is also discussed, before the problem of how the outputs of these models of atmospheric turbulence can be introduced correctly into the equations of motion is dealt with.

The interested reader is referred to Etkin (1980) for further discussion.

5.3 A DISCRETE GUST FUNCTION

That mathematical model, representing a sharp edged gust, which enjoys the most general acceptance for fixed-wing aircraft is the (1-cos) gust, defined thus:

$$x_g(t) = \frac{k}{T}\,(1\text{-}\cos\,(2\pi/T)t) \tag{5.1}$$

where the duration of the gust, denoted by T, is given by:

$$T = L/U_0 \tag{5.2}$$

The scale length L is the wavelength of the gust in metres; the equilibrium speed of the aircraft, U_0, is measured in metres per second. In eq. (5.1) k is a scaling factor which is selected to achieve the required gust intensity. The gust function is represented in Figure 5.1. The gust wavelength is traditionally taken to be equal to twenty-five times the mean aerodynamic chord of the wing of the aircraft being considered, i.e.:

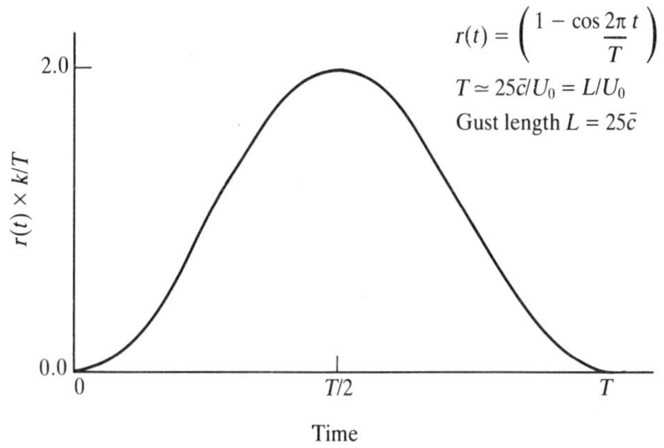

Figure 5.1 (1-cos) gust.

$$L = 25\bar{c} \tag{5.3}$$

This traditional value resulted because study showed that it coupled with the short period pitching and heaving motions of an aircraft to produce the greatest induced load factors. However, as aircraft have flown faster and, as a result of the consequent configuration changes, have become more flexible, it is possible for other gust wavelengths to couple with the flexible modes, thereby producing substantial load responses. When an attempt was made to consider all the possible gust wavelengths which could couple, it became necessary to use statistical methods, particularly the method involving the power spectral density which required a mathematical model to represent the atmospheric turbulence as a stationary, random process. Before dealing with that model, a brief review of the statistical theory associated with the power spectral density functions is presented.

5.4 POWER SPECTRAL DENSITY FUNCTIONS

The power spectral density (PSD) of any function, $x(t)$, is a real function, the knowledge of which affords the designer information of how the mean squared value of $x(t)$ is distributed with frequency. At any particular frequency, ω, the ordinate of the graph of the PSD versus frequency, is the mean squared value of that part of $x(t)$ whose frequency is within an infinitely narrow band, centred on ω. The PSD function is defined as:

$$\Phi(\omega) = \lim_{\substack{\Delta\omega \to 0 \\ T \to \infty}} \frac{1}{T\Delta\omega} \int_0^T x^2(t, \omega, \Delta\omega)\, dt \tag{5.4}$$

$\Phi(\omega)$ is the PSD function of the x and it has units of either m s^{-1} or rad s^{-2}. T is the duration, in seconds, of the record of $x(t)$, and $x(t, \omega, \Delta\omega)$ is the component of $x(t)$ which lies within the frequency band $\omega \pm \Delta\omega/2$. The total area under the curve is the mean squared value of $x(t)$, taken over all frequencies.

To remove the influence of the airspeed, when comparing one analysis with another, the PSD functions of atmospheric phenomena are usually calculated in terms of spatial frequency:

$$\Omega = \omega/U_0 \tag{5.5}$$

where Ω, the spatial frequency, is in rad m^{-1}, ω is the observed angular frequency in rad s^{-1}, and U_0 is the equilibrium speed of the aircraft, in m s^{-1}. The relationship between the original PSD function and one which has been transformed to the new spectral domain is given by:

$$\Phi(\omega) = \Phi(\Omega)/U_0 \tag{5.6}$$

While it is feasible to determine a PSD function directly from that definition, it is more convenient to first calculate the autocorrelation function, $R(T)$, for the complete record of $x(t)$, and thence to obtain the PSD function, $\Phi(\Omega)$, by taking the Fourier transform of $R(T)$. The steps involved are:

$$R(T) = \frac{1}{T}\int_0^T x(t)x(t + T)\mathrm{d}t \tag{5.7}$$

$$\Phi(\Omega) = \frac{1}{2\pi}\int_{-\infty}^{\infty} R(T)\mathrm{e}^{\mathrm{j}\Omega T}\mathrm{d}T \tag{5.8}$$

Some PSD functions, typical of those relating to atmospheric turbulence, are illustrated in Figure 5.2. The height of the curve is a measure of the intensity of turbulence at a particular frequency. The curves in Figure 5.2 show a feature which is characteristic of such atmospheric phenomena, namely as frequency increases, the intensity decreases. The square root of the area under the PSD curve is a measure of the overall r.m.s. gust velocity, σ. In theory, the PSD functions should extend from zero to infinite frequency; in practice, there exists a maximum frequency above which the power contained in the higher frequencies makes a negligible contribution to the aircraft's response to encountering turbulence. That maximum frequency is called the cut-off frequency, ω_c. However, it must be remembered that, if only the area under the frequency–limited power spectrum is included in an analysis, the r.m.s. value then obtained can be different from the value obtained by determining the area over all the frequencies 0 to ∞, by a factor of as much as 2 to 2.5.

5.5 CONTINUOUS GUST REPRESENTATIONS

There are two particular analytical representations for the PSD function of atmospheric turbulence which find extensive use in AFCS studies. The first, the

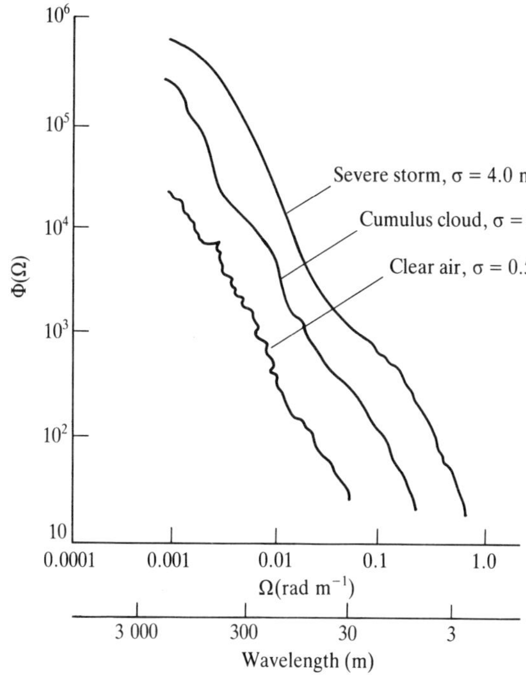

Figure 5.2 $\Phi(\Omega)$ vs Ω.

Von Karman spectrum, is the better fit to the spectrum obtained from records of atmospheric turbulence. However, it is the least favoured in analytical studies because it has a more complicated PSD function, its definition being:

$$\Phi_{VK}(\Omega) = \frac{\sigma^2 L}{\pi} \frac{[1 + 8/3(1.339 L\Omega)^2]}{1 + (1.339 L\Omega)^2]^{11/6}} \tag{5.9}$$

Because of the non-integer index, the Von Karman PSD function is difficult to simulate directly.

The second, the Dryden PSD function, is more favoured because it is simpler and, hence, more easily programmed:

$$\Phi_{Dry}(\Omega) = \frac{\sigma^2 L}{\pi} \frac{(1 + 3L^2\Omega^2)}{(1 + L^2\Omega^2)^2} \tag{5.10}$$

In Figure 5.3 are shown the graphs of the PSD functions for a reasonable range of frequency. The difference between them is not great, so that, when the handling qualities of a small, high performance aircraft are being considered, for example, when $0.1 < \omega < 5.0$, the two forms are within a few decibels of each other. In arriving at these representations a number of assumptions were involved. For the purposes of this review, the following are most significant:

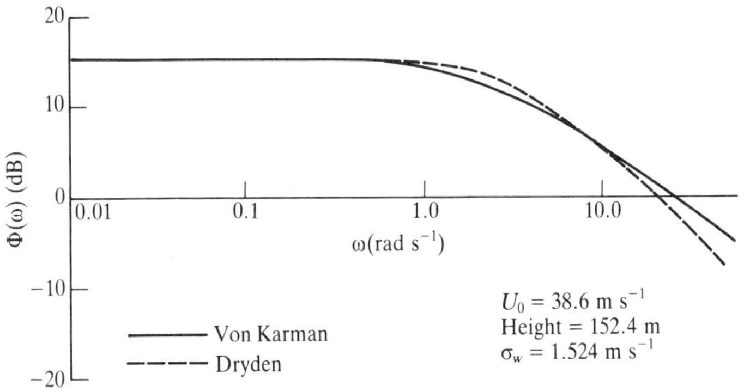

Figure 5.3 Von Karman and Dryden PSD.

1. The turbulence scale length varies with height. Chalk *et al.* (1969) provide information relating to the MIL-SPEC F-8785B (ASG); the dependence of scale length on height is defined in this manner:

At heights greater than 1750 ft (580 m)

$$L_u = L_v = L_w = 1750\,\text{ft (580 m)} \tag{5.11}$$

At heights lower than 1750 ft (580 m)

$$L_w = h_{cg}\,\text{ft (m)} \tag{5.12}$$

$$L_u,\ L_v = 145 h_{cg}\,\text{ft (m)} \tag{5.13}$$

where h_{cg} is the height of the aircraft encountering the turbulence.

2. Atmospheric turbulence is a stationary random process, i.e. its statistical properties are independent of time. Such an assumption is acceptable for AFCS studies since, in general, the duration of the automatically controlled response of any aircraft is less than one minute.

3. The turbulence field is frozen with respect to time. This is known as Taylor's hypothesis. It is as a consequence of this assumption that eq. (5.6) holds.

4. The statistical characteristics of turbulence are defined for the stability axis system of the aircraft.

5. The intensity of the three translational components of the turbulence are isotropic, i.e.:

$$\sigma_u^2/L_u = \sigma_w^2/L_w = \sigma_v^2/L_v \tag{5.14}$$

The corresponding intensities for the Von Karman spectrum are:

$$\sigma_u^2/L_u^{2/3} = \sigma_v^2/L_v^{2/3} = \sigma_w^2/L_w^{2/3} \tag{5.15}$$

For thunderstorms, at any height:

$$L_w = L_u = L_v = 1750\,\text{ft (580 m)} \tag{5.16}$$

$$\sigma_w = \sigma_u = \sigma_v = 21\,\text{ft s}^{-1}\ (7.0\,\text{m s}^{-1}) \tag{5.17}$$

For the Dryden PSD functions, however, the form for the horizontal speed gust is different from that given in eq. (5.10); it is shown in eq. (5.18):

$$\Phi_u(\Omega) = 2\sigma_u^2 \frac{L_u}{\pi} \frac{1}{(1 + L_u\Omega)^2} \tag{5.18}$$

For completeness, the PSD functions of the other, translational, gust velocities are quoted here:

$$\Phi_v(\Omega) = \sigma_v^2 \frac{L_v}{\pi} \frac{(1 + 3(L_v\Omega)^2)}{[1 + (L_v\Omega)^2]^2} \tag{5.19}$$

$$\Phi_w(\Omega) = \sigma_w^2 \frac{L_w}{\pi} \frac{(1 + 3(L_w\Omega)^2)}{[1 + (L_w\Omega)^2]^2} \tag{5.20}$$

where:

$$\sigma_i^2 \triangleq \int_0^\infty \Phi_i(\Omega)\mathrm{d}\Omega_{i\ =\ u,\ v\ \text{or}\ w} \tag{5.21}$$

Since:

$$\omega = U_0\Omega \tag{5.22}$$

$$\Phi_u(\omega) = \frac{2\sigma_u^2 L_u}{U_0\pi} \frac{1}{\{1 + (L_u/U_0)^2\omega^2\}} \tag{5.23}$$

$$\Phi_v(\omega) = \frac{\sigma_v^2 L_v}{\pi U_0} \frac{\{1 + 3(L_v/U_0)^2\omega^2\}}{\{1 + (L_v/U_0)^2\omega^2\}^2} \tag{5.24}$$

$$\Phi_w(\omega) = \frac{\sigma_w^2 L_w}{\pi U_0} \frac{\{1 + 3(L_w/U_0)^2\omega^2\}}{\{1 + (L_w/U_0)^2\omega^2\}^2} \tag{5.25}$$

To generate such gust signals with the required intensity, scale lengths and PSD functions for some given flight velocity and height, a wide-band noise source with a PSD function $\Phi_N(\omega)$, is used to provide the input signal to a linear filter, chosen such that it has an appropriate frequency response so that the output signal from the filter will have a PSD function $\Phi_i(\omega)$. The scheme is represented in the block diagram shown in Figure 5.4. The relationship of the PSD function of the output signal to the PSD function of the input signal is given by:

$$\Phi_i(\omega) = \left| G_i(s) \right|^2_{s\ =\ j\omega} \Phi_N(\omega) \tag{5.26}$$

When the noise source is chosen so that its power spectrum is similar to that of white noise, i.e.

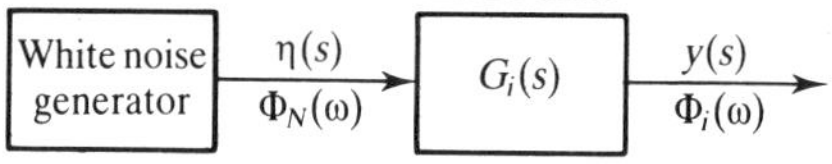

Figure 5.4 Block diagram.

$$\Phi_N(\omega) = 1.0 \tag{5.27}$$

it is found from eq. (5.26) that:

$$\Phi_i(\omega) = \left| G_i(s) \right|^2_{s = j\omega} \tag{5.28}$$

Thus, the filters needed to generate the appropriate spectral densities for the translational gust velocities, are easily seen to be:

$$G_u(s) = \frac{\sqrt{K_u}}{(s + \lambda_u)} \tag{5.29}$$

$$G_v(s) = \sqrt{K_v}\,\frac{(s + \beta_v)}{(s + \lambda_v)^2} \tag{5.30}$$

$$G_w(s) = \sqrt{K_w}\,\frac{(s + \beta_w)}{(s + \lambda_w)^2} \tag{5.31}$$

where:

$$K_u = \frac{2U_0\sigma_u^2}{L_u\pi} \tag{5.32}$$

$$K_v = \frac{3U_0\sigma_v^2}{L_v\pi} \tag{5.33}$$

$$K_w = \frac{3\sigma_w^2}{L_w\pi U_0} \tag{5.34}$$

$$\beta_v = \frac{U_0}{\sqrt{3}L_v} \tag{5.35}$$

$$\beta_w = \frac{U_0}{\sqrt{3}L_w} \tag{5.36}$$

$$\lambda_u = U_0/L_u \tag{5.37}$$

$$\lambda_v = U_0/L_v \tag{5.38}$$

$$\lambda_w = U_0/L_w \tag{5.39}$$

5.6 STATE VARIABLE MODELS

Take eq. (5.31) as an example. Then,

$$w_g(s) = \sqrt{K_w}\,\frac{(s + \beta_w)}{(s + \lambda_w)^2}\,\eta(s) \tag{5.40}$$

where $\eta(t)$ is the signal from the white noise source. From eq. (5.40) it can be derived that:

$$\ddot{w}_g + 2\lambda_w \dot{w}_g + \lambda_w^2 w_g = \sqrt{K_w}\beta_w \eta + \sqrt{K_w}\dot{\eta} \tag{5.41}$$

Set:

$$\frac{w_g(s)}{\eta(s)} = \frac{x(s)}{\eta(s)} \cdot \frac{w_g(s)}{x(s)} \tag{5.42}$$

and let:

$$\frac{x(s)}{\eta(s)} \triangleq \frac{1}{s^2 + 2\lambda_w s + \lambda_w^2} \tag{5.43}$$

then:

$$\frac{w_g(s)}{x(s)} = \sqrt{K_w}(s + \beta_w) \tag{5.44}$$

Thus,

$$\ddot{x} + 2\lambda_w \dot{x} + \lambda_w^2 x = \eta(t) \tag{5.45}$$

and:

$$w_g = \sqrt{K_w}\dot{x} + \sqrt{(K_w \beta_w)}x \tag{5.46}$$

Let:

$$d_g \triangleq w_g \qquad x_1 \triangleq x \qquad x_2 \triangleq x \tag{5.47}$$

then:

$$\begin{aligned} \dot{x}_1 &= x_2 \\ \dot{x}_2 &= -\,2\lambda_w x_2 - \lambda_w^2 x_1 + \eta(t) \end{aligned} \tag{5.48}$$

$$y \triangleq w_g \sqrt{K_w} x_2 + \sqrt{(K_w \beta_w)} x_1 \tag{5.49}$$

If:

$$\mathbf{x} \triangleq \begin{bmatrix} x_1 \\ x_2 \end{bmatrix} \tag{5.50}$$

then:

$$\dot{\mathbf{x}} = \begin{bmatrix} 0 & 1 \\ -\lambda_w^2 & -2\lambda_w \end{bmatrix} \mathbf{x} + \begin{bmatrix} 0 \\ 1 \end{bmatrix} \eta \tag{5.51}$$

$$d_g = \sqrt{K_w}[1 \;\; \beta_w]\mathbf{x} \tag{5.52}$$

Hence:

$$\begin{aligned} \dot{\mathbf{x}} &= A\mathbf{x} + B\eta \\ d_g &= F\mathbf{x} \end{aligned} \tag{5.53}$$

where

$$A = \begin{bmatrix} 0 & 1 \\ \dfrac{-U_0^2}{L_w^2} & \dfrac{-2U_0}{L_w} \end{bmatrix} \tag{5.54}$$

$$B = \begin{bmatrix} 0 \\ 1 \end{bmatrix} \tag{5.55}$$

$$F = \begin{bmatrix} \dfrac{3U_0\sigma_w^2}{L_w\pi} & \dfrac{\sqrt{3}U_0^2\sigma_w^2}{L_w\pi} \end{bmatrix} \tag{5.56}$$

An alternative derivation can be obtained, based upon eq. (5.41). Let:

$$d_2 \triangleq w_g \tag{5.57}$$

$$d_1 = \dot{w}_g - \sqrt{K_w}\eta \tag{5.58}$$

$$\therefore \quad \dot{w}_g = d_1 + \sqrt{K_w}\eta \tag{5.59}$$

$$\therefore \quad \dot{d}_1 = \ddot{w}_g - \sqrt{K_w}\dot{\eta} = -2\lambda_w\dot{w}_g - \lambda_w^2 w_g + \sqrt{K_w}\beta_w\eta \tag{5.60}$$

$$\begin{aligned} \therefore \quad \dot{d}_1 &= -2\lambda_w(d_1 + \sqrt{K_w}\eta) - \lambda_w^2 d_2 + \sqrt{K_w}\beta_w\eta \\ &= -2\lambda_w d_1 - \lambda_w^2 d_2 + \sqrt{K_w}(\beta_w - 2\lambda_w)\eta \end{aligned} \tag{5.61}$$

$$\dot{d}_2 = d_1 + \sqrt{K_w}\eta \tag{5.62}$$

Setting

$$\mathbf{d}_g = \begin{bmatrix} d_1 \\ d_2 \end{bmatrix} \tag{5.63}$$

$$\dot{\mathbf{d}}_g = F\mathbf{d}_g + D\eta \tag{5.64}$$

where

$$F = \begin{bmatrix} -2\lambda_w & -\lambda_w^2 \\ 1 & 0 \end{bmatrix} \tag{5.65}$$

$$D = \begin{bmatrix} \sqrt{(K_w(\beta_w - 2\lambda_w))} \\ \sqrt{K_w} \end{bmatrix} \tag{5.66}$$

5.7 ANGULAR GUST EQUATIONS

$$\frac{p_g(s)}{\eta(s)} = \frac{\sigma_w \sqrt{\pi}}{\sqrt{(L_w U_0)}} \frac{\sqrt{\left[0.8\left(\frac{\pi L_w}{4b}\right)^{1/3}\right]}}{\left(1 + \frac{4b}{\pi U_0}s\right)} \tag{5.67}$$

b is the semi-span of the wing.

$$\frac{r_g(s)}{\eta(s)} = \frac{-\ v_g(s)s}{U_0\left(1 + \frac{3b}{\pi U_0}s\right)} \tag{5.68}$$

$$v_g(s) = \sigma_v \sqrt{(L_v/U_0)} \frac{\left(1 + \sqrt{3}\frac{L_v}{U_0}s\right)}{\left(1 + \frac{L_v}{U_0}s\right)^2} \tag{5.69}$$

5.8 THE EFFECTS OF GUSTS ON AIRCRAFT MOTION

The components of translational velocity of turbulence are defined as positive along the positive body axes. Hence,

$$\alpha_g = -\ w_g/U_0 \tag{5.70}$$

$$\beta_g \simeq -\ v_g/U_0 \tag{5.71}$$

The gust velocities, u_g, w_g and v_g, may vary along the length and span of the aircraft. To account for that it is assumed that the exact distribution of the turbulence velocity over the airframe can be satisfactorily approximated by a truncated Taylor series expansion, i.e.:

$$u_g(x) = u_g(0) + \left.\frac{\partial u_g}{\partial x}\right|_0^x \tag{5.72}$$

$$v_g(y) = v_g(0) + \left.\frac{\partial v_g}{\partial y}\right|_0^y \tag{5.73}$$

$$w_g(x, y) = w_g(0, 0) + \left.\frac{\partial w_g}{\partial x}\right|_0^x + \left.\frac{\partial w_g}{\partial y}\right|_0^y \tag{5.74}$$

For small perturbation motion the gradient of $\partial w_g/\partial x$ is linear and can be taken as the aerodynamic equivalent to the inertial pitching velocity, q. Hence,

$$q_g = \partial w_g/\partial x \tag{5.75}$$

$$p_g = -\ \partial w_g/\partial y \tag{5.76}$$

$$r_g = \partial v_g/\partial x \tag{5.77}$$

$$\dot{\alpha}_g = \frac{d\alpha_g}{dt} = \frac{\partial\alpha_g}{\partial x}\cdot\frac{dx}{dt} = \frac{\partial}{\partial x}\left(-\,w_g/U_0\right)U_0 \tag{5.78}$$

$$= -\frac{\partial w_g}{\partial x} \tag{5.79}$$

$$\therefore\quad \dot{\alpha}_g = -\,q_g \tag{5.80}$$

For example, the equations of small perturbation longitudinal motion, with gust terms included, are given by:

$$\dot{u} = -\,g\theta + X_\delta\delta + X_u(u + u_g) + X_\alpha(\alpha + \alpha_g) \tag{5.81}$$

$$\begin{aligned}\dot{\alpha} = q + \frac{Z_u}{U_0}(u + u_g) + Z_\alpha(\alpha + \alpha_g) + Z_q(q + q_g)\\ + Z_{\dot{\alpha}}(\dot{\alpha} - q_g) + Z_\delta\delta\end{aligned} \tag{5.82}$$

$$\begin{aligned}\dot{q} = M_u(u + u_g) + M_\alpha(\alpha + \alpha_g) + M_{\dot{\alpha}}(\dot{\alpha} - q_g)\\ + M_q(q + q_g) + M_\delta\delta\end{aligned} \tag{5.83}$$

Thus, if:

$$x \triangleq \begin{bmatrix} u \\ \alpha \\ q \\ \theta \end{bmatrix}$$

then

$$\dot{\mathbf{x}} = A\mathbf{x} + B\delta + EV_g \tag{5.85}$$

where

$$V_g \triangleq \begin{bmatrix} u_g \\ \alpha_g \\ q_g \end{bmatrix}$$

5.9 TRANSIENT ANALOGUE

If the PSD function is rational and can be factorized, it is possible to calculate the corresponding steady state variance. This being so, it is then possible to represent any component of atmospheric turbulence by an equivalent deterministic signal.

Suppose that the longitudinal gust velocity is considered as an example,

then:

$$\Phi_u(\omega) = \left(\frac{2\sigma_u^2 L_u}{\pi U_0}\right)(1 + (L_u^2/U_0^2)\omega^2)^{-1} \quad (5.87)$$

$$G_U(s) = \sqrt{\left(\frac{2\sigma_u^2 U_0}{L_u \pi}\right)}\left(s + \frac{U_0}{L_u}\right)^{-1} \quad (5.88)$$

$$\sigma_u^2 = \frac{1}{2\pi}\int_{-\infty}^{\infty} \Phi(\omega)\mathrm{d}\omega \quad (5.89)$$

The gust component, which acts as an input to the aircraft equations, is now assumed to have as the probability distribution of its amplitude a Gaussian distribution, of zero mean.

The equivalent deterministic input (the *transient analogue*) is obtained by factorizing the PSD function representing the gust:

$$\Phi_u(s) = G_u(s)G_u(-s)\Big|_{s = \mathrm{j}\omega} \quad (5.90)$$

$$= \frac{\sigma_u \surd(2U_0/L_u\pi)}{(s + \lambda_u)}\,\frac{\sigma_u \surd(2U_0/L_u\pi)}{(-s + \lambda_u)} \quad (5.91)$$

i.e.:

$$G_u(s) = \frac{\surd K_u}{(s + \lambda_u)} \quad (5.92)$$

Suppose the equivalent to the white noise signal is a unit impulse function, then:

$$u_g(t) = \sigma_u \surd(2U_0/L_u\pi)\mathrm{e}^{-\lambda_u t} \quad (5.93)$$

Equation (5.93) represents the specific deterministic test input signal which can be substituted for the gust spectrum being considered. By using such an imput signal, the mean squared value of the output is obtained when the steady state conditions have been reached.

5.10 DETERMINATION OF THE R.M.S. VALUE OF ACCELERATION AS A RESULT OF ENCOUNTERING GUSTS

In CCV aircraft there is likely to be a ride control system (RCS) the purpose of which is to provide smoother ride qualities in the aircraft when it is flying in atmospheric turbulence (see Section 12.4 of Chapter 12).

To assess the effectiveness of such RCSs, it is necessary to know the r.m.s. values of acceleration at a number of locations on the aircraft and to decide if these are sufficiently reduced from the values which applied when the aircraft was not controlled by an RCS. Although r.m.s. values can be determined using PSD functions, a more efficient method for computation is now explained (Swaim *et al.*, 1977).

When the motion of an aircraft is to be studied in response to continuous atmospheric turbulence the suitable representation of the equation of motion is:

$$\dot{\mathbf{x}} = A\mathbf{x} + B\mathbf{u} + E\mathbf{d}_g \tag{5.94}$$

The gust vector can be obtained from eq. (5.64), i.e.:

$$\dot{\mathbf{d}}_g = F\mathbf{d}_g + D\eta \tag{5.64}$$

It is easy to drive the aircraft dynamics by means of the white noise input, η, to the Dryden filter, such that the motion of the aircraft will correspond to the motion caused by atmospheric disturbances, to the extent that eq. (5.64) represents a good mathematical model of continuous atmospheric turbulence.

Combining eqs (5.64) and (5.85) yields:

$$\begin{bmatrix} \dot{\mathbf{x}} \\ \dot{\mathbf{d}}_g \end{bmatrix} = \begin{bmatrix} A & E \\ 0 & F \end{bmatrix} \begin{bmatrix} \mathbf{x} \\ \mathbf{d}_g \end{bmatrix} + \begin{bmatrix} B \\ 0 \end{bmatrix} \mathbf{u} + \begin{bmatrix} O \\ D \end{bmatrix} \eta \tag{5.95}$$

In what follows the response of the aircraft to the control inputs u is ignored. If it is important to consider the response to both gusts and inputs simultaneously, the responses can be found independently and summed, since the aircraft dynamics are linear.

Equation (5.95) can be re-expressed as follows:

$$\dot{\mathbf{x}}^* = H\mathbf{x}^* + M\eta \tag{5.96}$$

where:

$$\mathbf{x}^* \triangleq \begin{bmatrix} \mathbf{x} \\ \mathbf{d}_g \end{bmatrix}$$

$$H = \begin{bmatrix} A & E \\ 0 & F \end{bmatrix}$$

$$M = \begin{bmatrix} 0 \\ D \end{bmatrix} \tag{5.99}$$

In Chapter 2, it was shown that acceleration, whether normal or lateral, can be represented in the form of an output equation:

$$\mathbf{y} = C\mathbf{x} + D\mathbf{u} \tag{5.100}$$

(See, for example, eq. (2.131) or (2.158).)

When the effects of control inputs are being ignored and only the gusts are present then:

$$y = C\mathbf{x}^* \triangleq a_x \tag*{(5.101)*}$$

The mean value of a_x^2 can be found by squaring a_x and averaging

$$a_x^2 = [C\mathbf{x}^*]\,[C\mathbf{x}^*]' \tag{5.102}$$

but $C\mathbf{x}^*$ is a scalar, therefore:

$$[C\mathbf{x}^*]' = [C\mathbf{x}^*] = [\mathbf{x}^{*\prime}C'] \tag{5.103}$$

$$\therefore \quad a_x^2 = [C\mathbf{x}^*]\,[\mathbf{x}^{*\prime}C'] = C\mathbf{x}^*x^{*\prime}C' \tag{5.104}$$

The mean squared value is then the expected value, $E\{a_x^2\}$, *i.e.*

$$E\{a_x^2\} = CE\{\mathbf{x}^*\mathbf{x}^{*\prime}\}C' \tag{5.105}$$

where $E\{\mathbf{x}^*\mathbf{x}^{*\prime}\}$ is a symmetric, square, state covariance matrix of order $(n + 2) \times (n + 2)$. Note that a_x represents either a_{z_x} or a_{y_x}.

If this covariance matrix can be evaluated, the mean squared value, and therefore the r.m.s. value, of a_x, can be found.

From eq. (5.96) we note that:

$$E\{\mathbf{x}^*\mathbf{x}^{*\prime}\} = HE\{\mathbf{x}^*\mathbf{x}^{*\prime}\} + ME\{\eta\mathbf{x}^{*\prime}\} \tag{5.106}$$

and that:

$$\mathbf{x}^{*\prime} = (H\mathbf{x}^*)' + (M\eta)' = \mathbf{x}^{*\prime}H' + \eta'M' \tag{5.107}$$

$$\therefore \quad \mathbf{x}^*\mathbf{x}^{*\prime} = \mathbf{x}^*\mathbf{x}^{*\prime}H' + \mathbf{x}^*\eta'M' \tag{5.108}$$

$$\therefore \quad \mathrm{E}\{\mathbf{x}^*\mathbf{x}^{*\prime}\} = E\{\mathbf{x}^*\mathbf{x}^{*\prime}\}H' + E\{\mathbf{x}^*\eta'\}M' \tag{5.109}$$

For a unit white noise input, the correlation between $\mathbf{x}^*$ and η is:

$$E[\eta\mathbf{x}^{*\prime}] = M'/2 \tag{5.110}$$

$$E[\mathbf{x}^*\eta'] = M/2 \tag{5.111}$$

When eqs (5.106) and (5.109) are added (making use of eqs (5.110) and (5.111)) it can be shown that:

$$E[\dot{\mathbf{x}}^*\mathbf{x}^{*\prime}] + E[\mathbf{x}^*\dot{\mathbf{x}}^{*\prime}] = HE[\mathbf{x}^*\mathbf{x}^{*\prime}] + E[\mathbf{x}^*\mathbf{x}^{*\prime}]H' + MM' \tag{5.112}$$

For a stationary random process, such as was assumed for the mathematical model representing the continuous atmospheric turbulence:

$$\frac{\mathrm{d}}{\mathrm{d}t}\{E[\mathbf{x}^*\mathbf{x}^{*\prime}]\} = 0 = E[\dot{\mathbf{x}}^*\mathbf{x}^{*\prime}] + E[\mathbf{x}^*\mathbf{x}^{*\prime}] \tag{5.113}$$

$$\therefore \quad HE[\mathbf{x}^*\mathbf{x}^{*\prime}] + E[\mathbf{x}^*\mathbf{x}^{*\prime}]H' + MM' = 0 \tag{5.114}$$

Given H and M, eq. (5.114) has a unique solution for the elements of the covariance matrix, $E[\mathbf{x}^*\mathbf{x}^{*\prime}]$. This matrix is then substituted in eq. (5.105); the square root of which yields the required r.m.s. value.

There are a number of algorithms available for solving the Lyapunov equation:

$$XA + A'X = -\,Q \tag{5.115}$$

Equation (5.114) is in the form:

$$BX' + XB' = -\,C \tag{5.106}$$

Therefore, if any of the Lyapunov algorithms are to be used, it is first necessary to arrange that the following are true:

$$Q = C = MM' \tag{5.116}$$

$$A = H' \tag{5.117}$$

Using these values of Q and A will result in a solution of $E[\mathbf{x}^* \mathbf{x}^{*\prime}]$.

Example 5.1

An aircraft has the following state equation and is disturbed by a vector, $\mathbf{n}_g$:

$$\dot{\mathbf{x}} = \begin{bmatrix} -0.806 & 824.2 \\ -0.011 & -1.34 \end{bmatrix} \mathbf{x} + \begin{bmatrix} 34.6 \\ -4.57 \end{bmatrix} \delta_E + \begin{bmatrix} -0.8 & 0.0 & 0.0 \\ -0.011 & 0.0 & -0.924 \end{bmatrix} \mathbf{n}_g$$

The disturbance dynamics are given by:

$$\dot{\mathbf{n}}_g = \begin{bmatrix} -0.47 & -0.24 & 0.0 \\ 0.0 & -0.47 & 0.0 \\ 0.0 & -0.0013 & -5.02 \end{bmatrix} \mathbf{n}_g + \begin{bmatrix} 1.19 \\ 1.0 \\ 0.0066 \end{bmatrix} \eta$$

A feedback control law is used:

$$\delta_E = [0.0021 \;\; 0.695]\mathbf{x}$$

and the output y is defined by:

$$y = 0.027x_1 + 0.748x_2 + 0.026n_{g_1}$$

Determine the r.m.s. value of y. The closed loop system can be represented by:

$$\begin{bmatrix} \dot{\mathbf{x}}_c \\ \dot{\mathbf{n}}_g \end{bmatrix} = \begin{bmatrix} (A + BK) & W \\ 0 & A_g \end{bmatrix} \begin{bmatrix} \mathbf{x}_c \\ \mathbf{n}_g \end{bmatrix} + \begin{bmatrix} 0 \\ W_g \end{bmatrix} \eta \tag{A}$$

where:

$$A = \begin{bmatrix} -0.806 & 824.2 \\ -0.011 & -1.34 \end{bmatrix}$$

$$B = \begin{bmatrix} 34.6 \\ -4.57 \end{bmatrix}$$

$$K = [0.0021 \;\; 0.695]$$

$$W = \begin{bmatrix} -0.8 & 0.0 & 0.0 \\ -0.011 & 0.0 & -0.924 \end{bmatrix}$$

$$A_g = \begin{bmatrix} -0.47 & -0.24 & 0.0 \\ 0.0 & -0.47 & 0.0 \\ 0.0 & -0.0013 & -5.02 \end{bmatrix}$$

$$W_g = \begin{bmatrix} 1.19 \\ 1.0 \\ 0.0066 \end{bmatrix}$$

$$\hat{\mathbf{x}} \triangleq \begin{bmatrix} \mathbf{x}_c \\ \mathbf{n}_g \end{bmatrix}$$

Then from eq. (A) $\dot{\hat{\mathbf{x}}} = D\hat{\mathbf{x}} + F\eta$ where

$$D = \begin{bmatrix} -0.878 & 800.15 & -0.81 & 0.0 & 0.0 \\ -0.02 & -4.52 & -0.011 & 0.0 & -9.24 \\ 0.0 & 0.0 & -4.7 & -0.24 & 0.0 \\ 0.0 & 0.0 & 0.0 & -0.47 & 0.0 \\ 0.0 & 0.0 & 0.0 & -0.0013 & -5.02 \end{bmatrix}$$

$$F = \begin{bmatrix} 0.0 \\ 0.0 \\ 1.19 \\ 1.0 \\ 0.0066 \end{bmatrix}$$

Let $y = C\hat{\mathbf{x}}$, then:

$$C = [0.027 \; 0.748 \; 0.026 \; 0.0 \; 0.0]$$

$$\therefore \quad \tilde{A} \equiv D$$

$$Q = \begin{bmatrix} 0 & 0 & 0 & 0 & 0 \\ 0 & 0 & 0 & 0 & 0 \\ 0 & 0 & 1.41 & 1.19 & 0.008 \\ 0 & 0 & 0.008 & 0.007 & 0.0004 \end{bmatrix}$$

From which it can be found, by solving the Lyapunov equation, that:

$$K = \begin{bmatrix} 0.393 & -0.00013 & -0.558 & -0.58 & -0.0002 \\ -0.00013 & 0.000001 & -0.0001 & -0.000025 & -0.0000013 \\ -0.558 & -0.0001 & 0.998 & 0.995 & 0.00114 \\ -0.58 & -0.00002 & 0.995 & 1.04 & 0.00095 \\ -0.0002 & -0.0000013 & 0.00114 & 0.00095 & 0.000004 \end{bmatrix}$$

Then $E[y^2] = 1.473 \times 10^{-4}$ and the r.m.s. value of y is 0.0126.

5.11 WIND SHEAR AND MICROBURSTS

Wind shear is a change in the wind vector in a relatively small amount of space. One of its consequences is a rapid change in the airflow over the aerodynamic surfaces of an aircraft.

Such rapid changes of airflow can be hazardous, particularly to aircraft flying at low altitudes and at low speeds. It is a particularly difficult phenomenon to detect since the effects of wind shear are transitory, and its nature and occurrence are random. A form of wind shear which is of particular concern is the microburst, in which a large mass of air is propelled downwards in a jet from some convective cloud system, or, perhaps, from a rapid build-up of small weather cells. A physical account of how such a microburst forms, acts and decays is given in Klehr (1986).

Thunderstorms, being highly variable and dynamic atmospheric occurrences, translate rapidly across the ground. As they travel, they grow and then decay. A thunderstorm results from the rapid growth and expansion in the vertical of a cumulus cloud. In its initial stages, such a storm comprises an updraft of warm, moist air with a velocity as great as $15\,\mathrm{m\,s^{-1}}$. In the updraft, moisture droplets are lifted until the temperature of the atmosphere causes freezing to occur. These droplets next grow into supercooled raindrops. However, the size of these raindrops is soon too large to be supported by the updraft, at which stage they fall, dragging air with them, which produces a strong downdraft. This stage is the most mature stage of any storm. The downdraft is strengthened by drier, outside air becoming entrained and then cooled as the raindrops evaporate. This reinforcing of the downdraft causes not only the wind to become stronger but also sudden, heavy precipitation, typified by a sudden downpour. As the thunderstorm abates, the downdraft becomes even more extensive and cuts off the downdraft from its inflow of warm, moist air. As a result, the storm begins to subside, the precipitation to lessen and then stop, and, soon after, the clouds begin to disperse. In the area separating the inflow and outflow, which is usually called the gust front, and which can extend for 20 km, wind shear may occur at low altitudes.

Since aircraft do not normally have sufficient specific excess power to counter the force of such a downwardly propelled air mass, the microburst is particularly dangerous. In such an atmospheric condition, within a period of one minute or less, an aircraft can be subjected to, say, a headwind, followed by a downdraft, and then succeeded by a tailwind. There has been observed in the performance of pilots flying in such conditions a consistent pattern of response; when an updraft is first experienced, the pilot lowers the nose of the aircraft and reduces thrust. Then follows a headwind, with a consequent increase in the air-speed of the aircraft, causing the pilot to further reduce thrust. From the microburst, there is next experienced a strong downdraft and tailwind, but the pilot's actions, already taken, have set the scene for further difficulty, since the thrust has been reduced and the nose lowered. In general, the performance of in-experienced pilots in wind shear situations is rarely adequate, manifesting itself (usually) in a failure to maintain the appropriate airspeed and the correct flight path.

Notwithstanding the evident importance for flight safety of the phenomenon of wind shear, standard representations for use in analytical studies are unsatisfactory, although Frost (1983) has recently provided a number of new models for consideration. Two important vortex models have been suggested (see Markov, 1981; Woodfield, 1985). Yet, there are but two official forms, one defined by the Federal Aviation Authority (FAA), and the other by the Air Registration Board (ARB) in the UK. Both are represented in Figure 5.5. The ARB profile is log-linear and, at the lower heights, its gradient becomes progressively steeper than that of the FAA profile. Neither is adequate for studying the microburst situation. The problem of how to adequately represent such a situation remains unsolved.

In any wind shear encounter it is the phugoid mode, the slow period response of the aircraft, which is most important because it depends upon the

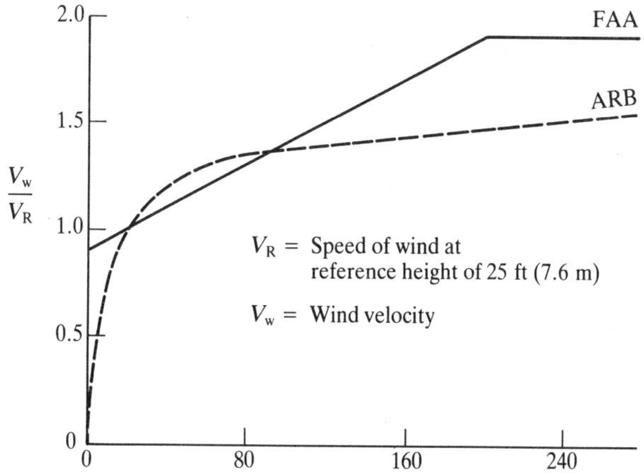

Figure 5.5 FAA/ARB wind shear profiles.

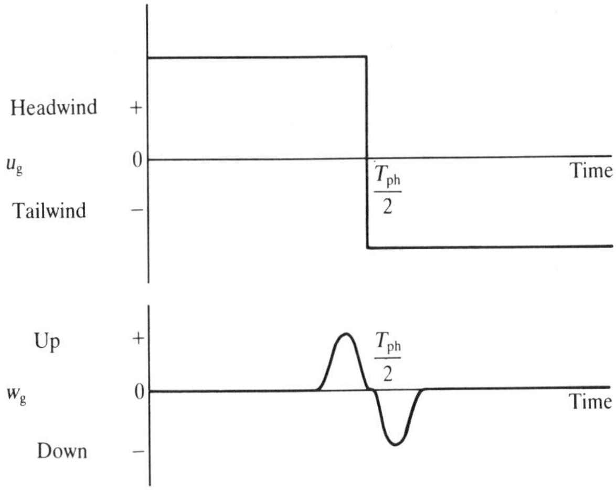

Figure 5.6 Square wave + (1-cos) wind shear.

interchange between the kinetic and the potential energy of the aircraft. In Chapter 2 it is shown that the phugoid mode is usually oscillatory and very lightly damped. In some cases it can be unstable. Significantly, the time involved in a microburst encounter is often about the same as the period of the phugoid mode, thereby making possible a resonant response in which the interchanged energy is amplified. Such amplification leads to a greater deviation from the intended flight path than would have occurred with a well-damped mode.

One form of representation of wind shear (Frost *et al.*, 1982), which takes these facts into account, is represented in Figure 5.6. It must be 'tuned' to accord with the flying characteristics of the aircraft being studied. In Figure 5.6, the square wave oscillation represents a head/tailwind combination: at the mid-point of the square wave, a $(1 - \cos)$ downdraft is introduced. The period of the square wave is adjusted to be the same as the period of the phugoid motion of the aircraft being investigated. Although the profile in Figure 5.6 has been presented as a function of time, it is intended to represent a physical phenomenon in which the velocity changes with height. There is an implicit assumption that during the period of the wind shear encounter the aircraft will be climbing or landing, i.e. changing height.

Another method of representation is to use any record of a wind shear which may have been obtained, either from meteorological studies or from flight records. A number of records are now available; the most discussed was obtained from a reconstruction of the available data relating to the crash of a Boeing 727 which occurred on 24 June 1975 at John F. Kennedy Airport in New York. The reconstructed data are shown in Figure 5.7(a) together with the aircraft trajectory. 00 seconds (2006 GMT) denotes the time when the aircraft reached the

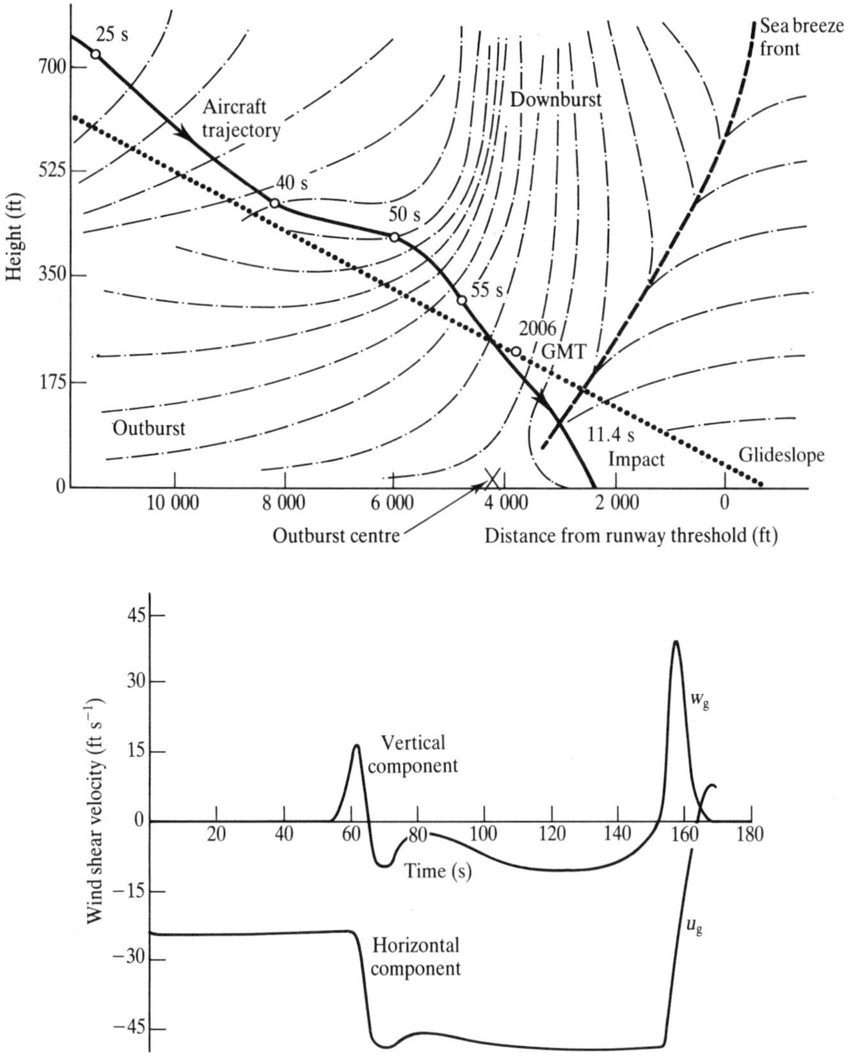

Figure 5.7 (a) JFK wind shear. (b) Components of the JFK wind shear.

outburst centre. Note how the characteristic 'ballooning' of the aircraft's path started 15 s before this point, and how some 11.5 s after its occurrence the severe downdraft caused the aircraft to crash some 2000 ft (600 m) short of the runway. Resolution of this wind shear into vertical and horizontal components results in the profiles for u_g and w_g shown in Figure 5.7(b). These can be used, with appropriate amplitude scaling, in wind shear studies.

5.12 SENSOR NOISE

Noise on the output signal, which is usually electrical, is regarded as a random signal. However, the properties of these uncertain signals are not well described in the literature and recourse is usually taken in analysis or simulation studies to representing such noise signals as random signals with a Gaussian distribution. They are usually regarded as having been generated as the output signals from linear first order filters which have been driven by white noise sources. The filter time constant is usually selected in the first instance, in the absence of specific knowledge of the power spectral density function relating to the noise, to ensure that the boundaries of the noise spectrum are at least an order greater than those of the AFCS. It is usual to regard the noise signal as being stationary and having zero mean value. But a number of common AFCS sensors are known to have drift rates which, fortunately, are very slow. For example, a typical attitude gyro may have a drift rate of $0.1° \text{ h}^{-1}$, $(4.84 \times 10^{-7} \text{ rad s}^{-1})$. The accuracy of gyroscopes is typically 0.1°, or $0.1° \text{ s}^{-1}$, if it is a rate gyroscope. Accelerometers have errors of, typically, 3×10^{-5} g $(3 \times 10^{-3} \text{ m s}^{-2})$, and barometric altimeters are subject to typical r.m.s. errors of 16 m. For accelerometers, a typical r.m.s. noise figure is 10^{-4} g $(10^{-3} \text{ m s}^{-2})$ with the corresponding power spectral density being approximately $3 \times 10^{-7} \text{ g}^2/\text{Hz}$.

5.13 CONCLUSIONS

This chapter presents some information about the disturbances which most affect the operation of AFCSs. The atmospheric turbulence phenomena considered were continuous gusts, defined by the mathematical model suggested by Dryden as a practical improvement on the Von Karman model, and the discrete (1 − cos) gust. Generating test signals by means of a transient analogue was also dealt with. An account of wind shear and some methods of representing such a phenomenon, particularly the microburst, was also given and the chapter closed with a brief note on the nature of representations of sensor noise.

5.14 EXERCISES

5.1 A particular representation of continuous atmospheric turbulence, of zero mean value, which affects the angle of attack of an aircraft, has a power spectral density given by:

$$\Phi_{\alpha_g}(\omega) = \sigma_w^2\left\{\frac{L_w}{U_0^3\pi}\right\}\frac{\left(1 + 3\left\{\frac{L_w}{U_0}\omega\right\}^2\right)}{\left(1 + \left\{\frac{L_w}{U_0}\omega\right\}^2\right)^2}$$

where: L_w is the scale length of 600 m; σ_w is the r.m.s. intensity of the gust, and is equal to $2\ \text{m s}^{-1}$; U_0 is the equilibrium airspeed of the aircraft, of $200\ \text{m s}^{-1}$.

(a) Show that the random gust signal, α_g, can be obtained as the output from a state variable model forced with white noise.

(b) By means of a block diagram, show how a gust generator, based on the model of part (a), may be synthesized.

(c) If the r.m.s. intensity of the gust is reduced to $0.5\ \text{m s}^{-1}$, and if:

$$L_w = h \qquad 30 \le h < 600$$

write down the transfer function of a filter which will generate α_g from a white noise input. The aircraft is assumed to be flying at the same steady airspeed, but at a lower height of 300 m.

5.2 Write down the conditions which obtain for the expected value of the state vector of an aircraft to be constant. Under what conditions can the covariance of the state vector take a constant value?

5.3 An RCS for a fighter aircraft is discussed in Section 6.6 of Chapter 12. Using the results obtained there, and noting that a vertical velocity gust of intensity of $0.3\ \text{m s}^{-1}$, represented by the gust disturbance dynamics shown:

$$\dot{\mathbf{n}}_g = \begin{bmatrix} -0.45 & -0.2 & 0.0 \\ 0.0 & -0.45 & 0.0 \\ 0.0 & -0.0011 & -5.6 \end{bmatrix} \mathbf{n}_g + \begin{bmatrix} 1.2 \\ 1.0 \\ 0.007 \end{bmatrix} \eta$$

(where η is a white noise source) has been encountered, determine the r.m.s. value of the normal acceleration of the controlled aircraft. Compare this value with the corresponding value for the aircraft without an RCS.

5.4 Derive a suitable state variable representation of the side gust, v_g, based upon the Dryden model.

5.5 (a) Using the aircraft ALPHA-3 write down the equations of short period motion for vertical gust input, w_g.

(b) If w_g is a $(1 - \cos)$ gust determine the corresponding responses of the aircraft's vertical velocity and its pitch rate.

(c) Calculate the peak value of the normal acceleration in response to the $(1 - \cos)$ gust.

5.6 The r.m.s. intensities of Dryden gusts are related by:

$$\sigma_u^2/L_u = \sigma_v^2/L_v = \sigma_w^2/L_w$$

The choice of σ_x (where x may be u, v or w) is, in general, arbitrary but ought to be related to the chances of its occurring.

There is a finite probability, P_0, of there being no turbulence, while there is also a probability, P_1, of turbulence being encountered. Consequently, the total probability density function for σ_x is given by:

$$\rho(\sigma_x) = P_0\delta(\sigma_x) + P_1\hat{p}(\sigma_x)$$

where $\delta(\sigma_x)$ is a Dirac delta function, i.e. $\delta(\sigma_x) = 0$ for $\sigma_x \neq 0$ and:

$$\int_0^\infty \delta(\sigma_x)d\sigma_x = 1.0$$

When turbulence is encountered, the probability density function for σ_x may be assumed to be of the Rayleigh form, i.e.:

$$\hat{p}(\sigma_x) = \frac{\sigma_x e^{-\sigma_x^2/2c^2}}{c^2} \qquad c > 0$$

and $\xi\{\sigma_x^2\} = 2c^2$ where $\zeta\{\quad\}$ denotes the expected value. Show that:

$$c = \sqrt{(1/2 L_x \xi(\sigma_x^2/L_x))}.$$

5.15 REFERENCES

CHALK, C.R., T.P. NEAL, T.M. HARRIS, *et al.* 1969. Background information and user guide for MIL-F-8785 (ASG) – military specification – flying qualities of piloted airplanes. AFFDL-TR-69-72, August.

ETKIN, B. 1980. The turbulent wind and its effect on flight (AIAA Wright Brothers Lecture, 1980). *UTIAS Review* no. 44, August. Inst. Aero. Studies, Univ. of Toronto, Canada.

FROST, W. 1983. Flight in low level wind shear. NASA CR-3678, March.

FROST, W., B.S. TURKEL and J. McCARTHY. 1982. Simulation of phugoid excitation due to hazardous wind shear. *AIAA 20th Aerospace Sciences Mtg, Orlando, Florida.*

KLEHR, J.T. 1986. Wind shear simulation enters the fourth dimension. *ICAO Bull.* May, 23–5.

MARKOV, B. 1981. The landing approach in variable winds: curved glidepath geometries and worst-case wind modelling. UTIAS Rpt 254, December. Toronto.

SWAIM, R.L., D.K. SCHMIDT, P.A. ROBERTS and A.J. HINSDALE. 1977. An analytical method for ride quality of flexible airplanes. *AIAA Journal.* 15(1): 4–7.

WOODFIELD, A.A. 1985. Wind-shear topics at RAE. FS Dept, TN FS132.

6

Flying and Handling Qualities

6.1 INTRODUCTION

A special issue of the influential *Journal of Guidance, Control and Dynamics* from the American Institute of Aeronautics and Astronautics was concerned with aircraft flying qualities which were defined in the editorial as 'those qualities of an aircraft which govern the ease and precision with which a pilot is able to perform his mission'. All the papers which made up that special issue refer to the handling qualities of the aircraft. It is helpful to those new to the field to distinguish between flying and handling qualities; with experience, the two will be seen to merge into a single topic.

Aircraft flying qualities are usually characterized by a number of parameters relating to the complex frequency domain, such as the damping ratio and undamped natural frequency of the short period longitudinal motion of the aircraft. Knowledge of these parameters allows a designer to imagine the nature of the aircraft's response to any command or disturbance; it allows a general notion of how the aircraft will fly in a controlled manner.

Handling qualities reflect the ease with which a pilot can carry out some particular mission with an aircraft which has a particular set of flying qualities. However, handling qualities depend not only upon flying qualities but also upon the primary flying controls, the visual and motion cues available, and the display of flight information in the cockpit. The importance of handling qualities is particularly marked when some aircraft exhibit such unwanted flight characteristics as pilot-induced oscillations or roll ratchet. It should always be remembered that a human pilot is a variable, dynamic element closing an outer loop around an AFCS. Handling qualities ought to be arranged, therefore, to suit the pilot, so that his adapted characteristic is best for the flight mission. Sometimes, special command input filters are added to AFCSs to assist in providing acceptable handling qualities. Since different types of aircraft can carry out similar missions, it follows that the required handling qualities also depend upon the type of aircraft.

Extensive research into flying and handling qualities has been carried out in many countries for a great number of years. Harper and Cooper (1986) provide an excellent account of this research. The results of these studies have been incorporated into specifications for aircraft flying qualities which have been laid down by the statutory bodies responsible for aviation in different countries. Although ten years ago, the UK specifications were in a number of respects different in expression from those laid down by the American authorities, it was decided by 1978 that the UK specifications (MoD, 1983) should correspond wherever possible with those used by the American authorities. For most classes of fixed wing aircraft, the most significant of these specifications is MIL-F-8785(ASG), Military Specification – Flying Qualities of Piloted Airplanes published in 1980. If general aviation aircraft are to be considered, the specification generally used is FAR 23 issued by the Federal Aviation Authority (FAA) in the USA. Whenever AFCS designs are to be studied, then it is necessary to consider, in conjunction with MIL-F-8785(ASG), other specifications laid down by the American military authorities, namely MIL-F-9490D (see references at end of chapter), which is the current USAF flight controls specification, and MIL-C-18244, which is a general specification for piloted airplanes with automatic control and stabilization systems. The appropriate specification defining the flying and ground handling qualities for military helicopters is MIL-H-8501A. When the concern is VSTOL aircraft then the appropriate specification is MIL-F-83300. Details can be found in the references at the end of this chapter.

In this book, it is essentially the recommendations of MIL-F-8785 which are followed for fixed wing aircraft, and those of MIL-H-8501A for rotary wing aircraft. Since many of the specifications in MIL-F-8785 are framed with reference to aircraft classes, flight phases, and levels of flying qualities, these terms are explained first before discussing the specifications.

6.2 SOME DEFINITIONS REQUIRED FOR USE WITH FLYING QUALITIES' SPECIFICATION

6.2.1 Aircraft Classes

An aircraft is considered to belong to one of the four classes shown in Table 6.1.

Table 6.1 Aircraft classification

Class	*Aircraft characteristics*
I	Small, light aircraft (max. weight $\simeq$ 5 000 kg)
II	Aircraft of medium weight and moderate manoeuvrability (weight between 5 000 and 30 000 kg)
III	Large, heavy aircraft with moderate manoeuvrability (30 000+ kg)
IV	Aircraft with high manoeuvrability

6.2.2 Flight Phases

Whatever mission an aircraft is used to accomplish, the mission is divisible into three phases of flight, as follows:

Phase A which includes all the non-terminal phases of flight such as those involving rapid manoeuvring, precision tracking, or precise control of the flight path. Included in phase A would be such flight phases as: air-to-air combat (CO), ground attack (GA), weapon delivery (WD), reconnaissance (RC), air-to-air refuelling in which the aircraft acts as the receiver (RR), terrain following (TF), maritime search and rescue (MS), close formation flying (FF), and aerobatics (AB).

Phase B involves the non-terminal phases of flight usually accomplished by gradual manoeuvres which do not require precise tracking. Accurate flight path control may be needed, however. Included in the phase would be: climbing (CL), cruising (CR), loitering (LO), descending (D), aerial delivery (AD) and air-to-air refuelling in which the aircraft acts as a tanker (RT).

Phase C involves terminal flight phases, usually accomplished by gradual manoeuvres, but requiring accurate flight path control. This phase would include: take-off (TO), landing (L), overshoot (OS) and powered approach (including instrument approach) (PA).

6.2.3 Levels of Acceptability

The requirements for airworthiness are stated in terms of three distinct, specified values of control (or stability) parameter. Each value is a limiting condition necessary to satisfy one of the three levels of acceptability. These levels are related to the ability to complete the missions for which the aircraft is intended. The levels are defined in Table 6.2.

Table 6.2 Flying level specification

Level	*Definition*
1	The flying qualities are completely adequate for the particular flight phase being considered.
2	The flying qualities are adequate for the particular phase being considered, but there is either some loss in the effectiveness of the mission, or there is a corresponding increase in the workload imposed upon the pilot to achieve the mission, or both.
3	The flying qualities are such that the aircraft can be controlled, but either the effectiveness of the mission is gravely impaired, or the total workload imposed upon the pilot to accomplish the mission is so great that it approaches the limit of his capacity.

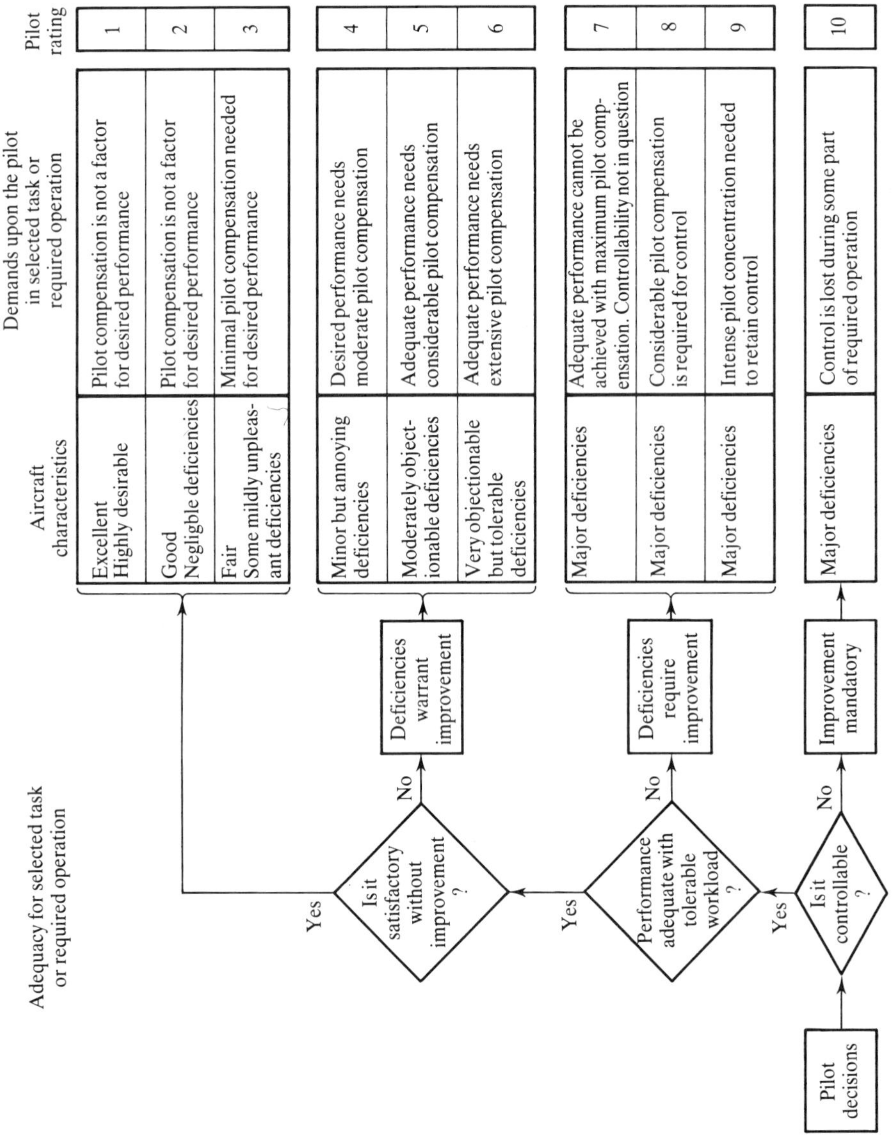

Figure 6.1 Cooper–Harper rating chart.

There is a direct relationship between these levels of acceptability and the pilot rating scale developed by Cooper and Harper (1986). The rating scale is shown in Figure 6.1 and a representation of the relationship between the rating scale and the levels of acceptability is illustrated in Figure 6.2

Pilot state	Pilot rating	Level	Definition
	1 3½	1	Clearly adequate for the mission flight phase
	6½	2	• Adequate to accomplish mission flight phase • Increase in pilot workload, or loss of effectiveness of mission, or both
	9 10	3	• Aircraft can be controlled • Pilot workload excessive – mission effectiveness impaired • Category A flight phases can be terminated safely

Figure 6.2 Acceptable level of flying qualities.

6.3 LONGITUDINAL FLYING QUALITIES

6.3.1 Static Stability

An aircraft should have no tendency for its airspeed to diverge aperiodically whenever it is disturbed from its trim condition and with its pitch control either free or fixed.

6.3.2 Phugoid Response

Provided that the frequencies of the phugoid and the short period modes of motion are widely separated, for the pitch control either being free or fixed, the values of damping ratio quoted in Table 6.3 must be achieved.

If the separation between the frequencies of the phugoid and short period modes is small, handling difficulties can arise. If $\omega_{ph}/\omega_{sp} < 0.1$ there may be some trouble with the handling qualities.

Table 6.3 Phugoid mode flying qualities

Level	*Damping ratio of phugoid mode*
1	$\geqq 0.04$
2	$\geqq 0.0$
3	An undamped oscillatory mode having a period of at least 55 s

6.3.3 Short Period Response

The flying qualities related to this work are governed by the parameters, ζ_{sp}, the short period damping ratio, and ω_{sp}/n_{z_α} where n_{z_α} is the acceleration sensitivity of the aircraft. The specified values of damping ratio are quoted in Table 6.4. At high speed, low values of short period damping ratio are less troublesome than at low speeds.

Table 6.4 Short period mode damping ratio specification

Flight phase category	*Level 1*		*Level 2*		*Level 3*	
	Min.	*Max.*	*Min.*	*Max.*	*Min.*	*Max.*
A	0.35	1.3	0.25	2.0	0.1	—
B	0.3	2.0	0.2	2.0	0.1	—
C	0.5	—	0.35	2.0	0.25	—

If the short period oscillations are non-linear with amplitude, then the flying qualities parameters quoted must apply to each cycle of the oscillation.

The specified limits for the undamped natural frequency are functions of the acceleration sensitivity, n_{z_α}, for any particular level category and phase; the specification is usually presented as a figure such as Figure 6.3.

The curves defining the upper and lower frequency limits are straight lines, each with a slope of + 0.5 on the log-log plot. The parameter $\omega_{sp}^2/n_{z_\alpha}$ is referred to as the control anticipation parameter (CAP) which relates initial pitch acceleration to steady state normal load factor, i.e.:

$$\text{CAP} = \dot{q}(0)/n_{z_{cg|ss}} \tag{6.1}$$

This parameter has been proposed upon the assumption that when a pilot initiates a manoeuvre the response of greatest importance to him is the initial pitch acceleration. In a pull-up manoeuvre, his concern is with the steady state normal acceleration. By assuming constant speed flight, and by applying to the approximate transfer function relating pitch acceleration to an elevator deflection

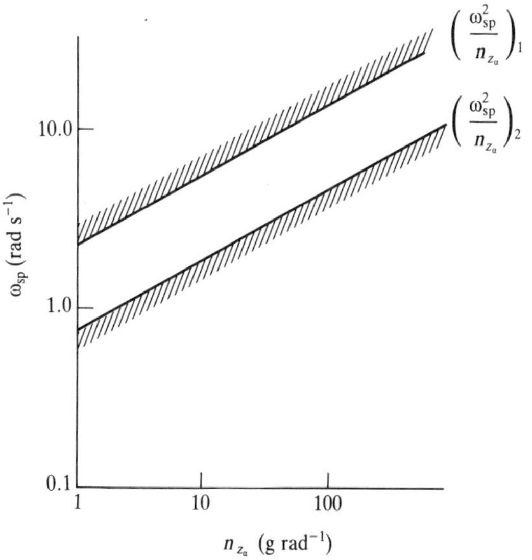

Figure 6.3 Handling qualities diagram.

the initial value theorem, and then the final value theorem to the transfer function relating normal acceleration, $n_{z_{cg}}$, to the same elevator input, an expression for the CAP can be written, if it is assumed that the elevator deflection is a step input:

$$n_{z_{cg}}\Big|_{ss} = U_0(Z_{\delta_E}M_w - M_{\delta_E}Z_w)/g\omega_{sp}^2$$
$$\simeq M_{\delta_E}n_{z_\alpha}/\omega_{sp}^2 \qquad (6.2)$$

If:

$$\frac{sq(s)}{\delta_E(s)} \triangleq \frac{M_{\delta_E}}{(s + (1/T_E))} \qquad (6.3)$$

where $T_E^{-1} \simeq -M_q$ then:

$$\dot{q}(0) \rightarrow M_{\delta_E} \qquad (6.4)$$

and the CAP defined in eq. (6.1) is obtained.

Figure 6.4 shows the specifications for levels 1, 2 and 3 for categories A, B, and C.

6.4 LATERAL/DIRECTIONAL FLYING QUALITIES

The specification of flying qualities for lateral/directional motion is more involved than for longitudinal motion and, consequently, requires more parameters.

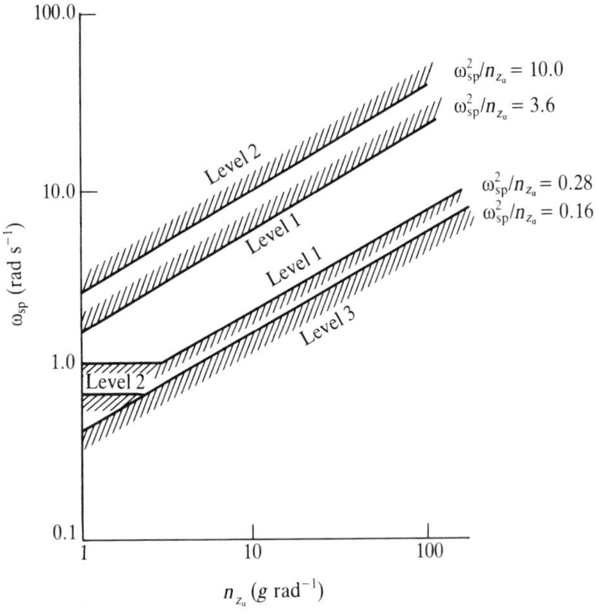
100.0
10.0
1.0
0.1
ω_{sp} (rad s^{-1})
1
10
100
n_{z_α} (g rad^{-1})
$\omega_{sp}^2/n_{z_\alpha} = 10.0$
$\omega_{sp}^2/n_{z_\alpha} = 3.6$
$\omega_{sp}^2/n_{z_\alpha} = 0.28$
$\omega_{sp}^2/n_{z_\alpha} = 0.16$
Level 2
Level 1
Level 1
Level 3
Level 2

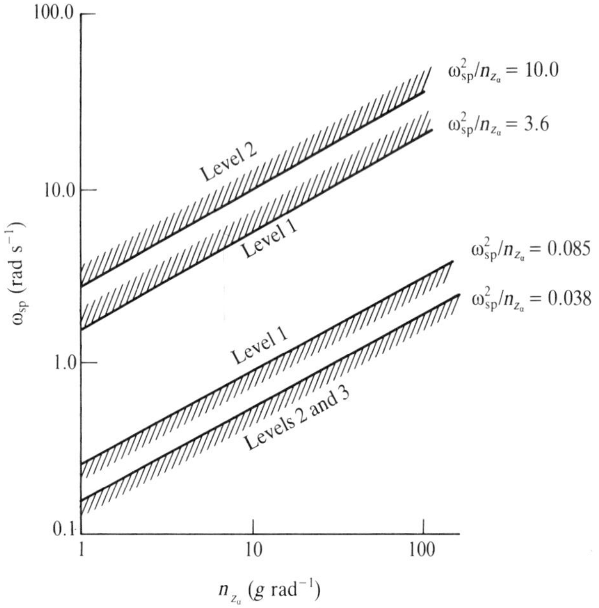
100.0
10.0
1.0
0.1
ω_{sp} (rad s^{-1})
1
10
100
n_{z_α} (g rad^{-1})
$\omega_{sp}^2/n_{z_\alpha} = 10.0$
$\omega_{sp}^2/n_{z_\alpha} = 3.6$
$\omega_{sp}^2/n_{z_\alpha} = 0.085$
$\omega_{sp}^2/n_{z_\alpha} = 0.038$
Level 2
Level 1
Level 1
Levels 2 and 3

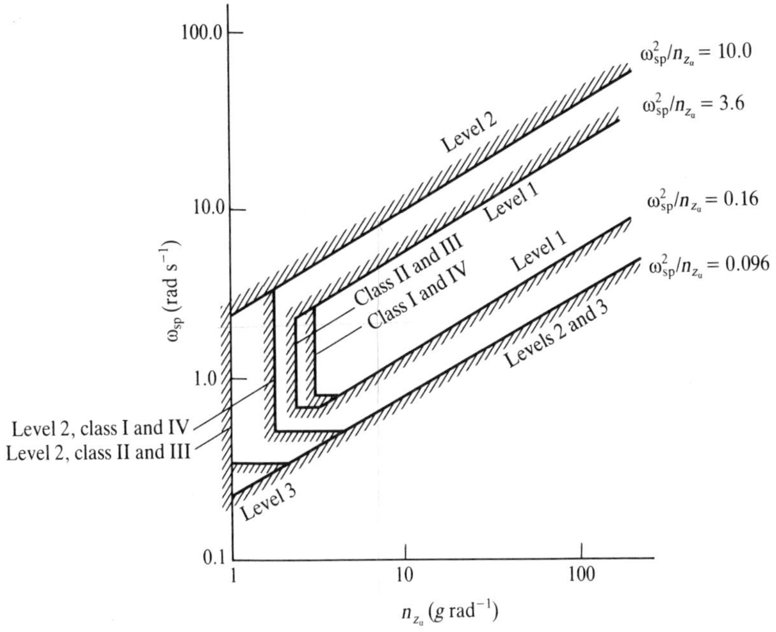

Figure 6.4 Short period frequency requirements. (a) CAT. A. (b) CAT. B. (c) CAT. C.

6.4.1 Rolling Motion

The time constant of the roll subsidence mode, T_R, is required to be less than the specified maximum values given in Table 6.5. It is customary to specify roll performance in terms of the change of bank angle achieved in a given time in response to a step function in roll command. The required bank angles and time are specified in Table 6.6.

Table 6.5 Roll mode time constant specification

Flight phase category	*Class*	*T_R (seconds)*		
		Level 1	*Level 2*	*Level 3*
A	I, IV	1.0	1.4	Not specified – limit is believed to lie within range 6–8 s
A	II, III	1.4	3.0	
B	All	1.4	3.0	
C	I, IV	1.0	1.4	
C	II, III	1.4	3.0	

Table 6.6 Bank angle specification

Class	*Flight phase category*	*Bank angle in fixed time*		
		Level 1	*Level 2*	*Level 3*
	A	60° in 1.3 s	60° in 1.7 s	60° in 2.6 s
I	B	60° in 1.7 s	60° in 2.5 s	60° in 3.4 s
	C	30° in 1.3 s	30° in 1.8 s	30° in 2.6 s
	A	45° in 1.4 s	45° in 1.9 s	45° in 2.8 s
II	B	45° in 1.9 s	45° in 2.8 s	45° in 3.0 s
	C	30° in 2.5 s	30° in 3.5 s	30° in 5.0 s
	A	30° in 1.5 s	30° in 2.0 s	30° in 3.0 s
III	B	30° in 2.0 s	30° in 3.0 s	30° in 4.0 s
	C	30° in 3.0 s	30° in 4.0 s	30° in 6.0 s
	A	90° in 1.3 s	90° in 1.7 s	90° in 2.6 s
IV	B	60° in 1.7 s	60° in 2.5 s	60° in 3.4 s
	C	30° in 1.0 s	30° in 1.3 s	30° in 2.0 s

For class IV aircraft, for level 1, the yaw control should be free. For other aircraft and levels it is permissible to use the yaw control to reduce any sideslip which tends to retard roll rate. Such yaw control is not permitted to induce sideslip which enhances the roll rate.

6.4.2 Spiral Stability

When specifying spiral stability it is assumed that the aircraft is trimmed for straight and level flight, with no bank angle, no yaw rate and with the flying controls free. The specification is given in terms of the time taken for the bank angle to double following an initial disturbance in bank angle of up to 20°. The time taken must *exceed* the values given in Table 6.7.

Table 6.7 Spiral mode stability specification

Flight phase category	*Level*		
	1	*2*	*3*
A and C	12 s	8 s	5 s
B	20 s	8 s	5 s

Table 6.8 Dutch roll mode specification

Flight phase category	Class	Level								
		1			2			3		
		ξ_D	$\xi_D\omega_D$	ω_D	ξ_D	$\xi_D\omega_D$	ω_D	ξ_D	$\xi_D\omega_D$	ω_D
A	I, IV	0.19	0.35	1.0	0.02	0.05	0.5	0	—	0.4
A	II, III	0.19	0.35	0.5	0.02	0.05	0.5	0	—	0.4
B	All	0.08	0.15	0.5	0.02	0.05	0.5	0	—	0.4
C	I, IV	0.08	0.15	1.0	0.02	0.05	0.5	0	—	0.4
C	II, III	0.08	0.1	0.5	0.02	0.05	0.5	0	—	0.4

6.4.3 Lateral/Directional Oscillations – Dutch Roll

Although the dutch roll mode has very little useful part to play in the control of an aircraft, it does have significant nuisance value. The values of the important dutch roll parameters, namely damping ratio, ξ_D, the dutch roll frequency, ω_D, are specified in Table 6.8.

It is usual to avoid coupled roll/spiral oscillation as its leads to inferior tracking performance.

For atmospheric turbulence the Tables 6.5, 6.7 and 6.8 are still valid. For bank angle, however, for a class IV aircraft, level 1, category A flight phase, the r.m.s. value of bank angle which arises in severe turbulence must be less than 2.7°.

6.5 THE C^* CRITERION

This criterion can be used to assess the dynamic response of the aircraft's longitudinal motion to a manoeuvre command. When an AFCS is used, it has been found that if the poles and zeros of the controller are located in the s-plane such that they are close in frequency to the resulting short period frequency, ω_{sp}, of the uncontrolled aircraft, the resulting dynamic response of the controlled aircraft is so altered that characterizing the response by specifying the short period damping ratio and undamped natural frequency is unsatisfactory. The C^* criterion is based upon the tailoring of the total response of the controlled aircraft to pilot inputs such that the defined output response lies between specific limits. The quantity C^* is a measure of a blended contribution to the total response from the normal acceleration, the pitch acceleration, and the pitch rate of the aircraft. That blend varies with airspeed; the acceleration measure, $C^*(t)$, is arranged so

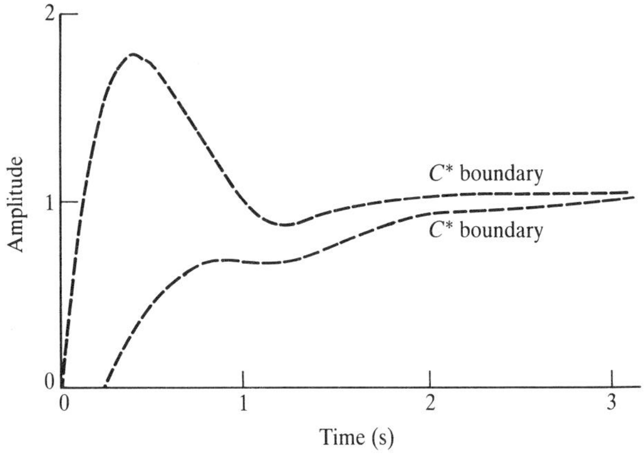

Figure 6.5 C^* time history for category A.

that when the crossover speed, U_c, is reached, the contributions to $C^*(t)$ from the normal acceleration term and the terms related to pitching motion are equal. The crossover speed is a weighting factor which reflects the change in emphasis which pilots place on motion cues at certain speeds, a change from controlling pitch rate at the lower speeds to an emphasis upon controlling normal acceleration at the higher speeds. One definition of $C^*(t)$ is:

$$C^*(t) = n_z l_{x_{\text{pilot}}} + (U_c/g) \tag{6.5}$$

The criterion adopted is that the normalized time response, $C^*(t)/C^*_{ss}$, shall lie between two specified boundaries. For as long as the $C^*(t)/C^*_{ss}$ response remains within the specified boundaries the AFCS designer may assume that the response of the controlled aircraft is satisfactory, without regard to the details of the control system or the aircraft dynamics being considered. Typical C^* boundaries are shown in Figure 6.5, for flight condition 1. Similar boundaries obtain for the other flight categories.

It must be remembered that C^* is a function of time and, consequently, the C^* criterion is a performance criterion for the time domain. It should be noted that C^* can be treated as an output variable of the aircraft. In Chapter 3 it is shown that n_{z_x} could be expressed as:

$$n_{z_x} = \frac{1}{g}\left\{a_{z_{cg}} - l_x\dot{q}\right\} \tag{6.6}$$

$$\therefore\ n_{z_{\text{pilot}}} = \frac{1}{g}\left\{Z_u u + Z_w w + Z_{\delta_E}\delta_E - l_{x_{\text{pilot}}}(\tilde{M}_u u + \tilde{M}_w w + \tilde{M}_q q + \tilde{M}_{\delta_E}\delta_E)\right\}$$

$$= \frac{1}{g}\left\{[Z_u - l_{x_{\text{pilot}}}\tilde{M}_u]u + [Z_w - l_{x_{\text{pilot}}}\tilde{M}_w]w - l_{x_{\text{pilot}}}\tilde{M}_q q + [Z_{\delta_E} - l_{x_{\text{pilot}}}\tilde{M}_{\delta_E}]\delta_E\right\} \tag{6.7}$$

Hence,

$$y \triangleq n_{z_{x_{\text{pilot}}}} = C\mathbf{x} + D\mathbf{u} \tag{6.8}$$

where:

$$\mathbf{x}' \triangleq [u \ w \ q \ \theta]$$

$$\mathbf{u} \triangleq \delta_E$$

$$C = \left[\frac{(Z_u - l_{x_{\text{pilot}}}\tilde{M}_u)}{g} \ \frac{(Z_w - l_{x_{\text{pilot}}}\tilde{M}_w)}{g} \ -\frac{l_{x_{\text{pilot}}}\tilde{M}_q}{g} \ 0 \right]$$

$$D = \left[\frac{Z_{\delta_E}}{g} \ \frac{l_{x_{\text{pilot}}}\tilde{M}_{\delta_E}}{g} \right]$$

There is still uncertainty about the general applicability of the C^* criterion, however. The problem can be seen from Figure 6.6 from which it is seen that system 1 has a number of overshoots, but lies wholly within the boundaries. System 2 infringes the boundary slightly at the initial part of the response. System 1 attracted a pilot rating of 8.5 and system 2 was awarded 2.5.

It is this difficulty of reconciling human prejudices with quantitative performance indices and parameters which makes the study of handling and flying qualities a most demanding and protracted technical problem. The single fact which it is essential for students to understand is that extensive studies related to the flying qualities specification must be undertaken, before being satisfied that any AFCS design is acceptable; it must never be forgotten that the motion of an aircraft is controlled by a number of control surfaces which a pilot, human or automatic, can operate simultaneously.

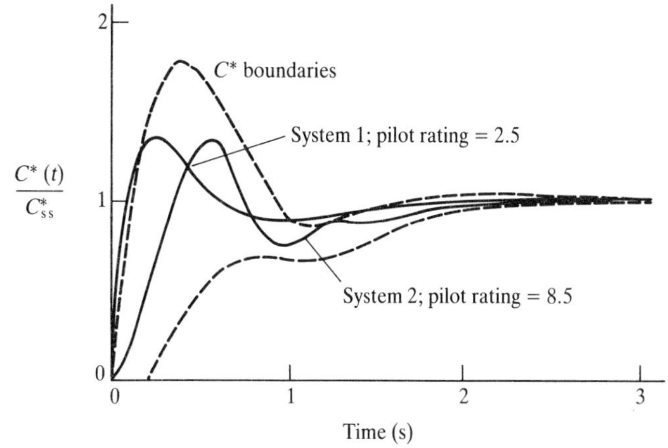

Figure 6.6 Different C^* responses with pilot rating.

6.6 RIDE DISCOMFORT INDEX

One of the proposed functions of active control technology is to provide on control configured vehicles ride control systems (RCSs) to reduce those vertical accelerations which are caused principally by atmospheric turbulence (see Chapter 12). Such a control system is expected to improve the comfort of crew and passengers. RCSs are important systems for strike aircraft which are required, for strategic reasons, to fly low, thereby avoiding detection by radar, and fast, thereby minimizing the chance of being shot down. RCSs also have a special importance for commuter aircraft in which much of the flight is spent at low heights where atmospheric turbulence is most likely to be encountered (see Chapter 5). A measure of the quality of an aircraft's ride, a ride discomfort index J_{RD}, has been proposed in the specification MIL-F-9490D. This index is the ratio of wing lift slope to wing loading, i.e.:

$$J_{RD} = \frac{kC_{L_\alpha}}{(W/S)} \tag{6.9}$$

where W/S is the wing loading of the aircraft, C_{L_α} is the wing lift slope, $\partial C_L/\partial\alpha$, and k is a constant of proportionality. The larger an aircraft is, the lower is its value of J_{RD}. It is easy to show that J_{RD} is inversely proportional to the aspect ratio of the aircraft's wing.

The stability derivative relating changes in the normal force to changes in the heave velocity, Z_w, can be shown (see MIL-F-9490D) to be given by:

$$Z_w = \frac{-\rho SV}{2m}(C_{L_\alpha} + C_D) \tag{6.10}$$

For the flight conditions of concern, it is generally true that:

$$C_D \ll C_{L_\alpha} \tag{6.11}$$

hence:

$$Z_w \simeq \frac{-\rho SV}{2m} C_{L_\alpha} = \frac{-\rho Vg}{2k} J_{RD} \tag{6.12}$$

Considering the short period approximation only, then:

$$\dot{w} = Z_w w + U_0 q + \sum_{j=i}^{m} Z_{\delta_i}\delta_i \tag{6.13}$$

and:

$$a_{z_{cg}} = \dot{w} - U_0 q = Z_w w + \sum_{j=i}^{m} Z_{\delta_j}\delta_j \tag{6.14}$$

Hence:

$$a_{z_{cg}} = \frac{-\rho U_0 g}{2k} J_{RD} w + \sum_{j=i}^{m} Z_{\delta_j}\delta_j \tag{6.15}$$

Thus, for any particular flight condition and control activity, if J_{RD} is minimized, then the normal acceleration at the aircraft's c.g. is also minimized, since all other terms are constant.

It is generally agreed that a ride discomfort index of less than 0.1 means that there will be very little, if any, degradation of the aircrew's performance, or of a passenger's comfort. If the value of J_{RD} is greater than 0.28 it may be necessary for a pilot to alter the aircraft's flight path, airspeed or height to reduce the effects of turbulence on his aircraft's motion.

In Chapter 3, in eq. (3.15), the static margin was defined as:

$$C_{m_\alpha}/C_{L_\alpha} = \frac{-x_{AC}}{\bar{c}} \tag{3.15}$$

where $\bar{c}$ represents the m.a.c., x_{AC} is the distance from the aerodynamic centre to the c.g., and C_{m_α} is the longitudinal static stability derivative. Therefore:

$$J_{RD} = \frac{-S}{W}\,\bar{c}\,\frac{C_{m_\alpha}}{x_{AC}} \tag{6.16}$$

However, it can be shown (see MIL-F-9490D) that:

$$C_{m_\alpha} = \frac{2I_{yy}}{\rho S U_0 \bar{c}} M_w \tag{6.17}$$

Hence:

$$J_{RD} = \frac{2I_{yy}}{\rho U_0 W} \frac{M_w}{x_{AC}} \tag{6.18}$$

Thus, if an RCS minimizes J_{RD}, it must also effectively reduce M_w and Z_w, which means that the dynamics of the short period mode of the aircraft are affected (for example, see eqs (3.91) and (3.92)). Obviously, an RCS has to be used in conjunction with a stability augmentation system (SAS). However, it cannot be forgotten that the control activity arising from the action of the SAS will affect the ride index: see eq. (6.16). It is shown in the succeeding chapter how an AFCS can be designed which will simultaneously minimize both J_{RD} and the control activity, with the stability of the closed loop system being assured.

There is no corresponding ride index for lateral motion, although it is known that human beings are more sensitive to the effects of lateral acceleration. If it is required to reduce the level of lateral acceleration occurring at some specific aircraft station, a control system is provided, the system usually having been designed to minimize the r.m.s. value of a_{y_x}, by using vertical canards or moving vertical fins. Combined axis accelerations are found to be particularly objectionable, and the effect of different levels of such combined motion upon the rating awarded by a pilot to such an aircraft may be judged from inspecting Figure 6.7.

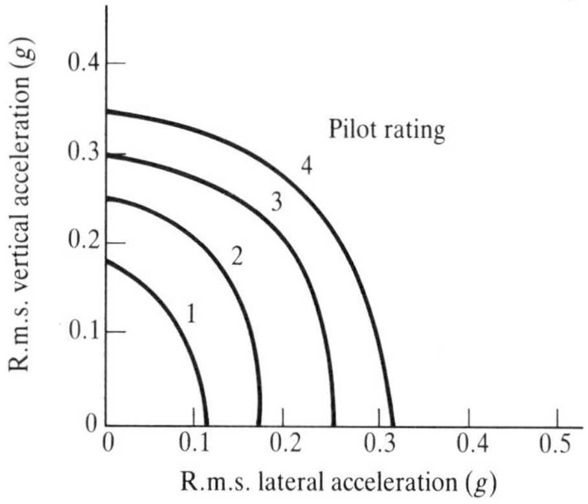

Figure 6.7 Pilot rating of acceleration levels.

6.7 HELICOPTER CONTROL AND FLYING QUALITIES

6.7.1 Introduction

The specifications for the flying qualities required in a helicopter depend very much upon how the vehicle is to be used, in a way rather similar to the distinctions which were necessary for fixed wing aircraft. However, the main differences in specification reside in the requirements for VFRs (visual flight rules) and IFRs (instrument flight rules) flight.

6.7.2 Control Efficiency and Sensitivity

In a helicopter, a control input causes the forces and moments on the rotor to change which causes the helicopter to translate and rotate. Therefore, for longitudinal motion, the change in normal acceleration in response to a cyclic pitch command is very important. Obviously the angular acceleration, $\dot{\omega}$, is

$$\dot{\omega} = M_{\text{control}}/J \tag{6.20}$$

If the efficiency of control, η_c, is defined as the angular acceleration produced by a unit displacement of the control stick, then η_c can be expressed in terms of the angular acceleration:

$$\eta_c \triangleq \frac{\dot{\omega}}{\delta_{\text{stick}}} = \frac{M_{\text{control}}}{J\delta_{\text{stick}}} \tag{6.21}$$

The control moment which is produced by a unit displacement is defined as the control power, i.e.:

$$P_c = M_{\text{control}}/\delta_{\text{stick}} \tag{6.22}$$

Hence,

$$\eta_c = P_c/J \tag{6.23}$$

The control sensitivity is the ratio of control power to rotor damping, i.e.:

$$S_c = \frac{P_c}{D_{rot}} = \frac{M_c/\delta_{stick}}{M_{damp}/\omega} \tag{6.24}$$

where ω is the angular velocity of the helicopter, i.e. the integral of the angular acceleration. In equilibrium flight the control moment should be equal and opposed to the damping moment so that:

$$S_c = \omega/\delta_{stick} \tag{6.25}$$

In other words, control sensitivity can be considered to be the angular velocity produced per unit displacement of the stick.

6.7.3 Normal Acceleration Response

When a step input displacement of the longitudinal cyclic pitch, θ_s, is applied to the rotor there is an immediate increment of thrust which produces a small vertical acceleration. The pitch rate is zero initially, but builds up to its corresponding steady state value. The transient response of the pitch rate is characterized by the second order mode associated with the short period motion; it is this pitch rate of the fuselage (about the body axis) which produces the major component of normal acceleration in forward flight. When the response is considered at times greater than the settling time of the short period mode, the long period motion predominates in the response. Such long period motion is typically a slowly growing (or decaying) oscillation. A typical response is illustrated in Figure 6.8.

To restore the helicopter to its equilibrium flight point a pilot must take corrective action, but it can be seen from Figure 6.8 that some time elapses before the maximum normal acceleration is achieved in response to a longitudinal cycle

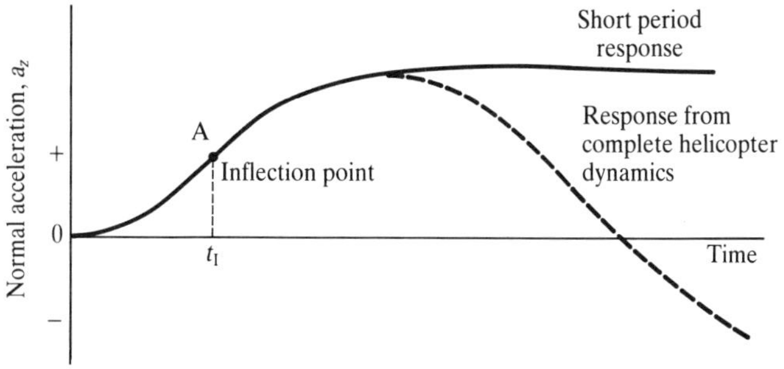

Figure 6.8 Helicopter response.

input. This time lag makes control difficult. Thus, one of the basic requirements for the flying qualities of a helicopter to be considered good is that $a_{z_{max}}$ shall be achieved by some specified time after the application of the step displacement of the cyclic control. This requirement is often met by using a horizontal tail which affects M_w, changing it (in the case of fuselage and rotor alone) from a positive to a negative value of about half its magnitude.

6.7.4 Dynamic Stability Specifications

The dynamic stability characteristics in forward flight are specified in MIL-H-8501A in terms of the period and damping of the long period modes. The requirements for VFR and IFR operations are summarized in Figure 6.9: the roots corresponding to the long period mode should not be to the right of the shaded boundaries.

Manoeuvrability of a helicopter in forward flight is specified in terms of normal acceleration. The specification uses the inflection point, i.e. point A on Figure 6.8, where da_z/dt changes from a positive to a negative value. The existence of this point means that the response of the normal acceleration will not diverge and that for times greater than t_I the response curve of the normal acceleration is concave (downwards). The specification which is used is that the time history of the normal acceleration in response to a step input displacement of longitudinal cyclic should be concave downwards within 2.0 s, i.e. $t_I \ngtr 2.0$.

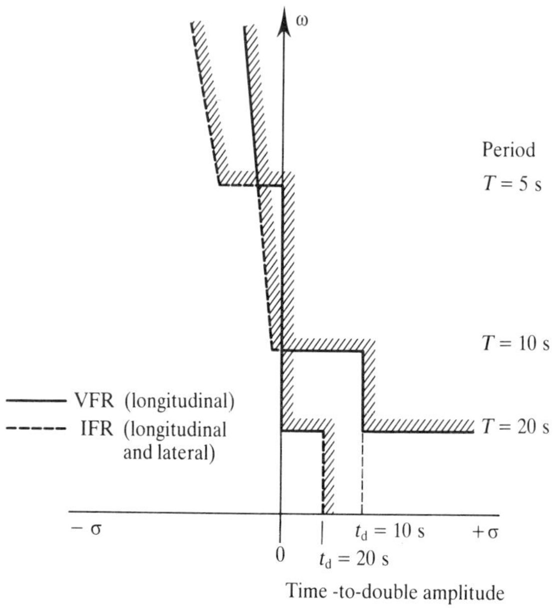

Figure 6.9 MIL-H-8501A specification – long period motion for forward flight.

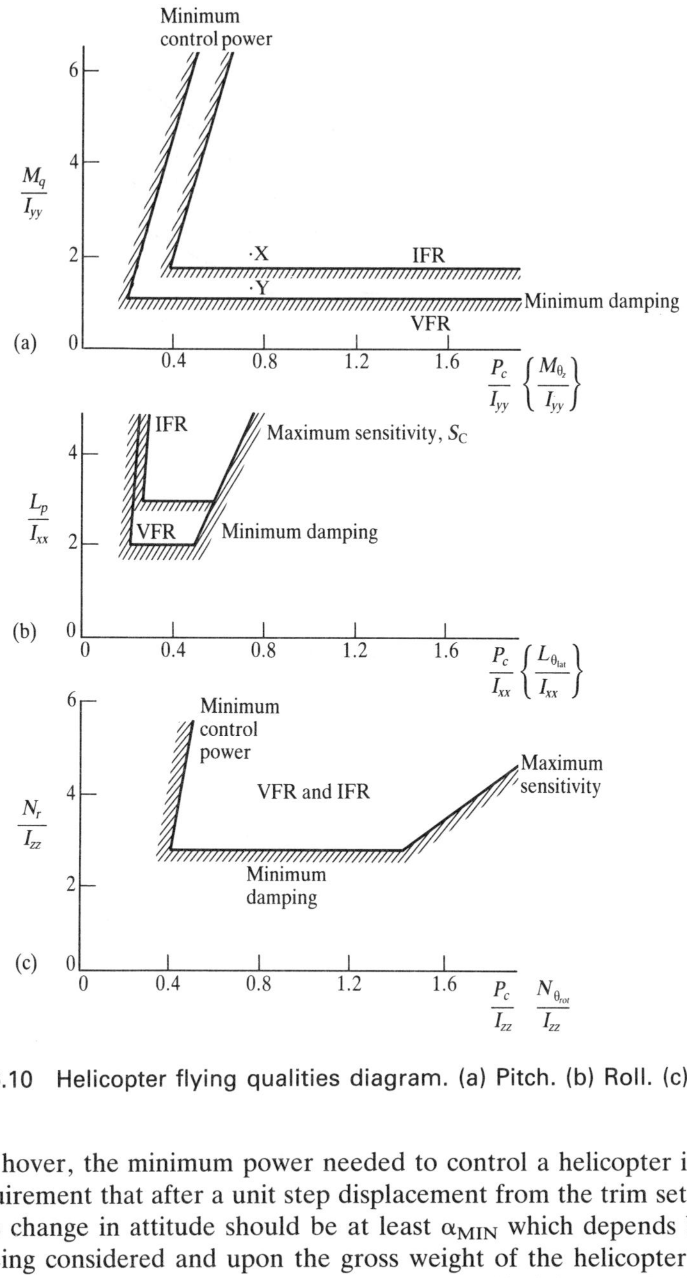

Figure 6.10 Helicopter flying qualities diagram. (a) Pitch. (b) Roll. (c) Yaw.

In hover, the minimum power needed to control a helicopter is specified by the requirement that after a unit step displacement from the trim setting of the control the change in attitude should be at least α_{MIN} which depends both upon the axis being considered and upon the gross weight of the helicopter.

The control characteristics required are specified in MIL-H-8501A and are summarized in Figure 6.10 which shows the boundaries of the effective time constant of the helicopter versus control efficiency, η_c, for pitch, roll and yaw axes. The more stringent requirements for an armed helicopter are presented in Figure 6.11 which shows the specified boundaries for hover control power,

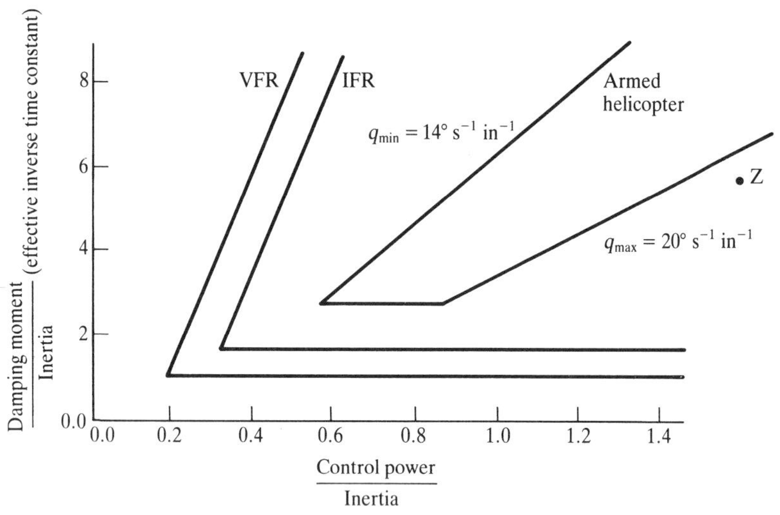

Figure 6.11 Helicopter flying qualities: IFR vs VFR.

damping and control sensitivity. In Figure 6.10, for example, a helicopter possessing an effective time constant and control efficiency which result in point X will be satisfactory for both IFR and VFR operations; that helicopter correponding to point Y will be acceptable for VFR operation only. In Figure 6.11, it can be seen that, although a helicopter with characteristics which place it at point Z has acceptable IFR and VFR values, it would be unsuitable for use as an armed helicopter.

6.8 CONCLUSIONS

This chapter introduces the important subjects of the flying and handling qualities of an aircraft. They are important because they involve a set of complex interactions between the pilot, the aircraft, the operational environment and the mission which is being flown. Since these qualities are what govern the ease, the accuracy, and the precision with which a pilot can carry out his flying task it is specially important for the designer of an AFCS to understand them, how they are specified and how they can be measured, for, if an aircraft has been found to have poor handling qualities, it is customary to recover the loss by introducing a control system. The importance of these aircraft qualities is not lessened by the introduction of modern technology; indeed, with the introduction of digital flight control systems the inevitable time delays involved in this form of control law generation invariably have a detrimental effect on aircraft handling.

The reader should regard this chapter as no more than a brief introduction to a complex scientific study which is more fully accounted for in the papers by Harper and Cooper (1986) and McRuer *et al.* (1962), and the special issue of the *Journal of Guidance, Control and Dynamics* (1986).

6.9 EXERCISES

6.1 The primary longitudinal control for a strike aircraft is represented in the schematic diagram of Figure 6.12.

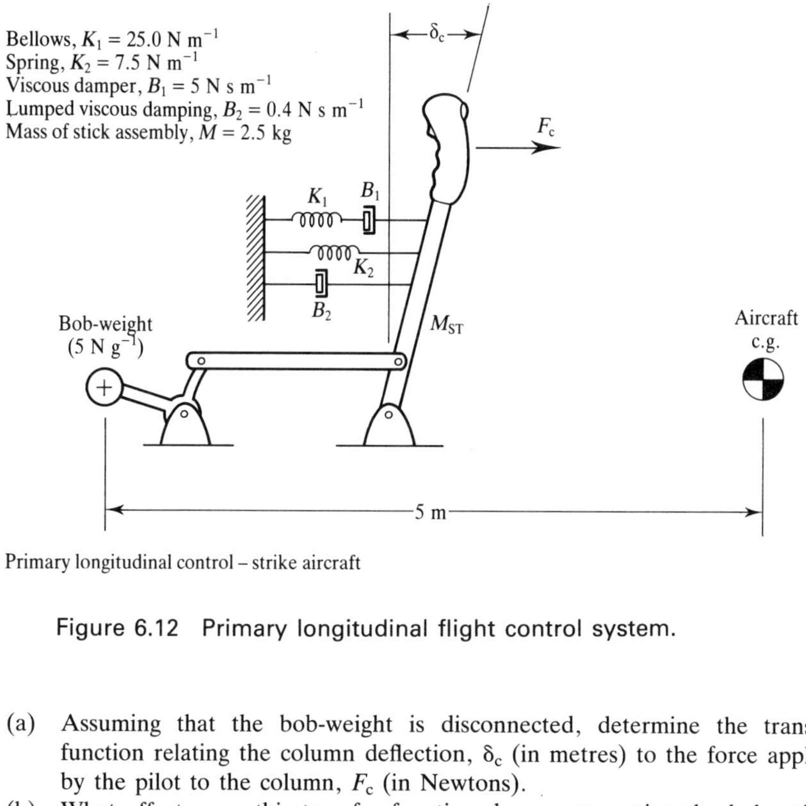

Figure 6.12 Primary longitudinal flight control system.

(a) Assuming that the bob-weight is disconnected, determine the transfer function relating the column deflection, δ_c (in metres) to the force applied by the pilot to the column, F_c (in Newtons).

(b) What effect upon this transfer function does reconnecting the bob-weight have?

(c) The following transfer functions relate to the aircraft:

$$\frac{a_{z_{cg}}(s)}{\delta_E(s)} = \frac{98(s - 0.005)(s + 0.03)(s^2 + 0.83s + 69)}{(s^2 + 2.6s + 6.8)(s^2 + 0.006s + 0.0009)}$$

$$\frac{q(s)}{\delta_E(s)} = \frac{-6.0(s + 0.002)(s + 0.2)}{(s^2 + 2.6s + 6.8)(s^2 + 0.006s + 0.0009)}$$

where $a_{z_{cg}}$ is the normal acceleration at the c.g. of the aircraft, and q is the pitch rate and δ_E is the elevator deflection.

If a column gearing of $5° \text{cm}^{-1}$ is used, determine the transfer function which relates $a_{z_{cg}}$ to the force, F_c, applied to the column by the pilot.

6.2 (a) The lateral stability quintic for an aircraft is given by:

$$\lambda^5 + 7.9\lambda^4 + 23.2\lambda^3 + 29.6\lambda^2 - 3.2\lambda$$

Two zeros of this polynomial are known to be + 0.1 and − 4.0. Identify the other roots and calculate their periodic times (if any) and the time-to-half amplitude. For the rolling subsidence mode it is known that the time-to-half amplitude is 0.3 s.

(b) From a knowledge of the roots of its characteristic equation assess whether this aircraft possesses satisfactory flying qualities in its lateral motion.

6.3 Flying at a height of 10 000 m and at Mach 0.84, a fighter aircraft has a transfer function:

$$\frac{q(s)}{\delta_E(s)} = \frac{-17.8(s + 0.014)(s + 0.43)s}{(s^2 + 1.2s + 12.11)(s^2 + 0.01s + 0.0026)}$$

(a) Find the short period frequency and damping ratio. Does the aircraft possess satisfactory flying qualities?

(b) From the point of view of flying qualities an acceptable closed loop transfer function is given by:

$$\frac{q(s)}{q_c(s)} = \frac{-4.4(s + 0.43)}{(s^2 + 5.6s + 14.0)}$$

If the structure of the flight control system is as indicated in Figure 6.13, find an appropriate transfer function, $C(s)$, for the controller.

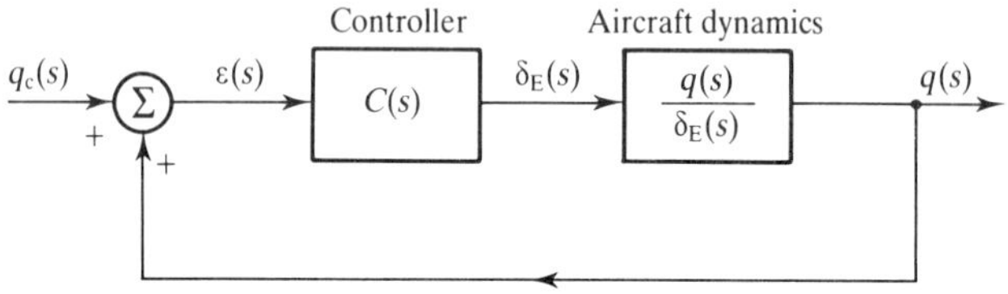

Figure 6.13 Pitch rate damper system block diagram for Exercise 6.3.

(c) Is the controller of part (b) physically realizable?

(d) Show that the parameters of the closed loop transfer function do correspond to acceptable flying qualities.

6.4 Show that the approximation of eq. (6.4) is a reasonable one and thence complete the derivation to show that the control anticipation parameter (CAP) is given by eq. (6.1).

6.5 For the short period motion of the aircraft BRAVO-3 in its role as an air-to-air combat aircraft, determine which level of flying qualities it possesses.

6.6 (a) Determine the output equation for FOXTROT-1 which represents the normal load factor at the pilot's station.

(b) Determine for the same aircraft the ride discomfort index at the pilot's station.

6.10 REFERENCES

Department of Defense. Flight control systems – general specification for design, installation and test of piloted aircraft. MIL-F-9490D. Washington, D.C.: DoD.

Department of Defense. 1961. Helicopter flying and ground qualities: general requirements. MIL-H-8501A. Washington, D.C.: DoD.

Department of Defense. 1970. Flying qualities of piloted VSTOL aircraft. MIL-F-83300. Washington, D.C.: DoD.

Department of Defense. 1980. Military specifications – flying qualities of piloted airplanes. MIL-F-8785C. Washington, D.C.: DoD.

HARPER, R.P. and G.E. COOPER. 1986. Handling qualities and pilot evaluation – 1984 Wright Bros. Lecture. *J. Guid. Cont.* 9(5): 515–29.

McRUER, D.T. and I.L. ASHKENAS. 1962. Design implications of the human transfer function. *Aerospace Eng.* 21: 76–7, 144–7.

Ministry of Defence, 1983. Design and airworthiness requirements for service aircraft. Def. Standard 00–970, Vol. 1, Aeroplanes. London: MoD.

J. Guid., Cont. and Dyn. 1986. 9(5). Special Issue on Aircraft Flying Qualities.

7

Control System Design Methods I

7.1 AFCS AS A CONTROL PROBLEM

Although it is difficult to define what a control system is, it can be said that its purpose is to alter the dynamical behaviour of a physical process so that the response from the controlled system more nearly corresponds with the user's requirements. The means by which the dynamical behaviour of an aircraft is usually altered is negative linear feedback. It is important to understand, however, that any linear control law, no matter what method was used in its derivation, can only provide the required closed loop response at the expense of permitting the occurrence of some unsatisfactory features in the response to disturbances. Whether the disturbances are extraneous to the aircraft, such as can occur when it encounters atmospheric turbulence, or are introduced by the AFCS itself through sensor noise, for example, the design of the linear control system is inevitably such that, if the AFCS has been specially arranged to minimize the effects of unwanted inputs, the desired dynamic performance of the closed loop system to command inputs is unavoidably impaired. Even if some compromise can be achieved, whereby the commanded closed loop response is tolerable and the effects of disturbances moderately alleviated, such a solution can only be obtained within a most restricted region of the aircraft's flight envelope. Consequently, when an aircraft is required to fly on some particular mission, through the extreme regions of its flight envelope, say, recourse is frequently taken to either gain-scheduling or self-adaptive control schemes in an attempt to retain some measure of the compromise solution at every flight condition to be encountered. Both gain-scheduling and adaptive control systems are dealt with later in this book.

How performance requirements can conflict may be seen if we consider the linear system represented by the block diagram of Figure 7.1. The feedback and automatic control elements are represented by the transfer function, $H(s)$. The transfer function, $G(s)$, represents the dynamics of both the aircraft and the control surface actuators. The command signal is $r(t)$; the corresponding motion variable is taken as the output signal, $c(t)$. The disturbance signals, corresponding to atmospheric turbulence and sensor noise, are denoted by $u(t)$ and $n(t)$, respectively. The system represented by Figure 7.1 is assumed to be single-input, single-output (s.i.s.o.), and all the dynamic elements to be time-invariant.

Let the response of the system to any command signal r be c'; to a disturbance u, c'' and to noise n, let the response be c'''. Then:

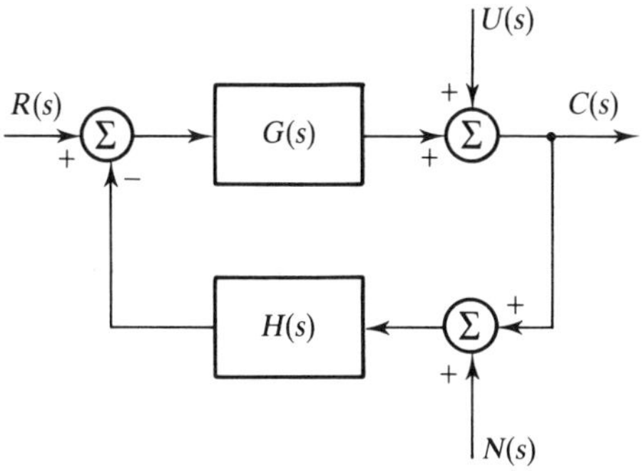

Figure 7.1 Linear time invariant control system.

$$\frac{c'(s)}{R(s)} = \frac{G(s)}{1 + G(s)H(s)} \tag{7.1}$$

$$\frac{c''(s)}{u(s)} = \frac{1}{1 + G(s)H(s)} \tag{7.2}$$

$$\frac{c'''(s)}{n(s)} = \frac{-\,G(s)H(s)}{1 + G(s)H(s)} \tag{7.3}$$

$$C(s) \triangleq c'(s) + c''(s) + c'''(s) \tag{7.4}$$

If it is required that the output response c'' be negligibly small for any disturbance u, $\{1 + G(s)H(s)\}$ should be large, which can be achieved if:

$$G(s)H(s) \gg 1 \tag{7.5}$$

In that situation:

$$c'(s) = R(s)/H(s) \tag{7.6}$$

However, if it is required that, for acceptable tracking of the command input, c' must be identically equal to r, then $H(s)$ must be unity. Consequently, the inequality (7.5) will be satisfied if and only if $G(s)$ is very much greater than unity. But $G(s)$ represents the dynamics of both the control surface actuator and of the aircraft and, therefore, as these are physical devices, $G(s)$ cannot be greater than unity over the entire complex frequency domain, i.e. for every value of s. Moreover, if the inequality (7.5) is valid, the measurement noise from the motion sensor will appear at the output completely undiminished.

It is these contradictory results which make the design of simple AFCSs difficult. When the multivariable nature of aircraft control is considered, the problems become markedly more difficult to solve.

For the simple s.i.s.o. case, a number of methods have been proposed to mitigate these performance conflicts; in practice, they are generally unsuccessful. One of the most common methods is to insert in series in the forward path a compensation element, such as a phase advance filter, for example, which is designed so that, over the frequency range of interest, the modulus of the frequency response function associated with the modified loop, $|G_c(j\omega)G(j\omega)H(j\omega)|$, is always greater than unity without the associated phase characteristic having an adverse influence on the closed loop stability. With the wide changes in the parameters of $G(s)$ which can occur over the flight envelope of any aircraft, it can become very difficult to design a fixed compensation element to fulfil the purpose for every condition. Generally more successful, in practical application, is the use of minor loop compensation since it provides a more satisfactory solution over a wider range of variation of aircraft dynamics (Bower and Schultheiss, 1958).

However, difficulty is often experienced in providing a sufficient gain–bandwidth product in the minor loop to achieve the specified performance. In addition, the minor loop compensation may require a function which is rather complicated for synthesis, or may just be physically unrealizable. Some benefit can be obtained, in a limited number of cases, by changing the structure of the control system, by introducing a feedforward path via the element, F, seen in Figure 7.2. Notice that the aircraft dynamics, represented by $G_A(s)$, have been separated from the forward transfer function, $G(s)$. $G_1(s)$ represents the controller, the actuator and any series compensation element which might also be employed. Thus, from Figure 7.2, it can be deduced that:

$$c'(s) = G_A(s)\{F(s)R(s) + G_1(s)[R(s) - H(s)c'(s)]\} \tag{7.7}$$

If:

$$G(s) \triangleq G_1(s)G_A(s) \tag{7.8}$$

then:

$$\frac{c'(s)}{R(s)} = \frac{G_A(s)F(s) + G_1(s)}{1 + G(s)H(s)} \tag{7.9}$$

If the inequality (7.5) is valid then:

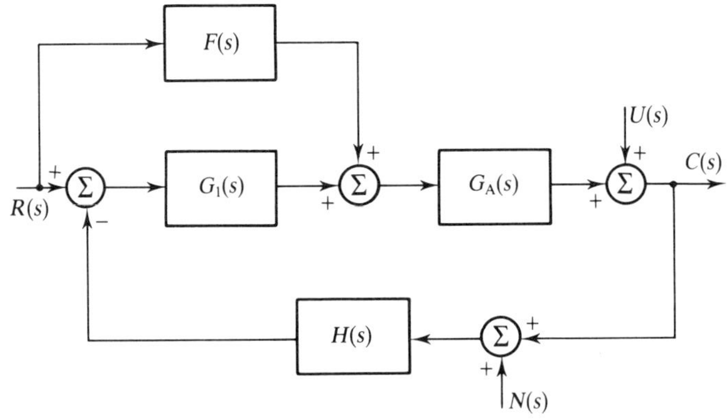

Figure 7.2 Linear system with feedforward added.

$$\frac{c'(s)}{R(s)} = \frac{G_A(s)F(s) + G(s)}{G_A(s)H(s)} \tag{7.10}$$

To ensure that c' is identically equal to r it is necessary to arrange that:

$$F(s) = G_1(s)[H(s) - 1] \tag{7.11}$$

There are several features of this result which merit comment:

1. When unity feedback is used, i.e. $H(s) = 1.0$, then $F(s)$ is zero and Figure 7.2 reverts to Figure 7.1.
2. Since F depends on G_1 and H, both of which can be chosen by the designer, once they have been settled, F is fixed.
3. Since $G(s)H(s)$ has been arranged to very much greater than unity, c'' is very small (as before).
4. $F(s)$ cannot be realized physically for every choice of $G_1(s)$ and $H(s)$. Consequently, some choices of G_1 and H are inadmissible.
5. Noise transmission is not modified by this scheme.

Most AFCSs have been designed using methods which are referred to generically as conventional control methods. Modern aircraft have greater need for more complex AFCSs and the use of modern control methods is more likely.

In this chapter some conventional control design methods are first outlined and discussed, followed by a number of algebraic methods which extend the conventional methods. Finally, an effective modern control method is detailed although a more extended treatment of such methods is given in the succeeding chapter.

7.2 GENERALIZED AFCS

A block diagram representing the most general structure for an AFCS using linear feedback control is shown in Figure 7.3. Note that the feedback controller is dynamic.

From Figure 7.3 it can be seen that the equations defining the aircraft dynamics are given by:

$$\dot{\mathbf{x}} = A\mathbf{x} + B\mathbf{u} + Hp_c \tag{7.12}$$

$$\mathbf{y} = C\mathbf{x} + D\mathbf{u} \tag{7.13}$$

where $\mathbf{x} \in R^n$ represents the state vector of the aircraft; $\mathbf{u} \in R^m$ represents the control vector. p_c is a scalar representing the pilot's (or navigation or weapons systems) command, and $\mathbf{y} \in R^p$ represents the output vector. The matrices A, B, H, C and D have the orders $(n \times n)$, $(n \times m)$, $(n \times 1)$, $(p \times n)$ and $(p \times m)$ respectively.

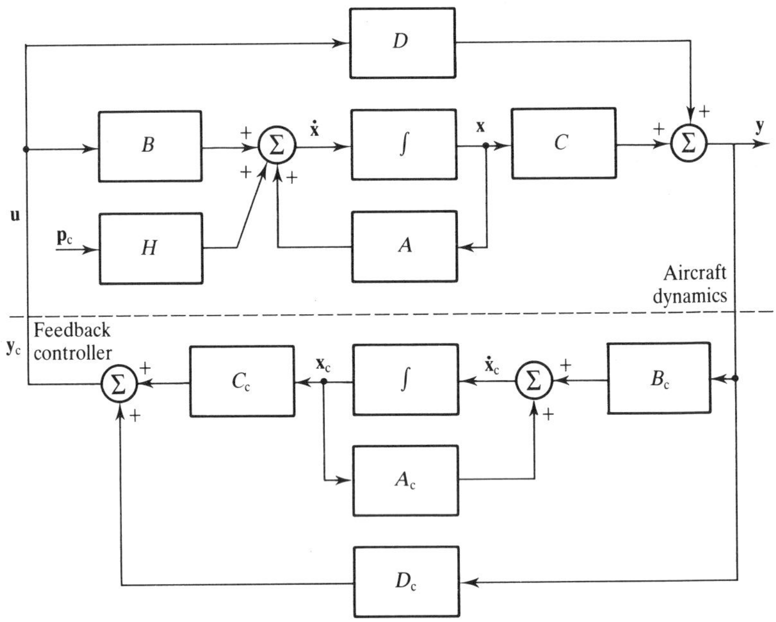

Figure 7.3 Generalized AFCS.

The equations governing the feedback controller are given by:

$$\dot{\mathbf{x}}_c = A_c\mathbf{x}_c + B_c\mathbf{y} \tag{7.14}$$

$$\mathbf{y}_c = C_c\mathbf{x}_c + D_c\mathbf{y} \tag{7.15}$$

and closed loop control is achieved when:

$$\mathbf{u} = \mathbf{y}_c \tag{7.16}$$

The vector $\mathbf{x}_c \in R^s$ represents the state vector of the controller and the matrices A_c, B_c, C_c and D_c have orders $(s \times s)$, $(s \times p)$, $(m \times s)$ and $(m \times p)$ respectively.

From eqs (7.12), (7.15) and (7.16):

$$\dot{\mathbf{x}} = A\mathbf{x} + B(C_c\mathbf{x}_c + D_c\mathbf{y}) + Hp_{\text{comm}} \tag{7.17}$$

$$\begin{aligned}\mathbf{y} &= C\mathbf{x} + DC_c\mathbf{x}_c + DD_c\mathbf{y} \\ &= [I - DD_c]^{-1}C\mathbf{x} + [I - DD_c]^{-1}DC_c\mathbf{x}_c\end{aligned} \tag{7.18}$$

$$\therefore \quad \dot{\mathbf{x}} = \{A + BD_c[I - DD_c]^{-1}C\}\mathbf{x} + \{BC_c + BD_c[I - DD_c]^{-1}DC_c\}\mathbf{x}_c \tag{7.19}$$

and

$$\dot{\mathbf{x}}_c = B_c[I - DD_c]^{-1}C\mathbf{x} + \{A_c + B_c[I - DD_c]^{-1}DC_c\}\mathbf{x}_c \tag{7.20}$$

Let:

$$\mathbf{z} \triangleq \begin{bmatrix} \mathbf{x} \\ \mathbf{x}_c \end{bmatrix} \tag{7.21}$$

then:

$$\dot{\mathbf{z}} = K\mathbf{z} + \Lambda p_c \tag{7.22}$$

where:

$$K = \begin{bmatrix} \{A + BD[I - DD_c]^{-1}C\} & \{BC_c + BD_c[I - DD_c]^{-1}DC_c\} \\ B_c[I - DD_c]^{-1}C & \{A_c + B_c[I - DD_c)^{-1}DC_c\} \end{bmatrix} \tag{7.23}$$

$$\Lambda = \begin{bmatrix} H \\ 0 \end{bmatrix} \tag{7.24}$$

$\mathbf{z} \in R^{n+s}$ and matrices K and Λ are of order $[(n + s) \times (n + s)]$ and $[(n + s) \times 1]$ respectively.

If the control law depends solely up on output feedback, i.e.:

$$\mathbf{u} \triangleq D_c\mathbf{y} \tag{7.25}$$

then:

$$A_c \triangleq 0,\ B_c \triangleq 0 \text{ and } C_c \triangleq 0 \tag{7.26}$$

and K reduces to:

$$K = \begin{bmatrix} A + BD_c[I - DD_c]^{-1}C & 0 \\ 0 & 0 \end{bmatrix} \tag{7.27}$$

If the control law depends solely on state feedback, i.e.:

$$\mathbf{u} \triangleq D_c\mathbf{x} \tag{7.28}$$

and if $\mathbf{y} \triangleq \mathbf{x}$, then eq. (7.27) obtains, but $D = 0$ and C is an identity matrix.

The dimension, p, of the output vector equals that of the state vector, namely n. Therefore, K reduces to:

$$K = \begin{bmatrix} A + BD_c & 0 \\ 0 & 0 \end{bmatrix} \tag{7.29}$$

i.e.

$$\dot{\mathbf{x}} = (A + BD_c)x + Hp_c \tag{7.30}$$

which is the most usual form for an AFCS with linear state variable feedback.

7.3 CONVENTIONAL CONTROL METHODS

7.3.1 Introduction

It is customary to regard conventional control methods as those appropriate to time-invariant, linear s.i.s.o. systems. When AFCSs have been designed using these conventional methods, the techniques employed have usually belonged to the class of frequency domain methods, which are essentially graphical. No method is inherently superior to any other: merits are usually advanced upon a basis of personal preference. Control textbooks such as those by Bower and Schultheiss (1958), d'Azzo and Houpis (1978), Kuo (1982), Takahashi *et al.* (1970), and Newton *et al.* (1957), give comprehensive accounts of the procedures for plotting the necessary graphs. However, students will probably find readily available in their colleges and institutions computer aided design packages such as ACSL, CTRL-C, $\mathrm{MATRIX_x}$, or TOTAL, which can provide such plots quickly and reliably. Consequently, the emphasis in this chapter is upon the interpretation of such graphic information as a means of effecting satisfactory AFCS designs quickly and reliably. The methods to be dealt with briefly are: pole-placement, model-following, root locus, and frequency response.

7.3.2 Pole Placement Methods

Introduction

The performance of a linear, time-invariant, s.i.s.o. system is usually assessed by considering the nature of the roots of its characteristic equation. For example, if the system under consideration was a simple, second order system with a large, negative real root and another, smaller, negative real root, then its response will be almost the same as if the system had been first order, with the value of its single root being nearly equal to that of the smaller root of the second order system. By knowing the values of the roots of such systems a designer can acquire insight into the nature of the corresponding dynamic response. The effective way of presenting information about the response of a system is to display in an s-plane diagram the location of the zeros of the characteristic polynomial (which are the poles) of the system. There are, obviously, regions of the s-plane which represent desirable locations for the roots of the systems. In essence, many of the parameter values specified for required flying qualities, which are discussed in Chapter 6, represent merely desirable pole locations which are known to result in acceptable flying qualities. Consequently, it is attractive for AFCS design to consider the use of methods which afford the designer the opportunity of precisely locating the poles of the resulting closed loop system so that they correspond with the specified locations.

Although the idea of pole location stems from the study of s.i.s.o. systems, it is an idea of such powerful intuitive appeal that it has been carried over to studies concerned with linear multivariable systems. Because some modes of an aircraft's motion can be reasonably represented by single transfer functions, and because other modes require full state variable descriptions to adequately represent the dynamic response, the pole placement methods, which relate to both s.i.s.o. and multivariable systems, find use in AFCS studies.

Simple Pole Placement Method

The simplest method involves using the specified values of the poles to form a characteristic polynomial which the closed loop system is required to have. Then negative feedback is used around the dynamics of the aircraft to alter the coefficients of the polynomial to those of the specified characteristic polynomial. A simple example is given to show the method.

Example 7.1

Suppose that it is required that the output from the system represented in Figure 7.4(a) in response to a particular deterministic input should be identical to that of the system represented in Figure 7.4(b), in response to the same input.

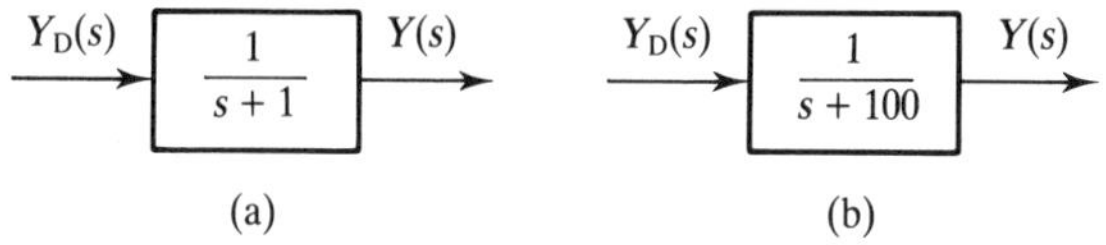

Figure 7.4 Block diagram for Example 7.1.

By using negative proportional feedback, in the manner illustrated in Figure 7.5, the characteristic polynomial of the newly closed loop system becomes $(s + 1 + K)$. Choosing K to have a value of 99 ensures that the dynamic response of the system of Figure 7.5 is identical to the required response: the pole of the closed loop system has been placed at the desired value of -100.

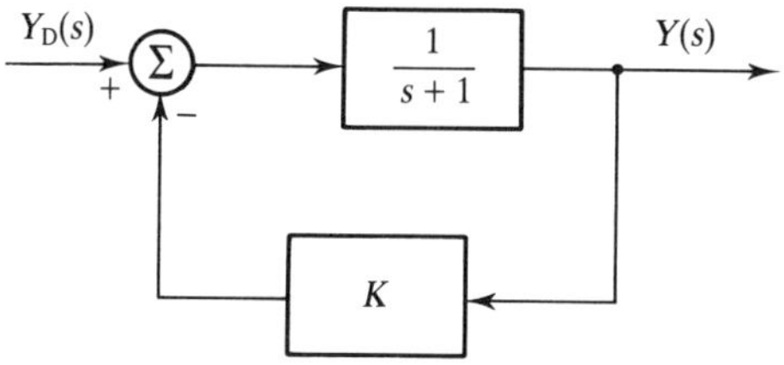

Figure 7.5 Closed loop system for Example 7.1.

Another example shows how effective the technique is in stabilizing unstable dynamics.

Example 7.2

The block diagram of the basic system, which is unstable, is shown in Figure 7.6. The poles have values of 0.0 and + 1.0; the specified values are given as − 5.0 and − 12.0, i.e. the characteristics polynomial desired for the closed loop system is $(s + 5)(s + 12) = s^2 + 17s + 60$.

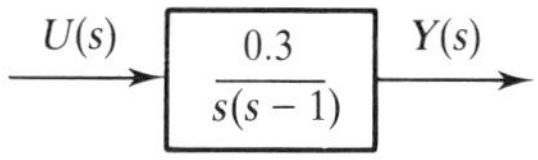

Figure 7.6 Block diagram of open loop system for Example 7.2.

The differential equation which governs the dynamic behaviour of the closed-loop system must be:

$$\frac{d^2y}{dt^2} + \frac{17dy}{dt} + 60y = y_D$$

whereas the differential equation which governs the basic system is:

$$\frac{d^2y}{dt^2} - \frac{dy}{dt} = 0.3u$$

By choosing u such that:

$$u = 3.333y_D - 200y - \frac{60dy}{dt}$$

the closed loop system must have the required response. How the closed loop system may be synthesized is shown in Figure 7.7.

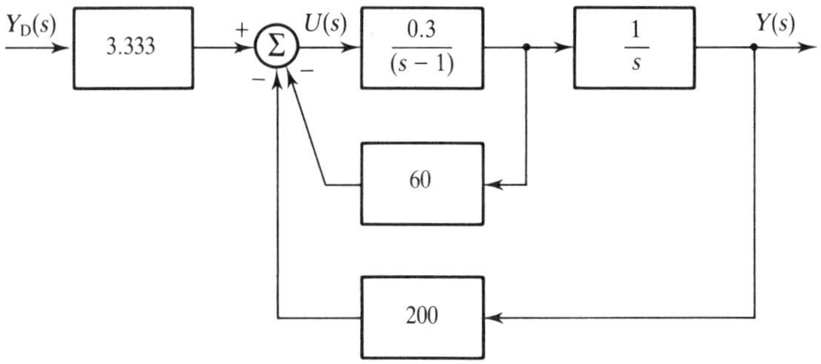

Figure 7.7 Closed loop system for Example 7.2.

Method of Eigenvalues Assignment

When the system being considered is linear and multivariable, the problem is more properly related to eigenvalue assignment, than to pole placement. If a transfer function of a system has a pole, λ, then λ is also an eigenvalue of the coefficient matrix, A, of that same system. It is possible, however, that some eigenvalues of A are not poles of the associated transfer function: it depends upon whether that particular transfer function has been derived from a minimal realization, which, in turn, requires that the particular state variable description used is both completely controllable and observable. To avoid any difficulties of that kind, it is proposed to consider here methods of assigning values to the eigenvalues of the closed loop system. Those will be the eigenvalues which will result when the appropriate feedback control has been applied to the completely controllable, and completely observable, basic system. For convenience, the problem of achieving eigenvalue assignment by means of complete, linear, state variable feedback (LSVF) is considered first.

Suppose that a system is defined by the vector equations:

$$\dot{\mathbf{x}} = A\mathbf{x} + B\mathbf{u} \tag{7.31}$$

$$\mathbf{y} = \mathbf{x} \tag{7.32}$$

where $\mathbf{x} \in R^n$, $\mathbf{u} \in R^m$ and $\mathbf{y} \in R^n$. The problem is that because of the values of some or all of the eigenvalues of matrix A, the dynamic response of the system is unacceptable. It is necessary to find a feedback gain matrix, K, to use in the control law:

$$\mathbf{u} = K\mathbf{x} \tag{7.33}$$

such that the eigenvalues, γ_i, of the closed loop system will be placed precisely at specified locations.

The closed loop system is defined by:

$$\dot{\mathbf{x}} = (A + BK)\mathbf{x} = \bar{A}\mathbf{x} \tag{7.34}$$

(compare eq. [7.30]). The eigenvalues, γ_i, are determined from the characteristic polynomial, $f(\gamma)$:

$$f(\gamma) \triangleq |\gamma I - \bar{A}| = |\gamma I - A - BK| \tag{7.35}$$

Many methods of determining the feedback matrix, K, have been proposed (see, for example, Tyler (1968), Wonham (1967), Munro (1973), Munro and Vardulakis (1973), and Patel (1974)). Three of those methods are dealt with next.

Equating Coefficients

The polynomial of eq. (7.35) can be evaluated, and the coefficients of that polynomial can then be equated with those of the desired polynomial, which is formed from the specified eigenvalues. From those equated coefficients, the matrix, K, can be determined. The concept, being straightforward, needs no further discussion; two simple examples indicate the procedures involved and, also, how successful the method can be.

Example 7.3

A basic system is characterized by the state equation:

$$\dot{\mathbf{x}} = \begin{bmatrix} -4 & 0 \\ 2 & -2 \end{bmatrix} \mathbf{x} + \begin{bmatrix} 4 \\ 0 \end{bmatrix} u$$

Its eigenvalues are, therefore, -4 and -2. It is desired to find a linear control law such that the eigenvalues of the closed loop system will be -5 and -12.

The desired characteristic polynomial of the closed loop system is therefore:

$$(\gamma + 5)(\gamma + 12) = \gamma^2 + 17\gamma + 60 = f(\gamma)$$

But

$$f(\gamma) \triangleq |\gamma I - A - BK|$$

$$= \begin{vmatrix} (\gamma + 4) & 0 \\ -2 & (\gamma + 2) \end{vmatrix} + \left| \begin{bmatrix} 4 \\ 0 \end{bmatrix} [k_1 \; k_1] \right|$$

$$= \begin{vmatrix} (\gamma + 4 - 4k_1) & -4k_2 \\ -2 & (\gamma + 2) \end{vmatrix}$$

$$= \gamma^2 + (6 - 4k_1)\gamma + 8(-k_1 + k_2 + 1)$$

Hence:

$$\gamma^2 + 17\gamma + 60 = \gamma^2 + (6 - 4k_1)\gamma + 8(-k_1 + k_2 + 1)$$

$$\therefore \quad 17 = 6 - 4k_1$$

Thus:

$$k_1 = -11/4, \text{ hence } k_2 = -15/4$$

Example 7.4

A basic system has the state equation:

$$\dot{\mathbf{x}} = \begin{bmatrix} -3 & 2 & 0 \\ 4 & -5 & 1 \\ 0 & 0 & -3 \end{bmatrix} \mathbf{x} + \begin{bmatrix} 0 \\ 1 \\ 1 \end{bmatrix} u$$

with corresponding eigenvalues of $\lambda_1 = -1$, $\lambda_2 = -3$ and $\lambda_3 = -7$.

If the closed loop eigenvalues are required to be: $\gamma_1 = -3$, $\gamma_2 = -5$ and $\gamma_3 = -10$ then it is necessary to find the required control law:

$$u = -[k_1 \; k_2 \; k_3]\mathbf{x} = \mathrm{K}x$$

The desired characteristic polynomial is:

$$f(\gamma) = (\gamma^3 + 18\gamma^2 + 95\gamma + 150) \tag{A}$$

$$f(\gamma) = |\gamma I - A - BK| = \begin{vmatrix} (\gamma + 3) & -2 & 0 \\ (k_1 - 4) & (\gamma + 5 + k_2) & (k_3 - 1) \\ k_1 & k_2 & (\gamma + 3 + k_3) \end{vmatrix}$$

from which:

$$f(\gamma) = \gamma^3 + (11 + k_2 + k_3)\gamma^2 + (2k_1 + 7k_2 + 8k_3 + 31)\gamma + (8k_1 + 12k_2 + 7k_3 + 21) \tag{B}$$

Equating coefficients of eqs (A) and (B) yields:

$$11 + k_2 + k_3 = 18$$

$$2k_1 + 7k_2 + 8k_3 + 31 = 95$$

$$8k_1 + 12k_2 + 7k_3 + 21 = 150$$

Thus $k_1 = 6.667$, $k_2 = 5.333$ and $k_3 = 1.667$. Therefore:

$$K = [6.667 \;\; 5.333 \;\; 1.667]$$

The Method of the Modal Matrix

This method was proposed by Widodo (1972) and is valid for any s.i.s.o., time-invariant, linear system. It works for desired eigenvalues which are simple, multiple, or complex conjugate. The design procedure is straightforward and is stated below:

1. The vector, **k**, is defined as:

$$\mathbf{k} \triangleq [k_1 \; k_2 \; . \; . \; . \; k_n] \tag{7.36}$$

2. The gain elements, k_i are determined from:

$$k_i = \frac{\prod_{j=1}^{n} (\lambda_i - \gamma_j)}{\prod_{j=1}^{n} (\lambda_j - \gamma_i)} \tag{7.37}$$

3. The feedback gain matrix, K, is defined as:

$$K = \mathbf{k}U^{-1} \tag{7.38}$$

where U is the modal matrix of the system. To illustrate Widodo's procedure consider Example 7.3 once again.

Example 7.5

$$\dot{\mathbf{x}} = \begin{bmatrix} -4 & 0 \\ 2 & -2 \end{bmatrix} \mathbf{x} + \begin{bmatrix} 4 \\ 0 \end{bmatrix} u$$

The modal matrix U is found to be:

$$U = \begin{bmatrix} 4 & 0 \\ -4 & 4 \end{bmatrix}$$

Hence

$$U^{-1} = \begin{bmatrix} 1/4 & 0 \\ 1/4 & 1/4 \end{bmatrix}$$

Also:

$$k_1 = \frac{(-4+5)(-4+12)}{-2} = +4$$

$$k_2 = \frac{(-2+5)(-2+12)}{2} = -15$$

i.e.:

$$\mathbf{k} = [+4 \quad -15]$$

Now:

$$K = \mathbf{k}U^{-1} = [+4 \quad -15] \begin{bmatrix} 1/4 & 0 \\ 1/4 & 1/4 \end{bmatrix}$$

$$= \begin{bmatrix} \frac{-11}{4} & \frac{-15}{4} \end{bmatrix}$$

This result is identical to that obtained in Example 7.3.

Example 7.6

Find the feedback gains which will result in the eigenvalues of the closed loop system having the following values: -2, -3 and -5. The basic system has a state equation:

$$\dot{\mathbf{x}} = \begin{bmatrix} 2 & -2 & 3 \\ 1 & 1 & 1 \\ 1 & 3 & -1 \end{bmatrix} \mathbf{x} + \begin{bmatrix} 0 \\ 0 \\ 1 \end{bmatrix} u$$

It has eigenvalues -2, 1 and 3, i.e. the basic system is unstable.

The modal matrix of the basic system can be found to be:

$$U = \begin{bmatrix} -1 & 11 & 1 \\ 1 & 1 & 1 \\ 1 & -14 & 1 \end{bmatrix}$$

Its inverse is:

$$U^{-1} = \frac{1}{30}\begin{bmatrix} -15 & 25 & -10 \\ 0 & 0 & -2 \\ 15 & 3 & 12 \end{bmatrix}$$

From eq. (7.37), $k_1 = -6$, $k_2 = -8$ and $k_3 = -2.4$, therefore:

$$\mathbf{k} = [-6 \ -8 \ -2.4]$$

$$K = \mathbf{k}U^{-1}$$

$$= -[6 \ 8 \ 2.4]\frac{1}{30}\begin{bmatrix} -15 & 25 & -10 \\ 0 & 2 & -2 \\ 15 & 3 & -12 \end{bmatrix}$$

$$= [1.8 \ -5.77 \ 1.57]$$

Output Feedback

When lsvf is used, then, provided that the system is completely controllable, the eigenvalues of the closed loop system can be located arbitrarily in the complex plane, the only restriction being that complex eigenvalues must occur in conjugate pairs.

If the poles of the closed loop system are to be located, by using *output* feedback, it is found that only some of these poles may be placed arbitrarily. The questions of how many poles, and which, are dealt with next, followed by an account of one procedure for achieving pole placement by using output feedback. An alternative method can be found in Shapiro *et al.* (1981).

The basic system is assumed to be defined by the equations:

$$\dot{\mathbf{x}} = A\mathbf{x} + B\mathbf{u} \tag{7.39}$$

$$\mathbf{y} = C\mathbf{x} \tag{7.40}$$

where $\mathbf{x} \in R^n$, $\mathbf{u} \in R^m$, and $\mathbf{y} \in R^p$. The matrices A, B and C, are of order $(n \times n)$, $(n \times m)$ and $(p \times n)$, respectively. Let the control law be given by:

$$\mathbf{u} = K\mathbf{y} \tag{7.41}$$

where the matrix K is of order $(m \times p)$.

There is a theorem (see Wonham (1967)) which states that linear output feedback, such as the control law of eq. (7.41), will always result in max(n, p)[1] eigenvalues of the closed loop system being placed arbitrarily close to the preassigned values, provided that the rank of matrix B is $m \leq n$, and the rank of the matrix C is $p \leq n$.

The method depends upon assuming that the feedback gain matrix, K, is a dyadic product of two vectors, i.e. that:

$$K = \mathbf{g}\mathbf{h}' \tag{7.42}$$

$\mathbf{g}$ is a column matrix, of m rows, and $\mathbf{h}$ is also a column matrix, but of p rows.

The ratio of the characteristic polynomials of the closed loop and the basic systems is given by:

$$\frac{|sI - A - BKC|}{|sI - A|} = 1 + \sum_{i=1}^{n} \frac{\alpha_i}{(s - \lambda_i)} \tag{7.43}$$

Equation (7.44) can be re-expressed as:

$$\frac{(s - \gamma_1)(s - \gamma_2) \ldots (s - \gamma_n)}{(s - \lambda_1)(s - \lambda_2) \ldots (s - \lambda_n)} = 1 + \sum_{i=1}^{n} \frac{\alpha_i}{(s - \lambda_1)} \tag{7.44}$$

When $p \leq m$, the vector $\mathbf{h}$ is calculated from:

$$\tilde{C}'\mathbf{h} = \boldsymbol{\alpha} \tag{7.45}$$

where

$$\tilde{C} = CU \tag{7.46}$$

U is the modal matrix.

$\boldsymbol{\alpha}$ is a column matrix, the elements of which take the form α_i/δ_i where:

$$\delta_i = \mathbf{b}_i\mathbf{g} \neq 0 \qquad i = 1, 2, \ldots, n \tag{7.47}$$

$\mathbf{b}_i$ is the ith row of a matrix, $B \triangleq U^{-1}B$. Therefore:

$$\mathbf{h} = C_p^{-1}\mathbf{a}_p \tag{7.48}$$

C_p is a matrix consisting of the p independent rows of $\tilde{C}'$; $\boldsymbol{\alpha}$ is the corresponding subset of α.

The choice of $\mathbf{h}$ (and any $\mathbf{g}$ which satisfies inequality (7.47) results in p eigenvalues being assigned to their arbitrary locations.

Example 7.7

A basic system has the state and output equations:

$$\dot{\mathbf{x}} = \begin{bmatrix} -3 & 2 & 0 \\ 4 & -5 & 1 \\ 0 & 0 & -3 \end{bmatrix} \mathbf{x} + \begin{bmatrix} 0 & 1 \\ 1 & 0 \\ 0 & 1 \end{bmatrix} \mathbf{u}$$

$$\mathbf{y} = \begin{bmatrix} 1 & 0 & 0 \\ 0 & 1 & 0 \end{bmatrix} \mathbf{x}$$

Since only two poles can be placed (why?), the desired closed loop eigenvalues are -10.0 and -5.0. The output feedback gain matrix is to be determined.

For the basic system the eigenvalues are: $\lambda_1 = -1$, $\lambda_2 = -3$ and $\lambda_3 = -7$. The modal matrix is:

$$U = \begin{bmatrix} 1 & 1 & 1 \\ 1 & -2 & 0 \\ 0 & 0 & -4 \end{bmatrix}$$

The choice of **g** can be arbitrary; for analytical convenience let:

$$\mathbf{g} = \begin{bmatrix} 1 \\ 1 \end{bmatrix}$$

Then:

$$h_1 - h_2 = \frac{18}{7}(\gamma_3 - 1)$$

$$\therefore \quad h_1 - 2h_2 = 3(7 - \gamma_3) \qquad \text{(P)}$$

$$h_1 = 7(\gamma_3 - 3)$$

γ_3 is the dependent pole. From eq. (P) $\gamma_3 = -4.18$ and:

$$\mathbf{h}' = [h_1 \; h_2] = \left[\frac{91}{11} \; \frac{-1}{11}\right]$$

$$\therefore \quad K = \mathbf{g}\mathbf{h}' = \begin{bmatrix} 1 \\ 1 \end{bmatrix} \left[\frac{91}{11} \; -\frac{1}{11}\right]$$

$$= \frac{1}{11}\begin{bmatrix} 91 & -1 \\ 91 & -1 \end{bmatrix}$$

The closed loop system with its coefficient matrix $(A + B\mathbf{g}\mathbf{h}'C)$ has eigenvalues of -5, -10 and -4.18.

7.3.3 Model Following

1. This method of control system design (Erzberger, 1968) might be regarded with greater meaning as 'model matching'. If the eigenvalues for the closed loop system can be specified, by using the parameters specified in the flying qualities specifications, for example, it is a simple matter to establish a matrix which possesses those eigenvalues.

   Such a matrix can be regarded as the coefficient matrix of a model system. If it is known that some aircraft has all the dynamic characteristics necessary to achieve the flying qualities, which the aircraft being considered does not, then the coefficient matrix of that other aircraft could be used as a model matrix, so that a linear control law can be found to produce a perfect match between the output variables of the closed loop controlled aircraft and those of the chosen, model aircraft. In other words, the model response, obtained from the model equation:

$$\dot{\mathbf{y}}_m = L\mathbf{y}_m \tag{7.49}$$

is expected to result when a control:

$$\mathbf{u} = K\mathbf{x} \tag{7.50}$$

is applied to the basic system given by:

$$\dot{\mathbf{x}} = A\mathbf{x} + B\mathbf{u} \tag{7.51}$$

$$\mathbf{y} = C\mathbf{x} \tag{7.52}$$

where $\mathbf{x} \in R^n$, $\mathbf{u} \in R^m$, $\mathbf{y} \in R^p$ and $\mathbf{y}_m \in R^p$. Now,

$$\dot{\mathbf{y}} = C\dot{\mathbf{x}} = CA\mathbf{x} + CB\mathbf{u} \tag{7.53}$$

and, if it is assumed that perfect matching is to be achieved, it follows that:

$$\mathbf{y} = \mathbf{y}_m \tag{7.54}$$

Therefore:

$$\dot{\mathbf{y}} = L\mathbf{y}_m = LC\mathbf{x} = CA\mathbf{x} + CB\mathbf{u} \tag{7.55}$$

and:

$$CB\mathbf{u} = (LC - CA)\mathbf{x} \tag{7.56}$$

i.e.:

$$\mathbf{u} = [CB]^{\dagger}(LC - CA)\mathbf{x} \tag{7.57}$$

$$= K\mathbf{x}$$

is the required control law where † denotes the generalized inverse of the matrix product $[CB]$. The feedback gain matrix, K, is given by:

$$K = [CB]^{\dagger}(LC - CA) \tag{7.58}$$

If perfect matching has been achieved then it can easily be shown that:

$$([CB][CB]^{\dagger} - I)(LC - CA)\mathbf{x} = 0 \tag{7.59}$$

If perfect matching is not achieved, the properties of the generalized inverse matrix involved in the feedback gain matrix, K, guarantee that any difference between the response of the closed loop system and the model system will result in the least squared value of the error which exists between the response from the model and that of the closed loop system.

2. How is such a generalized inverse matrix to be found? If a rectangular matrix, P, of order $(n \times m)$ is post-multiplied by some other rectangular matrix, G, of order $(m \times n)$, a new square matrix, of order $(n \times n)$ is formed:

$$S = PG \tag{7.60}$$

If $S = I$ then P is said to be the left inverse of the matrix, G.

Similarly, the result of post-multiplying the rectangular matrix, G, of order $(n \times m)$, by another rectangular matrix, Q, of order $(n \times m)$ is that a new square matrix of order $(m \times m)$, is formed:

$$T = GQ \tag{7.61}$$

If $T = I$ then Q is said to be the right inverse of matrix G.

If the rank of G is n then G possesses a left inverse; if its rank is m, G has a right inverse. If G is a square matrix, i.e. $m = n$, and consequently its rank is n, G has a right and a left inverse, which are identical: each is G^{-1}, i.e. G has a proper inverse. If G is singular, i.e. $\det G = 0$, G has neither a left, nor a right inverse.

Now:

$$GPG = G \tag{7.62}$$

or:

$$GG^{\dagger}G = G \tag{7.63}$$

so the left inverse is:

$$P = G^{\dagger} = (G'G)^{-1}G' \tag{7.64}$$

where $G^{\dagger}$ is of order $(n \times m)$. Also:

$$GQG = G = GG^{\dagger}G \tag{7.65}$$

$$\therefore \quad Q = G^{\dagger} = G'(GG')^{-1} \tag{7.66}$$

where $G^{\dagger}$ is of order $(m \times n)$.

If the rank of G is unknown, initially, how can one decide upon which generalized inverse to use? It follows from the dimensions of the matrices used in the problem, because if G is $m \times n$, $G^{\dagger}$ must be $n \times m$: use the right inverse, therefore. If G is $n \times m$, then $G^{\dagger}$ must be $m \times n$ and, consequently, the left inverse is used.

3. An identical result to eq. (7.57) can be obtained (Markland, 1970) by minimizing a weighted least squares error criterion, R, given by:

$$R = \mathbf{e}'Q\mathbf{e} \tag{7.67}$$

where Q is a symmetric, positive definite matrix and:

$$\mathbf{e} \triangleq \mathbf{y}_m - \mathbf{y} = (LC - CA)\mathbf{x} - CB\mathbf{u} \tag{7.68}$$

$$\therefore \quad \frac{\partial R}{\partial \mathbf{u}} = \left(\frac{\partial \mathbf{e}}{\partial \mathbf{u}}\right)' \left(\frac{\partial R}{\partial \mathbf{e}}\right) \tag{7.69}$$

but (because Q is symmetric):

$$\frac{\partial R}{\partial \mathbf{e}} = Q\mathbf{e} + Q'\mathbf{e} = 2Q\mathbf{e} \tag{7.70}$$

$$\frac{\partial \mathbf{e}}{\partial \mathbf{u}} = -\, CB \tag{7.71}$$

$$\therefore \quad \frac{\partial R}{\partial \mathbf{u}} = -\, B'C'\{2Q[(LC - CA)\mathbf{x} - CB\mathbf{u}]\} \tag{7.72}$$

Now, if $\partial R/\partial \mathbf{u} = 0$ then, because B, C and Q are not null matrices:

$$(LC - CA)\mathbf{x} - CB\mathbf{u} = 0 \tag{7.73}$$

$$\mathbf{u} = [CB]^{\dagger}(LC - CA)\mathbf{x} \tag{7.74}$$

Equation (7.70) has an alternative solution, i.e.:

$$\frac{\partial R}{\partial \mathbf{e}} = \mathbf{e}'(Q + Q') = \mathbf{e}'\,2Q \tag{7.75}$$

then

$$\frac{\partial R}{\partial \mathbf{u}} = \{\mathbf{x}'(CA - LC)' + \mathbf{u}B'C'\}\,2QCB = 0 \tag{7.76}$$

from which

$$\begin{aligned} \mathbf{u} &= -\,(B'C'QCB)^{-1}B'C'Q(CA - LC)\mathbf{x} \\ &= [CB]^{\dagger}(LC - CA)\mathbf{x} \end{aligned} \tag{7.77}$$

where

$$[CB]^{\dagger} = ([B'C'][CB])^{-1}B'C' \tag{7.78}$$

(Q is taken as the identity without any loss of accuracy), i.e.

$$[CB]^{\dagger} = ([CB]'[CB])^{-1}[CB]' \tag{7.79}$$

Example 7.8

Consider the aircraft CHARLIE, of Appendix B, for flight condition 4. The linearized equations of longitudinal motion are given by:

$$\begin{aligned} \dot{u} &= 0.0002u + 0.039w - 9.81\theta + 0.44\delta_E \\ \dot{w} &= -\,0.07u - 0.32w + 250q - 5.46\delta_E \\ \dot{q} &= 0.00006u - 0.34q - 1.16\delta_E \\ \dot{\theta} &= q \end{aligned}$$

The output variable to be controlled is the pitch rate, q, i.e.:

$$q \triangleq y = [0\ \ 0\ \ 1\ \ 0]\mathbf{x} = C\mathbf{x}$$

The uncontrolled aircraft has the following eigenvalues:

$$0.00 \pm j0.0147$$

$$-\ 0.328 \pm j0.865$$

Note that the aircraft has neutral static stability (i.e. $M_w = 0.0$) and is dynamically unstable. The design requirement for the closed loop system is that the pole associated with the pitch rate shall have a value of $-\ 1.0$, i.e. the pitch rate should match the model response defined by the equation: $\dot{y}_m = -\ y_m$. The problem is to determine a control law to achieve this requirement.

Using the method outlined in eqs (7.49) to (7.58), a feedback matrix K can be found to achieve the required result. Using eq. (7.58), and noting that $[CB] = -\ 1.16$ so that it is known that $[CB]$ possesses a unique inverse, namely $-\ 0.862$, it is easy to show that:

$$K = [0.0001\ \ -\ 0.0026\ \ 0.5698\ \ 0.0]$$

With this feedback control law the closed loop coefficient matrix $(A + BK)$ has eigenvalues 0.0, $-\ 0.0088$, $-\ 0.2938$ and $-\ 1.0$.

It can be seen that the result has been achieved. The response of the closed loop system to a unit step command for pitch rate is shown in Figure 7.8.

Example 7.9

The equations governing the lateral motion of a helicopter during hovering motion (see Chapter 13) are given by:

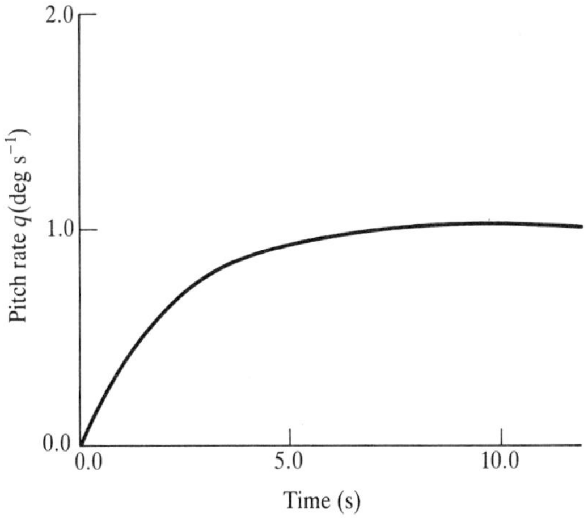

Figure 7.8 Pitch rate response of Example 7.8.

$$\dot{\beta} = -0.1\beta + 30.0\phi + 30.0\delta_A + 20.0\delta_T$$

$$\dot{p} = -0.05\beta + r - 3.0p + 30.0\delta_C + 10.0\delta_T$$

$$\dot{r} = 0.04\beta + 0.2p - r + 15.0\delta_T$$

where β is the sideslip angle in rad, p is the roll rate in rad s^{-1}, r is the yaw rate in rad s^{-1}, ϕ is the roll angle in rad, δ_A is the change in the lateral cyclic pitch in rad, and δ_T is the change in tail rotor pitch in rad.

Assume that every state variable is available for measurement, and that the output variables are the roll rate, p, and the sideslip angle, β. Design a feedback controller which will augment the flight dynamics of the helicopter so that the poles of the closed loop helicopter in hover are -0.5 and -0.1. The characteristic polynomial of the helicopter is:

$$(s + 0.244)(s + 3.282)(s^2 + 0.574s + 0.375)$$

The desired characteristic polynomial is:

$$(\gamma + 0.5)(\gamma + 0.1) = \gamma^2 + 0.6\gamma + 0.05$$

A matrix which has these eigenvalues is:

$$\begin{bmatrix} -0.5 & 0 \\ 0 & -0.1 \end{bmatrix}$$

and can be taken to be the model matrix, L. Now if

$$\mathbf{x} \triangleq [\beta \ p \ r \ \phi]'$$

$$\mathbf{u} \triangleq [\delta_A \ \delta_T]'$$

then

$$A = \begin{bmatrix} -0.1 & 0 & 0 & 30.0 \\ -0.05 & -3 & 1 & 0 \\ 0.04 & 0.2 & -1 & 0 \\ 0 & 1 & 0 & 0 \end{bmatrix}$$

$$B = \begin{bmatrix} 30 & 20 \\ 30 & 10 \\ 0 & -15 \\ 0 & 0 \end{bmatrix}$$

From the specification of the output variables it can be seen that:

$$C = \begin{bmatrix} 1 & 0 & 0 & 0 \\ 0 & 1 & 0 & 0 \end{bmatrix}$$

Using the procedure developed in eqs (7.49) to (7.58) a feedback matrix, K, can be found. Therefore:

$$[CB] = \begin{bmatrix} 30 & 20 \\ 30 & 10 \end{bmatrix}$$

Now $[CB]^{-1}$ has rank 2, so $[CB]^{-1}$ exists. Therefore:

$$[CB]^{-1} = -\frac{1}{300}\begin{bmatrix} 10 & -20 \\ -30 & 30 \end{bmatrix}$$

$$LC = \begin{bmatrix} -0.5 & 0 & 0 & 0 \\ 0 & -0.1 & 0 & 0 \end{bmatrix}$$

$$CA = \begin{bmatrix} -1 & 0 & 0 & 30 \\ -0.5 & -3 & 1 & 0 \end{bmatrix}$$

$$(LC - CA) = \begin{bmatrix} -0.4 & 0 & 0 & -30 \\ 0.05 & 2.9 & -1 & 0 \end{bmatrix}$$

$$\therefore \quad K = \begin{bmatrix} 0.0166 & 0.1933 & -0.067 & 1.0 \\ -0.045 & -2.9 & 0.1 & -3.0 \end{bmatrix}$$

The achieved closed loop eigenvalues are:

$\lambda_1 = -0.007 \; (\simeq -0.1)$

$\lambda_2 = -0.494 \; (\simeq -0.5)$

$\lambda_3 = -2.52$

$\lambda_4 = -26.19$

which are very close to the required values.

7.3.4 Root Locus

In the classical analysis of s.i.s.o. linear systems the description is predominantly by means of its transfer function. The open loop transfer function of the system, represented in Figure 7.1, is $G(s)$, which can be generally represented in the following form:

$$G(s) = \frac{K(1 + sT_A)(1 + sT_B) \ldots (s^2 + 2\zeta_A\omega_A s + \omega_A^2)}{s^m(1 + sT_1)(1 + sT_2) \ldots (s^2 + 2\zeta_1\omega_1 s + \omega_1^2)} \tag{7.80}$$

m is the type number of the system. Obviously, the characteristic equation of the system is given by:

$$1 + G(s)H(s) = 0 \tag{7.81}$$

or, from eq. (7.80),

$$s^m(1 + sT_1)(1 + sT_2) \ldots (s^2 + 2\zeta_1\omega_1 s + \omega_1^2) \ldots + K(1 + sT_A)(1 + sT_B) \ldots (s^2 + 2\zeta_A\omega_A s + \omega_A^2) \ldots = 0 \tag{7.82}$$

If the variation of the values of the roots of this characteristic equation, with changes in K, are plotted on an s-plane, the resulting diagram is a root locus diagram. Most elementary textbooks on control systems theory cover the root locus technique. Some typical root locus diagrams are shown in Figure 7.9.

In every case, it is possible for the closed loop system to be unstable with some inappropriate choice of K. Design of AFCSs using the root locus technique invariably involves either merely selecting an appropriate value for the gain of the closed loop system, such that the locations of the closed loop roots in the s-plane correspond to acceptable flying qualities, or introducing additional zeros and/or poles, thereby altering the dynamics of the closed loop system in a manner such that particular pole locations are achieved. Since the stability derivatives of any aircraft change with flight condition, it follows that the poles and zeros of the corresponding transfer function will also change, requiring a choice of gain, K, which will ensure acceptable flying qualities over as wide a range as possible. It is part of the challenge of designing AFCSs that such a range is invariably too

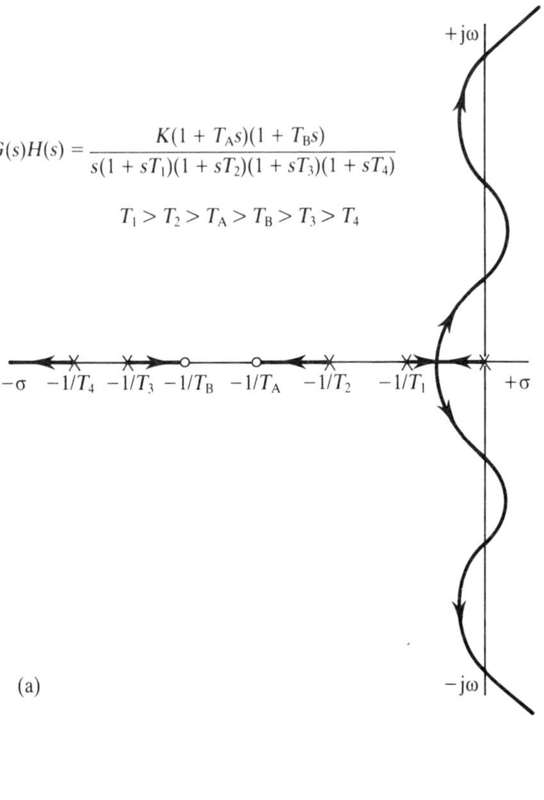

(a)

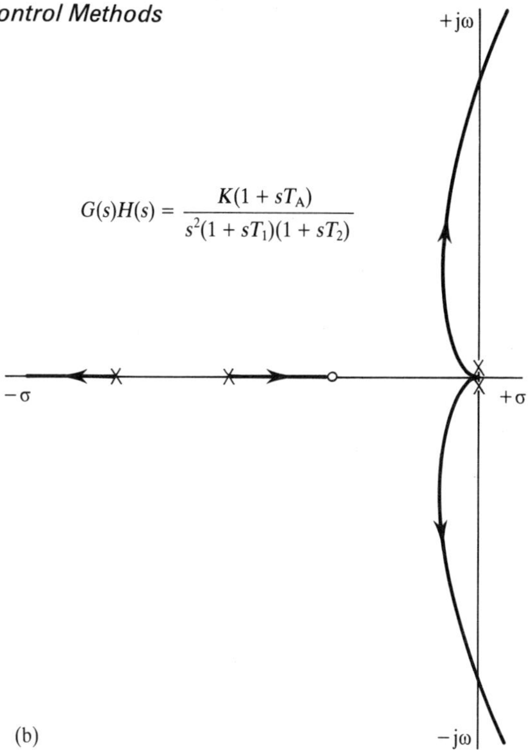
+jω
$G(s)H(s) = \frac{K(1 + sT_A)}{s^2(1 + sT_1)(1 + sT_2)}$
−σ
+σ
(b)
−jω

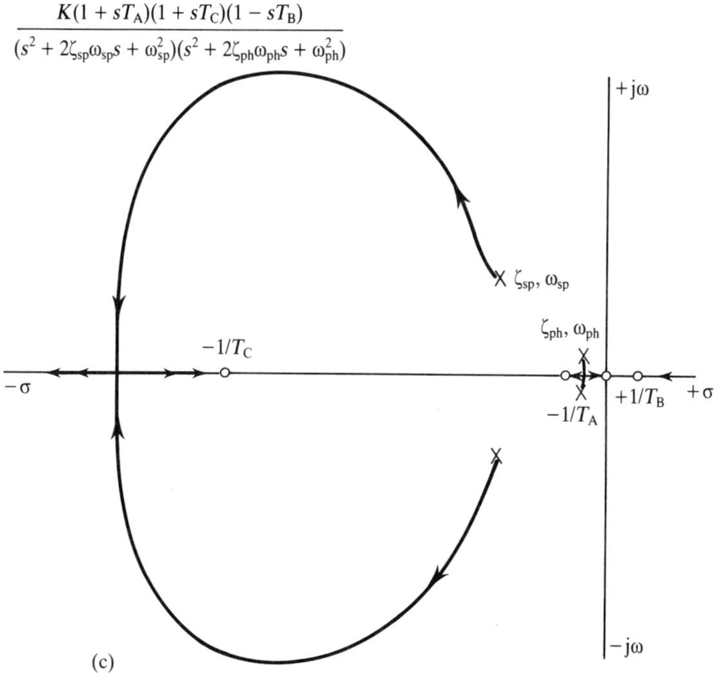
$\frac{K(1 + sT_A)(1 + sT_C)(1 - sT_B)}{(s^2 + 2\zeta_{sp}\omega_{sp}s + \omega_{sp}^2)(s^2 + 2\zeta_{ph}\omega_{ph}s + \omega_{ph}^2)}$
+jω
ζ_{sp}, ω_{sp}
ζ_{ph}, ω_{ph}
$-1/T_C$
−σ
$-1/T_A$
$+1/T_B$
+σ
(c)
−jω

Figure 7.9 Root locus diagrams.

restricted to be acceptable, and, consequently, further techniques have to be tried. If a pole is added then the locus branch is driven away from that pole, and if a zero is added, it tends to attract the locus branch towards it. These pole/zero effects tend to be stronger as the distance between the new singularity and the existing poles and zeros is reduced. The introduction of a zero can improve the stability of a closed loop system because it can attract the locus branch away from the imaginary axis, or even from the right-half of the s-plane itself to the far left of the s-plane.

An example of how such 'compensation' works is shown in Figure 7.10. The dotted line represents the root locus system of the basic system; adding a first order phase advance network introduces an extra zero and a pole, with the effect that the root locus diagram becomes that represented by the solid line. If the gain of the compensated system is adjusted to maintain the same frequency of the dominant closed loop complex poles, it can be seen from Figure 7.10 that the damping ratio of these dominant poles will be increased, since $\zeta = \cos^{-1}\phi$. However, such a simple compensation scheme is not always so effective. Consider the example of Figure 7.11 in which the basic system is shown with dotted lines. Introducing a compensation network with a transfer function:

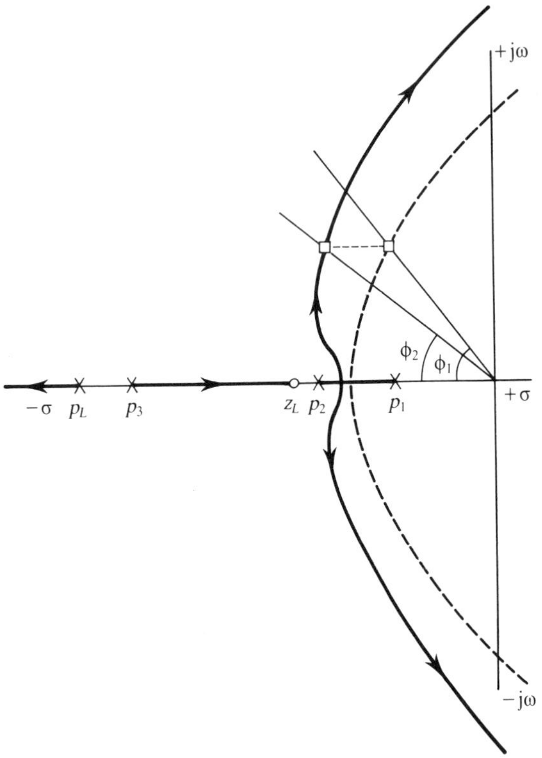

Figure 7.10 Root locus diagram.

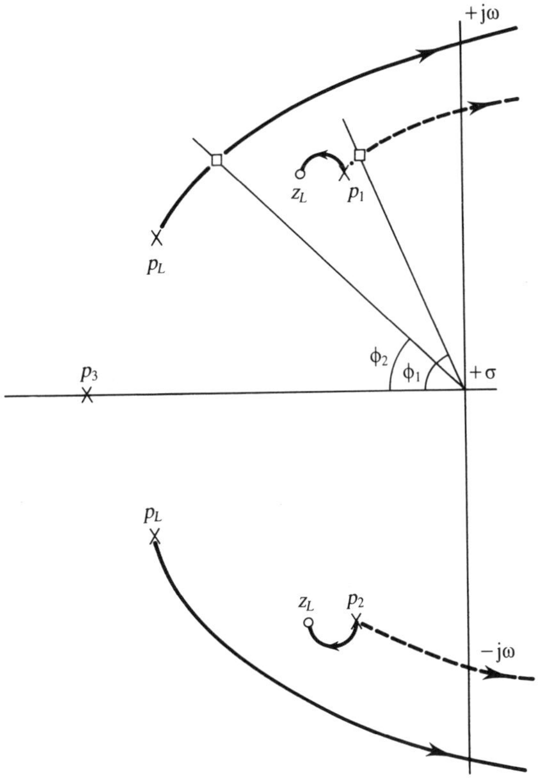

Figure 7.11 Root locus diagram.

$$G_c(s) = \frac{(s^2 + 2\zeta_z\omega_z s + \omega_z^2)}{(s^2 + 2\zeta_p\omega_p s + \omega_p^2)} \tag{7.83}$$

where $\omega_z < \omega_p$. The complex zero pair, z_L, effectively cancels the complex pole pair of the basic system and the complex pole pair of the compensation network is moved far to the left.

7.3.5 Frequency Response

1. Although the frequency response function of a system is a measure of the steady state response of a system to sinusoidal inputs, its principal usefulness rests in the ease with which a designer can assess the stability of the closed loop system from a knowledge of the open loop response. A number of easily determined frequency response parameters have been established as providing excellent guides to the resultant response in the time domain of the closed loop system. By considering only the steady

state response, the Laplace operator, s, can be replaced everywhere in a transfer function by $j\omega$; thus, the most general form of frequency response function is:

$$G(j\omega)H(\omega) = \frac{K(1 + j\omega T_A)(1 + j\omega T_B) \ldots (\omega_A^2 - \omega^2 + j2\zeta_A\omega_A\omega)}{(j\omega)^m(1 + j\omega T_1)(1 + j\omega T_2) \ldots (\omega_1^2 - \omega^2 + j2\zeta_1\omega_1\omega)} \quad (7.84)$$

To plot the frequency response function as a function of frequency, ω, requires either the calculation, over a range of frequencies, of the magnitude and phase of eq. (7.84), or the calculation of its real and imaginary parts. This is rarely done by hand and one of the many computer packages now available, such as ACSL, CTRL-C, TOTAL or MATRIX_x, is usually employed. The results are invariably plotted on a frequency response diagram. The diagrams which are most commonly used are:

(a) The Nyquist diagram, which is an Argand diagram, on which $G(j\omega)H(j\omega)$ is plotted over some desired range of ω.
(b) The Bode diagram, which shows a graph of $20 \log_{10}|G(j\omega)H(j\omega)|$ versus ω plotted on a logarithmic scale, together with a separate graph of the phase angle, $\arg\{G(j\omega)H(j\omega)\}$, plotted against ω on the same logarithmic scale.
(c) The Nichols diagram is a plot of $20 \log_{10}|G(j\omega)H(j\omega)|$ versus phase angle, $\arg\{G(j\omega)H(j\omega)\}$, with the particular points on the graph annotated with the frequency to which it relates. Usually the Nichols diagram is most easily obtained from the corresponding Bode diagram.

2. Some typical diagrams, corresponding to the root locus example shown earlier in Figure 7.9(a), are represented in Figure 7.12. The quantities G_{m_1}, G_{m_2} and ϕ_m denoted on these figures refer to the first and second gain margins and the phase margin, respectively. The gain margin is defined as the amount by which the gain curve must be raised (or lowered) to make the gain crossover coincide with the phase crossover. If the gain margin is positive (i.e. the gain curve is raised) the closed loop system will be stable.

The phase margin is defined as the negative of the additional phase shift needed to make the phase angle of the system be $-180°$ at the frequency at which the gain is 0 dB. A positive phase margin means that a negative phase shift is needed to make the phase angle $-180°$. A positive phase margin corresponds to a stable closed loop system. The usual specifications for an acceptable design are: minimum gain margin $\sim$ 6.0 dB, minimum phase margin $\sim$ 30°. A gain margin of 6 dB means that the open loop gain can be doubled before instability of the closed loop system results.

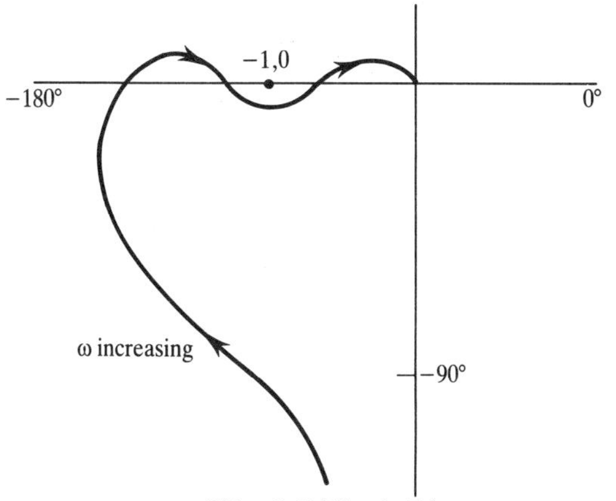

$$G(j\omega)H(j\omega) = \frac{K(1 + j\omega T_A)(1 + j\omega T_B)}{j\omega(1 + j\omega T_1)(1 + j\omega T_2)(1 + j\omega T_3)(1 + j\omega T_4)}$$

(a)

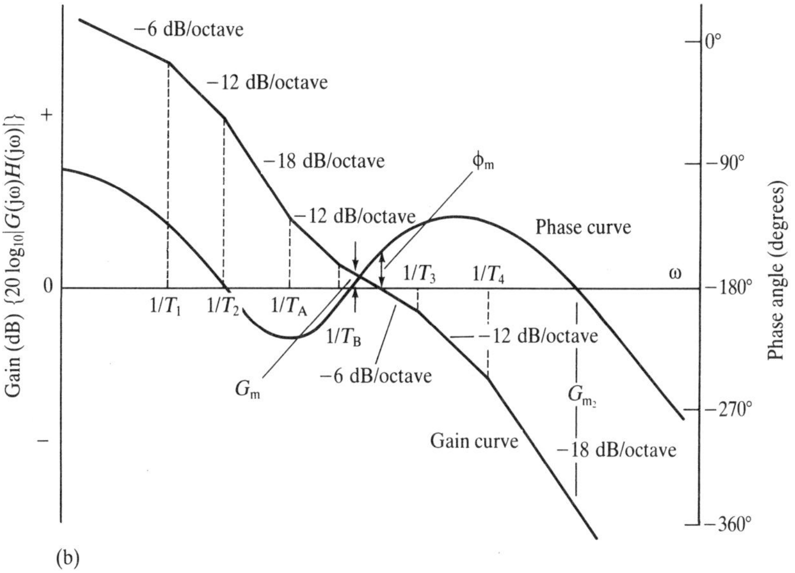

(b)

Figure 7.12 (a) Nyquist diagram; (b) Bode diagram.

Considerable care must be exercised, however, in the use of such margins. For example, for the system represented by Figure 7.12, G_{m_1} is negative, G_{m_2} is positive and ϕ_m is positive.

The point can be seen easily from the following simple example. The system represented by the Nichols diagram of Figure 7.13(a) has a gain margin of + 8 dB and a phase margin of + 60°.

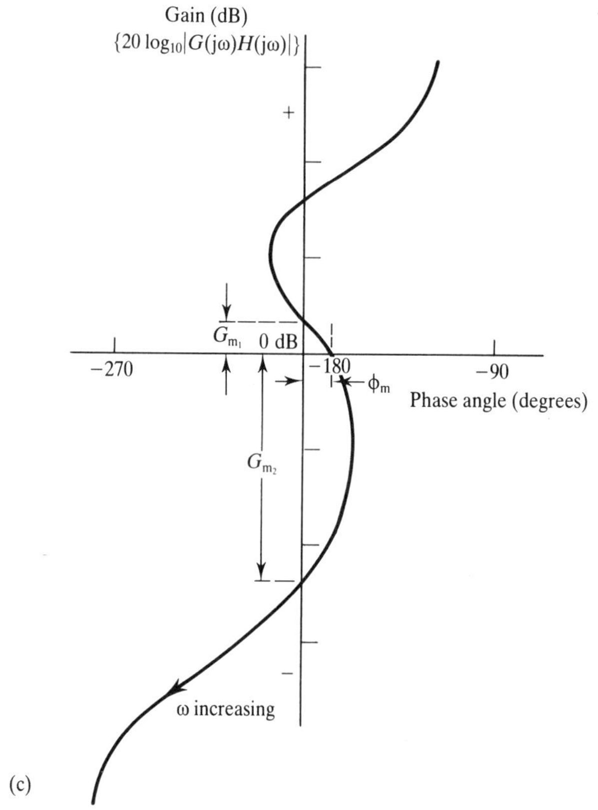

Figure 7.12 (c) Nichols diagram.

But consider a system with the Nichols diagram of Figure 7.13(b). It, too, has a gain margin of 8 dB, and a phase margin of + 50°. But this system is much less stable than its companion because any small variation in gain, 0.5 dB say, can make the closed loop system unstable.

3. For AFCSs, the basic design rules, using frequency response as a design method, can be summarized in the following way. At those frequencies where good manoeuvring and stabilization are required, use high loop gain, and at those frequencies, where noise rejection and insensitivity to changes in the aircraft dynamics are important, use low loop gains. (These rules do no more than reflect the situation discussed at eqs (7.5) and (7.6) in Section 7.1). These design rules can be shown graphically, as in Figure 7.14.

4. Figure 7.14 has the unfortunate effect that it leads to a general impression that the transient response of a linear s.i.s.o. closed loop system is determined chiefly by the nature of its Bode diagram near its crossover

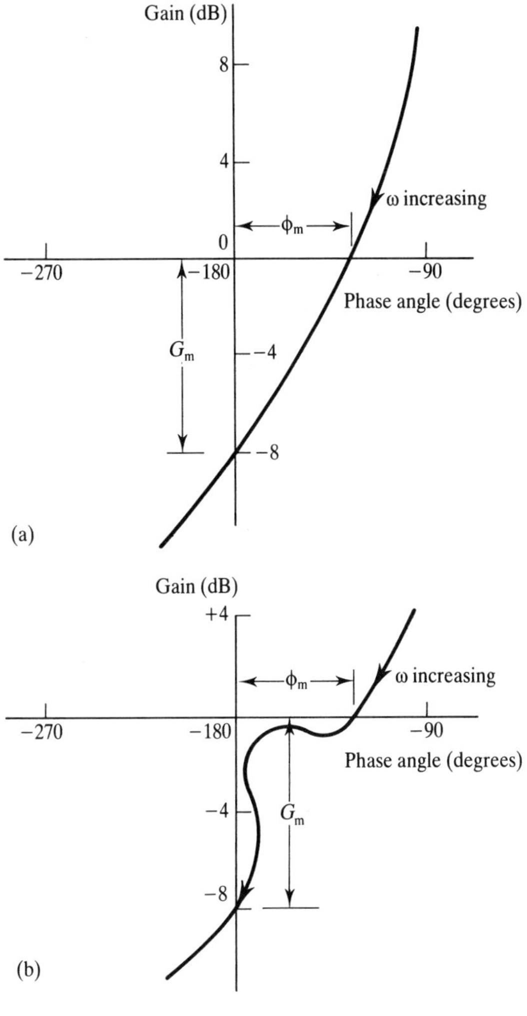

Figure 7.13 Nichols diagrams. (a) Gain curve. (b) Phase curve.

frequency. It is assumed that a designer need concentrate upon only the small section of the dynamics whose break frequencies occur in the vicinity of the crossover frequency. As an example, consider a (fictitious) aircraft transfer function:

$$G(s) = \frac{0.015865s^3 + 0.21023s^2 + 0.539s + 1}{0.015641s^3 + 0.2099s^2 + 0.827s + 1} \tag{7.85}$$

Most control engineers would regard that transfer function as being as good as unity. If it is factorized, it can be written as:

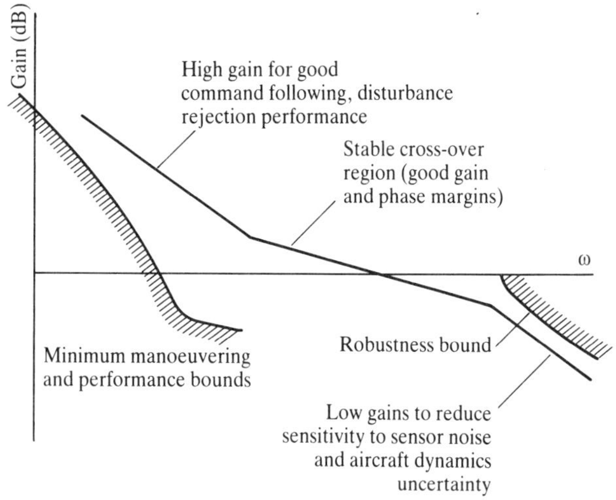

Figure 7.14 Design constraints on Bode diagram.

$$G(s) = \frac{(1 + 0.5s)(1 + 0.19s)(1 + 0.167s)}{(1 + 0.4s)(1 + 0.294s)(1 + 0.133s)} \tag{7.86}$$

which a designer might be less likely immediately to take as unity. If, however, the corresponding Bode diagram was plotted (see Figure 7.15) it is easy to see that if the unit approximation was taken, it would not result in any appreciable loss of accuracy.

The corresponding root locus diagram is shown in Figure 7.16 which does not indicate the easy nature of the approximation quite so readily. However, a state variable representation of the same transfer function is given thus:

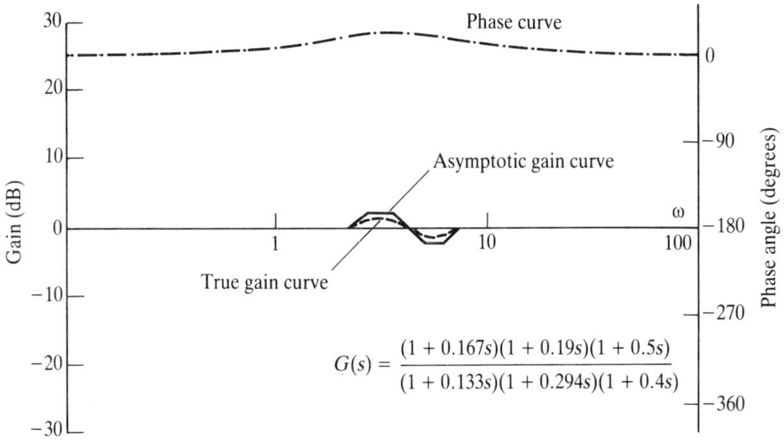

Figure 7.15 Bode diagram of unity gain network.

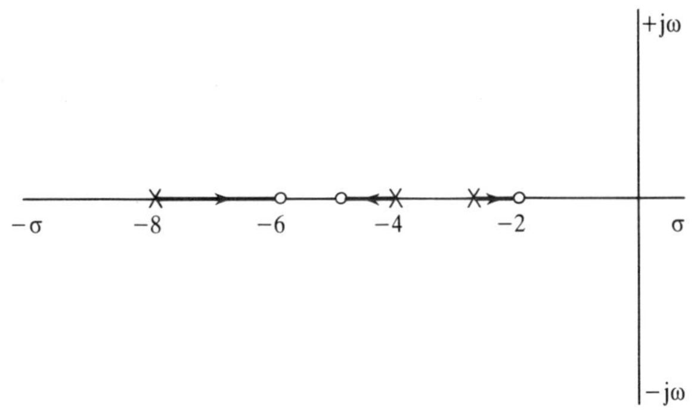

Figure 7.16 Root locus diagram of unity gain network.

$$\dot{\mathbf{x}} = \begin{bmatrix} 0 & 1 & 0 \\ 0 & 0 & 1 \\ -63.9345 & -52.8739 & -13.42 \end{bmatrix} \mathbf{x} + \begin{bmatrix} 0 \\ 0 \\ 65.9345 \end{bmatrix} u \qquad (7.87)$$

$$y = [-0.0432 \; 0.01816 \; -0.00268]\mathbf{x} + 1.041u \qquad (7.88)$$

From inspection of eq. (7.88) it can be deduced that the contribution of the state variables to the output, y, is very small. Consequently,

$$y = 1.014u \qquad (7.89)$$

i.e.:

$$y(s)/u(s) \simeq 1.0 \qquad (7.90)$$

5. One of the most common situations in AFCS design is the occurrence of transfer functions of the form:

$$G(s) = \frac{K(s^2 + 2\zeta_N\omega_N s + \omega_N^2)}{s(s^2 + 2\zeta_D\omega_D s + \omega_D^2)} \qquad (7.91)$$

When $\omega_N/\omega_D > 1$, there is a considerable dip in the phase angle curve when the crossover frequency is in the region of the dipole. This large phase lag at this frequency tends to have a destabilizing effect on the aircraft's response. When $\omega_N/\omega_D < 1$ there is a considerable upwards bulge in the phase angle curve when the crossover frequency is in the region of the dipole. The greater this bulge, the greater the phase lead effect; in effect, the phase margin is increased and the value of the damping ratio of the closed loop system tends to increase. Hence, the effect is a stabilizing one. In AFCS practice, these 'dipole' effects are commonly observed both in problems where roll control is effected by means of aileron deflection ($\omega_N/\omega_D > 1$) and in problems where yaw rate feedback to the rudder is involved ($\omega_N/\omega_D < 1$). The same phenomenon also occurs in the dynamics of any electrohydraulic actuator when the oil compressibility effects are significant, or when structural compliance exists.

For these AFCS problems, particular care must be exercised if the design is based upon transfer functions obtained from a mathematical representation of the aircraft's dynamics which approximated the degrees of freedom involved.

7.4 PARAMETER OPTIMIZATION

7.4.1 Introduction

It was shown in Chapter 6 how the flying qualities are specified in terms of parameters such as short period damping, natural frequency of yawing motion, roll subsidence time constant, and so on. These parameters refer to idealized, low order models of the aircraft dynamics and have been specified because the settling time, or peak overshoot, or time-to-first crossover of the time response, produced by the corresponding low order model, is close to what is required from the aircraft motion when the aircraft has been subjected to some similar forcing function. The conventional design methods for s.i.s.o. control systems, dealt with in the earlier sections of this chapter, provide adequate means of achieving these figures of merit but require considerable experience, skill and judgement to produce acceptable designs. It would be helpful to have a design method which provides as a solution the structure of the control system and the best values for the corresponding parameters. A method which does this depends upon a performance measure which is a member of a class of performance indices.

7.4.2 Performance Indices

For any control system, its output, y, is required to follow its input signal, r, as closely as possible. Any difference between the input and output is an error, e. If $e(t)$ is transient, by which it is meant that e gradually reduces to zero as time goes on, i.e. $e \rightarrow 0$ as $t \rightarrow \infty$, it is appropriate to adopt as a performance index the scalar, J, where:

$$J = \int_0^\infty j(e)\,\mathrm{d}t \tag{7.92}$$

in which $j(\bullet)$ is a non-negative, single valued function of error. Time, t, is measured from zero, the instant at which an input is applied. If it is assumed that $j(e)$ is of the form:

$$j(e) = |e|^{\upsilon} \qquad \upsilon \geq 0 \tag{7.93}$$

the performance index, J_{υ}, can be denoted as

$$J_\upsilon = \int_0^\infty |e|^\upsilon \mathrm{d}t \qquad \upsilon \neq 0 \tag{7.94}$$

where υ is a constant. When $\upsilon = 1$, J, is the integral of absolute error (i.a.e.); when $\upsilon = 2$, J_2 is the integral of squared error (i.s.e.).

The performance index, when $\upsilon = 0$, is defined as a special case, meaning that

$$J_0 = \int_0^\infty \left[\lim_{\upsilon \to 0} \left| e \right|^\upsilon \right] \mathrm{d}t \tag{7.95}$$

where

$$\lim_{\upsilon \to 0} \left| e^\upsilon \right| = \begin{cases} 1 & e \neq 0 \\ 0 & e = 0 \end{cases} \tag{7.96}$$

If it is supposed that $e(t)$ is non-zero throughout the interval $0\text{–}t_s$, except possibly at a finite number of points, and is uniformly zero for $t \geq t_s$, then t_s is the settling time of the system. Then it follows, from eqs (7.95) and (7.96) that:

$$J_0 = \int_0^{ts} 1\,\mathrm{d}t + \int_{t_s}^\infty 0\,\mathrm{d}t = t_s \tag{7.97}$$

J_0 is, therefore, the settling time of the system.

I.s.e. (J_2) is a much favoured performance index because it is easy to work with analytically, but the time response which results from an AFCS, designed on the basis of minimizing J_2, is often unsatisfactory and, consequently, alternative performance indices, such as i.a.e. (J_1) and i.t.a.e., (integral of the product of time and absolute error) are used, because they penalize large and persistent errors. Neither i.a.e. nor i.t.a.e. is easy to handle analytically, however, but design tables are readily available (see, for example, Newton *et al.*, 1957).

For further discussion of performance indices, the interested reader should consult Fuller (1967).

7.4.3 Parseval's Theorem and Definite Integral Table

Integrals of the form:

$$I = \int_{-\infty}^\infty f_1(t) f_2(t) \mathrm{d}t \tag{7.98}$$

often need to be solved in AFCS work. By means of Parseval's theorem, a solution to eq. (7.98) can be found by evaluating I in the domain of the complex frequency, s a procedure which is easier than solving for I directly in the time domain.

Parseval's theorem states that the integral defined in eq. (7.98) can be re-expressed as:

$$I = \frac{1}{2\pi j}\int_{-j\infty}^{j\infty} F_2(s)F_1(-s)\mathrm{d}s \tag{7.99}$$

Of particular interest to AFCS designers is the case when:

$$f_1(t) = f_2(t) = f(t) \tag{7.100}$$

for then:

$$I = \frac{1}{2\pi j}\int_{-j\infty}^{j\infty} F(s)F(-s)\mathrm{d}s \tag{7.101}$$

Of course, eq. (7.101) is still the Parseval equivalent to:

$$I = \int_0^{\infty} f(t)f(t)\mathrm{d}t \tag{7.102}$$

provided that, for $t < 0$, $f(t) = 0$.

Suppose there is a variable, $x(t)$, and it is necessary to evaluate its integral-squared value, I, where:

$$I = \int_0^{\infty} x^2\mathrm{d}t \tag{7.103}$$

Table 7.1 Phillips' integrals

Let:

$$I_n = \frac{1}{2\pi j}\int_{-j\infty}^{j\infty} \frac{c(s)c(-s)}{d(s)d(-s)}\mathrm{d}s$$

where the subscript n refers to the degree of the denominator polynomial, $d(s)$ where

$$c(s) = \sum_{j=0}^{n-1} c_j s^j \text{ and } d(s) = \sum_{k=0}^{n} d_k s^k$$

Then:

$$I_1 = \frac{c_0^2}{2d_0d_1}$$

$$I_2 = \frac{c_1^2d_0 + c_0^2d_2}{2d_0d_1d_2}$$

$$I_3 = \frac{c_2^2d_0d_1 + (c_1^2 - 2c_0c_2)d_0d_3 + c_0^2d_2d_3}{2d_0d_3(d_1d_2 - d_0d_3)}$$

$$I_4 = \frac{c_3^2(d_0d_1d_2 - d_0^2d_3) + (c_2^2 - 2c_1c_3)d_0d_1d_4 + (c_1^2 - 2c_0c_2)d_0d_3d_4 + c_0^2(d_2d_3d_4 - d_1d_4^2)}{2d_0d_4(d_1d_2d_3 - d_1^2d_4 - d_0d_3^2)}$$

A more extensive table can be found in Newton *et al.*, 1957.

Let $x(s)$ be a rational function of s of the form:

$$x(s) = \frac{N(s)}{D(s)} = \frac{c_0 + c_1 s + \ldots + c_{n-1} s^{n-1}}{d_0 + d_1 s + \ldots + d_n s^n} \tag{7.104}$$

If all the poles of the function in eq. (7.104) have negative values or, if any poles are complex with negative, real parts, then I exits, and can be expressed as an algebraic function of the coefficients c_j, where $j = 1, 2, \ldots, n-1$ and $i = 1, 2, \ldots, n$. The results are summarized in Table 7.1.

7.4.4 Design of Optimal s.i.s.o. Linear Systems

The method of achieving a design is procedural: a structure is assumed for example, series compensation element is inserted in the forward path of the closed loop system) and the i.s.e., in response to some specific input, is minimized by the appropriate choice of the unknown parameters of the compensation elements. Or it may possibly be as simple a problem as setting some gain to that value which results in the lowest value of i.s.e. The procedure and method are illustrated by means of two simple examples.

Example 7.10

A simple system is represented by the block diagram of Figure 7.17. The problems to be solved are:

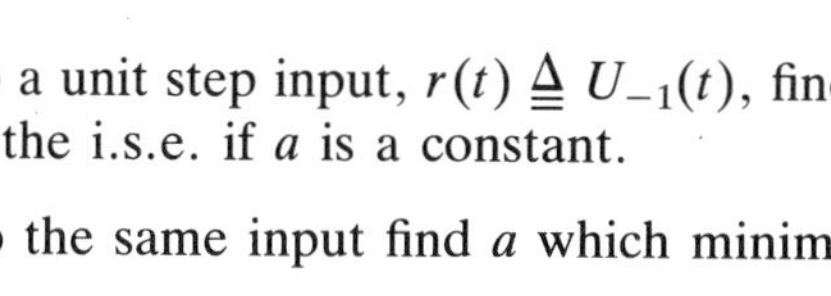

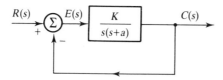

Figure 7.17 Block diagram for Example 7.10.

1. In response to a unit step input, $r(t) \triangleq U_{-1}(t)$, find the value of K which will minimize the i.s.e. if a is a constant.
2. In response to the same input find a which minimizes the i.s.e. if K is a constant.
3. If the forward transfer functions is re-expressed as $K/s(1 + sT)$, find the values of K and T which minimize the i.s.e. in response to a unit step input.

From Figure 7.17 it can be deduced that:

$$E(s) = \frac{s(s+a)}{s^2 + as + K} R(s)$$

and so for a unit step input $R(s) = 1/s$:

$$E(s) = \frac{s(s+a)}{(s^2 + as + K)} \quad \frac{1}{s}$$

Thus, for $E(s)$, referring to eq. (7.104): $c_0 = a$, $c_1 = 1$, $d_0 = K$, $d_1 = a$, $d_2 = 1$, and from Table 7.1:

$$I_2 = \frac{K + a^2}{2Ka}$$

Now, firstly:

$$\frac{\partial I_2}{\partial K} = \frac{2Ka - (K + a^2)\,2a}{4K^2a^2}$$

$$= \frac{-a}{2K^2} = 0$$

Therefore $K \rightarrow \infty$ yields minimum i.s.e. Secondly:

$$\frac{\partial I_2}{\partial \mathrm{a}} = 0 = \frac{1}{2K}\left\{\frac{a^2 - K}{a^2}\right\}$$

For minimum i.s.e. $a = \sqrt{K}$ and the optimum transfer function is:

$$\frac{C(s)}{R(s)} = \frac{K}{s2 + \sqrt{(Ks)} + K}$$

hence $\omega_n^2 = K$, giving:
$\zeta = 0.5$.

Thirdly:

$$E(s) = \frac{(Ts + 1)}{s^2T + s + K}$$

Thus: $c_0 = 1$, $c_1 = T$, $d_0 = K$, $d_1 = 1$, $d_2 = T$, and:

$$I_2 = \frac{T^2K + T}{2KT} = \frac{T}{2} + \frac{1}{2K}$$

$$\therefore \quad \frac{\partial I_2}{\partial K} = 0 = \frac{-2}{4K^2}$$

Therefore $K = \infty$ for minimum i.s.e. and $T = 0$.

Example 7.11

A unity feedback system has the closed loop transfer function:

$$\frac{C(s)}{R(s)} = \frac{1}{s^3 + a_2s^2 + a_1s + 1}$$

Find the values of a_1 and a_2 which minimize i.s.e. for a unit step input.

Now,

$$\frac{E(s)}{R(s)} = \frac{s^3 + a_2 s^2 + a_1 s}{(s^2 + a_2 s^2 + a_1 s + 1)}$$

Referring to eq. (7.104):

$$c(s) = \sum_{j=0}^{2} c_j s^j; \; d(s) = \sum_{k=0}^{3} d_k s^k$$

Therefore: $c_0 = a_1$, $c_1 = a_2$, $c_2 = 1$, $d_0 = 1$, $d_1 = a_1$, $d_2 = a_2$, and $d_3 = 1$. From Table 7.1:

$$I_3 = \frac{c_2^2 d_0 d_1 + (c_1^2 - 2c_0 c_2) d_0 d_3 + c_0^2 d_2 d_3}{2 d_1 d_3 (d_1 d_2 - d_0 d_3)}$$

$$\therefore \quad I_3 = \frac{a_1 + (a_2^2 - 2a_1) + a_1^2 a_2}{2(a_1 a_2 - 1)}$$

$$\therefore \quad I_3 = \frac{a_2^2 - a_1 + a_1^2 a_2}{2(a_1 a_2 - 1)}$$

and I_3 is a minimum with respect to a_1 when:

$$\frac{\partial I_3}{\partial a_1} = \frac{2a_2^3 - 2a_1^2 a_2^2 - 2 + 4a_1 a_2}{4(a_1 a_2 - 1)^2} = 0$$

$$\therefore \quad a_2^3 - a_1^2 a_2^2 - 1 + 2a_1 a_2 = 0$$

and I_3 is a minimum with respect to a_2 when:

$$\frac{\partial I_3}{\partial a_2} = \frac{-2a_1 a_2^2 + 4a_2}{4(a_1 a_2 - 1)^2} = 0$$

$$\therefore \quad 2 = a_1 a_2$$

$$\therefore \quad a_2^3 - 4 - 1 + 4 = 0$$

$$\therefore \quad a_2^3 = 1.0$$

$$a_2 = 1.0$$

$$\therefore \quad a_1 = 2.0$$

7.4.5 Lagrange Multipliers

Suppose that the variables, $x(t)$ and $u(t)$, are related by some differential equation, and let it be assumed that $u(t)$ is to be chosen to minimize:

$$J = \int_0^\infty x^2 \mathrm{d}t \tag{7.105}$$

subject to a constraint on $u(t)$, namely:

$$C = \int_0^{\infty} u^2 \mathrm{d}t \tag{7.106}$$

where C is some specified value which the integral on the r.h.s. must not exceed.

Suppose that $u(t)$ has been chosen, but does *not* satisfy eq. (7.106). For this particular $u(t)$, the difference between the right and the left sides of (7.106) is then defined as Z, i.e.:

$$Z = \int_0^{\infty} u^2 \mathrm{d}t - C \tag{7.107}$$

A new problem has now to be solved: to find that $u(t)$ which minimizes the scalar, K, where $K \triangleq J + \lambda Z$, i.e.:

$$K = \int_0^{\infty} x^2 \mathrm{d}t + \lambda \left\{ \int_0^{\infty} u^2 \mathrm{d}t - C \right\} \tag{7.108}$$

Note that in the new problem there is no constraint on $u(t)$. The control, $u(t)$, which minimizes eq. (7.108) is called the *optimal control function*, $u^{\mathrm{o}}(t)$. It depends upon the scalar, λ, i.e.:

$$u^{\mathrm{o}} = u^{\mathrm{o}}(\lambda, t) \tag{7.109}$$

With this special value of u, Z also depends upon λ. Thus,

$$Z(\lambda) = \int_0^{\infty} [u^{\mathrm{o}}(\lambda, t)]^2 \mathrm{d}t - C \tag{7.110}$$

If λ is chosen such that Z is zero, then

$$Z(\lambda) = 0 \tag{7.111}$$

and, of course,

$$K = J \tag{7.112}$$

Therefore, if K is minimized, J will be minimized too. Moreover, it will have been minimized subject to the constraint of eq. (7.106). Equation (7.106) is sometimes regarded as an 'energy' constraint, owing to its 'squared' nature.

Therefore, rather than finding some control, $u(t)$, from a class of control functions which satisfy the constraint, to minimize eq. (7.105), the equivalent problem which is solved is to choose $u(t)$ from the class of control functions which minimizes eq. (7.105), for some value of λ and which satisfies the constraint eq. (7.106).

The procedure which is used is illustrated in the three examples which follow.

Example 7.12

For the system represented by the block diagram in Figure 7.18 determine, for a unit step input, the values of K and T which minimize the i.s.e. *subject to the constraint* that

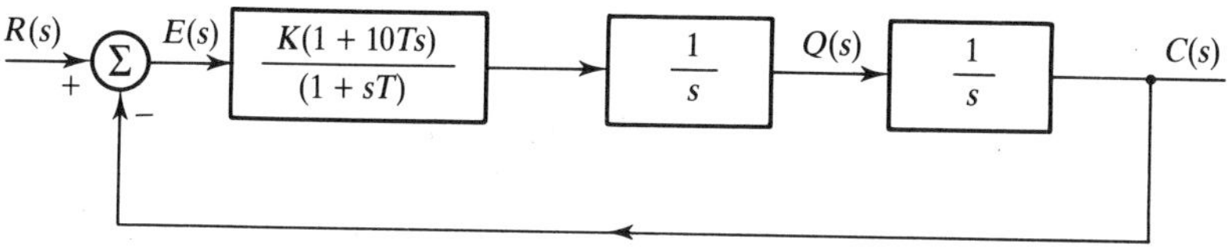

Figure 7.18 Block diagram for Example 7.12.

$$\int_0^{\infty} q^2 \mathrm{d}t \leq 100$$

i.e.:

$$J = \int_0^{\infty} (e^2 + \lambda q^2)\mathrm{d}t$$

For the specified input: $R(s) = 1/s$:

$$E(s) = \frac{s(Ts + 1)}{s^3T + s^2 + 10KTs + K}$$

$$Q(s) = \frac{K(10Ts + 1)}{s^3T + s^2 + 10KTs + K}$$

Therefore, for the error, e: $c_0 = 0$, $c_1 = 1$, $c_2 = T$, $d_0 = K$, $d_1 = 10KT$, $d_2 = 1$, and $d_3 = T$. Therefore:

$$I_{3_E} = \frac{10K^2T^3 + KT}{2KT(-KT + 10KT)} = \frac{10KT^2 + 1}{18KT}$$

and for the variable, q: $c_0 = K$, $c_1 = 10KT$, $c_2 = 0$, $d_0 = K$, $d_1 = 10KT$, $d_2 = 1$, $d_3 = T$. Hence,

$$I_{3_E} = \frac{K^2T(1 + 100KT^2)}{18K^2T^2} = \frac{1 + 100KT^2}{18T} = 100$$

$$\therefore \quad J = \frac{1}{18}\left\{\frac{1 + 10KT^2 + \lambda K + 100\lambda K^2T^2}{KT}\right\}$$

$$\therefore \quad \frac{\partial J}{\partial K} = \frac{1}{18}\left\{\frac{(KT)(10T^2 + \lambda + 200\lambda T^2K)}{K^2T^2} - \frac{(1 + 10KT^2 + \lambda K + 100\lambda K^2T^2)T}{K^2T2}\right\} = 0$$

i.e.:

$$10KT^3 + \lambda KT + 200\lambda K^2T^3 - T - 10KT^3 - \lambda KT - 100\lambda K^2T^3 = 0$$

$$\therefore \quad 100\lambda K^2T^2 = 1$$

$$\frac{\partial J}{\partial T} = 0$$

results in:

$$100\lambda K^2T^2 + 10KT^2 - 1 - \lambda K = 0$$

$$\therefore \quad \lambda = 10T^2$$

i.e.:

$$T = (\lambda/10)^{1/2}$$

hence:

$$K = \frac{1}{\sqrt{10\lambda}}$$

$$\therefore \quad 100 = \frac{1 + 100\dfrac{1}{\sqrt{10\lambda}} \cdot \dfrac{\lambda}{10}}{18\dfrac{\sqrt{\lambda}}{10}} = \frac{1 + \sqrt{10}}{1.8\sqrt{\lambda}}$$

$$\therefore \quad \lambda = \frac{10(1 + \sqrt{10})^2}{(180)^2}$$

$$= 0.0005347$$

$$\therefore \quad K = 591.4$$

$$T = 0.0073 \text{ s}$$

Example 7.13

For the system represented in Figure 7.19 choose K_1 and K_2 such that, in response to a unit step inupt, y_D, the performance index, J, is minimized.

$$J = \int_0^\infty \left\{25(y - y_D)^2 + u^2\right\} dt$$

$$\therefore \quad \frac{Y(s)}{Y_D(s)} = \frac{300}{s^4 + 184s^3 + 760.5s^2 + (162 + 300K_2)s + 300K_1}$$

If J is to be finite, there has to be zero steady state error in response to a unit step input. Hence K_1 must equal unity.

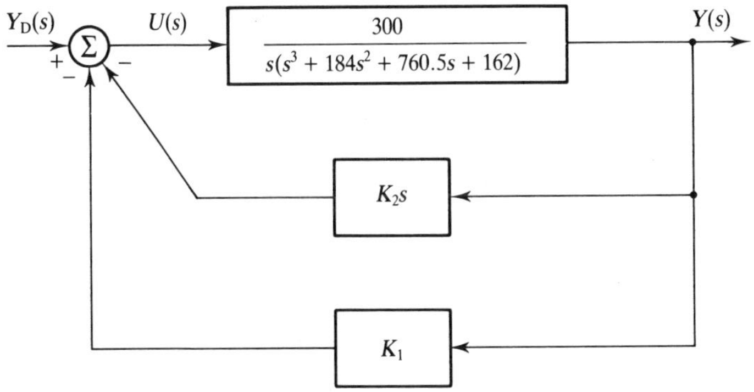

Figure 7.19 Block diagram for Example 7.13.

Now, from Figure 7.19:

$$E(s) \triangleq Y(s) - Y_D(s)$$

$$Y(s)/Y_D(s) \triangleq G_0(s)$$

$$\therefore \quad E(s) = -Y_D(s) + G_0(s)Y_D(s)$$

$$= Y_D(s)[-1 + G_0(s)]$$

$$= \frac{-s^2 + 184s^2 + 760.5s + 162 + 300K_2}{s^4 + 184s^3 + 760.5s^2 + 162s + 300K_2s + 300}$$

$$U(s) = \frac{Y(s)}{G_0(s)} = \frac{s^3 + 184s^2 + 760.5s + 162}{s^4 + 184s^3 + 760.5s^2 + (162 + 300K_2)s + 300}$$

$$\therefore \quad 25E(s)E(-s) + U(s)U(-s)$$

$$= \frac{26s^4 + 8.4 \times 10^5 s^4 + (2.76 \times 10^6 K_2 - 1.35 \times 10^7)s^2}{\text{denom }(s)\text{ denom }(-s)}$$

$$+ \frac{6.82 \times 10^5 + 2.43 \times 10^6 K_2 + 2.25 \times 10^6 K_2^2}{\text{denom }(s)\text{ denom }(-s)}$$

From Table 7.1:

$$J = 12.5\frac{(K_2^3 - 464K_2^2 - 392K_2 - 1305)}{(K_2^2 - 466K_2 - 139)}$$

$$\therefore \quad \frac{\partial J}{\partial K_2} = \frac{12.5(K_2^4 - 932K_2^3 + 21.7 \times 10^4 K_2^2 - 31.2 \times 10^4 K_2 - 55.35 \times 10^4)}{(K_2^2 - 466K_2 - 139)}$$

There are four solutions of K_2 in $\partial J/\partial K_2 = 0$. From a solution of the quartic, a positive real solution is found: $K_2 = 1.93$.

Note that the response of this system to a step input is very sluggish; it can be changed by increasing the weighting factor of 25 on the $(y - y_D)^2$ term.

Example 7.14

For the system represented in Figure 7.20 its bandwidth, BW, is defined as:

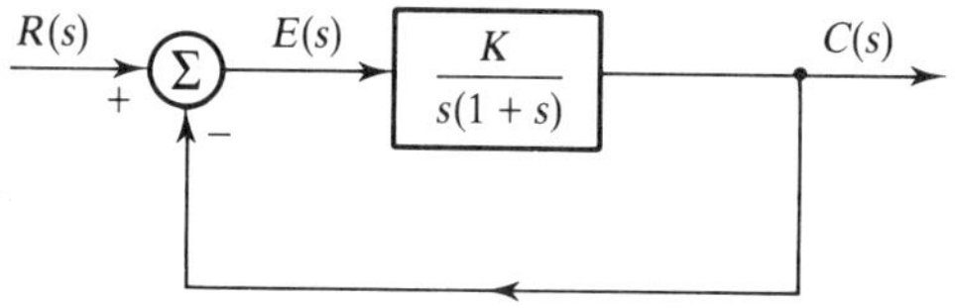

Figure 7.20 Block diagram for Example 7.14.

$$BW = \int_{-\infty}^{\infty} \left| \frac{C(j\omega)}{R(j\omega)} \right|^2 df$$

Determine the gain which will minimize the i.s.e., subject to the constraint that $BW \leq 1$.

Note that:

$$BW = \frac{1}{2\pi} \int_{-\infty}^{\infty} \left| \frac{C(j\omega)}{R(j\omega)} \right|^2 d\omega$$

$$\frac{C(s)}{R(s)} = \frac{K}{(s^2 + s + K)}$$

$$\frac{E(s)}{R(s)} = \frac{s(s+1)}{s^2 + s + K}$$

For i.s.e. $c_0 = 1$, $c_1 = 1$, $d_0 = K$, $d_1 = 1$, and $d_2 = 1$.

$$\therefore \quad \text{i.s.e.} = (K+1)/2K$$

For BW: $c_0 = K$, $c_1 = 0$, $d_0 = K$, $d_1 = 1$, and $d_2 = 1$.

$$BW = K^2/2K = K/2 = 1$$

$$\therefore \quad K = 2$$

$$\therefore \quad J = \frac{K+1}{2K} + \frac{\lambda K}{2}$$

$$\frac{\partial J}{\partial K} = \frac{(2K)(2\lambda K + 1) - (\lambda K^2 + K + 1)2}{4K^2}$$

$$4\lambda K^2 + 2K + 2\lambda K^2 - 2K - 2 = 0$$

$$\therefore \quad 2\lambda K^2 = 2$$

$$\therefore \quad \lambda = 1/4$$

The required gain is 2.0.

7.5 CONCLUSIONS

The chapter introduces the AFCS as a control problem and shows that, with linear feedback control, it is never possible to satisfy simultaneously the requirements for good stability, good tracking performance and good disturbance or noise rejection. The use of feedforward was discussed and the equations for a generalized AFCS, which allowed the linear feedback control to contain dynamic elements, were developed.

The chapter concentrates on the use of the conventional control methods, such as pole placement, model-following, root locus and frequency response, to design AFCSs which are essentially s.i.s.o., linear and time-invariant. This work is extended by considering parameter optimization techniques to achieve feedback controllers which optimize a performance index, usually the integral of error squared and subject to constraints on the control surface, some rate of change of a motion variable, or the bandwidth of the closed loop system. These methods are illustrated by a number of examples.

7.6 EXERCISES

7.1 Design a closed loop system using linear state variable feedback for the open loop system shown in Figure 7.21. The desired dominant complex poles of the closed loop system must have a damping ratio of not less than 0.45. And in response to a unit step input the peak overshoot of the response of the closed loop system must not exceed 20 per cent and must not occur later than 0.15 s after the step has been applied. The complete response must have settled in 0.4 s.

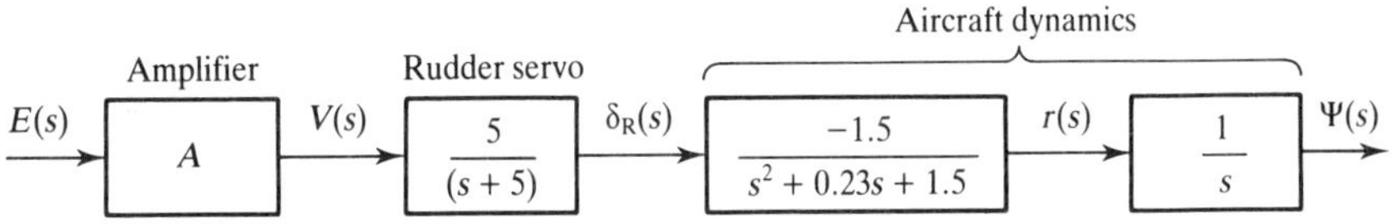

Figure 7.21 Open loop system for Exercise 7.1.

(a) Draw a root locus diagram for the aircraft system of Figure 7.21.
(b) If $A = 0.04$ calculate the values of the poles of the system with positive unity feedback.
(c) Use a pole placement method to obtain a feedback control law which will result in the required closed loop response.

7.2 The short period dynamics of an aircraft can be represented by the equations:

$$\dot{\alpha} = Z_{\alpha}\alpha + q + Z_{\delta_E}\delta_E$$

$$\dot{q} = M_{\alpha}\alpha + M_{\dot{\alpha}}\dot{\alpha} + M_q q + M_{\delta_E}\delta_E$$

(a) Plot the root locus diagram for the transfer function $q(s)/\delta_E(s)$ for the aircraft BRAVO-2.

(b) Repeat part (a) for the transfer function $\alpha(s)/\delta_E(s)$.
(c) Plot the corresponding Bode diagrams for both transfer functions.
(d) Generate the corresponding Nichols diagrams.
(e) Calculate the gain and phase margins for each transfer function.

7.3 Suppose that the elevator of the aircraft BRAVO is driven by an actuator which is characterized by the first order differential equation:

$$\dot{\delta}_E = -7.0\delta_E + 7.0\delta_{E_c}$$

where δ_{E_c} represents the commanded deflection. Determine what effect the actuator dynamics will have on the response of BRAVO-2 (see Exercise 7.2) to a commanded step of δ_E of $-2.0°$.

7.4 For the aircraft DELTA-3 plot the Nyquist diagram corresponding to the transfer function $\lambda(s)/\delta_R(s)$, where λ denotes the aircraft's heading, and δ_R the rudder deflection.

7.5 Plot the Nichols diagram corresponding to the transfer function $\gamma(s)/\delta_E(s)$ for GOLF-2. Plot its Bode diagram for $\theta(s)/\delta_E(s)$. Hence plot the Nyquist diagram for the transfer function $\gamma(s)/\theta(s)$. Is this diagram valid?

7.6 The lateral dynamics of a large cargo aircraft, DELTA, for flight condition 3, are augmented by the addition of the dynamics associated with the control surface actuators and with a washout filter which operates on the yaw rate. The transfer functions of these elements are:

$$\frac{\delta_A(s)}{\delta_{A_c}(s)} = \frac{20}{s + 20}$$

$$\frac{\delta_R(s)}{\delta_{R_c}(s)} = \frac{4}{s + 4}$$

$$\frac{e_{wo}(s)}{r(s)} = \frac{s}{s + 1}$$

The state vector is given by:

$$\mathbf{x}' = [\beta \; p \; r \; \phi \; e_{wo} \; \delta_A \; \delta_R]$$

and the control vector by:

$$\mathbf{u}' = [\delta_A \; \delta_R]$$

The output vector is defined as:

$$\mathbf{y}' = [\beta \; p \; e_{wo} \; \phi]$$

Use an eigenvalue assignment technique to obtain a feedback control law which will result in the closed loop system having the following eigenvalues:

$$\lambda_{dir_{1,2}} = -1.5 \pm j1.5$$

$$\lambda_{lat_{1,2}} = -2.0 \pm j1.0$$

7.7 A simple yaw damper is represented by the block diagram of Figure 7.22. The required transfer function $r(s)/\delta_R(s)$ can be found by using the two degrees of freedom approximation discussed in Section 3.10 of Chapter 3 and the stability derivatives corresponding to GOLF-4. Determine an appropriate value of K_c which will result in the integral of error squared being minimized, subject to the constraint $\delta_R \leq 15°$, for a unit step command.

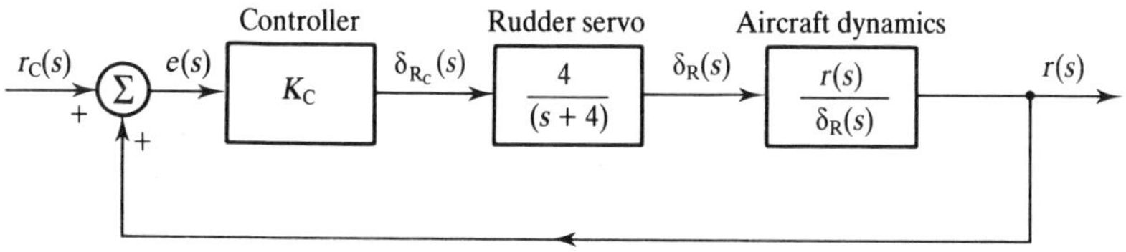

Figure 7.22 Yaw damper system for Exercise 7.7.

7.8 The block diagram of a roll attitude control system for CHARLIE-2 is shown in Figure 7.23. The gain, K_c, of the controller is to be found such that the integral of error squared is minimized subject to the constraint $\Delta\omega \leq 4.0$ where the system bandwidth $\Delta\omega$ is defined as:

$$\Delta\omega \triangleq \frac{1}{2\pi}\int_{-\infty}^{\infty}\left|\frac{\phi(j\omega)}{\phi_{comm}(j\omega)}\right|^2 d\omega$$

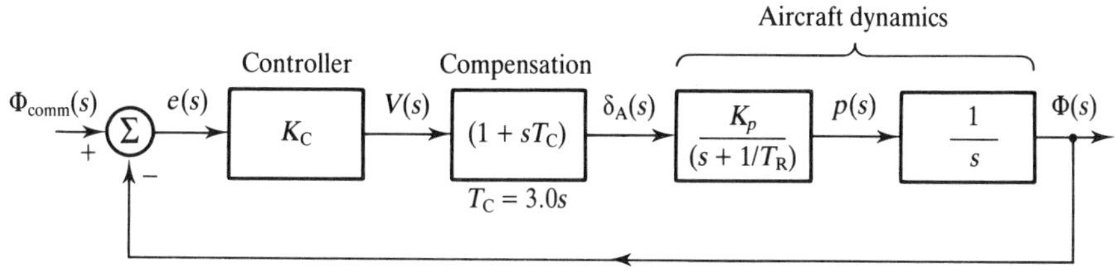

Figure 7.23 Roll attitude control system for Exercise 7.8.

7.9 The block diagram of a flight control system which is used to control the pitch rate of an aircraft is shown in Figure 9.10(b) in Chapter 9. The transfer function of the compensation network used with aircraft FOXTROT-3 is known to be:

$$G_c(s) = \frac{1 + s}{1 + 0.2s}$$

and the sensitivity, K_q, of the rate gyro is unity, and $K_{servo} = 2.0$.

(a) Show that the closed loop pitch rate control system can be represented by:

$$\dot{\mathbf{z}} = K\mathbf{z} + \Lambda q_{comm}$$

where

$$\mathbf{z}' \triangleq [\mathbf{x}\ \mathbf{x}_c]$$

(b) Evaluate the matrices K and Λ.

7.10 The rate of change of height in response to a change in the collective deflection of a hovering helicopter can easily be shown (see Chapter 13) to be governed by a transfer function:

$$\frac{sh(s)}{\delta_{\theta_0}(s)} = \frac{Z_{\delta_{\theta_0}}}{(s - Z_w)}$$

For a small helicopter with a single main rotor the values of the stability derivatives have been found to be:

$$Z_{\delta_{\theta_0}} = 4.0 \text{ and } Z_w = 1.4$$

When a simple height control system with a proportional controller, with a value $K = 6.0$, and with unity feedback is used it is found that the dynamic response of the closed loop system is unacceptable.

(a) Determine a feedback control law which will ensure that at hover the height control system will have a closed loop transfer function:

$$\frac{h(s)}{h_{\text{comm}}(s)} = \frac{36}{s^2 + 12s + 36}$$

(b) Compare the natural frequency and damping ratio of this system with the values which resulted with the simple height control system.

7.7 NOTE

1. $y = \max(a, b)$ means that y will take either the value a or b, whichever is the larger.

7.8 REFERENCES

BOWER, J.L. and P.M. SCHULTHEISS. 1958. *Introduction to the Design of Servomechanisms*. New York: Wiley.

d'AZZO, J.J. and C.H. HOUPIS. 1978. *Linear Control System Analysis and Design*. New York: McGraw-Hill.

ERZBERGER, H. 1968. On the use of algebraic methods in the analysis and design of model-following control systems. NASA TN-D4663, July.

FULLER, A.T. 1967. The replacement of saturation constraints with energy constraints in control optimization theory. *Int. J. Control*. 6(3): 201–27.

KUO, B.C. 1982. *Automatic Control Systems*. Englewood Cliffs, NJ: Prentice Hall.

MARKLAND, C.A. 1970. Optimal model-following control systems synthesis techniques. *Proc. IEE*. 117(3): 623–7.

MUNRO, N. 1973. Pole assignment. *Proc. IEE*. 120: 549–54.

MUNRO, N. and A.I.G. VARDULAKIS. 1973. Pole shifting using output feedback. *Int. J. Cont.* 18:1267–73.

NEWTON, G.C., L.A. GOULD and J.F. KAISER. 1957. *Analytical Design of Linear Feedback Controls*. New York: Wiley.

PATEL, R.V. 1974. Pole assignment by means of unrestricted rank output feedback. *Proc. IEE*. 121: 874–8.

SHAPIRO, E.Y., A.N. ANDRY and J.C. CHUNG. 1981. Pole-placement with output feedback. *J. Guid. Cont.* 4(4): 441–2.

TAKAHASHI, Y., M.J. RABINS and D.M. AUSLANDER. 1970. *Control and Dynamic Systems.* Reading, Mass.: Addison Wesley.

TYLER, J.S. 1968. The characteristics of model-following systems as synthesized by optimal control. *Trans IEEE.* AC-9: 485–98.

WIDODO, R.J. 1972. Design of optimal control systems with prescribed closed-loop poles. *Elec. Lett.* 8(13): 339–40.

WONHAM, W.M. 1967. On pole assignment in multi-input, controllable linear systems. *Trans IEEE.* AC-12: 660–5.

8

Control System Design Methods II

8.1 INTRODUCTION

Whenever a set of specifications has been laid down for the dynamic behaviour of an aircraft, and when those specifications cannot be met, an AFCS problem exists. If the required dynamic performance has to be achieved then additional equipment must be used in conjunction with the basic aircraft, in all but the most trivial cases. Those conventional control techniques, outlined in Chapter 7, all depend upon an interpretation of the system's dynamic response, in terms of such parameters as settling time, frequency of oscillation of the transient, value of the peak overshoot, time-to-half amplitude, gain margin, phase margin, and so on. Inevitably, the design which results from using such methods is obtained as a consequence of some compromise, and it may not be unique. By using the modern theory of optimal control, a specified performance criterion is met exactly and the corresponding control design is unique. How this unique solution may be found, and how the performance criterion can be chosen to reflect the handling and flying qualities criteria, are the subjects of this chapter.

8.2 THE MEANING OF OPTIMAL CONTROL

An optimal control system is one which provides the best possible performance from its class when it responds to some particular input. To judge whether the system's performance is optimal requires some means by which the quality of the performance can be measured, and for this it is customary to adopt an integral of the form:

$$J = \int_{t_0}^{T} \mathscr{L}\{\mathbf{x}, \mathbf{u}, t\}\mathrm{d}t \tag{8.1}$$

A system is normally considered to have been optimized if some control input, $\mathbf{u}^{\circ}$, has been used such that the value of J is least over the period from t_0, when the response is considered to have started, to T, when the response ceases. (In some cases J may be chosen so that it can be maximized over the chosen period: for example, this could be achieved by choosing the cost functional, $\mathscr{L}\{\,.\,\}$, in eq. (8.1) to be negative). Equation (8.1) is not the only type of performance index of use in aeronautical studies, of course, but it is the most common. $\mathscr{L}\{\mathbf{x}, \mathbf{u}, t\}$ is known as the cost, or pay-off, functional: it represents the cost of a system's having been at a particular point in the state space, corresponding to the particular control inputs, for the entire period of time $(T - t_0)$. Posing an optimal control problem in this way has considerable merit, because it includes in its statement most of the important problems relating to flight control, namely stability, the dynamic response of the closed loop system, and the determination of the required control law.[1] One of the chief problems in setting up an optimal control problem is the particular choice of performance index.

The significance of performance indices has been lucidly explained by Fuller (1959). His approach is used in Section 7.4 of Chapter 7. When an optimal problem involves control limits, such as limits on the permitted deflection of a control surface, or a limit on the rate of change of the position of a control surface actuator, it is often convenient to replace, say, the hard constraint, $|\delta_E| \leq 10°$ (for example) by an equivalent constraint on the energy being expended in the control activity. The replacement performance index then becomes:

$$J = \int_{t_0}^{T} (\mathbf{e}^2 + \lambda \mathbf{u}^2)\mathrm{d}t \tag{8.2}$$

where the error vector, $\mathbf{e}$, is defined as the difference between the actual state vector and the commanded value:

$$\mathbf{e} \triangleq (\mathbf{x} - \mathbf{x}_{\text{comm}}) \tag{8.3}$$

and λ is a Lagrange multiplier. If a different value of weighting is required on each of the elements of the error vector, a square matrix, denoted here as Q, is used to ensure that J is non-negative for all values of $\mathbf{e}$, but is zero when $\mathbf{x}$ and $\mathbf{x}_{\text{comm}}$ are equal.

It is important sometimes to place different weighting penalties on the cost of using each control input, u_j. In such a case, a square matrix, G, is associated with the control vector $\mathbf{u}$ and is used in the performance index, so that eq. (8.2) becomes:

$$J = \int_{t_0}^{T} (\mathbf{e}'Q\mathbf{e} + \mathbf{u}'G\mathbf{u})\mathrm{d}t \tag{8.4}$$

For each choice of Q and G, minimization of J corresponds to a unique choice of $\mathbf{u}(t)$.

In AFCS problems, the designer is usually concerned with controlling the motion of an aircraft about its trimmed flight state, $\mathbf{x}_{\text{comm}}$. Therefore, the equilibrium flight condition is taken, without any loss of accuracy, as the origin of the state space of the aircraft's dynamics, and the 'error' variables are identical to the state variables, i.e. eq. (8.4) can be written as:

$$J = \tfrac{1}{2}\int_{t_0}^{T} (\mathbf{x}'Q\mathbf{x} + \mathbf{u}'G\mathbf{u})\mathrm{d}t \tag{8.5}$$

(The multiplying factor, $\frac{1}{2}$, has been included merely for later analytical convenience.) If it is of particular importance to some design that the state vector should be as close as possible to the trimmed state, at the end of the interval, a heavy penalty is placed upon any finite values of the state variables which exist at T, by adding a special weighting term to the performance index. Thus:

$$J = \tfrac{1}{2}\mathbf{x}'(T)S\mathbf{x}(T) + \tfrac{1}{2}\int_{t_0}^{T} (\mathbf{x}'Qx + \mathbf{u}'G\mathbf{u})\mathrm{d}t \tag{8.6}$$

It has been assumed that Q, G and S are constant matrices: Q and G need not be, for the theory, yet to be developed, will still be valid for $Q(t)$ and $G(t)$. Most often, the problem is solved for a semi-infinite interval, i.e.:

$$J = \tfrac{1}{2}\mathbf{x}'(\infty)S\mathbf{x}(\infty) + \tfrac{1}{2}\int_{0}^{T} (\mathbf{x}'Q\mathbf{x} + \mathbf{u}'G\mathbf{u})\mathrm{d}t \tag{8.7}$$

If an optimal control can be found, then, by definition, it must work such that $\mathbf{x}(\infty)$ is zero. Consequently:

$$J = \tfrac{1}{2}\int_{0}^{\infty} (\mathbf{x}'Q\mathbf{x} + \mathbf{u}'G\mathbf{u})\mathrm{d}t \tag{8.8}$$

When the performance index of eq. (8.8) is minimized by choosing $\mathbf{u}$ subject to the constraint imposed by the aircraft's dynamic equation, namely

$$\dot{\mathbf{x}} = A\mathbf{x} + B\mathbf{u} \tag{8.9}$$

the problem is referred to in the technical literature as the linear quadratic problem (LQP). There are two great advantages to be gained from solving the LQP. Firstly, the control is in the form of a linear, constant feedback law, namely $\mathbf{u}^{\circ} = K\mathbf{x}$, and secondly, subject to a few conditions on the choice of the matrices Q and G, and some conditions relating to the aircraft dynamics (which are easily met in practice), the resulting feedback control law will ensure that the closed loop system is stable.

Example 8.1

This example is based upon Anderson and Moore (1971). Let $\dot{\mathbf{x}} = A\mathbf{x} + B\mathbf{u}$ where

$$A = \begin{bmatrix} 1 & 0 \\ 1 & 10 \end{bmatrix} \text{ and } B = \begin{bmatrix} 0 \\ 1 \end{bmatrix} \text{ and } \mathbf{x}(0) = \begin{bmatrix} 2 \\ 0 \end{bmatrix}$$

A block diagram, representing the state equation, is shown in Figure 8.1. If

$$J = \tfrac{1}{2}\int_{0}^{\infty} \{x_1^2 + x_2^2 + u^2\}\mathrm{d}t$$

then:

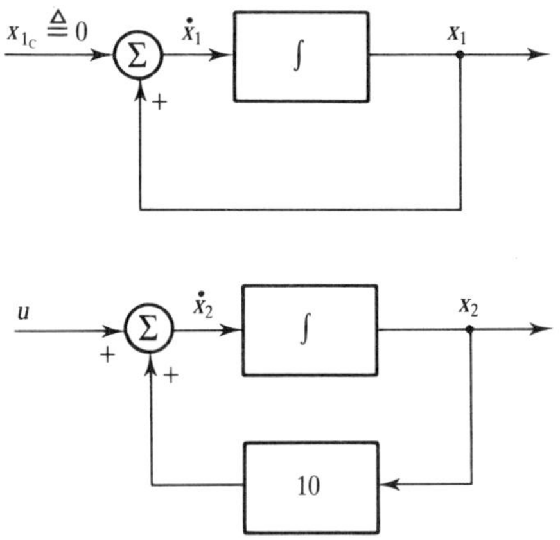

Figure 8.1 Simple unstable and uncontrollable system.

$$J = \tfrac{1}{2}\int_0^{\infty} (\mathbf{x}'Q\mathbf{x} + \mathbf{u}'G\mathbf{u})\mathrm{d}t$$

when:

$$Q = \begin{bmatrix} 1 & 0 \\ 0 & 1 \end{bmatrix} \text{ and } G = 1.0$$

However:

$$x_1(t) = x_1(0)e^t = 2\mathrm{e}^t$$
$$x_1^2 = 4\mathrm{e}^{2t}$$

thus:

$$J = \tfrac{1}{2}\int_0^{\infty} \{4\mathrm{e}^{2t} + x_2^2 + u^2\}\mathrm{d}t$$

But a choice of u of zero will minimize the performance index, since, if u is zero, there can be no value for x_2, $x_2(0)$ being zero. Therefore,

$$J_{\text{min}} = \tfrac{1}{2}\int_0^{\infty} 4\mathrm{e}^{2t}\mathrm{d}t = \infty$$

There are three reasons why the performance index is infinite:

1. The state variable x_1 is unaffected by the control u; there is no means, therefore, whereby x_1 can be altered.
2. The uncontrollable part of the dynamics is also unstable, i.e. $x_1 = 2\mathrm{e}^t$.
3. The unstable and uncontrollable part of the dynamics is included in the integrand and is integrated over the whole range of the integral, resulting in the value of infinity.

When a performance index has a finite time interval its value is always finite; when the interval is infinite, that may not be so.

8.3 CONTROLLABILITY, OBSERVABILITY AND STABILIZABILITY

8.3.1 Controllability

In Example 8.1 the state variable x_1 could not be altered by any control action. This is a condition of the state variable's being uncontrollable. The property of controllability is an important one: it must be checked and confirmed before attempting to find an optimal control by any of the methods to be described. It is important, however, for the reader to understand that controllability (and observability) are properties of the state space representation of the system dynamics, and not of the system (the aircraft) itself. This follows from the fact, which is pointed out in Section 3.3 of Chapter 3, that a state space representation of system dynamics is not unique.

Controllability is a property relating the effects of the control inputs to the changes in the state variables of some mathematical representation of the aircraft dynamics. The model of the aircraft dynamics is said to be completely controllable if any and only if all initial state variables, namely $x_i(0)$, can be transferred in finite time, by the application of some control function, $\mathbf{u}(t)$, to any final state, $\mathbf{x}(T)$. To be completely controllable, the structure of the mathematical model of the aircraft dynamics must be such that $\mathbf{u}$ can affect all the state variables. A number of excellent texts (Zadeh and Desoer, 1963; Desoer, 1970; Porter, 1966; Brockett, 1970; Kwakernaak and Sivan, 1972; Maybeck, 1979) provide comprehensive treatments of the theory, which provides the following result for a system described by eq. (8.9).

The system represented by eq. (8.9) is completely controllable if and only if the range space of the $(n \times mn)$ matrix W given by eq. (8.10), is R^n, i.e. if the rank of W is n, or equivalently, if W has n linearly independent columns. Each column of W then represents a vector in state space along which control is possible. But since the columns of W form a basis of R^n, it is therefore possible to control in all R^n. The matrix W is referred to as the controllability matrix and is given by:

$$W \triangleq [B:AB:A^2B: \ldots :A^{n-1}B] \tag{8.10}$$

Complete controllability is a sufficient condition for closed loop stability.

For a single-input system such as the longitudinal dynamics of an aircraft controlled by means of the elevator deflection, W becomes a square matrix, of order $(n \times n)$. In that case, the aircraft longitudinal dynamics are completely controllable if and only if W is non-singular, that is, if its determinant is non-zero. This means that $[sI - A]^{-1}B$ must have no pole-zero cancellations.

In the AFCS literature it is often said that for a completely controllable aircraft the pair $\{A, B\}$ is completely controllable. Sometimes, only some of the state variables are controllable, for example, some bending modes may not be directly controllable. In such situations it is convenient to express the state variable equation in controllability canonical form:

$$\dot{\hat{\mathbf{x}}} = \begin{bmatrix} \hat{A}_{11} & \hat{A}_{12} \\ 0 & \hat{A}_{22} \end{bmatrix} \hat{\mathbf{x}} + \begin{bmatrix} B_1 \\ 0 \end{bmatrix} \mathbf{u} \tag{8.11}$$

where:

$$\mathbf{x} \triangleq \begin{bmatrix} \mathbf{x}_1 \\ \mathbf{x}_2 \end{bmatrix}$$

$\mathbf{x}_1$ has dimension, say, q; therefore $\mathbf{x}_2$ has dimension $(n - q)$.

A_{11} is a matrix of order $(q \times q)$, and the pair $\{A_{11}, B\}$ is completely controllable. The eigenvalues of A_{11} are commonly referred to as the controllable poles of the system, while those of A_{22} are termed the uncontrollable poles.

A natural definition for the uncontrollable subspace of the system is that space which is spanned by the eigenvectors corresponding to the uncontrollable poles of the system.

The controllability canonical form is not unique.

8.3.2 Stabilizability

For AFCSs it is of fundamental importance that, if an aircraft is to be completely controlled, any unstable subspace must lie in a controllable subspace.

A system represented by eq. (8.9) is regarded as stabilizable if any vector, $\mathbf{x}$, contained in its unstable subspace is also contained in its controllable subspace.

Any asymptotically stable system is obviously stabilizable, and any completely controllable system must be stabilizable. Therefore, the pair (A, B) is stablizable when eq. (8.9) is stabilizable. If the controllability canonical form is considered, in which the pair $\{A_{11}, B\}$ is completely controllable, then eq. (8.9) is said to be stabilizable if and only if the matrix A_{22} is asymptotically stable, i.e. all the real parts of its eigenvalues are negative and finite.

8.3.3 Reconstructibility and Observability

An important property of a linear system is whether, from a knowledge of the output from the system, the behaviour of the state of the system can be determined. Suppose the output equation related to the system represented by eq. (8.9) is given by:

$$\mathbf{y} = C\mathbf{x} \tag{8.13}$$

where $\mathbf{y} \in R^p$, then the system will be completely reconstructible if and only if the row vectors of the reconstructibility matrix $\bar{R}$, order $(n \times np)$, spans the space R^n, that is, $\bar{R}$ has rank n.

$$\bar{\mathrm{R}} = \begin{bmatrix} C \\ CA \\ CA^2 \\ \cdot \\ \cdot \\ \cdot \\ CA^{n-1} \end{bmatrix} \tag{8.14}$$

Equation (8.14) is the transpose of the observability matrix, namely:

$$V = \bar{R}' = [C' : A'C' : (A')^2 C' : \ldots : (A')n^{-1} C'] \tag{8.15}$$

Observability means that it is possible to determine the state vector $\mathbf{x}(0)$, at time $t = 0$, from the output variables which (obviously) occur in the future. In AFCSs only output signals from the past are available; it is more natural in AFCS work to adopt the complementary idea of reconstructibility which is concerned with the problem of determining the present state of the aircraft from past observations. For linear time-invariant systems, such as eqs (8.9) and (8.13), complete reconstructibility implies and is, in turn, implied by, complete observability.

For systems in which only a single output is considered, $\bar{R}$ and V are square matrices, of order $(n \times n)$. The conditions for reconstructibility and observability simply require that $\bar{R}$ and V be non-singular, which is equivalent to the condition that $C[sI - A]'$ has no pole-zero cancellations.

8.3.4 Detectability

The reconstructible canonical form of eqs (8.9) and (8.13) is given by:

$$\dot{\hat{\mathbf{x}}} = \begin{bmatrix} \hat{A}_{11} & 0 \\ \hat{A}_{21} & \hat{A}_{22} \end{bmatrix} \hat{\mathbf{x}} + \begin{bmatrix} \hat{B}_1 \\ \hat{B}_2 \end{bmatrix} \mathbf{u} \tag{8.16}$$

$$\mathbf{y} = [\hat{C} \;\; 0]\hat{\mathbf{x}} \tag{8.17}$$

The matrix, $\hat{A}_{11}$, is of order $q \times q$ and the pair $\{\hat{A}_{11}, \hat{C}_1\}$ is completely reconstructible. When an unreconstructible subspace is contained in the stable subspace of a system it is said to be detectable. Any asymptotically stable system is detectable, as is any completely reconstructible system. For a system expressed in the reconstructible canonical form, when $\{\hat{A}_{11}, \hat{C}\}$ is completely reconstructible, the system will be detectable if and only if $\hat{A}_{22}$ is asymptotically stable.

Example 8.2

A linear system has the state equation:

$$\dot{\mathbf{x}} = \begin{bmatrix} 0 & 1 & 0 \\ 5 & 0 & 2 \\ -1.95 & 0 & -2 \end{bmatrix} \mathbf{x} + \begin{bmatrix} 0 \\ 0 \\ 0.473 \end{bmatrix} u$$

Its output equation is:

$$y = [-2 \ 1 \ 0]\mathbf{x}$$

The eigenvalues of the system are: $\lambda_1 = -1.0167$, $\lambda_2 = 2.0066$, $\lambda_3 = -2.9899$. Hence, the system is unstable, although it is controllable and observable. It can be checked by finding an orthogonal, similarity transformation, T, such that:

$$AA = TAT^{-1} \qquad BB = TB$$

The pair (AA, BB) form a quasi-lower triangular form:

$$\begin{bmatrix} Z & 0 & 0 & 0 \\ x & E_3 & 0 & 0 \\ x & x & E_2 & 0 \\ x & x & x & E_1 \end{bmatrix}$$

The submatrix, Z, if it exists, is a square matrix (followed by all zeros) which contains the uncontrollable modes of the system. By using this approach, the controllability indices can be determined and their sum equals the number of controllable modes. For the example:

$$T = \begin{bmatrix} 1 & 0 & 0 \\ 0 & -1 & 0 \\ 0 & 0 & -1 \end{bmatrix}$$

$$\therefore \quad BB = \begin{bmatrix} 0 \\ 0 \\ -0.473 \end{bmatrix}$$

$$AA = \begin{bmatrix} 0 & -1 & 0 \\ -5 & 0 & 2 \\ 1.95 & 0 & -2 \end{bmatrix}$$

The sum of the controllability indices is 3, hence the system is controllable.

For the observability check

$$AA = TAT^{-1}$$

$$CC = CT^{-1}$$

For the example:

$$T = \begin{bmatrix} 0.4364 & 0.8729 & -0.2182 \\ -0.0976 & -0.1952 & -0.9759 \\ -0.8944 & 0.4472 & 0 \end{bmatrix}$$

Hence:

$$AA = \begin{bmatrix} 1.9952 & -2.6822 & -4.089 \\ -0.0213 & -1.5952 & -0.8729 \\ 0 & -0.9165 & -2.4 \end{bmatrix}$$

$$CC = [0 \;\; 0 \;\; 2.2361]$$

The sum of the observability indices is 3, therefore the system is observable.

However, observability and controllability are fragile properties and small changes is a system's parameters can result in quite significant changes.

The transfer function relating to the completely controllable and observable system can be shown to be:

$$G(s) = \frac{(0.946s - 1.892)}{(s^3 + 2s^2 - 5s - 6.1)}$$

If the element a_{31} of the coefficient matrix decreases from -1.95 to -2.0 the eigenvalues of the system do not change very greatly, being $\lambda_1 = -1.0$, $\lambda_2 = 2.0$, $\lambda_3 = -3.0$.

The same orthogonal similarity transformation, T, results and the system remains completely controllable, as before. However, for observability:

$$T = \begin{bmatrix} -0.4364 & -0.8729 & 0.2182 \\ -0.0976 & -0.1952 & -0.9759 \\ -0.8944 & 0.4472 & 0 \end{bmatrix}$$

$$\begin{bmatrix} 2 & 2.6833 & 4.0988 \\ 0 & -1.6 & -0.9165 \\ 0 & -0.9165 & -2.4 \end{bmatrix}$$

$$CC = [0 \;\; 0 \;\; 2.2361]$$

The sum of the observability indices is 2 and the mode associated with the unstable eigenvalue, 2, is unobservable. The transfer function corresponding to this case is:

$$G(s) \equiv \frac{0.946}{(s^2 + 4s + 3)}$$

The transfer function does not contain the unstable mode corresponding to the eigenvalue equal to 2.0.

Example 8.3

Consider an object of unit mass in a circular orbit, with an angular velocity of 1 revolution per day. The object has been provided with two thruster jets which can be controlled such that a thrust force, u_1, can be exerted in the radial direction, and another force, u_2, can be exerted tangentially. The radius of orbit is constant and may be taken as unity without loss of generality. The equations of motion corresponding to the situation represented in Figure 8.2 are:

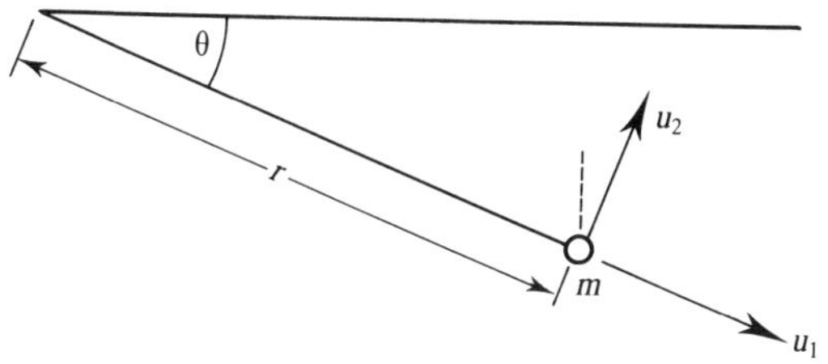

Figure 8.2 Object in orbit.

$$\ddot{r} = r\dot{\theta}^2 - \frac{\omega^2}{r^2} + u_1$$

$$\dot{\theta} = -\frac{2\ddot{\theta}r}{r} + \frac{1}{r}u_2$$

$$r(t) = 1.0 \text{ (by definition)}$$

$$\theta(t) = \omega t$$

Let $x_1 = r - 1$, $x_2 = \dot{r}$, $x_3 = \theta - \omega t$, $x_4 = \dot{\theta} - \omega$. Then:

$$\begin{bmatrix} \dot{x}_1 \\ \dot{x}_2 \\ \dot{x}_3 \\ \dot{x}_4 \end{bmatrix} = \begin{bmatrix} 0 & 1 & 0 & 0 \\ 3\omega^2 & 0 & 0 & 2\omega \\ 0 & 0 & 0 & 1 \\ 0 & -2\omega & 0 & 0 \end{bmatrix} \begin{bmatrix} x_1 \\ x_2 \\ x_3 \\ x_4 \end{bmatrix} + \begin{bmatrix} 0 & 0 \\ 1 & 0 \\ 0 & 0 \\ 0 & 1 \end{bmatrix} u$$

then:

$$3\omega^2 = 1.5865 \times 10^{-8} \text{ since } \omega = 2\pi \text{ rad per day}$$

$$2\omega = 1.4544 \times 10^{-4} \text{ since } \omega = 0.00007272 \text{ rad s}^{-1}$$

Using A and B it is relatively easy to show that since the rank of

$$W = [B{:}AB{:}A^2B{:}A^3B]$$

is 4, the system is completely controllable. If the tangential thrust rocket is lost, $u_2 = 0$ and B becomes

$$B|_{u_2=0} = \begin{bmatrix} 0 \\ 1 \\ 0 \\ 0 \end{bmatrix}$$

and then the rank of W can be shown to be only 3, i.e. the system is no longer controllable. If u_1 is lost then:

$$B|_{u_1=0} = \begin{bmatrix} 0 \\ 0 \\ 0 \\ 1 \end{bmatrix}$$

but the rank remains at four and the system can be controlled. Hence, it is essential to have available for control at all times tangential thrust.

8.4 THEORY OF THE LINEAR QUADRATIC PROBLEM

The problem is to determine an optimal control, **u**, which will minimize the performance index, J, given by:

$$J = \tfrac{1}{2}\int_0^\infty \{\mathbf{x}'Q\mathbf{x} + \mathbf{u}'G\mathbf{u}\}dt \tag{8.18}$$

and will control the aircraft whose dynamics are described by eq. (8.9), i.e.

$$\dot{\mathbf{x}} = A\mathbf{x} + B\mathbf{u} \tag{8.19}$$

where $\mathbf{x} \in R^n$ and $\mathbf{u} \in R^m$. The matrices A and Q are of order $(n \times n)$, B is of order $n \times m$, and G is of order $(m \times m)$.

The Hamiltonian associated with this system is given by:

$$H = \tfrac{1}{2}\mathbf{x}'Q\mathbf{x} + \tfrac{1}{2}\mathbf{u}'G\mathbf{u} + \boldsymbol{\Psi}'(A\mathbf{x} + B\mathbf{u}) \tag{8.20}$$

$\boldsymbol{\Psi}$ is the co-state vector, defined by:

$$\dot{\boldsymbol{\Psi}} = -\frac{\partial H}{\partial \mathbf{x}} \tag{8.21}$$

i.e.:

$$\dot{\boldsymbol{\Psi}} = -Q\mathbf{x} - A' \tag{8.22}$$

If H is to be minimized with respect to control function $\mathbf{u}$, i.e.:

$$\frac{\partial H}{\partial \mathbf{u}} = 0 = - G\mathbf{u}^{\circ} - B'\boldsymbol{\Psi} \qquad (8.23)$$

Hence:

$$\mathbf{u}^{\circ} = - G^{-1}B'\boldsymbol{\Psi} \qquad (8.24)$$

If G^{-1} is to exist it is necessary to restrict the choice of G to being positive definite (p.d.).[2]

For eq. (8.23), and therefore eq. (8.24), to be true, i.e. for the system to be optimal – at least locally – the $m \times m$ matrix $\partial^2 H/\partial \mathbf{u}^2$ must be p.d.

Since

$$\partial^2 H/\partial \mathbf{u}^2 = G \qquad (8.25)$$

and since G is restricted to be p.d., it follows that $\mathbf{u}$ does minimize H.

Furthermore, if $\mathbf{u}$ is locally optimal, the matrix Y of eq. (8.26) must also be positive definite:

$$Y = \begin{bmatrix} \dfrac{\partial^2 H}{\partial \mathbf{x}^2} & \dfrac{\partial^2 H}{\partial \mathbf{x}\partial \mathbf{u}} \\ \dfrac{\partial^2 H}{\partial \mathbf{u}\partial \mathbf{x}} & \dfrac{\partial^2 H}{\partial \mathbf{u}^2} \end{bmatrix} \qquad (8.26)$$

$$\frac{\partial^2 H}{\partial \mathbf{x}^2} = Q \qquad (8.27)$$

$$\frac{\partial^2 H}{\partial \mathbf{x}\partial \mathbf{u}} = \frac{\partial^2 H}{\partial \mathbf{u}\partial \mathbf{x}} = 0 \qquad (8.28)$$

From eq. (8.25):

$$\frac{\partial^2 H}{\partial \mathbf{u}^2} = G \qquad (8.25)$$

$$\therefore Y = \begin{bmatrix} Q & 0 \\ 0 & G \end{bmatrix} \qquad (8.29)$$

Since G is chosen to be p.d., if Q is also chosen to be p.d., then Y is p.d. However, if Q is indefinite, then it is possible that Y might not be p.d. To guarantee the required p.d. property for Y it is necessary that Q be chosen to be non-negative-definite (n.n.d.). This can be assured by choosing Q to be p.s.d. (positive-semi-definite). Substituting eq. (8.24) into eqs (8.19) and (8.22) yields:

$$\dot{\mathbf{x}} = A\mathbf{x} - BG^{-1}B\boldsymbol{\Psi} \qquad (8.30)$$

$$\dot{\boldsymbol{\Psi}} = - Q\mathbf{x} - A'\boldsymbol{\Psi} \qquad (8.31)$$

Let:

$$F = BG^{-1}B' \qquad (8.32)$$

then:

$$\begin{bmatrix} \dot{\mathbf{x}} \\ \dot{\boldsymbol{\Psi}} \end{bmatrix} = \begin{bmatrix} A & -F \\ -Q & -A' \end{bmatrix} \begin{bmatrix} \mathbf{x} \\ \boldsymbol{\Psi} \end{bmatrix} \tag{8.33}$$

Let:

$$\mathbf{z} \triangleq \begin{bmatrix} \mathbf{x} \\ \boldsymbol{\Psi} \end{bmatrix} \tag{8.34}$$

and

$$N = \begin{bmatrix} A & -F \\ -Q & -A' \end{bmatrix} \tag{8.35}$$

and is of order $(2n \times 2n)$. Then

$$\dot{\mathbf{z}} = N\mathbf{z} \tag{8.36}$$

This is the canonical equation of the optimal control system.

If eq. (8.36) is to be solved, then $2n$ boundary conditions need to be known. Of these, n are given by the state vector, $\mathbf{x}(0)$; the remainder are found from the transversality condition, which means that, at some terminal time, T, because $\mathbf{x}(T)$ has not been specified, it is necessary for the co-state vector $\boldsymbol{\Psi}(T)$ to satisfy the relationship:

$$\boldsymbol{\Psi}(T) = \frac{\partial}{\partial \mathbf{x}(T)} \{\tfrac{1}{2}\mathbf{x}'(T)S\mathbf{x}(T)\} \tag{8.37}$$

i.e.:

$$\boldsymbol{\Psi}(T) = S\mathbf{x}(T) \tag{8.38}$$

When T is ∞:

$$\boldsymbol{\Psi}(\infty) \triangleq [0] \tag{8.39}$$

Supposing that $\mathbf{x}$ and $\boldsymbol{\Psi}$ are related by an equation of the form (8.38), say:

$$\boldsymbol{\Psi}(t) = P(t)\mathbf{x}(t) \tag{8.40}$$

where P is of order $n \times n$. Then:

$$\dot{\boldsymbol{\Psi}}(t) = \dot{P}(t)\mathbf{x}(t) + P(t)\dot{\mathbf{x}}(t) \tag{8.41}$$

But $\mathbf{x}$ and $\boldsymbol{\Psi}$ are known from eqs (8.19) and (8.22) respectively. Hence:

$$\dot{\mathbf{x}} = [A - FP]\mathbf{x} \tag{8.42}$$

and:

$$\dot{\boldsymbol{\Psi}} = \{\dot{P} + PA - PFP\}\mathbf{x} \tag{8.43}$$

Also:

$$\dot{\boldsymbol{\psi}} = \{-Q - A'P\}\mathbf{x} \tag{8.44}$$

Hence:

$$[\dot{P} + PA + A'P - PFP + Q]\mathbf{x} = 0 \tag{8.45}$$

Since $\mathbf{x}$ is the perturbed motion of the aircraft, it is obvious that eq. (8.45) must hold for any value of $\mathbf{x}$. Hence:

$$\dot{P} + PA + A'P - PFP + Q = 0 \tag{8.46}$$

If P is a constant (which it must be for constant A, B, Q and G) then $\dot{P}$ is zero. Hence:

$$PA + A'P - PBG^{-1}B'P + Q = 0 \tag{8.47}$$

Equation (8.47) is known as the algebraic Riccati equation (ARE). Solving eq. (8.47) for P provides the optimal control law from eq. (8.24):

$$\mathbf{u}^{o} = -G^{-1}B'P\mathbf{x} = K\mathbf{x} \tag{8.48}$$

where K is the feedback gain matrix. Thus, the solution of the linear quadratic problem reduces to solving the ARE, provided that G is p.d., Q is p.s.d., and the pair $\{A, B\}$ are completely controllable.[3]

One of the most effective methods of evaluating P (see Marshall and Nicholson, 1970) is to determine the eigenvectors of the matrix N, given in eq. (8.35). These eigenvectors are then used to form the columns of a modal matrix U. Hence:

$$NU = U\Lambda \tag{8.49}$$

where Λ is a diagonal matrix, the elements on its diagonal being the eigenvalues of the eq. (8.36). Hence:

$$\mathbf{z}(t) = Ue^{\Lambda t}U^{-1}\mathbf{z}(0) \tag{8.50}$$

If the Λ is partitioned such that:

$$\Lambda = \begin{bmatrix} \Lambda_1 & 0 \\ 0 & \Lambda_2 \end{bmatrix} \tag{8.51}$$

where:

$$\Lambda_1 = \text{diag}(\lambda_i) \qquad i = 1, 2, \ldots, n \tag{8.52}$$

$$\Lambda_2 = \text{diag}(\lambda_j) \qquad j = n + 1, n + 2, \ldots, 2n \tag{8.53}$$

then the real parts of λ_i are all negative (being associated with the stable optimal, closed loop state variables), whereas the real parts of λ_j are all positive (being associated with the co-state variables of the optimal system). Partitioning eq. (8.50) in a similar way leads to:

$$\begin{bmatrix} \mathbf{x} \\ \mathbf{\Psi} \end{bmatrix} = \begin{bmatrix} U_{11} & U_{12} \\ U_{21} & U_{22} \end{bmatrix} \begin{bmatrix} e^{\Lambda_1 t} & 0 \\ 0 & e^{\Lambda_2 t} \end{bmatrix} \begin{bmatrix} V_{11} & V_{12} \\ V_{21} & V_{22} \end{bmatrix} \begin{bmatrix} \mathbf{x}(0) \\ \mathbf{\Psi}(0) \end{bmatrix} \tag{8.54}$$

V_{ij} represents a submatrix of the inverse of the modal matrix U. Therefore:

$$\mathbf{x} = U_{11}e^{\Lambda_1 t}\{V_{11}\mathbf{x}(0) + V_{12}\mathbf{\Psi}(0)\} + U_{12}e^{\Lambda_2 t}\{V_{21}\mathbf{x}(0) + V_{22}\mathbf{\Psi}(0)\} \tag{8.55}$$

The divergent modes must be eliminated from this equation to satisfy the condition of stability for the optimal closed loop system. From eq. (8.54) it can be deduced that:

$$\mathbf{\Psi}(0) = U_{21}U_{11}^{-1}\mathbf{x}(0) \tag{8.56}$$

(since $VU \triangleq I$) hence:

$$\begin{aligned} \mathbf{x} &= U_{11}e^{\Lambda_1 t}\{V_{11} + V_{12}U_{21}U_{11}^{-1}\}\mathbf{x}(0) \\ &= U_{11}e^{\Lambda_1 t}U_{11}^{-1}\mathbf{x}(0) \end{aligned} \tag{8.57}$$

Similarly:

$$\mathbf{\Psi} = U_{21}e^{\Lambda_1 t}U_{11}^{-1}\mathbf{x}(0) = U_{21}U_{11}^{-1}\mathbf{x} \tag{8.58}$$

$$\begin{aligned} \therefore \quad u^o &= -G^{-1}B'U_{21}U_{11}^{-1}\mathbf{x} \\ &= -G^{-1}B'P\mathbf{x} = K\mathbf{x} \end{aligned} \tag{8.59}$$

where:

$$P = U_{21}U_{11}^{-1} \tag{8.60}$$

Hence, the required solution of the ARE can be obtained by first forming the canonical matrix, N, then determining the corresponding eigenvectors, which are next used to form the modal matrix, which is then partitioned to form U_{21} and U_{11}. U_{11} is inverted, and U_{21} post-multiplied with this inverse to form the matrix P. A number of packages are available for solving the ARE, including MATRIX_x and CTRL-C.

Although the method is very efficient in obtaining the solution to the ARE it has one disadvantage: it cannot work unless the eigenvectors of the canonical matrix are independent. In AFCS work, such a situation can arise when the full five-state variable vector, namely:

$$\mathbf{x}' = [\beta \; p \; r \; \phi \; \Psi] \tag{8.61}$$

is used to define the lateral dynamics. One of the eigenvalues of the coefficient matrix A is zero and, consequently, the eigenvalue associated with the corresponding co-state vector is also zero; therefore, the eigenvectors cannot be independent. Either the reduced state vector with the first four elements should be used, or the method proposed by Laub (1979), involving Schur vectors instead of eigenvectors, should be employed to determine the matrix P.

A block diagram representation of the optimal state regulator is shown in Figure 8.3.

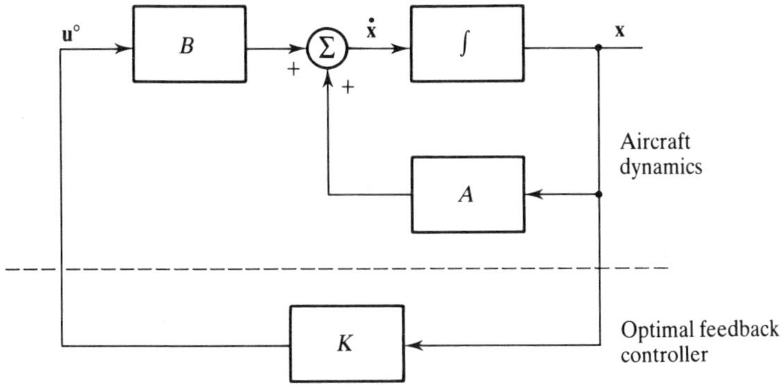

Figure 8.3 Optimal state regulator system.

Example 8.4

For the aircraft BRAVO, at flight condition 4, the equations of longitudinal motion are given by:

$$\dot{u} = -0.007u + 0.012\alpha - 9.81\theta$$

$$\dot{\alpha} = -0.128u - 0.54\alpha + q - 0.06\delta_E$$

$$\dot{q} = 0.69\alpha - 0.51\dot{\alpha} - 0.48q - 12.6\delta_E$$

$$\dot{\theta} = q$$

U_0 is 240 m s^{-1}. The corresponding matrices A and B are:

$$A = \begin{bmatrix} -0.007 & 0.012 & 0 & -9.81 \\ -0.128 & -0.54 & 1 & 0 \\ 0.064 & 0.96 & -0.99 & 0 \\ 0 & 0 & 1 & 0 \end{bmatrix}$$

$$B = \begin{bmatrix} 0 \\ -0.036 \\ -12.61 \\ 0 \end{bmatrix}$$

Suppose the weighting matrices are chosen as follows:

$$Q = \begin{bmatrix} 1 & 0 & 0 & 0 \\ 0 & 10 & 0 & 0 \\ 0 & 0 & 50 & 0 \\ 0 & 0 & 0 & 1 \end{bmatrix}$$

$G = [5.0]$

This choice means that q_{22} and q_{33} penalize any persistent transient motion of the angle of attack and pitch rate, and the weighting factor of 5.0 on the control ensures that only moderate deflection of the elevator results. Then by solving the ARE of eq. (8.47) and using eq. (8.59), the following feedback gain matrix, K, is obtained:

$$K = [-\ 0.475\ \ 0.387\ \ 3.2253\ \ 5.35]$$

The resulting eigenvalues of the closed loop system are: $\lambda_1 = -\ 0.774$, $\lambda_2 = -\ 39.91$, and λ_3, $\lambda_4 = -\ 0.764 \pm j0.73$.

The response of the optimal system to an initial angle of attack of 1° is shown in Figure 8.4.

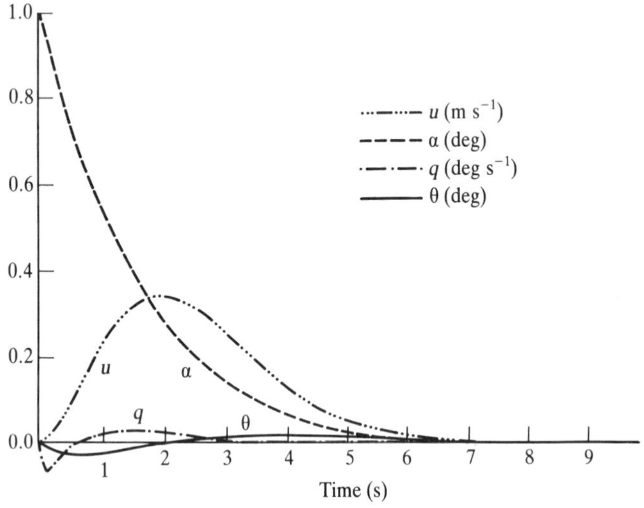

Figure 8.4 Optimal AFCS for BRAVO-4 – response to $\alpha(0) = 1°$.

The interested reader should refer to Athans and Falb (1966) for further discussion of the theory of the linear quadratic problem.

8.5 OPTIMAL OUTPUT REGULATOR PROBLEM

It is frequently required in AFCS work to control motion variables, such as normal acceleration at the pilot's station, or height, which are not themselves state variables. An optimal control formulation can be found such that its solution provides a unique and stabilizing control law. The performance index is chosen to be:

$$J = \tfrac{1}{2}\int_0^\infty \{\mathbf{y}'Q\mathbf{y} + \mathbf{u}'G\mathbf{u}\}\mathrm{d}t \tag{8.62}$$

with:

$$\dot{\mathbf{x}} = A\mathbf{x} + B\mathbf{u} \tag{8.63}$$

and:

$$\mathbf{y} = C\mathbf{x} + D\mathbf{u} \tag{8.64}$$

where:

$\mathbf{x} \in R^n$, $\mathbf{u} \in R^m$ and $\mathbf{y} \in R^p$

A is a matrix of order $(n \times n)$, B is of order $(n \times m)$, C is of order $(p \times n)$, D is of order $(p \times m)$, Q is of order $(p \times p)$, and G is of order $(m \times m)$.

In addition to the requirement that the pair $\{A, B\}$ be completely controllable, it is necessary that the pair $\{A, C\}$ be completely reconstructible.

$$J = \tfrac{1}{2}\int_0^\infty \{[C\mathbf{x} + D\mathbf{u}]'Q[C\mathbf{x} + D\mathbf{u}] + \mathbf{u}'G\mathbf{u}\}\mathrm{d}t \tag{8.65}$$

The Hamiltonian is:

$$H = \tfrac{1}{2}\{[C\mathbf{x} + D\mathbf{u}]'Q[C\mathbf{x} + D\mathbf{u}] + \mathbf{u}'G\mathbf{u}\} + \boldsymbol{\Psi}'(A\mathbf{x} + B\mathbf{u}) \tag{8.66}$$

$$\frac{\partial H}{\partial \mathbf{u}} = 0 = D'QC\mathbf{x} + (G + D'QD)\mathbf{u} + B'\boldsymbol{\Psi} \tag{8.67}$$

from which the optimal control $\mathbf{u}^{\mathrm{o}}$ is found to be:

$$\mathbf{u}^{\mathrm{o}} = -\,(G + D'QD)^{-1}[D'QC\mathbf{x} + B'\boldsymbol{\Psi}] \tag{8.68}$$

Furthermore,

$$-\frac{\partial H}{\partial \mathbf{x}} = \dot{\boldsymbol{\Psi}} = -\,C'\mathrm{QC}\mathbf{x} - C'\mathrm{QD}\mathbf{u} - A'\boldsymbol{\Psi} \tag{8.69}$$

The canonical equation of the optimal system is, therefore:

$$\begin{bmatrix} \dot{\mathbf{x}} \\ \dot{\boldsymbol{\Psi}} \end{bmatrix} = \begin{bmatrix} A - B(G + D'QD)^{-1}D'QC & -\,B(G + D'QD)^{-1}B' \\ -\,C'[Q - QD(G + D'QD)^{-1}D'Q]C & -\,[A - B(G + D'QD)^{-1}D'QC]' \end{bmatrix} \begin{bmatrix} \mathbf{x} \\ \boldsymbol{\Psi} \end{bmatrix} \tag{8.70}$$

or

$$\dot{\mathbf{z}} = \hat{N}\mathbf{z} \tag{8.71}$$

The ARE associated with this optimal control problem can be shown to be:

$$\hat{P}\hat{A} + \hat{A}'\hat{P} - \hat{P}B\hat{G}^{-1}B'\hat{P} + \hat{Q} = 0 \tag{8.72}$$

where:

$$\hat{A} \triangleq A - B\hat{G}^{-1}D'QC \tag{8.73}$$

$$\hat{G} \triangleq G + D'QD \tag{8.74}$$

$$\hat{Q} \triangleq C'[Q - QDG^{-1}D'Q]C \tag{8.75}$$

Since:

$$\mathbf{\Psi} = \hat{P}\mathbf{x} \tag{8.76}$$

$$\mathbf{u}^{o} = -(G + D'QD)^{-1}[D'QC + B'\hat{P}]\mathbf{x} \tag{8.77}$$

Note that the control law involves full state variable feedback. If only the output variables are available for feedback, then some form of reconstruction of the state vector is required before it is used in the optimal feedback controller. For example:

$$\mathbf{x} = C^{\dagger}[\mathbf{y} - D\mathbf{u}] \tag{8.78}$$

Depending upon the rank of C, either the left or right generalized inverse should be used in eq. (8.78).[4]

$$\mathbf{u}^{o} = KC^{\dagger}[\mathbf{y} - D\mathbf{u}^{o}] \tag{8.79}$$

i.e.:

$$\mathbf{u}^{o} = [I + KC^{\dagger}D]^{-1}KC^{\dagger}\mathbf{y} \tag{8.80}$$

If the matrix $[I + KC^{\dagger}D]$, of order $(m \times m)$, is singular, then its generalized inverse must be used leading to a further loss of accuracy in the reconstruction of the state vector. Alternatively, use could be made of the state estimation theory, which is outlined and explained in Section 8.9 of this chapter.

If the output vector depends solely upon the state vector, i.e. if eq. (8.64) becomes:

$$\mathbf{y} = C\mathbf{x} \tag{8.81}$$

then the results given earlier still obtain, but with the matrix D taken as a null matrix.

The results become:

$$\mathbf{u}^{o} = -G^{-1}B'P\mathbf{x} \tag{8.82}$$

where P is the solution of the ARE given by eq. (8.83) namely:

$$\hat{P}A + A'\hat{P} - \hat{P}BG^{-1}B'\hat{P} + \tilde{Q} = 0 \tag{8.83}$$

where:

$$\tilde{Q} = C'QC \tag{8.84}$$

These results could be obtained directly from recognizing that the performance index in this case can be written as follows:

$$J = \tfrac{1}{2}\int_0^\infty (\mathbf{y}'Q\mathbf{y} + \mathbf{u}'G\mathbf{u})\mathrm{d}t = \tfrac{1}{2}\int_0^\infty \{\mathbf{x}'C'QC\mathbf{x} + \mathbf{u}'G\mathbf{u}\}\mathrm{d}t$$

$$= \tfrac{1}{2}\int_0^\infty \{\mathbf{x}'\tilde{Q}\mathbf{x} + \mathbf{u}'G\mathbf{u}\}\mathrm{d}t \tag{8.85}$$

By the simple substitution, the problem is rendered back to a linear quadratic problem.

Even the performance index of eq. (8.65) can be re-expressed in a form which will transform the problem to a linear quadratic state regulator problem:

$$J = \tfrac{1}{2}\int_0^\infty \{\mathbf{x}'C'QC\mathbf{x} + \mathrm{u}'D'QC\mathbf{x} + \mathbf{x}'C'QD\mathbf{u} + \mathbf{u}'[G + D'QD]\mathbf{u}\}\mathrm{d}t \tag{8.86}$$

Since $\mathbf{x}'C'QD\mathbf{u}$ is the transpose of $\mathbf{u}'D'QC\mathbf{x}$ and since it is a scalar, and the transpose of a scalar is the same scalar, the sum of these terms can be expressed as:

$$\mathbf{x}'C'QD\mathbf{u} + \mathbf{u}'D'QC\mathbf{x} = 2\mathbf{x}'C'QD\mathbf{u} \tag{8.87}$$

Now:

$$\begin{aligned}\mathbf{x}'\tilde{Q}\mathbf{x} + 2\mathbf{x}'W\mathbf{u} + \mathbf{u}'\hat{G}\mathbf{u} &= [\mathbf{u} + \hat{G}^{-1}W'\mathbf{x}]'G[\mathbf{u} + \hat{G}^{-1}W'\mathbf{x}] \\ &\quad + \mathbf{x}'[\tilde{Q} - W\hat{G}^{-1}W']\mathbf{x}\end{aligned} \tag{8.88}$$

where:

$$W = C'QD \tag{8.89}$$

Hence:

$$J = \tfrac{1}{2}\int_0^\infty \{\mathbf{x}'\hat{Q}\mathbf{x} + \mathbf{u}'\hat{G}\mathbf{u}\}\mathrm{d}t \tag{8.90}$$

where:

$$\hat{\mathbf{u}} = \mathbf{u} + \hat{G}^{-1}W'\mathbf{x} \tag{8.91}$$

$$\begin{aligned}\hat{Q} &= \tilde{Q} - W\hat{G}^{-1}W' = C'QC - C'QD\hat{G}^{-1}D'QC \\ &= C'[Q - QD\hat{G}^{-1}D'Q]C\end{aligned} \tag{8.92}$$

$$\therefore \quad \dot{\mathbf{x}} = (A - B\hat{G}^{-1}W')\mathbf{x} + B\hat{\mathbf{u}} = \hat{A}\mathbf{x} + B\hat{\mathbf{u}} \tag{8.93}$$

From eqs (8.93) and (8.90) it is evident that the problem is now a linear quadratic state regulator. Note that $\hat{A}$ defined in eq. (8.73) is identical to that defined in eq. (8.93); eqs (8.75) and (8.92) are also identical.

The optimal control law obtained from the linear quadratic problem (LQP) state regulator is:

$$\hat{\mathbf{u}}^{\mathrm{o}} = -\hat{G}^{-1}B'\hat{P}\mathbf{x} \tag{8.94}$$

where:

$$\hat{P}\hat{A} + \hat{A}'\hat{P} - \hat{P}B\hat{G}^{-1}B'\hat{P} + \hat{Q} = 0 \tag{8.95}$$

$$\mathbf{u}^o = \hat{\mathbf{u}}^o - \hat{G}^{-1}W'\mathbf{x} = -\hat{G}^{-1}(B'P + D'QC')\mathbf{x} \tag{8.96}$$

which is identical to eq. (8.77).

8.6 STATE REGULATORS WITH A PRESCRIBED DEGREE OF STABILITY

Consider the aircraft dynamics:

$$\dot{\mathbf{x}} = A\mathbf{x} + B\mathbf{u} \tag{8.97}$$

which is completely controllable. What is sought is a feedback control law which will ensure that the real part of every eigenvalue of the closed loop system lies to the left of a prescribed value in the left-hand s-plane. To achieve this the performance index chosen is:

$$J = \tfrac{1}{2}\int_0^\infty e^{2\alpha t}\{\mathbf{x}'Q\mathbf{x} + \mathbf{u}'G\mathbf{u}\}\mathbf{d}t \tag{8.98}$$

G is p.d. and Q is at least n.n.d. Let:

$$\hat{\mathbf{x}}(t) = e^{\alpha t}\mathbf{x}(t) \tag{8.99}$$

$$\hat{\mathbf{u}}(t) = e^{\alpha t}\mathbf{u}(t) \tag{8.100}$$

$$\begin{aligned}\therefore\quad \dot{\hat{\mathbf{x}}}(t) &= \alpha e^{\alpha t}\mathbf{x}(t) + e^{\alpha t}\dot{\mathbf{x}}(t) = \alpha e^{\alpha t}\mathbf{x}(t) + e^{\alpha t}A\mathbf{x}(t) + e^{\alpha t}B\mathbf{u}(t)\\ &= [A + \alpha I]\hat{\mathbf{x}}(t) + B\hat{\mathbf{u}}(t)\end{aligned} \tag{8.101}$$

$$\therefore\quad \hat{J} = \tfrac{1}{2}\int_0^\infty \{\hat{\mathbf{x}}'Q\hat{\mathbf{x}} + \hat{\mathbf{u}}'G\hat{\mathbf{u}}\}\mathrm{d}t \tag{8.102}$$

Hence the ARE becomes for eqs (8.97) and (8.98):

$$PA + A'P + e^{2\alpha t}Q - PBe^{-2\alpha t}G^{-1}B'P = 0 \tag{8.103}$$

$$\therefore\quad \mathbf{u}^o = -G^{-1}B'Pe^{2\alpha t}\mathbf{x}(t) \tag{8.104}$$

From eqs (8.101) and (8.102):

$$P(A + aI) + (A' + aI)P - PBG^{-1}B'P + Q = 0 \tag{8.105}$$

$$\hat{\mathbf{u}}^o = -G^{-1}B'P\hat{\mathbf{x}} \tag{8.106}$$

But:

$$\begin{aligned}\mathbf{u}^o &= e^{-\alpha t}\hat{\mathbf{u}}^o = -e^{-\alpha t}G^{-1}B'Pe^{\alpha t}\mathbf{x}(t)\\ &= -G^{-1}B'P\mathbf{x}(t) = K\mathbf{x}(t)\end{aligned} \tag{8.107}$$

This is a constant feedback control law. Using this control:

$$\hat{\mathbf{x}} = (A + aI - BG^{-1}B'K)\hat{\mathbf{x}} \tag{8.108}$$

which is asymptotically stable, since (A, B) is controllable. Hence if $\hat{\mathbf{x}}(t)$ is stable,

$\mathbf{x}(t)$ must be stable, since:

$$\mathbf{x}(t) = e^{-\alpha t}\hat{\mathbf{x}}(t) \tag{8.109}$$

$\mathbf{x}(t)$ approaches zero as fast as $e^{-\alpha t}$, as $t \to \infty$.

8.7 EXPLICIT MODEL FOLLOWING

In Section 7.6 of Chapter 7, the idea was explained of finding a feedback control law which would ensure that the output response of a closed loop control system would match the response of some model system defined by the equation:

$$\dot{\mathbf{y}}_m = L\mathbf{y}_m \tag{8.110}$$

An alternative method of obtaining an optimal model following control is to define a performance index:

$$J = \tfrac{1}{2}\int_0^\infty \{(\dot{\mathbf{y}} - L\mathbf{y})'Q(\dot{\mathbf{y}} - L\mathbf{y}) + \mathbf{u}'G\mathbf{u}\}dt \tag{8.112}$$

$\dot{\mathbf{y}}$ can be shown to be:

$$\dot{\mathbf{y}} = CA\mathbf{x} + CB\mathbf{u} \tag{8.113}$$

It can easily be shown that the performance index of eq. (8.112) is minimized when the control of eq. (8.114) is used:

$$\mathbf{u}^o = K\mathbf{x} = [K_1 \vdots K_2]\mathbf{x} \tag{8.114}$$

where:

$$K_1 = -(B'C'QCB + G)^{-1}B'P \tag{8.115}$$

$$K_2 = -(B'C'QCB + G)^{-1}B'C'Q(CA - LA) \tag{8.116}$$

The matrix P is obtained as the solution of the ARE given by:

$$PA_m + A'_mP + Q_m - KBG_m^{-1}B'K = 0 \tag{8.117}$$

where:

$$A_m = \{A - B[(B'C'QCB + G)^{-1}B'C'Q(CA - LA)]\} \tag{8.118}$$

$$G_m = \{G + B'C'QCB\} \tag{8.119}$$

$$Q_m = (CA - LA)'\{Q - QCB(B'C'QCB + G)^{-1}B'C'Q\}(CA - LA) \tag{8.120}$$

A_m, G_m and Q_m are pre-computed and then the standard LQP is solved to obtain P, after which K_1 and K_2, and hence K, are calculated.

Example 8.5

Suppose it is required to find a feedback control law to make the longitudinal motion of the aircraft BRAVO-1 have closed loop characteristics similar to those of an aircraft, a model, with a coefficient matrix, L, namely:

$$L = \begin{bmatrix} -0.02 & -0.02 & 0 & -9.81 \\ -0.002 & -1.85 & 1 & 0 \\ 0 & -1.86 & -1.4 & 0 \\ 0 & 0 & 1 & 0 \end{bmatrix}$$

From Appendix B, it can be shown that BRAVO-1 can be represented by:

$$\dot{\mathbf{x}} = A\mathbf{x} + Bu$$

where:

$$\mathbf{x} \triangleq \begin{bmatrix} u \\ \alpha \\ q \\ \theta \end{bmatrix}$$

$$u = [\delta_E]$$

$$A = \begin{bmatrix} -0.017 & 0.026 & 0 & -9.81 \\ -0.0143 & -1.02 & 1.0 & 0 \\ 0 & 2.06 & -1.12 & 0 \\ 0 & 0 & 1 & 0 \end{bmatrix}$$

$$B = \begin{bmatrix} 0 \\ -0.064 \\ -11.56 \\ 0 \end{bmatrix}$$

The output matrix is the identity matrix I_4:

$$C = \begin{bmatrix} 1 & 0 & 0 & 0 \\ 0 & 1 & 0 & 0 \\ 0 & 0 & 1 & 0 \\ 0 & 0 & 0 & 1 \end{bmatrix}$$

The eigenvalues of BRAVO-1 are:

$\lambda_1 = 0.6091$
$\lambda_2 = -\ 2.5219$
$\lambda_3 = -\ 0.122 + j0.4162$
$\lambda_4 = -\ 0.122 + j0.4162$

The aircraft is unstable; the eigenvalues of the stable, model aircraft are:

$\lambda_{x_m} = -\ 0.007 + j0.09$
$\lambda_{2_m} = -\ 0.007 - j0.09$
$\lambda_{3_m} = -\ 1.628 + j1.3457$
$\lambda_{4_m} = -\ 1.628 - j1.3457$

If weighting matrices Q and G are chosen as follows:

$$Q = \begin{bmatrix} 0.1 & 0 & 0 & 0 \\ 0 & 10.0 & 0 & 0 \\ 0 & 0 & 100.0 & 0 \\ 0 & 0 & 0 & 0.1 \end{bmatrix}$$

where the choice of q_{22} and q_{33} reflects the importance placed upon the closed loop responses in α and q being close to the required responses. Then, evaluating A_m, Q_m and G_m as in eqs (8.118)–(8.129), will allow an optimal feedback control law:

$$\mathbf{u}^o = K\mathbf{x}$$

to be evaluated by solving the LQP. From this approach a feedback matrix of:

$$K = [-\ 0.0002\ \ 0.3242\ \ 0.0344\ \ 0.0297]$$

is obtained; the eigenvalues of the resulting closed loop system are easily shown to be:

$\lambda_{1_c} = -\ 0.036 + j0.281$

$\lambda_{2_c} = -\ 0.036 + j0.281$

$\lambda_{3_c} = -\ 1.252 + j1.35$

$\lambda_{4_c} = -\ 1.252 - j1.35$

which are close to those of the model matrix.

8.8 OPTIMAL COMMAND CONTROL SYSTEM

The theory will provide a control law which will ensure that the AFCS provides optimal command response: it is an optimal servomechanism problem.

The aircraft dynamics are represented by eq. (8.121):

$$\dot{\mathbf{x}} = A\mathbf{x} + B\mathbf{u} \tag{8.121}$$

and the output equation is taken to be

$$\mathbf{y} = C\mathbf{x} \tag{8.122}$$

If the desired output is the command input, $\mathbf{y}_{\text{comm}}$, the system error can be defined as

$$\mathbf{e} \triangleq \mathbf{y}_{\text{comm}} - \mathbf{y} \tag{8.123}$$

It is required to minimize the performance index of eq. (8.122):

$$J = \tfrac{1}{2}\mathbf{e}'(T)S\mathbf{e}(T) + \tfrac{1}{2}\int_0^T \{\mathbf{e}'(t)Q\mathbf{e} + \mathbf{u}'G\mathbf{u}\}\mathbf{d}t \tag{8.124}$$

Because the system is a command system, the system response cannot take infinite time to respond; hence, the upper limit of the integral is T. However:

$$\mathbf{e} \triangleq \mathbf{y}_{\text{comm}} - C\mathbf{x} \tag{8.125}$$

$$\begin{aligned}\therefore\quad J = {} & \tfrac{1}{2}\{\mathbf{y}_{\text{comm}}(T) - C\mathbf{x}(T)\}'S\{\mathbf{y}_{\text{comm}}(T) - C\mathbf{x}(T)\} \\ & + \tfrac{1}{2}\int_0^T \{[\mathbf{y}_{\text{comm}} - C\mathbf{x}]'Q[\mathbf{y}_{\text{comm}} - C\mathbf{x}] + \mathbf{u}'G\mathbf{u}\}\mathrm{d}t\end{aligned} \tag{8.126}$$

$$\therefore\quad H = \tfrac{1}{2}\{[\mathbf{y}_{\text{comm}} - C\mathbf{x}]'Q[\mathbf{y}_{\text{comm}} - C\mathbf{x}] + \mathbf{u}'G\mathbf{u}\} + \boldsymbol{\Psi}'(A\mathbf{x} + B\mathbf{u}) \tag{8.127}$$

$$\partial H/\partial \mathbf{u} \triangleq 0 = G\mathbf{u} + B'\boldsymbol{\Psi} \tag{8.128}$$

from which:

$$\mathbf{u}_o = -G^{-1}B'\boldsymbol{\Psi} \tag{8.129}$$

But:

$$\dot{\boldsymbol{\Psi}} = -\partial H/\partial \mathbf{x} = -C'QC\mathbf{x} - A'\boldsymbol{\Psi} + C'Q\mathbf{y}_{\text{comm}} \tag{8.130}$$

$$\dot{\mathbf{x}} = A\mathbf{x} - BG^{-1}B'\boldsymbol{\Psi} \tag{8.131}$$

Let:

$$F = BG^{-1}B' \tag{8.132}$$

$$\tilde{Q} = C'QC \tag{8.133}$$

$$T = C'Q \tag{8.134}$$

Hence, the canonical equation becomes:

$$\begin{bmatrix}\dot{\mathbf{x}} \\ \dot{\boldsymbol{\Psi}}\end{bmatrix} = \begin{bmatrix} A & -F \\ -V & -A'\end{bmatrix}\begin{bmatrix}\mathbf{x} \\ \boldsymbol{\Psi}\end{bmatrix} + \begin{bmatrix}0 \\ T\end{bmatrix}\mathbf{y}_{\text{comm}} \tag{8.135}$$

At $t = 0$:

$$\mathbf{x} = \mathbf{x}(0) \tag{8.136}$$

at $t = T$:

$$\mathbf{\Psi}(T) = \frac{\partial}{\partial \mathbf{x}(T)} \{\tfrac{1}{2}\mathbf{e}'(T)S\mathbf{e}(T)\} \tag{8.137}$$

$$= C'SC\mathbf{x}(T) - C'S\mathbf{y}_{\text{comm}}(T) \tag{8.138}$$

This is the transversality condition. Hence:

$$\mathbf{\Psi} = P\mathbf{x} - \mathbf{g}(t) \tag{8.139}$$

$$\therefore \quad \dot{\mathbf{\Psi}} = \dot{P}\mathbf{x} + P\dot{\mathbf{x}} - \dot{\mathbf{g}}(t) \tag{8.140}$$

Hence:

$$\begin{aligned}\dot{\mathbf{x}} &= A\mathbf{x} - BG^{-1}B'P\mathbf{x} + BG^{-1}B'\mathbf{g}(t) \\ &= [A - FP]\mathbf{x} + F\mathbf{g}(t)\end{aligned} \tag{8.141}$$

and:

$$\dot{\mathbf{\Psi}} = [\dot{P} + PA - PFP]\mathbf{x} + PF\mathbf{g}(t) - \dot{\mathbf{g}}(t) \tag{8.142}$$

However:

$$\begin{aligned}\dot{\mathbf{\Psi}} &= -V\mathbf{x} - A'\mathbf{\Psi} + T\mathbf{y}_{\text{comm}} \\ &= -V\mathbf{x} - A'[P\mathbf{x} - \mathbf{g}(t)] + T\mathbf{y}_{\text{comm}}\end{aligned} \tag{8.143a}$$

$$\therefore \quad [-V - A'P]\mathbf{x} + A'\mathbf{g}(t) + T\mathbf{y}_{\text{comm}} = \dot{\mathbf{\Psi}} \tag{8.143b}$$

Equating coefficients of eqs (8.142) and (8.143b):

$$-V - A'\dot{P} = P + PA - PFP \tag{8.144}$$

$$A'\mathbf{g}(t) + T\mathbf{y}_{\text{comm}} = PF\mathbf{g}(t) - \dot{\mathbf{g}} \tag{8.145}$$

Equation (8.144) is a matrix Riccati equation, namely:

$$\dot{P} + PA + A'P - PFP + V = 0 \tag{8.146}$$

$$\dot{\mathbf{g}} = [PF - A']\mathbf{g} - T\mathbf{y}_{\text{comm}} \tag{8.147}$$

Both equations must be solved to obtain P and $\mathbf{g}(t)$ required for the optimal control:

$$\mathbf{u}^{\text{o}} = -G^{-1}B'P(t)\mathbf{x}(t) - G^{-1}B'\mathbf{g}(t) \tag{8.148}$$

The necessary boundary conditions for eqs (8.146) and (8.147) are:

$$P(T) = C'SC \tag{8.149}$$

$$\mathbf{g}(T) = C'S\mathbf{y}_{\text{comm}}(T) \tag{8.150}$$

The block diagram representation of the optimal command system is shown in Figure 8.5.

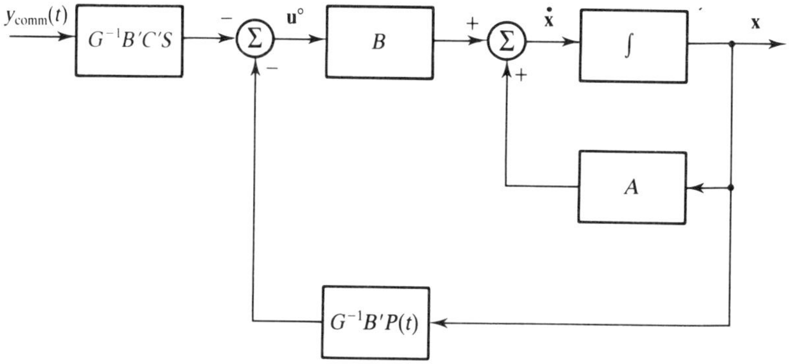

Figure 8.5 Optimal command control system.

8.9 USE OF INTEGRAL FEEDBACK IN LQP

In AFCS the control laws often involve integral terms. This section shows how such terms in the feedback controller can be dealt within the framework of the LQP.

The aircraft is represented by the usual equations:

$$\dot{\mathbf{x}} = A\mathbf{x} + B\mathbf{u} \tag{8.151}$$

$$\mathbf{y} = C\mathbf{x} \tag{8.152}$$

Let:

$$\mathbf{z} \triangleq \begin{bmatrix} \dot{\mathbf{x}} \\ \mathbf{y} \end{bmatrix} \tag{8.153}$$

then:

$$\dot{\mathbf{z}} \triangleq \begin{bmatrix} \ddot{\mathbf{x}} \\ \dot{\mathbf{y}} \end{bmatrix} = \begin{bmatrix} A & 0 \\ C & 0 \end{bmatrix} \begin{bmatrix} \dot{\mathbf{x}} \\ \mathbf{y} \end{bmatrix} + \begin{bmatrix} B \\ 0 \end{bmatrix} \dot{\mathbf{u}} \tag{8.154}$$

Now let:

$$\mathbf{v} = \dot{\mathbf{u}} \tag{8.155}$$

then:

$$\dot{\mathbf{z}} = \tilde{A}\mathbf{z} + \tilde{B}\mathbf{v} \tag{8.156}$$

If the performance index to be minimized is chosen to be:

$$J = \tfrac{1}{2}\int_0^{\infty} \{\mathbf{z}'Q\mathbf{z} + \mathbf{v}'G\mathbf{v}\}dt$$

and the control is subject to the constraint of eq. (8.156), then by solving the LQP the optimal control can easily be shown to be:

$$\mathbf{v}^o = K\mathbf{z} = -G^{-1}\tilde{B}'P\mathbf{z} \quad (8.157)$$

where P is the solution of the ARE given in eq. (8.158):

$$P\tilde{A} + \tilde{A}'P - P\tilde{B}G^{-1}\tilde{B}'P + Q = 0 \quad (8.158)$$

$$\mathbf{v}^o = \dot{\mathbf{u}}^o \triangleq K_I\dot{\mathbf{x}} + K_2\mathbf{y} \quad (8.159)$$

i.e.:

$$\mathbf{u}^o = K_1\mathbf{x} + K_2\int_0^t \mathbf{y}(\lambda)d\lambda + K_2\mathbf{c} \quad (8.160)$$

where $\mathbf{c}$ represents the initial condition vector of the m integrators (frequently taken as zero).

In Section 7.2 of Chapter 7, a generalized AFCS was presented in which a dymamic feedback controller was used. In Section 8.8 an optimal command control system is examined, in which it is arranged for the output to follow the command input closely over some period of time, T. This present section deals with the same problem, but adds the requirement that the command system must have zero steady state error.

In the steady state:

$$\dot{\mathbf{x}} \triangleq 0 \quad (8.161)$$

$$\therefore \quad 0 = A\mathbf{x}_{ss} + B\mathbf{u}_{ss} \quad (8.162)$$

$$\mathbf{y}_{ss} = C\mathbf{x}_{ss} \quad (8.163)$$

$$\therefore \quad \mathbf{y}_{ss} = -CA^{-1}B\mathbf{u}_{ss} \quad (8.164)$$

Equation (8.164) depends upon the non-singularity of A; if it is singular then $A^{\dagger}$ should be used.

If zero steady state error is achieved then:

$$\mathbf{y}_{ss} = \mathbf{y}_{comm_{ss}} \quad (8.165a)$$

$$\therefore \quad \mathbf{y}_{comm_{ss}} = -CA^{-1}B\mathbf{u}_{ss} \quad (8.165b)$$

$$\mathbf{y}_{comm} \in R^p; \ \mathbf{u} \in R^m$$

If $m < p$ there is generally no $\mathbf{u}_{ss}$ to be satisfied: this means that a command AFCS cannot track (follow) more variables than the aircraft has effective control surfaces.

If $m \geq p$, and $\mathbf{y}_{comm}$ is non-zero, there will be a non-zero $\mathbf{u}_{ss}$ which will satisfy eq. (8.165b). In general, therefore, $\mathbf{y}_{ss}$ and $\mathbf{x}_{ss}$ are non-zero. In the LQP, however, $\mathbf{x}$ and $\mathbf{u}$ have to tend towards zero over the control interval. Quadratic forms in $\mathbf{x}$, $\mathbf{y}$ and $\mathbf{u}$ cannot be used in the cost functional because of these non-zero, steady state values. What is done usually is to choose.

$$\bar{\mathbf{x}} = \mathbf{x} - \mathbf{x}_{ss}$$

$$\bar{\mathbf{y}} = \mathbf{y} - \mathbf{y}_{ss} \tag{8.166}$$
$$\bar{\mathbf{u}} = \mathbf{u} - \mathbf{u}_{ss}$$

and then to proceed to solve the corresponding LQP, in the usual way. However, $\mathbf{x}_{ss}$, $\mathbf{u}_{ss}$ and $\mathbf{y}_{ss}$ depend upon the parameters of the system and, since these may change, or may not be well known, it is often more helpful to follow this approach (see Parker, 1972). Let:

$$\mathbf{e}(t) \triangleq \mathbf{y}_{comm}(t) - \mathbf{y}(t) \tag{8.167}$$

and let it be assumed that, as $t \to \infty$:

$$\mathbf{e}(t) \to 0 \tag{8.168}$$

$$\therefore \quad \lim_{t \to \infty} \mathbf{e}(t) \to 0 \tag{8.169}$$

Further, let:

$$\boldsymbol{\xi} \triangleq \begin{bmatrix} \mathbf{y} \\ \boldsymbol{\eta} \end{bmatrix} \tag{8.170}$$

where:

$$\begin{aligned} &\boldsymbol{\eta} \in R^{(n-p)} \\ &\boldsymbol{\xi} = T\mathbf{x} \end{aligned} \tag{8.171}$$

where T is non-singular and is defined as:

$$T \triangleq \begin{bmatrix} C \\ \hdashline L \end{bmatrix} \tag{8.172}$$

where L is an arbitrary marix, of order $(n - p) \times n$, but it must be chosen such that T is non-singular:

$$\therefore \quad \dot{\boldsymbol{\xi}} = TAT^{-1}\boldsymbol{\xi} + TB\mathbf{u} = F\boldsymbol{\xi} + H\mathbf{u} \tag{8.173}$$

where:

$$F = \begin{bmatrix} F_{11} & F_{12} \\ F_{21} & F_{22} \end{bmatrix} \tag{8.174}$$

$$H = \begin{bmatrix} H_1 \\ H_2 \end{bmatrix} \tag{8.175}$$

Thus:

$$\dot{\mathbf{y}} = F_{11}\mathbf{y} + F_{12}\boldsymbol{\eta} + H_1\mathbf{u} \tag{8.176}$$

$$\dot{\boldsymbol{\eta}} = F_{21}\mathbf{y} + F_{22}\boldsymbol{\eta} + H_2\mathbf{u} \tag{8.177}$$

Now, if the following vectors are defined:

$$\boldsymbol{\sigma}_1 \triangleq \boldsymbol{\xi} \qquad \boldsymbol{\sigma}_2 \triangleq \dot{\boldsymbol{\xi}} \qquad \boldsymbol{\sigma}_3 \triangleq \dot{\boldsymbol{\eta}} \tag{8.178}$$

where $\boldsymbol{\sigma}_1$ and $\boldsymbol{\sigma}_2 \in R^p$ and $\boldsymbol{\sigma}_3 \in R^{n-p}$ and also the following:

$$\mathbf{v} \triangleq \dot{\mathbf{u}} \text{ (as before)} \tag{8.179}$$

$$\boldsymbol{\Sigma} = \begin{bmatrix} \boldsymbol{\sigma}_1 \\ \boldsymbol{\sigma}_2 \\ \boldsymbol{\sigma}_3 \end{bmatrix} \tag{8.180}$$

$$\dot{\boldsymbol{\sigma}}_1 \triangleq \boldsymbol{\sigma}_2 \tag{8.181}$$

$$\boldsymbol{\sigma}_2 = \frac{\mathrm{d}}{\mathrm{d}t}(\mathbf{y}_{\text{comm}} - \mathbf{y}) \simeq -\dot{\mathbf{y}} \text{ (for constant } \mathbf{y}_{\text{comm}}) \tag{8.182}$$

$$\dot{\boldsymbol{\sigma}}_2 = -\ddot{\mathbf{y}} \tag{8.183}$$

However:

$$\ddot{\mathbf{y}} = F_{11}\dot{\mathbf{y}} + F_{12}\dot{\boldsymbol{\eta}} + H_1\dot{\mathbf{u}} \tag{8.184}$$

$$\therefore \quad \dot{\boldsymbol{\sigma}}_2 = F_{11}\boldsymbol{\sigma}_2 - F_{12}\boldsymbol{\sigma}_3 - H_1\mathbf{v} \tag{8.185}$$

$$\begin{aligned} \dot{\boldsymbol{\sigma}}_3 = \ddot{\boldsymbol{\eta}} &= F_{21}\dot{\mathbf{y}} + F_{22}\dot{\boldsymbol{\eta}} + H_2\dot{\mathbf{u}} \\ &= -F_{21}\boldsymbol{\sigma}_2 + F_{22}\boldsymbol{\sigma}_3 + H_2\mathbf{v} \end{aligned} \tag{8.186}$$

Hence:

$$\dot{\boldsymbol{\Sigma}} = \Phi\boldsymbol{\Sigma} + \Gamma\mathbf{v} \tag{8.187}$$

where:

$$\Phi \triangleq \begin{bmatrix} 0 & I & 0 \\ 0 & F_{11} & -F_{12} \\ 0 & -F_{21} & F_{22} \end{bmatrix} \tag{8.188}$$

$$\Gamma = \begin{bmatrix} 0 \\ H_1 \\ H_2 \end{bmatrix} \tag{8.189}$$

Letting:

$$J = \tfrac{1}{2}\int_0^\infty \{\boldsymbol{\Sigma}'Q\boldsymbol{\Sigma} + \mathbf{v}'G\mathbf{v}\}\mathrm{d}t \tag{8.190}$$

allows the determination of the optimal feedback control law:

$$\mathbf{v}^{\mathrm{o}} = -G^{-1}\Gamma'P\boldsymbol{\Sigma} = K\boldsymbol{\Sigma} \tag{8.191}$$

where P is the solution of the corresponding ARE eq. (8.192):

$$P\Phi + \Phi'P - P\Gamma G^{-1}\Gamma'P + Q = 0 \tag{8.192}$$

The optimal feedback laws can be re-expressed as:

$$\mathbf{v}^{\text{o}} = K_1\boldsymbol{\sigma}_1 + K_2\boldsymbol{\sigma}_2 + K_3\boldsymbol{\sigma}_3 \tag{8.193}$$

or:

$$\dot{\mathbf{u}}^{\mathbf{o}} = K_1\boldsymbol{\xi} + K_2\dot{\boldsymbol{\xi}} + K_3\dot{\boldsymbol{\eta}} \tag{8.194}$$

hence:

$$\mathbf{u} = K_1 \int_0^{\infty} [\mathbf{y}_{\text{comm}} - \mathbf{y}]\text{d}t + K_2[\mathbf{y}_{\text{comm}} - \mathbf{y}] + K_3\boldsymbol{\eta} \tag{8.195}$$

Example 8.6

Consider the simple second order system shown in Figure 8.6.

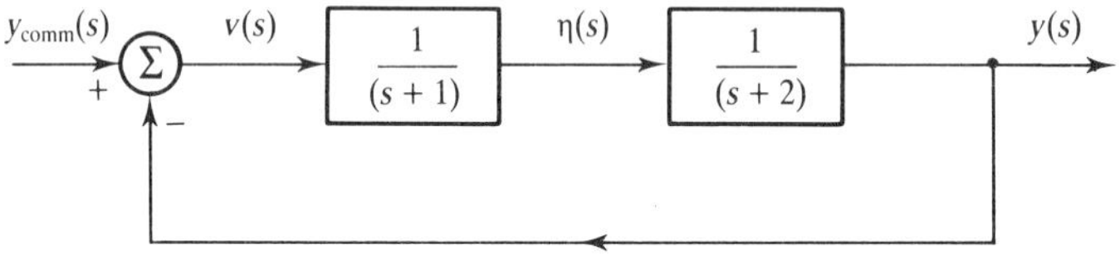

Figure 8.6 Simple second order system.

$$\frac{y(s)}{y_{\text{comm}}(s)} = \frac{1}{(s^2 + 3s + 3)}$$

If $y_{\text{comm}}(t)$ is a unit step input, $y_{ss} = 0.333$ and there is a steady state error of 0.666. Choose:

$$\boldsymbol{\xi} = \begin{bmatrix} y \\ \eta \end{bmatrix}$$

then:

$$F = \begin{bmatrix} -2 & 1 \\ 0 & -1 \end{bmatrix}$$

$$H = \begin{bmatrix} 0 \\ 1 \end{bmatrix}$$

hence:

$$\Phi \triangleq \begin{bmatrix} 0 & 1 & 0 \\ 0 & -2 & -1 \\ 0 & 0 & -1 \end{bmatrix}$$

$$\Gamma \triangleq \begin{bmatrix} 0 \\ 0 \\ 1 \end{bmatrix}$$

If:

$$J = \tfrac{1}{2}\int_0^\infty \{10y^2 + 0.01v^2\}\mathrm{d}t$$

then it can be shown that:

$$v = 10\sigma_1 + 4.15\sigma_2 - 2.05\sigma_3$$

and the optimal system is shown in Figure 8.7. Therefore:

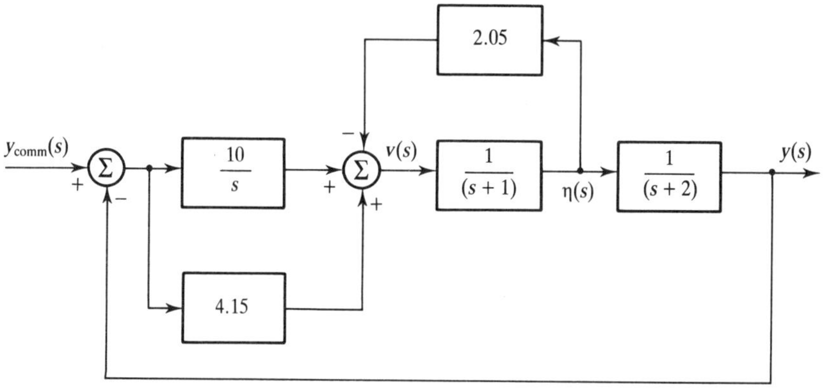

Figure 8.7 Optimal control system with integral action.

$$\frac{y(s)}{y_{comm}(s)} = \frac{10 + 4.15s}{s^3 + 5.05s^2 + 10.25s + 10.0}$$

$$\therefore \quad \mathbf{y}_{ss} = \mathbf{y}_{comm_{ss}} \quad \text{(no steady state error)}$$

8.10 STATE RECONSTRUCTION

8.10.1 Introduction

Most of the control laws derived from the methods outlined in this chapter involve full state variable feedback. Two situations can arise which makes it difficult to implement a feedback control law once it has been determined: the first is the case where only p output variables can be measured, and not the full n state variables, i.e.:

$$\mathbf{y} \triangleq C\mathbf{x} \tag{8.196}$$

where $\mathbf{y} \in R^p$, $\mathbf{x} \in R^n$ and $p < n$.

The second is the case where there are measurements of the state variables which are corrupted by noise. This situation can be represented by:

$$\mathbf{y} = C\mathbf{x} + \mathbf{n} \tag{8.197}$$

where $\mathbf{n}$ is a vector $\in R^p$ and representing sensor noise.

What is wanted is the best estimate of $\mathbf{x}$, given the set of measurements, $\mathbf{y}$ (the sense of best is yet to be defined). There are two methods commonly used, the difference between which depends upon what is known *a priori* about the probability characteristics of the signals involved.

Readers are referred to Curry (1970) for further discussion.

8.10.2 Weighted Least Squares Method

In this method the only assumptions are that, on the average, $\mathbf{n}$ is zero and $\mathbf{x}$ is near the equilibrium flight value, $\mathbf{x}_E$.

What is taken as the best estimate is the value of the state vector $\mathbf{x}$ which minimizes the performance index:

$$\begin{aligned} J &= (\mathbf{x} - \mathbf{x}_E)'Q(\mathbf{x} - \mathbf{x}_E) + \mathbf{n}'G\mathbf{n} \\ &= (\mathbf{x} - \mathbf{x}_E)'Q(\mathbf{x} - \mathbf{x}_E) + (\mathbf{y} - C\mathbf{x})'G(\mathbf{y} - C\mathbf{x}) \end{aligned} \tag{8.198}$$

Q and G are selected to be symmetric and p.d. matrices. In eq. (8.198), $\mathbf{y}$ represents a constant vector, as it represents the measurement. What is significant about choosing eq. (8.198) as the performance index is that the weighting can be arranged so that the situations can be avoided where $\mathbf{x}$ is close to $\mathbf{x}_E$, but $\mathbf{n}$ has large values, or $\mathbf{n}$ is near zero, but the difference between $\mathbf{x}$ and $\mathbf{x}_E$ is substantial. The value of the state vector, $\mathbf{x}^o$, which minimizes eq. (8.198) is the weighted least squares estimate of $\mathbf{x}$.

Using the chain rule of differentiation for vectors it can be shown that:

$$\partial J/\partial \mathbf{x} = -2(\mathbf{y} - C\mathbf{x})'GC + 2(\mathbf{x} - \mathbf{x}_E)'Q \tag{8.199}$$

$$\therefore \quad (\mathbf{y} - C\mathbf{x}^o)'GC = (\mathbf{x}^o - \mathbf{x}_E)'Q$$

$$C'G(\mathbf{y} - C\mathbf{x}^o) = Q(\mathbf{x}^o - \mathbf{x}_E) \tag{8.200}$$

i.e.:

$$\mathbf{x}^o = (Q + C'GC)^{-1}C'G\mathbf{y} + (Q + C'GC)^{-1}Q\mathbf{x}_E \tag{8.201}$$

Let:

$$Z = \begin{bmatrix} Q & C' \\ C & -G^{-1} \end{bmatrix} \tag{8.202}$$

$$Z^{-1} = \begin{bmatrix} L & N \\ O' & M \end{bmatrix} \tag{8.203}$$

$$Z^{-1}Z \triangleq I = \begin{bmatrix} (QL + C'O') & (QN + C'M) \\ (CL - G^{-1}O') & (CQ^{-1} - G^{-1}M) \end{bmatrix} \tag{8.204}$$

Hence:

$$QL + C'O' = I \tag{8.205}$$

$$CL - C^{-1}O' = 0 \tag{8.206}$$

$$\therefore \quad O' = GCL \tag{8.207}$$

$$\therefore \quad QL + C'GCL = I \tag{8.208}$$

from which:

$$L = (Q + C'GC)^{-1} \tag{8.209}$$

However, from eq. (8.205):

$$L = (Q^{-1} - Q^{-1}C'O') \tag{8.210}$$

$$\therefore \quad CQ^{-1} - CQ^{-1}C'O' - G^{-1}O' = 0 \tag{8.211}$$

i.e.:

$$CQ^{-1} - (CQ^{-1}C' + G^{-1})O' = 0$$

$$\therefore \quad O' = (CQ^{-1}C' + G^{-1})^{-1}CQ^{-1} \tag{8.212}$$

$$\therefore \quad L = Q^{-1} - Q^{-1}C'(CQ^{-1}C' + G^{-1})^{-1}CQ^{-1}$$

i.e.:

$$(Q + C'GC)^{-1} = Q^{-1} - Q^{-1}C'(CQ^{-1}C' + G^{-1})^{-1}CQ^{-1} \tag{8.213}$$

Equation (8.213) is a matrix inversion lemma; when substituted in eq. (8.201) it yields:

$$\begin{aligned} \mathbf{x}^{o} = {} & Q^{-1}C'G\mathbf{y} - Q^{-1}C'(CQ^{-1}C' + G^{-1})^{-1}CQ^{-1}C'G\mathbf{y} \\ & + \mathbf{x}_E - Q^{-1}C'(CQ^{-1}C' + G^{-1})^{-1}C\mathbf{x}_E \end{aligned} \tag{8.214}$$

i.e.:

$$\begin{aligned} \mathbf{x}^{o} = {} & \mathbf{x}_E + Q^{-1}C'(CQ^{-1}C' + G^{-1})^{-1}[\{(CQ^{-1}C' + G^{-1})G \\ & - CQ^{-1}C'\mathrm{G}\}\mathbf{y} - C\mathbf{x}_E] \end{aligned} \tag{8.215}$$

from which it can be shown that:

$$\mathbf{x}^{o} = \mathbf{x}_E + H(\mathbf{y} - C\mathbf{x}_E) \tag{8.216}$$

where:

$$H - Q^{-1}C'(CQ^{-1}C' + G^{-1})^{-1} \tag{8.217}$$

Equation (8.216) indicates that the estimate of the state vector, $\mathbf{x}^o$, is given by the equilibrium state vector plus a linear combination of the difference of the measured values from their nominal values, $C\mathbf{x}_E$. The matrix H is an indication of how important the measurements are relative to the quality of the estimated value. For example, suppose it is known for an AFCS that the sensors are not good and that the resulting measurements are poor. G should be chosen so that its norm is small; hence, its inverse will be large. As a consequence, H will be small and the contribution of the measurements to the estimate in eq. (8.216) will be small.

8.10.3 Optimal Linear Estimation

Given eq. (8.197), assume that for the random vectors $\mathbf{x}$ and $\mathbf{n}$ the following first and second order probability characteristics are known:

$$\bar{x} = \xi(\mathbf{x}) \tag{8.218}$$

$$J = \xi\{(\mathbf{x} - \bar{\mathbf{x}})(\mathbf{x} - \bar{\mathbf{x}})'\} \tag{8.219}$$

$$\xi(\mathbf{n}) = 0 \tag{8.220}$$

$$N = \xi\{\mathbf{nn}'\}$$

where $\xi(\ )$ is expectation (or averaging) operator, $\bar{\mathbf{x}}$ is the mean of the vector $\mathbf{x}$ and J is a covariance matrix. The sensor noise has zero mean and its covariance is N. The optimum linear estimator is of the form:

$$\hat{\mathbf{x}} = \bar{\mathbf{x}} + \hat{K}(y - C\bar{\mathbf{x}}) \tag{8.221}$$

where $\hat{\mathbf{x}}$ is the estimated vector, based upon the sensor measurements, $\mathbf{y}$. The gain matrix K is chosen to minimize the mean square error in the estimate. It is easy to show that the correct choice of K for this criterion is:

$$\hat{K} = JC'(CJC' + N)^{-1} \tag{8.222}$$

Comparing eqs (8.217) and (8.222), the gain matrices $\hat{K}$ and L must be different unless the matrices in the least squares cost function are chosen such that:

$$Q^{-1} = J \tag{8.223}$$

$$G^{-1} = N \tag{8.224}$$

When eqs (8.217) and (8.224) apply, the estimated vectors will be identical although the criteria and the basic assumptions are wholly different.

8.10.4 State Estimation – Observer Theory

The theory of observers is due to Luenberger (1966); it is used where the available measurements are not heavily corrupted by noise, which is the usual situation prevailing in AFCSs. Its merit is that the state estimator which results is a dynamic system with a lower order than the system whose state vector is being reconstructed.

For a system defined by eqs (8.225) and (8.226):

$$\dot{\mathbf{x}} = A\mathbf{x} + B\mathbf{u} \tag{8.225}$$

$$\mathbf{y} = C\mathbf{x} \tag{8.226}$$

where $\mathbf{x} \in R^n$, $\mathbf{u} \in R^m$ and $\mathbf{y} \in R^p$. Luenberger showed that an observer of order $(n - p)$ can be constructed with a state vector, $\mathbf{z}$, such that the observer state vector is related to the true state vector by:

$$\mathbf{z} = S\mathbf{x} \tag{8.227}$$

where $\mathbf{z} \in R^{n-p}$ and S is a matrix of order $[(n - p) \times n]$. The observer is defined by:

$$\dot{\mathbf{z}} = E\mathbf{z} + F\mathbf{y} + J\mathbf{u} \tag{8.228}$$

where E is a matrix of order $[(n - p) \times (n - p)]$, F is of order $[(n - p) \times n]$, and J is of order $[(n - p) \times m]$.

Suppose a transformation matrix S can be found which satisfies:

$$SA - ES = FC \tag{8.229}$$

and the matrix J is arranged to be:

$$J = SB \tag{8.230}$$

If:

$$\mathbf{z}(0) = S\mathbf{x}(0) \tag{8.231}$$

then:

$$\mathbf{z}(t) = S\mathbf{x}(t) \tag{8.232}$$

$$\begin{aligned} \therefore\quad \dot{\mathbf{z}} - S\dot{\mathbf{x}} &= E\mathbf{z} + F\mathbf{y} + J\mathbf{u} - SA\mathbf{x} - SB\mathbf{u} \\ &= E\mathbf{z} + F\mathbf{y} - SA\mathbf{x} \end{aligned} \tag{8.233}$$

But, substituting for SA from eq. (8.229), yields:

$$\dot{\mathbf{z}} - S\dot{\mathbf{x}} = E(\mathbf{z} - S\mathbf{x}) \tag{8.234}$$

which has a solution:

$$\mathbf{z}(t) = S\mathbf{x}(t) + e^{Et}[\mathbf{z}(0) - S\mathbf{x}(0)] \tag{8.235}$$

If E is chosen such that the eigenvalues of the observer are more negative than those of the aircraft dynamics, the observer state, $\mathbf{z}$, will converge rapidly to the aircraft state $\mathbf{x}$.

Once E is chosen, methods are available for solving for S and F, thus completing the design of the observer.

The required estimate $\hat{\mathbf{x}}$ of the aircraft state vector $\mathbf{x}$ is reconstructed from the measured output vector, $\mathbf{y}$, and the observer state $\mathbf{z}$, i.e.:

$$\hat{\mathbf{x}} = D_1\mathbf{y} + D_2\mathbf{z} \tag{8.236}$$

where

$$D_1C + D_2S = I \tag{8.237}$$

A block diagram representation of the observed aircraft is given in Figure 8.8.

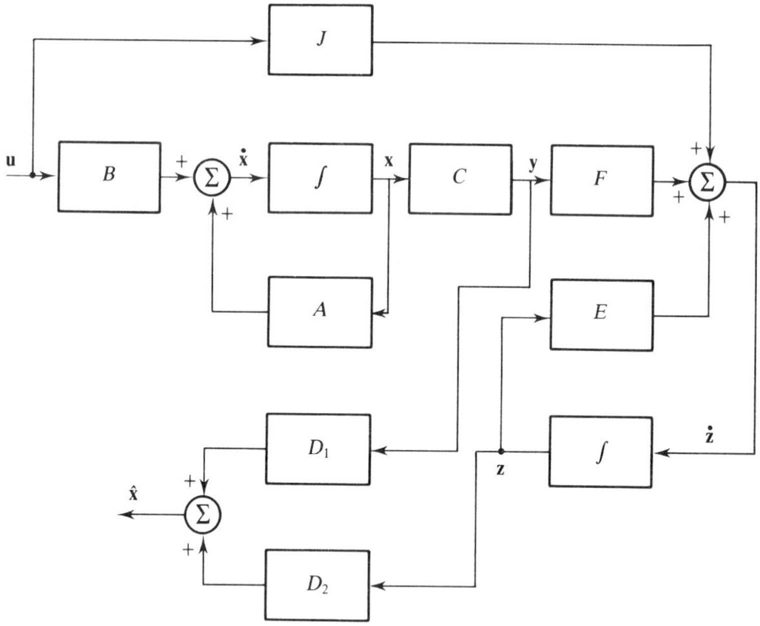

Figure 8.8 Observer system.

8.10.5 Optimal Observer

Suppose that the dynamics of some aircraft are defined by the state and output eqs (8.238) and (8.239):

$$\dot{\mathbf{x}} = A\mathbf{x} + B\mathbf{u} \tag{8.238}$$

$$\mathbf{y} = C\mathbf{x} \tag{8.239}$$

It is intended to design an observer to provide an estimated state vector $\mathbf{x}_E$ which will be close to the original state vector $\mathbf{x}$, but requires as its inputs only the control vector $\mathbf{u}$ and another vector $\mathbf{w}$ which is related to the output vector $\mathbf{y}$ of the aircraft, i.e.:

$$\dot{\mathbf{x}}_E = F\mathbf{x}_E + G\mathbf{u} + \mathbf{w} \tag{8.240}$$

The forcing vector, **w**, is chosen to be:

$$\mathbf{w} \triangleq K(\mathbf{y} - \mathbf{y}_E) \tag{8.241}$$

where:

$$\mathbf{y}_E \triangleq C\mathbf{x}_E \tag{8.242}$$

$$\therefore \quad \dot{\mathbf{x}}_E = (F - KC)\mathbf{x}_E + G\mathbf{u} + KC\mathbf{x} \tag{8.243}$$

However, from eq. (8.238):

$$B\mathbf{u} = \dot{\mathbf{x}} - A\mathbf{x} \tag{8.244}$$

and if:

$$G \triangleq B \tag{8.245}$$

then:

$$\dot{\mathbf{x}}_E = (F - KC)\mathbf{x}_E + \dot{\mathbf{x}} - (A - KC)\mathbf{x} \tag{8.246}$$

i.e.:

$$\dot{\mathbf{x}}_E - \dot{\mathbf{x}} = (F - KC)\mathbf{x}_E - (A - KC)\mathbf{x} \tag{8.247}$$

By choosing the coefficient matrix F of the observer to be identical to that of the aircraft, namely:

$$F \triangleq A \tag{8.248}$$

and by defining any difference between the estimated and actual state vector as an error vector, **e**, it can easily be shown that:

$$\dot{\mathbf{e}} = (A - KC)\mathbf{e} \tag{8.249}$$

Provided that $\lambda(A - KC) < 0$, then as $t \to \infty$, the error vector **e** will tend to zero and the observer's vector $\mathbf{x}_E$ will correspond to the state vector **x** of the aircraft. To secure this desirable condition requires only that K be determined.

As a first step, let K be chosen to be a stabilizing matrix. Imagine that the observer dynamics are defined by:

$$\dot{\mathbf{x}}_E = F\mathbf{x}_E + G\mathbf{u} + K\mathbf{y} \tag{8.250}$$

Letting $G \triangleq B$ (as before) results in:

$$\dot{\mathbf{x}} - \dot{\mathbf{x}}_E = A\mathbf{x} - F\mathbf{x}_E - KC\mathbf{x} = (A - KC)\mathbf{x} - F\mathbf{x}_E \tag{8.251}$$

If F is chosen to be $(A - KC)$, and:

$$\mathbf{e} \triangleq \mathbf{x} - \mathbf{x}_E \tag{8.252}$$

then:

$$\dot{\mathbf{e}} = (A - KC)\mathbf{e} = F\mathbf{e} \tag{8.253}$$

Suppose that we have a system defined by:

$$\dot{\mathbf{e}} = M\mathbf{e} + N\mathbf{v} \tag{8.254}$$

then if we choose as a performance index:

$$J = \tfrac{1}{2}\int_0^{\infty} (\mathbf{e}'Q\mathbf{e} + \mathbf{v}'G\mathbf{v})\mathrm{d}t \tag{8.255}$$

then minimizing eq. (8.255) subject to eq. (8.254) will result in a control law:

$$\mathbf{v} = H\mathbf{e} \tag{8.256}$$

Hence:

$$\dot{\mathbf{e}} = (M + NH)\mathbf{e} \tag{8.257}$$

If it can be arranged that:

$$\lambda(A - KC) = \lambda(M + NH) \tag{8.258}$$

then the optimal closed loop observer will be the required observer provided that:

$$M' = A,\ N' = C \text{ and } H' = -K \tag{8.259}$$

A block diagram representing the optimal closed-loop observer is shown in Figure 8.9.

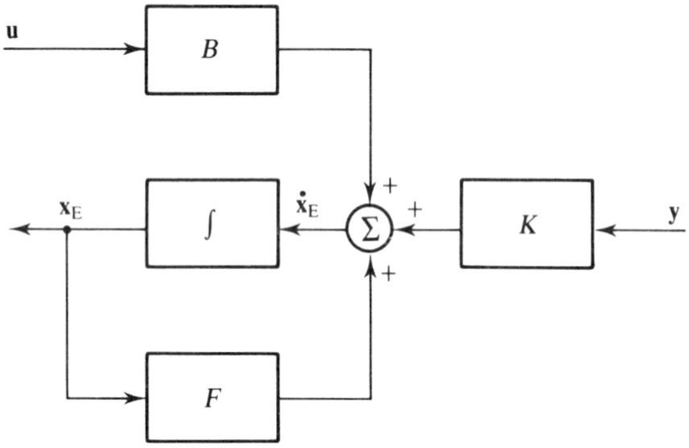

Figure 8.9 Optimal observer.

Example 8.7

For the aircraft DELTA, at flight condition 2, the equation of motion representing the aircraft's dynamics, including the flexibility effects, is given by $\dot{\mathbf{x}} = A\mathbf{x} + B\mathbf{u}$ where

$$\mathbf{x}' \triangleq [w\ \bar{q}\ \dot{\lambda}_1\ \dot{\lambda}_2\ \dot{\lambda}_3\ \dot{\lambda}_4\ \dot{\lambda}_5\ \dot{\lambda}_6\ \lambda_1\ \lambda_2\ \lambda_3\ \lambda_4\ \lambda_5\ \lambda_6\ \delta_A\ \delta_{E_i}\ \delta_{E_o}]$$

and

$$\mathbf{u} = \begin{bmatrix} \delta_{A_c} \\ \\ \delta_{E_{i_c}} \end{bmatrix}$$

δ_{E_i} and δ_{E_o} denote the respective deflections of the inboard and outboard sections of the elevator. λ_i represents the displacement of the ith bending modes.

The corresponding matrix A is shown in Figure 8.10; matrices B and C are shown in Figure 8.11. Note that C results because the output is assumed to be solely the vertical velocity w. It is from this solitary measurement that the state vector is to be reconstructed. The resulting optimal gain matrix for the observer is:

$$K = [32.2\ 229.0\ -291.0\ 24.0\ 170.0\ 171.0\ 44.5\ -41.8\ -2.24\ 0.486\ 2.64\ 8.32\ 1.99\ -3.44\ -0.88\ -2.26\ -0.0318]$$

$$A = \left[\begin{array}{ccccccccccccccccc}
-0.68 & -3.28 & -0.04 & -0.01 & -0.02 & -0.02 & -0.02 & 0.05 & -0.64 & -0.65 & -1.71 & 4.5 & -1.36 & 1.85 & -2.30 & -190 & -30.1 \\
-0.55 & -1.17 & 0.04 & -0.04 & -0.33 & -0.32 & -0.12 & 0.25 & -0.11 & -1.68 & -10.3 & -5.7 & -4.94 & 9.11 & -576 & -2500 & -440 \\
-1.49 & 0.11 & -0.99 & -0.02 & -0.15 & 0.51 & 0.02 & -0.26 & -29.9 & -4.09 & -16.6 & -40.6 & -5.84 & -6.69 & 3400 & 1420 & 260 \\
0.05 & -0.09 & 0.01 & -0.47 & -0.07 & -0.06 & -0.01 & 0 & 0.27 & -124.0 & -0.87 & -1.58 & -0.16 & 1.51 & -133 & -292 & -63.9 \\
0.05 & -0.85 & 0.05 & -0.07 & -1.29 & -0.41 & -0.03 & -0.06 & 1.4 & -0.65 & -193 & -15.4 & -0.98 & -3.15 & -1420 & -2570 & -582 \\
-1.11 & -0.99 & 0.08 & -0.04 & -0.27 & -1.09 & -0.18 & 0.44 & -0.2 & -0.68 & -9.37 & -243 & -7.18 & 17 & 804 & -2530 & -625 \\
-0.2 & -0.24 & 0.06 & -0.02 & -0.05 & -0.11 & -0.86 & 0.12 & 0.23 & -0.75 & -1.3 & -3.23 & -306 & 6.08 & -13.1 & -653 & -179 \\
0.46 & 0.42 & -0.11 & 0.02 & 0.04 & 0.18 & 0.1 & -1.15 & -0.12 & 2.01 & 1.5 & 4.5 & 4.77 & -352 & -411 & 1120 & 323 \\
0 & 0 & 1 & 0 & 0 & 0 & 0 & 0 & 0 & 0 & 0 & 0 & 0 & 0 & 0 & 0 & 0 \\
0 & 0 & 0 & 1 & 0 & 0 & 0 & 0 & 0 & 0 & 0 & 0 & 0 & 0 & 0 & 0 & 0 \\
0 & 0 & 0 & 0 & 1 & 0 & 0 & 0 & 0 & 0 & 0 & 0 & 0 & 0 & 0 & 0 & 0 \\
0 & 0 & 0 & 0 & 0 & 1 & 0 & 0 & 0 & 0 & 0 & 0 & 0 & 0 & 0 & 0 & 0 \\
0 & 0 & 0 & 0 & 0 & 0 & 1 & 0 & 0 & 0 & 0 & 0 & 0 & 0 & 0 & 0 & 0 \\
0 & 0 & 0 & 0 & 0 & 0 & 0 & 1 & 0 & 0 & 0 & 0 & 0 & 0 & 0 & 0 & 0 \\
0 & 0 & 0 & 0 & 0 & 0 & 0 & 0 & 0 & 0 & 0 & 0 & 0 & 0 & -6 & 0 & 0 \\
0 & 0 & 0 & 0 & 0 & 0 & 0 & 0 & 0 & 0 & 0 & 0 & 0 & 0 & 0 & -7.5 & 0 \\
0 & 0 & 0 & 0 & 0 & 0 & 0 & 0 & 0 & 0 & 0 & 0 & 0 & 0 & 0 & 0 & -7.5
\end{array}\right]$$

Figure 8.10 Coefficient matrix, A, for DELTA-2 (with flexibility effects).

$$B' = \left[\begin{array}{ccccccccccccccccc}
0 & 0 & 0 & 0 & 0 & 0 & 0 & 0 & 0 & 0 & 0 & 0 & 0 & 0 & 6.0 & 0 & 0 \\
0 & 0 & 0 & 0 & 0 & 0 & 0 & 0 & 0 & 0 & 0 & 0 & 0 & 0 & 0 & 7.5 & 0
\end{array}\right]$$

$$C = \left[\begin{array}{ccccccccccccccccc}
1 & 0 & 0 & 0 & 0 & 0 & 0 & 0 & 0 & 0 & 0 & 0 & 0 & 0 & 0 & 0 & 0
\end{array}\right]$$

Figure 8.11 Driving matrix, B, for flexible DELTA-2.

This corresponds to the choice of weighting matrices $\hat{Q}$ and $\hat{G}$ of:

$$\hat{Q} = \text{diag}[5\ 5\ 0.01\ 0.01\ 0.01\ 0.01\ 0.01\ 0.01\ 0.01\ 0.01\ 0.01\ 0.01\ 0.01\ 0.01\ 10\ 10\ 10]$$

$$\hat{G} = 2.0$$

in the performance index:

$$J = \tfrac{1}{2}\int_0^\infty (\mathbf{e}'\hat{Q}\mathbf{e} + \mathbf{v}'\hat{G}\mathbf{v})\mathrm{d}t$$

where $\mathbf{e} \triangleq \mathbf{x} - \mathbf{x}_E$ and $\mathbf{v} = K\mathbf{e}$.

Some results of applying an optimal control law to the aircraft, assuming that every state variable is available for measurement, are shown in Figure 8.12. Also shown there are the results of applying the same control law, but with the state vector having been entirely reconstructed in the observer from the solitary, continuous measurement of w.

8.10.6 The Kalman–Bucy Filter

In situations where noise contaminated measurements must be used (where for example, radio or radar receivers are used as sensors) then a Kalman–Bucy filter

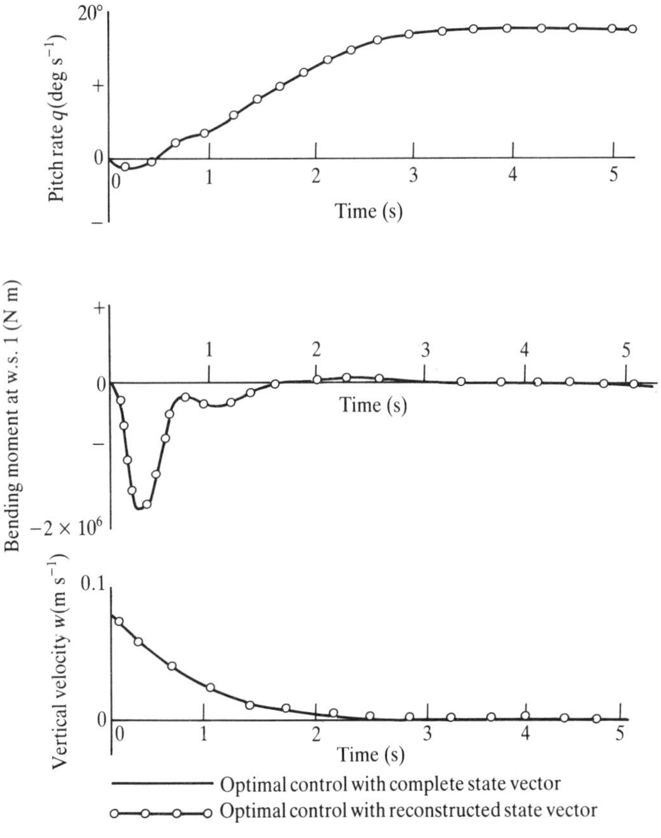

Figure 8.12 Response of optimally controlled DELTA-2 to initial angle of attack.

may be used to reconstruct the state vector from the noisy output signals. Although its use results in optimal rejection of the noise signals which corrupt the measurement, it requires a dynamic system of the same order (usually) as the aircraft dynamics.

The aircraft's linearized motion is assumed to be affected by the control surface deflections, $\mathbf{u}$, and atmospheric turbulence, $\mathbf{w}_g$. The output signals, $\mathbf{y}$, are affected by sensor noise, $\mathbf{n}$. Hence:

$$\dot{\mathbf{x}} = A\mathbf{x} + B\mathbf{u} + E\mathbf{w}_g \tag{8.260}$$

$$\mathbf{y} = C\mathbf{x} + \mathbf{n} \tag{8.261}$$

where:

$$\xi\{\mathbf{x}_0\mathbf{x}_0'\} = X_0 \tag{8.262}$$

$$\xi\{\mathbf{w}_g(t)\mathbf{w}_g'(t)\} = S(t)\delta(t - T) \tag{8.263}$$

where $\delta(\ )$ is a unit impulse function.

$$\xi\{\mathbf{n}(t)\mathbf{n}'(t)\} = T(t)\delta(t - T) \tag{8.264}$$

$$\xi\{\mathbf{w}_g(t)\mathbf{n}'(t)\} = 0 \tag{8.265}$$

where $\xi\{\ \}$ is the expectation operator.

The solution is obtained when a control $\mathbf{u}(t)$ has been found to minimize the performance index:

$$J = \tfrac{1}{2}E\{\mathbf{x}'(T)S\mathbf{x}(T) + \int_{t_0}^{T} [\mathbf{x}'(t)Q(t)\mathbf{x}(t) + \mathbf{u}'(t)G(t)\mathbf{u}(t)]dt\} \tag{8.266}$$

The separation theorem proposed by Lee (1964) allows the optimal control law to be found first. It can be shown to be:

$$\mathbf{u}^o = -G^{-1}B'P(t)\hat{\mathbf{x}}(t) \tag{8.267}$$

where $P(t)$ is the *time-varying* solution of the matrix Riccati equation:

$$\dot{P}(t) = P(t)A + A'P(t) + Q - P(t)BG^{-1}B'P(t) \tag{8.268}$$

where:

$$P(0) = S \tag{8.269}$$

Equation (8.267) depends upon the best estimate of $\mathbf{x}$ which is obtained from the Kalman–Bucy filter defined by:

$$\dot{\hat{\mathbf{x}}}(t/t) = A\hat{\mathbf{x}}(t/t) + \hat{K}(t)[\mathbf{y} - C\hat{\mathbf{x}}(t/t)] \tag{8.270}$$

The notation $\hat{\mathbf{x}}(t/t)$ means the estimate of $\mathbf{x}(t)$ based upon measurements up to and including $\mathbf{y}(t)$. $\hat{K}(t)$ is the gain matrix of the Kalman–Bucy filter and is given by:

$$\hat{K}(t) = W(t/t)C'T^{-1}(t) \tag{8.271}$$

where the error covariance, $W(t/t)$, is obtained from:

$$\dot{W}(t/t) = AW(t/t)(t) + W(t/t)A' + ES(t)E' - W(t/t)C'T^{-1}(t)CW(t/t) \quad (8.278)$$

with:

$$W(0|0) = X_0 \quad (8.273)$$

Example 8.8

An integrated flight control system has a height hold mode which can be represented by the transfer function:

$$\frac{h(s)}{h_{\text{comm}}(s)} = \frac{0.3(s + 0.01)}{(s^2 + 0.006s + 0.003)}$$

i.e. $\omega_{\text{ph}} = 0.055$ rad s^{-1} and $\zeta_{\text{ph}} = 0.055$.

The commanded height signal, h_{comm}, is composed of h_{comm_0}, which is taken to be a random variable, with normal probability distribution and a mean value of 10 000 ft, and a variance of 2.5×10^5 ft^2, plus δh_{comm} of white noise. Thus $h_{\text{comm}} = h_{\text{comm}_0} + \delta h_{\text{comm}}$.

The statistical characteristics of the noise in the command channel are defined by:

$$\xi\{h_{\text{comm}}\} = 0.0$$

$$\xi\{\delta h_{\text{comm}}(t)\delta h_{\text{comm}}(v)\} = N_{\text{comm}}\delta(t - v)$$

N_{comm} is defined as 400 ft^2 s. Height is measured continuously, but these measurements contain white noise, i.e.:

$$h_{\text{m}} = h + \delta_{\text{m}}$$

where

$$\xi\{\delta_{\text{m}}\} = 0$$

$$\xi\{\delta_{\text{m}}(t)\delta_{\text{m}}(v)\} = N_{\text{m}}\delta(t - v)$$

N_{m} is taken as 900 ft^2 s.

The requirement is to design a system which will provide an estimate of height with the least possible variance.

The height hold system can be represented in state variable form as:

$$\begin{bmatrix} \dot{x}_1 \\ \dot{x}_2 \end{bmatrix} = \begin{bmatrix} 0 & 1 \\ -0.003 & -0.006 \end{bmatrix} \begin{bmatrix} x_1 \\ x_2 \end{bmatrix} + \begin{bmatrix} 0 \\ 1 \end{bmatrix} h_{\text{c}}$$

$$h \triangleq y = [0.003 \ \ 0.3] \begin{bmatrix} x_1 \\ x_2 \end{bmatrix} = C\mathbf{x}$$

Let $h_{\text{comm}_0} \triangleq x_3$. Then, since $h_{\text{comm}} = h_{\text{comm}_0} + \delta h_{\text{comm}}$, the complete state representation becomes:

$$\begin{bmatrix} \dot{x}_1 \\ \dot{x}_2 \\ \dot{x}_3 \end{bmatrix} = \begin{bmatrix} 0 & 1 & 0 \\ -0.003 & -0.006 & 1 \\ 0 & 0 & 0 \end{bmatrix} \begin{bmatrix} x_1 \\ x_2 \\ x_3 \end{bmatrix} + \begin{bmatrix} 0 \\ 1 \\ 0 \end{bmatrix} \delta h_{\text{comm}}$$

and:

$$h_{\text{m}} \triangleq y = [0.003 \;\; 0.3 \;\; 0]\mathbf{x} + \delta_{\text{m}}$$

i.e.:

$$y = C\mathbf{x} + \mathbf{n}$$

$$\dot{\mathbf{x}} = A\mathbf{x} + E\mathbf{w}_{\text{g}}$$

then:

$$\dot{\mathbf{x}} = A\mathbf{x} + WC'T^{-1}[y - C\mathbf{x}]$$

where W is the solution from:

$$0 = AW + WA' + ESE' - WC'T^{-1}CW \qquad \text{(A)}$$

From the problem statement:

$$S = N_{\text{comm}} = 400$$

$$T = N_{\text{m}} = 900$$

Now:

$$W = \begin{bmatrix} W_{11} & W_{12} & W_{13} \\ W_{12} & W_{22} & W_{23} \\ W_{13} & W_{23} & W_{33} \end{bmatrix}$$

$$WC' = \begin{bmatrix} 0.003\,\mathrm{W}_{11} + 0.3\,W_{21} \\ 0.003\,W_{12} + 0.3\,W_{22} \\ 0.003\,W_{13} + 0.3\,W_{23} \end{bmatrix}$$

Hence:

$$\dot{\hat{x}}_1 = \hat{x}_2 + \left[\frac{0.003\,W_{11} + 0.3\,W_{12}}{900}\right]\left[h_{\text{m}} - 0.003\hat{x}_1 - 0.3\hat{x}_2\right]$$

$$\dot{\hat{x}}_2 = -0.003\hat{x}_1 - 0.006\hat{x}_2 + \hat{x}_3 + \left[\frac{0.003\,W_{12} + 0.3\,W_{12}}{500}\right]\left[h_{\text{m}} - 0.003\hat{x}_1 - 0.3\hat{x}_2\right]$$

$$\dot{\hat{x}}_3 = \left[\frac{0.003\,W_{13} + 0.3\,W_{23}}{900}\right]\left[h_{\text{m}} - 0.003\hat{x}_1 - 0.3\hat{x}_2\right]$$

$$\hat{h} = 0.003\hat{x}_1 + 0.3\hat{x}_2$$

The coefficients W_{ij} are obtained from a solution of the ARE eq. (A). Steady state starting conditions are usually assumed, such as:

$$\mathbf{x}(0) = \begin{bmatrix} 3.3 \times 10^6 \\ 0 \\ 10^4 \end{bmatrix}$$

8.11 CONCLUSIONS

This chapter introduces the important topics of linear optimal control, controllability and observability, which are very important properties of the mathematical models of the aircraft upon which the designs of effective AFCSs are based. In such advanced systems as AFCSs with analytical redundancy (a topic which is not covered in this book) these subjects are of considerable importance and need to be thoroughly understood by the control system designer. The solution of the linear quadratic optimal problem by means of the algebraic Riccati equation (ARE) is presented, with particular reference to effective methods of obtaining the required feedback control law. Based upon this work, methods of designing an optimal output regulator, or a system with a prescribed degree of stability, or one which explicitly follows a model response are also presented. In all the methods, the result depends upon solving an ARE. Furthermore, an optimal command control system was presented, which is also based on the work of the LQP. The use of a dynamic feedback controller is also dealt with, before concluding the chapter with a study of a few techniques for satisfactorily reconstructing a complete state vector from measurements of a few, or even a single, output variable.

8.12 EXERCISES

8.1 For a system defined by the state and output equations $\dot{\mathbf{x}} = A\mathbf{x} + B\mathbf{u}$ and $\mathbf{y} = C\mathbf{x} + D\mathbf{u}$ the following matrices apply:

$$A = \begin{bmatrix} 0 & 1 & 0 \\ 4 & 0 & 2 \\ -2 & 0 & -2 \end{bmatrix} \qquad \begin{aligned} B' &= [-1 \ 1 \ -1] \\ C &= [-1 \ 2 \ 0] \\ D &= [0] \end{aligned}$$

Is the system controllable and observable?

8.2 A system has two components represented by the transfer functions:

$$G_1(s) = \frac{s+2}{s+4} \qquad G_2(s) = \frac{s+2}{s+4}$$

The components can be connected in any one of three possible ways:

1. Cascade: $G_1(s)G_2(s)$
2. Parallel: $G_1(s) + G_2(s)$
3. In a closed loop configuration:

$$\frac{G_1(s)}{1 + G_1(s)G_2(s)}$$

Discuss the controllability and observability for each connection.

8.3 Write down an appropriate state equation and the corresponding output equation for the lateral acceleration at the pilot's station for the aircraft ALPHA-4. Is the aircraft completely controllable? Is it completely observable? What effect would losing rudder action have on the controllability?

8.4 Write down the state equation corresponding to the lateral motion of DELTA-1. If a performance index, J, is chosen to be:

$$J = \tfrac{1}{2}\int_0^\infty (\beta^2 + p^2 + r^2 + 2\phi^2 + 0.1\delta_A^2 + 10.0\delta_R^2)dt$$

Establish:
(a) Whether the feedback control law obtained as a solution to this linear quadratic problem can stabilize the aircraft.
(b) The gains of the optimal feedback control law.
(c) The eigenvalues of the closed loop flight control system.

8.5 The executive jet, ALPHA, is cruising at an altitude of 6100 m and a forward speed of 237 m s^{-1}. The aircraft is controlled by means of its elevator and by changing its thrust. For the longitudinal motion the output vector has as its elements the pitch rate and pitch attitude, i.e. $\mathbf{y}' \triangleq [q \ \ \theta]$
(a) Compute the steady state response to a unit step change in thrust.
(b) For $Q = \text{diag}[1 \ \ 1 \ \ 1 \ \ 1]$ and $G = \text{diag}[1 \ \ 100]$ find the optimal feedback gain matrix.

8.6 For the aircraft detailed in Exercise 2.5 determine a feedback control law which will result in the acceleration response of the controlled aircraft being identical to that obtained from an aircraft which has been idealized and modelled by the equation:

$$a_{y_{\text{mod}}} = -10a_{y_{\text{mod}}} + 10\delta_A + \dot{\delta}_A$$

Show that the feedback control law found does indeed provide model matching.

8.7 The aircraft BRAVO-3 is represented by the following state equation $\dot{\mathbf{x}} = A\mathbf{x} + B\mathbf{u}$ where:

$$\mathbf{x}' \triangleq [u \ \ w \ \ q \ \ \theta]$$

$$\mathbf{u}' \triangleq [\delta_E]$$

(a) Using weighting matrices:

$$Q = \text{diag}[1 \ \ 1 \ \ 1 \ \ 1]$$

$$G = [1]$$

determine the optimal feedback control law.

(b) Find the eigenvalues of the optimal closed loop system and compare them with those of the uncontrolled aircraft.

(c) Calculate the response of the optimal flight control system for a period of 15.0 s to an initial angle of attack of 1°.

8.8 A pitch rate damper is represented by the block diagram of Figure 8.13. It is observed that in response to a step command of q_{comm} of $10° \, s^{-1}$ there is a steady state error of 8.88°.

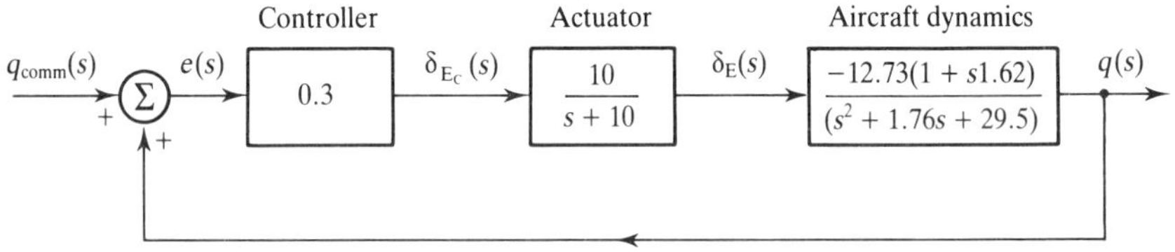

Figure 8.13 Pitch rate damping system for Exercise 8.8.

Use the method outlined in Section 8.9 to obtain an optimal control law which will both minimize the performance index:

$$J = \tfrac{1}{2}\int_0^{\infty} (10q^2 + 0.1e^2)\mathrm{d}t$$

and will result in there being zero steady state error in the optimal closed loop flight control system.

8.9 The aircraft FOXTROT-3, using only its elevator for control, has an optimal pitch control system for which the feedback gain matrix, K, is given by:

$$K = [0.0184 \ \ -0.0855 \ \ -2.905 \ \ -14.035]$$

The actuator dynamics have been ignored. It is found, however, that only the pitch rate and pitch attitude can be measured on the aircraft.

(a) Show how the motion variables u and w may be reconstructed if the elevator deflection can be measured also.

(b) Draw a block diagram of this complete flight control system. Include all the gains involved in your scheme.

8.13 NOTES

1. The pay-off functional is introduced as a postulate. The reader may like to be reminded of the view of the postulating method, expressed by the philosopher Bertrand Russell: it has a great many advantages, all of which coincide exactly with those of theft in comparison with honest labour.

2. A necessary condition that a matrix Z be positive definite is det $Z > 0$; hence Z is non-singular.
3. This restriction is required only when the upper limit of the integral is ∞. If it is finite, then the pair $\{A, B\}$ does not need to be completely controllable.
4. If rank of C is p then $C^{\dagger} = [C'(CC')^{-1}]$. If rank of C is m then $C^{\dagger} = [(C'C)^{-1}C']$.

8.14 REFERENCES

ANDERSON, B.D.O. and J.B. MOORE. 1971. *Linear Optimal Control.* Englewood Cliffs, NJ: Prentice Hall.

ATHANS, M. and P.L. FALB. 1966. *Optimal Control.* New York: McGraw-Hill.

BROCKETT, R.W. 1970. *Finite Dimensional Linear Systems.* New York: Wiley.

CURRY, R.E. 1970. A brief introduction to estimation for dynamic systems. In *Education in Creative Engineering*, edited by Y.T. Li, pp. 140–50. Cambridge, Mass.: MIT Press.

DESOER, C.A. 1970. *Notes for a Second Course on Linear Systems.* Princeton, NJ: Van Nostrand Reinhold.

FULLER, A.T. 1959. Performance criteria for control systems. *J. Elec. and Cont.* 7(3): 456–62.

KWAKERNAAK, H. and R. SIVAN. 1972. *Linear Optimal Control Theory.* New York: Wiley.

LAUB, A.J. 1979. A Schur method for solving algebraic Riccati equations. *Trans IEEE Auto. Cont.* AC-24(6): 913–21.

LEE, R.C.K. 1964. *Optimal Estimation, Identification and Control.* Cambridge, Mass.: MIT Press.

LUENBERGER, D.G. 1966. An introduction to observers. *Trans IEEE Auto. Cont.* AC-11(4): 190–7.

MARSHALL, S.A. and H. NICHOLSON. 1970. Optimal control of linear multivariable systems with quadratic performance criteria. *Proc. IEE.* 117(8): 1705–13.

MAYBECK, P.S. 1979. *Stochastic Models, Estimation and Control.* Vols 1, 2, 3. New York: Academic Press.

PARKER, K.T. 1972. Design of PID controllers by the use of optimal linear regulator theory. *Proc. IEE.* 119(7): 911–14.

PORTER, W.A. 1966. *Modern Foundations of Systems Engineering.* New York: MacMillan.

ZADEH, L.A. and C.A. DESOER. 1963. *Linear System Theory.* New York: McGraw-Hill.

9

Stability Augmentation Systems

9.1 INTRODUCTION

The term 'stability augmentation system' came into use in the USA about 1950. At that time, Northrop, an American manufacturer, was famous for its 'flying wing' aircraft, being the leading exponent of such designs. It was known from the outset, however, that such designs would provide most unsatisfactory flying qualities due to the absence of any suitable control action being provided by an AFCS. What Northrop called the kind of AFCS it proposed to use to remedy the poor, inherent flying qualities of its YB-49, a flying wing bomber aircraft, was a 'stability derivative augmentor'. However, on the standard form for installation drawings, the title block was insufficiently wide, so that the name was reduced by a draughtsman to 'stability augmentor' to fit the available space (McRuer and Graham, 1981). All similar systems have been called stability augmentation systems (SASs) ever since, although their purpose remains as it was originally: the values of a number of specific stability derivatives of an aircraft are to be increased by means of negative feedback control.

Although all stability derivatives could be so altered, only a few are usable candidates, since it is only by means of their alteration that any required change in the flying qualities of an aircraft can be effected. In general, SASs are concerned with the control of a single mode of an aircraft's motion.

The general structure of such an SAS is shown in the block diagram of Figure 9.1, in which it can be seen there are four principal elements: aircraft dynamics, actuator dynamics, sensor dynamics and flight controller. These elements are essential and are always present in any SAS. When the SAS is switched off, the aircraft can be controlled directly by the pilot moving the appropriate control surface(s) through his cockpit controls. The flight controller, of course, is not then active. When the SAS is switched on, the control surface is driven by its actuator which is controlled by the flight controller.

In SAS studies, command inputs are usually considered only secondarily; the flying qualities of the aircraft are enhanced by the control action of the feedback control system in such a manner that the effects of atmospheric, or other disturbances upon the aircraft's motion are suppressed. Sensor noise also affects the quality of control. However, many types of SAS cannot be switched off by a pilot, but always remain active, from the moment the master electrical switch is on. In the event of any failure of the SAS, the aircraft has then to be controlled solely by means of inputs from the pilot's cockpit controls. If an aircraft has a

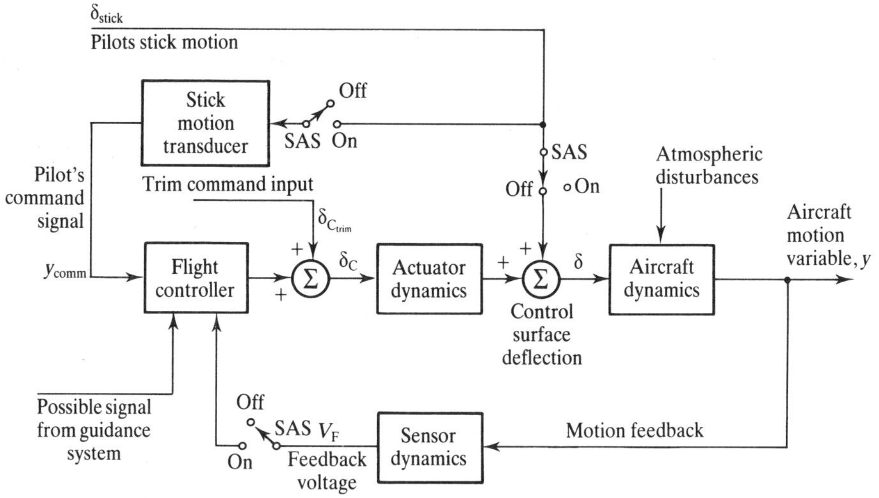

Figure 9.1 Stability augmentation system.

direct link between some particular cockpit control and its corresponding control surface, then the aircraft is said to possess, in the event of an AFCS failure, the property of manual reversion. In some cases, the forces which need to be supplied by the pilot are beyond the limits of human performance. In some modern aircraft, particularly CCVs, which depend upon active control technology for their successful operation, no such manual reversion is provided, reliance being placed upon some form of redundancy in the AFCS to ensure continuous operation of the SAS. Sometimes when SASs admit pilots' or guidance systems' command signals, the system may be referred to as a command and stability augmentation system (CSAS). The principal SAS functions which are found on modern aircraft are: pitch rate SAS, yaw damper, roll rate damper, and relaxed static stability SAS.

Essentially, certain desirable values of the non-dimensional stability derivatives, C_{m_α}, C_{m_q}, C_{n_β}, C_{n_r}, C_{n_p}, and C_{l_β}, can be obtained more effectively using automatic control than by physical sizing of aerodynamic surfaces.

9.2 ACTUATOR DYNAMICS

Actuators used in combat and transport aircraft are generally electrohydraulic.[1] General aviation aircraft sometimes use electric actuators. Such actuator systems have their own dynamic characteristics which affect the performance of the closed loop SAS. In Appendix A, some information on the nature of the dynamic characteristics of such actuators is presented. When the design of an SAS (or any AFCS mode) is initially being considered it may be assumed, as a first approximation, that the dynamic response of the actuator, in comparison with that of the mode of flight of the aircraft which is being controlled, is so rapid that it can be regarded as instantaneous.

Making that assumption means that the actuator dynamics can be considered to be represented by a very simple transfer function:

$$\delta(s)/\delta_c(s) = K \tag{9.1}$$

K is taken as the gain of the actuator: it is dimensional, usually degrees per volt. If the aircraft is large, then it is known that the actuator must provide large hinge moments for control. It is improbable in such a case that the response can then be instantaneous and, consequently, the transfer function usually assumed in this situation is:

$$\delta(s)/\delta_c(s) = K\lambda/(s + \lambda) \tag{9.2}$$

Typically, λ lies in the range 5–10.0 s^{-1}; λ is the inverse time constant of the actuator.

Even when it is known that the SAS design is likely to be much affected by the nature of the actuator's performance, it is customary to proceed with the design on the basis of either representation eqs (9.1) or (9.2) and then to simulate the final design, including the complete known description of the dynamic characteristics of the actuator, noting any loss of SAS performance as a result of including the more representative actuator dynamics. If a significant change is noted then some adjustment in the control law is normally tried in order to minimize the loss of dynamic performance.

It is more important to realize that this final test must always be made, particularly to confirm that the existence of the higher order terms in the actuator dynamics do not cause instability in the SAS. Another feature of the actuator dynamics, which can sometimes have very grave effects on the SAS performance, is the existence of non-linearities. Such effects should be accounted for in the simulation study.

There is a semantic difference which occurs between British and American usage; in British work, the actuator is usually taken to mean the device which converts electrical signals to mechanical signals, of low power, but of sufficient power to drive the hydraulic valve which controls the flow of hydraulic fluid to the powered flying control, which deflects the control surface. In American work, 'actuator' covers the whole system from the command voltage, δ_c, to the control surface deflection, δ. This is the usage followed in this book.

When an electric actuator is used, the representation of eq. (9.2) is normally employed; the values of K and λ will depend upon the actuator's characterization. It should also be remembered that the hinge moment is not a linear function; large deflections cause considerable loading of the actuator which affects the dynamic performance. For flight critical conditions, such effects should be studied by means of the simulation of the system, before committing to a final design.

Finally, it must be remembered that no AFCS is generally allowed to make use of the full range deflection of the control surfaces: it is usually limited to deflections ± 10 per cent of the trimmed value (although even this limited range of deflection is not allowed at the limits of the control surface deflection). It is then said that the SAS has 10 per cent control authority. Such limits on control authority were set by aviation authorities to ensure the safety of the aircraft in the event of AFCS failures which cause the actuator to be driven 'hardover'. The unwanted acceleration about the c.g. of the aircraft which could result was, therefore, strictly limited. This safety measure is inimical of good manoeuvring performance, however, and on military combat aircraft and CCVs considerably greater authority – sometimes 100 per cent – is now allowed, and is, in a few cases, essential.

9.3 SENSOR DYNAMICS

Every sensor used in an AFCS is a transducer. In modern aircraft, its purpose is to measure motion variables and to produce output voltages or currents which correspond to these motion variables. Some of the electronic sensors, such as radar altimeters, or radar, process the information so quickly in comparison with the aircraft's response that it is customary to regard their transducing action as instantaneous. Often, however, such sensors have in-built filters to improve their noise characteristics, and the time constant of such filters is often considered as representing that of the sensor. The inertial instruments, such as gyroscopes and accelerometers, do have well defined dynamics characteristics (see Appendix A), but the sensors employed in AFCS are chosen to have bandwidths and damping such that they can be considered to be instantaneous in their action. A sensor is frequently represented, then, by its sensitivity, i.e.:

$$v_f/y = K_s \tag{9.3}$$

K_s can have units, such as V rad^{-1} for an attitude gyro, V rad^{-1} s^{-1} for a rate gyro, and V m^{-1} s^{-2} for an accelerometer (more commonly: V g^{-1}). If the problem is concerned with an elastic aircraft, in which structural bending is significant, then sensor dynamics can be significant and the full representation should be used. For SASs, the most common sensors are gyroscopes and accelerometers.

What usually affects the performance of the SAS more strongly than a sensor's dynamics is its location on the fuselage.

9.4 LONGITUDINAL CONTROL (Use of Elevator Only)

9.4.1 Introduction

In Section 2.8 of Chapter 2 the state and output equations used with aircraft dynamics are presented. In SASs, the controller output is the command voltage to the control surface actuator which provides the appropriate deflection. If the actuator dynamics are to be represented by, say, eq. (9.1) no change to the form of the state equation is required but, if eq. (9.2) is used to represent the actuator dynamics, there is an additional differential equation to be accounted for, namely:

$$\dot{\delta}_j = -\lambda\delta_j + K\lambda\delta_{c_j} \tag{9.4}$$

where δ_j is, of course, u_j, one of the control surface deflections. This additional equation is usually made to augment the state equation by choosing x_{n+1} to be u_j. For example, consider the state equation for longitudinal motion with a single control input, δ_E – i.e. eq. (2.108). Let:

$$x_5 \triangleq \delta_E \tag{9.5}$$

$$\bar{\mathbf{u}} \triangleq \delta_{E_c} \tag{9.6}$$

then:

$$\dot{x}_5 = -\lambda x_5 + K\lambda\bar{\mathbf{u}} \tag{9.7}$$

hence:

$$\bar{\mathbf{x}}' \triangleq [u, w, q, \theta, \delta_E] \tag{9.8}$$

$$\bar{\mathbf{u}} \triangleq [\delta_{E_c}] \tag{9.10}$$

$$\bar{A} = \begin{bmatrix} X_u & X_w & 0 & -g & 0 \\ Z_u & Z_w & U_0 & 0 & Z_{\delta_E} \\ \tilde{M}_u & \tilde{M}_w & \tilde{M}_q & 0 & \tilde{M}_{\delta_E} \\ 0 & 0 & 0 & 0 & -\lambda \end{bmatrix} \tag{9.11}$$

$$\bar{B} = \begin{bmatrix} 0 \\ 0 \\ 0 \\ 0 \\ K\lambda \end{bmatrix} \tag{9.12}$$

When the control **u** depends solely upon time, we speak of it as being the control function; when it depends upon the motion (or other) variables of the aircraft, we refer to it as the control law, namely:

$$\mathbf{u} = \mathbf{f}(\mathbf{y}) \tag{9.13}$$

The control law of eq. (9.13) means that the control is based on output feedback; whether the control law is linear or non-linear depends upon the nature of the functional, **f**( ).

The customary forms of feedback control for AFCSs, and hence an SAS, are linear, i.e. the control takes the form:

$$\mathbf{u} = K\mathbf{y} \tag{9.14}$$

When:

$$\mathbf{y} = \mathbf{x} \tag{9.15}$$

then full state variable feedback is involved. If:

$$\mathbf{y} = C\mathbf{x} \tag{9.16}$$

applying a control law such as eq. (9.14) to the aircraft dynamics represented by eq. (2.108) results in the controlled aircraft, the closed loop dynamics taking the form:

$$\dot{\mathbf{x}} = (A + BKC)\mathbf{x} \tag{9.17}$$

Obviously, use of the control law has resulted in a change in the dynamic response of the controlled aircraft.

From experiment and practice, it has emerged that only a limited number of forms of linear control law are effective for stability augmentation. This number includes the following:

$$\delta_E = K_q q \tag{9.18}$$

$$\delta_E = K_{a_z} a_z \tag{9.19}$$

$$\delta_E = K_\alpha \alpha \tag{9.20}$$

Other control laws, involving such motion variables as pitch attitude, θ, change in forward speed u, height h, and flight path angle γ, are dealt with in Chapter 10. It should be noted here that control designs involving full state variable feedback are a mixture of SAS and attitude control; they are dealt with, therefore, in the next chapter. There are two methods excepted: pole placement and model-following, for, even though the resulting control law in each case is one involving full state variable feedback (FSVF), the design intention is to improve the basic stability of the aircraft dynamics.

It should be noted also that the control law of eq. (9.19) involves the feedback of more than a single motion variable:

$$a_{z_{cg}} = \dot{w} - U_0 q \tag{9.21}$$

$$= Z_u u + Z_w w + Z_{\delta_E}\delta_E \tag{9.22}$$

$$\therefore \quad \delta_E = K_{a_z} Z_u u + K_{a_z} Z_w w + K_{a_z} Z_{\delta_E}\delta_E \tag{9.23}$$

$$\therefore \quad \delta_E = (1 - K_{a_z} Z_{\delta_E})^{-1} K_{a_z} Z_u u + K_{a_z} Z_w w (1 - K_{a_z} Z_{\delta_E})^{-1} \tag{9.24}$$

Of course, if the normal acceleration is not measured at the aircraft's c.g. but at some other station, x_A, then:

$$a_{z_A} = a_{z_{cg}} - x_A \dot{q}$$

$$= Z_u u + Z_w w + Z_{\delta_E}\delta_E - x_A \tilde{M}_u u - x_A \tilde{M}_w w - x_A \tilde{M}_q q - x_A \tilde{M}_{\delta_E}\delta_E$$

$$= (Z_u - x_A\tilde{M}_u)u + (Z_w - x_A\tilde{M}_w)\dot{w} - x_A\tilde{M}_q q + (Z_{\delta_E} - x_A\tilde{M}_{\delta_E})\delta_E \quad (9.25)$$

Obviously, from eq. (9.25) the choice of location from the sensor measuring normal acceleration can have a profound influence on the control law, eq. (9.19), and hence upon the stability of the controlled aircraft.

9.4.2 Pitch Rate SAS

The stability derivative which such systems try to augment is M_q, and, thereby, the damping ratio of the short period motion is increased. The block diagram of a typical, conventional pitch rate SAS is shown in Figure 9.2. The feedback signal is obtained from the rate gyro used to measure pitch rate, q. Since there is a sign change present inherently in the aircraft dynamics associated with the relationship of pitch rate to elevator deflection, the feedback signal is added to the command signal, q_{comm}. A number of books and papers show a sign change between the signal representing commanded elevator deflection, δ_{E_c}, and the actual angular displacement of the elevator, δ_E. In such cases, the feedback voltage, v_f, is shown to be subtracted from the command signal.

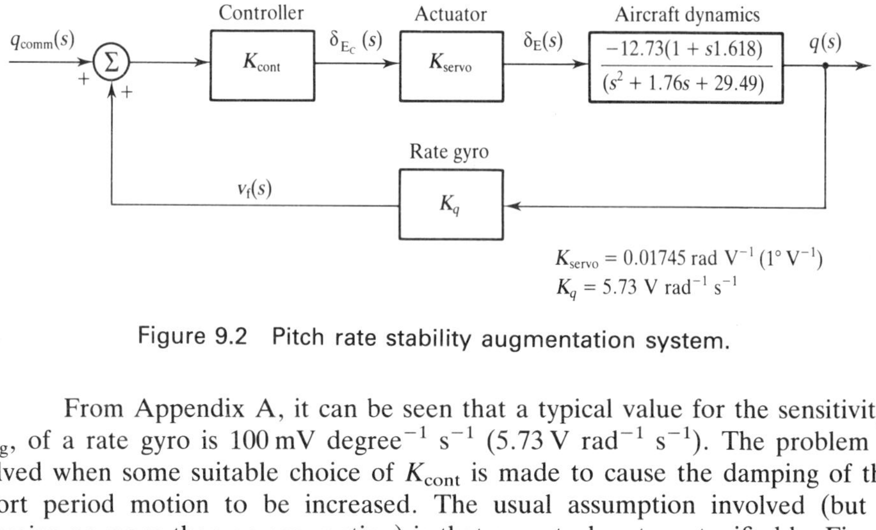

Figure 9.2 Pitch rate stability augmentation system.

From Appendix A, it can be seen that a typical value for the sensitivity, K_{rg}, of a rate gyro is 100 mV degree^{-1} s^{-1} (5.73 V rad^{-1} s^{-1}). The problem is solved when some suitable choice of K_{cont} is made to cause the damping of the short period motion to be increased. The usual assumption involved (but it remains no more than an assumption) is that a control system, typified by Figure 9.2, affects only the short period motion of the aircraft. Its phugoid motion is assumed to be unaffected by the control and its is also assumed that the phugoid motion does not affect the operation of the SAS. As a consequence, only the short period approximation needs to be used to represent the aircraft dynamics. The transfer function shown in the block representing aircraft dynamics in Figure 9.2 corresponds to aircraft FOXTROT at flight condition 3. The actuator dynamics are assumed to be represented by a fixed gain (servo gearing), K_{servo}: a value of 1° V^{-1} has been assumed. It can be deduced from the short period dynamics that

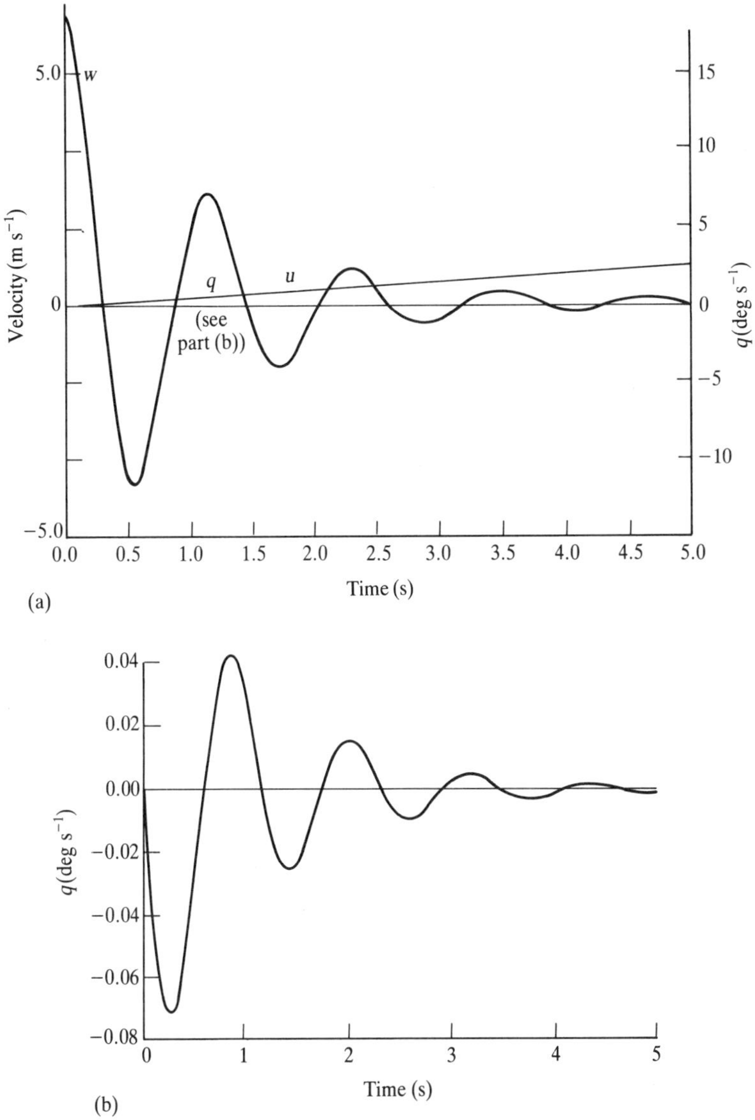

Figure 9.3 (a) Response of FOXTROT-3 to $\alpha(0) = 1°$.
(b) Pitch rate response of FOXTROT-3 (vertical scale expanded).

the damping ratio of the uncontrolled aircraft's motion is 0.16 and its frequency is 5.34 rad s^{-1}. The response of the uncontrolled aircraft to an initial disturbance in its angle of attack of 1° is shown in Figure 9.3. Note how the phugoid mode is evident chiefly in the speed response. The aircraft's rating is shown in the handling qualities diagram of Figure 9.4; on the same diagram the desired handling qualities point is shown as point Z. This point corresponds to a need to

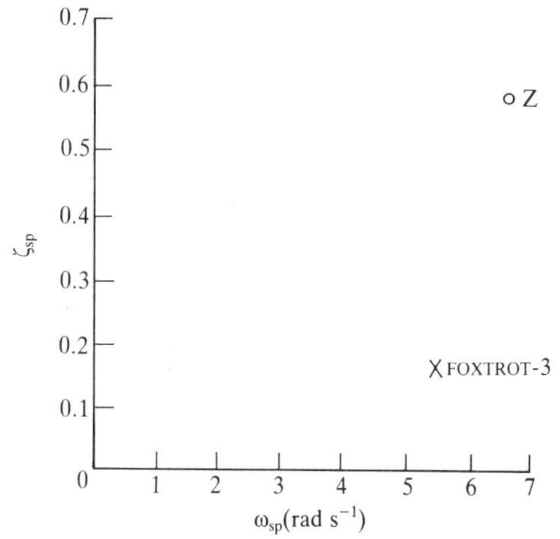

Figure 9.4 Handling qualities diagram.

increase the damping ratio to 0.6 and to ensure that the short period frequency is not less than 6.0 rad s^{-1}. These increases must be achieved by an appropriate choice of K_{cont} (which effectively results in M_q being augmented).

The control law of the SAS is, therefore:

$$\delta_E = K_q q = K_A K_{rg} K_{serv} K_{cont} q \tag{9.26}$$

A root locus diagram corresponding to the system represented by Figure 9.2 is shown in Figure 9.5. It can be calculated from that diagram that the required system gain K_q is + 0.36. Hence:

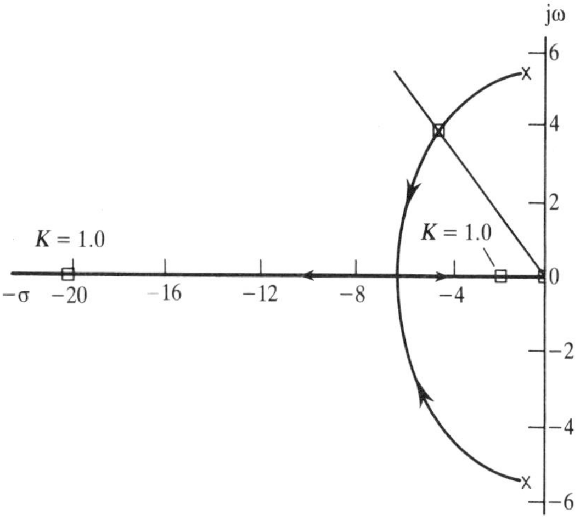

Figure 9.5 Root locus diagram for $q(s)/\delta_E(s)$ for FOXTROT-3.

$$K_{\text{cont}} = \frac{+\,0.36}{K_A K_{\text{servo}} K_{rg}} = \frac{0.36}{0.1 K_A} = 0.283 \tag{9.27}$$

The Bode diagram corresponding to the system is shown in Figure 9.6(a); the gain margin is infinite. It should be appreciated that for the aircraft dynamics there is a 180° shift of phase introduced at all frequencies, corresponding to the negative sign in the numerator of the transfer function. Consequently, the change in phase angle due to the dynamic terms is about + 130° to − 90° over the range of frequencies. Figure 9.6(b) shows the Nichols diagram corresponding to Figure 9.6(a). The gain margin, being infinite, means that any value of K_{cont} will obtain,

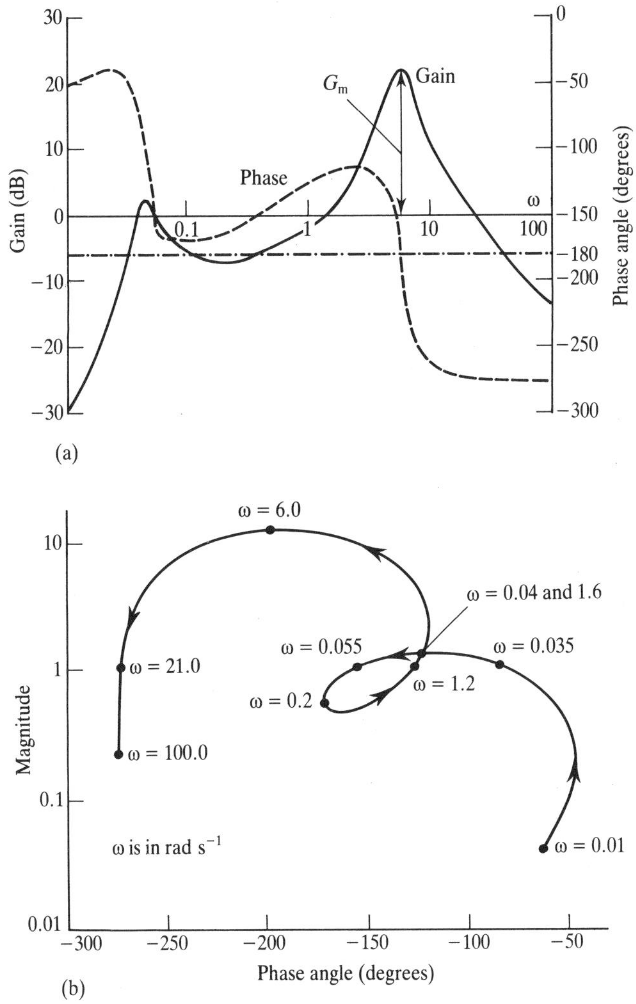

Figure 9.6 (a) Bode diagram for FOXTROT-3.
(b) Nichols diagram for FOXTROT-3.

from the standpoint of the stability of the closed loop system. However, to satisfy the handling qualities specification (point Z) only a single value will suit.

Any of the other methods of Chapter 8 can be used, but these methods require FSVF for their synthesis. Hence, the basic uncontrolled system is better represented as in Figure 9.7, and the problem is merely to determine the feedback gain matrix, K, in the control law:

$$\delta_E = Kx \tag{9.28}$$

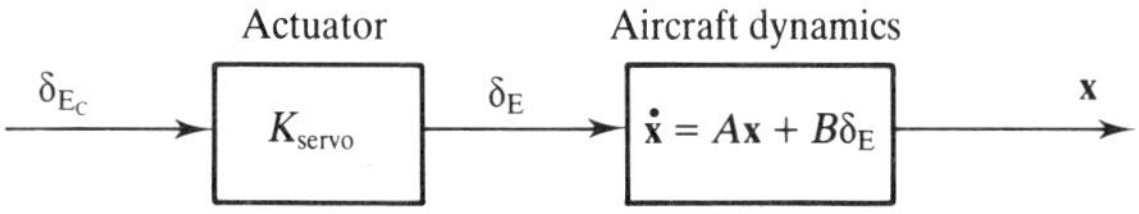

Figure 9.7 Open loop control system.

For example, using the pole placement technique of Section 7.3 of Chapter 7, if the desired closed loop poles are chosen to be:

$$\begin{aligned} \text{phugoid: } \lambda_1, \lambda_2 &= -0.004 \pm j0.04 \\ \text{short period: } \lambda_3, \lambda_4 &= -5.0 \pm j8.0 \end{aligned} \tag{9.29}$$

it is easy to determine the required matrix of feedback gains, namely:

$$K = [-0.002 \;\; 0.0023 \;\; 0.3824 \;\; -0.05] \tag{9.30}$$

From an examination of the relative magnitude of the elements of K it is tempting to consider that the feedback control law can be represented by:

$$\delta_E = K_q q \tag{9.31}$$

as before, but now K_q has the value of 0.3824. That this approximation is inappropriate can be seen from considering the closed loop poles, defined in eq. (9.32), which are achieved when the control law of eq. (9.31) is used, instead of eq. (9.30), which produces the desired closed loop poles of eq. (9.29).

$$\begin{aligned} \text{phugoid: } \lambda_1, \lambda_2 &= -0.0075 \pm j0.04 \\ \text{short period: } \lambda_3, \lambda_4 &= -4.9 \pm j3.3 \end{aligned} \tag{9.32}$$

If, however, eq. (9.30) is approximated to:

$$K = [0 \;\; 0.0023 \;\; 0.3824 \;\; 0]$$

the closed loop poles corresponding to the short period mode are not greatly affected being:

$$\begin{aligned} \text{phugoid: } \lambda_1, \lambda_2 &= -0.007 \pm j0.025 \\ \text{short period: } \lambda_3, \lambda_4 &= -5.0 \pm j8.1537 \end{aligned} \tag{9.33}$$

Equation (9.33) should be compared with the desired closed loop poles of eq. (9.29).

The response to an initial angle of attack of the controlled aircraft, using the control law defined in eqs (9.28) and (9.30), is shown by the dashed line in Figure 9.8; the solid line represents the same response for the control law defined by eqs (9.28) and (9.31).

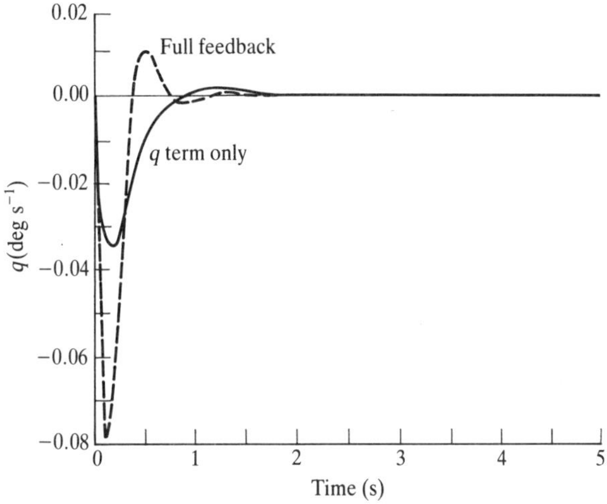

Figure 9.8 Pitch rate response for pole placement system.

Using the LQP solution is relatively straightforward but depends, of course, upon the choice of weighting matrices, Q and G. For the choice of eqs (9.34) and (9.35), namely:

$$Q = \text{diag}[0.01\ \ 0.01\ \ 0.5\ \ 0.2] \tag{9.34}$$

$$G = [2.5] \tag{9.35}$$

the resulting feedback matrix, obtained from solving the ARE, is:

$$K = [-\ 0.056\ \ 0.046\ \ 2.4\ \ 18.144] \tag{9.36}$$

Using the optimal control law results in the controlled aircraft having roots of:

$$\begin{aligned} \text{phugoid: } \lambda_1, \lambda_2 &= -\ 0.0934 \pm \text{j}0.0915 \\ \text{short period: } \lambda_3, \lambda_4 &= -\ 28.134 \pm \text{j}27.556 \end{aligned} \tag{9.37}$$

The closed loop response to an initial change of angle of attack of 1° is shown in Figure 9.9. Note how large changes of pitch rate have been penalized: the peak value at 0.2 s is only $-$ 0.013° compared to a peak value of $-$ 0.07 at 0.3 s for the uncontrolled aircraft. However, the long, drooping response, which has not settled by 5.0 s and which has arisen because of the dominant effect of the pitch attitude feedback, can only be reduced by penalizing the use of the elevator less heavily and allowing greater peak values of q. Other choices of Q and G matrices are needed. The dotted curve in Figure 9.9 shows the closed loop response which obtained for an arbitrary choice of weighting matrices:

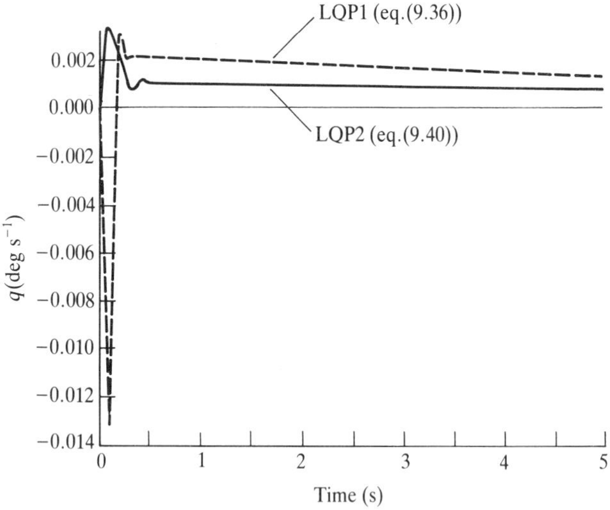

Figure 9.9 LQP response for FOXTROT-3.

$$Q = \text{diag}[0.003 \;\; 0.05 \;\; 0.4 \;\; 0.2] \tag{9.38}$$

$$G = [5.0] \tag{9.39}$$

The corresponding feedback gain matrix, K, was:

$$K = [0.0184 \;\; -0.0855 \;\; -2.905 \;\; -14.035] \tag{9.40}$$

9.4.3 Phase Advance Compensation

One common form of an SAS for pitch rate is to use a dynamic control law defined by:

$$\delta_{E_c}(s) = K_q G_c(s) q(s) \tag{9.41}$$

Either form (a) or (b) of Figure 9.10 may be used: their characteristic equations will be identical. Consequently, they have identical responses to initial conditions and to atmospheric turbulence. The SAS function is identical whichever structure is adopted. However, the command function will be affected. Figure 9.10(b) is preferred whenever the aircraft has manual reversion in the event of any SAS failure: it permits a direct input, p_c, from the primary flight control.

For the aircraft FOXTROT at flight conditions 3 (see Appendix B) the corresponding Bode diagram is shown as Figure 9.11, from which it can be seen that the gain and phase margins are both infinite. A phase advance network can safely be introduced; its transfer function is chosen to be:

$$G_c(s) = (1 + s)/(1 + s0.1) \tag{9.42}$$

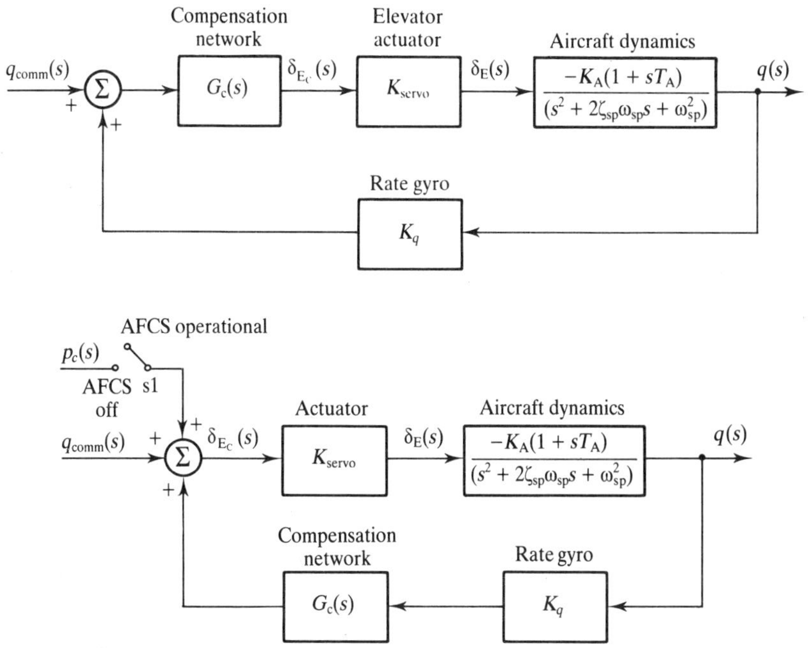

Figure 9.10 Pitch rate SAS. (a) Series Compensation. (b) Compensation in feedback.

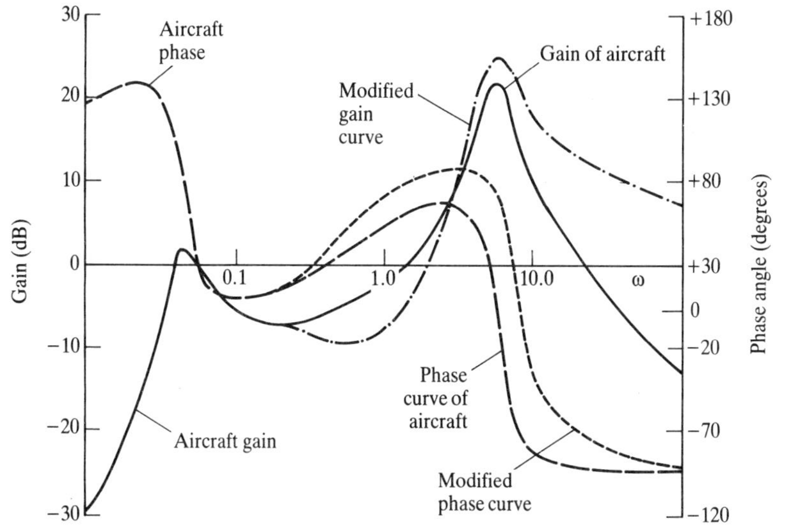

Figure 9.11 Bode plot of FOXTROT-3.

When K_q is chosen to be 0.5 the modified Bode diagram that is also shown in Figure 9.11 applies. The dynamic response of the closed-loop system to an initial change of angle of attack of + 1° is shown in Figure 9.12. The use of this phase advance network has added damping to the short-period response, but has reduced the frequency. Generally, phase advance networks tend to make the closed loop system perform less well in the presence of sensor noise.

It has been shown in Section 7.2 of Chapter 7 how dynamic feedback controllers may be represented in state variable form. The procedure can be used with the phase advance compensation scheme:

$$\delta_E(s) = K_q \frac{(1 + sT_1)}{(1 + sT_2)} q(s) \tag{9.43}$$

Then:

$$\frac{\delta_E(s)}{q(s)} = \frac{\delta_E(s)}{x(s)} \cdot \frac{x(s)}{q(s)} \tag{9.44}$$

Let:

$$\frac{x(s)}{q(s)} = \frac{1}{(1 + sT_2)} \tag{9.45}$$

$$\delta_E(s)/x(s) = K_q(1 + sT_1) \tag{9.46}$$

From eq. (9.45):

$$T_2\dot{x} + x = q$$

$$\therefore \quad \dot{x} = \frac{-1}{T_2} x + \frac{1}{T_2} q \tag{9.47}$$

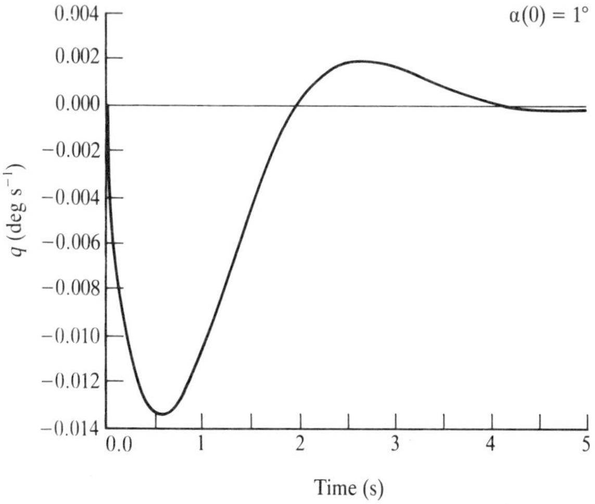

Figure 9.12 Pitch rate response with phase advance compensation.

$$\delta_E = K_q x + T_1 K_q \left\{ \frac{-1}{T_2} x + \frac{1}{T_2} q \right\} = K_q\left(1 - \frac{T_1}{T_2}\right)x + K_q \frac{T_1}{T_2} q \tag{9.48}$$

Let:

$$x \triangleq x_5 \qquad (\text{Note } q = x_3) \tag{9.49}$$

then:

$$\dot{x}_5 = \frac{-1}{T_2} x_5 + \frac{1}{T_2} x_3 \tag{9.50}$$

$$\delta_E = K_q \frac{T_1}{T_2} x_3 + K_q \left(1 - \frac{T_1}{T_2}\right) x_5 \tag{9.51}$$

$$\therefore \quad \delta_E = K\hat{\mathbf{x}} \tag{9.52}$$

where:

$$\dot{\hat{\mathbf{x}}} = \hat{A}\hat{\mathbf{x}} + \hat{B}\delta_E \tag{9.53}$$

$$K = \left[0 \; 0 \; \frac{K_q T_1}{T_2} \; 0 \; K_q\left(1 - \frac{T_1}{T_2}\right)\right] \tag{9.54}$$

$$\hat{A} = \begin{bmatrix} X_u & X_w & 0 & g & 0 \\ Z_u & Z_w & U_0 & 0 & 0 \\ \tilde{M}_u & \tilde{M}_w & \tilde{M}_q & 0 & 0 \\ 0 & 0 & 1 & 0 & 0 \\ 0 & 0 & \frac{1}{T_2} & 0 & -\frac{1}{T_2} \end{bmatrix} \tag{9.55}$$

$$\hat{B} = \begin{bmatrix} X_{\delta_E} \\ Z_{\delta_E} \\ \tilde{M}_{\delta_E} \\ 0 \\ 0 \end{bmatrix} \tag{9.56}$$

9.4.4 Additional Feedback Terms

Sometimes, to achieve required handling qualities, an additional feedback term based upon the normal acceleration measured at the c.g. is included in the feedback control law used in pitch SAS thus:

$$\delta_E = K_q q + K_{a_z} a_{z_{cg}} \tag{9.57}$$

From the point of view of modern control theory, eq. (9.57) is no more than another expression of a full state variable feedback control law. From the point of

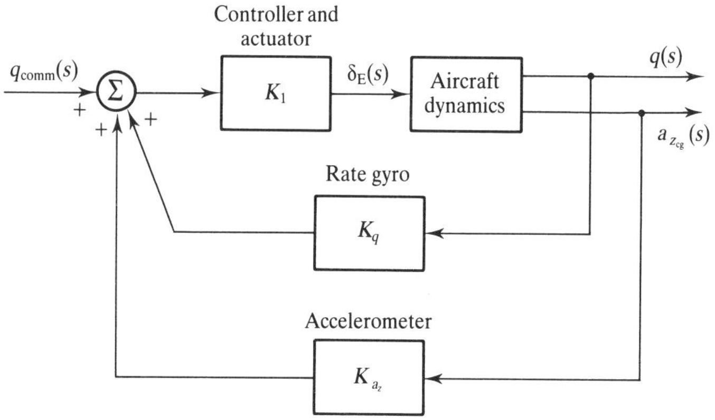

Figure 9.13 Pitch rate and acceleration feedback SAS.

view of a flight control engineer, eq. (9.57) is the practical alternative, requiring only pitch rate and normal acceleration to be measured. Both variables are relatively straightforward to measure using rate gyros and accelerometers located at the aircraft's c.g. The block diagram of a SAS, using the control law of eq. (9.57), is represented in Figure 9.13, with its corresponding dynamic response shown in Figure 9.14. This response should be compared with that of the uncontrolled aircraft which is shown in Figure 9.3(b). The closed loop responses shown in Figures 9.8, 9.9 and 9.12 should also be inspected for comparison purposes. Acceleration feedback is generally considered to 'stiffen' the system, i.e. the short period frequency is invariably increased. This can be appreciated easily by considering FOXTROT-3 controlled by the law of eq. (9.57), where:

$$K_q = 0.1753 \qquad K_{a_z} = -0.012 \tag{9.58}$$

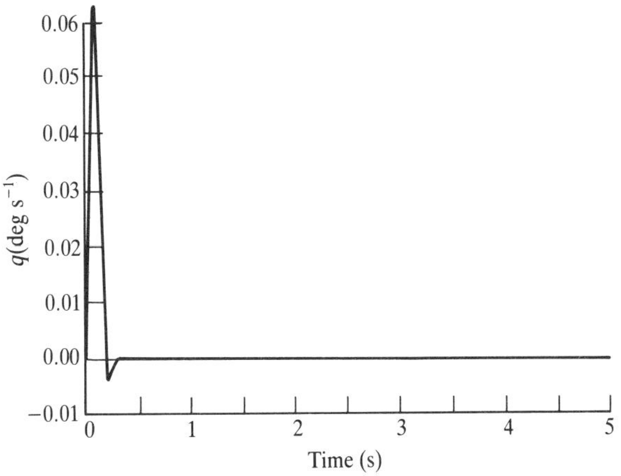

Figure 9.14 Response of blended control to $\alpha(0) = 1°$.

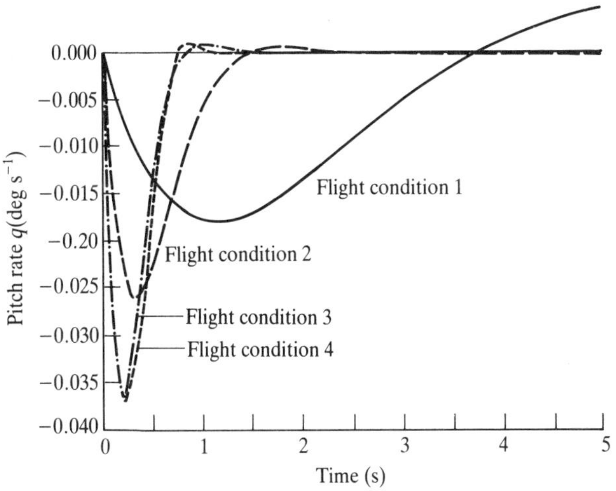

Figure 9.15 Response of pitch rate SAS for four flight conditions.

The corresponding eigenvalues of the controlled system are:

$$\begin{aligned} \text{phugoid: } \lambda_1, \lambda_2 &= -\ 0.0066 \pm j0.005 \\ \text{short period: } \lambda_3, \lambda_4 &= -\ 26.4 \pm j43.55 \end{aligned} \qquad (9.59)$$

In American papers, a control law such as eq. (9.57) is often referred as 'blended feedback control'; such a control law is usually used to achieve, as nearly as possible, invariant flying qualities throughout the flight envelope of the aircraft. The closeness with which this ideal is approached depends upon the ratio of the feedback gains, K_q and K_{a_z}. Usually, at low dynamic pressures (i.e. $1/2\rho U_0^2$ being not very large) the controlled aircraft is arranged to behave as if it were a pure pitch rate SAS; at high dynamic pressures, the system behaves more noticeably as a normal acceleration control system. Such blended feedback systems can 'mask' the natural ability of an aircraft to provide a 'stall warning'. This occurs because the control system tries to maintain good flying qualities until close to the point of the aircraft's stalling. To provide an illustration of this point, Figure 9.15 shows the transient response of the aircraft FOXTROT for all four flight conditions using the same fixed pitch rate feedback control law devised for flight condition 3. The transient responses for the same four flight conditions of the same aircraft, for the fixed blended feedback control designed for flight condition 3, are shown in Figure 9.16. It can be seen how effectively the blended control law of eq. (9.57) has provided invariant response, and this would ensure that the aircraft's handling qualities would remain acceptable as the aircraft traversed the region confined in the flight envelope.

The performance of such systems is greatly affected by the sensor locations; it has been supposed, for the present, that both sensors were located at the c.g. of the aircraft. The matter is considered anew in Section 9.12.

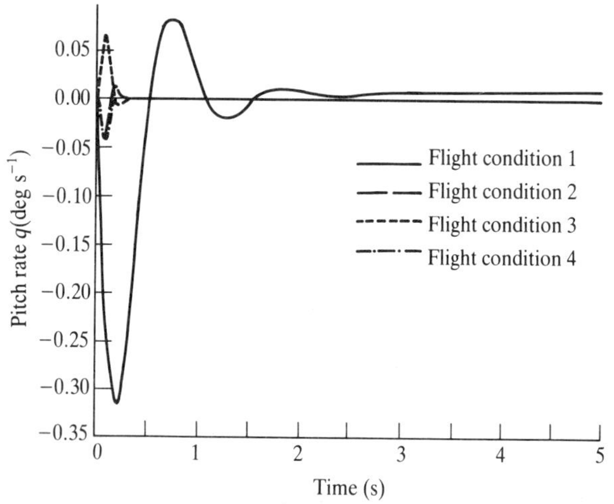

Figure 9.16 Blended control – pitch rate response for four flight conditions.

The importance of pitch rate command and stability augmentation systems cannot be overemphasized. It can be debated with considerable force that pilots rarely, if ever, require from an aircraft a particular value of pitch rate; rather they demand that the AFCS assist the aircraft to respond in some acceptable way to a manoeuvre command. In the UK, what is referred to as the RAE principle (since the idea was developed in the 1970s in the Flight Systems Division of the Royal Aircraft Establishment at Farnborough) shows that a manoeuvre demand, essentially a commanded acceleration, is simply a scaled version of a pitch rate command. A block diagram of the principle is shown in Figure 9.17, from which it is easily seen that:

$$q_{\text{comm}}/n_{z_{\text{comm}}} = K \tag{9.60}$$

However:

$$n_z = \frac{U_0}{g}(\dot{\alpha} - q) \tag{9.61}$$

If the aircraft is stable $\dot{\alpha} \rightarrow 0$ as $t \rightarrow \infty$. Therefore:

$$\left| n_{z_{\text{ss}}} \right| = \left| \frac{U_0}{g} q_{\text{ss}} \right| \tag{9.62}$$

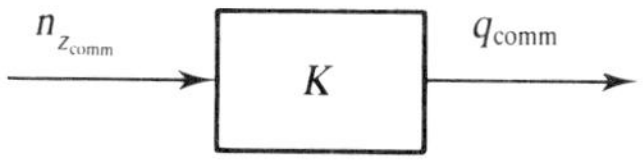

Figure 9.17 Manoeuvre demand.

i.e.:

$$\frac{q_{\text{comm}}}{n_{z_{\text{comm}}}} = \frac{g}{U_0} = K \tag{9.63}$$

Earlier in this section, in the discussion on blended feedback control, it was remarked how pitch rate response was dominant at low dynamic pressures, whereas at high q, the chief response was in acceleration. To maintain the relationship of (9.60) over the range of flight conditions, it is necessary to arrange that:

$$K \propto U_0^{-1} \tag{9.64}$$

In other words, the scaling factor, K, must be scheduled.

9.4.5 SAS for Relaxed Static Stability Aircraft

By relaxing the static stability of an aircraft it becomes possible to effect a considerable improvement in the manoeuvring performance of an aircraft. The improvement arises from the change in the load experienced by the tail which occurs where the c.g. of the aircraft shifts aft (see Figure 9.18). Were a gust to cause the nose of the aircraft in Figure 9.18(a) to move upwards, the angle of attack of the wing would increase, and that increase would result in an increase in the lift. Since this lift would be acting *behind* the aircraft's c.g., the resulting moment would cause the aircraft to rotate to bring the nose down once more. Such downloads upon a tail, however, produce considerable drag. Reduced static stability makes better use of the aircraft's lifting forces and it would result in less drag, greater manoeuvrability, and, because the stability requirements have been eased resulting in smaller control surfaces with less weight, better fuel efficiency. In Section 3.3 of Chapter 3 it is shown that:

$$C_{m_\alpha} = C_{L_\alpha}(\bar{x}_{\text{cg}} - \bar{x}_{\text{ac}}) \tag{9.65}$$

where $\bar{x}_{\text{cg}}$ is the location of the aircraft's c.g. (expressed usually as a percentage of the m.a.c.) and $\bar{x}_{\text{ac}}$ is the location of the aerodynamic centre (also expressed as a percentage of the m.a.c.). As long as C_{m_α} is negative, the aircraft is statically stable; as the c.g. moves further aft, C_{m_α} becomes positive and the static stability is lost. For the fighter aircraft BRAVO, of Appendix B, the following parameters relate to the statically stable state:

$$C_{L_\alpha} = 3.27 \qquad \bar{x}_{\text{cg}} = 0.255 \qquad \bar{x}_{\text{ac}} = 0.3112 \tag{9.66}$$

In Appendix B it is seen that for aircraft BRAVO flight conditions 2 and 3 are identical, except that the location of the c.g. for flight condition 2 is forward of the aerodynamic centre, whereas for flight condition 3 it is aft. BRAVO-2 is statically stable; BRAVO-3 is statically unstable. The corresponding eigenvalues are:

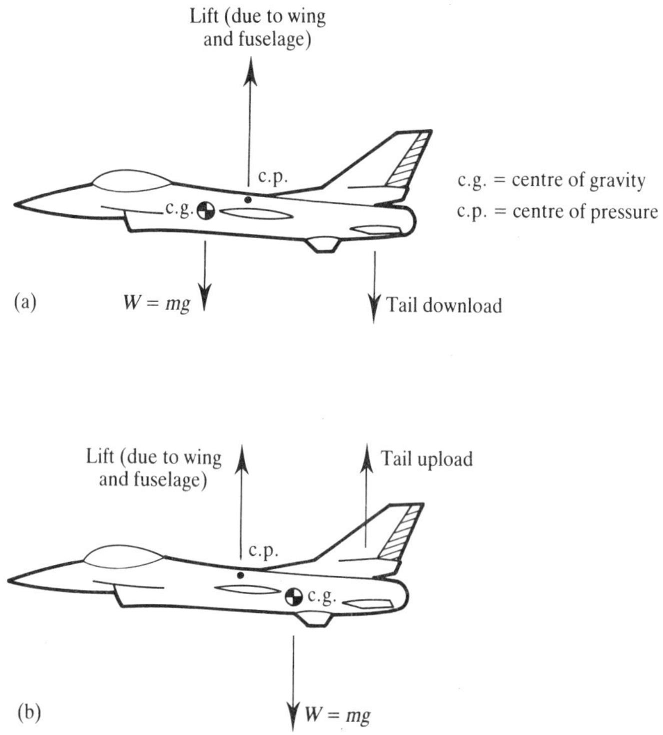

Figure 9.18 Static stability. (a) Conventional. (b) Relaxed.

BRAVO-2

$$\begin{aligned} \text{phugoid: } \lambda_1, \lambda_2 &= -\ 0.005 \pm j0.068 \\ \text{short period: } \lambda_3, \lambda_4 &= -\ 0.99 \pm j1.47 \end{aligned} \tag{9.67}$$

BRAVO-3

$$\begin{aligned} \text{phugoid: } \lambda_1, \lambda_2 &= -\ 0.014,\ \lambda_3 = -\ 0.326 \\ \text{short period: } \lambda_4 &= +\ 2.139 \end{aligned} \tag{9.68}$$

It can be seen how the short period mode has ceased to be oscillatory, and has become an unstable motion, comprising two real modes, one convergent and the other divergent. In this condition, the phenomenon of 'pitch-up' is likely to occur: any tendency of the angle of attack to increase goes on increasing rapidly until the aircraft stalls, with the pilot unable to control the corresponding pitch-up. A more complicated SAS is then required, and one type which is effective is that referred to as a pitch orientation control system. Another system, which is effective in overcoming the effects of changes of control effectiveness over the flight

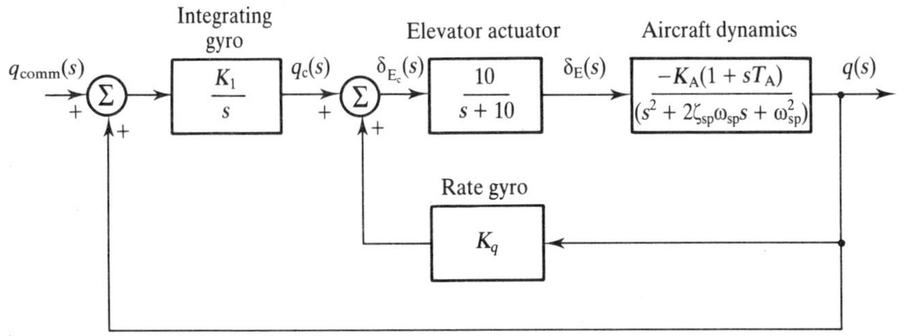

Figure 9.19 Pitch orientation control system.

envelope, is to 'wash out' both the proportional feedback and the integral term which operates on the washed-out pitch rate. Washing-out is a method of permitting to be transmitted only the changes which are occurring in some variable, and blocking any steady value. A block diagram of a pitch orientation control system is shown in Figure 9.19. Note that the inner loop is a conventional pitch rate SAS, but its command voltage is arranged to be proportional now to the integral of the sum of the commanded and the achieved pitch rates. Any of the methods of Chapter 7 can be used to obtain suitable values of K_q and K_1. Using:

$$K_q = 1.5 \qquad K_1 = 10.0 \tag{9.69}$$

then, from Figure 9.19:

$$\dot{\delta}_E = -20\delta_E + 20\delta_{E_c} \tag{9.70}$$

$$\delta_{E_c} = q_c + 1.5q \tag{9.71}$$

$$\dot{q}_c = 10q + 10q_{comm} \tag{9.72}$$

Let:

$$\delta_E \triangleq x_5 \tag{9.73}$$

$$q_c \triangleq x_6 \tag{9.74}$$

then, if:

$$\tilde{\mathbf{x}} \triangleq [u \;\; \alpha \;\; q \;\; \theta \;\; \delta_E \;\; q_c]' \tag{9.75}$$

$$\mathbf{u} \triangleq q_{comm} \tag{9.76}$$

then:

$$\dot{\tilde{\mathbf{x}}} = \tilde{A}_2\tilde{\mathbf{x}} + \tilde{B}_2\mathbf{u} \tag{9.77}$$

where:

$$\tilde{A}_2 = \begin{bmatrix} -0.0114 & 0.0179 & 0 & -9.81 & 0 & 0 \\ -0.113 & -0.723 & 1 & 0 & -0.0475 & 0 \\ 0.07 & -2.26 & -1.28 & 0 & -13.01 & 0 \\ 0 & 0 & 1 & 0 & 0 & 0 \\ 0 & 0 & 30 & 0 & -20 & 20 \\ 0 & 0 & 10 & 0 & 0 & 0 \end{bmatrix} \tag{9.78}$$

$$\tilde{B}_2 = [0\ 0\ 0\ 0\ 0\ 10]' \tag{9.79}$$

For flight condition 3:

$$\tilde{A}_3 = \begin{bmatrix} -0.0116 & 0.017 & 0 & -9.81 & 0 & 0 \\ -0.113 & -0.723 & 1 & 0 & -0.0475 & 0 \\ 0.06 & 1.4772 & -1.11 & 0 & -12.225 & 0 \\ 0 & 0 & 1 & 0 & 0 & 0 \\ 0 & 0 & 30 & 0 & -20 & 20 \\ 0 & 0 & 10 & 0 & 0 & 0 \end{bmatrix} \tag{9.80}$$

$\tilde{B}_3$ is identical to $\tilde{B}_2$.

The two responses, obtained for the values of gains quoted and for a commanded step pitch rate of $1°\,s^{-1}$, are shown in Figure 9.20. Note how the control provides good dynamic response for the two cases of static stability.

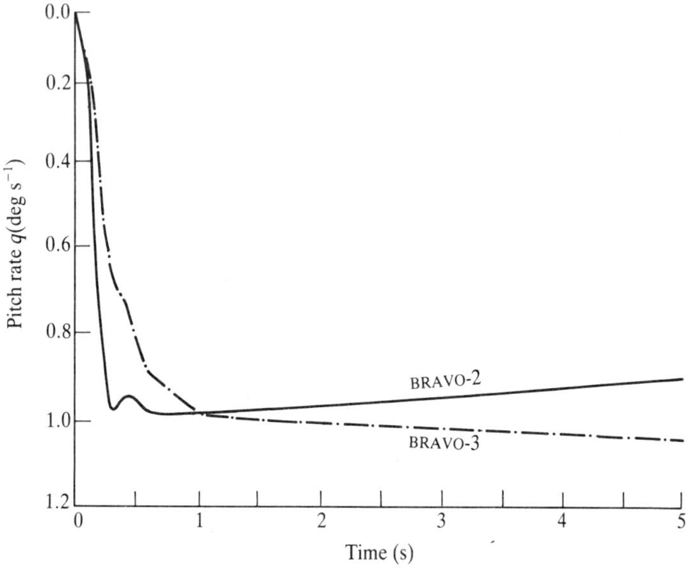

Figure 9.20 Step response of pitch orientation system.

9.5 OTHER LONGITUDINAL AXIS SASs

Since it is known from the short peroid approximation that:

$$2\zeta_{sp}\omega_{sp} = -(Z_w + M_q + U_0 M_{\dot{w}}) \tag{9.81}$$

$$\omega_{sp}^2 = (Z_w M_q - U_0 M_w) \tag{9.82}$$

then if M_w and $M_{\dot{w}}$ are both augmented, ζ_{sp} and ω_{sp} can be increased.

One of the easiest ways of augmenting M_w and $M_{\dot{w}}$ is to use as an elevator control signal a feedback signal based upon the angle of attack and its derivative:

$$\delta_E = K_\alpha \alpha + K_{\dot{\alpha}}\dot{\alpha} = \tilde{K}_\alpha w + \tilde{K}_{\dot{\alpha}}\dot{w} \tag{9.83}$$

Provided that the stability derivative, $M_{\dot{w}}$ is negligible, use of eq. (9.83) as a control law will have little effect on the phugoid mode. The method is not used very much, despite its effectiveness in augmenting both the damping and the frequency of the short period mode, since the stabilization reference for the system is the relative wind, i.e. the control system would cause an aircraft to rotate after a disturbance into a new relative wind direction. Essentially, the system tends to hold constant both the load factor and the angle of attack of an aircraft. Furthermore, it is relatively difficult to satisfactorily sense α and $\dot{\alpha}$; usually an accelerometer is used as the primary feedback sensor since:

$$a_{z_{cg}} \simeq Z_w w + Z_{\delta_E}\delta_E \tag{9.84}$$

However, it is rarely possible to measure the normal acceleration at precisely the c.g. of an aircraft: it is usually measured at some other location, x_A. Hence,

$$a_{z_A} = a_{z_{cg}} - x_A\dot{q} \simeq Z_w w + Z_{\delta_E}\delta_E - x_A\dot{q} \tag{9.85}$$

By manipulation of the appropriate transfer functions it is easy to show that acceleration and angle of attack are directly related by a simple proportionality factor:

$$a_{z_A}/\alpha \simeq [Z_w - (Z_{\delta_E}/M_{\delta_E})M_w]U_0 \tag{9.86}$$

It must be understood that this proportional relationship holds over only a limited range of frequency.

If the accelerometer is located at:

$$x_A = Z_{\delta_E}/M_{\delta_E} \tag{9.87}$$

it has been placed at an instantaneous centre of rotation, i.e. it is a point, a centre of percussion, at which, as a result of some deflection of the elevator, the centre of pressure of the aerodynamic force occurs. A step deflection of the elevator results in an initial vertical acceleration (owing to $Z_{\delta_E}\delta_E$) which is just balanced by the pitching acceleration term, $x_A\dot{q}$. However, this centre of rotation will shift as the aircraft's c.g. shifts in flight, so that a location close to x_A, as defined by eq. (9.87), is the best possible practical solution.

If, instead of angle of attack, normal acceleration is used in a feedback control law, it should be appreciated that the phugoid mode will also be affected. Usually the undamped natural frequency of the phugoid mode is decreased. If the aircraft is operating at some flight condition at which one of the zeros of the transfer function relating normal acceleration and elevation deflection is negative then, if the acceleration feedback signal is not washed out, instability (of the phugoid motion) may occur.

Angle of attack sensors are available, but their use is confined chiefly to military aircraft at present. However, at high speeds, angle of attack can be computed using the signals from a vertical accelerometer and from the air data unit, if the aircraft is equipped with one. The method is also used in aircraft with angle of attack sensors to give some redundancy to a signal of primary importance.

The lift coefficient of the aircraft is given by:

$$C_L = \frac{n_{z_{cg}}}{\bar{q}} \frac{mg}{S} = \frac{a_{z_{cg}}}{\bar{q}} \frac{m}{S} \tag{9.88}$$

where $\bar{q}$, m and S denote the usual quantities. But:

$$C_L = C_{L_0} + C_{L_\alpha}\alpha \tag{9.89}$$

i.e.

$$\alpha = \frac{C_{L_0}}{C_{L_\alpha}} + \frac{C_L}{C_{L_\alpha}} = \frac{a_{z_{cg}}}{\bar{q}} \frac{m}{SC_{L_\alpha}} - \frac{C_{L_0}}{C_{L_\alpha}} \tag{9.90}$$

If the parameters m, S, C_{L_0} and C_{L_α} are stored in a computer, the angle of attack can be computed using the measurements of normal acceleration, obtained from the accelerometer, and dynamic pressure, $\bar{q}$, from the air data unit.

9.6 SENSOR EFFECTS

It is important to understand that the SASs dealt with so far have all used sensors to provide the required feedback signals. In every case it has been assumed that the sensor location has been precisely at the aircraft's c.g. and that its orientation has been entirely correct. Since the most usual sensors for SASs are linear accelerometers or rate gyros, and, in the case of the pitch orientation control, an integrating rate gyro, it is essential to know what are the effects upon the AFCS performance if the assumptions do not hold.

9.6.1 Rate Gyro

It is usually quite simple to locate and align pitch rate gyros, except when the aircraft structure deforms easily, in which case special care must be taken to avoid locating the rate gyro where its output will be greatly affected by the structural bending rates. Also it must be remembered that the correct value of pitch rate, which is measured by the rate gyro, is given by:

$$q = \dot{\theta} \cos \phi + \dot{\Psi} \cos \theta \sin \phi \tag{9.91}$$

If a vertical attitude gyro is used it measures the Euler axis rate (not the body-fixed rate) and measures:

$$\dot{\theta} = q \cos \phi - r \sin \phi \tag{9.92}$$

At large bank angles, the rates measured in body-fixed axis and Euler axis systems are not equivalent and cannot be zero simultaneously. This fact has great importance for pitch attitude control (see Chapter 10).

Of great signficance, however, to the performance of SASs is what happens when the sensor saturates, i.e. its output signal is limited. This can result in special problems if the command and rate feedback do not limit at the same value. If the pitch rate saturates (the gyro limits), but the command signal does not simultaneously saturate, there results a sudden error command (see Figure 9.1) which, provided the control surface actuator is not saturated, increases the manoeuvre. This can result in pitch-up, an attendant loss of pitch rate damping and, of equal significance, the stick force per g is reduced. Such an effect is sensed by the pilot as an impairment of the aircraft's handling quality. Similarly, if the AFCS commands a control surface deflection greater than its authority, there is also an impairment of the flying qualities. In effect, both these limiting phenomena cause the aircraft to revert to open loop operation with unwanted inputs.

This sensor limitation problem is very much worse for the pitch orientation control, since the integration in the forward loop continues to increase the command signal to the feedback-limited inner loop SAS.

9.6.2 Linear Accelerometer

Such accelerometers are usually mounted rigidly in an aircraft with the sensitive axis perpendicular to an axis usually chosen to be nearly horizontal when the aircraft is in cruise flight. It is necessary to bias the output signal from the accelerometer to allow for the acceleration component of 1 g due to gravity; otherwise the accelerometer will not be properly sensing changes from level flight, which is at 1 g.

The static output from the accelerometer is approximately:

$$n \simeq 1 - \Theta_0 \cos \phi_0 \tag{9.93}$$

Θ_0 is the steady value of the pitch angle of the accelerometer relative to the gravity vector. Therefore, in unaccelerated, non-level flight the feedback signal which results from the accelerometer is $(1 - \cos \Theta \cos \phi)$; a command signal is then needed to prevent the feedback signal from producing, via the controller, a control surface deflection which will return the aircraft to a level flight path, i.e. at 1 g. When the value of the normal acceleration being sensed is less than 1 g it must be arranged that the sign of the feedback signal from the accelerometer is such that the control surface deflection produced will result in the aircraft having a nose-up attitude. When the value of the normal acceleration being sensed is greater than 1 g a control surface deflection to produce a nose-down manoeuvre is arranged. For unaccelerated descent (i.e. nose-down attitude) such a feedback arrangement tends to make the aircraft level out. For an unaccelerated climb, however, such a feedback arrangement tends to increase further the climb attitude. If any integration is present in the forward loop, or if there is automatic trim actuation available, the effect of the acceleration feedback can be hazardous since a divergence in both flight path and speed can obtain which, if uncorrected, can lead to the aircraft's stalling.

Obviously, it is an unsatisfactory arrangement to provide command inputs, via the stick, say, in steady flight conditions; in general aviation aircraft and commercial airliners this need is circumvented by adding an electrical trim command input to the SAS (see Figure 9.1). In high performance military aircraft, when manoeuvring flight is the principal means of accomplishing the aircraft's mission, it is impractical to use an electrical trim signal to offset every change in the gravity component: stick commands are used, and, in constant g manoeuvres, such as 360° rolls, the accelerometer feedback results in the pilots having to provide considerable longitudinal motion of the control stick.

In Section 9.4 it is pointed out how the performance of SAS can be greatly affected by sensor location, particularly location of the accelerometer. Assuming a rigid aircraft, the full output (in units of g) from a biased accelerometer, expressed in terms of a stability axis system is given by:

$$n_z = 1 - \cos\theta\cos\phi + \frac{a_{z_{cg}} + (pr - \dot{q})l_x + (qr + \dot{p})l_y + (q^2 + p^2)l_z}{g} \tag{9.94}$$

l_x, l_y and l_z are the distances between the sensor's location and the c.g. of the aircraft.[2] Generally, the lateral offset, l_y, is usually small and can be neglected. The troublesome terms in eq. (9.94) which are significant are $-\dot{q}l_x$ and p^2l_x. If the accelerometer is located at the point where elevator deflection produces pitch rotation of the aircraft without translation, i.e. at:

$$l_x = Z_{\delta_E}/M_{\delta_E} \tag{9.95}$$

then the high frequency zeros in the aircraft's transfer function relating normal acceleration to elevator deflection are effectively moved to infinity in the s-plane which makes simpler the task of maintaining stability of the closed loop system.

The effects caused by l_z can also be great, surprisingly so when rolling manoeuvres are considered, for there may result an appreciable amount of coupling of lateral motion into the longitudinal motion.

If a highly manoeuvrable aircraft, flown at a high angle of attack, is considered, with an accelerometer located forward of the aircraft's c.g. along its

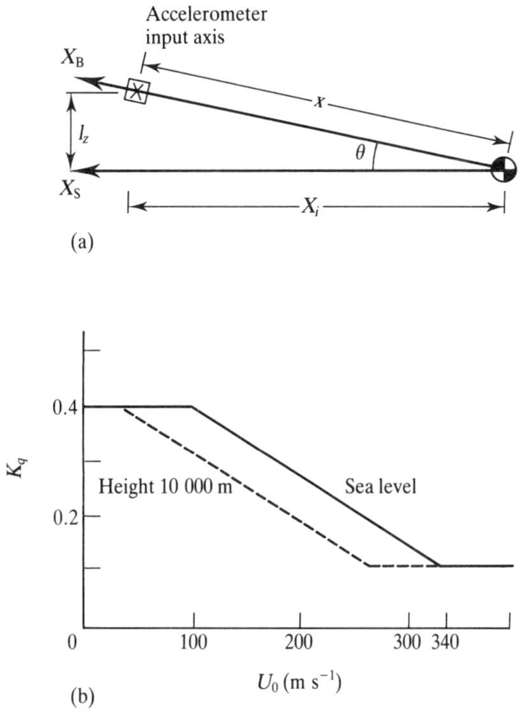

Figure 9.21 (a) Location geometry for accelerometer.
(b) A typical gain schedule.

fuselage reference axis, the distance of the accelerometer above the axis about which the aircraft rolls, the stability axis OX, can be very large. See Figure 9.21(a). From the figure it is evident that:

$$l_z = x \cos \theta \tag{9.96}$$

In the sensor's axis the acceleration is given by:

$$n_z = p^2 l_z \cos \theta = p^2 x \cos^2 \theta \tag{9.97}$$

If the roll rate is oscillatory, the output signal from the accelerometer will be rectified because $\cos^2 \theta$ and p^2 are both even functions. Thus, whenever the accelerometer is located above the roll axis, OX, of the aircraft, the term of eq. (9.97) will cause a feedback signal which will result in an upward deflection of the elevator. At large values of angle of attack such a tendency results in pro-stall, a condition of wing rock. It is also inimical of recovery in oscillatory spins.

9.7 SCHEDULING

It can be seen from the data presented in Appendix B how the characteristics of an aircraft change with height and speed. But, from the point of view of flying, it is preferred that an aircraft exhibits a response as nearly invariant as possible throughout its flight envelope. Consequently, the use of the types of SAS discussed in this chapter, with fixed gains and forms, is unlikely to satisfy this preference. If the gains, for example, are left fixed at values designed for one condition, then the closed loop response at the other flight conditions will be different from what is required (see Figure 9.15, for example). To overcome this deficiency, gain or sensor scheduling is frequently used.

Gain scheduling means that the gain in a control law, say K_q, is changed as height or speed, or (rarely) both, change. How the gain is 'scheduled' will depend upon the aircraft, and the AFCS function, but a representative 'schedule' is shown in Figure 9.21(b). The gain, K_q, is seen to be constant at a value of 0.4 for S.L. (sea level) operation from take-off to a value of U_0 of 100 m s^{-1}. Thereafter, it reduces uniformly at 0.00125 m^{-1} s^{-1} until the forward speed reaches a value corresponding to Mach 1.0, at which K_q reaches a value of 0.1, remaining constant at that value as the aircraft speed increases. At 10 000 m the same constant value of 0.1 is reached again at Mach 1.0, which corresponds to a forward speed of 300 m s^{-1}. The same slope is used so that the gain schedule starts to operate at 60 m s^{-1} for this aircraft height. It is quite common to schedule either the gain of the controller, or the sensor sensitivities, with dynamic pressure, $q(= 1/2\rho U_0^2)$, rather than with just speed or height, thereby compensating for density as well as forward speed.

9.8 LATERAL CONTROL

9.8.1 Introduction

In conventional aircraft, there are usually three, relatively independent modes of lateral motion: roll, spiral and dutch roll. These modes correspond to a well damped response in roll rate, p, to a long term tendency either to maintain the wings level or to 'roll off' in a divergent spiral, and to 'weather cocking' directional stability. However, if the dihedral effect of an aircraft is high, the roll damping is low, i.e. $L'_p \rightarrow 0$ and, as a consequence, the corresponding roll and spiral modes may converge into that single, roll/spiral, oscillatory mode referred to as the lateral phugoid (see Section 3.7). If the dutch roll mode of such an aircraft is also very lightly damped, then its piloting can become very difficult, particularly in the execution of co-ordinated turns, for which there must not exist sideslip motion. It is evident, therefore, that if an aircraft is deficient in good flying qualities, for any of these modes, some SAS is needed to remedy the deficiencies. Three types of SAS are commonly used for lateral motion: yaw damper, roll damper and spiral mode SAS.

Because lateral motion in conventional aircraft is controlled by the simultaneous use of two independent control surfaces – the ailerons[3] and the rudder – lateral motion studies are more involved than those involving longitudinal motion only. The results obtained as a result of idealizations and approximations are, consequently, less satisfactory than those obtained in studies of longitudinal motion. Nevertheless, such approximations provide useful insight into the physical problem. However, the three SASs mentioned involve the use of only one control surface, either the ailerons, or the rudder, according to the function of the SAS. Simultaneous use of both control surfaces is dealt with in Chapter 10.

9.8.2 The Yaw Damper

Few aircraft have a degree of inherent damping of the dutch roll motion adequate to satisfy the handling qualities enumerated in Chapter 6. As a result, whenever their rudders are used, the lack gives rise to oscillatory yawing motion, with some coupling into the rolling motion, the significance of which depends upon the relative size of the stability derivative, L'_r (see, for example, Figure 9.23(a)). The use of an SAS to artificially increase the damping, by augmenting N'_r, is universal. A block diagram of such a yaw damper, using proportional feedback, is shown in Figure 9.22. The aircraft dynamics correspond to CHARLIE-4 of Appendix B and were obtained from the two degrees of freedom approximation. Once again the actuator's dynamics have been assumed to be less complicated than they are in reality; they have been represented here by a simple, first order, transfer function. Such an approximation is very much less satisfactory than in the case of the pitch rate SAS, for example, since the response of the rudder actuator is less rapid than those of the other control surface actuators. The hinge moment of the rudder is very much larger than the moments associated with the other surfaces, and a more powerful, but consequently more sluggish, actuator is required to be used. Rarely should a mathematical model of the dynamics of a rudder actuator of order less than two be used. For verisimilitude, the actuator may be required to be represented by a fourth or fifth order transfer function and it may possibly have to include a number of significant, non-linear characteristics. To illustrate the principles of operation of the yaw damper, however, the gross simplification used in Figure 9.22 will be retained, for a little while. The actuator has been assumed to provide one degree of rudder deflection per 1 V input, and to have a time constant of 0.25 s. The effects upon the response of the yaw damper of a higher order representation of actuator dynamics are shown later in this section.

The sensitivities of the rate gyro used in the feedback is 0.1 V deg^{-1}. The controller gain, K_c, has to be chosen to ensure that the closed loop response results in dutch roll motion which corresponds to acceptable flying qualities. The transfer function, resulting from the two degrees of freedom approximation, relating yaw rate, r, to rudder deflecction, δ_R, for CHARLIE-4 is given by:

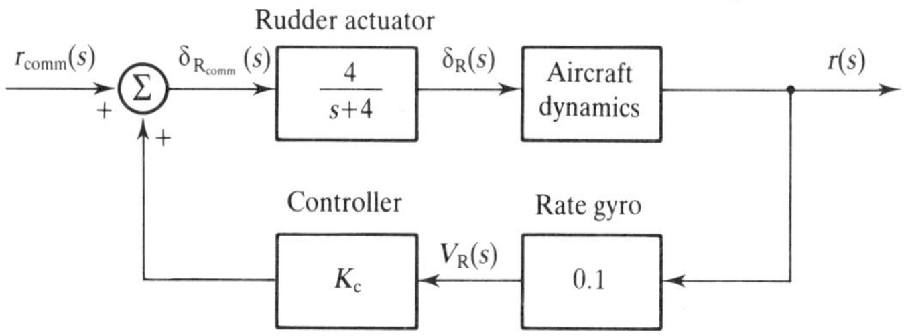

Figure 9.22 Yaw damper block diagram.

$$\frac{r(s)}{\delta_R(s)} = \frac{-0.442}{(s^2 + 0.19s + 1.04)} \tag{9.98}$$

It can be seen that the damping ratio is less than 0.1 which is too small a value to result in acceptable dutch roll motion. The objective of using the yaw damper is to ensure that the damping ratio of the resulting controller motion is much larger, say about 0.4 or 0.5, with possibly an increase in the corresponding natural frequency.

The dynamic response of the uncontrolled aircraft CHARLIE-4 to an initial disturbance in the yaw rate of $1° \, s^{-1}$ was obtained from a simulation of the complete equations of lateral motion and is shown in Figure 9.23(a). The response of the same uncontrolled aircraft to an initial disturbance in roll rate of $1° \, s^{-1}$ is shown in Figure 9.23(b). Note the oscillatory response which is predominant in all the motion variables shown in Figure 9.23(a). The absence of such oscillatory motion in the same variables shown in part (b) arises solely because the mode which was initialy disturbed was the roll mode. Since L'_r for CHARLIE-4 is negligible, there has been no significant coupling of the dutch roll into the rolling subsidence motion. This observation supports the use of approximations in deriving transfer functions for

$r(s)/\delta_R(s)$ and (later) for $p(s)/\delta_A(s)$

The responses from the yaw damper to the same initial disturbance of $r(0) = 1° \, s^{-1}$, but for a range of values of controller gains, K_c, are shown in Figure 9.24. Note that, although the most rapid response corresponds to $K_c = 15$ V/V, it is the one with the lowest damping (although the value is acceptable, being 0.4). Increasing K_c to 196.875 rcsults in the yaw damper's response being unstable. A K_c value of 10 provides a well damped and reasonably rapid response. The effect of the dynamics of the actuator on the performance of the yaw damper can be assessed by considering Figure 9.25, in which is shown the response of the yaw damper with $K_c = 10$, but with the transfer function for the actuator replaced by:

$$\frac{\delta_R(s)}{\delta_{R_{comm}}(s)} = \frac{16}{s^2 + 5.6s + 16}$$

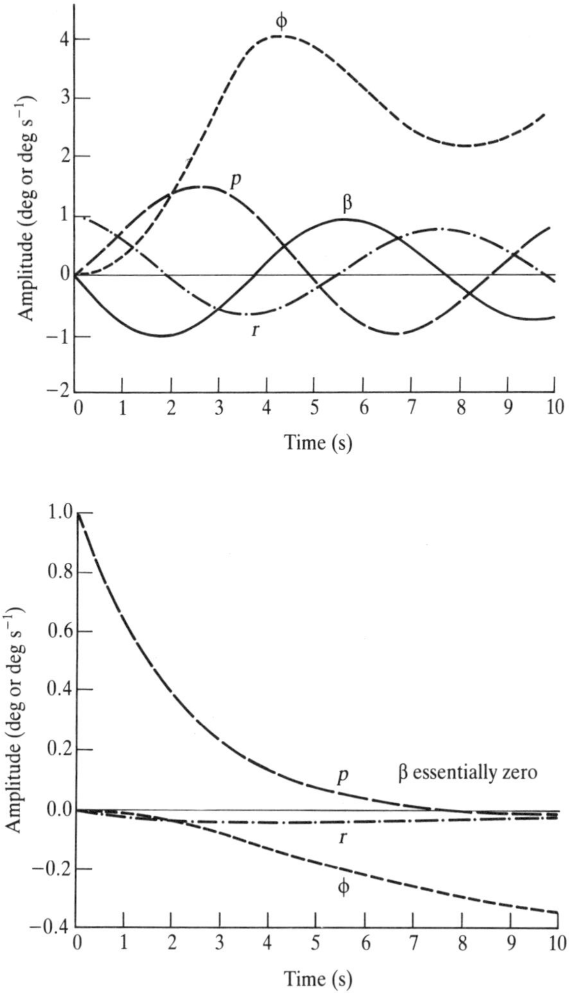

Figure 9.23 Response of uncontrolled aircraft: (a) to $r(0) = 1° s^{-1}$, (b) to $p(0) = 1° s^{-1}$.

Note how the response has been slowed and the damping has been reduced.

However, it should be noted that the yaw damper of Figure 9.22 does not completely remove the effect of the initial disturbance in yaw rate: there are non-zero steady state values. In addition, such a system tends to oppose any change in yaw rate, even if it has been commanded, in order to change the aircraft's heading, for example.[4] To avoid such opposition, the signal proportional to yaw rate, being used as feedback signal to the controller, is first passed through a wash-out network for the purpose of differentiating the signal from the yaw rate gyroscope (see Figure 9.26). Such a filter is easily synthesized by means of active electronic components, such as operational amplifiers. A block diagram

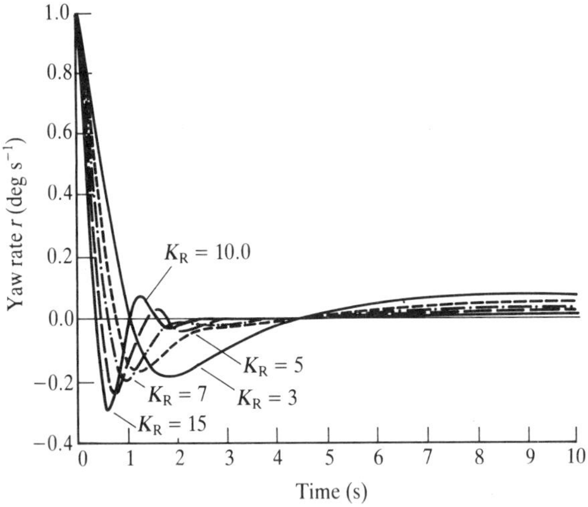

Figure 9.24 Response of yaw damper for various values of K_c.

representation of such a wash-out filter is shown in Figure 9.27. Values of K_c and T_{wo} are easy to obtain from any of the conventional control system design methods (see Chapter 7). To illustrate a number of features of the results which can be obtained, values of K_c and T_{wo} of 100.0 and 1.0 respectively, were used. The following differential equations resulted:

$$\dot{\delta}_R = -4\delta_R + 4e_{wo} + 4r_{comm} \tag{9.99}$$

$$\begin{aligned}\dot{e}_{wo} &= e_{wo} + 0.1K_c\dot{r} \\ &= -e_{wo} + 0.06K_c\beta - 0.0032K_{cp} - 0.0115K_c r - 0.0475\,K_{cr}\delta_R\end{aligned} \tag{9.100}$$

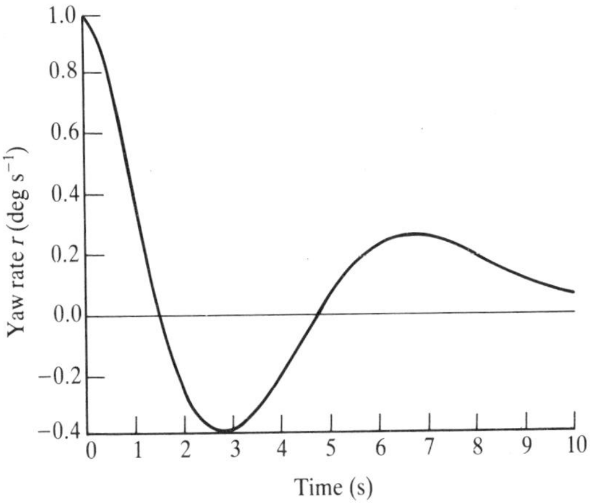

Figure 9.25 Response of yaw damper with second order rudder actuator.

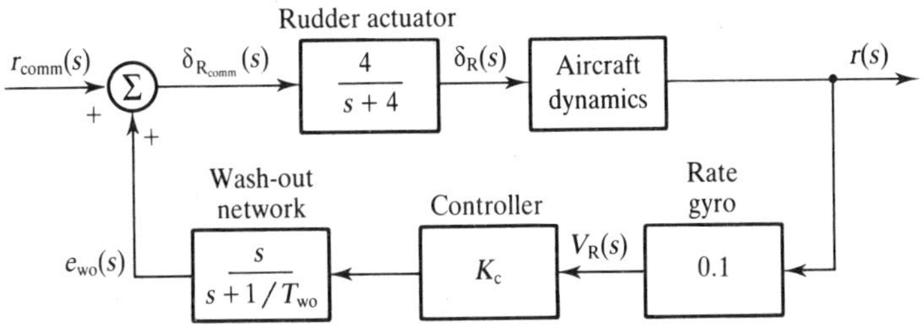

Figure 9.26 Yaw damper with wash-out in feedback.

Letting:

$$\mathbf{x}' = [\beta \; p \; r \; \phi \; \delta_R \; e_{wo}] \tag{9.101}$$

$$\mathbf{u} = r_{comm} \tag{9.102}$$

then the yaw damper, with wash-out network, can be represented as:

$$\dot{\mathbf{x}} = A\mathbf{x} + B\mathbf{u} \tag{9.103}$$

where:

$$A = \begin{bmatrix} -0.056 & 0 & -1 & 0.042 & 0.0022 & 0 \\ -1.05 & -0.465 & 0.39 & 0 & 0.153 & 0 \\ 0.6 & -0.032 & -0.115 & 0 & -0.475 & 0 \\ 0 & 1 & 0 & 0 & 0 & 0 \\ 0 & 0 & 0 & 0 & -4 & 4 \\ 6.0 & -0.32 & -1.15 & 0 & -4.75 & -1.0 \end{bmatrix} \tag{9.104}$$

$$B' = [0 \; 0 \; 0 \; 0 \; 4 \; 0] \tag{9.105}$$

Step responses for this yaw damper to a commanded yaw rate of $1^\circ \, s^{-1}$ for a range of values of controller gain are shown in Figure 9.28. Note that the washed-out

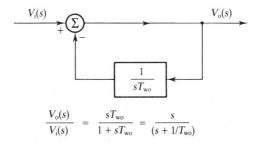

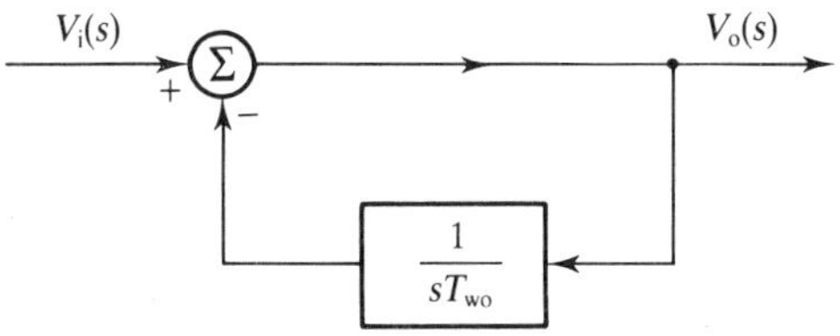

$$\frac{V_o(s)}{V_i(s)} = \frac{sT_{wo}}{1 + sT_{wo}} = \frac{s}{(s + 1/T_{wo})}$$

Figure 9.27 Block diagram of wash-out network.

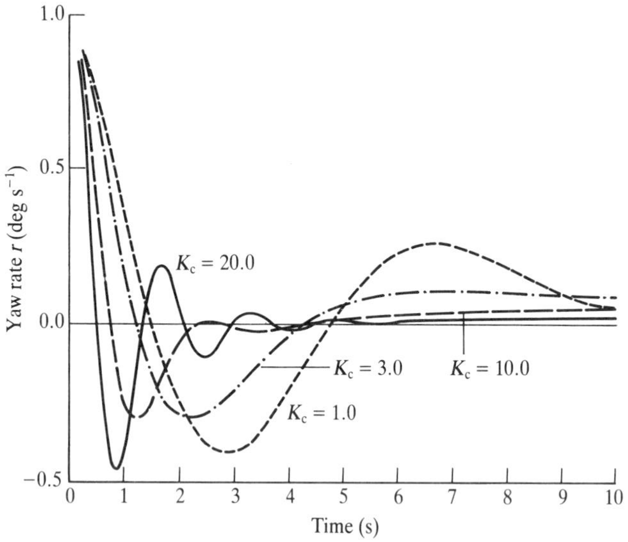

Figure 9.28 Response of yaw damper with wash-out.

feedback does not oppose the commanded input in the steady state. In designing such yaw dampers care must be taken with the choice of value of the time constant of the wash-out network, for, if it is too short, the yaw damper, having less time to act, is less effective. If it is too long, then stability problems arise.

In aircraft of the general aviation (GA) type, arrangements are usually made to allow the pilot to switch out the yaw damper so that it does not operate. In this way the pilot can carry out landing manoeuvres without the rudder pedals being moved automatically and continuously as a result of the action of the yaw damper. Such pedal motion is particularly distracting to a pilot during a flight phase as busy as the approach, and it would occur in GA aircraft since it is customary, as a weight reducing measure, to install any AFCS with the actuator of each control surface in series with the control runs from the primary flying controls. In combat aircraft and large transport aircraft the surface actuators are usually installed in parallel with the control cables or rods. Consequently, it is rare in such aircraft for a means of switching out the yaw damper in flight to be provided: it operates continuously throughout the flight.

9.8.3 Effect of Tilt Angle of the Rate Gyro Upon the Performance of the Yaw Damper

Although the usual assumption of perfect placement of the sensor has been used so far, the effects of sensor characteristics being deferred until the end of the chapter, the effect of gyro tilt will be considered here since it is an effect which may be used deliberately by a designer to enhance the dynamic performance of a yaw damper.

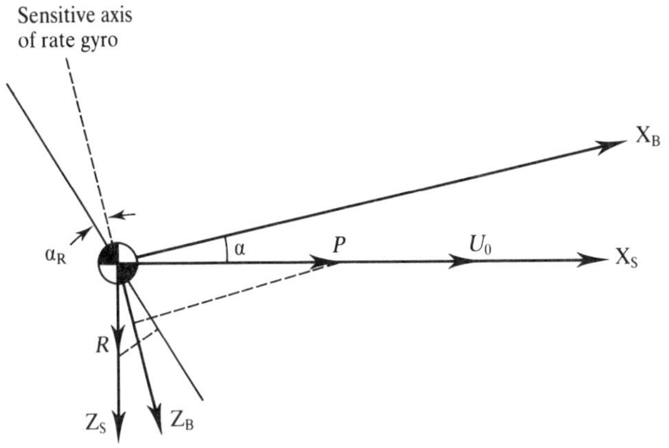

Figure 9.29 Geometry for tilted yaw rate gyro.

Normally, a rate gyro measuring yawing motion will have its sensitive axis aligned with the axis OZ at the c.g. However, this will hold at only a single flight condition; at others, the gyro will be aligned in the fashion represented in Figure 9.29. The output signal from such a rate gyro, usually a voltage, may be denoted as:

$$v_r = 0.1\{r\cos(\alpha + \alpha_R) + p\sin(\alpha + \alpha_R)\} \tag{9.106}$$

In a yaw damper this signal is used for feedback: a block diagram is shown in Figure 9.30. By increasing the tilt angle (α_R) more aftwards (i.e. α_R is increasingly negative) the dutch roll damping may be further increased. The technique is

$$\frac{r(s)}{\delta_R(s)} = \frac{-0.442}{(s^2 + 0.19s + 1.04)}$$

$$\frac{p(s)}{\delta_R(s)} = \frac{0.1(s - 2.83)}{(s^2 + 0.19s + 1.04)}$$

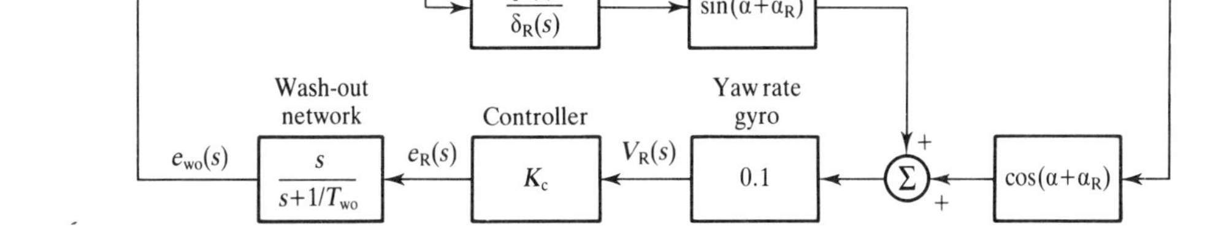

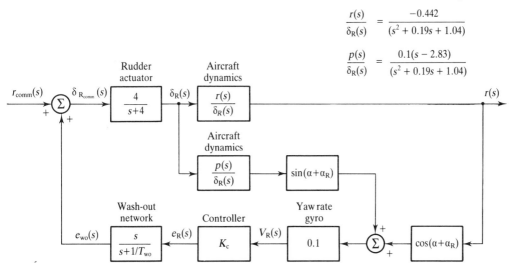

Figure 9.30 Block diagram of yaw damper with tilted gyro.

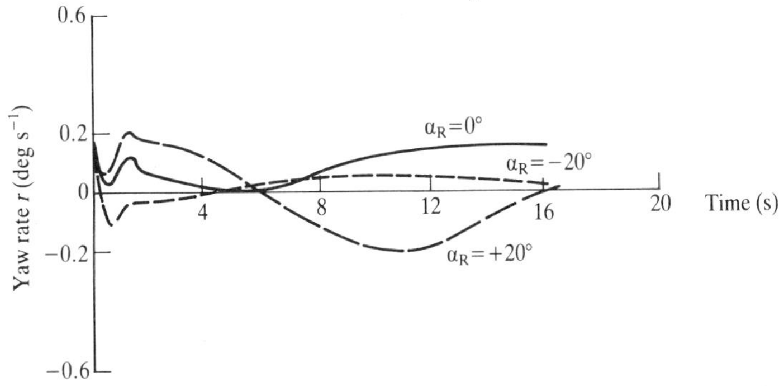

Figure 9.31 Response of yaw damper with tilted gyro.

often used in high performance aircraft. The effect can be seen in the transient response shown in Figure 9.31 which relates to the system of Figure 9.26 for $K_c = 10$, but with the gyro tilted aft by 20°. When the gyro tilt angle is reduced to zero the response of the system of Figure 9.30 is identical to that shown for $K_c = 10$ in Figure 9.28.

9.8.4 Roll Rate Damper

This type of AFCS is usually fitted when the roll performance of an aircraft is considered to be inadequate, by which it is meant that the time to attain a desired value of roll rate is too long. The roll rate damper augments the stability derivative, L'_p, thereby reducing the response time of the aircraft. This SAS is seldom used as a command controller on its own, but rather as an essential inner loop of another lateral AFCS.

The customary assumptions about the dynamics of aileron actuator and the associated rate gyroscope are involved: both are assumed to act instantaneously, the aileron actuator having a gain, K_{act}, and the rate gyro a sensitivity of K_p. A block diagram of a typical roll rate damper is shown in Figure 9.32. The aircraft dynamics have been represented by a transfer function relating the roll rate, p, and the aileron deflection, δ_A, and derived from the single degree of freedom approximation. From the block diagram it can easily be shown that:

$$\frac{p(s)}{p_c(s)} = \frac{K_{act} L'_{\delta_A}}{\left(s + \dfrac{1}{T_R}\right) + K_{act} L'_{\delta_A} K_p K_c} \tag{9.107}$$

i.e.:

$$\frac{p(s)}{p_c(s)} = \frac{\hat{K}}{1 + s\hat{T}} \tag{9.108}$$

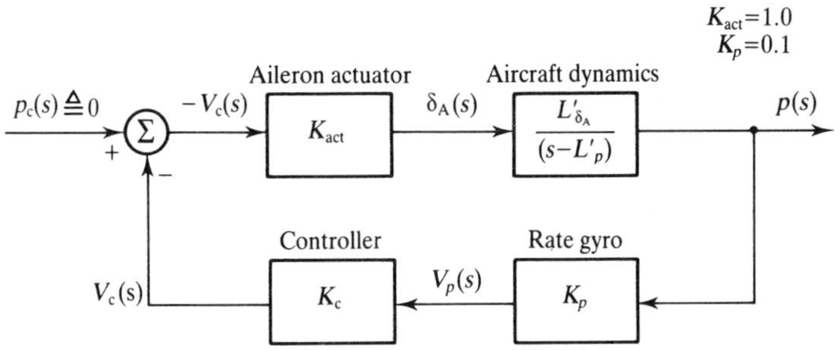

Figure 9.32 Roll rate damper block diagram.

where:

$$\hat{K} = \frac{K_{act}L'_{\delta_A}}{K_{act}L'_{\delta_A}K_pK_c + \dfrac{1}{T_R}} \tag{9.109}$$

$$\hat{T} = \frac{T_R}{K_{act}L'_{\delta_A}K_pK_cT_R + 1} \tag{9.110}$$

If the designer can arrange that $K_{act}L'_{\delta_A}K_cK_p > 1/T_R$ then:

$$\hat{K} \simeq 1/K_pK_c \tag{9.111}$$

$$\hat{T} \simeq \frac{1}{K_pK_{act}K_cL'_{\delta_A}} \tag{9.112}$$

Such a reduction in the time constant of the system results in an improvement of the dynamic response of the aircraft's rolling motion, which often also has a beneficial effect upon the dutch roll motion.

The practice of using the single degree of freedom approximation to represent the aircraft dynamics is almost universal; how justified it is depends upon the nature of the aircraft being studied. Figure 9.33 shows the roll rate responses of CHARLIE-4 to an initial disturbance in roll rate of $1° s^{-1}$; one response relates to the single degree of freedom approximation, the other to the motion variable, p, obtained as a result of solving the full, linearized equations of lateral motion. It is apparent that not much is lost in using the simpler form to represent the aircraft. The corresponding roll rate response obtained from the roll rate damper, with a value of controller gain of 30.0, is shown in Figure 9.34; the other curve – (a) – is the roll rate response curve of the uncontrolled aircraft dynamics shown in Figure 9.32. The settling time for the basic aircraft is 10 s; for the roll damper, the response is an order faster. However, it must be appreciated that the roll rate damper does *not* affect the initial rolling acceleration which is available, although it does reduce the maximum roll rate which the aircraft can produce. Hence, the bank angle reached in some specified time is also reduced, thereby causing the aircraft, perhaps, to fail to meet the specification of flying

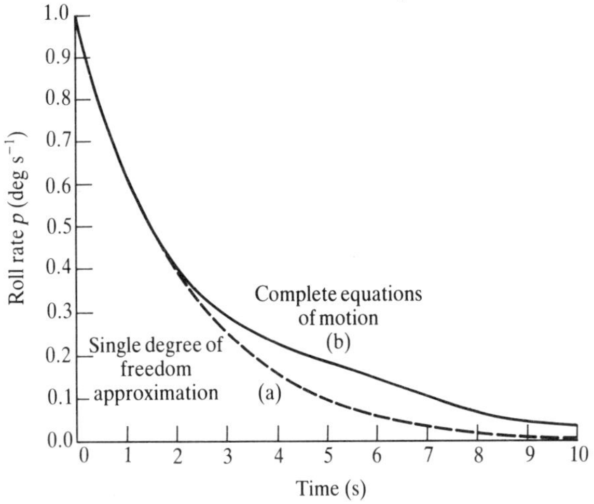

Figure 9.33 Roll rate response for CHARLIE-4.

qualities. In such a case, more aileron control power is needed, i.e. the product $L'_{\delta_A}\delta_A$ must be increased.

Care must be exercised in locating the rate gyro on the aircraft. Usually it is mounted with its sensitive axis aligned with the centreline of the aircraft. However, since an aircraft rolls about its velocity vector, there is a misalignment between this roll axis and the gyro's input axis, which is directly related to the aircraft's angle of attack. The voltage output signal from a rate gyro being used to sense roll rate is given by:

$$v_p = p_s \cos\alpha - r_s \sin\alpha \tag{9.113}$$

where the subscript 's' is used to denote that the variable has been measured in the stability axis system.

Generally, it is true for conventional aircraft that:

$$p_s \cos\alpha \gg r_s \sin\alpha \tag{9.114}$$

Hence:

$$v_p \simeq p_s \cos\alpha \tag{9.115}$$

and the effect upon the operation of the roll rate damper of such a misalignment is that the feedback gain is modulated by the instantaneous value of the aircraft's angle of attack.

9.8.5 Spiral Mode Stabilization

The method to be described is particularly effective in stabilizing a spiral mode. The three degrees of freedom approximation relating yaw rate, r, to aileron

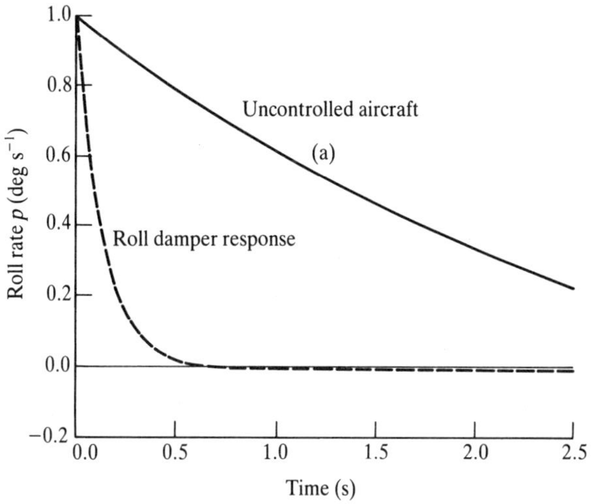

Figure 9.34 Roll damper and uncontrolled roll rate response.

deflection, δ_A, is usually used, i.e.:

$$\frac{r(s)}{\delta_R(s)} = \frac{\frac{g}{U_0}(N'_\beta L'_{\delta_A} - L'_\beta N'_{\delta_A}) + Y^*_{\delta_A}(L'_\beta N'_p - L'_p N'_\beta)s + N'_\beta Y^*_{\delta_A} s^2}{s^2 N'_\beta - \left(N'_\beta L'_p - L'_\beta N'_p + \frac{g L'_\beta}{U_0}\right)s + g/U_0(L'_\beta N'_r - N'_\beta L'_r)} \qquad (9.116)$$

For a number of aircraft types, however, the stability derivatives N'_{δ_A} and $Y^*_{\delta_A}$ are negligible. Hence, the approximation is more often expressed in the form:

$$\frac{r(s)}{\delta_R(s)} = \frac{\left(\frac{g}{U_0}\right)N'_\beta L'_{\delta_A}}{s^2 N'_\beta - (N'_\beta L'_p - L'_\beta N'_p + \left(\frac{g}{U_0}\right)L'_\beta)s + g/U_0(L'_\beta N'_r - N'_\beta L'_r)} \qquad (9.117)$$

The spiral mode stabilization system is represented in the block diagram of Figure 9.35 in which the aileron actuator is assumed to be adequately represented by a simple gain of $1°\,V^{-1}$ so that the actuator block is subsumed in the controller. Furthermore, the yaw rate gyro is assumed to have a sensitivity of K_R V/°/s. It can then be deduced from Figure 9.35 that:

$$\frac{r(s)}{r_{comm}(s)} = \qquad (9.118)$$

$$\frac{\left(\frac{g}{U_0}\right)K_{cont}N'_\beta L'_{\delta_A}}{N'_\beta s^2 - (N'_\beta L'_p - L'_\beta N'_p + \left(\frac{g}{U_0}\right)L'_\beta)s + \left(\frac{g}{U_0}\right)(L'_\beta N'_r - N'_\beta L'_r + K_{cont}N'_\beta L'_{\delta_A})}$$

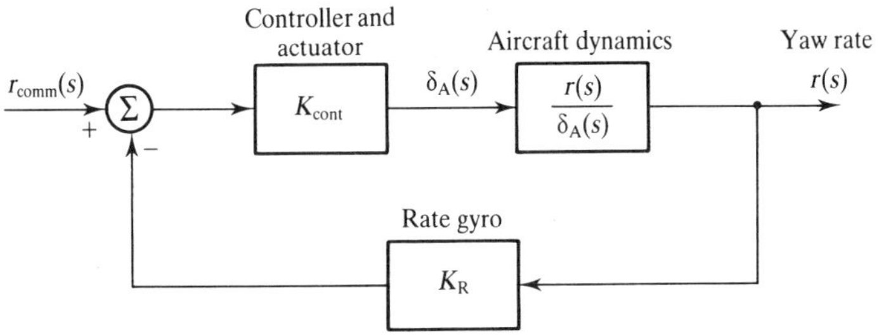

Figure 9.35 Spiral mode stabilization system.

Hence, the natural frequency of the closed loop system is reduced, thereby increasing the damping, which is the desired result. Note that if, for some particular aircraft, N'_{δ_A} and $Y^*_{\delta_A}$ are not negligible, every coefficient of the denominator polynomial of eq. (9.118) would be altered. If N'_{δ_A} is negative (i.e. an adverse yaw effect), the gain $(K_{cont}K_R)$ cannot be made arbitrarily large without causing the dutch roll motion to be unstable. If, however, a proverse yaw effect is evident, i.e. N'_{δ_A} is positive, the damping of the dutch roll motion is augmented by the spiral mode stabilization. Often spiral mode stabilization is obtained by means of a kind of 'piggy-back' operation involving the yaw damper: the feedback signal from the yaw rate gyro is also used to drive the ailerons. That technique is referred to as aileron/rudder interconnection (ARI) or control crossfeed (see Section 10.6.5).

9.9 CONCLUSIONS

This chapter deals with stability augmentation systems which are closed loop control systems used on aircraft to remedy those deficiencies in flying quality which are due to basic aerodynamic or geometric inadequacies in the aircraft. Feedback control is used to augment some particular stability derivatives, thereby improving the parameters which directly govern the flying qualities.

Both lateral and longitudinal motion systems have been considered and the most common types of SAS, such as pitch, roll and yaw dampers, are treated. A number of methods of designing such SASs have been discussed and the effects on the closed loop performance of actuator and sensor dynamics have also been dealt with.

SAS are important since they invariably form the innermost loop of an integrated AFCS.

9.10 EXERCISES

9.1 The linearized equations of perturbed lateral motion for a Tristar (L-1011) passenger aircraft in a cruising flight condition are given by:

$$\dot{\beta} = -0.13\beta - r + 0.04\phi + 0.02\delta_R$$

$$\dot{p} = -4.28\beta - p + 0.25r - 0.9\delta_A + 0.34\delta_R$$

$$\dot{r} = -1.2\beta - 0.004p - 0.178r - 0.58\delta_R$$

$$\dot{\phi} = p$$

Using appropriate approximations, design a yaw damper to increase the damping of the dutch roll mode from its uncontrolled value of 0.14 to a new value of 0.67. Calculate the natural frequency of the yaw damper.

9.2 The short period dynamics of a fighter aircraft are represented in the s-plane diagrams of Figure 9.36.

Design an SAS (ignoring actuator dynamics) to obtain a closed loop damping ratio of 0.6.

9.3 A VTOL aircraft of the AV8B type has the following linearized equations of motion:

$$\dot{u} = X_u u - g\theta + X_{\delta_E}\delta_E + X_{\delta_T}\delta_T + X_{\delta_N}\delta_N$$

$$\dot{w} = Z_w w + (U_0 + Z_q)q + Z_{\delta_E}\delta_E + Z_{\delta_T}\delta_T + Z_{\delta_N}\delta_N$$

$$\dot{q} = M_w w + M_q q + M_{\delta_E}\delta_E + M_{\delta_T}\delta_T + M_{\delta_N}\delta_N$$

$$\dot{\theta} = q$$

where u, w, q and θ represent the changes in forward velocity, vertical velocity,

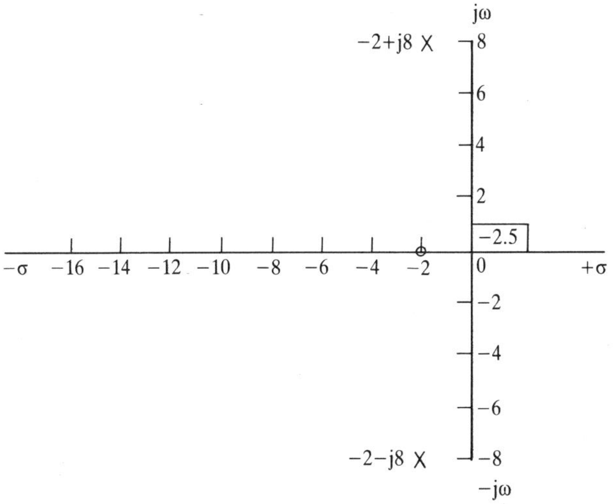

Figure 9.36 Pole zero map for Exercise 9.2.

pitch rate and pitch attitude respectively. The control inputs are represented by the elevator deflection, δ_E, the change in thrust, δ_T, and the deflection of the reaction nozzles, δ_N.

At hover, the corresponding stability derivatives are as follows:

$X_u = -0.045$	$Z_w = -0.02$	$M_w = 0.004$
$g = 32.2$	$Z_q = -0.05$	$M_q = -0.056$
$X_{\delta_E} = -0.16$	$Z_{\delta_E} = -0.4$	$M_{\delta_E} = 0.23$
$X_{\delta_T} = 0.34$	$Z_{\delta_T} = -2.00$	$M_{\delta_T} = -0.036$
$X_{\delta_N} = -0.56$	$Z_{\delta_N} = -0.1$	$M_{\delta_N} = 0.0$

It is required that in hover the vertical velocity be controlled such that it has a characteristic equation of motion of the form $\dot{w} + 5w = 0$.

(a) Design a feedback control system to achieve this requirement.

(b) Sketch a block diagram of the resulting control scheme.

(c) If the aircraft is equipped with sensors for pitch rate and angle of attack, discuss the consequences for the synthesis of the control law determined in part (a).

9.4 A strike aircraft has the following linearized equations of lateral motion:

$$\dot{\beta} = -0.1\beta - r + 0.1\phi + 0.04\delta_R$$

$$\dot{p} = -3\beta - 0.2r - 0.04p + 0.33\delta_A - \delta_R$$

$$\dot{r} = -12\beta + r - 4p - 21\delta_A + 3.33\delta_R$$

$$\dot{\phi} = p$$

β is the sideslip angle, in radians

p is the roll rate (rad s^{-1})

r is the yaw rate (rad s^{-1})

ϕ is the roll rate (rad)

δ_A is the aileron deflection (rad)

δ_R is the rudder deflection (rad)

Only the roll and yaw rates of the basic aircraft are to be directly controlled to improve the handling qualities. The desired handling qualities are assumed to be those obtained from the dynamics of some ideal aircraft which has the model equation:

$$\dot{\mathbf{z}} = \begin{bmatrix} -5.0 & 0 \\ 0 & -3.0 \end{bmatrix} \mathbf{z}$$

where

$$\mathbf{z} = \begin{bmatrix} p_{\text{ideal}} \\ r_{\text{ideal}} \end{bmatrix}$$

Assume that the dynamics associated with the measurement of any motion variable, and also those associated with the control surface actuators, are negligible.

(a) Obtain a feedback control law which will provide the required handling qualities.
(b) Show that this law results in perfect matching.
(c) By means of a block diagram show how the control law of part (a) could be implemented.

9.5 The state vector of an oblique-winged research aircraft is defined as

$$\mathbf{x}' = [u\ h\ \alpha\ \beta\ \phi\ \theta\ \psi\ p\ q\ r]$$

The aircraft has been provided with five controls such that

$$\mathbf{u}' = [\delta_{E_L}\ \delta_{E_R}\ \delta_{A_L}\ \delta_{A_R}\ \delta_R]$$

where δ_{E_L} denotes left stabilizer deflection, δ_{E_R} right stabilizer deflection, δ_{A_L} left aileron deflection, δ_{A_R} right aileron deflection and δ_R rudder deflection. For a particular flight condition the corresponding matrices A and B are:

$$A = \begin{bmatrix} -0.0075 & 0 & 0.19 & 0 & 0 & -32.2 & 0 & 0 & 0 & 0 \\ 0 & 0 & -634.4 & 0 & 0 & 634.4 & 0 & 0 & 0 & 0 \\ 0 & 0 & -1.0 & 0 & 0 & 0 & 0 & 0 & 1.0 & 0 \\ 0 & 0 & 0 & -0.24 & 0.05 & 0 & 0 & 0.006 & 0 & -1.0 \\ 0 & 0 & 0 & 0 & 0 & 0 & 0 & 1.0 & 0 & 0 \\ 0 & 0 & 0 & 0 & 0 & 0 & 0 & 0 & 1.0 & 0 \\ 0 & 0 & 0 & 0 & 0 & 0 & 0 & 0 & 0 & 1.0 \\ 0 & 0 & 0 & -24.39 & 0 & 0 & 0 & -5.86 & -0.03 & 0.84 \\ 0 & 0 & -6.3 & 0 & 0 & 0 & 0 & 0.002 & -0.71 & 0.1 \\ 0 & 0 & 0 & 6.14 & 0 & 0 & 0 & -0.13 & -0.1 & -0.67 \end{bmatrix}$$

$$B = \begin{bmatrix} 1.734 & 1.734 & -0.77 & -0.77 & 0 \\ 0 & 0 & 0 & 0 & 0 \\ -0.09 & -0.09 & -0.04 & -0.04 & 0 \\ -0.012 & 0.012 & 0 & 0 & 0.054 \\ 0 & 0 & 0 & 0 & 0 \\ 0 & 0 & 0 & 0 & 0 \\ 8.0 & -8.0 & 19.18 & -19.18 & 6.1 \\ -6.53 & -6.53 & -0.012 & -0.012 & 0 \\ 1.075 & -1.075 & 0.585 & -0.585 & -4.3 \end{bmatrix}$$

(a) Find the eigenvalues corresponding to the phugoid, the short period and the convergent modes of longitudinal motion, and also those corresponding to the heading, spiral convergence, roll subsidence and dutch roll modes of the aircraft's lateral motion.

(b) Find an optimal feedback control law for the weighting matrices:

$$Q = \text{diag}[1\ \ 10\ \ 0.1\ \ 0.1\ \ 10\ \ 10\ \ 1\ \ 1\ \ 1\ \ 1]$$

$$G = \text{diag}[10\ \ 10\ \ 5\ \ 5\ \ 1]$$

(c) Calculate the corresponding closed loop eigenvalues.

9.6 For the oblique winged aircraft of Exercise 9.5 it is desired to have the closed loop dynamics match those characterized by the vector differential equation $\dot{\mathbf{x}}_m = L\mathbf{x}_m$ where L is defined as:

$$L = \text{diag}[-2.0\ \ -0.5\ \ -1.0\ \ -4.0\ \ -10.0\ \ -10.0\ \ -3.5\ \ -3.5\ \ -5.0\ \ -5.0]$$

(a) Find a feedback control law to achieve these model dynamics.
(b) Calculate the eigenvalues of the resulting closed loop system.
(c) How do these values compare with the eigenvalues of the model aircraft?

9.7 A hypothetical aircraft is considered to have the following matrices when it is flying at a height of 6 000 m and a Mach number of 0.8.

$$A = \begin{bmatrix} 0 & 1 & 0 & 0 & 0 \\ 0 & 0 & 0.882 & 0 & 0 \\ 0 & 0 & -0.882 & 0 & 254.4 \\ 0 & 0 & 0 & 0 & 1 \\ 0 & 0 & -0.008 & 0 & -1.22 \end{bmatrix}$$

$$B = \begin{bmatrix} 0 & 0 \\ 60.4 & 47.4 \\ -60.4 & -47.4 \\ 0 & 0 \\ -2.34 & -22.1 \end{bmatrix}$$

The state vector is defined as:

$$\mathbf{x}' = [h\ \ U_0\gamma\ \ w\ \ \theta\ \ q]$$

and the control vector as:

$$\mathbf{u}' = [\delta_F\ \ \delta_E]$$

The output vector is defined as:

$$\mathbf{y} \triangleq \mathbf{x}$$

Suppose that the equations characterizing the required stability augmentation system are given by:

$$\dot{\mathbf{x}}_m = A\mathbf{x}_m + Hp_{\text{comm}}$$

$$\mathbf{y}_m = \mathbf{y}$$

The matrices A_m and H' are given as:

$$A_m = \begin{bmatrix} 0 & 1 & 0 & 0 & 0 \\ -9 & -6 & 0 & 0 & 0 \\ 0 & 0 & -10 & 0 & 0 \\ 0 & 0 & 0 & 0 & 1 \\ 0 & 0 & 0 & -9 & -6 \end{bmatrix}$$

$$H' \triangleq [1\ 0\ 0\ 0\ 0]$$

Find a suitable feedback control law.

9.8 A prototype fighter aircraft has been built with a vertical fin of reduced size such that the directional stability derivative, N'_β, becomes negative and the derivatives N'_r, N'_{δ_R} and L'_β are reduced in amplitude. The change of sign of N'_β makes the aircraft directionally unstable.

(a) Show that for such an aircraft there must always be two unstable roots.

(b) The prototype aircraft has been flight tested at sea level and at a Mach number of 0.4 and the following stability derivatives were determined:

$$\begin{array}{lll} Y_v = -0.2 & N'_\beta = -2.03 & N'_r = -0.2 \\ L'_\beta = -5.0 & N'_p = -0.07 & N'_{\delta_A} = 0.3 \\ L'_p = -2.5 & L'_{\delta_A} = 20.0 & N'_{\delta_R} = -3.0 \\ L'_r = 3.0 & L'_{\delta_R} = 1.4 & \end{array}$$

Find the eigenvalues of the aircraft.

(c) Using the two degrees of freedom approximation evaluate the transfer function, $r(s)/\delta_R(s)$, and thence design a yaw damper to improve the dutch roll mode. (Note that the stable roots of the corresponding stability quartic are both real).

(d) Will the feedback control scheme devised in part (c) stabilize all the aircraft's modes?

(e) Using any suitable method determine a feedback control law which will result in the controlled aircraft being stable.

(f) Discuss in operational terms the benefits which relaxed static stability (see Chapter 12) is likely to bring.

9.9 (a) A flight control system has been designed for the aircraft ALPHA-2 to reduce the acceleration experienced as a result of encountering turbulence. It is necessary to provide as a feedback signal some measure of the angle of attack, but no suitable sensor is available. An accelerometer is used, but it has to be located 1.55 m ahead of the aircraft's c.g. Show that the measured acceleration is approximately equal to 3.2α.

(b) If the accelerometer is placed as detailed in part (a) what is the measured value of the initial normal acceleration in response to a step deflection of the elevator?

9.11 NOTES

1. All-electric airplanes, proposed by the Americans for development by the year 2000, will remove such actuators and use electric actuators in their place. The aircraft will have no hydraulic supply.
2. These distances should not be confused with the distances l_{x_p} and l_{z_p}, quoted in Appendix B, which represent the distances between the pilot and the c.g. of the aircraft.
3. In a number of high speed aircraft, spoilers are used instead of the ailerons; the principles to be discussed are not materially affected, whichever is used.
4. In some of the earlier, single-axis, autopilots which consisted solely of yaw rate feedback to the rudder, it was because they *did* oppose the almost steady turn associated with an unstable spiral mode that they were successful.

9.12 REFERENCE

McRUER D.T. and D.C. GRAHAM. 1987. Eighty years of flight control: triumphs and pitfalls of the systems approach. *J. Guid. Cont.* 4(4): 353–62.

10

Attitude Control Systems

10.1 INTRODUCTION

Attitude control systems find extensive employment on modern aircraft. They form the essential functions of any AFCS, in that they allow an aircraft to be placed, and maintained, in any required, specified orientation in space, either in direct response to a pilot's command, or in response to command signals obtained from an aircraft's guidance, or weapons systems. It is through their agency that unattended operation of an aircraft is possible. In AFCS work, attitude hold, the commonest function, is often referred to, especially in the USA, as a control wheel steering (CWS) mode.

Stability augmentation systems, which are dealt with in Chapter 9, often form the inner loops of attitude control systems; the attitude control systems then form the inner loops for the path control systems, which are discussed in Chapter 11. It is often the case that attitude control systems need to use simultaneously several of the aircraft's control surfaces, or they may require the use of feedback signals which depend upon motion variables other than those being controlled directly. Attitude control systems are, consequently, more complex in their operation than stability augmentation systems.

10.2 PITCH ATTITUDE CONTROL SYSTEMS

Pitch attitude control systems have traditionally involved the use of elevator only as the control in the system. A block diagram of a typical system is shown in Figure 10.1; the assumptions adopted in Chapter 9 about the representations of the dynamics of both the elevator's actuator and the sensor of pitch attitude are still maintained here. Therefore, the feedback control law being considered in this section can be generally expressed in the form:

$$\delta_E = K_c K_\theta \theta \tag{10.1}$$

As the feedback gain, $K_c K_\theta$, is increased, it is found that the aircraft's short period frequency ω_{sp}, also increases, although its damping ratio, ζ_{sp}, decreases; however, the damping ratio of the phugoid, ζ_{ph}, increases. The period of the phugoid motion also increases until the mode becomes over-damped and, consequently non-oscillatory. An early view (c. 1940) that the best results are

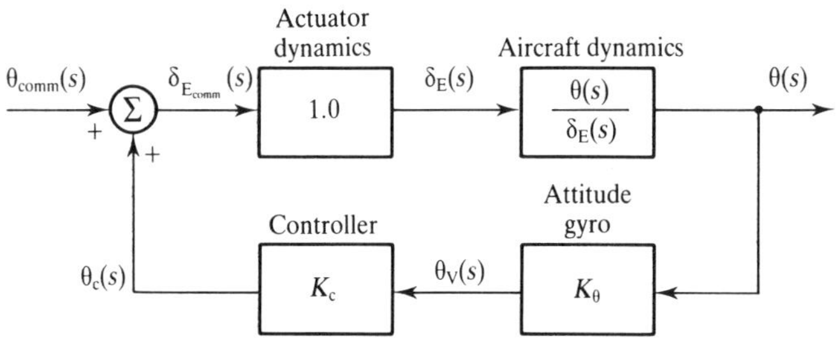

Figure 10.1 Block diagram of pitch attitude control system.

obtained when the value of the feedback gain is chosen such that the phugoid mode is critically damped, thereby making the phugoid motion aperiodic, will be seen to be incorrect. In general, feedback of pitch attitude causes the damping of the phugoid mode to increase at the expense of the damping of the short period mode. Whenever the feedback signals, being used in an AFCS for longitudinal motion, depend solely upon motion variables which *do not* result in the augmenting of the stability derivatives X_u, Z_w, M_α, or M_q, then the total damping of the system is unchanged by the application of feedback. Consequently, the total damping of an open loop system can then be redistributed only among the resulting closed loop modes as a result of linear feedback control. If the phugoid damping is increased, for example, it can only be at the expense of the short period damping. If K_c is so chosen that the phugoid mode is heavily damped then, in the pitch attitude response of the controlled aircraft, the phugoid motion will be almost completely absent. The response of a pitch attitude control system used for FOXTROT-2 is shown in Figure 10.2. The controller gain, K_c, was chosen to be 1.0 V/V, with the sensitivity of the attitude gyro, K_θ, being taken as 1 V/deg. It has sometimes been claimed that whenever the pitch attitude of an aircraft is tightly controlled the phugoid mode cannot exist; but such a claim is incorrectly expressed (Stengel, 1983). What is meant is that, with such control, the roots of the phugoid mode are usually real and negative. When the phugoid mode is so heavily damped, any changes, which occur in other motion variables (such as speed and height) as a result of the pitch command signal, are small and the responses associated with such variables are well damped, with long period. It is for such reasons that the use of pitch attitude feedback to the elevator has been, and will go on being, one of the most successful feedback control techniques used in AFCSs. However, such a system is said to be type O – see Figure 10.1 – and there must then exist, in response to any step command or disturbance, a steady state error – see Figure 10.2. Moreover, the loss of short period damping to augment the damping of the phugoid mode has resulted in a rather unsatisfactory dynamic response because the stability margins have been degraded. The steady state error can be removed by including an integral term in the control law; the inclusion of this additional term, however, may further reduce the damping of the short period motion. A third term is then added to the control law, one involving feedback of the pitch rate (thereby implementing an SAS function) such that:

$$\delta_E = K_c K_\theta \theta + K_b K_I \int \theta dt + K_d K_q q \qquad (10.2)$$

$$= K_2 \theta + K_0 \int \theta dt + K_1 q$$

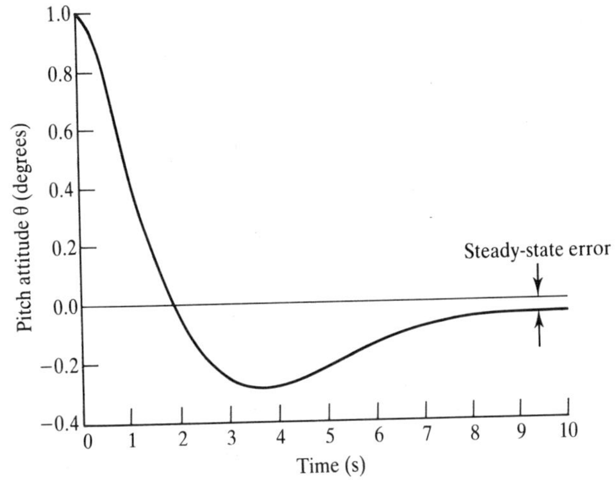

Figure 10.2 Response of system of Figure 10.1.

A block diagram of a pitch attitude control system using such a control law is shown in Figure 10.3. The use of such a three-term controller is not universal, however, and in many systems the degree of steady state error which exists with

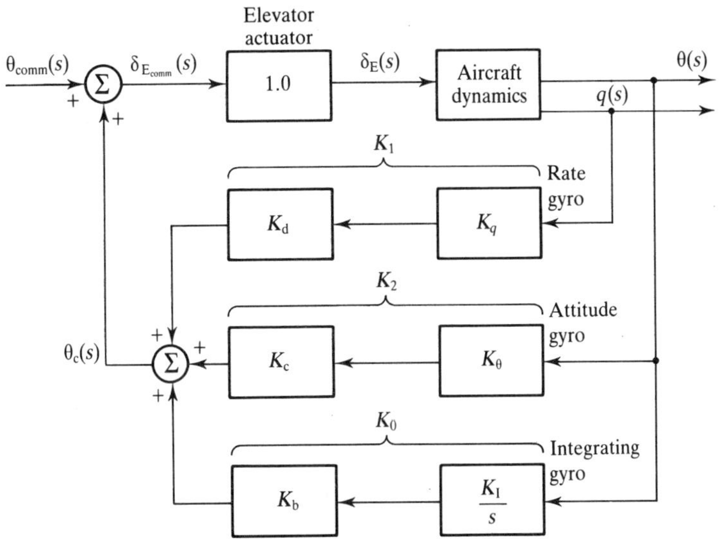

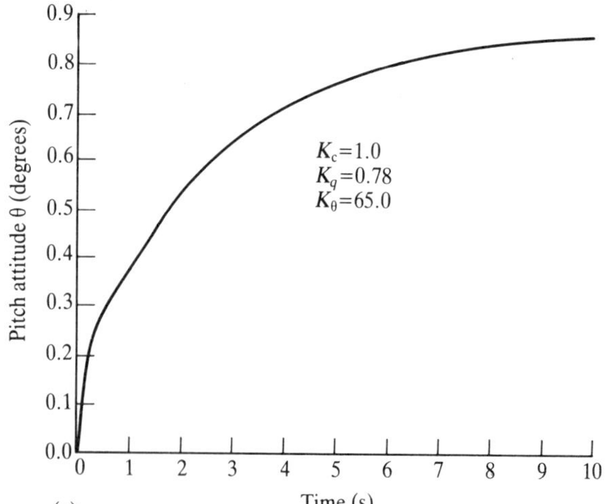

(a)

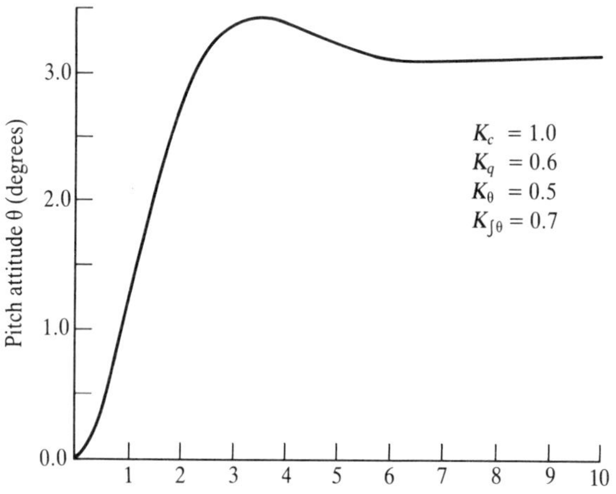

(b)

the chosen values of controller gains, K_c and K_d, is acceptable. As a result, many pitch attitude control systems have a control law which consists of only two terms:

$$\delta_E = K_2\theta + K_1 q \tag{10.3}$$

This feedback control is very effective in general use. Step responses for a pitch attitude control system for FOXTROT-2 are shown in Figures 10.4(a) and (b) for the control laws:

$$\delta_E = 65.0\theta + 0.78q \tag{10.4a}$$

$$\delta_E = 0.5\theta + 0.6q + 0.7\int \theta dt \tag{10.4b}$$

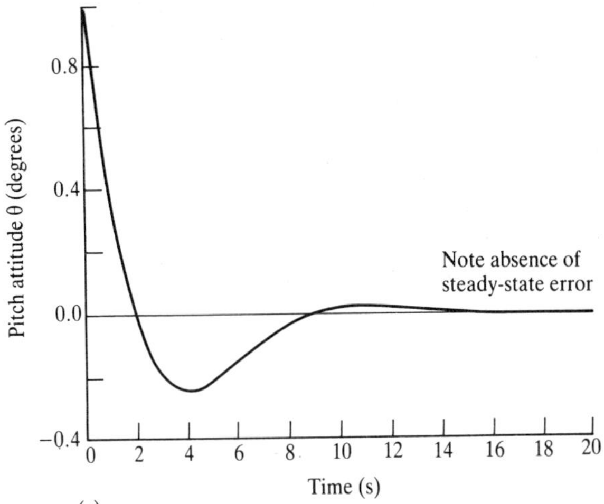

(c)

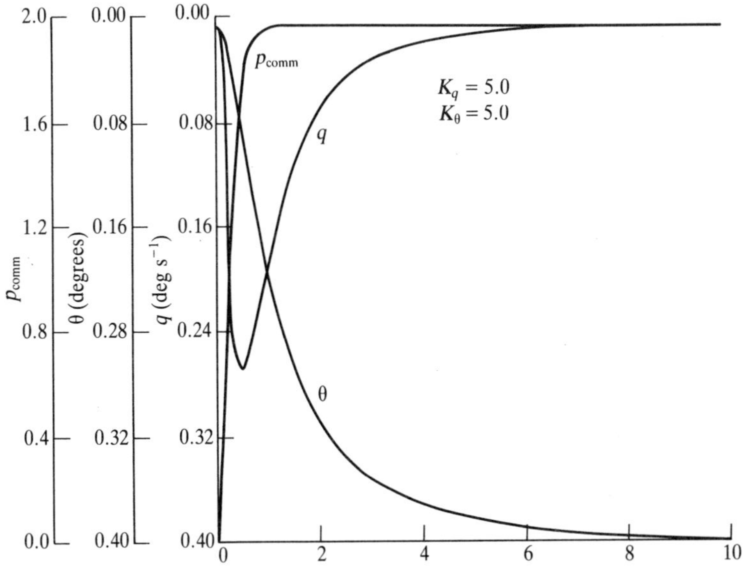

(d)

Figure 10.4 (a) Step response of system of Figure 10.1.
(b) Step response of system of Figure 10.3.
(c) Response of system of Figure 10.3 to initial pitch attitude.
(d) Step response of pitch attitude control with C^* pre-filter.

Figure 10.4(c) shows the transient response of the same system for the same aircraft and flight condition using control law (10.4b). Note that the steady state error has been removed. These responses should be compared with that shown in Figure 10.2. The improvements, which the use of an integral term and pitch rate feedback have made in the dynamic response, are evident from comparing these figures.

A pitch attitude control system using a control law such as (10.3) can produce a better command response by first generating the command signal, θ_{comm}, from a pre-filter which follows the stick input, p_c. One form of pre-filter is the C^* criterion filter which has as transfer function:

$$\frac{\theta_{comm}(s)}{p_c(s)} = \frac{(1 + 0.45s)}{(1 + 0.1s)(1 + 0.2s)} \tag{10.5}$$

where the time constants have been chosen to suit the aircraft being dealt with. The resulting step response of the pitch attitude control system which uses this pre-filter will correspond to the C^* criterion discussed in Section 6.5 of Chapter 6. With the use of this pre-filter it is often possible to change the values of K_q and K_θ so that the transient response to disturbances can also be improved. Figure 10.4(d) shows the step response of the system whose response without pre-filter was given in Figure 10.4(a). For the system corresponding to Figure 10.4(d) the feedback gains were changed to $K_q = 5.0$ and $K_\theta = 5.0$. Note the improved response of Figure 10.4(d).

There is, however, a common flight situation in which too tight control of pitch attitude can be disadvantageous: when an aircraft is flying in the presence of atmospheric turbulence, the pitch attitude control system tends to hold the pitch angle at a constant value. This fixity of attitude opposes the natural tendency of an aircraft to nose into the wind, thereby reducing the acceleration being experienced by the aircraft. It also results in the angle of attack coinciding with the gust. The net result of these two effects is that the accelerations experienced in gusty conditions are higher than they would be otherwise, with a consequent increase of the load being imposed upon the structure of the aircraft.

When a pitch attitude control system is operating a problem can arise if the aircraft is banked at some large angle. The problem depends upon whether a rate gyro or a vertical gyro has been used as the means of providing the feedback signal representing pitch attitude rate in the control law. The rate gyro produces a signal which is related to the body axis system, the vertical gyro signal is related to the Euler axis system, i.e.:

$$q = \dot{\theta} \cos \phi + \dot{\Psi} \cos \theta \sin \phi \tag{10.6}$$

$$\dot{\theta} = q \cos \phi - r \sin \phi \tag{10.7}$$

At large bank angles these signals q and $\dot{\theta}$ cannot both be zero simultaneously. Nor are they equivalent signals. For the wings-level flight situation, either gyro can be used with no discernible difference in performance; but in turning flight the system performance will be quite different, depending upon which gyro has been used. If the vertical gyro is used, the operation of the pitch attitude system must be restricted to a limited range of bank angles.

10.3 ROLL ANGLE CONTROL SYSTEMS

10.3.1 Introduction

Roll angle is generally controlled simply and effectively by the ailerons at low-to-medium speeds on all types of aircraft; on military aircraft, at high speed, spoilers are used. Such spoilers, on the wing of an aircraft, are a very effective means of producing roll moments, but these moments are generally very non-linear, and are quite often accompanied by a proverse yaw moment as well as producing considerable drag.

Roll control for swing-wing aircraft is usually produced by means of control surfaces, moving differentially, and located at the tail. Swing-wings generally contain spoilers to augment the roll control power of the tail surfaces. These spoilers are activated whenever the wings are forward of some value of sweep angle, typically 40–45°. Except at high speed, a differential tail is not very effective at producing rolling moments, since the differential deflection which can be applied is necessarily restricted to allow the same surfaces to be used (symmetrically) for longitudinal control. Associated with the rolling moments produced by this method is a large, adverse yawing moment. Unless particular care is exercised in the design of the basic aircraft, it is possible for the spoilers and the differential tail to produce rolling moments which oppose, and yawing moments which aid. In this section the symbol δ_A will be used to denote any means of producing rolling moments.

The complete transfer function relating bank angle to aileron deflection is given by:

$$\frac{\phi(s)}{\delta_A(s)} = \frac{K_\phi(s^2 + 2\zeta_\phi\omega_\phi s + \omega_\phi^2)}{\left(s + \dfrac{1}{T_s}\right)\left(s + \dfrac{1}{T_R}\right)(s^2 + 2\zeta_D\omega_D s + \omega_D^2)} \tag{10.8}$$

Typically, T_s can be very large; see Table 10.1. Therefore, the spiral mode can correspond to either a slow convergent or a divergent motion. In an early (and excellent) textbook Langeweische (1944) on flying, stated that 'any aircraft which was spirally stable was unpleasant to fly in rough air, for it was wallowy and unsteady and wore you out'. However, for unattended operation, neutral and divergent stability are undesirable since any disturbance can cause an aperiodic, divergent motion of the aircraft, which pilots have referred to as the 'graveyard spiral'. One of the most important functions of any AFCS operating on lateral motion must be, therefore, to attain to a high degree of spiral stability, but it must also improve the other lateral flying qualities so that a pilot is not 'worn out'

Table 10.1 Spiral mode time constants

Aircraft	T_s			
	FC1	*FC2*	*FC3*	*FC4*
ALPHA	− 85.28	2 849.00	534.76	− 5 000.00
CHARLIE	23.42	111.11	97.09	− 128.20
DELTA	35.34	97.09	126.58	− 37.88
FOXTROT	68.03	103.20	534.76	1 792.10

whenever he is flying in atmospheric turbulence. An effective technique of achieving good spiral stability is to provide the aircraft with good lateral static stability. To achieve the degree of dynamic stability desired in roll requires the use of a roll attitude control system. Such a control system is a feedback control system which maintains the roll attitude in the presence of disturbances and responds rapidly and accurately to roll commands from the pilot or a guidance system. For most aircraft, the following assumptions hold: (1) $T_R \ll T_s$, and (2) the quadratic term in the numerator of eq. (10.8) cancels the quadratic term in the denominator.

When these assumptions are true, or are nearly so, the aircraft's roll dynamics may be represented by a single degree of freedom approximation:

$$\frac{p(s)}{\delta_A(s)} = \frac{K_\phi}{(s + (1/T_R))} \tag{10.9}$$

where:

$$K_\phi = L'_{\delta_A} \qquad T_R = -(L'_p)^{-1} \qquad p = d\phi/dt \tag{10.10}$$

10.3.2 A Typical System

A block diagram representation of a typical, roll attitude control system, in which the actuator response is assumed to be instantaneous, is shown in Figure 10.5. It can easily be shown that:

$$\frac{\phi(s)}{\phi_{comm}} = \frac{K_c K_\phi}{s^2 + \dfrac{1}{T_R}s + K_c K_\phi} \tag{10.11}$$

Hence:

$$\zeta = \frac{1}{2T_R(K_c K_\phi)^{1/2}} \tag{10.12}$$

$$\omega_n = (K_c K_\phi)^{1/2} \tag{10.13}$$

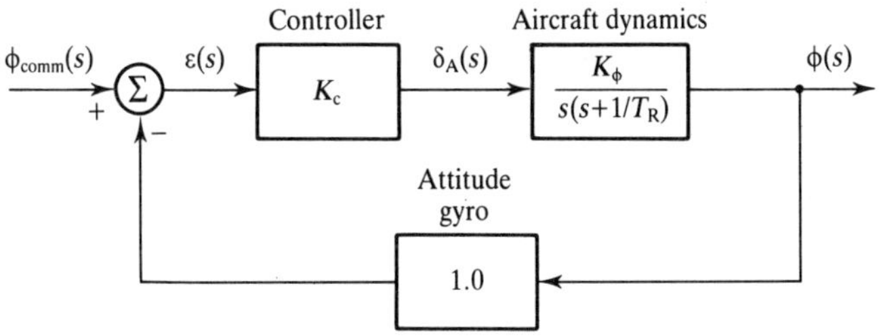

Figure 10.5 Bank angle control system.

For a specific damping ratio of this roll attitude control system, the value of controller gain needed is given by:

$$K_c = \frac{1}{K_\phi (2\zeta T_R)^2} = \frac{L_p'^2}{4\zeta^2 L'_{\delta_A}} \tag{10.14}$$

It is interesting to consider what must be done to this value of controller gain if it is hoped to maintain the damping ratio of the closed loop system at a constant value throughout the flight envelope of the aircraft. In Section 2.10 of Chapter 2 it is noted that the stability derivatives L'_p and L'_{δ_A} could be expressed as:

$$L'_p = \frac{\rho S U_0 b^2}{4 I_{xx}} C_{L_p} \tag{10.15}$$

$$L'_{\delta_A} = \frac{\rho S U_0 b}{2 I_{xx}} C_{L_{\delta_A}} \tag{10.16}$$

Consequently:

$$K_c = \frac{\rho S U_0 b^3}{32 \zeta^2 I_{xx}} \frac{C^2_{L_p}}{C_{L_{\delta_A}}} \tag{10.17}$$

Therefore, the gain must be steadily increased with increase in forward speed.

* * *

Example 10.1

For CHARLIE-2 it can be shown that:

$$\frac{p(s)}{\delta_A(s)} = \frac{0.21(s - 0.002)(s^2 + 0.32s + 1.2)}{(s + 0.01)(s + 0.9)(s^2 + 0.16s + 1.2)} \simeq \frac{0.21}{(s + 0.09)}$$

$$\therefore \frac{\phi(s)}{\phi_c(s)} = \frac{0.21 K_c}{(s^2 + 0.9s + 0.21 K_c)}$$

Suppose $\zeta = 0.6$ is required. Therefore:

$$\frac{\phi(s)}{\phi_c(s)} = \frac{\omega_n^2}{s^2 + 1.2\omega_n s + \omega_n^2}$$

where:

$$\omega_n^2 \triangleq 0.21 K_c$$

But $\omega_n = 0.74$ rad s^{-1}, hence:

$$K_c = 2.6\text{V/V}$$

Figure 10.6 shows the step response of this example system.

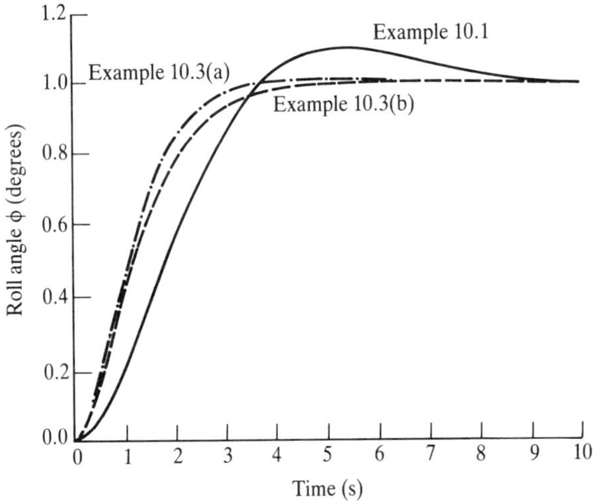

Figure 10.6 Step response of bank angle control system.

10.3.3 Phase Advance Compensation

Sometimes the cancellation of the numerator and denominator quadratics is inexact. In that case, the rolling motion contains a significant component of dutch roll oscillation which may lead to serious difficulties for a pilot flying that aircraft. Whenever this situation is likely to arise, the control law is changed from $\delta_A = K_c\varepsilon$ to:

$$\delta_A = K_c\varepsilon + K_c T_c \dot{\varepsilon} \tag{10.18}$$

where:

$$\varepsilon \triangleq (\phi_{\text{comm}} - \phi) \tag{10.19}$$

The additional rate term in eq. (10.18) introduces damping and corresponds to a phase advance term. The corresponding block diagram is represented in Figure 10.7. With a control law such as eq. (10.18), the closed loop system has a transfer function given by:

$$\frac{\phi(s)}{\phi_{\text{comm}}(s)} = \frac{K_c K_\phi(1 + sT_c)}{s^2 + \left(\dfrac{1}{T_R} + T_c K_c K_\phi\right) s + K_c K_\phi} \tag{10.20}$$

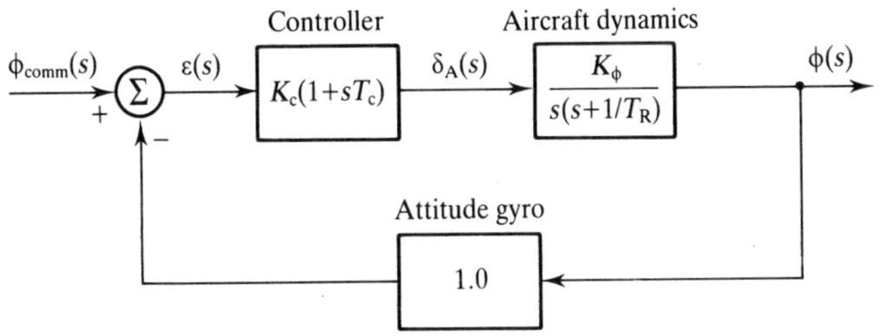

Figure 10.7 Bank angle control system with phase advance.

By proper selection of values of K_c and T_c it is possible to achieve the transfer function of eq. (10.21):

$$\frac{\phi(s)}{\phi_{\text{comm}}(s)} = \frac{K_c K_\phi(1 + sT_c)}{T_c T_\phi(1 + sT_c)(1 + sT_\phi)}$$

$$= \frac{K}{1 + sT_\phi} \tag{10.21}$$

where:

$$K = \frac{K_c K_\phi}{T_c T_\phi} \tag{10.22}$$

* * *

Example 10.2

Consider CHARLIE-2 once more.

$$\frac{\phi(s)}{\phi_{\text{comm}}(s)} = \frac{0.21 K_c(1 + sT_c)}{s^2 + (0.9 + 0.21 T_c)s + 0.21 K_c}$$

Let:

$$s^2 + (0.9 + 0.21 T_c)s + 0.21 K_c \triangleq \left(s + \frac{1}{T_c}\right)\left(s + \frac{1}{T_\phi}\right)$$

$$\therefore \quad s^2 + (0.9 + 0.21 T_c)s + 0.21 K_c = s^2 + \left(\frac{1}{T_c} + \frac{1}{T_\phi}\right)s + \frac{1}{T_c T_\phi}$$

Hence:

$$0.21 K_c = 1/T_c T_\phi$$

$$(0.9 + 0.21T_c) = \frac{T_\phi + T_c}{T_c T_\phi}$$

Since there are three unknowns, T_c, T_ϕ and K_c, and only two equations it is necesssary to choose one and evaluate the others. Suppose K_c is chosen to be 10.0, then, by elementary algebra, it can be found that there are two possible values of T_c which can be used, namely $T_c = 3.107$s or $T_c = 0.2742$s. If the former value is used, the resulting value of T_ϕ is 0.1633, whereas, when T_c is chosen to be 0.2742, the corresponding value for T_ϕ becomes 1.737, i.e when $T_c = 3.107$s then:

$$\frac{\phi(s)}{\phi_{comm}(s)} = \frac{4.41}{(1 + s0.153)} \tag{A}$$

When $T_c = 0.2742$ the result is:

$$\frac{\phi(s)}{\phi_{comm}(s)} = \frac{4.41}{(1 + s1.737)} \tag{B}$$

The response of the system corresponding to eq. (A) is ten times faster than the response obtained from a system corresponding to eq. (B). Hence, system (A) would be the preferred system because the quality of rolling motion from the aircraft would be better than the flying qualities specified in Chapter 6.

10.3.4 The Use of a Roll Damper as an Inner Loop

Using phase advance compensation is often unsuccessful in practice, in situations where the feedback, or the command signals, are subject to noise interference. An alternative scheme, which permits a designer to use considerable freedom in arriving at the required dynamic performance of the roll angle system, is to employ as an inner loop the roll damper SAS discussed in Section 9.5. The roll damping of the aircraft can be considerably augmented by such an inner loop, to values even greater than that needed by the roll angle system, in order to sacrifice some in the outer loop, thereby achieving good steady state performance and the required transient response. A block diagram representing a typical system is shown in Figure 10.8; the actuator dynamics are represented as a simple first order lag. It should be noted that using this technique requires that there be available another motion sensor, namely, a rate gyroscope, for use in the roll damper, or, alternatively, the signal from the roll attitude gyroscopc must be washed-out in an appropriate filter.

From Figure 10.8 it can be established that the closed loop transfer function of the roll angle control system is:

$$\frac{\phi(s)}{\phi_{comm}(s)} = \frac{L'_{\delta_A} K_{c_2}}{\{s^2 + s(L'_p + 0.1K_{c_1}L'_{\delta_A}) + K_{c_2}L'_{\delta_A}\}} \tag{10.23}$$ [1]

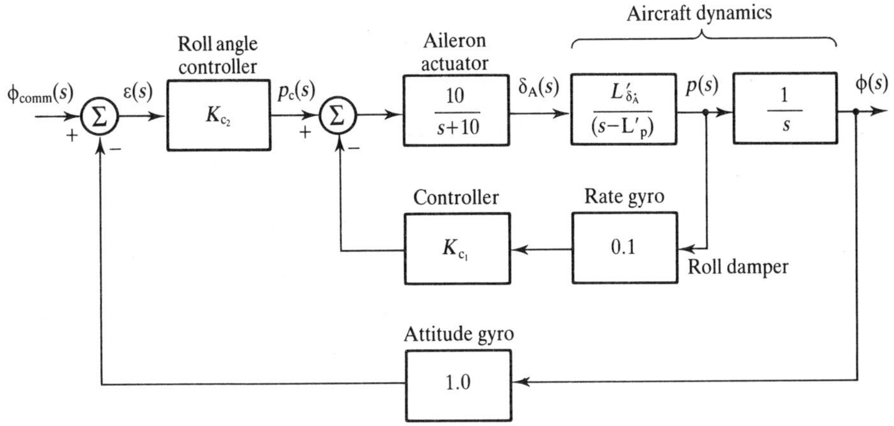

Figure 10.8 Bank angle control system with roll rate inner loop damper.

By using the roll damper as an inner loop, the frequency of the roll angle system can be controlled by K_{c_2} and the damping by K_{c_1}.

The chief difficulty experienced with such systems is associated with locating the sensors to avoid the unwanted effects of structural flexibility. The effect of the aircraft's angle of attack should also be considered. (See the discussion on the roll rate gyro in Section 9.5 of Chapter 9).

* * *

Example 10.3

For CHARLIE-2 the single degree of freedom approximation for rolling motion as a result of aileron deflection can be approximated by the transfer function:

$$\frac{p(s)}{\delta_A(s)} = \frac{0.21}{(s + 0.9)}$$

If the system used as a roll angle control system is that represented by Figure 10.8, then the corresponding closed loop transfer function is:

$$\frac{\phi(s)}{\phi_{comm}(s)} = \frac{0.21 K_{c_2}}{s^2 + (0.1 \times K_{c_1} \times 0.21 + 0.9)s + 0.21 K_{c_2}}$$

K_{c_1} and K_{c_2} can be obtained from any of the methods outlined in Chapter 7.

System A. If K_{c_2} is chosen to be, say, 10.0 and K_{c_1} is selected to be 31.55, then the characteristic polynomial of the roll angle system becomes:

$$(s^2 + 1.5625s + 2.1) = (1 + s3.107)(1 + s0.1533)$$

which is identical to the polynomial which obtained for Example 10.2.

However, since phase-advance is not being used, there is no numerator term and the factor $(1 + s3.107)$ is not cancelled. As a result, the response of this system, although heavily damped, is sluggish.

System B. A better choice of K_{c_1} is 95.156 (K_{c_2} remains fixed at 10.0), for this results in the system being critically damped, i.e.:

$$\frac{\phi(s)}{\phi_{comm}(s)} = \frac{1.0}{(1 + 0.69s)^2}$$

The step responses for systems A and B are shown in Figure 10.6; the superiority of B is evident from inspection.

10.3.5 Use of a Yaw Term in the Roll Control Law

If the control law being used in a roll angle control system is modified to become:

$$\delta_{A_{comm}} = K_{c_1}\phi + K_{c_2}\Psi \tag{10.24}$$

The mode associated with the 'yawing' motion of the aircraft can then become a subsidence mode, with its damping being increased substantially, as K_{c_2} is increased. The dutch roll damping is decreased, however. From experiment and flight tests, it has been found (McRuer and Johnston, 1975) that the best practical arrangement results when:

$$K_{c_1}/K_{c_2} = 1.0 \tag{10.25}$$

The step responses of a roll angle control system, used with CHARLIE-2, and using the control law eq. (10.24) for three values of the ratio, K_{c_1}/K_{c_2}, are shown in Figure 10.9. These results should be compared with those shown in Figure 10.6. It is evident from Figure 10.9 that the best choice is a ratio, K_{c_1}/K_{c_2}, of unity.

10.3.6 Some Problems Arising with Roll Control

In fighter aircraft, the pilot usually controls the roll angle indirectly through a CSAS, a commanded role damper, since such CSASs are necessary to assist the aircraft to provide the rapid roll performance which is essential for modern aerial combat, or for evasive manoeuvres during low level strike missions. To achieve the performance required inevitably means the use of high loop gains. Such high values of gain cause a number of problems, although it is worth noting that the gains of such CSASs are often fixed throughout the flight envelope. Among the problems are the following:

1. The command signal from the pilot must usually be 'damped'. If the input signal to the CSAS corresponding to a small deflection of the pilot's stick is too large then pilot-induced oscillations may result. This is particularly

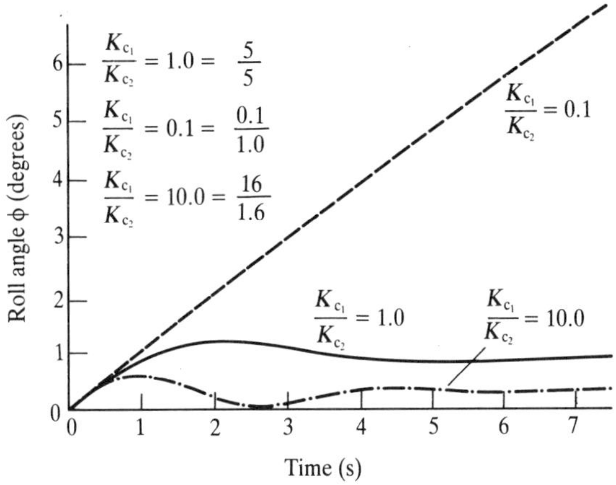

Figure 10.9 Step response of bank angle control system with yaw term added.

likely when the aircraft is being used on a precision tracking task. This problem is general for any high gain CSAS. The obvious remedy of reducing the value of input signal corresponding to the stick deflection often results in the system's performance being inadequate.

2. When the speed of the aircraft is low, and the dynamic pressure is relatively small, such as during a landing approach, the response of the aircraft is sluggish. To achieve the roll response required in this condition means that a pilot has to apply large deflections to the control stick. These large values can result in limiting of the command signals. At high speeds, when the dynamic pressure is large, the much more rapid response of the aircraft, in association with the high loop gain, can result in limiting of the feedback signal. Both limiting conditions can result in degraded roll performance if the roll control system is not well designed.

3. A system with a too high value of loop gain precludes control of bank angle by use of the rudder, which is a technique often used by pilots in making S-turns during landing, or during manoeuvres in aerial combat. This problem can be overcome by carefully scheduling the control gains with the correct flight parameter.

4. On swept-wing aircraft, as the stall condition is approached, it is essential to reduce the value of the loop gain by a substantial amount to avoid very large deflections of the control surfaces. Such large deflections lead to the aircraft's rapidly departing from its trimmed state into a stall.

10.3.7 Roll Ratchet Caused by Excessive Roll Damping

In-flight experiments with modern fighter aircraft have indicated that excessive values of rolling accelerations are experienced by pilots when trying to reach some desired value of roll rate. To avoid such accelerations the pilot must apply more slowly, through the primary flying control, the input to the roll control system. But, frequently, a pilot's reaction is instinctive and sudden, with the result that the closed loop system, formed by the pilot and the aircraft dynamics, oscillates in roll. The oscillatory motion is typically of high frequency (1.8–3.0 Hz) and when it occurs is referred to as 'roll ratchet'. The phenomenon arises with aircraft in which the roll damping is excessive.

Suppose the closed loop transfer function of a roll damper system is given by:

$$\frac{\phi(s)}{P_{\text{comm}}(s)} = \frac{K}{s(1 + sT)} \tag{10.26}$$

If the damping is large $T \rightarrow 0$ and eq. (10.26) can be approximated to:

$$\frac{\phi(s)}{P_{\text{comm}}(s)} = \frac{K}{s} \tag{10.27}$$

When a pilot closes the command loop around a roll damper SAS the system may be represented as shown by Figure 10.10. The form of mathematical model used to represent the pilot is explained in Appendix C; the model used represents a proportional gain, K_p, followed by a pure time delay, τ (representing the pilot's reaction time) of about 0.13 s. Therefore:

$$\frac{\phi(s)}{\phi_{\text{comm}}(s)} = \frac{\hat{K}e^{-s\tau}}{s + \hat{K}e^{-s\tau}} \tag{10.28}$$

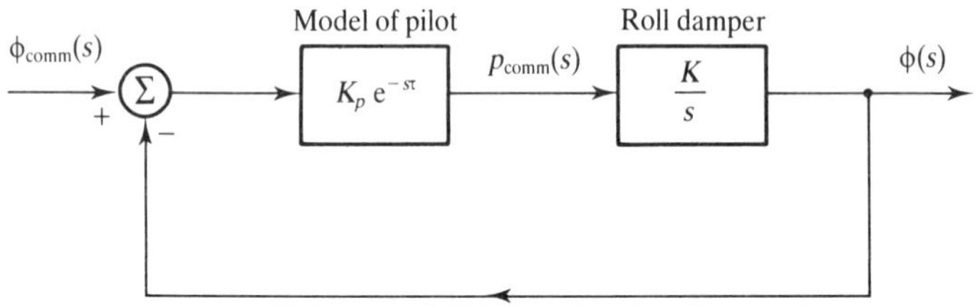

Figure 10.10. Pilot-in-the-loop roll ratchet.

When the loop gain (K_pK) has a value of, say, 12, and the time delay function is approximated by $e^{-s\tau} = (2 - \tau s)/(2 + \tau s)$, then:

$$\frac{\phi(s)}{\phi_{\text{comm}}(s)} = \frac{92.512(2 - 0.13s)}{s^2 + 3s + 185}$$

Therefore, the system will oscillate with very little damping ($\zeta \simeq 0.01$) at a frequency of 13.6 rad s^{-1} in response to a unit step function.

The result of applying a unit step function to a digital simulation of eq. (10.28) is shown in Figure 10.11(a). The roll ratchet oscillation is clearly evident, at a frequency of 13 rad s^{-1}. Figure 10.11(b) shows two step responses for the

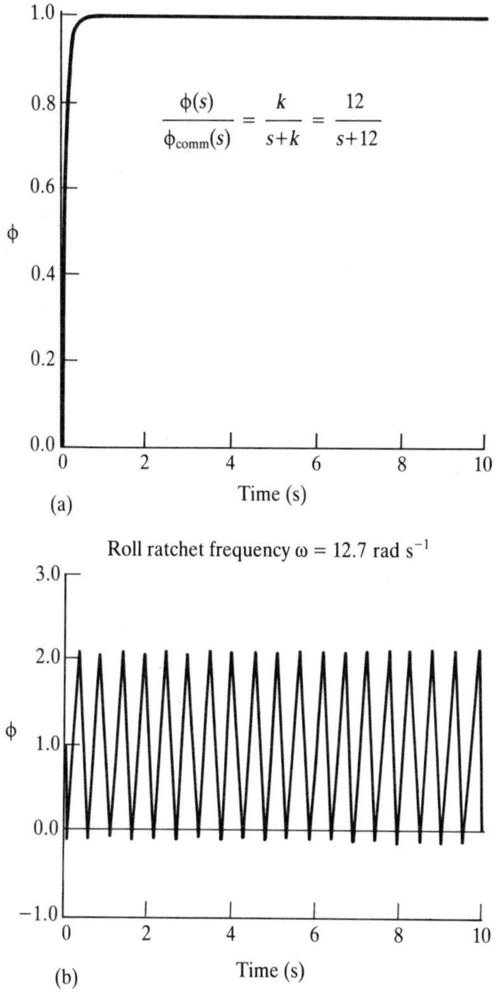

Figure 10.11 (a) Bank angle control system: pilot reaction instantaneous. (b) Bank angle response with pilot reaction time of 0.3 s.

same simulation, but for the situations where T in eq. (10.26) is not entirely negligible, T being 0.01 in case A and 0.2 in case B. From the figure it can be seen that roll ratchet is only evident in case A; in case B, where T has increased, i.e. the roll damping has been reduced, the roll ratchet vanishes.

Readers should refer to Chalk (1983) for further discussion of these topics.

10.3.8 Unwanted Pitching Motion Caused by Rolling Motion

In Section 2.6 of Chapter 2 it is shown that, in a steady turn, there occurs a steady pitch rate, the value of which is:

$$q_{ss} = \frac{g}{U_0} \tan\phi \sin\phi = r \sin\phi \tag{10.29}$$

It is necessary to use as feedback a signal proportional to this steady state pitch rate, to oppose the pitch rate signal being used in the pitch attitude control system, otherwise the pitch attitude control system will not perform properly in banked turns. This matter is discussed in Section 10.2. To obtain this signal, q_{ss}, requires that the output signal from the yaw rate gyroscope be multiplied with that from a resolver driven by a bank angle servomechanism (or the product can be determined in an on-board digital computer).

10.4 WING LEVELLER

In small, general aviation aircraft there is a need, sometimes, for a regulating system which will hold the wings level in the presence of atmospheric disturbances. Although any roll angle control system performs this function, in such a class of aircraft the use of a roll attitude gyro may be avoided by means of setting the command signal, ϕ_{comm} to zero and using a tilted rate gyro in a wing leveller system such as that represented in Figure 10.12. This system has proved to be very effective. The principle of the tilted gyro is the same as that explained in Section 9.8.

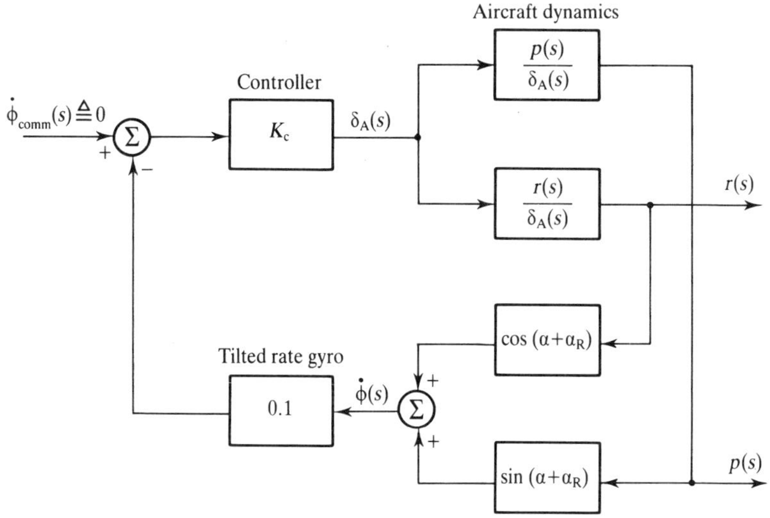

Figure 10.12 Roll rate system with tilted gyro.

10.5 CO-ORDINATED TURN SYSTEMS

10.5.1 Introduction

A co-ordinated turn is one in which both the lateral acceleration, $a_{y_{cg}}$, and the sideslip velocity, v, are zero. In such a turn the lift vector is perpendicular to the aircraft axis OY. Co-ordinated turns reduce adverse sideslip and, therefore, roll hesitation. In such turns, there is minimum coupling of rolling and yawing motions. Provided that the side force due to aileron, $Y^*_{\delta_A}$, and the side force due to the yaw rate, Y_r, are both negligible, then zero sideslip angle ($\beta = 0$), zero sideslip velocity ($v = \beta/U_0 = 0$), and zero lateral acceleration ($a_{y_{cg}} = 0$) are all equivalent conditions. Sometimes, particularly in early textbooks on flying techniques, a co-ordinated turn was assumed to be one in which the lateral acceleration experienced in the cockpit was zero – a condition displayed to pilots by the turn-and-bank indicator, with its black ball centred between the vertical lines. However, this condition is not one which finds much use in AFCS studies since the acceleration at the cockpit is a function of the distance from the aircraft's c.g. Generally, the acceleration at the pilot's station features in AFCS work only in relation to ride control systems, which are dealt with in Chapter 12.

10.5.2 Conditions Needed for a Co-ordinated Turn

For a body axis system the side force equation is:

$$Y = m(\dot{V} - WP + UR) \tag{10.30}$$

Following the development detailed in Section 2.4 of Chapter 2, it can be seen that the rate of change of sideslip angle can be expressed as in eq. (2.75), i.e.:

$$\dot{\beta} = -r + \frac{pW_0}{U_0} + \frac{g}{U_0}\sin\phi\cos\Theta_0 + \frac{g}{U_0}\sin\psi\sin\Theta_0 \tag{10.31}$$

If $\Theta_0 = 0$,

$$W_0/U_0 = \alpha_0 \tag{10.32}$$

and, if a co-ordinated turn is achieved, i.e. if:

$$\dot{\beta} = 0 \tag{10.33}$$

then:

$$r = p\alpha_0 + \frac{g}{U_0}\sin\phi \tag{10.34}$$

If the aircraft has been trimmed so that α_0 is zero, then:

$$r = \frac{g}{U_0}\sin\phi \tag{10.35}$$

Therefore, in a co-ordinated turn, the rate of turn develops in proportion to the bank angle, ϕ. Of course, neither Y_v nor $Y^*_{\delta_A}$ is generally zero, nor may they be neglected. Consequently, if β is to be zero, so that eq. (10.35) obtains, a steady deflection of the ailerons is required to maintain the co-ordinated turn. The value of aileron deflection required is given by:

$$\delta_A = \frac{Y_v}{Y^*_{\delta_A}} \beta \tag{10.36}$$

There are a number of factors which may delay the establishment of a co-ordinated turn. They include the following:

1. An aileron deflection usually induces a yawing moment.
2. The build-up of yaw rate, as a result of any change in bank angle, is delayed by aerodynamic lag.
3. The action of the yaw damper, which is commonly fitted to aircraft, tends to reduce any transient yaw rate.

As an illustration of how these factors affect the turn, consider an aircraft, such as CHARLIE in Appendix B, in which:

$$N'_{\delta_A} > 0 \tag{10.37}$$

Whenever a positive roll rate is required i.e. $\delta_A < 0$, a negative (*adverse*) yawing moment results. This can be seen from eq. (2.85):

$$\dot{r} = N'_v\beta + N'_r r + N'_p p + N'_{\delta_A}\delta_A + N'_{\delta_R}\delta_R \tag{2.85}$$

For all aircraft, N'_r and N'_{δ_R} are both negative. If the yawing moment is negative, the sideslip is positive.

10.5.3 Sideslipping as a Result of Sensor Signals in Lateral AFCSs

If the rate gyro used to measure the yaw rate in a yaw damper is of the strap-down variety (i.e. it is fixed to the aircraft and is not mounted on gimbals) its signal is a measure of the body rate, rather than of a wind/body rate (i.e. one which has been measured in relation to the stability axes). However, the equations used in the yaw damper design have been derived using stability axes, so that there is a discrepancy when a strap-down gyro is used. The output signal produced by such a gyro is given by:

$$r_{\text{body}} = r_s \cos\alpha_0 + p_s \sin\alpha_0 \tag{10.38}$$

In a rolling manoeuvre, with a positive angle of attack, the component due to roll rate in the signal from the strap-down gyro will increase. But if this signal is used as the feedback signal in a yaw damper, that feedback signal will be increased, causing further rudder action, which results in an increased sideslip angle. For negative angle of attack in a rolling manoeuvre, the effect is to reduce the sideslip motion.

10.5.4 Horizontal Acceleration During a Turn

The situation is represented in Figure 10.13: f_c denotes the centripetal force, V_T the tangential velocity, ω the angular velocity, m the mass of the aircraft, and R the radius of the turn.

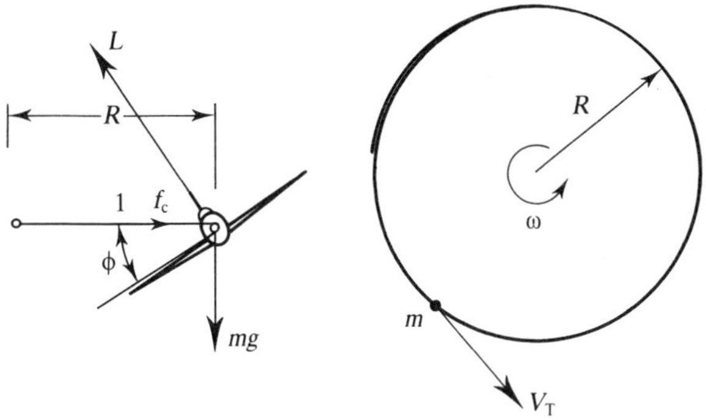

Figure 10.13 Aircraft turn geometry.

$$f_c = m\omega^2 R = m\omega V_T \tag{10.39}$$

$$\therefore \quad a_{y_{cg}} = \omega V_T \tag{10.40}$$

However:

$$r = \omega \cos \phi \tag{10.41}$$

$$\therefore \quad a_{y_{cg}} = (V_T/\cos \phi) r = V_T r \sec \phi \tag{10.42}$$

But:

$$\omega = (g/V_T) \tan \phi \tag{10.43}$$

$$\therefore \quad a_{y_{cg}} = g \tan \phi \tag{10.44}$$

The total acceleration is the vector sum of $a_{y_{cg}}$ and the acceleration due to gravity. The maximum value of acceleration is always experienced at the same bank angle, irrespective of aircraft velocity, V_T. If the aircraft, however, is subject to some maximum value of r, then the lateral acceleration is limited to some maximum value which corresponds to V_T. For a given speed, U_0, and a constant rate of turn, ω, the bank angle required for a co-ordinated turn is given by:

$$\phi_0 = \tan^{-1}(U_0\omega/g) \tag{10.45}$$

Although turns are invariably made at values of bank angle too large for the linearization of $\sin \phi$ and $\cos \phi$ to hold, the results obtained above are correct.[2] The number of turns which are completed in a manoeuvre may be calculated from:

$$N = \frac{1}{2\pi}\int r\,dt = \frac{1}{2\pi}\int \dot{\Psi}\,dt \tag{10.46}$$

10.5.5 A Steady Sideslip Manoeuvre

This flight condition of non-symmetric, rectilinear translation is often used in light aircraft to correct for the presence of a cross-wind on the landing approach. At *large values of sideslip angle*, the drag on the aircraft increases; as a result, the aircraft's lift/drag ratio decreases. In this flight condition, rates of change are zero, i.e.:

$$\dot{\beta} = p = r = 0 \tag{10.47}$$

$$Y_v\beta + \frac{g}{U_0}\cos\Theta_0\phi + Y^*_{\delta_A}\delta_A + Y^*_{\delta_R}\delta_R = 0 \tag{10.48}$$

$$L'_\beta\beta + L'_{\delta_A}\delta_A + L'_{\delta_R}\delta_R = 0 \tag{10.49}$$

$$N'_\beta\beta + N'_{\delta_A}\delta_A + N'_{\delta_R}\delta_R = 0 \tag{10.50}$$

$$\begin{bmatrix} Y_v & Y^*_{\delta_A} & Y^*_{\delta_R} \\ L'_\beta & L'_{\delta_A} & L'_{\delta_R} \\ N'_\beta & N'_{\delta_A} & N'_{\delta_R} \end{bmatrix} \begin{bmatrix} \beta \\ \delta_A \\ \delta_R \end{bmatrix} = \begin{bmatrix} -\frac{g}{U_0}\cos\Theta_0\phi \\ 0 \\ 0 \end{bmatrix} \tag{10.51}$$

i.e. $A\mathbf{u} = \mathbf{c}$.

If, say, a value of bank angle is chosen, arbitrarily, the resulting sideslip angle β and the control surface deflections δ_A and δ_R required for the manoeuvre can easily be found, provided that the matrix A is non-singular. The control deflections required tend to be very large, since powerful controls are needed to sideslip an aircraft at large angles. If A is singular, it implies that the bank angle required for the manoeuvre is zero. In this situation, the bank angle term on the r.h.s. should be transferred to the l.h.s. of eq. (10.51) and the β term should be transferred from the l.h.s. to r.h.s. The new matrix A which results is then non-singular.

The control deflections required to produce the specified sideslip angle can then be determined, along with the resulting bank angle.

10.6 SIDESLIP SUPPRESSION SYSTEMS

10.6.1 Introduction

It can be deduced from the discussion on co-ordinated turns that sideslip angle is the motion variable whose control is central to the achievement of a co-ordinated turn. There is no particularly good method of measuring sideslip; the vane sensors which are used in some low speed aircraft are affected by problems concerning the local aerodynamic flow around the vane. They are also physically vulnerable. Some types of stagnation point sensor are useful for sensing flow direction, but have not yet found general application for AFCSs. Thus, the obvious means of controlling sideslip angle, by using a feedback control law based on sideslip sensing, is rarely used on high performance aircraft. However, its design and use will be covered first, to indicate the effectiveness of such systems, before presenting some other methods which are commonly used. These include: lateral acceleration feedback, computed yaw rate feedback, and control cross feeds.

Further discussion of this topic can be found in McRuer and Johnston (1975).

10.6.2 Sideslip Feedback

Figure 10.14 shows a typical system in which the sideslip angle, β, is sensed and used as a feedback signal to drive the rudder so that the sideslip motion is eliminated.

Note that the system includes a yaw damper as its inner loop. For example, the yaw damper system for CHARLIE-4 used a yaw rate gyro with a sensitivity, K_R, of 0.1 V deg^{-1}, a value of controller gain, K_{c_1}, of 10, and a wash-out time constant of 1.0 s. The state equation for the yaw damper was defined in eqs (9.74)–(9.76). The command input there was taken as r_{comm}; from Figure 10.14 it can be seen that when the sideslip suppression system is added, the command input to the yaw damper is now:

$$r_{comm} = p_c - K_{c_2} K_\beta \beta \tag{10.52}$$

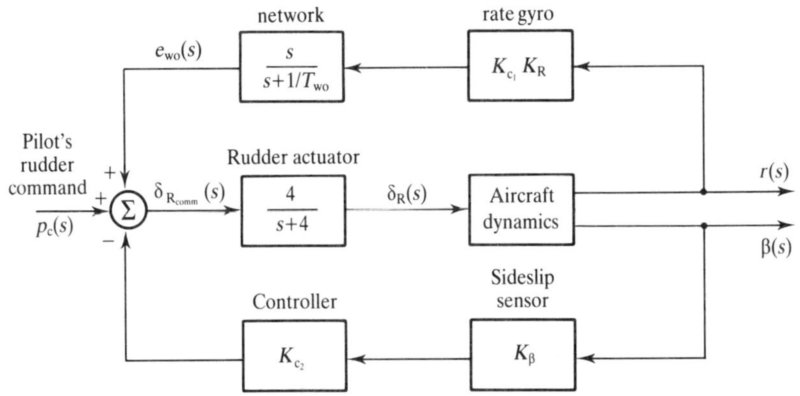

Figure 10.14 Sideslip suppression system.

Hence the state equation for the controlled aircraft, with both yaw damper and sideslip suppression system, may be written as:

$$\dot{\mathbf{x}} = A_1\mathbf{x} + B\mathbf{u} \tag{10.53}$$

where:

$$\mathbf{x}' \triangleq [\beta \;\; p \;\; r \;\; \phi \;\; \delta_R \;\; e_{wo}] \tag{10.54}$$

(as before – see eq. (9.72))

$$\mathbf{u} \triangleq p_c \tag{10.55}$$

$$\mathbf{B}' = [0 \;\; 0 \;\; 0 \;\; 0 \;\; 4 \;\; 0] \tag{10.56}$$

$$A_1 = \begin{bmatrix} -0.056 & 0 & -1 & 0.042 & 0.0022 & 0 \\ -1.05 & -0.465 & 0.39 & 0 & 0.153 & 0 \\ 0.6 & -0.032 & -0.115 & 0 & -0.47 & 0 \\ 0 & 1 & 0 & 0 & 0 & 0 \\ -K_{c_2}K_\beta 4 & 0 & 0 & 0 & -4 & 4 \\ 6 & -3.2 & -1.15 & 0 & -4.75 & -1.0 \end{bmatrix} \tag{10.57}$$

Because of the perturbed airflow surrounding the vane of a sideslip sensor, the output signal is prone to contamination by noise. Consequently, to avoid feedback of local flow disturbances, it is customary to use vane sensors of low sensitivity. To illustrate the effectiveness of the system, a value of sensitivity, K_β, for the sideslip sensor in Figure 10.14 of 0.05 V deg^{-1} has been chosen. Figure 10.15 shows the system responses to an initial sideslip disturbance of 1°, (K_{c_2} = 100.0, K_{c_1} = 10.0, K_β = 0.05) for the sideslip controller. The response, corresponding to Kc_2 = 0, is the response of the yaw damper only: the other responses should be compared to this one to observe the relative effectiveness of the sideslip suppression system. The effect of the sideslip suppression system can also be appreciated from an examination of the system eigenvalues. Table 10.2 shows the eigenvalues of the basic uncontrolled aircraft (CHARLIE-4), the yaw damper only, and the combined system with sideslip suppression. The corresponding values of controller gains K_{c_1} and K_{c_2} are indicated. From Table 10.2 it can be seen how the sideslip suppression system has increased the stability of the spiral mode, thereby reducing the sideslip transient more effectively. It is worth appreciating, finally, that a considerable degree of sideslip suppression results from the action of the yaw damper on its own.

10.6.3 Lateral Acceleration Feedback

When an accelerometer is located at the centre of percussion, an instantaneous centre of rotation at which occurs the centre of pressure of the aerodynamic force

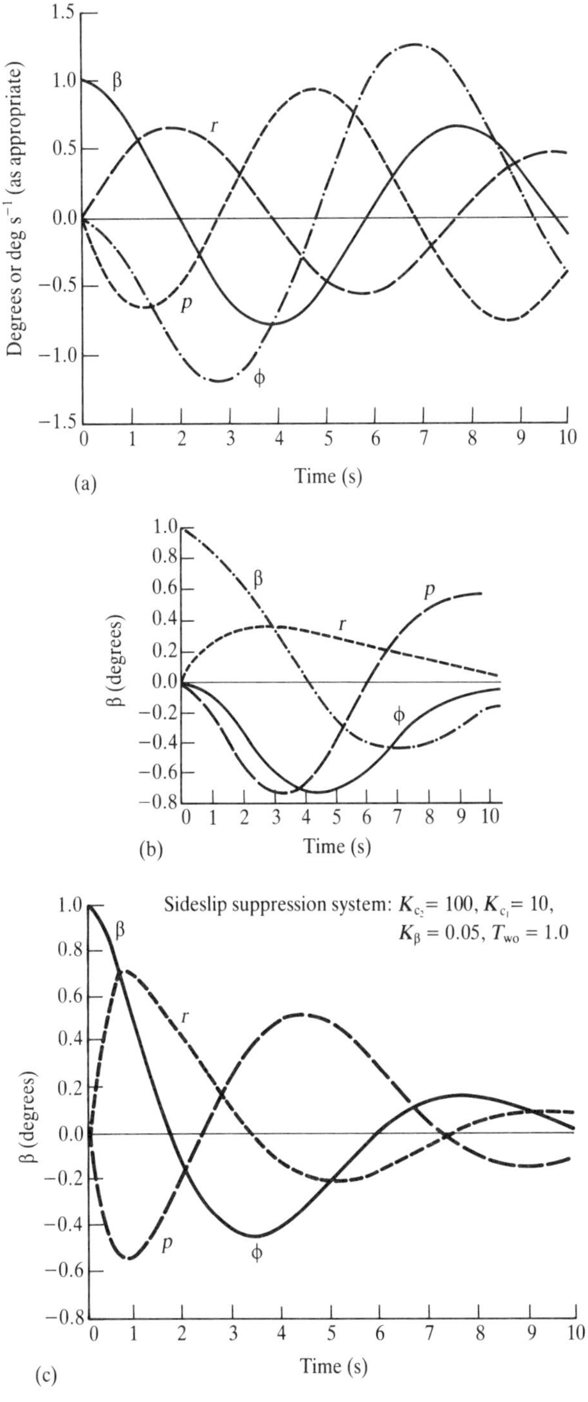

Figure 10.15 Response to $\beta(0) = 1°$. (a) Uncontrolled aircraft. (b) Yaw damper system – wash-out time constant = 1 s. (c) Sideslip suppression system.

Table 10.2 Eigenvalues of sideslip suppression systems

Eigenvalue	*Uncontrolled aircraft*	*Yaw damper and wash-out network*	*Sideslip suppression – sideslip feedback*
λ_1	0.0129	0.0089	0.0227
λ_2	-0.5617	-0.586	-0.564
λ_3	$-0.0436 \pm j0.81$	$-0.0398 \pm j0.394$	$-0.2408 \pm j0.727$
λ_4	$-0.0436 \pm j0.81$	$-0.0398 \pm j0.394$	$-0.2408 \pm j0.727$
λ_5	—	$-2.49 \pm j4.149$	$-2.307 \pm j4.006$
λ_6	—	$-2.49 \pm j4.149$	$-2.307 \pm j4.006$
			$K_{C_1} = 10.0$
			$K_{C_2} = 100.0$
			$K_\beta = 0.05$

as a result of the rudder deflection, the acceleration which is sensed (assuming linear relationships) is:

$$a_y = Y_v\beta \qquad (10.58)^3$$

Thus, the sideslip suppression system can now have a block diagram like that shown in Figure 10.16. The system requires, however, that the sensitivity of the accelerometer be high, since Y_v is usually small, e.g. for CHARLIE-4, $Y_v = -0.056$. In addition, the acceleration threshold of the accelerometer must be low if the sideslip suppression system is to be effective for small values of sideslip angle. This low threshold value means that the system is subject to spurious inputs from structural effects, and, possibly in very high performance aircraft, from the effects of Coriolis acceleration. The state equation of eq. (10.53) also applies for this system, and for the example of CHARLIE-4, the only change which occurs is to the element a_{51} of A. It now becomes:

$$a_{51} = (-4K_{a_y}K_{c_2}Y_v) \qquad (10.59)$$

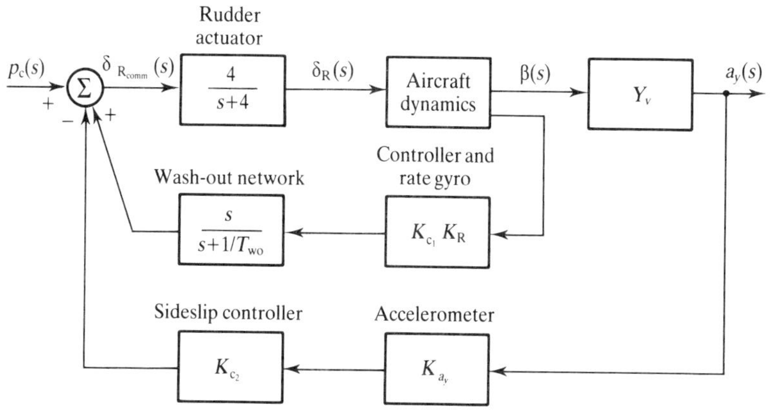

Figure 10.16 Block diagram of lateral acceleration control system.

This type of sideslip suppression system is sometimes referred to as 'directional stiffening' (see McRuer and Johnston, 1975) since it augments N'_{β}.

10.6.4 Sideslip Suppression Using Computed Yaw Rate

It is shown in Section 10.5 that, in a co-ordinated turn, the rate of turn develops in proportion to the bank angle, i.e.

$$r = \frac{g}{U_0} \sin \phi \qquad (10.35)$$

By using this signal as a feedback signal in the system (the block diagram of which is given in Figure 10.17) unwanted sideslip motion can be suppressed. The system causes the rudder to be deflected to change the sideslip angle only if eq. (10.35) does not hold. In other words, if the sideslip angle has a value other than zero, the feedback operates. The error signal in Figure 10.17 is given by:

$$e_{ss} = K_{c_2} K_{res} \left\{ r - \frac{g}{U_0} \sin \phi \right\} \qquad (10.60)$$

The system is effective, if the resolver is accurate; with modern, airborne digital computers computing equations such as eq. (10.35) can be carried out to very good accuracy. With old-fashioned, electromechanical resolvers, the accuracy was often difficult to achieve and, as a result, the rudder could be held over at either extreme of its range of deflection during a turn. This tendency was objectionable to many pilots and, although its use was confined to high performance, military

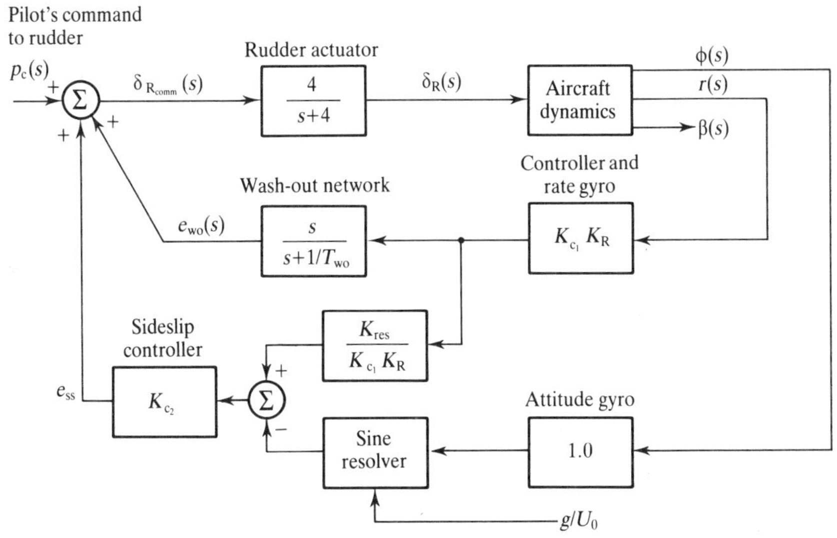

Figure 10.17 Block diagram of computed yaw rate sideslip suppression.

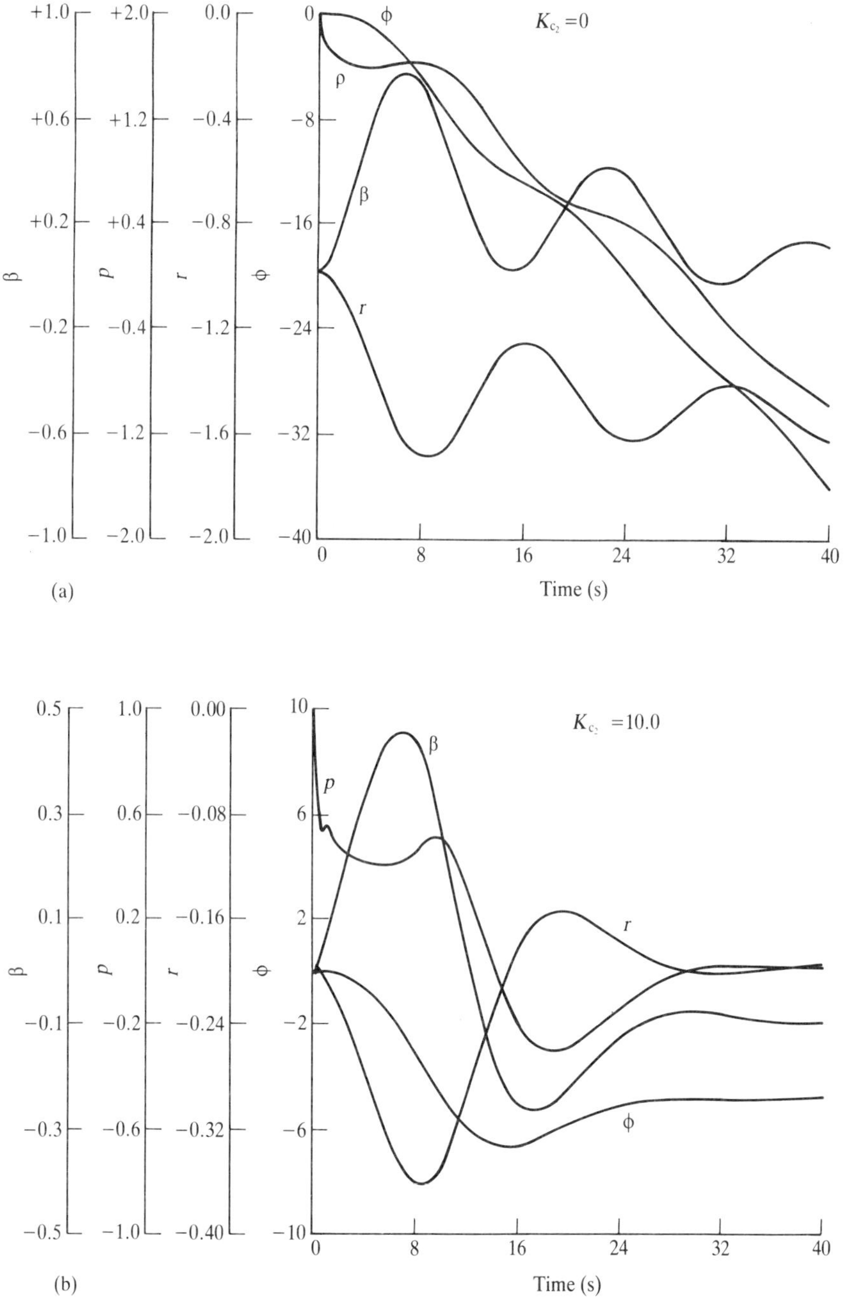

Figure 10.18 Response to β(0) = 1°.
(a) Computed yaw rate system $K_{c_2} = 0$.
(b) Computed yaw rate system $K_{c_2} = 10.0$.

aircraft, the system never enjoyed much popularity. The responses of such a system, for CHARLIE-4, using the same parameters for the inner loop as were used in the yaw damper discussed in Chapter 9, are shown in Figure 10.18. The sensitivity of the resolver was chosen to be 1 V deg^{-1}. The value of the gain of the controller is indicated at the appropriate response curve in Figure 10.18.

10.6.5 Control Crossfeeds

Introduction

It must be remembered that turn co-ordination is most often required when either stopping or completing a lateral manoeuvre during the final approach. Such manoeuvres are usually controlled by use of the ailerons; however, the use of ailerons can result in a significant yawing moment if the stability derivative, N'_{δ_A}, is relatively large. This yawing moment can make a substantial contribution to the sideslip which can arise in manoeuvres of this kind. As a result, it has long been a practice in lateral/directional control systems to incorporate a control crossfeed to remove that source of sideslip. There are two types of crossfeed (sometimes referred to as 'interconnects'): aileron-to-rudder interconnect (ARI) and bank angle-to-rudder crossfeed. ARI is the most common, being the most effective.

ARI

A control system, which uses ARI to maintain at zero the sideslip induced by both aileron deflection and roll rate (N'_p) is represented in Figure 10.19. The most suitable value of the crossfeed gain, K_{cf}, has been found from flight studies (see McRuer and Johnston, 1975) to be:

$$K_{cf} = N'_{\delta_A}/N'_{\delta_R}L'_p \tag{10.61}$$

However, the student should understand that if the ARI is to be a permanent connnection throughout the flight envelope, and not active just at the terminal phases of flight, being switched in, say, when the flaps are deployed, or when the landing gear is lowered, gain scheduling of K_{cf} will be needed (it should vary inversely with the forward speed of the aircraft). Additionally, if the structural modes of the aircraft are significant, then some form of frequency compensation must be used. In aircraft with a variable configuration, such as a swing wing, the sign of the crossfeed signal may also need to be changed as a function of the sweep angle to maintain dynamic stability of the system. The presence of the wash-out network in the crossfeed path is required to permit the aircraft to produce steady sideslipping manoeuvres, unopposed by the system. Such manoeuvres are most frequently required in cross-wind landings. One concern of flight control system designers using ARI, to suppress sideslip to improve turn co-ordination, must be the situation when the aircraft is subjected to asymmetric thrust when an engine (or engines) has failed. In such a situation, the pilot will need to command a constant aileron deflection to counter the resulting yawing motion caused by the engine failure. The ARI system may aggravate this control problem.

From Figure 10.19 the following relationships can be established:

$$\delta_{R_{comm}} = e_{wo} - e_{cf} \tag{10.62}$$

$$\delta_{A_{comm}} = K_{c_2}\phi_{comm} - 0.1K_{c_1}p - K_{c_2}\phi \tag{10.63}$$

$$\dot{\delta} = -10\delta_A + 10\delta_{A_{comm}}$$
$$= -10\delta_A + 10K_{c_2}\phi_{comm} - K_{c_1}p - 10K_{c_2}\phi \tag{10.64}$$

$$\dot{e}_{cf} = -\frac{1}{T_2}e_{cf} - K_{cf}\dot{\delta}_A$$
$$= -\frac{1}{T_2}e_{cf} - 10F_{cf}\delta_A + 10K_{c_2}K_{cf}\phi_{comm} - K_{c_1}K_{cf}p - 10K_{c_2}K_{cf}\phi \tag{10.65}$$

$$\dot{e}_{wo} = -e_{wo} + K_R r \tag{10.66}$$

For CHARLIE-4 (see Appendix B):

$$\dot{\beta} = -0.056\beta - r + 0.042\phi + 0.0022\delta_R$$

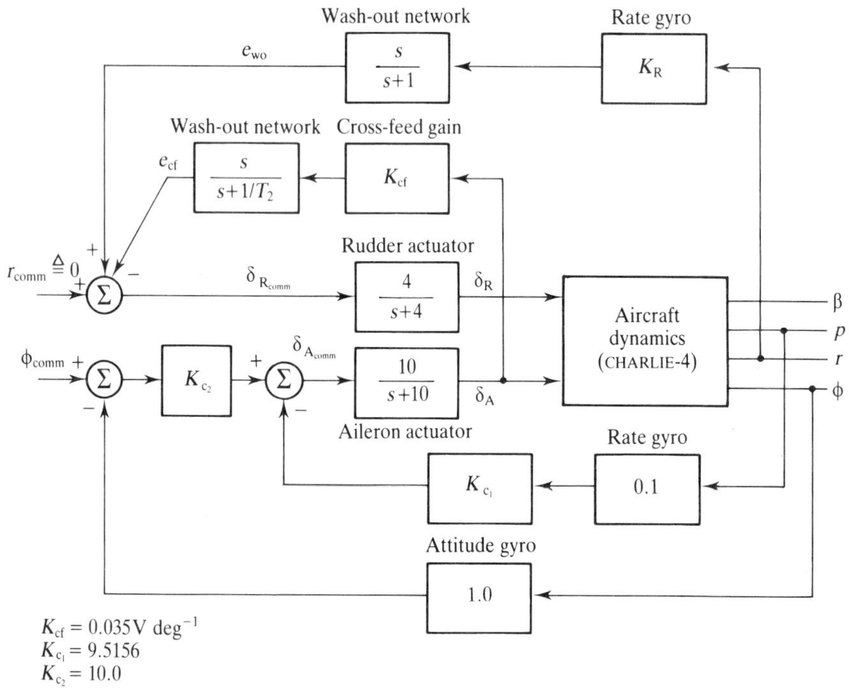

Figure 10.19 Block diagram of ARI system.

$$\dot{p} = -1.05\beta - 0.465p + 0.39r + 0.14\delta_A + 0.153\delta_R$$
$$\dot{r} = 0.6\beta - 0.032p - 0.115r + 0.008\delta_A - 0.475\delta_R \qquad (10.67)$$
$$\dot{\phi} = p$$

Let:

$$\mathbf{x}' \triangleq [\beta\ p\ r\ \phi\ \delta_A\ \delta_R\ e_{wo}\ e_{cf}] \qquad (10.68)$$

$$\mathbf{u} \triangleq \phi_{comm} \qquad (10.69)$$

From Figure 10.19, the following values are found: $K_{c_1} = 9.5156$ V/V, $K_{c_2} = 10.0$ V/V, $K_{cf} = 0.035$ V deg^{-1}, $K_R = 10$ V deg^{-1} s^{-1}. Therefore, the system can be represented as:

$$\dot{\mathbf{x}} = A\mathbf{x} + B\mathbf{u} \qquad (10.70)$$

where:

$$A = \begin{bmatrix} -0.056 & 0 & -1 & 0.042 & 0 & 0.0022 & 0 & 0 \\ -1.05 & -0.465 & 0.39 & 0 & 0.14 & 0.153 & 0 & 0 \\ 0.6 & -0.032 & -0.115 & 0 & 0.008 & -0.475 & 0 & 0 \\ 0 & 1 & 0 & 0 & 0 & 0 & 0 & 0 \\ 0 & -95.156 & 0 & -100.0 & -10.0 & 0 & 0 & 0 \\ 0 & 0 & 0 & 0 & 0 & -4 & 4 & -4 \\ 6 & -0.32 & -1.15 & 0 & 0.08 & -4.75 & -1 & 0 \\ 0 & -3.328 & 0 & -3.5 & -0.35 & 0 & 0 & -\frac{1}{T_2} \end{bmatrix} \qquad (10.71)$$

$$B' = [0\ 0\ 0\ 0\ 100.0\ 0\ 0\ 0\ -3.5] \qquad (10.72)$$

The response of the system depends critically upon the values chosen for T_2 and K_{cf}. For this particular aircraft and its flight condition, $K_{cf} = 0.035$ is the best choice. Large values of T_2 (slow wash-out) result in poor sideslip response. A value of $T_2 = 0.05$s, very short, gives good response for this example. The step responses of this system are shown in Figure 10.20. It is evident how effectively the sideslip has been suppressed, and it can be seen that the bank angle response has not been seriously affected by the crossfeed (cf. Figure 10.6).

Roll Angle to Rudder Crossfeed

This type of control crossfeed is used most with large transport aircraft, which tend to be flexible. For such aircraft, the time constant needed for the wash-out network in the yaw damper is frequently unsuitable to achieve the required value of damping ratio for the closed loop system. The situation arises because the

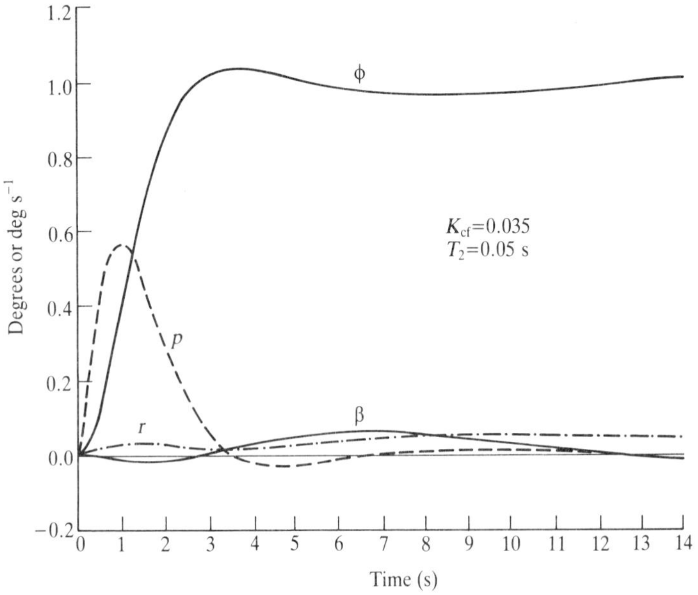

Figure 10.20 Step response of Figure 10.19.

frequency of the dutch roll mode is very low, as are the frequencies of the structural bending modes, so that feedback of lateral acceleration cannot be used, otherwise there would be considerable coupling of the rigid body and structural motion. Furthermore, the relatively slow response of the rudder fitted to such large aircraft precludes the use of high loop gain to suppress unwanted sideslip motion. Consequently the following technique is employed. (See Figure 10.21.) The crossfeed signal, e_{cf}, is introduced into the summing junction of the yaw damper as if it were a command signal for some value of yaw rate which corresponds to zero sideslip angle. It has already been shown in this chapter that in a co-ordinated turn the yaw rate is given by:

$$r = \frac{g}{U_0}\sin\phi \tag{10.73}$$

However, for small bank angles (which is likely to be the case for large transport aircraft) the command signal for yaw rate can be taken as:

$$r = \frac{g}{U_0}\phi \triangleq K_{cf}\phi \tag{10.74}$$

In using such a crossfeed to the rudder channel some phase advance compensation is introduced into the system which causes an increase in the damping of the dutch roll motion. The state equation which corresponds to the system of Figure 10.21 can be represented once more by eqs (9.74)–(9.76) save that the fifth row of the matrix A, now becomes

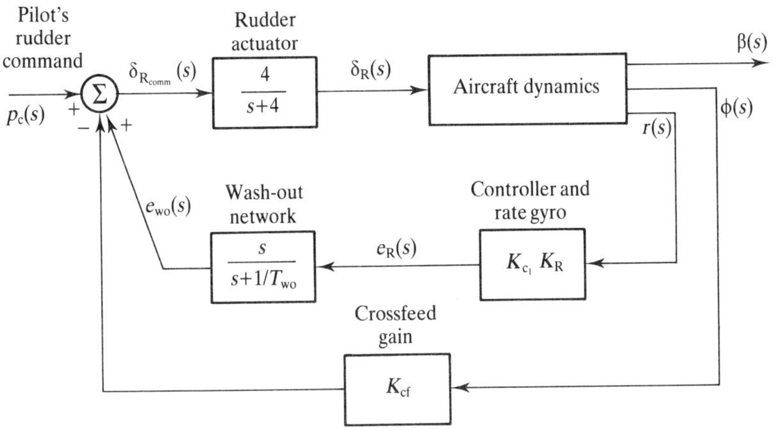

Figure 10.21 Block diagram of roll angle to rudder interconnect centre system.

$$A_{5,i} = [0\ 0\ 0\ -4K_{cf}\ -4\ 4] \qquad (i = 1, \ldots, 5) \tag{10.75}$$

For CHARLIE-4, it can be shown that:

$$K_{cf} = 0.041 \tag{10.76}$$

Hence:

$$A_{5,i} = [0\ 0\ 0\ -0.164\ -4\ 4] \qquad (i = 1, \ldots, 5) \tag{10.77}$$

The response of this system to an initial value of sideslip angle of 1° is shown in Figure 10.22 where the responses of the yaw damper and the ARI system to the

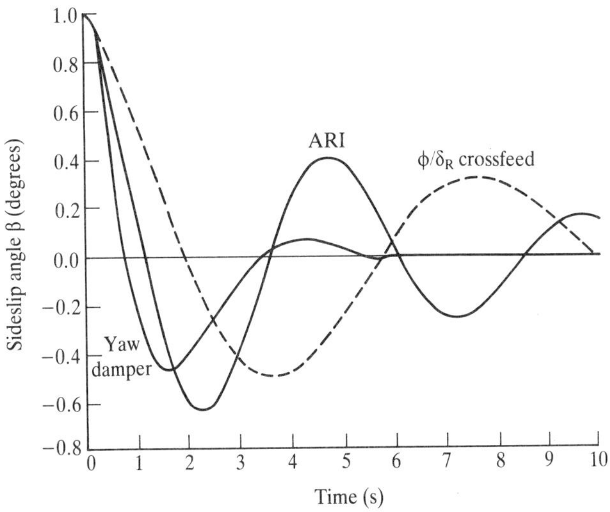

Figure 10.22 Sideslip response of yaw damper, ARI and Φ/δ_R crossfeed.

same initial condition are also shown for comparison. Bank angle to rudder crossfeed is evidently less effective at suppressing sideslip than ARI. Its use results in the stability of the spiral mode of the aircraft being reduced. If this type of crossfeed is used to suppress sideslip, it is usually necessary, therefore, to use a roll angle control system of the kind discussed in Section 10.3 to augment the stability of the spiral mode. When this is done, there is a marked improvement in the sideslip suppression capacity of this type of crossfeed.

Reliability

Although reliability is of the greatest importance in AFCS work, there are situations in which the loss of a feedback path will result in no more than a downwards change of level of an aircraft's flying qualitites. In other situations, the dynamic stability of the aircraft can be impaired to such a degree that the safety of the aircraft and its occupants is imperilled. In AFCSs employing crossfeeds, if failure occurs in any feedback path, the flying qualities of the aircraft are usually so drastically impaired that it becomes necessary to disconnect at once the other feedbacks so that the aircraft is no longer under automatic control. This is the case for the bank angle to rudder crossfeed. Hence, if the yaw damper should fail, it is necessary to immediately disconnect the bank angle signal from the rudder. This is a difficult engineering problem and its partial solution is to be found in the technique of using redundancy in the feedback paths.

Readers should refer to McRuer and Johnston (1975) for further discussion of control crossfeeds.

10.7 DIRECTIONAL STABILITY DURING GROUND ROLL

The geometry of the situation is represented in Figure 10.23 in which y denotes the lateral displacement from the desired track (the runway centre-line), λ is the azimuth angle, Ψ is the heading angle of the aircraft, β is the sideslip angle and σ is the gear slip angle. Now:

$$\sigma = \Psi - \lambda \tag{10.78}$$

$$\therefore \quad \beta = \lambda - \Psi \tag{10.79}$$

The lateral acceleration which the aircraft experiences during its ground roll is:

$$\ddot{y} = V\dot{\lambda} \tag{10.80}$$

With this acceleration being used as a negative feedback signal, and with the feedback gain represented by K_{a_y}, then:

$$\ddot{\Psi}I_{yy} = N_\beta\beta + N_\sigma\sigma - K_{a_y}V\dot{\lambda} \qquad (10.81)^4$$

The sideforce equation is given by:

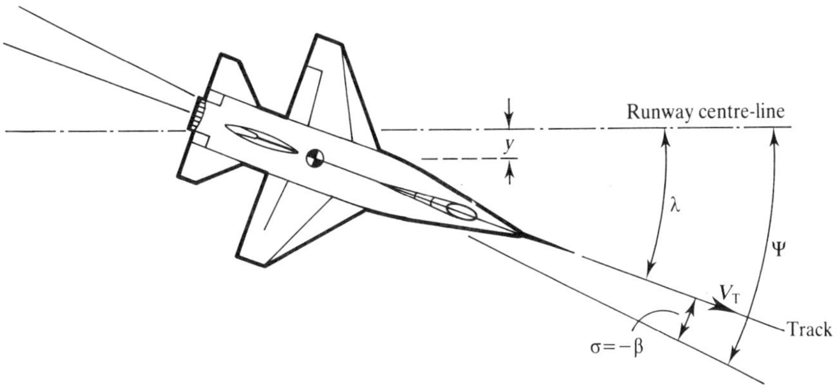

Figure 10.23 Ground run geometry.

$$mV\dot{\lambda} = Y_\beta\beta + Y_\sigma\sigma \tag{10.82}$$

where N_β is the aerodynamic weathercock stability, N_σ is the contribution of the undercarriage to the track stability, Y_β is the aerodynamic sideforce stability derivative and Y_σ is the combined sideforce stability derivative from the tyres of the undercarriage.

$$\therefore \quad \ddot{\Psi} = N'_\beta\beta + N'_\sigma\sigma - \frac{K_{a_y}}{I_{yy}}V\dot{\lambda} \tag{10.83}$$

$$= N'_\beta\beta + N'_\sigma\sigma - \hat{K}_{a_y}V\dot{\lambda}$$

$$\dot{\lambda} = Y^*_\beta\beta + Y^*_\sigma\sigma \tag{10.84}$$

where:

$$N'_\beta \triangleq \frac{N_\beta}{I_{yy}} \qquad N'_\sigma \triangleq \frac{N_\sigma}{I_{yy}} \qquad \hat{K}_{a_y} \triangleq \frac{K_{a_y}}{I_{yy}} \qquad Y^*_\beta = \frac{Y_\beta}{mV} \qquad Y^*_\sigma = \frac{Y_\sigma}{mV} \tag{10.85}$$

Taking Laplace transforms, eq. (10.83) and (10.84) can be re-expressed as:

$$\begin{bmatrix} (s^2 + N'_\beta - N_\sigma) & (s\hat{K}_{a_y}V + N'_\sigma - N'_\beta) \\ (Y^*_\beta - Y^*_\sigma) & (s - Y^*_\beta + Y^*_\sigma) \end{bmatrix} \begin{bmatrix} \Psi(s) \\ \lambda(s) \end{bmatrix} = [0] \tag{10.86}$$

where [0] represents a null matrix. From this equation, the characteristic equation can easily be shown to be:

$$\begin{aligned} &s^3 + [Y^*_\sigma - Y^*_\beta]s^2 + [N'_\beta - N'_\sigma - \hat{K}_{a_y}V(Y^*_\beta - Y^*_\sigma)]s = \\ &\qquad s\{s^2 + [Y^*_\sigma - Y^*_\beta]s + [N'_\beta - N'_\sigma \quad \hat{K}_{a_y}V(Y^*_\beta - Y^*_\sigma)]\} = 0 \end{aligned} \tag{10.87}$$

The zero root means that if the aircraft is disturbed from its track there is no inherent restoring moment unless the pilot applies rudder correction or nose wheel steering or asymmetric thrust.

Examining the quadratic term, and noting that $Y^*_\beta < 0$, $N^*_\sigma < 0$, $Y^*_\sigma > 0$ and $N^*_\beta > 0$, it is then evident that the sideforce contributions of the tyres of the undercarriage contribute to the damping of the motion during ground roll.

However, suppose V represents the ground speed and V_w represents the component of headwind which arises when the aircraft is moving on the runway in the presence of a wind. Equation (10.79) then becomes:

$$\beta = -\Psi + \frac{\lambda}{1 + (V_w/V)} \simeq -\Psi + \lambda\left(1 - \frac{V_w}{V}\right) \tag{10.88}$$

The presence of the headwind now results in the real root of the characteristic cubic being finite, rather than zero, with the possibility of some stability in track. When the headwind is positive, the real root is stable if:

$$N'_\beta Y^*_\sigma > N'_\sigma Y'_\beta \tag{10.89}$$

Therefore, it can be deduced that N'_β stabilizes the ground tracking mode whereas N'_σ destabilizes it.

A discussion of the dynamics of aircraft rotation and lift-off can be found in Pinsker (1967).

10.8 CONCLUSIONS

Automatic control systems for maintaining the attitude angles of an aircraft, or for changing an aircraft's attitude to a new commanded value, are introduced. To emphasize the principles of negative feedback control which are common to the many varieties of attitude control system used on aircraft, the pitch attitude control system is dealt with extensively. The use of a pre-filter in conjunction with these types of AFCS to obtain the required handling qualities in the controlled aircraft is briefly dealt with, before a roll angle control system is considered. The use in such systems of phase advance compensation networks, or a roll rate damper as an inner loop to achieve the required dynamic response is dealt with and gain scheduling as a means of maintaining the same closed loop performance over as much of the flight envelope as possible is also treated. The unwanted results of tight roll control, such as roll ratchet or pitching motion due to rolling, are treated briefly before the means of achieving automatically controlled co-ordinated turns by a variety of methods is explained. The chapter concluded with the important subject of controlling direction stability during ground roll.

10.9 EXERCISES

10.1 A transport aircraft, flying at a Mach number of 0.8 and a height of 10 000 m has as its transfer function, relating bank angle, ϕ, to aileron deflection, δ_A, $G_1(s)$ as as defined below. When the aircraft flies at half the height and at a Mach number of 0.4 its transfer function becomes $G_2(s)$.

$$G_1(s) = \frac{-2.3(s^2 + 0.35s + 2.62)}{(s + 0.004)(s + 1.36)(s^2 + 0.33s + 2.67)}$$

$$G_2(s) = \frac{-1.62(s^2 + 0.33s + 1.39)}{(s + 0.005)(s + 1.33)(s^2 + 0.3s + 1.4)}$$

The block diagram of the bank angle control system used on the aircraft is shown in Figure 10.24.

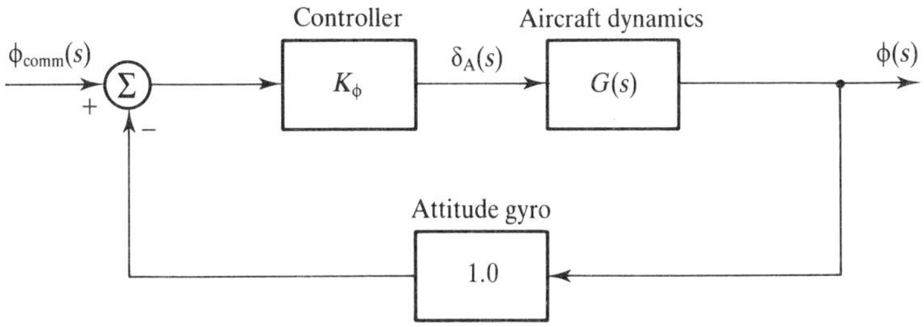

Figure 10.24 Block diagram of a bank angle control system for Exercise 10.1.

(a) Determine the closed loop transfer function relating the bank angle, ϕ, to the commanded bank angle, ϕ_{comm}, for flight condition 1. (Hint: make reasonable simplifying assumptions.)

(b) What is the effect upon the dynamic response of the bank angle control system if the aircraft flies at flight condition 2? Assume the controller gain, K_ϕ, remains unchanged.

(c) If the value of K_ϕ is 2.5, and if the value of the commanded bank angle is 5.0°, sketch the closed loop response for both flight conditions.

10.2 If the experimental VTOL aircraft of Exercise 2.7 is flying at 15 m s^{-1}, and has the same stability derivatives that were listed in that question, calculate the lateral acceleration at its c.g. for a flat, co-ordinated turn in which the yaw rate is 0.33 rad s^{-1}. (The aircraft may be assumed to have zero sideslip velocity.)

10.3 In the sideslip suppression system, represented by the block diagram in Figure 10.25 a sideslip signal is used as feedback to drive the rudder so that sideslip is eliminated. The wash-out filter in the inner loop can be regarded as a blocking filter for constant manoeuvre commands, i.e. yaw rate feedback operates only during changes of the flight state. The dynamics associated with the rudder servo are negligible.

The equations of motion of the aircraft are:

$$\dot{\beta} = -0.1\beta - r - 0.014\delta_R$$

$$\dot{r} = 5.2\beta - 0.25r - 2.6\delta_R$$

The sideslip suppression system is to be designed so that its closed loop response resembles closely that obtained from an idealized model system governed by the

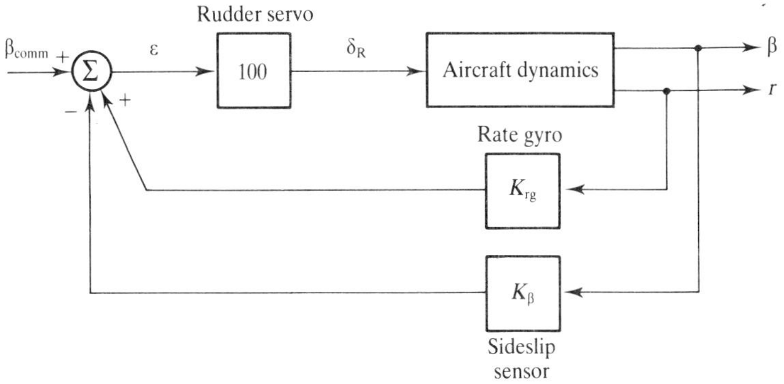

Figure 10.25 Block diagram of a sideslip control system for Exercise 10.3.

characteristic equation $\dot{\beta}_m + 5.0\beta_m = 0$.

(a) By means of any suitable analytical method determine suitable values of the sensitivities of the rate gyro and the sideslip sensor.

(b) Show that use of the values of K_{rg} and K_β obtained in part (a) results in the sideslip motion being suppressed in any manoeuvre.

10.4 For the aircraft detailed in Exercise 3.5 design a simple bank angle control system, with full wing-tip fuel tanks, which will ensure that the aircraft can roll through a bank angle of 30° in 1.225 s in response to a step command.

10.5 (a) In a co-ordinated turn the lift vector is perpendicular to the aircraft axis OY and the lateral acceleration at the c.g., $a_{y_{cg}}$, and the sideslip velocity, β, are both zero. The situation is represented in Figure 10.26. Derive, for small angles, a transfer function relating yaw rate, r, to bank angle, ϕ.

(b) For an aircraft on approach, with a flight path angle of 2°, the appropriate lateral stability derivatives are:

(Height = SL; Speed = 37.73 m s^{-1}):

$Y_v = -8.0 \qquad Y^*_{\delta_A} = 0$

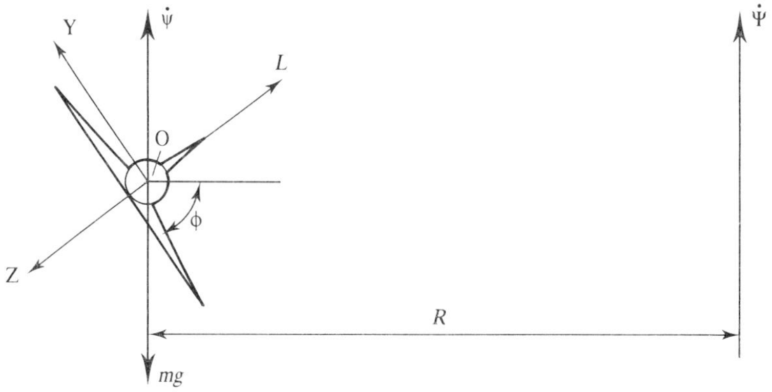

Figure 10.26 Geometry of a co-ordinated turn for Exercise 10.5.

$L'_\beta = -2.0 \qquad L'_{\delta_A} = 4.0$

$L'_p = -0.8 \qquad N'_{\delta_A} = 0.05$

$L'_r = 0.42 \qquad Y^*_{\delta_R} = 0.05$

$N'_\beta = 1.0 \qquad L'_{\delta_R} = 0.1$

$N'_p = -0.2 \qquad N'_{\delta_R} = -1.0$

$N'_r = -0.24$

If the aircraft has been commanded to produce a steady sideslip at a constant bank angle of 10° determine the steady deflections of the ailerons and rudder required to be maintained by the pilot. The sideslip is to occur to starboard. What value of sideslip angle is produced?

(c) What numerical difficulty would occur in your calculation if the bank angle was to be zero during the sideslip manoeuvre?

10.6 The high speed reconnaisance aircraft described in Exercise 3.9 is to be controlled such that its transient roll rate response is close to that shown in Figure 10.27. (Compare this response with that determined for the uncontrolled aircraft in Exercise 3.9.) Determine a suitable feedback control law.

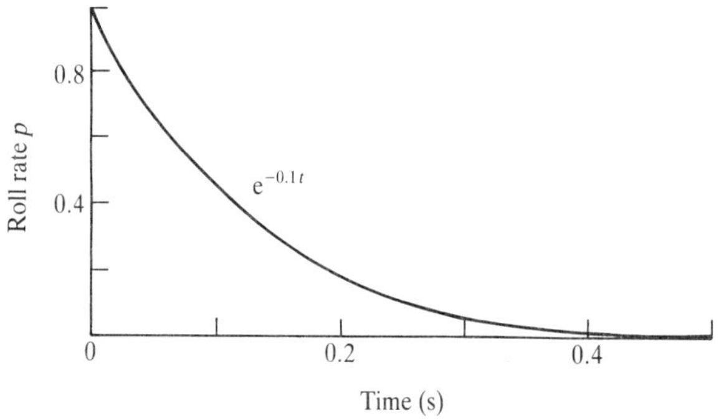

Figure 10.27 Model roll rate response for Exercise 10.6.

10.7 (a) For the L-1011 detailed in Exercise 9.1 the rudder is deflected to 'hold' the side force due to yaw rate when a co-ordinated turn is being executed under 'manual' control. If the steady sideslip angle is 5.73°, calculate the lateral acceleration at the instantaneous centre of rotation of the aircraft. (Note: the equations of Exercise 9.1 were derived using SI units.)

(b) Suppose the aircraft is flying over the North Pole at the cruising speed which corresponds to the equations of motion given in Exercise 9.1. Calculate the value of the Coriolis acceleration to which the aircraft will be subjected. Comment upon whether there would be any significant effect upon the performance of the aircraft's yaw damper if the aircraft were to carry out over the North Pole a co-ordinated turn of the kind defined in part (a).

10.8 A transport aircraft with twin piston engines has the following equations of lateral motion:

$$\dot{\beta} = -8.6\beta - 0.25\phi + 0.04\delta_R + F_T$$

$$\dot{p} = -2.0\beta - 6.5p + 2.5r + 4.0\delta_A + 0.08\delta_R + L_T$$

$$\dot{r} = \beta - 0.2p - 0.6r + 0.05\delta_A - \delta_R + (N_T + \Delta D)$$

β, p, r, δ_A and δ_R denote the sideslip angle, roll rate, yaw rate, aileron and rudder deflections respectively. The terms F_T, L_T and N_T represent, respectively, the changes in sideforce, rolling and yawing moments which occur when an engine fails. ΔD is the yawing moment due to drag caused principally by the feathered propeller. When both engines are operating satisfactorily the four terms are zero. When the starboard engine fails these terms have the following values:

$$F_T = -0.01 \qquad L_T = -0.005 \qquad N_T = -0.015 \qquad \Delta D = -0.015.$$

(a) If the pilot takes no corrective action when the starboard engine fails determine the approximate maximum angle of sideslip which develops.
(b) Calculate the aileron deflection needed to counteract the rolling moment induced by the sideslip.
(c) With the starboard engine failed, determine the aileron and rudder deflections needed to maintain straight and level flight with a bank angle not exceeding 5°. Calculate the sideslip angle which results from this manoeuvre.

10.9 A training aircraft, with a roll control system, is flown by a novice pilot. The transfer function of the roll system is given by:

$$\phi(s)/\phi_{comm}(s) = 4.5/(1 + 0.01s)$$

Whenever the novice pilot commands a bank angle, roll ratcheting is observed in the aircraft's motion. From several assessments of his tracking performance it has been established that his performance can be reasonably represented by the following transfer function:

$$G_{np}(s) = 2.67\,e^{-0.32s}$$

(a) When the same aircraft is flown by an experienced test pilot whose mathematical representation is

$$G_{tp}(s) = 3.2^{-0.12s}$$

will the phenomenon of roll ratchet be observed once again?
(b) At what frequency did the roll ratchet occur when the aircraft was flown by the novice pilot?

10.10 A sideslip suppression system is to be designed for the aircraft FOXTROT-4 using computed yaw rate as the feedback signal. The sensitivity of the resolver is $1\,\text{V deg}^{-1}$ and the product of the values of the gain of the controller and the sensitivity of the rate gyro used in the yaw damper is 1.0. A time constant of 1.0 s is employed in the wash-out network used in the feeback path of the yaw damper. If the dynamics of the rudder actuator can be represented by the first order transfer function:

$$\delta_R(s)/\delta_{R_c}(s) = 4/(s + 4)$$

(a) Find a suitable value for the gain, K_{c_2}, of the controller of this sideslip suppression system;
(b) Determine the response of the system to a commanded change in yaw rate.

10.11 A wing leveller is required for the aircraft GOLF. Design a suitable system such that it can produce almost the same performance at flight condition 1 as at flight condition 4. Discuss what you mean by 'almost'.

10.10 NOTES

1. For the purpose of comparison with results presented earlier, the actuator dynamics here have been assumed to be instantaneous, and represented by a transfer function of unity.
2. The same results are obtained using the non-linear equations of motion.
3. If $x_A = -Y^*_{\delta_R}/N'_{\delta_R}$, then $a_y = a_{y_{cg}} + x_A\dot{r}$

$$a_y = Y_v\beta + Y^*_{\delta_R}\delta_R - \frac{Y^*_{\delta_R}}{N'_{\delta_R}} N'_\beta\beta - \frac{Y'_{\delta_R}}{N'_{\delta_R}} N'_p p - N'_r \frac{Y^*_{\delta_R}}{N'_{\delta_R}} - Y^*_{\delta_R}\delta_R \simeq Y_v\beta$$

4. Primed stability derivatives are not involved since it is assumed that during ground roll any rolling motion is negligible.

10.11 REFERENCES

CHALK, C.R. 1983. Excessive roll damping can cause roll ratchet. *J. Guid. and Cont.* 6(3): 218–9.

LANGEWEISCHE, W. 1944. *Stick and Rudder.* New York: McGraw-Hill, p. 133.

McRUER, D.J. and D.E. JOHNSTON. 1975. Flight control systems properties and problems. Vol. I. NASA CR-2500.

PINSKER, W.G. 1967. The dynamics of aircraft rotation and lift-off. *ARC R & M 3560.*

STENGEL, R.F. 1983. A unifying framework for longitudinal flying qualities criteria. *J. Guid., Cont and Dyn.* 6(2): 84–90.

11

Flight Path Control Systems

11.1 INTRODUCTION

There are a number of flight missions which require that an aircraft be made to follow with great precision some specially defined path. For fixed-wing aircraft there are four positioning tasks which must be performed with extreme precision. These tasks are: air-to-ground weapons delivery, air-to-air combat, in-flight refuelling and all-weather landing.[1]

Whenever a conventional aircraft is to be controlled, a pilot can command rates of rotation in any or all of three axes: pitch, roll and yaw. On such aircraft his direct control of translation is restricted to the control of airspeed either by means of changing the thrust being delivered by the engines, or by the use of any speed brakes or drag modulators. Conventional aircraft have no special control surfaces to permit the control of translation in either the normal or lateral directions. Consequently, the reduction of an inadvertent lateral displacement from some desired track, for example, has to be achieved indirectly by means of a controlled change of aircraft heading. As another example, consider how the height of an aircraft is altered. To change its height means adjusting the aircraft's flight path angle by altering its pitch attitude.

As a consequence of such limitations, a number of the attitude control systems which are discussed in Chapter 10 find general application as necessary inner loops in flight path control systems. In Chapter 12, active control technology (ACT) is discussed and its use with control configured vehicles (CCVs) is dealt with. Because such CCVs are provided with many more control surfaces than are usually to be found on a conventional aircraft, aircraft positioning control systems are dealt with more appositely in that chapter. The systems treated in this chapter are restricted to those most commonly to be found on modern, conventional fixed-wing aircraft of every class.

In Chapter 1, it is stated that the control of the attitude angles of an aircraft is the special function of flight control, whereas the control of its path through space is more properly a guidance function. But path variables, such as heading and pressure altitude, need to be measured in the aircraft; there is some logic, then, in considering their control in a treatment of flight control. Automatic tracking and terrain-following will be shown to involve merely linear approximations to those kinematic transformations in the guidance loops which place an aircraft and its destination (or target) on comparable terms. Since these approximations are linear as well as sufficient, such systems can be regarded as members of the class of flight path control systems, and are so treated in this book.

11.2 HEIGHT CONTROL SYSTEMS

11.2.1 Introduction

When a system is used to control the height at which an aircraft is flying, it acts as a feedback regulator to maintain the aircraft's height at a reference (or set) value, even in the presence of disturbances. The pilot can either fly the aircraft by manual control or use the pitch attitude control system to control the climb (or descent) of the aircraft until it has reached the required height. When that height has been reached, the height control system is selected to maintain that height thereafter. There are two important exceptions to that usage, however, which merit distinct treatment: automatic landing and terrain following. In each of those special cases, the height control system is required to control the aircraft in a manner which will cause the aircraft's path to follow closely, and with good dynamic response, a particular height profile. In general use, a height control system is often referred to as a 'height hold' system.

Supersonic transport (SST) aircraft are known to have phugoid modes of very long period and it has been observed that pilots of such SST caused their aircraft to deviate from a pre-assigned height, in about 80 per cent of the flights that were studied, by as much as 160 m. Upset recovery is also known to be prolonged and as much as 5000 m may be needed to recover the aircraft's attitude and height after an upset. For such SST aircraft, a height hold system is a necessity.

11.2.2 Height Hold System

A block diagram representing a typical height hold system is shown in Figure 11.1. The height of the aircraft can be seen to be controlled by means of elevator deflection; that deflection is produced by an actuator, the dynamics of which have been represented as a first approximation by a first order transfer function, with a value of time constant of 0.1 s. The dynamics of the altimeter have also been assumed to be linear and first order, with the same value of time constant. For its successful operation, the system requires a longitudinal accelerometer to provide a feedback signal proportional to $\dot{u}$. The sensitivity of the altimeter, denoted by K_h, can be taken to be unity without loss of generality. Obviously, being a closed loop feedback control system, the height hold system may be stable, unstable, oscillatory or over-damped depending upon the aircraft dynamics and the values of the controller gains, $K_{\dot{u}}$ and K_c. With $K_{\dot{u}}$ being selected at -200.0, it is found that a somewhat oscillatory, but very slow, response results with an evident error

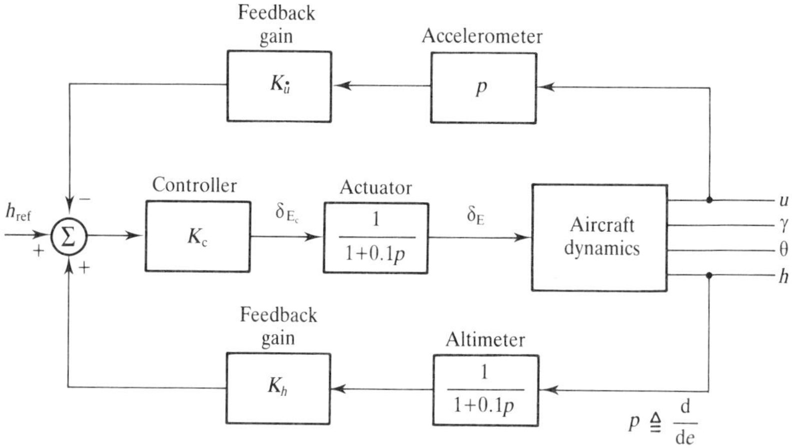

Figure 11.1 Height hold system I.

in the steady state value of the height (compared to the reference height) when the controller gain is chosen to be $0.08\,\text{mV m}^{-1}$. It is obvious from an inspection of the response shown in Figure 11.2 how large are the variations in flight path angle and for how long they persist. Doubling the value of K_c leads to obvious dynamic instability – see Figure 11.3. With the value of the controller gain reduced once more to $0.08\,\text{mV m}^{-1}$, but with the value of the gain of the accelerometer increased to – 300.0, the dynamic reponse can be seen from Figure 11.4 to be much better damped, and that very much smaller values of flight path

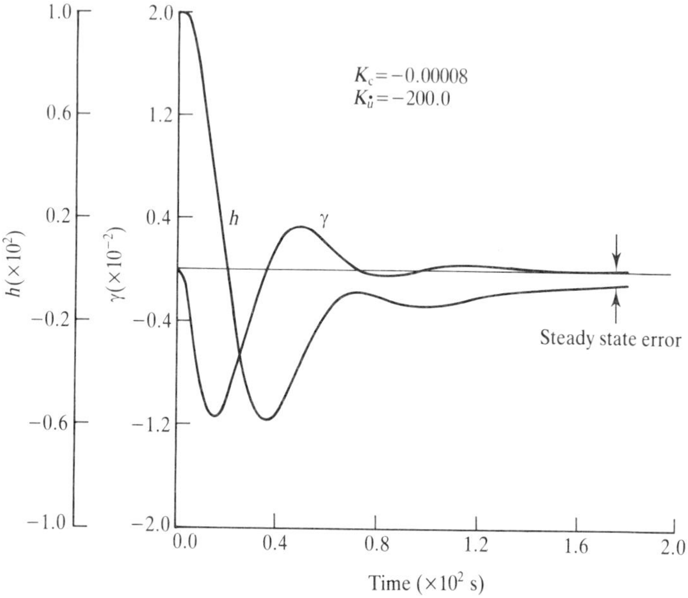

Figure 11.2 Response of height hold system I.

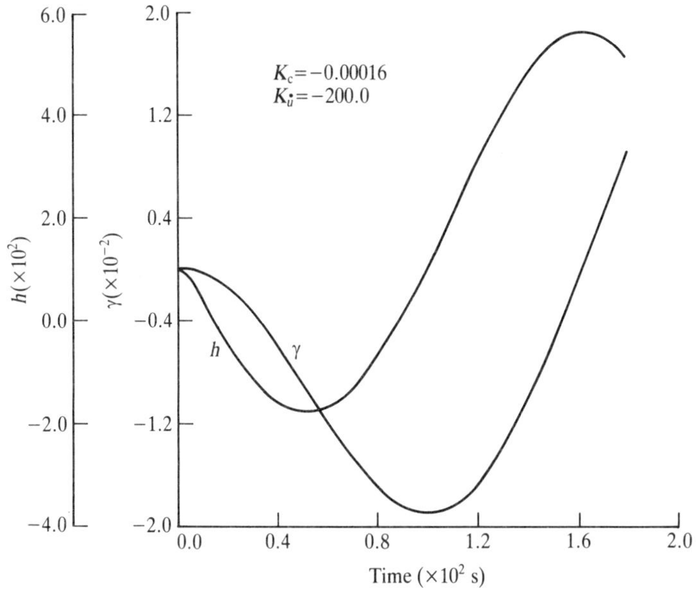

Figure 11.3 Response of height hold system I – increased gain.

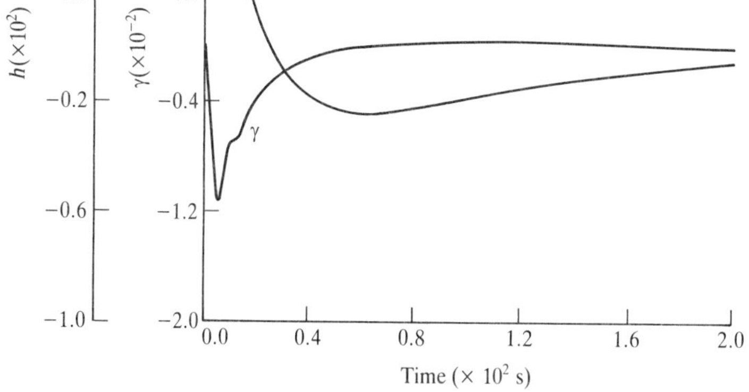

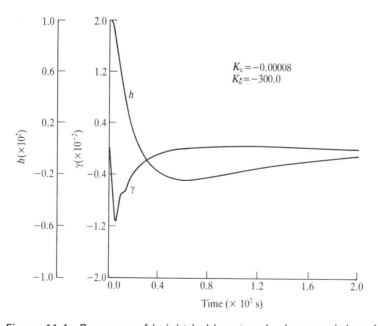

Figure 11.4 Response of height hold system I – increased damping.

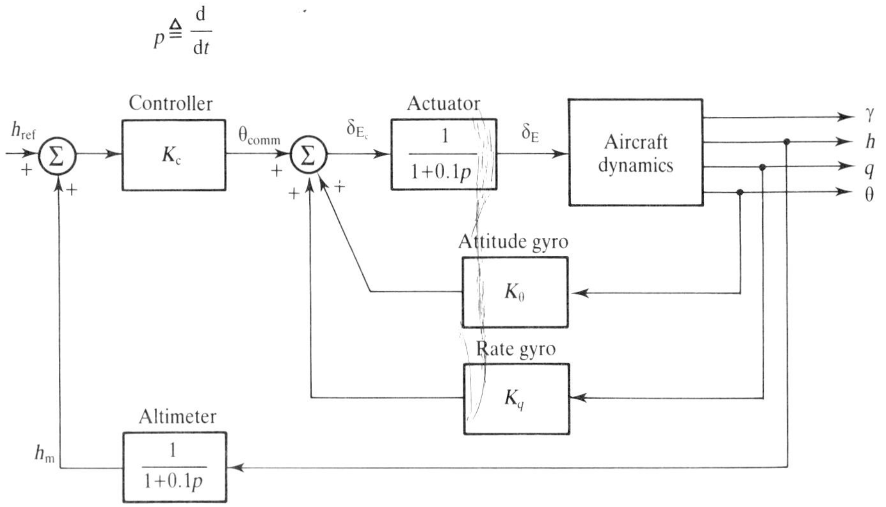

Figure 11.5 Height hold system II.

The block diagram of an alternative height hold system is shown in Figure 11.5. Notice that it represents a pitch attitude control system, with a pitch rate SAS as its inner loop. An outer loop, involving the use of an altimeter to provide a feedback signal proportional to height, is used to achieve the height hold function. It can be seen from Figure 11.6 how much improved is the dynamic reponse and how the steady state error has been very nearly eradicated. The amplitude of the necessary changes in flight path angle has also been reduced.

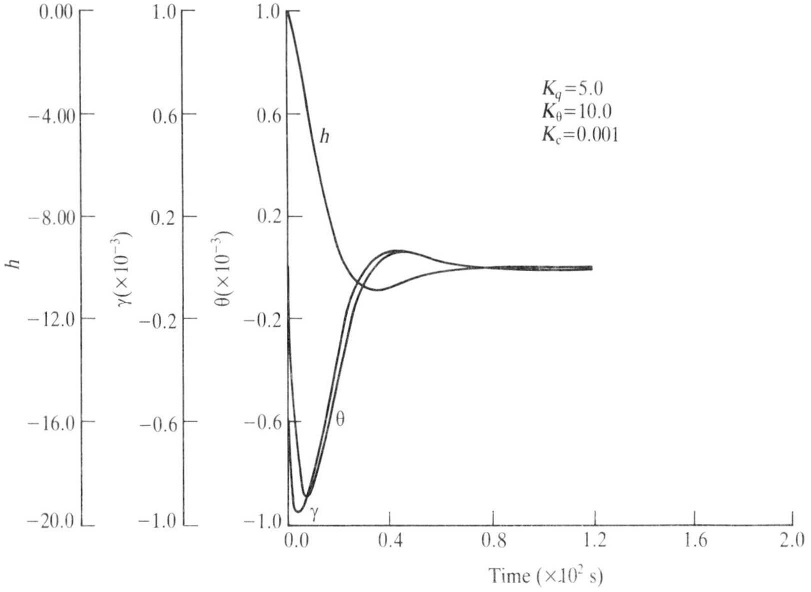

Figure 11.6 Response of height hold system II.

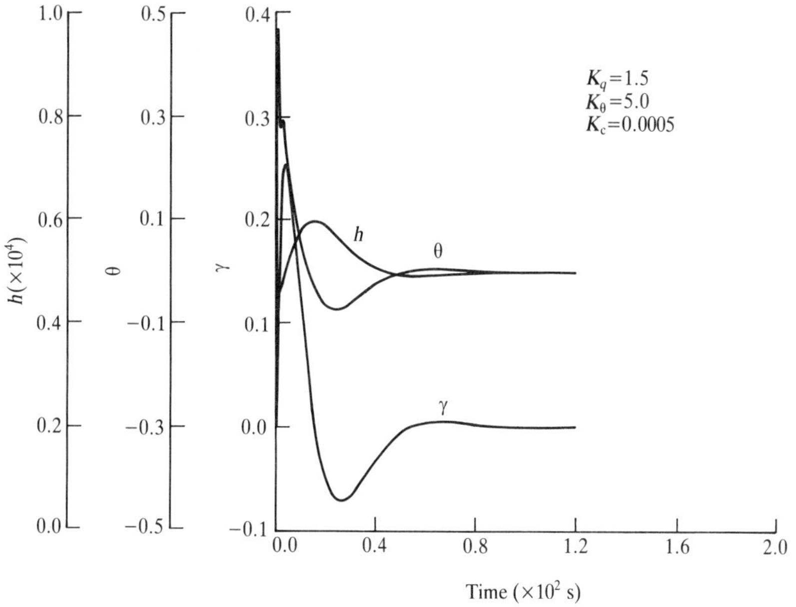

Figure 11.7 Commanded step response of height hold system II.

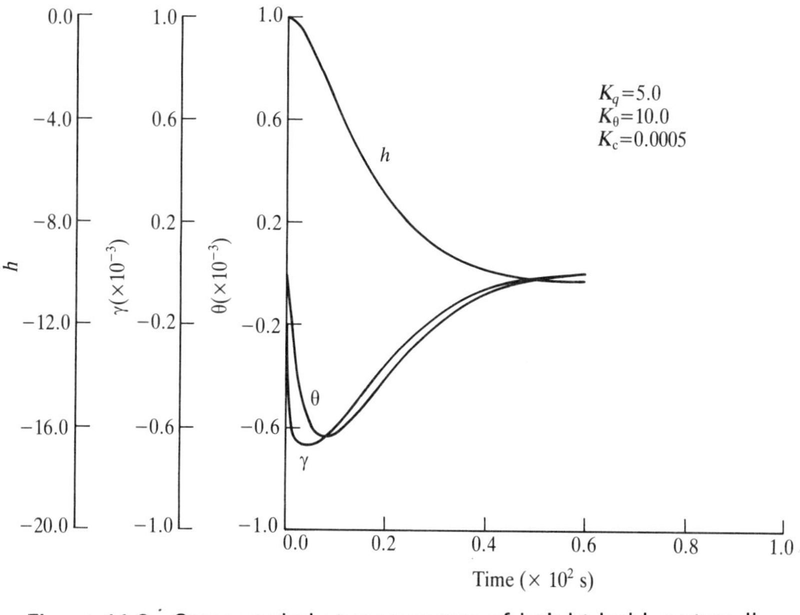

Figure 11.8 Commanded step response of height hold system II.

angle are called for. Nevertheless, the slow response and the sizeable steady state error still remain. A different control structure is needed to avoid this steady state error.

There is some scope, however, for choosing different values for the sensitivities of the rate and attitude gyros, and of the controller gain, too. Note how in Figure 11.7 (in which the values of K_q, K_c and K_θ differ from those relating to Figure 11.6), in changing from the first set height of 4 000 ft to be the reference height of 5 000 ft, there is a peak height of 6 000 ft at about 15 s. This large peak, which occurs in an oscillatory but heavily damped, response, comes about as a result of the existence of a significant zero in the transfer function relating the change in height to the elevator deflection which caused it.

Other choices for the values of the controller gain lead to improved dynamic reponse. The dynamic response for a commanded change of height of − 10 ft is shown in Figure 11.8. It can be seen from that figure that the dynamic response is non-oscillatory, smooth, and rapid.

There is a pronounced difference in the effectiveness of the two systems. Since

$$h = U_0 \int \theta \mathrm{d}t - \int w \mathrm{d}t \tag{11.1}$$

any feedback control, of the form,

$$\delta_E = K_h h \tag{11.2}$$

must inevitably reduce the damping ratio of phugoid mode, although the period of the phugoid oscillation is itself reduced. For really quite moderate values for K_h, instability results. Consequently, the second type of height hold system is preferred.

One of the most difficult design problems likely to be met in this type of system relates to the 'backside' parameter, a, namely:

$$a = \frac{1}{m}\left(\frac{\partial D}{\partial u} - \frac{\partial T}{\partial u}\right) \tag{11.3}$$

where D represents the aircraft's drag force, and T is its thrust.

The parameter a is one of the zeros of the transfer function relating height to elevator deflection. In certain aircraft, a performance reversal can arise (on the backside of the power curve) in which $\partial T/\partial u \gg \partial D/\partial u$; a is then negative. When this happens it is difficult to find a suitable value for the gain of the controller to assure stability of the height hold system. In that case a more complex form of control law than the simple proportional feedback control being used in these two systems is required.

The interested reader should refer to McRuer *et al.* (1973) for further discussion of this topic.

11.3 SPEED CONTROL SYSTEMS

Although speed is not truly a path variable, its exact control is essential for many tasks related to the control of an aircraft's flight path. Consequently, speed control systems are treated in this present chapter. If speed can be controlled, the position of an aircraft, in relation to some reference point, can also be controlled.

A block diagram representing a typical airspeed control system is shown in Figure 11.9. Speed is controlled by changing the thrust, δ_{th}, of the engines; such a change in thrust is obtained by altering the quantity of the fuel flowing to the engines by means of the throttle actuator. Typical values for the time constant, T_E, of a jet engine lie in the range 0.3–1.5 s, depending on the thrust setting and the flight condition. For the purposes of illustration, T_E will be assigned a value of 0.5 s. Although the thrust/throttle angle relationship is not linear, in practice, it will be assumed to be so here. The system depends upon a feedback signal based on sensed airspeed and sensed longitudinal acceleration. However, the dynamics of the accelerometer are such that its bandwidth is much greater than that of the aircraft system so that its response in this application can be assumed to be instantaneous. Since the airspeed sensor is usually a barometric device, it has been represented by a first order transfer function, with a time constant of T_p. The controller is a proportional plus integral type; the integral term has been added to remove, if required, any steady state error in the response of the airspeed system to constant airspeed command. If it is assumed, in the first place, that the aircraft is to be maintained at its equilibrium airspeed, U_0, then no significant changes in airspeed, u, should persist, Hence u_{ref} if taken to be zero. The dynamic response of the system of Figure 11.9 to an initial airspeed error of $+\ 10\ \text{m s}^{-1}$ in the equilibrium (approach) airspeed of $75\ \text{m s}^{-1}$, for CHARLIE-1, is shown in Figure 11.10. The time constant of the airspeed sensor was taken to be 0.1 s, and the controller gain K_{c_L} was chosen to be 2.0. The sensitivity of the accelerometer $K_{\dot{u}}$, was $2.0\ \text{V m}^{-1}\ \text{s}^{-2}$. The integral term was omitted. Note the small error at values of time greater than 12 s. In Figure 11.10 the longitudinal acceleration, $\dot{u}$, is also shown. The key factor in the response of this speed control system is the authority allowed over the engines' thrust. However, if 10 per cent authority is allowed, say, then it is possible to evaluate K_E by knowing that for steady flight:

$$T = W(D/L) \tag{11.4}$$

For the approach flight condition, the weight and lift/drag ratio of CHARLIE are known to be:

$$W = 2\,450\,000\ \text{N} \tag{11.5}$$

$$L/D = 8.9 \tag{11.6}$$

$$T_{max} = 800\ \text{kN} \tag{11.7}$$

Hence the available excess thrust on approach is 525 000 N. Only 10 per cent of that excess thrust can be changed by the actuator (since the control authority is

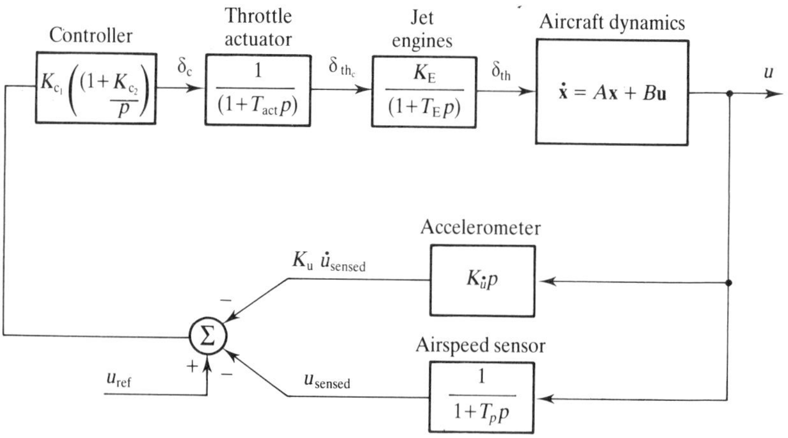

Figure 11.9 Airspeed control system.

only 10 per cent). It is assumed that the maximum throttle deflection is 86° (1.5 rad). Hence:

$$K_E = 35\,000\ \text{N rad}^{-1}$$

The dynamic performance of this system is very greatly affected by the actuator dynamics. In Figure 11.11 are shown the speed responses which result for the same conditions and values of parameters that were used for the response shown in Figure 11.10, except that, in case A, the time constant of the actuator has been

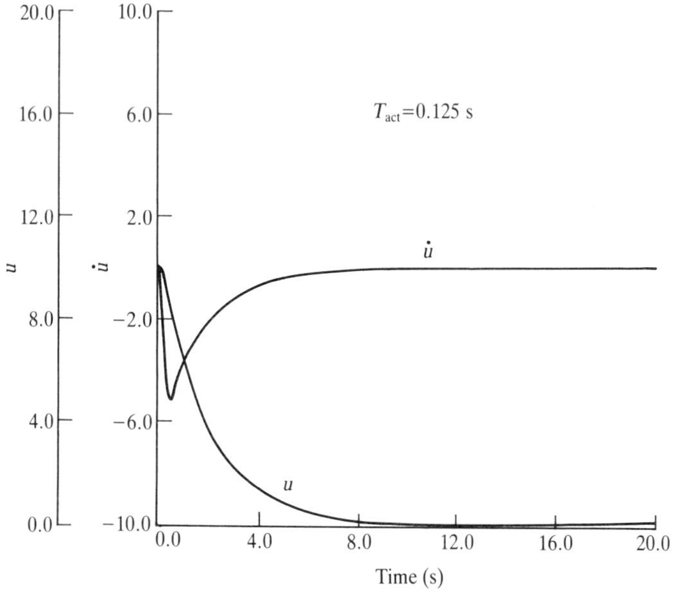

Figure 11.10. Response to initial airspeed error.

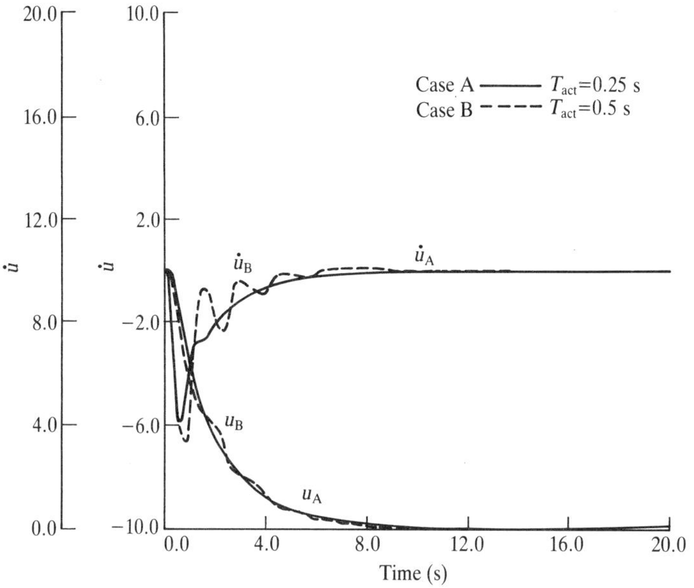

Figure 11.11 Response to initial $u(0)$ – effects of actuator time constant.

doubled ($T_{act} = 0.25$ s) and, in case B, the actuator's response is four times slower than the standard case, when $T_{act} = 0.125$ s. It can be seen how the response is beginning to be oscillatory. Further increases in the time constant of the actuator will lead to instability of the speed control system. Similarly, the dynamics of the airspeed sensor are crucial.

Figure 11.12 shows the dynamic responses to the same initial airspeed error, with the same flight condition and control parameters (the value of the time constant of the actuator being restored to 0.125 s). Case A represents the response when the value of time constant of the airspeed sensor was increased to 0.4 s and case B when its value was increased further, by a factor of 10. With the value of the proportional gain of the controller set at 25.0, and the sensitivity of the accelerometer reduced to 1 V m^{-1} s^{-2}, the response of the system to a reference speed command, which is a linear change of airspeed from 75.0 m s^{-1} to 70.0 m s^{-1} in 20 s, is shown in Figure 11.13. The resulting steady state speed error of approximately 0.3 m s^{-1} can be reduced by increasing K_{c_1} but the dynamic response will be destabilized by such an increase.

The improved dynamic response of the system can be clearly seen in Figure 11.14 which shows the responses to the same initial speed error of + 10 m s^{-1} but, in case A, with $K_{c_1} = 10.0$, and $K_{\dot{u}} = 2.0$, and, in case B, with $K_{c_1} = 25.0$, and $K_{\dot{u}} = 1.0$. Case B is the case used to obtain the ramp response shown in Figure 11.13. In Figure 11.14 the incipient oscillatory response with increased values of K_{c_1} can be seen in the acceleration ($\dot{u}$) responses.

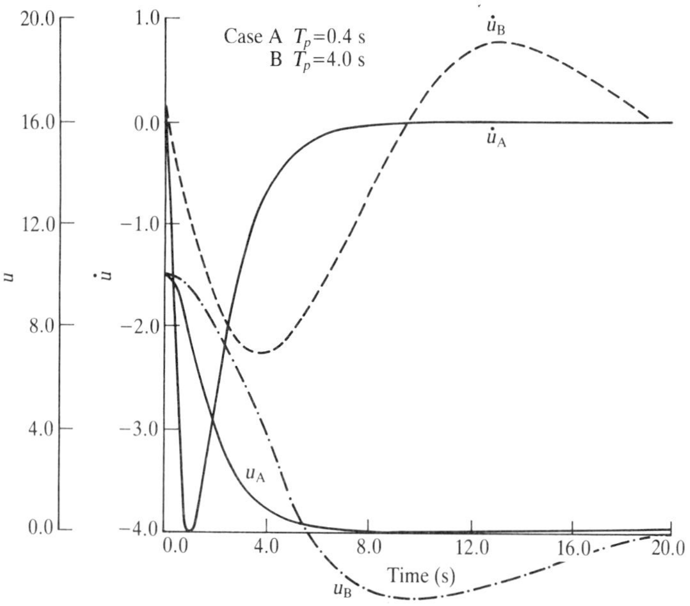

Figure 11.12 Response to $u(0)$ – effects of sensor time constant.

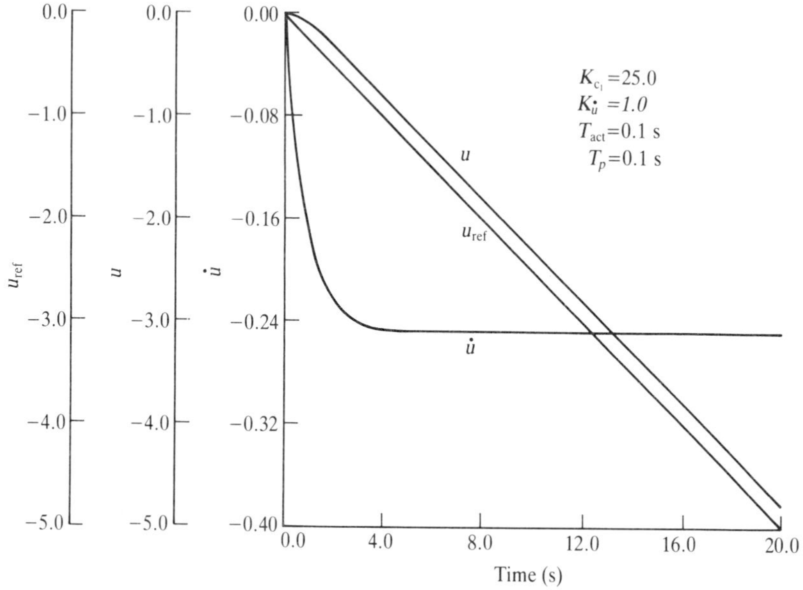

Figure 11.13 Ramp response of airspeed system.

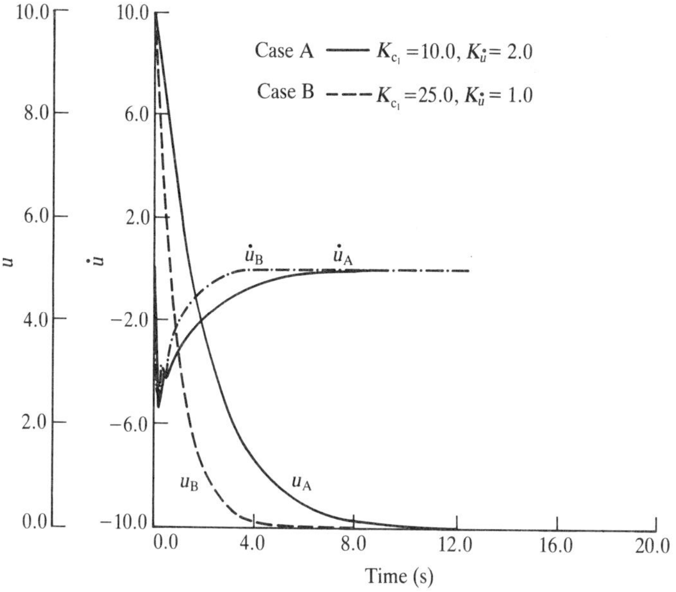

Figure 11.14 Response to $u(0)$ of modified airspeed system.

Further discussion of speed control systems can be found in McRuer *et al.* (1973) and Blakelock (1965).

11.4 MACH HOLD SYSTEM

Modern jet aircraft are often fitted with such a control system; its purpose is to hold the set Mach number in the presence of disturbances, provided that the change in height is not very great. Variations in Mach number can be represented by variations in velocity since:

$$M = V/a = (U_0 + u)/a \tag{11.8}$$

A block diagram of a typical system is shown in Figure 11.15. Note that speed is being controlled in this system by using elevator deflection. Since the elevator is being used, and the aircraft will be flying at large subsonic, or even supersonic, Mach numbers, the basic short period dynamics usually have to be augmented. A pitch rate SAS has been used as an inner loop in the system represented by Figure 11.15. For BRAVO-4, of Appendix B, the aircraft has a Mach number of 0.8. To illustrate how effective the system is, Figure 11.16 shows the results of a digital simulation of the system of Figure 11.15, with $T = 7.0$, $K_q = 5.0$ and $K_{c_1} = 10.0$, and being subjected to a horizontal wind shear, u_g, defined by:

$$u_g = -t \tag{11.9}$$

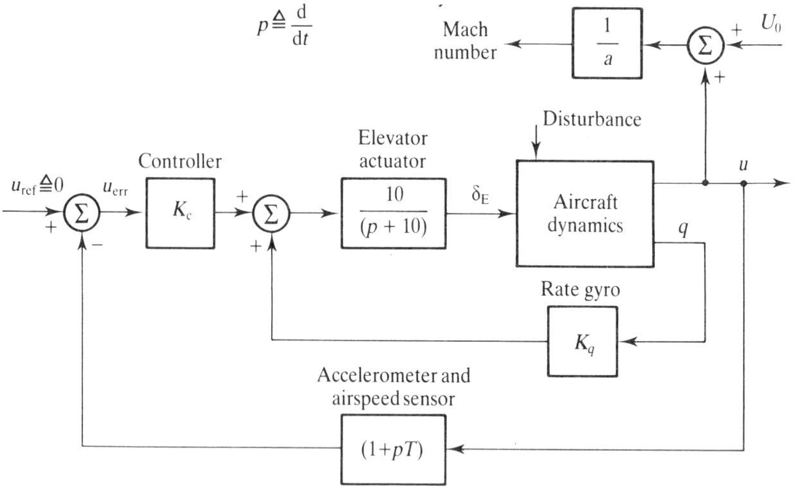

Figure 11.15 Mach hold system.

(i.e. u_g changes from 0 to $-20\,\text{m s}^{-1}$ in 20 s). It is evident from Figure 11.16 how effectively the speed and Mach number have been held nearly constant.

This splendid regulatory performance is not achieved, however, without adjustment of other motion variables of the aircraft. It can be seen, for example, from Figure 11.17, that the aircraft climbs by approximately 1 800 m to a new

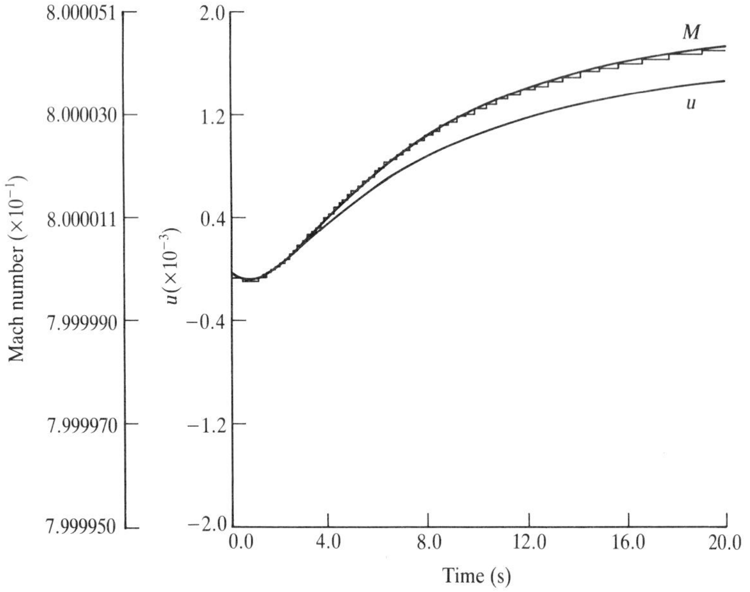

Figure 11.16 Response of Mach hold to horizontal shear.

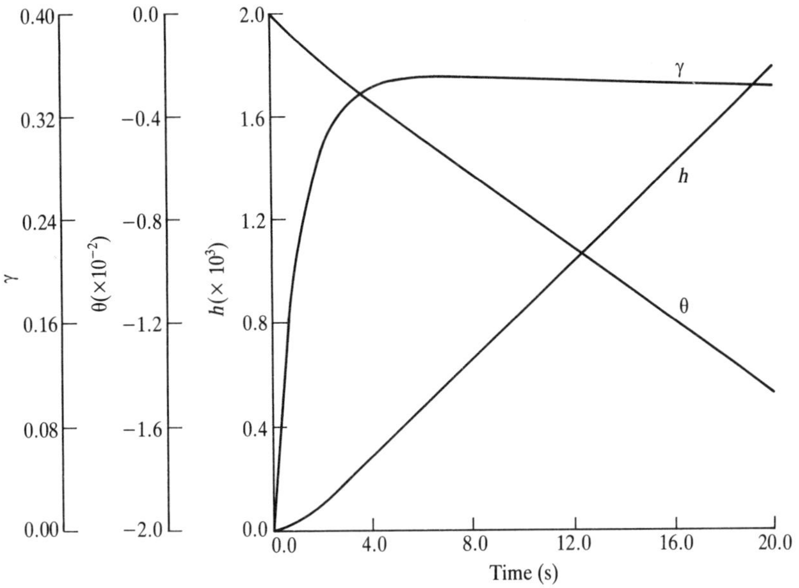

Figure 11.17 Response of motion variables to Mach hold shear.

height of 11 000 m. This dramatic climb occurs because the aircraft being studied is a very high performance fighter.

11.5 DIRECTION CONTROL SYSTEM

The purpose of such a system is to allow an aircraft to be steered automatically along some set direction. A block diagram representation of a typical system is shown in Figure 11.18. The heading of the aircraft is taken as its yaw angle, since it is assumed that any turn the aircraft makes under automatic control will be co-ordinated. Hence, any sideslip angle, β, is zero. It is shown in Section 10.5 of Chapter 10 that for small bank angles:

$$r = (g/U_0)\phi = \dot{\psi} \tag{11.10}$$

This equation is represented in Figure 11.18 by the blocks which have been labelled 'aircraft kinematics'. The aircraft heading is assumed to be sensed by a gyrocompass of sensitivity 1 V deg^{-1}, hence providing a unity feedback path. The control law for this direction control system is simply:

$$\phi_{comm} = K_{\Psi}(\psi_{ref} - \psi) \tag{11.11}$$

where the value of the controller gain, K_{Ψ}, can be determined by any of the appropriate design methods discussed in Chapter 7. The system shown relates to CHARLIE-2 and the bank angle control system being used is that derived as system B

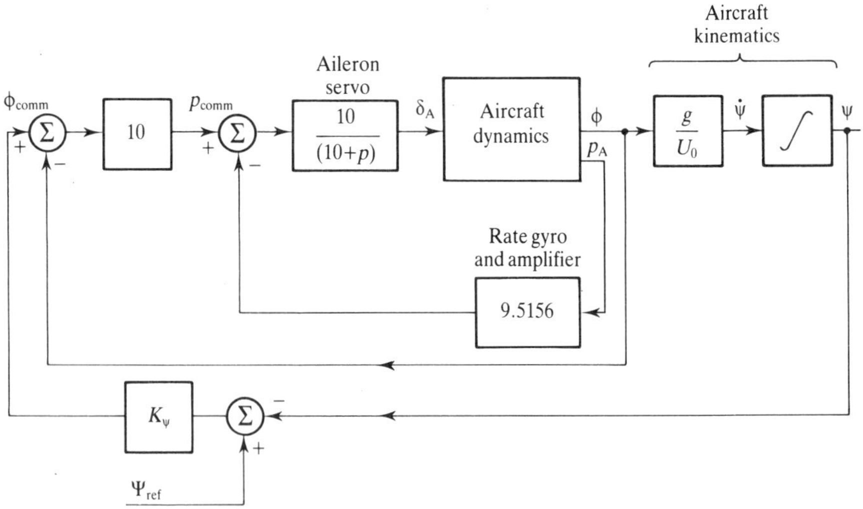

Figure 11.18 Direction control system.

in Example 10.3. An appropriate value for K_Ψ was selected to be:

$$K_\Psi = 2\,\text{deg/deg}$$

The unit step response of the system is shown in Figure 11.19 in which the corresponding bank angle, ϕ, and aileron deflection, δ_A are also shown. The long settling time required to achieve the new heading should be noted. Although it has been assumed that the turn was co-ordinated, there is some residual sideslip angle, β, with a peak deviation of 0.38°; see Figure 11.20. The response of the system can be made more rapid by using an improved value of K_Ψ. Figure 11.21 shows the step responses of the system to a 1° direction change command, for different values of controller gain, K_Ψ. From that figure it is obvious that $K_\Psi = 8.0$ is the best value. Using this value, the system was subjected to a sideslip crosswind with a profile similar to that shown in Figure 11.22. The heading reference was 0°, and the response to this crosswind disturbance is shown in Figure 11.23. Note that the peak heading deviation was merely 0.0085 degrees, which caused a bank angle change of 0.013°. The effectiveness of this direction control system can also be seen by considering how well it performs to suppress the effects of a sideslip shear. Figure 11.24 shows the response of the system when subjected to a sideslip shear with the profile represented by BCW in Figure 11.24, a change in sideslip of 3.5° in 3.5 s. The peak deviation in heading was 0.012°, and the set heading was regained in about 12 s after the onset of the shear. There is an associated peak bank angle of 0.2°. This direction control system forms the basis of the automatic azimuth tracking systems (to be discussed) which use guidance commands from the VOR (VHF ommi range) and ILS (instrument landing system) localizer systems.

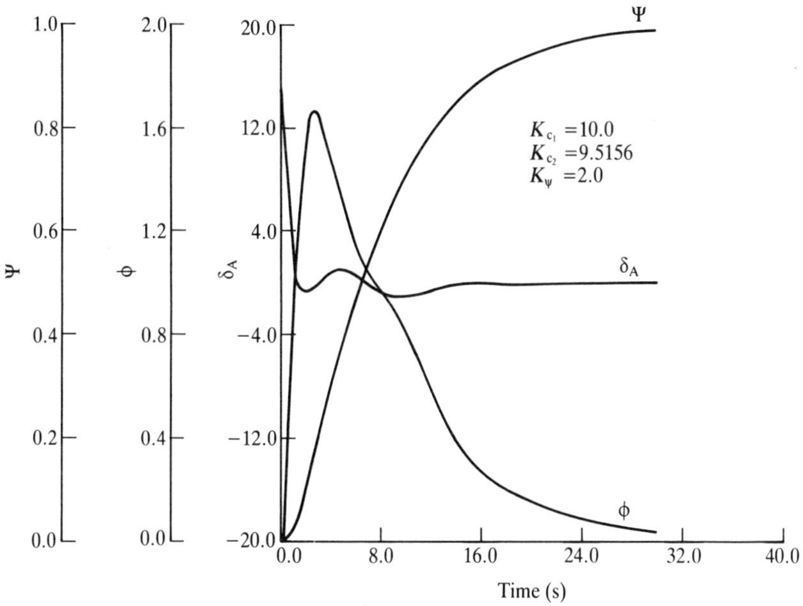

Figure 11.19 Step response of direction control system.

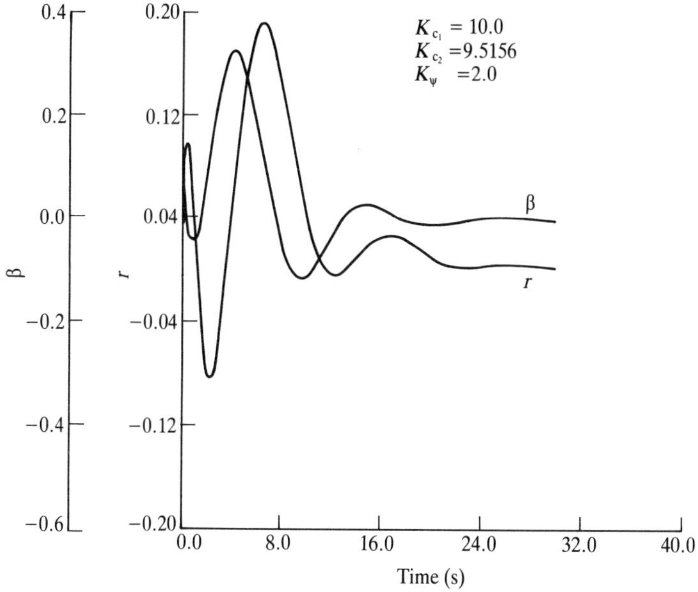

Figure 11.20 Yaw and sideslip response to step change in direction.

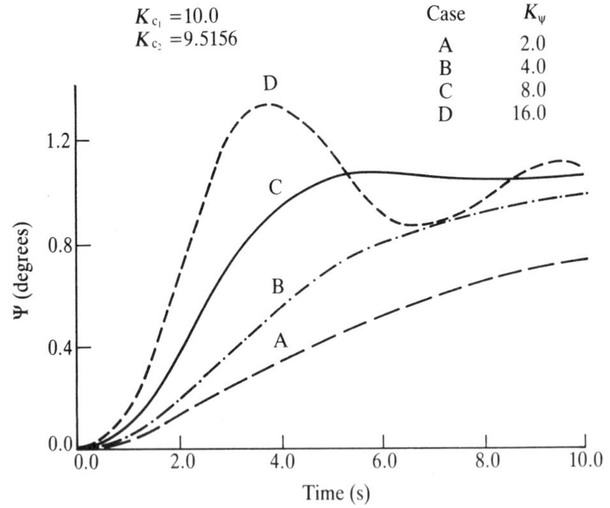

Figure 11.21 Step response of direction control system – different controller gains.

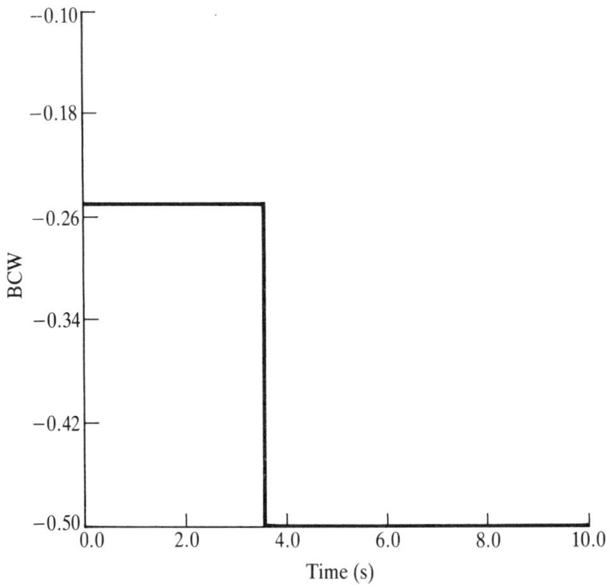

Figure 11.22 Sideslip cross-wind profile.

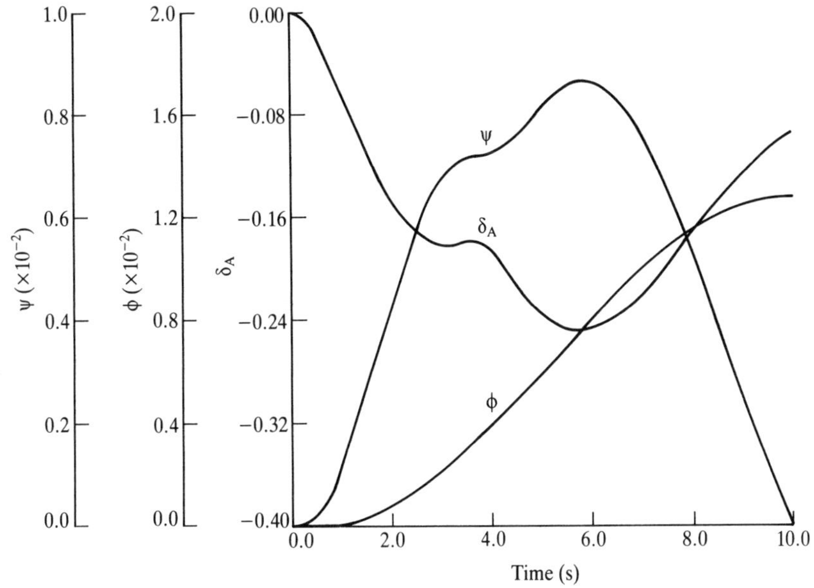

Figure 11.23 Response of direction control system to cross-wind.

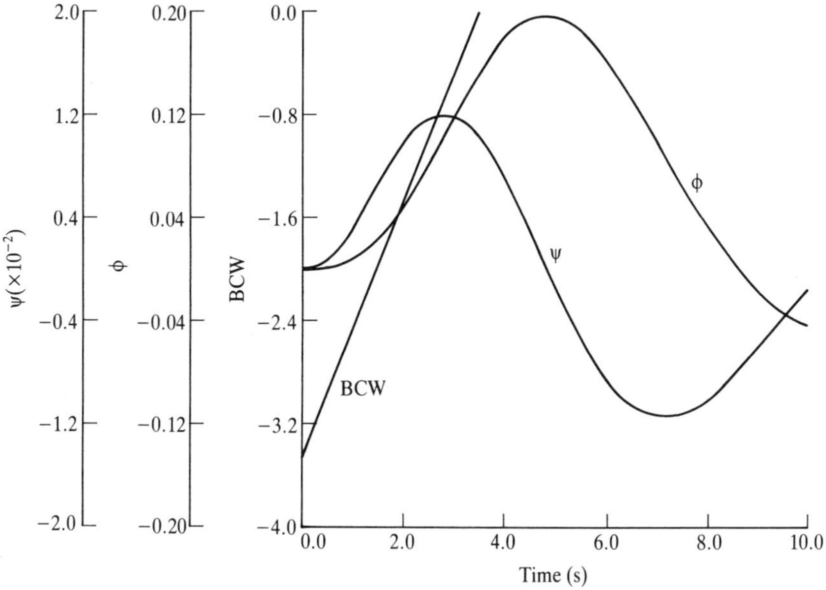

Figure 11.24 Response of direction control system to sideslip shear.

11.6 HEADING CONTROL SYSTEM

The heading angle, λ, of an aircraft is defined by:

$$\lambda = \beta + \Psi \tag{11.12}$$

In the preceding section, the direction control system operated by means of co-ordinated turns, thereby ensuring that the sideslip angle, β, was effectively zero. To do that, however, required the turning manoeuvre to be effected by means of the ailerons. If rudder use is involved, then it would seem that the yaw angle, Ψ, could be controlled by means of a yaw damper system, and with sufficient sideslip suppression could provide the basis of a heading control system. However, there are fundamental control problems involved with this approach and it is not much used. Nevertheless, for the purpose of instruction, a heading control system, with a block diagram like that shown in Figure 11.25, can be considered. For CHARLIE-4, and using the yaw damper of Section 9.8.2 of Chapter 9, it can be shown that if the state vector is defined as:

$$\mathbf{x}' = [\beta \; p \; r \; \phi \; \psi \; \delta_R \; e_{wo}] \tag{11.13}$$

and the control vector is defined as:

$$u = r_{comm} \tag{11.14}$$

the corresponding coefficient and driving matrices, A and B, for $K_A = 1.0$ and $T_{wo} = 3.0$, are given by:

$$A = \begin{bmatrix} -0.056 & 0 & -1 & 0.042 & 0 & 0.0022 & 0 \\ -1.05 & -0.465 & 0.39 & 0 & 0 & 0.153 & 0 \\ 0.6 & -0.032 & -0.115 & 0 & 0 & -0.475 & 0 \\ 0 & 1 & 0 & 0 & 0 & 0 & 0 \\ 0 & 0 & 1 & 0 & 0 & 0 & 0 \\ 0 & 0 & 0 & 0 & 0 & -4 & 4 \\ 0.6 & -0.032 & -0.115 & 0 & 0 & -0.0475 & -0.33 \end{bmatrix} \tag{11.15}$$

$$B' = [0 \; 0 \; 0 \; 0 \; 0 \; 4 \; 0] \tag{11.16}$$

For the heading angle, λ, the output matrix, C, becomes:

$$C = [1 \; 0 \; 0 \; 0 \; 1 \; 0 \; 0] \tag{11.17}$$

The response to an initial error of 1° in heading is shown in Figure 11.26 for two values of yaw damper gain, K_r, namely 1.0 and 0.5. The yaw rate response is identical for both cases, but the heading angle, λ, has a different steady state value in each case. To remove such steady state errors normally requires the use of an integral term in the controller.

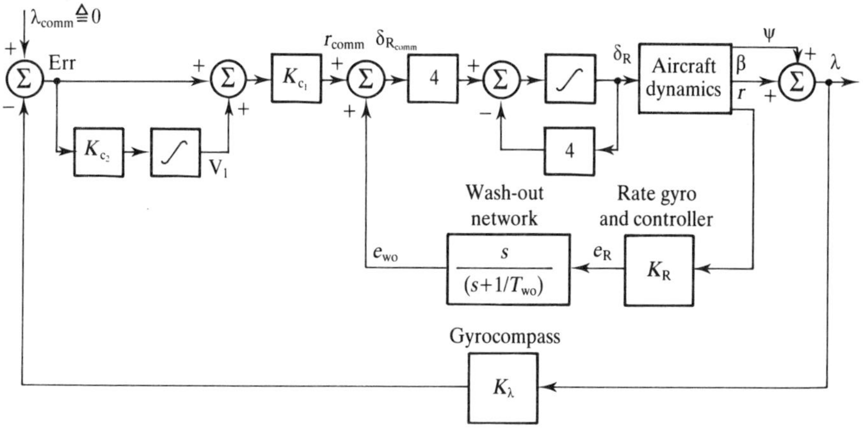

Figure 11.25 Heading control system.

From Figure 11.25 it can be seen that the control law for the heading control system is given by:

$$r_{comm} = -K_\lambda K_{c_1}\lambda - K_{c_1}K_\lambda K_{c_2}\int \lambda dt$$

$$= -K_\Lambda K_{c_1}(\beta + \Psi) - K_\lambda K_{c_1}K_{c_2}\int (\beta + \Psi)dt \qquad (11.18)$$

If we let:

$$\beta = x_1 \triangleq \dot{x}_8 \qquad (11.19)$$

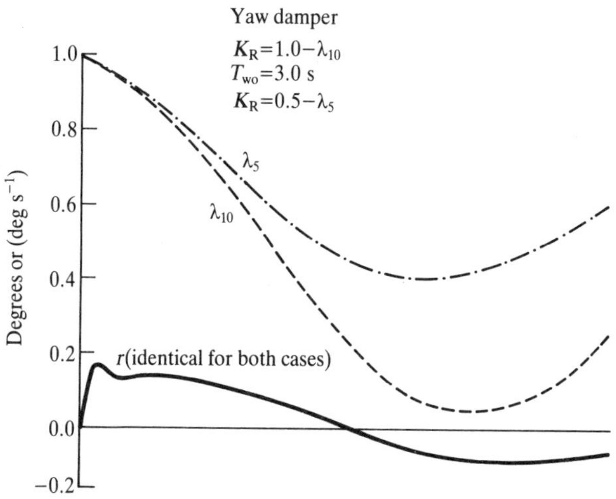

Figure 11.26 Response of heading control system to $\Psi(0)$.

then:

$$x_8 = \int \beta \mathrm{d}t \tag{11.20}$$

And if we let:

$$\psi = x_5 \triangleq \dot{x}_9 \tag{11.21}$$

then:

$$x_9 = \int \psi \mathrm{d}t \tag{11.22a}$$

$$r_{\mathrm{comm}} = -K_\lambda K_{c_1} x_1 - K_\lambda K_{c_1} x_5 - K_\lambda K_{c_1} K_{c_2} x_3 - K_\lambda K_{c_1} K_{c_2} x_9 \tag{11.22b}$$

Hence, the state vector of the closed loop heading control system becomes:

$$\mathbf{x}'_{\mathrm{H}} = [\beta \; p \; r \; \phi \; \psi \; \delta_{\mathrm{R}} \; e_{\mathrm{wo}} \int \beta \mathrm{d}t \int \psi dt] \tag{11.23}$$

and the corresponding coefficient matrix, A_{H}, can be written as:

$$A_{\mathrm{H}} = \begin{bmatrix} -0.056 & 0 & -1 & 0.042 & 0 & 0.0022 & 0 & 0 & 0 \\ -1.05 & -0.465 & 0.39 & 0 & 0 & 0.153 & 0 & 0 & 0 \\ 0.6 & -0.032 & -0.115 & 0 & 0 & -0.48 & 0 & 0 & 0 \\ 0 & 1 & 0 & 0 & 0 & 0 & 0 & 0 & 0 \\ 0 & 0 & 1 & 0 & 0 & 0 & 0 & 0 & 0 \\ 4K_{c_1}K_\lambda & 0 & 0 & 0 & 4K_{c_1}K_\lambda & -4 & 4 & a & b \\ 0.6 & -0.032 & -0.115 & 0 & 0 & -0.48 & 0.33 & 0 & 0 \\ 1 & 0 & 0 & 0 & 0 & 0 & 0 & 0 & 0 \\ 0 & 0 & 0 & 0 & 1 & 0 & 0 & 0 & 0 \end{bmatrix} \tag{11.24}$$

where

$$a = b = 4K_{c_1}K_{c_2}K_\lambda \tag{11.25}$$

A heading signal is usually obtained from a gyrocompass and it is considered here, for the purposes of illustration, that its sensitivity, K_λ, is 1 V deg^{-1}. It can easily be shown that, if K_{c_2} is zero, the maximum permissible value of controller gain, K_{c_1}, for closed loop stability is 1.1. Using a value of K_{c_1} of 0.875, with $K_{c_2} = 0.01$ results in a stable, but lightly damped and oscillatory, closed loop system with the following eigenvalues:

$$\lambda_1 = 0.0 \qquad \lambda_5, \lambda_6 = -0.02 \pm j0.26$$

$$\lambda_2 = -0.01 \qquad \lambda_7 = -0.59$$

$$\lambda_3, \lambda_4 = -0.01 \pm j0.154 \qquad \lambda_8, \lambda_9 = -2.16 \pm j4.02$$

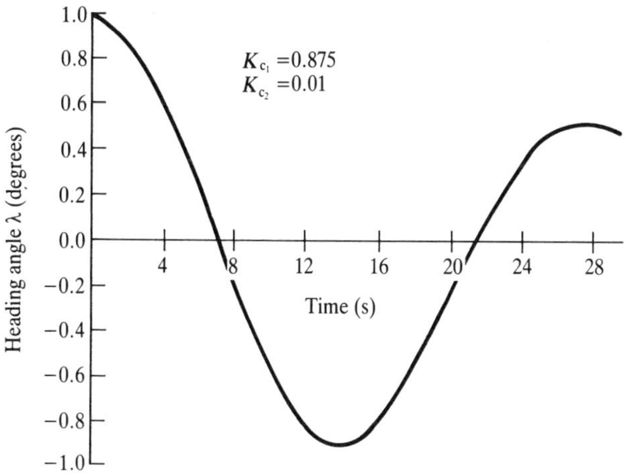

Figure 11.27 Response to initial heading error.

The response of this closed loop system to an initial error of 1° in heading is shown in Figure 11.27. It is worth noting that the choice of K_{c_2} is most important. It can easily be shown that for stability the value of K_{c2} must not be greater than 0.0222.

Much of the difficulty of designing a heading control system, of the type being considered, relates to the presence of the wash-out network in the feedback path of the yaw damper. If it is removed, then the yaw system shown in Figure 11.28 can be represented by the following state equation:

$$\dot{\mathbf{x}} = A\mathbf{x} + B\mathbf{u} \tag{11.26}$$

where:

$$\mathbf{x}' \triangleq [\beta \ p \ r \ \phi \ \psi \ \delta_R] \tag{11.27}$$

$$\mathbf{u} = \mathrm{e} \tag{11.28}$$

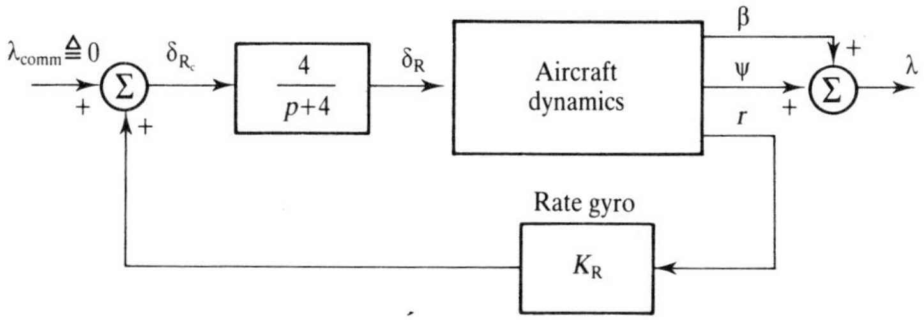

Figure 11.28 Block diagram of heading control system.

For CHARLIE-1

$$A = \begin{bmatrix} -0.189 & 0 & -1 & 0.146 & 0 & 0.005 \\ -1.33 & -0.98 & 0.33 & 0 & 0 & 0.06 \\ 0.17 & -0.17 & -0.217 & 0 & 0 & -0.15 \\ 0 & 1 & 0 & 0 & 0 & 0 \\ 0 & 0 & 1 & 0 & 0 & 0 \\ 0 & 0 & -60 & 0 & 0 & -4 \end{bmatrix} \tag{11.29}$$

$$B = [0\ 0\ 0\ 0\ 0\ 4]' \tag{11.30}$$

$$C = [1\ 0\ 0\ 0\ 1\ 0\ 0] \tag{11.31}$$

$$D = [0] \tag{11.32}$$

Using LQP, or pole placement, or any other appropriate method outlined in Chapter 8, provides a feedback control law. One such law is:

$$u = e = -2.844\beta + 11.80p + 53.16r + 23.5\phi + 47.16\psi \tag{11.33}$$

With attitude, and rate gyros, and a radio compass, it is possible to measure p, r, ϕ, ψ and λ. Measuring sideslip angle is not particularly simple or successful. However, using the radio compass to measure heading, λ, means that the control law of eq. (11.33) can be re-expressed as:

$$e = -2.884\lambda + 11.80p + 53.16r + 23.5\phi + 50\psi \tag{11.34}$$

The step response of the system is shown in Figure 11.29. Case A represents the

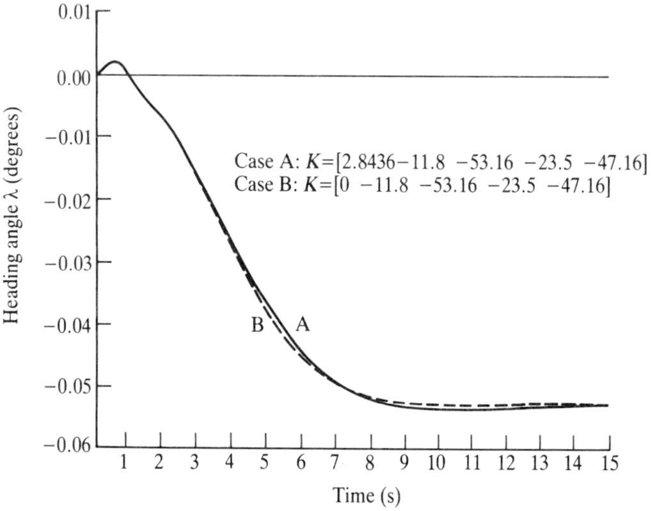

Figure 11.29 Step responses of radio compass heading control system.

response to the complete state feedback represented by eq. (11.34); case B shows how little affected is the response if eq. (11.33) is synthesized, but omitting the first term completely, thereby avoiding the need to measure sideslip, or to carry a radio compass.

11.7 VOR-COUPLED AUTOMATIC TRACKING SYSTEM

To achieve automatic tracking of an aircraft's lateral path requires the use of a navigation system to provide the AFCS with the appropriate steering commands. Radio navigation systems are very commonly used and the VOR system is one of the most popular and effective of these systems. It is used in conjunction with DME (distance measuring equipment) transmissions so that both, working together, provide a rho/theta navigation system. VOR provides the bearing (θ) information.

The VOR system operates in the frequency range of 108–135 MHz; DME operates at UHF, in the range 960–1 215 MHz. The principle of providing bearing information by means of VOR is relatively simple (see Kayton and Freid, 1969). The ground transmitter has an antenna system which is so arranged that the transmission pattern is a cardioid rotating at 30 rev s^{-1}. When this signal is received in the airborne receiver, the resulting output signal is a 30 Hz sine wave. There is also transmitted from the ground station an omni-directional signal which has been modulated with a 30 Hz tone. When this signal is simultaneously received on the airborne receiver, the output signal is demodulated 30 Hz tone. There is a phase difference between these two 30 Hz output signals which depends upon the bearing of the aircraft in relation to the transmitter. The beam width of the VOR transmission is relatively coarse, being about $\pm$ 10°. However, it should be remembered that even when a navigation system has a large bearing error it does not mean that an aircraft cannot home onto the source of the bearing information. Accuracy of bearing of 1° is achieved with operational airborne VOR systems. Therefore, VOR guidance can be regarded as accurate for the reception range which, because the transmission is VHF, is line-of-sight, i.e. about one hundred miles. But as an aircraft nears a particular transmitter the system inherently becomes more sensitive. It can easily be understood, from studying Figure 11.30(a) why this comes about. Obviously, the greater the displacement, d, from the beam's centre-line the greater is the error angle, Γ, as range reduces. The output voltage from an airborne VOR receiver is proportional to the measured error angle Γ. Such an increase in the sensitivity of the receiving system, as the aircraft flies nearer the transmitter, will have a destabilizing effect on the closed loop VOR-coupled system. Consequently, it is customary to schedule the gain of the system, using the DME to reduce the gain as the distance to the transmitter reduces. The basic geometry of the navigation system is represented in Figure 11.30(b).

The output signal from the VOR receiver is proportional to Γ. It is this

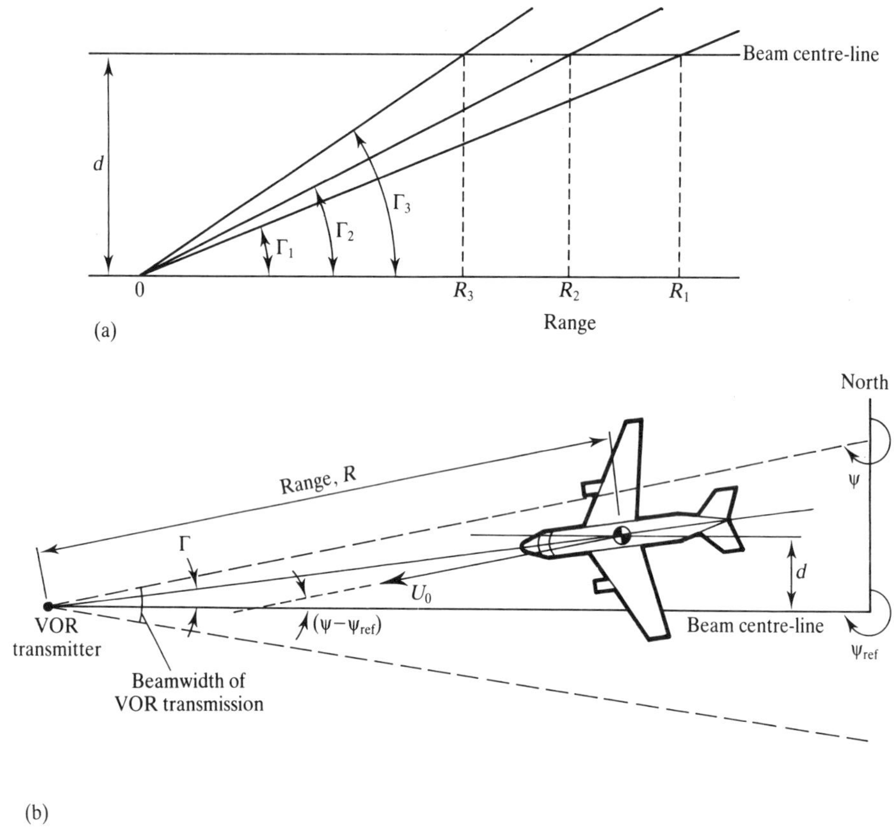

Figure 11.30 (a) Change of error angle with range for fixed displacement. (b) Geometry of VOR system.

signal which is used as a command signal for the direction control system to drive the aircraft back on to the centre-line of the VOR beam, thereby reducing Γ to zero.

From Figure 11.30(b) it can be deduced that:

$$\Gamma = 57.3d/R \qquad (11.35)$$

The error angle, Γ, is assumed to be not greater than 15°, i.e. small. It can also be seen that:

$$\dot{d} = U_0 \sin(\psi - \psi_{ref}) \simeq U_0(\psi - \psi_{ref}) \qquad (11.36)$$

If Laplace transforms are taken then:

$$sd(s) = (U_0/57.3)(\psi(s) - \psi_{ref}(s)) \qquad (11.37)$$

where ψ and ψ_{ref} are in degrees.

A block diagram representation of eqs (11.35) and (11.37) is shown as

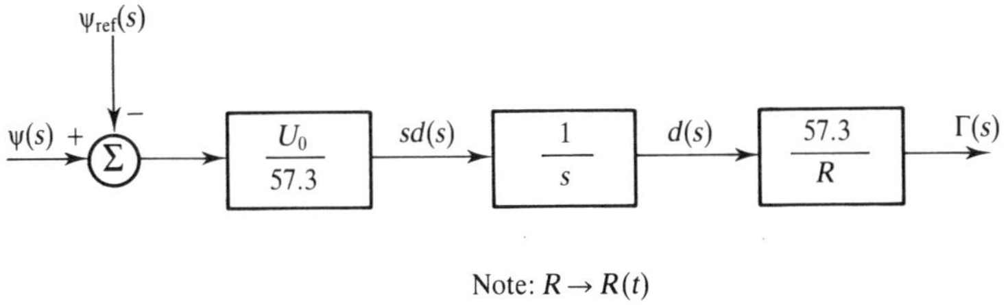

Figure 11.31 Block diagram of VOR geometry.

Figure 11.31. For analytical simplicity, ψ_{ref} can be taken as zero without loss of generality.

It is supposed that if the VOR-coupled system causes the aircraft to change direction to restore its path along the centre-line of the VOR beam, it will do so in a manner that results in any turn being a co-ordinated one. Consequently, the direction control system of Section 11.5 can be used to provide the required heading, ψ.

It is the function of the flight controller and the VOR receiver to provide the command signal, ψ_{ref}. The signal provided by the VOR receiver is proportional to the angular deviation, Γ. As a result of the comparison of the receiver's output signal with Γ_{ref} (which is zero, by definition) the controller (sometimes referred to as the coupling unit) provides the required command signal, ψ_{ref}. However, to ensure that the complete system performs correctly, even in the presence of a severe cross-wind, there must be an integral term in the control law. Consequently, the controller must have a transfer function at least of the form:

$$G_c(s) = K_c\left\{1 + \frac{K_{c_I}}{K_c s}\right\} \tag{11.38}$$

Of course, G_c may also have a rate term, or a phase advance compensation term, depending upon the nature of the aircraft's dynamics.

Note that if the initial capture of the VOR beam is at some large angular deviation, say ± 20°, then if the proportional gain, K_c, in the controller is large the bank angle initially commanded will be excessive. To avoid this, practical systems have limiting circuits on the roll rate and also on the commanded bank angle. In the example which follows, only a simple proportional plus integral controller is used, but the reader should remember that these limiting circuits are necessary for practical applications.

A block diagram of this system is shown in Figure 11.32. Obviously, there is a minimum value of range R below which the VOR-coupled system will become unstable, since R contributes to the open loop gain. In some systems, the loop gain is scheduled with range measured from the DME system. No such scheduling is assumed in this system, although it has been arranged for R to reduce linearly with time from R_0 to R_{min} (actually R_{min} + 200 m). The response

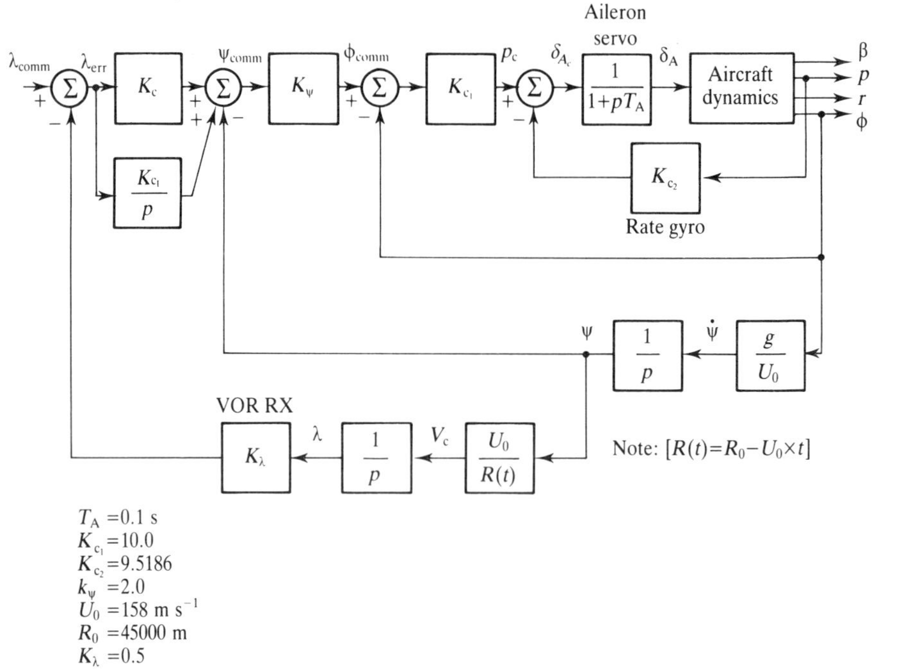

Figure 11.32 Block diagram of VOR-coupled system.

of the VOR coupled system to an initial bearing error, for a variety of controller gains, is shown in Figure 11.33. Note that an overshoot occurs when the gain, K_c, is increased from 20 to 30 (with the gain of the integral term being zero). With some integral action present, i.e. $K_{c_I} = 0.025\,s^{-1}$, and with $K_c = 25$, the resulting response has reduced the overshoot and has 'locked on' to the VOR bearing in about 80 s. The same response is shown in Figure 11.34 from which it can be seen how the system holds the aircraft on the VOR radial until minimum range, R_{min}, is reached at which point the system becomes unstable.

11.8 ILS LOCALIZER-COUPLED CONTROL SYSTEM

ILS equipment is located only at airports in which the runway length is greater than 1 800 m. ILS is often referred to as the instrument landing system, but should more correctly be called the instrument low approach system. It is an important distinction since the system is insufficiently accurate (owing to the nature of the propagation characteristics corresponding to the transmission frequencies) to permit its use by an aircraft right down to touchdown,[2] even though the system does form an essential element of all aircraft automatic landing systems. The ILS involves a number of independent low-power radio transmissions:

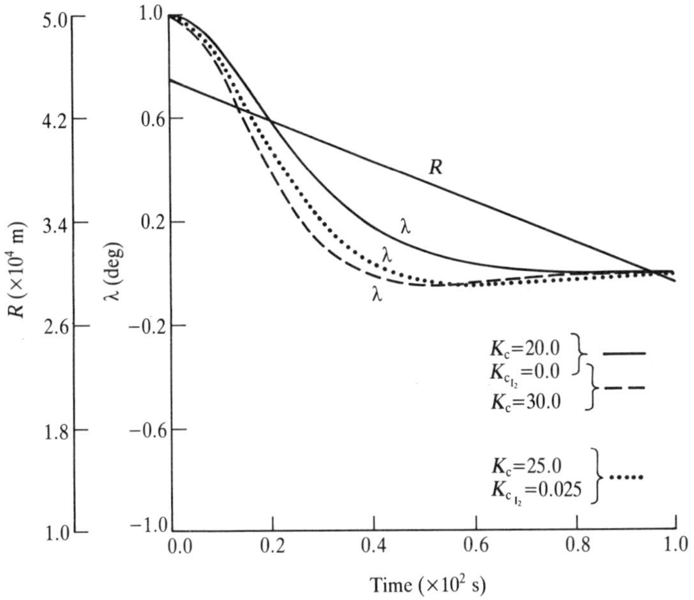

Figure 11.33 Response of VOR-coupled system to initial error.

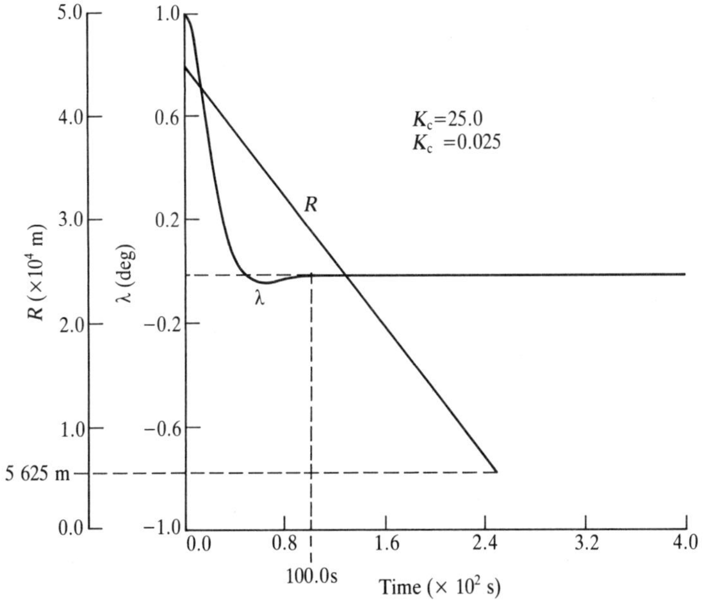

Figure 11.34 Complete VOR-coupled approach response.

Table 11.1 ILS transmitter characteristics

Localizer Transmitter (VHF)	
Carrier frequency	108–122 MHz (USA)
Radiation:	
Polarization	Horizontal
Power	100 W
Modulation:	
Frequencies	90 Hz and 150 Hz
Depth (on course)	20% for each frequency
Code identification:	
Frequency (tone)	1 020 Hz
Depth	5%
Voice communication	
Depth	50%
The transmitter building is offset by a minimum of 80 m from the centre of the localizer aerial system.	
Glide Slope Transmitter (UHF)	
Carrier frequency	329.3–335 MHz (USA)
Radiation:	
Polarization	Horizontal
Power	5 W
Modulation:	
Frequencies	90 Hz and 150 Hz
Depth (on path)	40% for each frequency
Marker Transmitters (VHF)	
All marker frequencies	75 MHz
Radiation:	
Polarization	Horizontal
Power	2 W
Modulation:	
Frequencies	400 Hz (outer marker) 1 300 Hz (middle marker) 3 000 Hz (inner marker)
Depth	95%

1. The localizer which provides information to an aircraft about whether it is flying to the left or the right of the centre-line of the runway towards which it is heading.

2. The glide path (or slope, in American usage) which provides an aircraft with information about whether it is flying above or below a preferred descent path (nominally 2.5°) for the airport at which the aircraft intends to land.

3. Marker beacons which indicate to an aircraft its precise location at fixed points from the runway threshold.

The characteristics of the radio transmitters involved are summarized in Table 11.1.

A representation of the transmission characteristics of the ILS localizer and glide path systems is shown as Figure 11.35 and the locations of the transmitter and aerial systems in relation to the runway are represented in Figure 11.36. It will be noted that reference was made in Table 11.1 to an inner marker which is *not* shown in Figure 11.35. When an airport runway is fitted with an ILS system which is certified to provide category III landing information, the third marker is used. It is located at a distance of 305 m (1 000 ft) from the runway threshold: for a touchdown point some 366 m (1 200 ft) from the runway threshold this location of the inner marker means that an aircraft correctly positioned on the glide path will be at a height of 100 ft above the ground. This height is the decision height for a category III landing (see Section 11.10).

Provided an aircraft is equipped with the necessary airborne receivers and aerials for the localizer, glide path and marker transmissions, it has available signals which indicate its location left/right of runway centre-line or whether it is above/below the glide slope, depending upon whether the demodulated 90 Hz signal is greater than the 150 Hz signal or vice versa (see Figure 11.35).

A different method of using the ILS has been under consideration for many years: it is known as the two-segment approach system. In it an aircraft is required to descend at a rate of about 1 400 ft min^{-1} along a glide path of 6° before intercepting, at a height of 800 ft, some 5 000 m from touchdown, the normal glide path of 2.5°. There has been considerable pilot opposition to the scheme, not least because a failure to effect the transition from steep to normal segment could result in ground impact as much as 2 400 m short of the runway. Nevertheless, the principles involved in the proposed system are the same as those just discussed, apart from the glide path angles and the transition point.

Using such output signals as guidance signals, an ILS localizer-coupled control system can be arranged which will steer an aircraft automatically towards a runway, minimizing any deviations from the centre-line of the runway. The block diagram of the system is essentially the same as that given in Figure 11.32

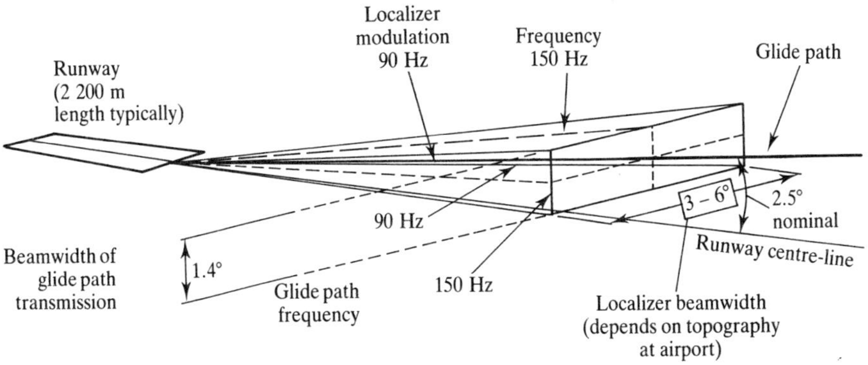

Figure 11.35 ILS localizer and glide slope transmissions.

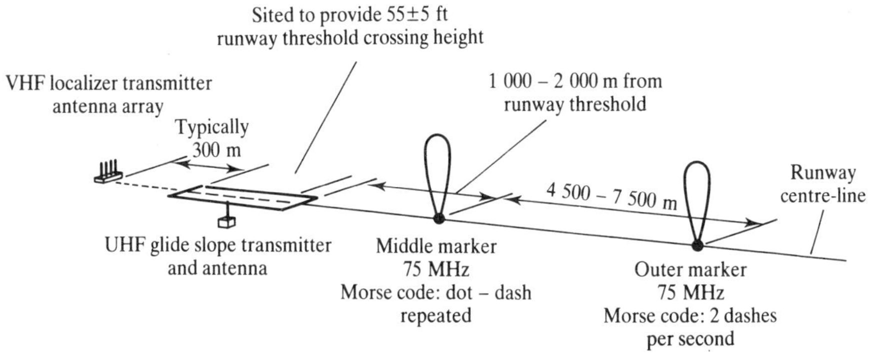

Figure 11.36 Location of ILS ground transmitters and antennas.

except that Γ represents the angular deviation from the localizer centre-line, and a localizer receiver is used, not the VOR receiver denoted. More care must be exercised with the controller gains since the beamwidth of the system is less (~ 3°). There are also present in the transfer function representing the localizer receiver, the dynamics associated with the low-pass filters needed to remove the 90 and 150 Hz modulation tones from the output signals. The range involved in this system is much less than that which obtains with VOR coupling, being not greater than about fifteen miles, usually less. However, like the VOR hold system, the localizer-coupled control system cannot operate below a certain minimum value of range, otherwise the open loop gain will increase beyond the critical value and the closed loop system will become unstable. The response of a digital simulation of an ILS localizer-coupled control system to an initial angular displacement of 1° to the right, at a range of 15 000 m, for CHARLIE-1, is shown in Figure 11.37(a). The corresponding values of gains are shown in Table 11.2. The minimum value of range for stability is approximately 200 m; the simulation was stopped when the range reached 1 800 m. This simulation was only illustrative since the airspeed was maintained at a constant value of $U_0 = 60.0 \text{ m s}^{-1}$. The response of the same system to a crosswind corresponding to a side gust of ± 1° in 10 s, and with the airspeed being reduced steadily from 60 to 40 m s^{-1} throughout the approach, is shown in Figure 11.37(b). Note how effectively the system restores the aircraft to the localizer centre-line and maintains it there: the peak displacement in heading is only 8×10^{-4} degrees. The dotted line represents the trajectory corresponding to $K_{c_{I_2}} = 0.25 \text{ s}^{-1}$. In Figure 11.37(c) the trajectory is shown for an initial range of 40 000 m and a constant speed of 158 m s^{-1}; the purpose of including this trajectory is to show the behaviour of the system when minimum range is approached and reached: the system becomes unstable.

11.9 ILS GLIDE-PATH-COUPLED CONTROL SYSTEM

This system uses the output signal from the airborne glide path receiver as a guidance command to the attitude control system of the aircraft. The loop is

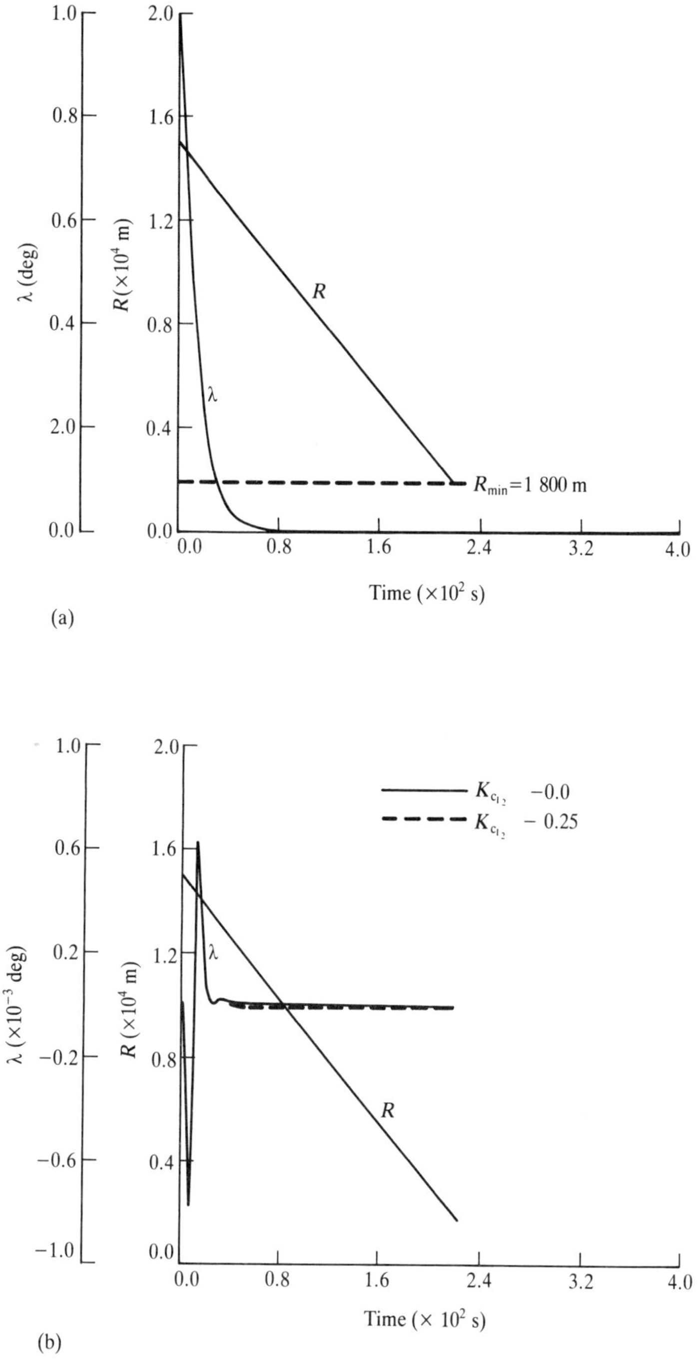

Figure 11.37 (a) ILS-coupled trajectory. (b) Response to side gust.

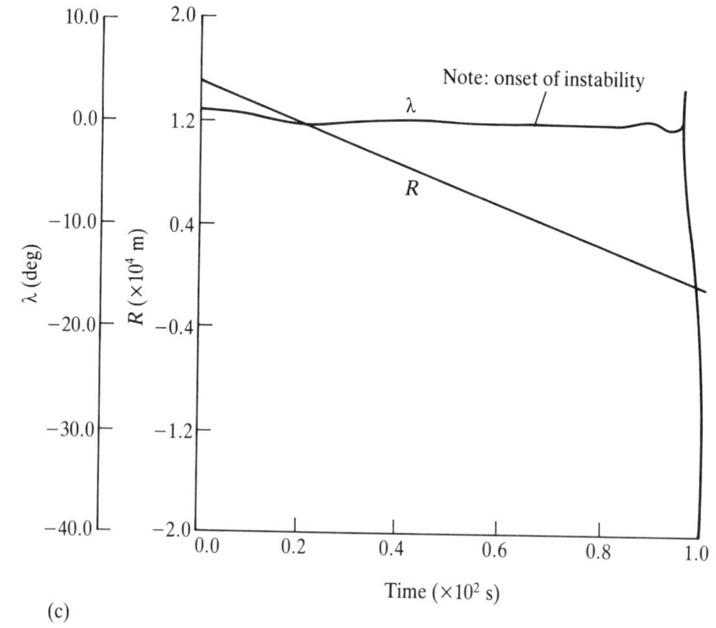

(c) Unstable response.

Table 11.2 Gains for ILS localizer-coupled system

$K_\lambda = 1.0$	$K_c = 15.0$	$K_{c_{I_2}} = 0.0$
$U_0 = 60\ \text{m s}^{-1}$	$R_0 = 15 \times 10^3\ \text{m}$	

closed via the aircraft kinematics which transform the pitch attitude of the aircraft into a displacement from the preferred descent path (the glide path) into the airport. The situation is represented in Figure 11.38(a). The glide path angle is denoted by γ_G and its nominal value is $-2.5°$. If an aircraft is flying into an airport, but it is displaced below the glide path by a distance, d, that distance is negative. The geometry is shown in Figure 11.38(b). If the value of the aircraft's own flight path angle is $-2.5°$, the displacement is 0. Any angular deviation from the centre-line of the glide path transmission is measured by the airborne glide path receiver: that deviation depends upon both the displacement, d, and the slant range from the transmitter. Since the value of γ_G is so small, it is customary to regard the slant and horizontal ranges, R and x, repectively, as identical; the correct relationship is, of course:

$$x = R \cos 2.5° \tag{11.39}$$

In this section, x and R are taken as identical. Therefore, the angular deviation, Γ, is defined as:

$$\Gamma = d/R \tag{11.40}$$

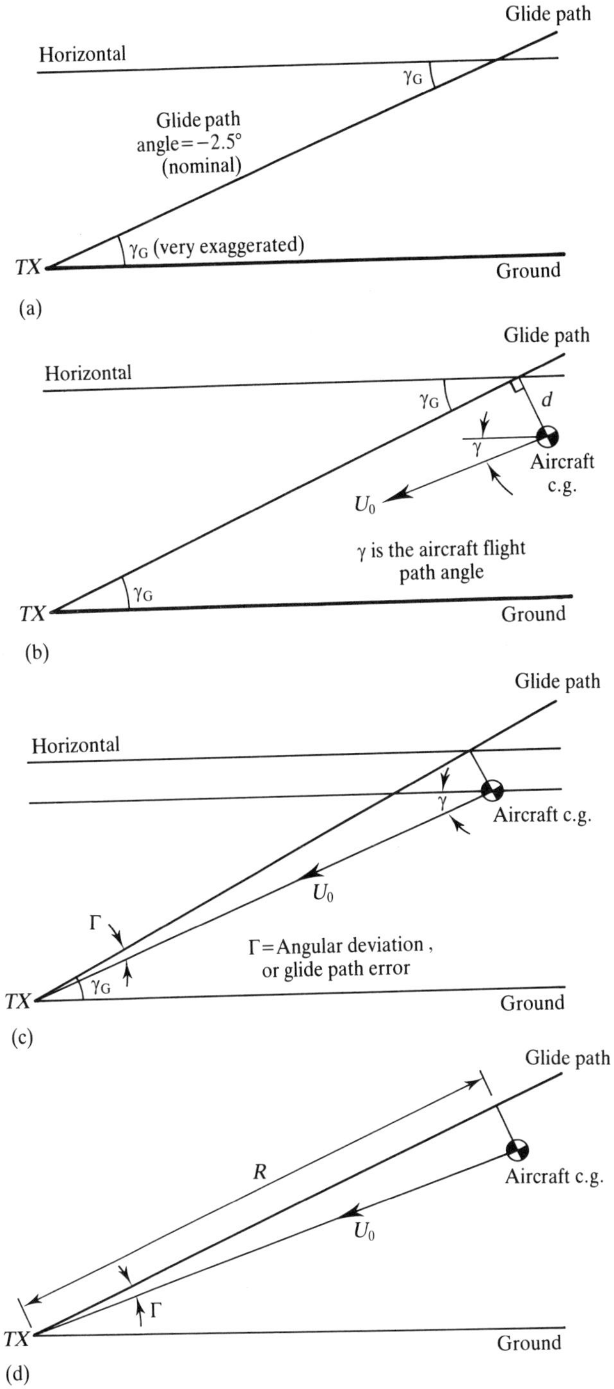

Figure 11.38 (a) The glide path geometry.
(b) Aircraft below glide path – geometry.
(c) Angular deviation from glide path – geometry.
(d) Slant range definition.

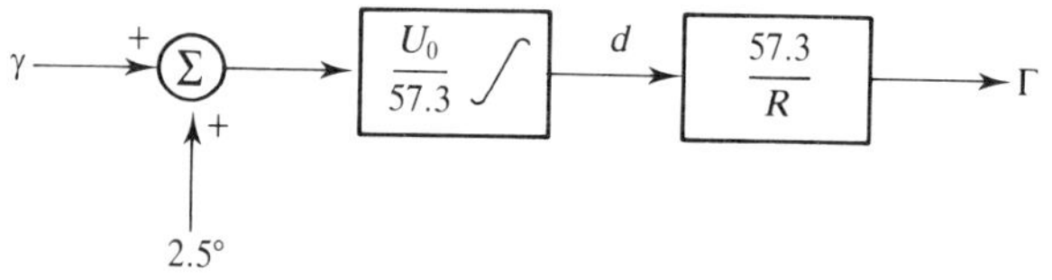

Figure 11.39 Block diagram of glide path measurement.

where Γ is in radians.

The component of the airspeed which is perpendicular to the glide path is $U_0 \sin \Gamma$; this quantity represents the rate of change of the displacement, i.e.:

$$\dot{d} = U_0 \sin \Gamma \simeq (U_0/57.3)\Gamma \tag{11.41}$$

However, for the situation shown in Figure 11.38 the aircraft's flight path angle is less than 2.5°, therefore Γ is positive (note that $\Gamma = \gamma + 2.5°$) and $\dot{d}$ is positive. As the initial displacement was negative, and its rate of change is positive, the situation shown in Figure 11.38(c) represents the case when the aircraft is approaching the glide path from below:

$$d = (U_0/57.3)\int(\gamma + 2.5°)\mathrm{d}t = (U_0/57.3)\int\Gamma\mathrm{d}t \tag{11.42}$$

The block diagram representing eq. (11.42) is shown in Figure 11.39.

The aircraft flight path angle, γ, is defined by:

$$\gamma = (\theta - \alpha) \tag{11.43}$$

Consequently, the flight path angle is most effectively controlled by using a pitch attitude control system, with a pitch rate SAS as an inner loop, to effectively

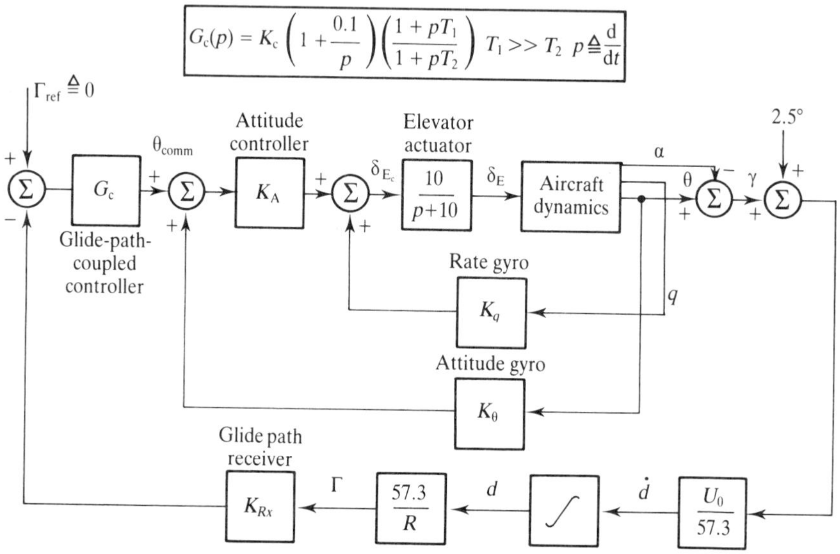

Figure 11.40 Glide-path-coupled control system.

control any changes in the angle of attack which may arise as a result of the elevator's being used to drive the aircraft back onto the glide path. The block diagram of a typical glide path control system is shown in Figure 11.40. The gain of the glide path receiver, K_{R_x}, can be considered, without loss of generality, to be 1 V deg^{-1}. The control law used is then:

$$\theta_{\text{comm}} = -G_c(p)\Gamma \tag{11.44}$$

The transfer function, G_c, of the glide-path-coupled controller represents essentially a proportional plus integral term controller. The phase advance term has been added to provide extra stabilization, if required. So far it has been presumed that the airspeed, U_0, is constant throughout the coupled trajectory, but this is never the case. A speed control system, used in conjunction with the glide-path-coupled system, is essential to ensure that the aircraft's flight path angle, γ, in the steady state, has the same sign as the commanded pitch angle. The speed control system also ensures that the airspeed of the aircraft is reduced from U_{01} at the start of the approach to a lower value, U_{02}, at its finish, the change in speed corresponding to the appropriate speed schedule, $U_{\text{ref}}(t)$. A typical speed schedule, for CHARLIE-1, is given in Figure 11.41. At the start of the coupled glide path descent, the airspeed, U_{01}, is 85.0 m s^{-1}; thirty seconds later, it is 65.0 m s^{-1}. During that time the aircraft will have travelled a slant distance of:

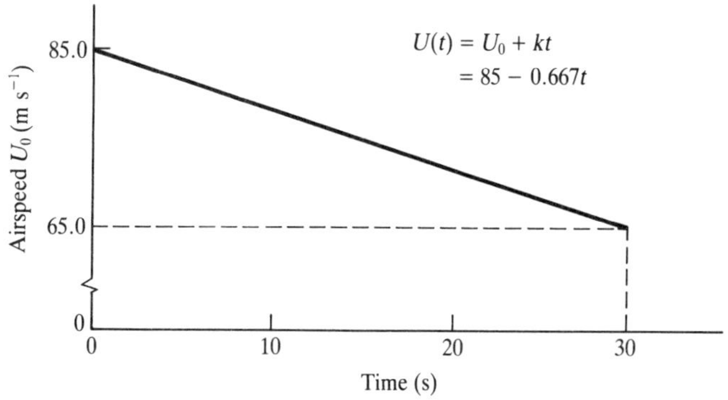

Figure 11.41 Airspeed schedule for CHARLIE-1.

$$R = \int_0^{30} (85 - 0.667t)\mathrm{d}t = 2\,250\ \mathrm{m} \tag{11.45}$$

The horizontal distance covered is actually 2 248 m (assuming aircraft descends along the glide path). The height at the start of this manoeuvre is 320 ft. A typical set of parameters, corresponding to CHARLIE-1, is given in Table 11.3 and the corresponding dynamic response to an initial displacement, d, of 100 ft above the glide path, is shown in Figure 11.42. It is evident how effective the system is in restoring the aircraft to the glide path and maintaining it there subsequently.

Table 11.3 Parameters of glide-path-coupled system

$K_\theta = 1.0$	$K_A = 3.1$	$T_1 = 0.4$
$K_q = 1.9$	$K_c = -20.00$	$T_2 = 0.04$

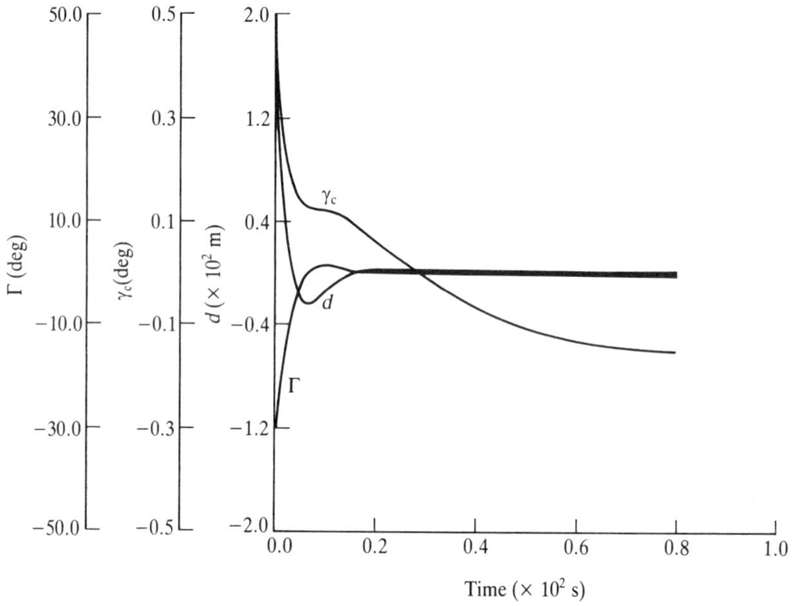

Figure 11.42 Response of glide-slope-coupled system.

For the system represented in Figure 11.40, and using the values of parameters listed in Table 11.3,[3] it can be shown that the closed loop dynamics can be represented in that form, representing a generalized AFCS, which was explained in Section 7.2 of Chapter 7.

Aircraft dynamics

$$\dot{\mathbf{x}} = A\mathbf{x} + B\mathbf{u} \tag{11.46}$$

where:

$$\mathbf{x}' \triangleq [u \; w \; q \; \theta \; \delta_E] \tag{11.47}$$

$$\mathbf{u} \triangleq [\delta_{E_c}] \tag{11.48}$$

$$A = \begin{bmatrix} -0.021 & 0.122 & 0 & -9.81 & 0.292 \\ -0.2 & -0.512 & 65.1 & 0 & -1.96 \\ 0.00004 & -0.006 & -0.402 & 0 & -0.4 \\ 0 & 0 & 1 & 0 & 0 \\ 0 & 0 & 0 & 0 & -10 \end{bmatrix} \quad \text{for CHARLIE-1} \tag{11.49}$$

$$B' = [0\ 0\ 0\ 0\ 10] \tag{11.50}$$

Output equation

$$\mathbf{y} = C\mathbf{x} \tag{11.51}$$

where:

$$\mathbf{y} \triangleq [\alpha\ q\ \theta] \tag{11.52}$$

$$C = \begin{bmatrix} 0 & 0.015 & 0 & 0 & 0 \\ 0 & 0 & 1 & 0 & 0 \\ 0 & 0 & 0 & 1 & 0 \end{bmatrix} \tag{11.53}$$

Controller dynamics

$$\dot{\mathbf{x}}_c = A_c\mathbf{x}_c + B_c\mathbf{y} + E \tag{11.54}$$

Controller output equation is:

$$\mathbf{y}_c = C_c\mathbf{x}_c + D_c\mathbf{y} \tag{11.55}$$

with:

$$\delta_{E_c} \triangleq y_c \tag{11.56}$$

From Figure 11.40 and Table 11.3 it can be deduced that for the glide path coupled control system the control law is:

$$\begin{aligned} \delta_{E_c} &= K_q q + K_\theta K_A \theta - K_A K_c \frac{(1 + pT_1)}{(1 + pT_2)} \left\{ 1 + \frac{0.1}{p} \right\} \Gamma \\ &= 1.9q + 3.1\theta + 62.0 \frac{(1 + p0.4)}{(1 + p0.04)} \left\{ 1 + \frac{0.1}{p} \right\} \Gamma \end{aligned} \tag{11.57}$$

Furthermore, it can be seen that:

$$\begin{aligned} \Gamma &= \frac{U_0}{R} \int \theta \mathrm{d}t - \frac{1}{R} \int w \mathrm{d}t + 2.5 \frac{U_0}{R} t \\ &= \frac{65.1}{R} \int \theta \mathrm{d}t - \frac{1}{R} \int w \mathrm{d}t + \frac{162.75}{R} t \end{aligned} \tag{11.58}$$

If we let:

$$\int \theta \mathrm{d}t \triangleq x_{c_1} \tag{11.59}$$

$$\int w \mathrm{d}t \triangleq x_{c_2} \tag{11.60}$$

$$t \triangleq x_{c_3} \tag{11.61}$$

then

$$\Gamma = \frac{65.1}{R} x_{c_1} - \frac{1}{R} x_{c_2} + \frac{162.75}{R} x_{c_3} \tag{11.62}$$

If the third term on the r.h.s. of eq. (11.57) is denoted by $-K_A K_c g(p)$ then:

$$\frac{g(p)}{\Gamma(p)} = \frac{p^2 T_1 + (1 + 0.1 T_1)p + 0.1}{p^2 T_2 + p}$$

$$= \frac{0.4p^2 + 1.04p + 0.1}{0.04p^2 + p} \tag{11.63}$$

Let:

$$\frac{g(p)}{\Gamma(p)} = \frac{g(p)}{z(p)} \cdot \frac{z(p)}{\Gamma(p)} = (0.4p^2 + 1.04p + 0.1) \frac{1}{0.04p^2 + p} \tag{11.64}$$

Then:

$$0.04\ddot{z} + z = \Gamma \tag{11.65}$$

$$0.4\ddot{z} + 1.04\dot{z} + 0.1z = g \tag{11.66}$$

Let:

$$z \triangleq x_{c_4} \tag{11.67}$$

$$\dot{z} \triangleq x_{c_5} = \dot{x}_{c_4} \tag{11.68}$$

Hence:

$$\dot{x}_{c_5} = -25x_{c_5} + 25\Gamma \tag{11.69}$$

$$g = 0.1x_{c_4} + 1.04x_{c_5} - 10x_{c_5} + \frac{651}{R} x_{c_1} - \frac{10}{R} x_{c_2} + \frac{1627.5}{R} x_{c_3} \tag{11.70}$$

Hence, the third term on the r.h.s. of eq. (11.57) can be written as:

$$\delta_{E_c} = 1.9y_2 + 3.1y_3 + 62 \left\{ \frac{651}{R} \quad -\frac{10}{R} \quad \frac{1627.5}{R} \quad 0.1 \quad -8.96 \right\} \mathbf{x}_c$$

$$y_c \triangleq \delta_{E_c} = \left[\frac{40362}{R} \quad -\frac{620}{R} \quad \frac{100905}{R} \quad 6.2 \quad -555.52 \right] \mathbf{x}_c + [0 \ 1.9 \ 3.1]\mathbf{y} \tag{11.71}$$

Hence:

$$A_c = \begin{bmatrix} 0 & 0 & 0 & 0 & 0 \\ 0 & 0 & 0 & 0 & 0 \\ 0 & 0 & 0 & 0 & 0 \\ 0 & 0 & 0 & 0 & 0 \\ \frac{1627.5}{R} & \frac{-25}{R} & \frac{40687.5}{R} & 0 & -25 \end{bmatrix} \qquad (11.72)$$

$$B_c = \begin{bmatrix} 0 & 0 & 1 \\ 65.1 & 0 & 0 \\ 0 & 0 & 0 \\ 0 & 0 & 0 \\ 0 & 0 & 0 \end{bmatrix} \qquad (11.73)$$

$$C_C = \begin{bmatrix} \frac{40362}{R} & \frac{-620}{R} & \frac{100905}{R} & 6.2 & -555.5 \end{bmatrix} \qquad (11.74)$$

$$D_c = [0 \;\; 1.9 \;\; 3.1] \qquad (11.75)$$

$$E = \begin{bmatrix} 0 \\ 0 \\ 1 \\ 0 \\ 0 \end{bmatrix} \qquad (11.76)$$

Let:

$$\mathbf{v} = \begin{bmatrix} \mathbf{x} \\ \mathbf{x}_c \end{bmatrix} \qquad (11.77)$$

then the closed loop dynamics of the glide-path-coupled control system can be expressed as:

$$\dot{\mathbf{v}} = K\mathbf{v} + L \qquad (11.78)$$

where:

$$K = \begin{bmatrix} (A + BD_cC) & BC_c \\ B_cC & A_c \end{bmatrix} \qquad (11.79)$$

Table 11.4 Eigenvalues of glide-path system at two values of range

Range = 4 000 m	*Range = 200 m*
$\lambda_1 = 0.0$	$\lambda_{1,2} = 0.0$
$\lambda_2 = -0.005$	$\lambda_{3,4} = 0.026 \pm j0.024$
$\lambda_3 = -0.013$	$\lambda_5 = -4.004$
$\lambda_4 = -0.12$	$\lambda_6 = -8.91$
$\lambda_{5,6} = -0.186 \pm j0.325$	$\lambda_{7,8} = -1.57 \pm j4.105$
$\lambda_7 = -2.027$	$\lambda_{9,10} = +2.58 \pm j4.77$
$\lambda_{8,9} = -4.21 \pm j6.76$	
$\lambda_{10} = -24.944$	

$$L \triangleq \begin{bmatrix} 0 \\ E \end{bmatrix} \tag{11.80}$$

The eigenvalues of the closed loop system just described, which correspond to values of range, R, of 4 000 m and 200 m, are shown in Table 11.4. It can be deduced from these values of the closed loop roots that at a range of 4 000 m the glide-path-coupled system is stable, but when the range has reduced to 200 m it is unstable. In fact, there is a critical value of range below which the system is unstable.

The treatment above supposes that the glide slope receiver is located at the c.g. of the aircraft, and measures the aircraft's angular deviation from the glide path at the c.g. However, if the aircraft receiver is installed at, say, the nose of the aircraft, the dynamics of the system are affected, as follows. From Figure 11.43, the height measured at the receiver is:

$$h_A \simeq h + x_A\theta \tag{11.81}$$

(assuming θ is small). Therefore the flight path angle at the receiver is:

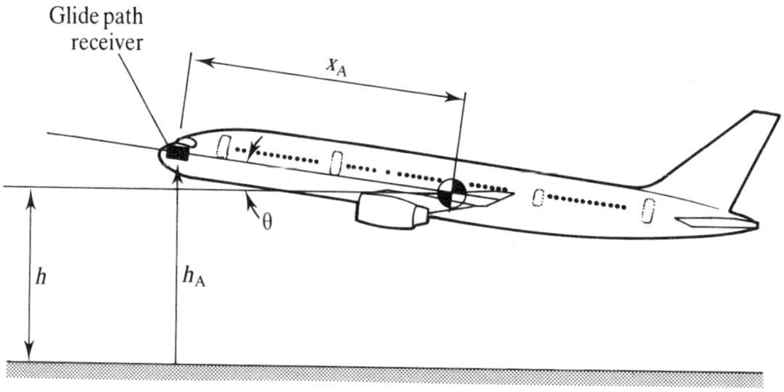

Figure 11.43 Glide path receiver located in aircraft nose.

$$\gamma' = \frac{\dot{h}_A}{U_0} = \frac{\dot{h}}{U_0} + \frac{x_A\dot{\theta}}{U_0} = \gamma + x_A\frac{\dot{\theta}}{U_0} \tag{11.82}$$

$$\therefore \quad \frac{\gamma'(s)}{\theta(s)} = \frac{\gamma(s)}{\theta(s)} + \frac{sx_A}{U_0} \tag{11.83}$$

Thus, the effect of locating the glide path receiver in the aircraft's nose is to introduce a phase advance term into the closed loop dynamics.

11.10 AUTOMATIC LANDING SYSTEM

Although the contribution to the development of airborne automatic landing systems has been international, the basis of most of the operational systems in service is the system developed in the UK by the Blind Landing Experimental Unit (now disbanded) of the Royal Aerospace Establishment. It makes use of the ILS, and the entire automatic landing segment is made up of a number of phases which are shown in Figure 11.44. At the start of the final approach phase (point 1 in Figure 11.44), the aircraft being considered is assumed to be guided on the glide path by a glide-path-coupled control system of the type described in Section 11.9, and to be steered onto the runway centre-line by means of the ILS localizer-coupled control system described in Section 11.8.

What has been described above is a category II automatic landing. What distinguishes landings into the various categories are the conditions of visibility. These categories are summarized in Figure 11.45; it can be seen that each category is defined as a combination of the decision height (DH), i.e. the minimum

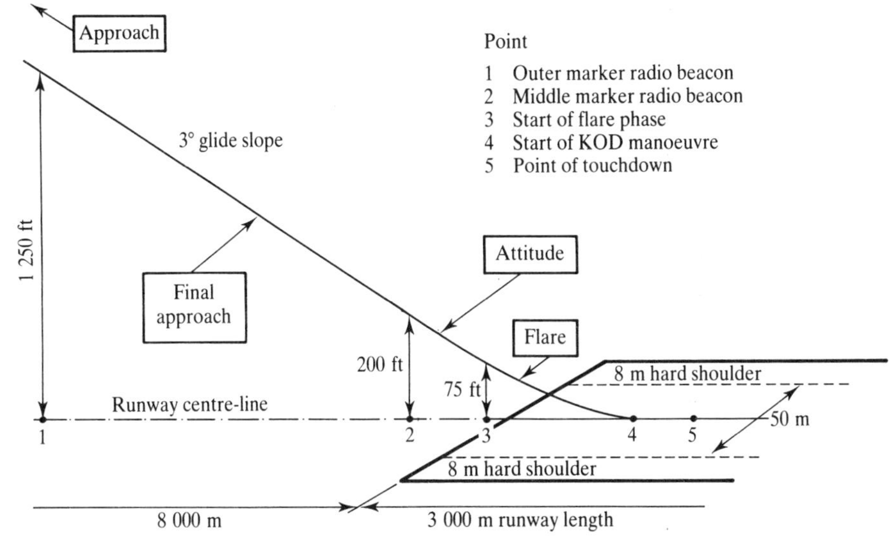

Figure 11.44 BLEU aircraft automatic landing.

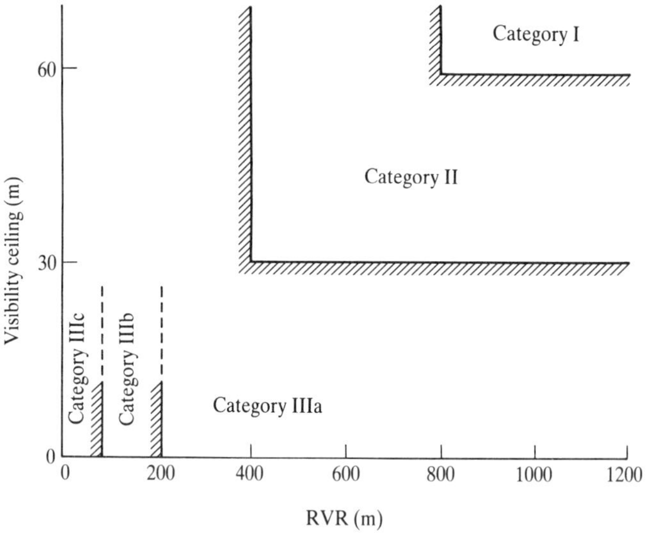

Figure 11.45 Definition of landing categories.

permitted ceiling for vertical visibility for the landing to proceed, and the runway visual range (RVR). Categories I and II allow only coupled glide path approaches down to the DH/RVR combinations defined in Figure 11.45. At the DH, the pilot either continues the flight under manual control to land, or executes a go-around manoeuvre either to attempt once more to land at the airport, or to divert to an alternative. Category IIIa allows the aircraft to make an automatic landing by providing an automatically controlled flare phase, with the pilot taking over control of the aircraft at the point of touchdown. Category IIIb allows the aircraft to use automatic flare and roll-out, with the pilot assuming control only at some distance along the runway after touchdown. Category IIIc is totally automatic landing with automatic taxi-ing: no system has yet been certified as being able to provide category IIIc performance. The DHs which obtain for categories IIIa and IIIb vary with airline and aircraft type. A summary of some airlines and aircraft is given, merely for illustration, with no intention of being definitive, in Table 11.5.

The automatic flare control system is arranged to provide a flare trajectory corresponding to that shown in Figure 11.46(a). The trajectory represents the path of the aircraft's wheels as the landing is carried out. During this flare manoeuvre, the flight path angle of the aircraft has to be changed from $-2.5°$ to the positive value which is recommended for touchdown; in other words, during the flare manoeuvre the control system must control the height of the aircraft's c.g. and its rate of change such that the resulting trajectory correponds as nearly as possible to the idealized exponential path shown in Figure 11.46(a), while at the same time causing the aircraft to rotate in a fashion similar to the representation of Figure 11.46(b). The equation which governs the idealized, exponential flare trajectory shown in Figure 11.46(a) is

Table 11.5 Landing categories for different airlines

Airline	*Aircraft types*	*Minimum values*	
		RVR (m)	*DH (ft)*
British Airways	Trident 3	100	12
	Tristar	200	15
	Concorde	250	15
	B-757		
Lufthansa	A300	300	20
Air France	A300	125	25
	Concorde[a]	200	35
Swiss Air[b]	DC-10	200	15
KLM	B-747	300	20
DELTA	Tristar	200	50
TWA	Tristar	200	50

[a] At Paris, Charles de Gaulle, only.
[b] At Zurich only.

$$h = h_0 e^{-t/\tau} \tag{11.84}$$

The distance from h_0 to the point of touchdown depends on the value of h_0, the flare entry height, and the approach speed of the aircraft, U_0. Usually the point of touchdown, which is aimed for, is 300 m from the runway threshold which is the nominal location of the glide path transmitter (see Figure 11.35). Assuming that the airspeed does not change significantly throughout the flare trajectory (a not unreasonable assumption), then:

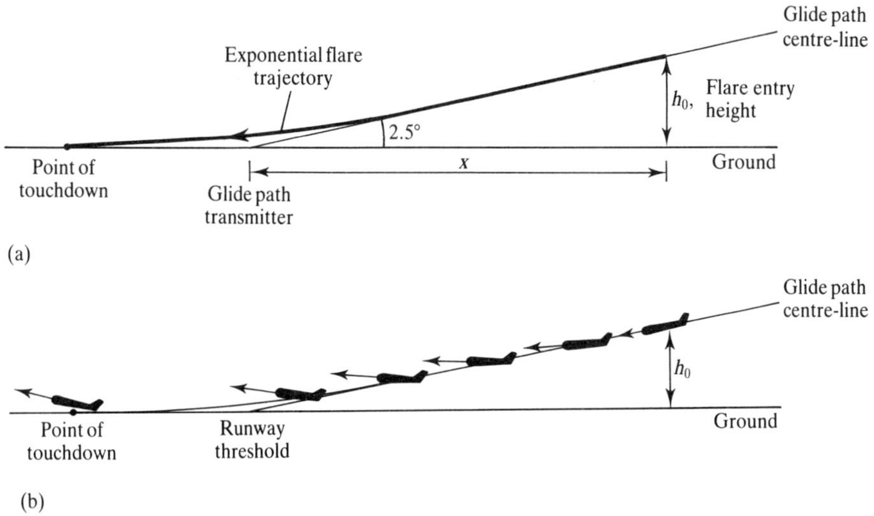

Figure 11.46 (a) Flare trajectory. (b) Rotation of aircraft during flare.

$$\dot{h}_0 = U_0 \sin\gamma = U_0 \sin(-2.5°)$$

$$\simeq \frac{-2.5}{57.3} \times 57.3 = -2.5 \text{ m s}^{-1} \tag{11.85}$$

(assuming landing speed for CHARLIE-1 of 57.3 m s^{-1}). From eq. (11.84) it can easily be shown that:

$$\dot{h} = \frac{-h_0}{\tau} e^{-t/\tau} = \frac{-h}{\tau} \tag{11.86}$$

If the time to complete the exponential flare is taken as 5τ then:

$$(x + 300) = U_0 5\tau = 286.5\tau \tag{11.87}$$

From eq. (11.86):

$$\dot{h}_0 = -h_0/\tau \tag{11.88}$$

hence:

$$-2.5 = -h_0/\tau$$

$$\therefore \quad h_0 = 2.5\tau \tag{11.89}$$

From Figure 11.46(a), $h_0 = x \tan 2.5° = 0.0435x$, therefore:

$$\tau = (0.0435/2.5)x \tag{11.90}$$

Hence, substituting eq. (11.90) in eq. (11.89) yields:

$$x + 300 = (286.5 \times 0.0435/2.5)x$$

$$\therefore \quad x = 75.3 \text{ m} \tag{11.91}$$

$$\therefore \quad h_0 = 3.25 \text{ m} \simeq 10.65 \text{ ft} \tag{11.92}$$

$$\tau = 1.3 \text{ s} \tag{11.93}$$

Hence, the ideal flare manoeuvre is assumed to take 6.5 s to completion. The law which governs the flare trajectory is given by:

$$\dot{h} = -0.77h \tag{11.94a}$$

A block diagram of an automatic flare control system is shown in Figure 11.47.

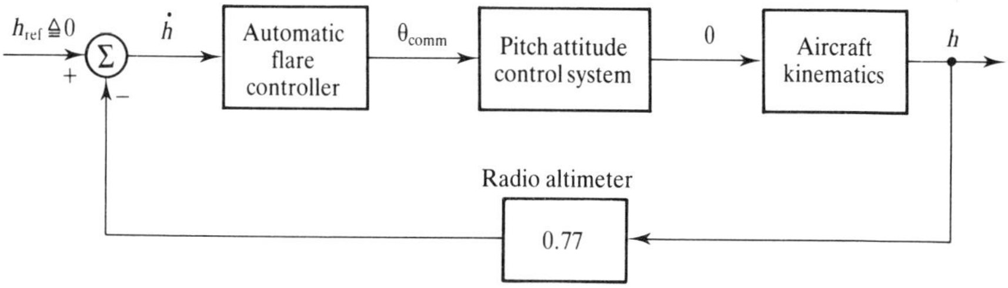

Figure 11.47 Block diagram of automatic flare control.

Note that the pitch attitude control system is used: changing θ results in a change in flight path angle, and consequently, a change in height. Because the heights involved are very low, an accurate measurement of height is necessary for this control system: a low range altimeter is used. The control law used can be simply:

$$\theta_{\text{comm}} = -K_c\dot{h} \tag{11.94b}$$

but, to ensure accuracy, it is usual to add an integral to the proportional term so that:

$$\theta_{\text{comm}} = -K_{c_1}\dot{h} - K_{c_2}h \tag{11.95}$$

The addition of the integral term, and the need to remove, by filtering, any noise from the height signal obtained from the radio altimeter, tends to destabilize the closed loop system. Consequently, it is customary to include a phase advance network with the feedback terms to improve the stability, i.e.:

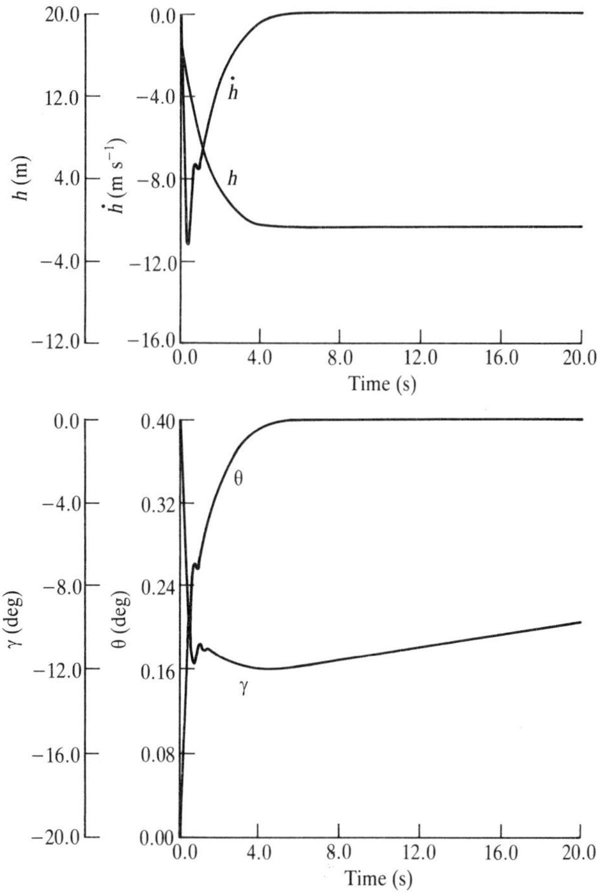

Figure 11.48 Flare trajectory response.

$$\theta_{\text{comm}} = -K_{c_1}\left(1 + \frac{K_{c_2}}{K_{c_1}} \cdot \frac{1}{p}\right)\left(\frac{1 + pT_1}{1 + pT_2}\right)\dot{h} \tag{11.96}$$

where $p = \mathrm{d}/\mathrm{d}t$ and $T_1 \gg T_2$. The results of a digital simulation of such an automatic flare control system for a particular flare entry condition is shown in Figure 11.48. Because the model flare trajectory is exponential it takes infinite time to reach zero height. In the UK, h_{ref} is taken as -1.5 ft, thereby ensuring that the wheels will touch the runway at a time much nearer 5τ s.

Obviously the methods of modern control theory can as easily provide a feedback control law to achieve automatic flare control. Either model following, or solving a LQP, will provide effective feedback control laws.

11.11 A TERRAIN-FOLLOWING CONTROL SYSTEM

11.11.1 Introduction

The terrain following situation is represented in the sketch shown as Figure 11.49. A change of range, the horizontal distance, is denoted by Δx; Δh denotes a change of the height of the aircraft. The reference height (of the obstacle to be cleared) is denoted by h_0 and the flight path angle is denoted by γ, as usual. For the aircraft to be considered, which is a representative (or generic) strike aircraft, there are two controls, namely a commanded change in normal acceleration measured at the aircraft's centre of gravity, $a_{z_{cg}}$, which is denoted u_1, and a change in the rate of opening or closing of the throttle which is denoted by u_2. It is customary in terrain-referenced navigation to use, as a technique for determining the aircraft's position, a comparison of the return signals of the radar

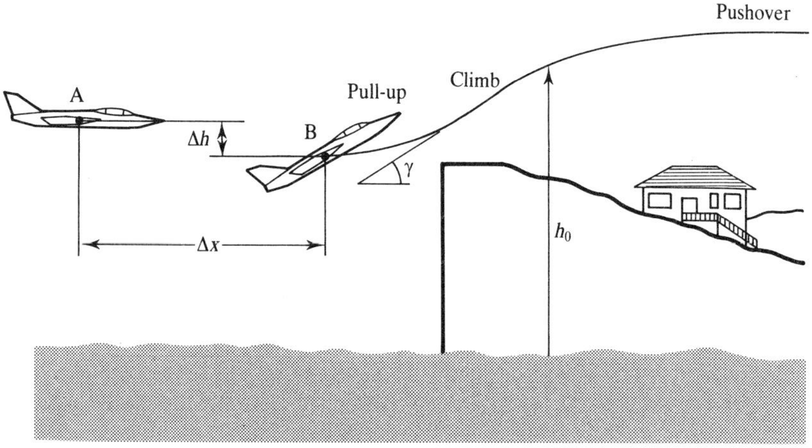

Figure 11.49 Terrain following geometry.

altimeter, (an accurate, short range, vertical radar system), with those obtained from a three-dimensional terrain model which has been digitized and stored on an on-board computer; this complex method is used to avoid, as much as possible, active sensing of the terrain, thereby reducing the chances of being detected. However, there may be unmapped obstacles, so that terrain-following by looking ahead in a map database is not wholly safe and recourse to briefly scanning the terrain ahead using a laser rangefinder, or a forward-looking infra-red (FLIR) system, is often taken. For the purposes of explaining the terrain-following control system it will be assumed that range can be measured by FLIR or laser rangefinder and that changes in height are measured using a radio altimeter.

11.11.2 Equations of Motion

The aircraft's equations of motion, assuming a stability axis system and small perturbations, can be expressed as:

$$\dot{u} = X_u u + X_w w - g\theta + X_{\delta_{th}}\delta_{th} \tag{11.97}$$

$$\dot{w} = Z_u u + Z_w w + U_0\dot{\theta} \tag{11.98}$$

Note that the elevator is not being used as a control. To relate the aircraft's motion at point A to the obstacle, and thereby to design an effective control system to control the aircraft automatically to avoid the obstacle, it is necessary to transform these equations into earth-fixed horizontal and vertical axes. For the linearized situation being studied, the flight path angle at point A is assumed to be zero. Hence:

$$\dot{u}_{\text{horiz}} = \dot{u}_{\text{stab}} \tag{11.99}$$

$$\dot{h} \triangleq U_0\theta - w \tag{11.100}$$

$$\therefore \quad \theta = (\dot{h} + w)/U_0 \tag{11.101}$$

$$\therefore \quad \ddot{h} = U_0\dot{\theta} - \dot{w} = -a_{z_{cg}} \tag{11.102}$$

Therefore:

$$Z_u u + Z_w w + U_0\dot{\theta} - \dot{w} = Z_u u + Z_w + \ddot{h} = 0 \tag{11.103}$$

from which:

$$w = -(Z_u u - \ddot{h})/Z_w \tag{11.104}$$

and

$$\theta = \frac{\dot{h}}{U_0} - \frac{Z_u u}{Z_w U_0} - \frac{\ddot{h}}{U_0 Z_w} \tag{11.105}$$

Therefore:

$$\dot{u} = X_u - \left(X_w\frac{Z_u}{Z_w} + \frac{Z_u}{U_0 Z_w}\,g\right)u - \left(\frac{X_w}{Z_w} - \frac{g}{Z_w U_0}\right)\ddot{h} - \frac{g}{U_0}\dot{h} + X_{\delta_{th}}\delta_{th} \tag{11.106}$$

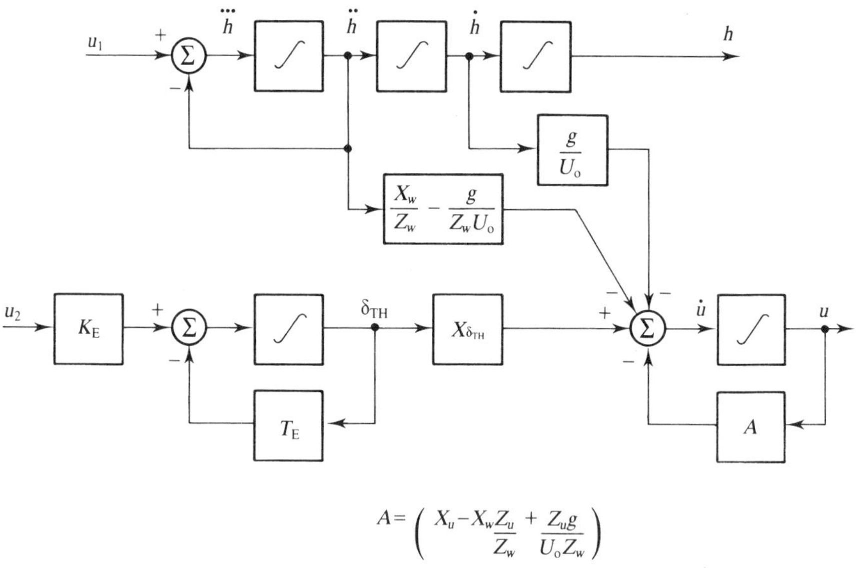

Figure 11.50 Block diagram of terrain following system.

Any change in thrust depends upon u_2, and, as a first approximation, the aircraft engines are represented by a simple, linear model, namely:

$$\delta_{th}(s)/u_2(s) = K_E/(1 + T_E s) \tag{11.107}$$

The system is represented in the block diagram shown as Figure 11.50; K_E represents the gain of the engine and T_E its time constant. From Figure 11.50 it may also be deduced that:

$$\dddot{h} = u_1 - \ddot{h} \tag{11.108}$$

By defining state variables in the way shown in Table 11.6 it is possible to obtain as a mathematical representation of the aircraft dynamics involved in the terrain-following situation a state equation, namely:

$$\dot{\mathbf{x}} = A\mathbf{x} + B\mathbf{u} \tag{11.109}$$

Table 11.6 State variables definition for terrain-following system

State variable	*Motion variable*	*Denotation*
x_1	Vertical acceleration	$\ddot{h}$
x_2	Rate of change of height	$\dot{h}$
x_3	Height	h
x_4	Thrust commanded	δ_{TH_c}
x_5	Change in thrust	δ_{TH}
x_6	Change in airspeed	u

The coefficient and driving matrices for the generic strike aircraft are given as follows:

$$A = \begin{bmatrix} -1 & 0 & 0 & 0 & 0 & 0 \\ 1 & 0 & 0 & 0 & 0 & 0 \\ 0 & 1 & 0 & 0 & 0 & 0 \\ 0 & 0 & 0 & 0 & 0 & 0 \\ 0 & 0 & 0 & 1 & -1 & 0 \\ \dfrac{g}{Z_w U_0} & \dfrac{g}{U_0} & 0 & 0 & 1 & \left\{ X_u + \dfrac{Z_u g}{Z_w U_0} - \dfrac{X_w Z_u}{Z_w} \right\} \end{bmatrix} \tag{11.110}$$

$$B = \begin{bmatrix} 1 & 0 \\ 0 & 0 \\ 0 & 0 \\ 0 & K_E X_{\delta_{th}} \\ 0 & 0 \\ 0 & 0 \end{bmatrix} \tag{11.111}$$

If the output variables are defined in the manner indicated in Table 11.7, then the output matrix, C, is given by:

$$C = \begin{bmatrix} 1 & 0 & 0 & 0 & 0 & 0 \\ 0 & 0 & 1 & 0 & 0 & 0 \\ 0 & 0 & 0 & 1 & -1 & 0 \\ 0 & 0 & 0 & 0 & 1 & 0 \\ 0 & 0 & 0 & 0 & 0 & 1 \end{bmatrix} \tag{11.112}$$

The following parameters and coefficients obtain for the strike aircraft at Mach 0.85 at a height of 40 000 ft.

Table 11.7 Output variables definition for terrain-following system

Output variable		*Output equation*	*Motion variable*
y_1	=	x_1	Vertical acceleration
y_2	=	x_3	Height
y_3	=	$x_4 - x_5$	Thrust rate
y_4	=	x_5	Change in thrust
y_5	=	x_6	Change in airspeed

$$X_{\delta_{th}} = 0.9 \times 10^{-4} \qquad g/Z_w U_0 = -0.088$$

$$K_E = 1010 \qquad g/U_0 \qquad +0.0345$$

$$\left(X_u + \frac{Z_u g}{Z_w U_0} - \frac{X_w Z_u}{Z_w}\right) = -0.0032 \tag{11.113}$$

Hence:

$$A = \begin{bmatrix} -1 & 0 & 0 & 0 & 0 & 0 \\ 1 & 0 & 0 & 0 & 0 & 0 \\ 0 & 1 & 0 & 0 & 0 & 0 \\ 0 & 0 & 0 & 0 & 0 & 0 \\ 0 & 0 & 0 & 1 & -1 & 0 \\ -0.088 & 0.0345 & 0 & 0 & 1 & -0.0032 \end{bmatrix} \tag{11.114}$$

$$B' = \begin{bmatrix} 1 & 0 & 0 & 0 & 0 & 0 \\ 0 & 0 & 0 & 0.09 & 0 & 0 \end{bmatrix} \tag{11.115}$$

The aircraft dynamics are represented in Figure 11.50.

11.11.3 The Control System

By framing the terrain-following problem as a LQP, with an appropriate performance index to be minimized, the feedback control is found as a solution to the LQP.

The performance index is chosen to be:

$$J = \frac{1}{2}\int_0^{\infty} (\mathbf{e}'Q\mathbf{e} + \mathbf{u}'G\mathbf{u})\mathrm{d}t \tag{11.116}$$

where:

$$\mathbf{e}' \triangleq [e_1\ e_2\ e_3\ e_4\ e_5] \tag{11.117}$$

$$\mathbf{e} \triangleq \mathbf{z} - \mathbf{y} \tag{11.118}$$

$\mathbf{z}$ denotes the vector defining the desired flight path. This vector is defined in terms of vertical acceleration, height, required thrust rate, thrust and set speed. These desired inputs have to be available as instantaneous functions of time. Therefore: e_1 denotes the error in the vertical acceleration, e_2 the deviation in the aircraft's height from the desired path, e_3 the error in the thrust rate, e_4 the error in the thrust being developed, and e_5 the deviation in the aircraft's speed from the reference value.

A method of solving such an LQP was discussed in Section 8.4 of Chapter 8, from which it can be learned that the required feedback control is given by:

$$\mathbf{u}^{o} = -G^{-1}B'[K\mathbf{x}(t) + \mathbf{h}(t)] \tag{11.119}$$

where:

$$\dot{\mathbf{h}} = (A - BG^{-1}B'K)'\mathbf{h} - C'Q\mathbf{z} \tag{11.120}$$

with:

$$\mathbf{h}(\infty) \triangleq 0 \tag{11.121}$$

K is the solution of the corresponding ARE. It should be appreciated that the feedforward function, $\mathbf{h}(t)$, involves $\mathbf{z}$ as a forcing function and is obtained by solving eq. (11.120) in 'reverse' time (i.e. by starting at $t = \infty$ and returning to $t = 0$).

To illustrate one particular solution, for the strike aircraft defined by eqs (11.109), (11.112), (11.114) and (11.115), the parameters given in Table 11.8 were used.

Table 11.8 Elements for weighting matrices in LQP

q_{11}	=	9.0			
q_{22}	=	6.0			
q_{33}	=	300.0	g_{11}	=	1.0
q_{44}	=	275.0	g_{22}	=	300.0
q_{55}	=	5.0			

The reference vector, $\mathbf{z}$, is chosen to be:

$$\mathbf{z}' = [0 \;\; 200.0 \;\; 0 \;\; 0 \;\; 0] \tag{11.122}$$

i.e. the aircraft path requires constant speed, no change in thrust, no vertical acceleration and a constant height of 200 ft, i.e. the aircraft encounters a sudden step change in the terrain of 200 ft.

Using matrices A, B, C, Q and G so far given, the resulting control law is given by:

$$\mathbf{u} = \begin{bmatrix} -1.4 & -1.9314 & -0.7743 & -0.06 & -0.0244 & -0.02 \\ -0.0002 & -0.011 & +0.004 & -1.91 & -0.12 & -0.1226 \end{bmatrix}\mathbf{x} + \begin{bmatrix} -0.1 & 0 & 0 & 0 & 0 & 0 \\ 0 & 0 & 0 & -0.0003 & 0 & 0 \end{bmatrix}\mathbf{h} \tag{11.123}$$

The appropriate variables, h_1, h_2, h_3, h_4, h_5, h_6, which make up the vector, $\mathbf{h}$, are shown in Figure 11.51. These represent the solutions to eq. (11.120) for the forcing vector $\mathbf{z}$ given in eq. (11.122). The resulting terrain following response for an initial aircraft height of 300 ft is shown in Figure 11.52; the variables, y_i, correspond to the definitions given in Table 11.6. Note how height (y_2) changes from 300 to 95 ft and then to a peak height of 350 ft before settling to the required height of 200 ft, after 1 minute of flight time. In executing that manoeuvre the

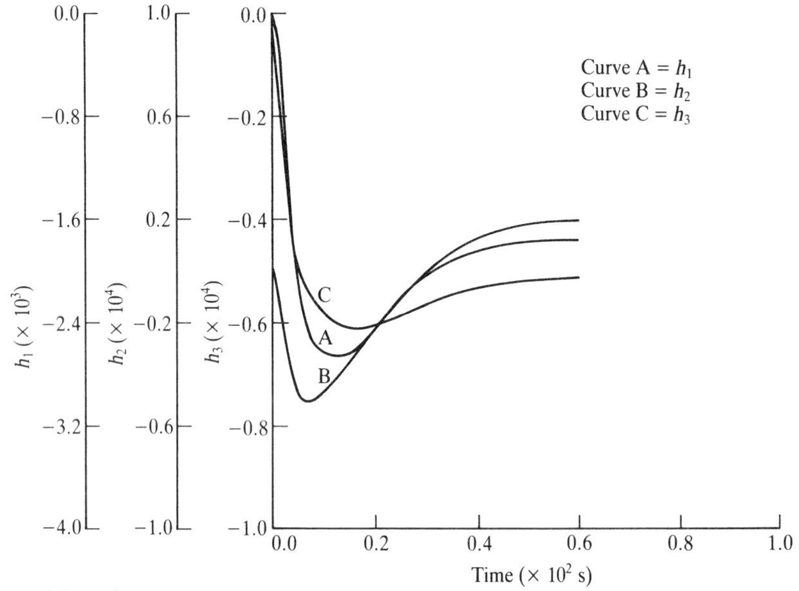

(a)

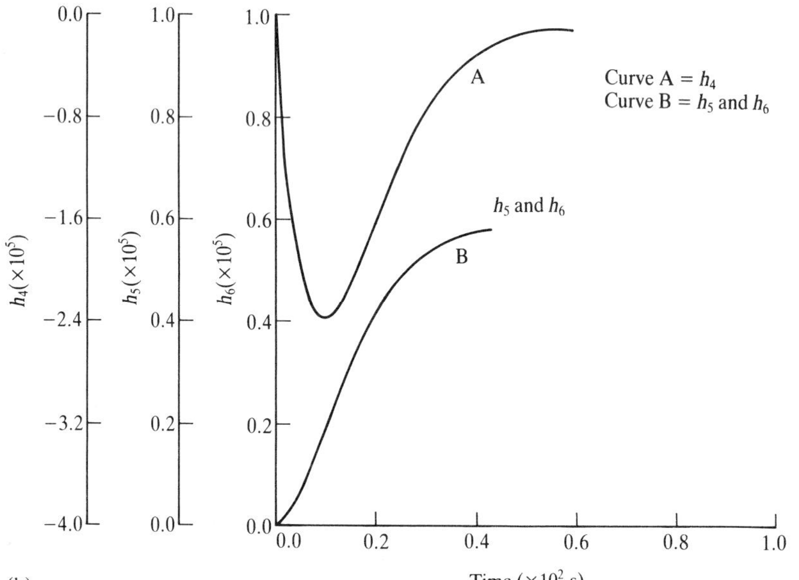

(b)

Figure 11.51 Solution of eq. (11.120) for given **z**.

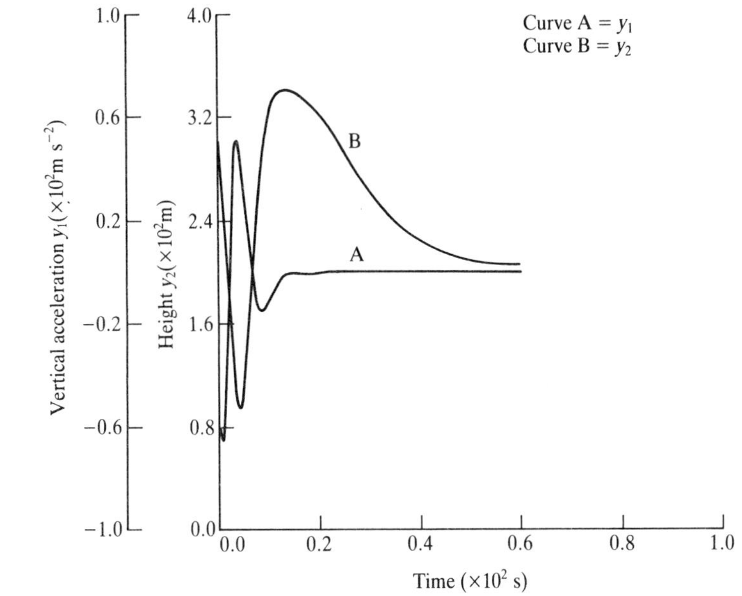

(a)

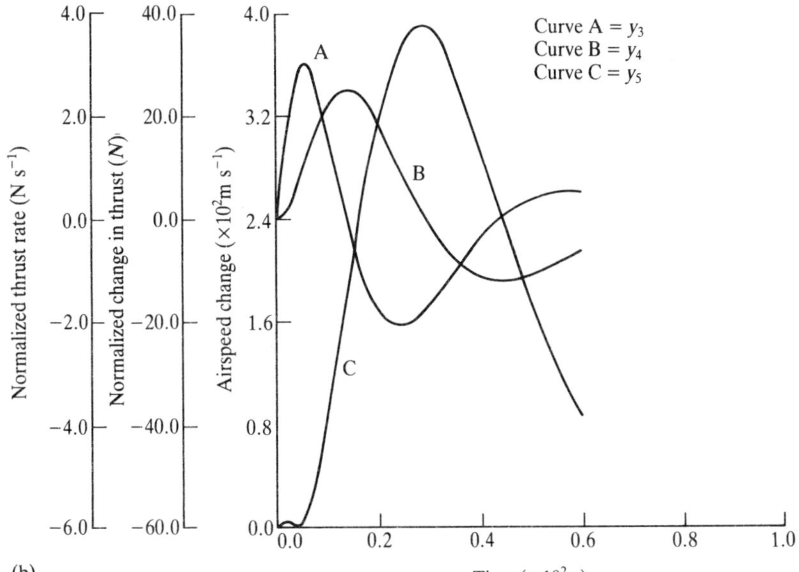

(b)

Figure 11.52 Response of terrain following system.

aircraft has to undergo a $-2g$ to $+2g$ (approximately) change in about 10 s. The airspeed is also required to increase from the equilibrium value of 933.3 to 1 303.33 ft s^{-1}, i.e. the aircraft is required to go supersonic at $t = 30$ s: this is most improbable. To avoid such a speed excursion it is necessary to solve the problem again with a much larger value of q_{55} to penalize such deviations in airspeed.

11.12 CONCLUSIONS

Although the chapter is devoted to path control systems, it is opened with detailed studies of automatic control systems which control aircraft flight variables such as airspeed, Mach number and height, rather than path variables such as heading or bearing to a transmitter. Direction and heading control are treated next, so that they can be used as elements in the automatic tracking systems which depend upon the radio transmissions and appropriate airborne receivers for VOR, ILS localizer and glide path to obtain the appropriate guidance commands for these tracking systems. From a detailed consideration of ILS localizer and ILS glide-path-coupled systems it was the next step to consider automatic landing, including a flare phase, and then finally a terrain following system which allows an aircraft to be guided automatically over ground obstacles.

11.13 EXERCISES

11.1 A business jet aircraft uses a speed hold system to assist the pilot with ILS coupled approaches. The block diagram of the system is shown in Figure 11.53. The following parameters and stability derivatives relate to the aircraft:

$U_0 = 72$ m s^{-1} $\quad$ $W = 98\,065$ N

Maximum thrust $= 54\,655$ N $\quad$ $X_u = -0.0166$

L/D (on approach) $= 8.0$ $\quad$ $Z_u = -0.175$

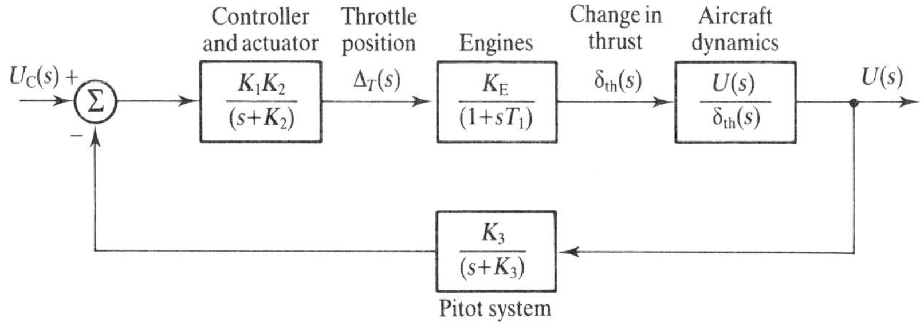

Figure 11.53 Block diagram of a speed control system for Exercise 11.1.

(a) If the system has 20 per cent authority, calculate the gain of the engines, K_E.
(b) If the time constants associated with the engine, the throttle actuator and pitot system are all negligible show that it takes 167 s to achieve a new commanded speed when $K_1 = 1.0$.
(c) If the effective time constant of the engines is 1.0 s, $K_2 = 7.5$ and $K_3 = 5.0$ what is the maximum value that K_1 can take before the closed loop system becomes unstable?

11.2 (a) For the landing approach represented in Figure 11.54 an aircraft is coupled to the glide path via its receiver and its AFCS. For any given departure from the glide path measured by the perpendicular distance, d, show that the angular error of the aircraft from the nominal glide slope increases with the integral of the flight path angle. Assume the airspeed is constant.

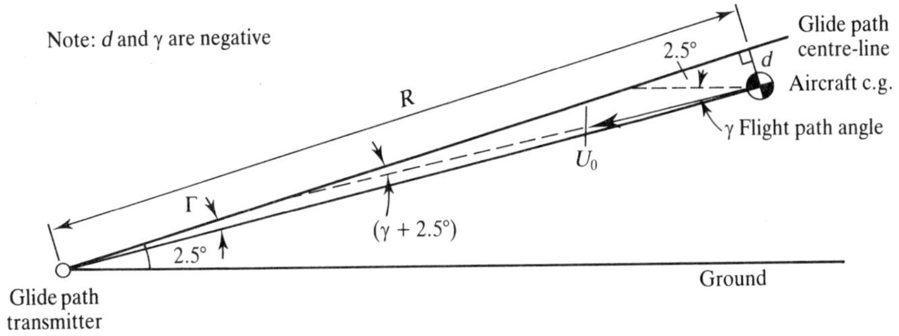

Figure 11.54 Glide path geometry for Exercise 11.2.

(b) The flare manoeuvre, performed at touchdown, results in the rate of descent of an aircraft being decreased in an exponential manner. If an aircraft has a contstant forward speed of 80 m s^{-1} and the distance to the touchdown point from the runway threshold, at which the glide path transmitter is located, is 500 m, calculate the following for a glide path angle of 2.5°:
(i) The approximate time to execute the flare manoeuvre.
(ii) The height of the aircraft at the start of the flare manoeuvre.
(iii) The ground distance travelled during the manoeuvre.
(c) Draw a block diagram of a complete automatic landing system which uses the glide path transmission to measure the departure of the aircraft from the approach trajectory. Show clearly all the significant variables of the system and indicate the function of each block. *Detailed transfer functions need not be shown.*

11.3 The bank angle control system developed in Section 10.3 of Chapter 10 for CHARLIE-2 is used as the inner loop of the direction control system whose block diagram is shown in Figure 11.18. With a value of controller gain, K_Ψ, of 2.0 the response was very slow, the settling time being about 28.0 s, although the response was well damped with no oscillation in the aircraft's heading being evident. It is known that the increasing the value of K_Ψ to 16.0 leads to an oscillatory response, which is unacceptable.
(a) Find a value for the gain, K_Ψ, of the controller of the direction control

system such that the direction response to a step command exhibits no overshoot and settles within 7.0 s.

(b) What is the maximum value which K_Ψ can take before the direction control system becomes unstable?

(c) If the controller gain, K_Ψ, is set to a value of 8.0 determine the response of the system to the sideslip cross-wind profile shown in Figure 11.22.

11.4 A cargo aircraft, with four turboprop engines, has been proposed for use as a gunship for counter-insurgency (COIN) operations. A control system is to be used so that the errors in positioning the aircraft in relation to its target are minimized, even in the presence of head and cross-winds. Three aerodynamic control surfaces – elevator, ailerons and rudder – are to be used. The state variables of the aircraft have been defined as follows:

x_1 change in airspeed, u
x_2 change in angle of attack, α
x_3 change in pitch rate, q
x_4 change in sideslip angle, β
x_5 change in roll rate, ρ
x_6 change in yaw rate, r
x_7 change in bank angle, ϕ
x_8 change in pitch attitude, θ
x_9 target attitude error, ε_{T_h}
x_{10} target elevation error, ε_{T_θ}
x_{11} target azimuth error, ε_{T_Ψ}
x_{12} head-wind component, u_g
x_{13} cross-wind component, v_g
x_{14} integral of target elevation error $\int \varepsilon_{T_\theta} dt$
x_{15} integral of target azimuth error $\int \varepsilon_{T_\Psi} dt$

The controls are defined as:

$$u_1 = \delta_A$$
$$u_2 = \delta_E$$
$$u_3 = \delta_R$$

The corresponding coefficient matrix, A, and the driving matrix, B, are:

$$A = \begin{bmatrix}
-0.013 & 21.35 & -8.17 & -15.11 & 0 & 0 & 0 & -32.2 & 0 & 0 & 0 & 0 & 0 & 0 & 0 \\
-0.001 & -0.95 & 1.0 & 0 & 0 & 0 & 0.05 & 0.007 & 0 & 0 & 0 & 0 & 0 & 0 & 0 \\
0.0003 & -2.53 & -1.57 & 0 & -0.042 & -0.005 & -0.025 & -0.0003 & 0 & 0 & 0 & 0 & 0 & 0 & 0 \\
0.0002 & 0.001 & 0 & -0.1 & 0.03 & -1 & 0.1 & 0.001 & 0 & 0 & 0 & 0 & 0 & 0 & 0 \\
0 & 0 & 0.045 & -0.55 & -1.51 & 0.7 & 0 & 0 & 0 & 0 & 0 & 0 & 0 & 0 & 0 \\
0 & 0 & 0.003 & 0.64 & -0.11 & -0.24 & 0 & 0 & 0 & 0 & 0 & 0 & 0 & 0 & 0 \\
0 & 0 & -0.01 & 0 & 1 & 0.022 & 0 & -0.06 & 0 & 0 & 0 & 0 & 0 & 0 & 0 \\
0 & 0 & 0.883 & 0 & 0 & 0.47 & 0.06 & 0 & 0 & 0 & 0 & 0 & 0 & 0 & 0 \\
0 & -0.26 & 0 & 0.14 & 0 & 0 & -0.004 & 0.3 & 0 & 0 & 0 & 0 & 0 & 0 & 0 \\
0 & 0.023 & 0 & 0.01 & -1 & 0 & -0.001 & 0 & -0.0002 & -0.001 & -0.04 & 0 & 0 & 0 & 0 \\
-0.0001 & 0 & -0.5 & 0 & 0 & -1 & 0.027 & 0 & 0.004 & 0.08 & 0.001 & 0.00001 & 0 & 0 & 0 \\
0 & 0 & 0 & 0 & 0 & 0 & 0 & 0 & 0 & 0 & 0 & -0.058 & 0 & 0 & 0 \\
0 & 0 & 0 & 0 & 0 & 0 & 0 & 0 & 0 & 0 & 0 & -0.06 & -0.0001 & 0 & 0 \\
0 & 0 & 0 & 0 & 0 & 0 & 0 & 0 & 1 & 0 & 0 & 0 & 0 & -0.001 & 0 \\
0 & 0 & 0 & 0 & 0 & 0 & 0 & 0 & 0 & 0 & 1 & 0 & 0 & 0 & -0.0002
\end{bmatrix}$$

$$B = \begin{bmatrix} 0 & 0 & 0 \\ 0 & -0.145 & 0 \\ 0 & -2.993 & 0 \\ 0 & 0 & 0.035 \\ -0.8 & 0 & 0.28 \\ -0.022 & 0 & -0.75 \\ 0 & 0 & 0 \\ 0 & 0 & 0 \\ 0 & 0 & 0 \\ 0 & 0 & 0 \\ 0 & 0 & 0 \\ 0 & 0 & 0 \\ 0 & 0 & 0 \\ 0 & 0 & 0 \\ 0 & 0 & 0 \end{bmatrix}$$

(a) If state and control weighting matrices Q and G, respectively, are:

$Q = \text{diag}[0.1\ 0.1\ 1.0\ 0.1\ 0.1\ 0.1\ 10.0\ 10.0\ 10.0\ 10.0\ 10.0\ 0.01\ 0.01\ 100\ 100]$

$G = \text{diag}[1.0\ 1.0\ 1.0]$

for a performance index:

$$J = \tfrac{1}{2}\int_0^\infty \{\mathbf{x}'Q\mathbf{x} + \mathbf{u}'G\mathbf{u}\}dt$$

determine the corresponding feedback gain matrix.

(b) Determine the eigenvalues of the closed loop system. Compare these with the values corresponding to the uncontrolled aircraft. Comment upon whether the closed loop system has been beneficial in making the cargo aircraft an effective COIN aircraft.

(c) Does the closed loop system reduce the target errors in response to a cross-wind?

11.5 The following stability derivatives relate to a VTOL aircraft in hovering motion:

$X_u = -0.06 \qquad M_u = 0.001$

$Z_w = -0.02 \qquad M_q = -0.05$

$Z_{\delta_T} = -36.0 \qquad M_{\delta_T} = 0.2$

If a feedback control law, $\delta_T = h_{comm} - 2.78 \times 10^{-6}h$ is used to control the aircraft, show that its change of height is characterized by a critically damped transient mode. At what time after a step input of h_{comm} does the rate of change of height reach its maximum value?

11.6 The block diagram of a speed control system used with the aircraft described in Exercise 2.9 is shown in Figure 11.55.

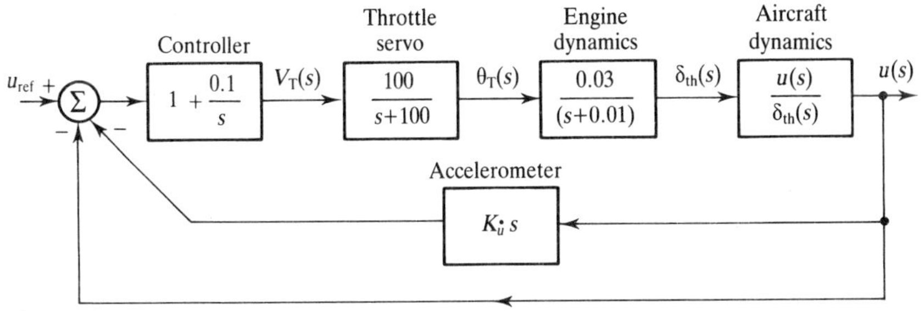

Figure 11.55 Block diagram of a speed control system for Exercise 11.6.

Making use of appropriate numerical approximations determine the maximum permissible value of accelerometer sensitivity for stability of the closed loop speed control system.

11.7 The glide slope receiver in the aircraft CHARLIE measures the angular deviation of the aircraft from the glide slope. The receiver is mounted in-line with the aircraft's c.g., but directly below the pilot.

(a) Determine the transfer function $\gamma'(s)/\theta(s)$ which is appropriate to this location of the receiver.

(b) Show how Figure 11.40 must be modified to take account of this new location of the receiver.

(c) Is the location of the receiver beneficial, or otherwise, to the performance of the coupled system?

11.8 For BRAVO-3, using the system represented in Figure 11.5 with $K_q = 1.5$ and an accelerometer time constant of 0.5 s, find a suitable value for the gain of the controller such that the Mach hold system is effective. What happens to the system's performance if the accelerometer fails in service?

11.9 Design a flight control system, suitable for localizer coupling, for the aircraft ALPHA's approach. It can be assumed that over the approach phase the aircraft speed is constant. At what range from the runway threshold will your system become unstable? Show how your system performs in the presence of a constant cross-wind from the right (i.e. from starboard) of 20 knots.

11.10 The VOR-coupled control system, represented by the block diagram of Figure 11.32, uses the directional control system of Figure 11.18 as its inner loop. The value of gain chosen for the directional controller was 2.0. Use the value of K_Ψ, evaluated in answer to Exercise 11.3(a), with the system of Figure 11.32, when the value of the gain of the VOR coupling unit is chosen to be 25.0 and the value of the gain associated with the integral term is 0.025. Compare the response obtained with that shown in Figure 11.33. Which is better? Suppose K_{c_I} is increased to 0.25. What is the likely effect upon the performance of the VOR-coupled control system? Is the integral term necessary?

11.14 NOTES

1. 'All-weather' is merely a euphemism used in aviation circles to describe the bad weather which the British habitually enjoy.
2. ILS is being replaced by MLS, the microwave landing system, which involves the use of transmission frequencies which avoid those errors which limit the ILS. However, the principles involved in providing the guidance signals are sufficiently similar for the account being given here based on the ILS to suffice.
3. Although it is not shown in the diagram, the speed control system (of the type represented in Figure 11.9) is assumed to operate and it has the following parameter values: $K_E = 30\,000$, $K_{c_u} = 3.0$, $K_{u_I} = 0.4$.

11.15 REFERENCES

BLAKELOCK, J. 1965. *Automatic Control of Aircraft and Missiles.* New York: Wiley.

KAYTON, M. and W.R. FREID. 1969. *Avionics Navigation Systems.* New York: Wiley.

McRUER, D.T., I.L. ASHKENAS and D.C. GRAHAM. 1973. *Aircraft Dynamics and Automatic Flight Control.* Princeton University Press.

ROSKAM, J. 1979. *Airplane Flight Dynamics.* Kansas: Roskam Publishing.

12

Active Control Systems

12.1 INTRODUCTION

Although there is now available a large amount of published material relating to active control technology (ACT), which is being added to continuously, there are few satisfactory definitions of what ACT is. It has been called an extension of conventional feedback control systems which provides a multi-input, multi-output capability to allow full exploitation of the complete six degrees of freedom of an aircraft (Ostgaard and Swortzel, 1977). A later definition proposed, however, that ACT should be considered to be 'the use of motion feedback control systems, in the absence of passive design features, to achieve specific design objectives' (Roughton, 1978). Neither definition is complete. In this textbook, it is proposed to use a definition which is based upon those earlier versions, namely:

> Active control technology is the use of a multivariable AFCS to improve the manoeuvrability, the dynamic flight characteristics and, often, the structural dynamic properties of an aircraft by simultaneously driving an appropriate number of control surfaces and auxiliary force or moment generators in such a fashion that either the loads which the aircraft would have experienced as a result of its motion without an ACT system are much reduced, or the aircraft produces a degree of manoeuvrability beyond the capability of a conventional aircraft.

The purpose of ACT is to provide AFCS with the additional means to increase the performance and operational flexibility of an aircraft. Modern aircraft are designed to attain maximum aerodynamic efficiency with considerably reduced structural weight, an achievement owing much to the use of new materials. The current design requirements for many aircraft, and for the missions they are to perform, are such that the resulting configurations are considerably changed from the familiar designs of earlier times. In meeting the new requirements, the designs have typically employed the following: thin, lifting surfaces, a long, slender fuselage, a low mass fraction structure, a design admitting a high level of stress, and low load factors.

These features have resulted in aircraft which are of the required structural lightness, but which, consequently, exhibit considerable flexibility. Such aircraft can develop structural displacement and accelerations of large amplitude as a result of the structural deflections and the rigid body motion of the aircraft. The structural deflections can arise either as a result of some manoeuvre command from the pilot, or from a guidance or weapons system, or from encountering atmospheric disturbances. The structural vibration which results can impair the life of the airframe because of the repeated high levels of stress and the peak loads to which the aircraft is subjected. With such new aircraft, a new class of flight control problems has emerged, including: the need to minimize the loads experienced by the aircraft, either completely or at just a few specific locations; the particular requirement for transport aircraft to precisely control the location of an aircraft's c.g. over its entire flight envelope; the suppression of flutter; the reduction of the amplitude of the disturbed motion of an aircraft which is caused when it encounters turbulence. To solve such problems by using modifications of the components of the airframe, such as increasing the damping or stiffness of the structure, or modifying the planform and the size of the conventional control surfaces, usually by increasing them, even in the few cases where there are feasible solutions, would impose severe economic penalties upon the aircraft's operation, mostly in terms of reduced payload, or reduced performance in terms of range or speed. Consequently, ACT was proposed to meet the evolving demands for more effective and efficient aircraft.

12.2 ACT CONTROL FUNCTIONS

It is generally agreed that the most beneficial effects of using ACT will be secured by using any, or all, of these six ACT functions: relaxed static stability (RSS), manoeuvre load control (MLC), ride control (RC), flutter mode control (FMC), gust load alleviation (GLA), and fatigue reduction (FR).

12.2.1 RSS

By relaxing the requirement for static stability it is possible to achieve better dynamic response to the aerodynamic controls and to reduce the trim drag and thereby enhance the aircraft's manoeuvrability. It is necessary when doing this to restore the aircraft's dynamic stability and its handling qualities by using an ACT system. When the need for static stability is relaxed, the empennage required on the aircraft is smaller: an empennage is sized to provide the aircraft's trim and manoeuvre requirements. With a small empennage, some savings in the weight of the aircraft are possible. An SAS for an aircraft with RSS – aircraft BRAVO of Appendix B – is discussed in detail in Section 9.4 of Chapter 9. By using RSS on an aircraft it becomes feasible to provide 'carefree manoeuvring'; sometimes the RSS function is an element of an aircraft's 'enhanced manoeuvre demand' systems.

12.2.2 MLC

MLC is a technique of redistributing the lift generated by the wing of an aircraft during a manoeuvre. By the symmetrical deflection of control surfaces, mounted at proper stations on the trailing edge of the wing, in response to load factor commands, it is possible to reduce the increments in the stress by arranging for an inboard shift of the centre of lift of the wing. This shift also reduces the bending moment at the wing root, which is a major factor in the fatigue life of a wing. MLC is sometimes referred to as active lift distribution control (ALDC), or a structural mode control (SMC) system, which it is called on the USAF bomber, the B-1. Occasionally such systems are provided simply to ensure that any loads which arise from the execution of some particular manoeuvre do not exceed some specific limit.

12.2.3 RC

The purpose of the RC system is to improve ride comfort for the crew or passengers by the reduction of objectionable levels of acceleration which are caused by the rigid body and/or structural motion of the aircraft. For an aircraft, such as a bomber, an RC system is required to reduce the accelerations only at the crew stations, but for a transport aircraft carrying passengers the requirement may be for a reduction in accelerations to be achieved over the whole length of the passenger cabin. For an interdiction aircraft, carrying out high speed strike missions at low level, the principal need is to prevent the pilot's ability to track his target from being impaired by the accelerations at the cockpit which are a result of flying in turbulence. Obviously the mission requirements considerably influence the purpose and the design of the system used to improve an aircraft's ride characteristics.

12.2.4 GLA

GLA is a technique which controls the contribution of the rigid body and the bending modes to the complete dynamic response of an aircraft to a gust encounter. Its purpose is to reduce the transient peak loads which arise from such encounters. Since their purpose is similar in nature to that of RC, the two functions are often achieved by a single system. Moreover, a successful GLA system will contribute to the reduction in structural loading so that MLC and GLA are quite likely to be used in conjunction with each other.

12.2.5 FMC

By properly controlled deflection of certain auxiliary control surfaces it is possible to damp the flutter modes of an aircraft without having to increase structural weight. There may also be an attendant increase in flutter speed. The principal benefit of FMC in fighter and strike aircraft is a resulting increase in the permissible wing-mounted stores which can be carried within the same speed envelope. The benefit for bomber and transport aircraft cannot be so direct, and it may be limited on those aircraft to a possible reduction in the weight of the wing. Of all the ACT functions, FMC is the most sensitive to configuration, particularly to planform and thickness of the wing.

12.2.6 FR

To reduce the rate of fatigue damage, FR systems minimize the amplitude and/or the number of transient bending cycles to which the structure may be subjected during flight in turbulence. This ACT function has not yet been implemented physically on any aircraft, and, at present, its objective is achieved indirectly as a result of the combined action of the other five ACT functions. It remains, however, as potentially one of the most economically advantageous ACT functions.

12.3 SOME BENEFITS EXPECTED FROM ACT

The potential benefits from applying ACT functions depend upon several aircraft parameters. However, the only function which will provide its benefits independent of the speed range of the aircraft is ride control. GLA, MLC and FR will be particularly beneficial for STOL aircraft because of the low wing-loading which such aircraft have, presuming that the STOL aircraft being considered are provided with aerodynamic rather than propulsive lift. To obtain the performance needed for commercial operation, supersonic transport aircraft must operate over a very wide range of dynamic pressure which greatly affects the handling qualities. Some form of stability augmentation is required. If RSS is decided upon to obtain a reduction in drag, thereby conserving the fuel consumption, the SAS is required to provide the dynamic stability in addition to improving the handling qualities. SST, and modern bombers such as the B-1, have a long slender fuselage, the forward position of which acts as a cantilevered beam mounted forward of the stiff structure. This configuration results in the lateral and vertical accelerations in the forebody having natural frequencies of about 1 Hz which is a vibration frequency causing considerable discomfort to passengers and crew alike. Hence, on such aircraft, an RC system is needed. On the B-1, the SMC system also acts as a ride control system at low altitudes; the function is referred to in this aircraft as a low altitude ride control system. The cruise phase of flight usually takes place at high altitude, over long stage lengths. Consequently, new transport aircraft have their configurations designed particularly for energy conservation. High aspect ratio wings and RSS will be employed to effect some drag reduction. As a result, the aircraft's handling qualities in high altitude turbulence will be poor and, therefore, a GLA system will be required. The principal area in which the many benefits of ACT will be seen to greatest advantage is that of aerial combat. Some present-day fighters require co-ordination of eight to eleven control surfaces to provide the aircraft with the conventional four degrees of freedom. With ACT, additional controls are required to provide six degrees of freedom, even though the two extra degrees of freedom in translation will inevitably be limited. Figure 12.1 represents the six degrees of freedom which ACT can provide. The extra degrees of freedom in translation provide that improvement in manoeuvrability which can lead to superior combat tactics.

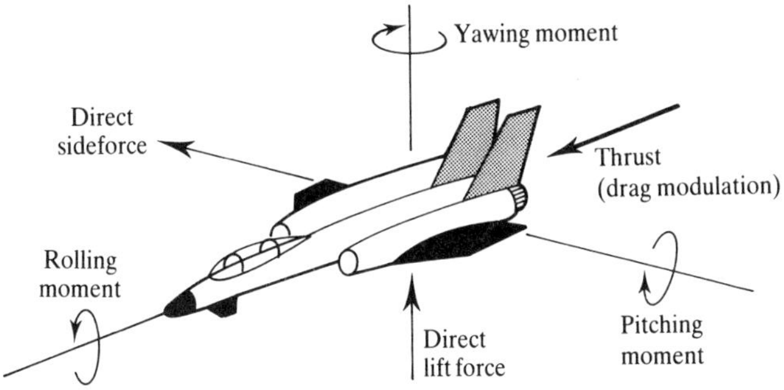

Figure 12.1 Six degrees of freedom of an aircraft.

12.4 GUST ALLEVIATION

12.4.1 Introduction

In Chapter 5 it is pointed out that the air through which an aircraft flies is constantly in turbulent motion. Consequently, the aircraft's aerodynamic forces and moments fluctuate about their equilibrium (trimmed) values. These changes cause the aircraft to heave up or down, to pitch its nose up or down, to roll about the axis OX, or to yaw from side to side about the aircraft's heading. These motions result in accelerations which are experienced by passengers and crew as unpleasant effects. To reduce these accelerations it is necessary to cancel the gust effects by other forces.

The general principle of gust alleviation is that specially located sensors provide motion signals to a controller which causes appropriate deflections of suitable control surfaces to generate additional aerodynamic forces and moments to cancel the accelerations caused by the gust. Several methods of achieving such alleviation have been proposed – almost since the beginning of manned flight – since early aircraft were particularly susceptible to being upset by gusts. One of the earliers pioneers of flight, Lillienthal, was killed in 1896 when his glider was so upset. A patent was granted in 1914 in the USA to a Mr A. Sprater for a 'stabilizing device for flying machines'. The device was claimed 'to counteract the disturbance and to prevent it from having an injurious effect on the stability of the machine'. In 1915 the very first NACA report by Hunsaker and Wilson (1915) contains a reference to the problem. Continual reference to the problem was made by early British workers in aircraft stability and control from 1914 up to the Second World War. The foundation papers which established the basis for suitable mathematical representations of turbulence were published by Von Karman (1937) and Taylor (1937). There was a proposal for a gust alleviation system in 1938 by a Frenchman which was eventually flight tested in the USA in 1954.

In 1949, the Bristol Brabazon aircraft (then the largest in the world) was fitted from the design stage with a GLA/MLC system whose purposes was to reduce the loads induced as a result of wing bending. Because the GLA/MLC system was provided, the wing structure of the prototype aircraft was 20 per cent weaker than the design figure required to meet the specified discrete gust levels (with a GLA system). The Brabazon system used symmetrical deflections of the ailerons in response to signals from a gust vane mounted on the aircraft's nose. The system was not proven in flight before the project was scrapped in 1953. A series of flight tests with other aircraft types were carried out in the USA in the period 1950–1956 and experiments were carried out from 1955 to 1960 by the RAE in England using an AVRO Lancaster.

All these attempts, except the Brabazon, were concerned solely with alleviating the effects of gusts on the rigid body motion. In every case, however, the results achieved were unsatisfactory. In the case of the RAE experiments with the Lancaster, a considerable loss of stability was observed which arose as a result of the larger pitching moment which was created by the symmetrical aileron deflection. This moment led to a decrease in the effectiveness of the alleviation system at large gust gradient distances.

The American systems, like the Brabazon system, depended upon a gust vane to detect the aircraft's entry into the gust field by sensing either changes of pressure or a change of direction of the relative wind. They were unsatisfactory chiefly because it was not appreciated that any gust has components normal to the plane of symmetry of an aircraft and because secondary effects, such as changes in flight condition, downwash effects on the tailplane, the time delay between the wing's encountering the gust and then the tail, were not considered. Thus, gust vane systems tried, in effect, to provide control correction in advance of the actual gust and were really feed forward systems. They were unsuccessful because the control system could not be designed then to provide the necessary speed of response, nor made insensitive enough to the secondary effects mentioned earlier. In many of these tests, the operation of the GLA systems actually caused a deterioration in the gust behaviour of the aircraft to which they were fitted.

The fundamental problem with GLA systems is that, when a gust has been sensed, the system cannot take action until it is too late to achieve much effect. These defects were noted and avoided by Attwood *et al.* (1961) who proposed in their patent application of 1955, which was granted in 1961, that the GLA should sense linear and angular accelerations and should use auxiliary control surfaces to produce the countering forces and moments required to minimize the unwanted accelerations.

Some further developments continued from that work including, notably, the prototype UK fighter-bomber, the TSR-2, which depended upon augmented static directional stability to reduce its sensitivity to side gusts in its high speed, low altitude role; and also the prototype American bomber, the XB-70. It was an event in 1964, however, which accelerated the present interest in gust alleviation. A B-52E bomber of the Strategic Air Command of the USAF encountered severe turbulence, with an estimated peak velocity of 35 m s^{-1}, on a low-level mission over territory in the western USA. Approximately 6 s after penetrating the gust field its yaw damper was saturated and the response of the then 'unaugmented' rigid body dynamics was such that about 80 per cent of the fin broke off. This event led in 1965 to an extensive flight development programme, known as the load alleviation and mode suppression (LAMS) program, being carried out by the USAF and its contractors. The results of the programme was presented in the report of Burris and Bender (1969). The work was extended in 1973 and the GLA function was used in the RCS which was developed to provide improved ride quality (Stockdale and Poyneer, 1973).

12.4.2 Gust Alleviation Control

The amplitude of the response caused by the structural vibration excited by turbulence may be reduced if either the amount of energy transferred from the gust to the bending modes is reduced or any energy which is absorbed by the bending modes is rapidly dissipated. Both methods should be employed simultaneously for optimal effectiveness. To reduce the energy being transferred requires a countering moment (or force) from the deflection of some control surface. The method requires an accurate knowledge of the aircraft's stability derivatives. Of course, these derivatives change with flight condition, with mass and the mass distribution of the aircraft, with changes in dynamic pressure, etc. Consequently, the aircraft dynamics are known too imperfectly to admit of perfect cancellation of any gust forces or moments. Once the energy has been absorbed, its dissipation can be controlled by augmenting the damping of the elastic modes. It is difficult, however, to achieve a sufficient increase in structural damping by such a method if the structural modes are close in frequency, for then they are usually closely coupled, and there is then a periodic exchange of energy between the modes which corresponds to the behaviour of very lightly damped structures.

To actively suppress the bending of a structure it is necessary to be able to sense either the structural displacements or the associated rates of change. It is possible to sense these quantities to provide motion signals for feedback in the GLA control system. However, as it had been discovered in the early GLA tests, the control surfaces suitable for controlling the rigid body motion are unsuitable for controlling the aircraft's bending modes and, consequently, auxiliary control surfaces are required.

12.4.3 Ride Quality

Almost every modern aircraft has an SAS which is used to control its rigid body motion, and for which the locations of the sensors are carefully chosen to pick up the minimum of spurious signals from any structural motion. Such SASs do not control or deliberately alter the structural vibration of the aircraft. Yet it should be remembered that such SASs do provide a large amount of reduction of the unwanted motion produced by an aircraft in response to any gust disturbance. However, from operational records and simulations, it is known that those symmetrical structural modes with the lowest natural frequencies contribute substantially to the levels of acceleration which are present at various points of the fuselage, such as the cockpit. For example, it has been found that at the crew stations on the B-52E, without any SAS, 60 per cent of the total normal acceleration measured at those locations could be attributed to the first three longitudinal bending modes; of the remaining 40 per cent, three-quarters was due to rigid body motion and the other quarter was caused by the structural modes of highter frequency. If the accelerations are unacceptable, resulting in discomfort for passengers or crew or impairment of the pilot's ability to fly, then an RC system is needed to reduce the accelerations being experienced at particular locations. One of the best methods of designing such a system is to solve the LQP, discussed in Chapter 8, by minimizing the ride discomfort index dealt with in Section 6.6 of Chapter 6.

12.5 LOAD ALLEVIATION SYSTEM FOR A BOMBER AIRCRAFT

12.5.1 The Aircraft Dynamics

The differential equations which represent the B-52E heavy bomber can be expressed as:

$$\dot{\mathbf{x}} = A\mathbf{x} + B\mathbf{u} \tag{12.1}$$

$$\dot{\mathbf{x}}_1 = A_1\mathbf{x}_1 + B_1\mathbf{u}_1 \tag{12.2}$$

where $\mathbf{x}$ represents the state vector relating to longitudinal motion, and $\mathbf{x}_1$ is that relating to lateral motion. In deriving the longitudinal equations it was assumed that the rigid body motion of the aircraft was adequately represented by the short period approximation. Included in both sets of equations were the dynamics associated with five structural bending modes: in the longitudinal set there were modes 1, 5, 7, 8 and 12, and in the lateral set they were 1, 2, 3, 9 and 10. The control inputs which were employed for longitudinal motion were the deflections of the elevator and a horizontal canard; for lateral motion the three control inputs were the deflections of aileron, rudder and vertical canard. For longitudinal motion, the state vector $\mathbf{x}$ is defined as:

$$\mathbf{x}' = [\alpha \; q \; \lambda_1 \; \dot{\lambda}_1 \; \lambda_5 \; \dot{\lambda}_5 \; \lambda_7 \; \dot{\lambda}_7 \; \lambda_8 \; \dot{\lambda}_8 \; \lambda_{12} \; \dot{\lambda}_{12}] \tag{12.3}$$

α and q have their usual meanings of angle of attack and pitch rate, respectively. λ_i represents the vertical displacement of the ith bending mode. The corresponding control vector, $\mathbf{u}$, is defined as:

$$\mathbf{u} = \begin{bmatrix} \delta_E \\ \delta_{c_{hor}} \end{bmatrix} \tag{12.4}$$

For lateral motion, the corresponding vectors are defined as:

$$\mathbf{x}_1' = [v \; p \; r \; \phi \; \psi \; \gamma_1 \; \dot{\gamma}_1 \; \gamma_2 \; \dot{\gamma}_2 \; \gamma_3 \; \dot{\gamma}_3 \; \gamma_9 \; \dot{\gamma}_9 \; \gamma_{10} \; \dot{\gamma}_{10}] \tag{12.5}$$

$$\mathbf{u}_1 = \begin{bmatrix} \delta_A \\ \delta_R \\ \delta_{c_v} \end{bmatrix} \tag{12.6}$$

The corresponding matrices A and B and A_1 and B_1 are defined in eqs (12.7) to (12.10) (given in Figures 12.2 and 12.3).

Since load alleviation is being considered, normal and lateral acceleration are motion variables of primary concern. If the measured normal acceleration at the pilot's station, location A, is taken as the output variable, y, it is easy to show, from the material presented in Section 2.7 of Chapter 2, that:

$$y \triangleq a_{z_A} = C_A\mathbf{x} + D_A\mathbf{u} \tag{12.11}$$

where the state vector in (12.11) comprises solely the short period motion variables.

$$A = \begin{bmatrix}
-1.6 & 1 & -1.81 & -0.18 & 0 & 0 & 0 & 0 & 0 & 0 & 0 & 0 \\
6.57 & -2.45 & -1.81 & 1.18 & 0 & 0 & 0 & 0 & 0 & 0 & 0 & 0 \\
0 & 0 & 0 & 1 & 0 & 0 & 0 & 0 & 0 & 0 & 0 & 0 \\
-7.2 & -0.45 & -56.82 & -5.53 & 0 & 0 & 0 & 0 & 0 & 0 & 0 & 0 \\
0 & 0 & 0 & 0 & 0 & 1 & 0 & 0 & 0 & 0 & 0 & 0 \\
-1.35 & 0.25 & 0 & 0 & -231.52 & -1.71 & 0 & 0 & 0 & 0 & 0 & 0 \\
0 & 0 & 0 & 0 & 0 & 0 & 0 & 1 & 0 & 0 & 0 & 0 \\
-2.1 & 0.24 & 0 & 0 & 0 & 0 & -409.0 & -2.7 & -10.71 & -0.52 & 0 & 0 \\
0 & 0 & 0 & 0 & 0 & 0 & 0 & 0 & 0 & 1 & 0 & 0 \\
0.31 & 0.06 & 0 & 0 & 0 & 0 & -1.24 & -0.18 & -390.1 & -0.47 & 0 & 0 \\
0 & 0 & 0 & 0 & 0 & 0 & 0 & 0 & 0 & 0 & 0 & 1 \\
-3.74 & 0.13 & 0 & 0 & 0 & 0 & 0 & 0 & 0 & 0 & -1466.1 & -1.75
\end{bmatrix} \tag{12.7}$$

$$B' = \begin{bmatrix}
-0.07 & 3.73 & 0 & 0.57 & 0 & -0.47 & 0 & -0.58 & 0 & -0.11 & 0 & 0.93 \\
-0.006 & -0.28 & 0 & 0.02 & 0 & -0.054 & 0 & -0.053 & 0 & -0.035 & 0 & 0.1
\end{bmatrix} \tag{12.8}$$

Figure 12.2 Matrices A and B.

$$A_1 = \begin{bmatrix} -0.18 & 0.12 & 171.0 & 9.81 & 0 & 0 & 0 & 0 & 0 & 0 & 0 & -103.6 & 5.5 & 0 & 0 \\ -0.02 & -2.26 & -0.47 & -0.01 & 0 & 0 & 0 & 0 & 0 & 0 & 0 & 34.41 & 1.79 & 0 & 0 \\ -0.02 & -0.03 & -0.54 & -0.01 & 0 & 0 & 0 & 0 & 0 & 0 & 0 & -15.57 & 0.02 & 0 & 0 \\ 0 & 1 & 0 & 0 & 0 & 0 & 0 & 0 & 0 & 0 & 0 & 0 & 0 & 0 & 0 \\ 0 & 0 & 1 & 0 & 0 & 0 & 0 & 0 & 0 & 0 & 0 & 0 & 0 & 0 & 0 \\ 0 & 0 & 0 & 0 & 0 & 0 & 1 & 0 & 0 & 0 & 0 & 0 & 0 & 0 & 0 \\ -0.01 & -7.92 & -10.73 & -0.01 & 0 & -97.67 & -1.9 & 0 & 0 & 0 & 0 & 0.06 & -0.003 & 0 & 0 \\ 0 & 0 & 0 & 0 & 0 & 0 & 0 & 0 & 1 & 0 & 0 & 0 & 0 & 0 & 0 \\ -0.003 & -32.3 & -1.63 & -0.001 & 0 & 0 & 0 & -151.0 & -3.57 & 150.1 & 3.73 & 0.015 & -0.001 & 0 & 0 \\ 0 & 0 & 0 & 0 & 0 & 0 & 0 & 0 & 0 & 0 & 1 & 0 & 0 & 0 & 0 \\ 0.004 & 0.17 & 0.11 & 0.002 & 0 & 0 & 0 & 8.71 & 0.6 & -160.0 & -1.54 & -0.02 & 0.001 & 0 & 0 \\ 0 & 0 & 0 & 0 & 0 & 0 & 0 & 0 & 0 & 0 & 0 & 0 & 1 & 0 & 0 \\ 0.003 & 0.11 & 0.14 & 0.001 & 0 & 0 & 0 & 0 & 0 & 0 & 0 & -532.6 & -1.72 & 3.25 & 0.36 \\ 0 & 0 & 0 & 0 & 0 & 0 & 0 & 0 & 0 & 0 & 0 & 0 & 0 & 0 & 1 \\ -0.02 & -0.06 & -0.51 & -0.01 & 0 & 0 & 0 & 0 & 0 & 0 & 0 & 1.64 & 0.93 & -930.3 & -2.3 \end{bmatrix} \quad (12.9)$$

$$B_1' = \begin{bmatrix} 0.4 & -0.8 & 0.06 & 0 & 0 & 0 & -2.14 & 0 & -0.4 & 0 & -0.12 & 0 & 0.01 & 0 & -0.02 \\ -7.0 & -0.22 & -4.31 & 0 & 0 & 0 & 23.7 & 0 & 4.32 & 0 & -0.18 & 0 & -0.16 & 0 & 0.61 \\ -0.48 & 0.01 & 0.05 & 0 & 0 & 0 & -0.04 & 0 & 0.63 & 0 & 0.002 & 0 & 0.06 & 0 & 0.05 \end{bmatrix} \quad (12.10)$$

Figure 12.3 Matrices A_1 and B_1.

When bending effects are included in the aircraft dynamics, the accelerations due to the structural motion have to be added, so that the true normal acceleration becomes:

$$\begin{aligned} y \triangleq a_{z_A} \\ &= U_0(\dot{\alpha} - q) - x_A\dot{q} + \Phi_{A,1}\ddot{\lambda}_1 + \Phi_{A,5}\ddot{\lambda}_5 + \Phi_{A,7}\ddot{\lambda}_7 \\ &\quad + \Phi_{A,8}\ddot{\lambda}_8 + \Phi_{A,12}\ddot{\lambda}_{12} \end{aligned} \quad (12.12)$$

where $\Phi_{A,i}$ is the ith bending mode slope at body station A. Consequently, the matrices C_A and D_A in eq. (12.11) must be altered to account for the structural motion augmenting the state vector by the variables associated with the bending modes. For B-52E, location A is 4.4 m from the tip of the nose of the aircraft (hence $x_A = 17.48$ m)[1] and it can be shown (see Burris *et al.*, 1969) that:

$$\begin{aligned} C_A = [&-32.65\ -28.04\ 49.93\ 2.37\ -1\,405.41\ -10.39\ -1\,707.61 \\ &-13.09\ -4\,472.18\ -7.53\ 4\,876.78\ 5.83] \end{aligned} \quad (12.13)$$

$$D_A = [-12.55\ -1.02] \quad (12.14)$$

It can also be shown from the work presented in Section 2.7 of Chapter that, at body station A, the lateral acceleration, with structural bending effects included, is given by:

$$\begin{aligned} y_1 \triangleq a_{y_A} \\ &= \dot{v} - g\phi + U_0 r + x_A\dot{r} + \Gamma_{A,1}\ddot{\gamma}_1 + \Gamma_{A,2}\ddot{\gamma}_2 + \Gamma_{A,3}\ddot{\gamma}_3 \\ &\quad + \Gamma_{A,9}\ddot{\gamma}_9 + \Gamma_{A,10}\ddot{\gamma}_{10} + \dots \end{aligned} \quad (12.15)$$

where $\Gamma_{A,j}$ is the slope of the jth bending mode curve at body station A.

Table 12.1 Eigenvalues of uncontrolled aircraft

Longitudinal motion	*Lateral motion*
$\lambda_1 = -0.073 + j2.68$	$\lambda_1 = 0.0$
$\lambda_2 = -0.073 - j6.68$	$\lambda_2 = -0.024$
$\lambda_3 = -2.982 + j6.99$	$\lambda_3 = -2.264$
$\lambda_4 = -2.98 - j6.99$	$\lambda_4 = -0.36 + j1.58$
$\lambda_5 = -0.046 + j15.21$	$\lambda_5 = -0.36 - j1.58$
$\lambda_6 = -0.046 - j15.21$	$\lambda_6 = -0.094 + j9.84$
$\lambda_7 = -1.35 + j18.65$	$\lambda_7 = -0.094 - j9.84$
$\lambda_8 = -0.23 + j19.73$	$\lambda_8 = -0.48 + j10.95$
$\lambda_9 = -0.23 + j19.73$	$\lambda_9 = -0.48 - j10.95$
$\lambda_{10} = -0.89 + j38.28$	$\lambda_{10} = -0.28 + j13.63$
$\lambda_{11} = -0.89 + j38.28$	$\lambda_{11} = -2.08 - j13.63$
$\lambda_{12} = -0.89 - j38.28$	$\lambda_{12} = -0.86 + j23.07$
	$\lambda_{13} = -0.86 - j23.07$
	$\lambda_{14} = -1.16 + j30.47$
	$\lambda_{15} = -1.16 - j30.47$

Note: Eigenvalues have been denoted by λ_i; the symbol λ_i does not denote here the displacement of the ith bending mode.

For the B-52E, at the pilot station:

$$C_{1_A} = [-0.072 \;\; -3.56 \;\; 34.6 \;\; 0.98 \;\; 0 \;\; 14.94 \;\; 0.29 \;\; -181.77 \;\; -4.1 \;\; 100.5 \;\; 3.8 \;\; -7\,531.0 \;\; -18.54 \;\; -3\,321.35 \;\; -3.18] \tag{12.16}$$

$$D_{1_A} = [-1.401 \;\; -0.94 \;\; -1.043] \tag{12.17}$$

The eigenvalues corresponding to the matrices A and A_1 are given in Table 12.1.

12.5.2 Alleviation Control System Designed as Optimal Control System

Since both the normal and lateral accelerations are linear functions of both state and control vectors, it is possible to use in a gust alleviation system the feedback control which results from minimizing the performance index, J, where:

$$J = \tfrac{1}{2}\int_0^\infty (\mathbf{x}'Q\mathbf{x} + \mathbf{u}'G\mathbf{u})\mathrm{d}t \tag{12.18a}$$

The performance index in eq. (12.18a) corresponds to longitudinal motion; if lateral motion was being considered, the appropriate performance index would be:

$$J = \tfrac{1}{2}\int_0^\infty (\mathbf{x}_1'Q_1\mathbf{x}_1 + \mathbf{u}_1'G_1\mathbf{u}_1)\mathrm{d}t \tag{12.18b}$$

$$K = \begin{bmatrix} 0.094 & -0.52 & 1.87 & -0.26 & -0.48 & 1.18 & 4.54 & 0.88 & -1.2 \\ 0.64 & -4.63 & -1.77 & & & & & & \\ 0.02 & 0.044 & -0.07 & -0.034 & -0.112 & 0.13 & 0.05 & 0.05 & -0.49 \\ 0.35 & -0.1 & -1.2 & & & & & & \end{bmatrix} \quad (12.19)$$

$$K_1 = \begin{bmatrix} 0.2 & 4.83 & 7.9 & 1.61 & -0.97 & 5.27 & -1.43 & 14.37 & -1.0 & -4.43 & -2.38 & -8.46 \\ 0.27 & -0.85 & -0.001 & & & & & & & & & \\ 0.95 & 0.24 & 19.85 & 0.78 & 0.24 & 18.84 & -0.01 & -5.67 & -0.12 & -18.62 & 0.5 & -9.36 \\ -0.47 & 12.67 & -0.06 & & & & & & & & & \\ 0.02 & -0.56 & -1.3 & -0.13 & -0.003 & -2.49 & 0.09 & -0.2 & 0.68 & 6.29 & 0.59 & 1.25 \\ 0.13 & -0.47 & 0.12 & & & & & & & & & \end{bmatrix} \quad (12.20)$$

Figure 12.4 Feedback matrices.

and Q (Q_1) is a symmetric, non-negative definite matrix, weighting the elements of the state vector, $\mathbf{x}(x_1)$, and G (G_1) is a symmetric, positive definite matrix weighting the elements of the control vector, $\mathbf{u}(\mathbf{u}_1)$. (See Section 8.4 of Chapter 8.)

When Q (Q_1) was chosen to be a diagonal matrix such that the state variables corresponding to rigid body motion were weighted at unity, while those state variables associated with the flexible modes were weighted at 10.0, then when G (G_1) was taken as I_2 (I_3), the resulting feedback control matrix, obtained by solving the associated LQP, for longitudinal motion, is given by eq. (12.19) and for lateral motion by eq. (12.20). Both are shown in Figure 12.4.

The eigenvalues corresponding to the closed loop alleviation control system are shown in Table 12.2.

Note from a comparison of Tables 12.1 and 12.2 how, for longitudinal motion, the damping ratio of the first bending mode (λ_3, λ_4) is unaltered in the closed loop system whereas the damping of every other mode is affected: in every case increased, except for the seventh mode, where it is actually very much

Table 12.2 Eigenvalues of closed loop gust alleviation optimal control system

$\lambda_1 = -2.91 + j1.92$	$\lambda_1 = -0.06$
$\lambda_2 = -2.91 - j1.92$	$\lambda_2 = -0.314$
$\lambda_3 = -2.92 + j6.94$	$\lambda_3 = -2.09$
$\lambda_4 = -2.92 - j6.94$	$\lambda_4 = -1.20$
$\lambda_5 = -1.14 + j15.18$	$\lambda_5 = -1.30$
$\lambda_6 = -1.14 - j15.18$	$\lambda_6 = -14.21$
$\lambda_7 = -0.23 + j19.72$	$\lambda_7 = -75.03$
$\lambda_8 = -0.23 - j19.72$	$\lambda_8 = -2.9 + j8.21$
$\lambda_9 = -1.65 + j20.18$	$\lambda_9 = -2.9 - j8.21$
$\lambda_{10} = -1.65 - j20.18$	$\lambda_{10} = -1.7 + j11.93$
$\lambda_{11} = -1.7 + j38.25$	$\lambda_{11} = -1.7 - j11.93$
$\lambda_{12} = -1.7 - j38.25$	$\lambda_{12} = -3.17 + j23.1$
	$\lambda_{13} = -3.17 - j23.1$
	$\lambda_{14} = -0.87 + j30.46$
	$\lambda_{15} = -0.87 - j30.46$

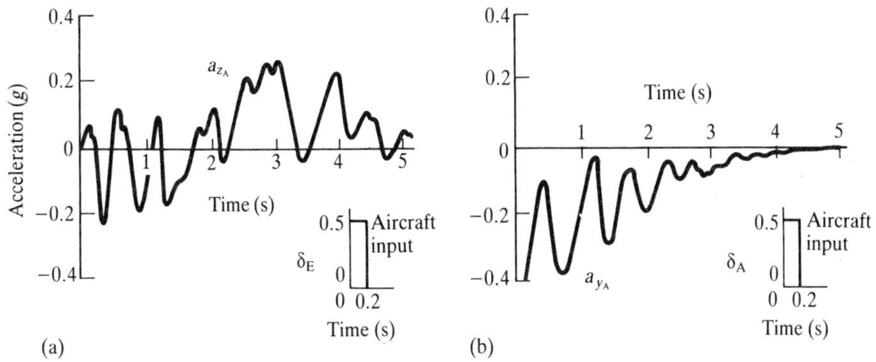

Figure 12.5 Acceleration responses of uncontrolled aircraft. (a) Normal acceleration. (b) Lateral acceleration.

reduced. For lateral motion, the damping of the rigid body motion is very much augmented. Note how the dutch roll mode, for example, has been changed from a very lightly damped, oscillatory mode to become two real modes (λ_3, λ_4). The same effect has occurred with the first bending mode (λ_5, λ_6). This substantial increase in the damping of the first bending mode has been achieved at the expense of the damping of the third and tenth lateral bending modes.

Some acceleration responses as a result of an initial disturbance are shown in Figure 12.5 for the uncontrolled aircraft and in Figure 12.6 for the aircraft when fitted with the optimal gust alleviation control system. It is evident that the accelerations occurring at the pilot's station have been reduced by the optimal control systems.

With another choice of weighting matrix for the state vector, namely:

$$Q = C_A C'_A \tag{12.21}$$

for longitudinal motion, and:

$$Q_1 = C_{A_1} C'_{A_1} \tag{12.22}$$

for lateral motion, it is found that the control law, which results from minimizing the performance index, depends almost entirely on the state variables which

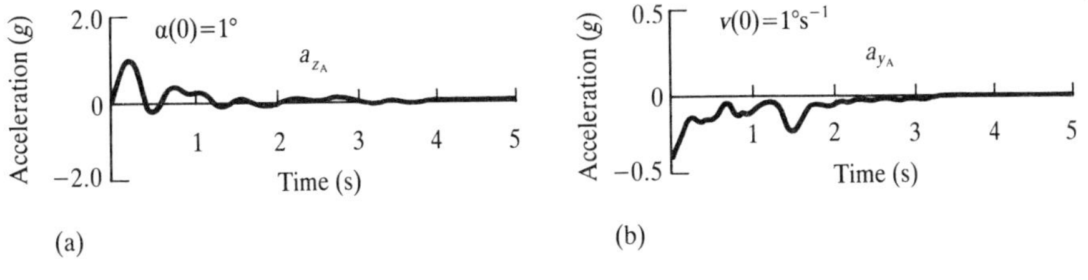

Figure 12.6 Optimal responses of gust alleviation system. (a) Normal acceleration. (b) Lateral acceleration.

contribute most to the output a_{z_A} (or a_{y_A}), e.g. for longitudinal motion, using C_A defined in eq. (12.13), the resulting feedback matrix, K, was found to be:

$$K = \begin{bmatrix} -0.12 & -0.5 & 0.41 & * & * & * & * & 1.2 \times 10^{-8} \\ * & -1.26 \times 10^{-8} & * & & & & & \\ 0.017 & 0.04 & 0.0015 & * & * & * & * & * \\ * & * & * & & & & & \end{bmatrix} \quad (12.23)$$

G was again taken as I_2. The elements denoted by the symbol $*$ were all less than 1×10^{-8} and consequently can be neglected. The only gain associated with variables of the bending motion is the 0.41 associated with the vertical displacement of the first longitudinal bending mode. The practical problem arises of how to gain a measure of λ_1 without fitting a sensor specifically to measure it. If no measure can be found the feedback gain matrix of eq. (12.23) cannot be synthesized directly and the optimal control law to achieve gust alleviation cannot be implemented. Some method of estimating x_3 from other measurements would be required. A number of estimation methods were outlined in Chapter 8.

12.5.3 Sensor Blending

Suppose an attitude gyro is located somewhere on an aircraft to measure pitch attitude. If the aircraft is flexible, the output signal from the attitude gyro will contain components proportional to the displacement of each significant bending mode. Assuming, for simplicity, that only the first two bending modes are significant, the output signal from an attitude gyro located at point number 1 will be given by:

$$v_1 = k_{11}\theta + k_{12}\lambda_1 + k_{13}\lambda_5 \quad (12.24)$$

If two more attitude gyros, are located on the same aircraft, but at points number 2 and 3, say, their output signals can be represented as:

$$v_2 = k_{21}\theta + k_{22}\lambda_1 + k_{23}\lambda_5 \quad (12.25)$$

$$v_3 = k_{31}\alpha + k_{32}\lambda_1 + k_{33}\lambda_5 \quad (12.26)$$

Let:

$$\mathbf{v} \triangleq \begin{bmatrix} v_1 \\ v_2 \\ v_3 \end{bmatrix} \quad (12.27)$$

$$\mathbf{x} = \begin{bmatrix} \theta \\ \lambda_1 \\ \lambda_5 \end{bmatrix} \quad (12.28)$$

then:

$$\mathbf{V} = K_{\mathrm{m}}\mathbf{x} \tag{12.29}$$

where:

$$K_{\mathrm{m}} = \begin{bmatrix} k_{11} & k_{12} & k_{13} \\ k_{21} & k_{22} & k_{23} \\ k_{31} & k_{32} & k_{33} \end{bmatrix} \tag{12.30}$$

Hence:

$$\mathbf{x} = K_{\mathrm{m}}^{-1}\mathbf{V} = M\mathbf{V} \tag{12.31}$$

The elements of M are the blending gains. For example:

$$\lambda_1 = M_{21}v_1 + M_{22}v_2 + M_{23}v_3 \tag{12.32}$$

By combining the signals obtained from these three, independently located, attitude gyros in the correct proportions it is possible to obtain the displacement of the first bending mode which may then be used with the feedback control corresponding to eq. (12.23). Note that the dynamics associated with each gyro have been considered to be negligible: this is a very important assumption for sensor blending.

12.5.5 Model-following control for gust alleviation

It has been shown how an optimally controlled gust alleviation control system can be found by using LQP theory. But if it was required that all the state variables, including the bending modes, of the gust alleviation system were to behave as first order modes, of rapid subsidence, then the technique of implicit model-following dealt with in Section 7.3 of Chapter 7 can be easily applied to obtain the required control law. To recapitulate:

$$\dot{\mathbf{y}}_{\mathrm{m}} = T\mathbf{y}_{\mathrm{m}} \tag{12.33}$$

and:

$$\mathbf{y} = \mathbf{x} \tag{12.34}$$

Then, from Chapter 7, it can be shown that:

$$K = [CB]^{\dagger}\,(TC - CA) \tag{12.35}$$

For longitudinal motion of the B-52E, suppose that the model matrix, T, was chosen to be:

$$T = \mathrm{diag}[-1.0\ \ -2.5\ \ 1\ \ -5.0\ \ 1\ \ -8.0\ \ 1\ \ -10.0\ \ 1\ \ -15.0\ \ 1\ \ -20.0] \tag{12.36}$$

The resulting feedback matrix K can easily be found to be given by:

$$K = \begin{bmatrix} 0.152 & 0.06 & 5.82 & -0.13 & -29.11 & 0.79 & -57.36 & 1.02 \\ -23.6 & 0.75 & 356.9 & -4.44 \\ 24.07 & 0.83 & 59.03 & 23.43 & -396.21 & 10.76 & -751.14 & 13.27 \\ -363.77 & 1.87 & 4\,809.3 & -59.85 \end{bmatrix} \quad (12.37)$$

It is most obvious from inspection that an arbitrary choice of model matrix has resulted in a feedback control law which depends very heavily on the rates and displacements of the bending modes: if sensor blending were required to obtain the feedback signals required, the design would be far too expensive, involving thirty attitude and rate gyros. A far better approach is to restrict the definition of the output matrix, C, to be

$$C_4 = [I_4 : 0] \quad (12.38)$$

so that only the rigid body motion and the first bending mode are controlled.

Let:

$$T \triangleq \text{diag}[-10.0 \; -5.0 \; -1.0 \; -4.0] \quad (12.39)$$

The corresponding feedback matrix, obtained by using implicit model-following theory, is now given by:

$$K = \begin{bmatrix} 9.68 & 0.95 & 66.6 & 1.67 & 0 & 0 & 0 & 0 & 0 \\ 0 & 0 & 0 \\ 52.47 & 10.35 & 879.35 & 26.44 & 0 & 0 & 0 & 0 & 0 \\ 0 & 0 & 0 \end{bmatrix} \quad (12.40)$$

The acceleration response to an initial disturbance in angle of attack for this model-following control is represented in Figure 12.7. The feedback control derived by this method is seen to be as effective for gust alleviation as that obtained from solving the LQP.

Interested readers can find further discussion of load alleviation systems in Burris *et al.* (1969).

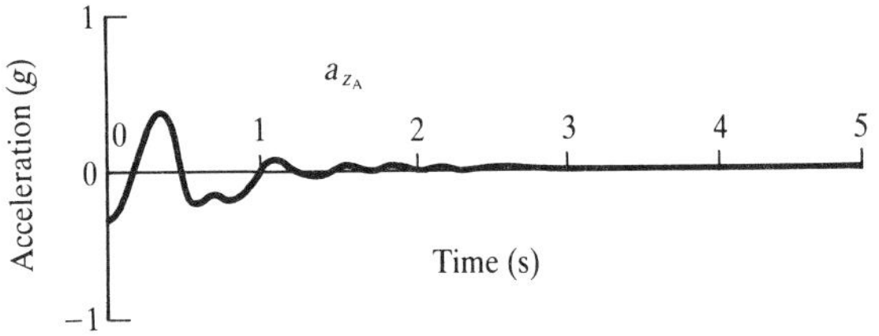

Figure 12.7 Model-following control system response to normal acceleration.

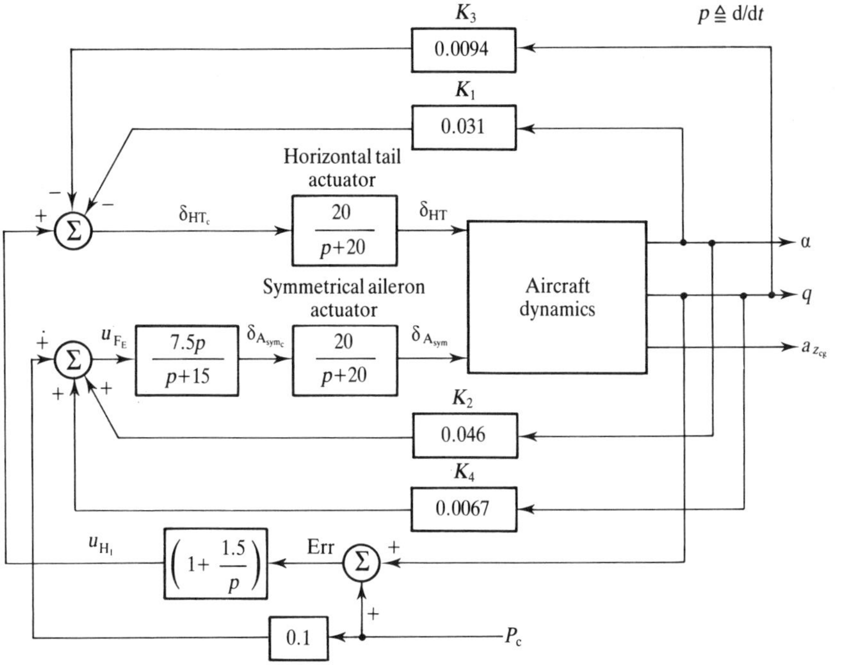

Figure 12.8 Ride control system.

12.6 A RIDE CONTROL SYSTEM FOR A MODERN FIGHTER AIRCRAFT

A modern fighter aircraft of the type represented by aircraft ECHO of Appendix B has an RCS fitted to provide a better aircraft path through low level turbulence so that the pilot's weapons tracking ability is not impaired by the accelerations which arise at the cockpit. A block diagram is shown in Figure 12.8 from which the following features will be noted:

1. There are two control surfaces employed: the horizontal all-moving tail and the symmetrical ailerons.
2. The motion variables sensed are angle of attack and pitch rate.
3. The control law being used in the pitch rate SAS is a proportional plus integral control.
4. The loop which acts through the symmetrical ailerons is washed out.
5. The control surface actuators are very rapid, both having a time constant of 0.05 s.

The equations of short period, longitudinal motion for the ECHO-2 (at Mach 0.81 at 4 600 m) are:

$$\dot{\alpha} = -0.018\alpha + 1.0q - 0.528\delta_{HT} - 0.734\delta_{A_{sym}}$$
$$\dot{q} = 0.007\alpha - 0.45q - 0.18\delta_{HT} + 0.2\delta_{A_{sym}} \tag{12.41}$$

The feedback control gains K_1 to K_4 may be found by using any of the design methods outlined in Chapters 7 and 8, but the preferred method is to use the LQP technique of Chapter 8 to minimize the performance index which results from considering the ride discomfort (RD) index (of Section 6.6). It is shown there that:

$$a_{z_{cg}} = -\frac{\rho U_0}{2k} g I_{RD} w + \sum_{j=HT}^{A_{sym}} Z_{\delta_j} \delta_j \tag{12.42}$$

where the subscript $_{HT}$ signifies horizontal tail. Thus, if $a_{z_{cg}}$ and the control deflections are minimized by the optimal control system, then I_{RD} will also be minimized. Thus, if the normal acceleration is taken as the system output, then it can be shown (see eq. (2.130)) that:

$$y = C\mathbf{x} + D\mathbf{u} \tag{12.43}$$

For ECHO-2, C and D can be shown to be:

$$C = [-4.644 \ \ 0.0] \tag{12.44}$$

$$D = [-134.16 \ \ -189.372] \tag{12.45}$$

From eq. (12.41) it can be shown that:

$$A = \begin{bmatrix} -0.018 & 1.00 \\ 0.007 & -0.45 \end{bmatrix} \tag{12.46}$$

$$B = \begin{bmatrix} -0.52 & -0.734 \\ -0.18 & 0.2 \end{bmatrix} \tag{12.47}$$

Thus, minimizing:

$$J = \tfrac{1}{2} \int_0^{\infty} (y'Qy + \mathbf{u}'G\mathbf{u})\mathrm{d}t \tag{12.48}$$

where:

$$Q = 100.0 \qquad G = \begin{bmatrix} 0.1 & 0.0 \\ 0.0 & 0.1 \end{bmatrix} \tag{12.49}$$

results in the control law:

$$\mathbf{u} = K\mathbf{x} \tag{12.50}$$

where:

$$K = \begin{bmatrix} K_1 & K_3 \\ K_2 & K_4 \end{bmatrix} = \begin{bmatrix} -0.0308 & -0.0094 \\ 0.0462 & 0.0063 \end{bmatrix} \tag{12.51}$$

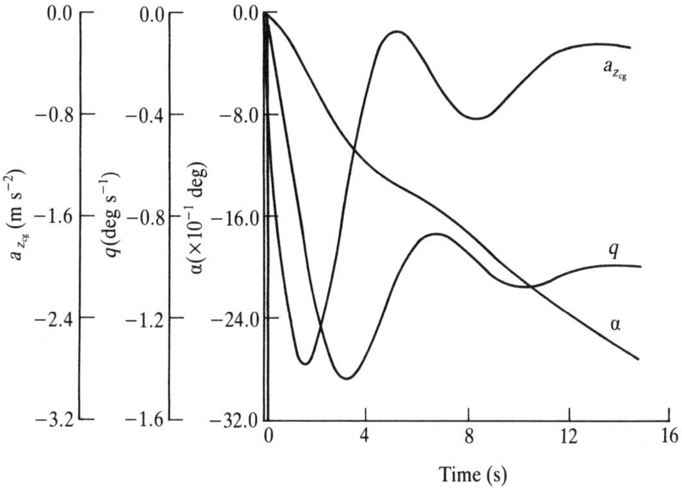

Figure 12.9 Acceleration step response for RCS.

The response of the controlled aircraft to a step command in P_c is shown in Figure 12.9. The response to low-level turbulence is shown in Figure 12.10. The r.m.s. value of the intensity of the vertical velocity gust was 0.3 m s^{-1}.

12.7 AIRCRAFT POSITIONING CONTROL SYSTEMS

12.7.1 Direct Lift Control and Sideforce Generation

There are four positioning tasks which require great precision in aircraft: air-to-ground weapons delivery; air-to-air combat; in-flight refuelling, and all-weather landing.

By using direct lift control (DLC) and direct sideforce generation (DSFG) it is possible to furnish an aircraft with additional degrees of freedom. Using DLC considerably enhances an aircraft's capability to manoeuvre; with the use of DSFG it is possible to turn an aircraft with its wing level. See Figure 12.11.

By this stage of his reading, the reader will be familiar with the idea that, in controlling conventional aircraft, a pilot can command angular rates in the three axes of pitch, roll and yaw. Such angular rates are achieved by means of the moments generated by the existing surfaces. But the direct control of translation in such conventional aircraft is restricted to what can be achieved by using the throttles or any speed brakes. And the use of these controls inevitably also generates moments simultaneously. There are no dedicated control surfaces fixed in the aircraft to achieve control of translation in the normal and lateral direction but, by using DLC and DSFG, complete control of the six degrees of freedom

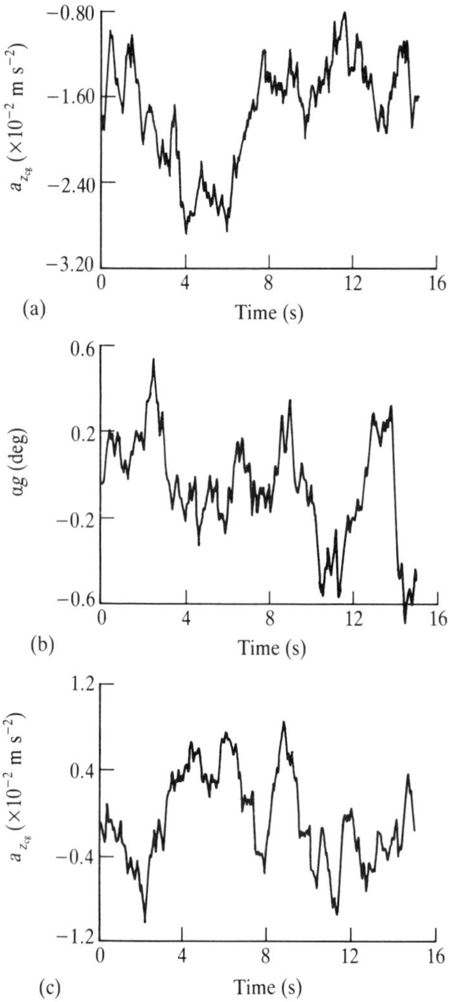

Figure 12.10 Response to turbulence of RCS. (a) Uncontrolled aircraft. (b) Gust. (c) Aircraft with RCS.

can be achieved. However, it needs extra control forces in pitch and yaw and these can be generated by either aerodynamic or propulsive means. Aerodynamic methods are the more efficient. However, even with conventional aircraft, some degree of DLC and DSFG is possible by using such auxiliary control surfaces as flaps, slats and drag petals.

12.7.2 Longitudinal Control System

The equation of short period longitudinal motion can be written as:

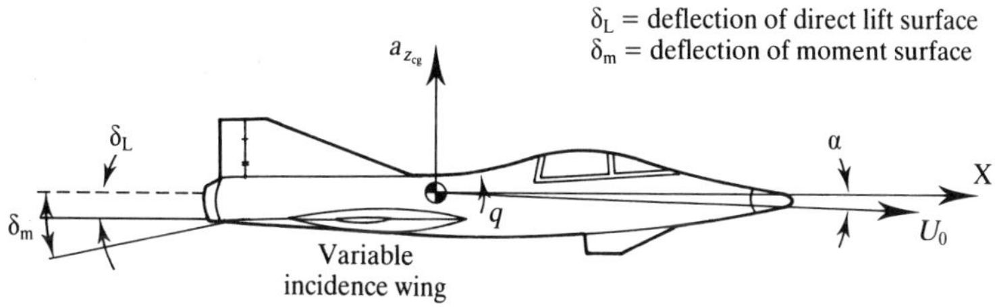

Figure 12.11 DLC aircraft.

$$\begin{bmatrix} \dot{\alpha} \\ \dot{q} \end{bmatrix} = \begin{bmatrix} Z_\alpha & 1 \\ M_\alpha & M_q \end{bmatrix} \begin{bmatrix} \alpha \\ q \end{bmatrix} + \begin{bmatrix} Z_m & Z_L \\ M_m & M_L \end{bmatrix} \begin{bmatrix} \delta_m \\ \delta_L \end{bmatrix} \tag{12.52}$$

If constant angle of attack flight is required, it is necessary to remove the influence of pitch rate from both the α and q equations. Thus, if a control function, say u_1, can be found such that:

$$u_1 = -Z_L\delta_L - Z_m\delta_m \tag{12.53}$$

and if another control, say u_2, can be found such that:

$$M_q u_2 = -M_m\delta_m - M_L\delta_L \tag{12.54}$$

then if a proportional feedback control law is used in which:

$$u_1 = u_2 = q \tag{12.55}$$

then:

$$\dot{\alpha} = Z_\alpha \alpha \qquad \dot{q} = M_\alpha \alpha \tag{12.56}$$

which is the desired result. How can the control be synthesized? From eqs (12.53)–(12.55) it can be shown that:

$$\begin{bmatrix} Z_m & Z_L \\ M_m & M_L \end{bmatrix} \begin{bmatrix} \delta_m \\ \delta_L \end{bmatrix} = \begin{bmatrix} -1 \\ -M_q \end{bmatrix} q \tag{12.57}$$

$$\begin{bmatrix} \delta_m \\ \delta_L \end{bmatrix} = \begin{bmatrix} Z_m & Z_L \\ M_m & M_L \end{bmatrix}^{-1} \begin{bmatrix} -1 \\ -M_q \end{bmatrix} q \tag{12.58}$$

i.e.:

$$\mathbf{u} = K\mathbf{x} \tag{12.59}$$

a feedback control law. How eq. (12.59) is mechanized is shown in Figure 12.12.

It is sometimes preferred to emphasize the 'over the nose' visibility of the aircraft in flight, or, perhaps, to control the 'tail scrape' angle at take-off. For such flight situations, constant pitch attitude is preferred, with a constant maintenance of the stability requirements on the flight path. Thus it is necessary to remove the influence of the angle of attack from the equations by using a

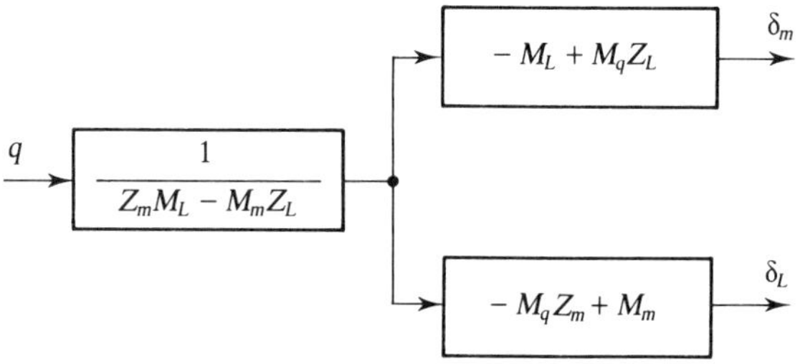

Figure 12.12 Controller/surface interconnect for constant α.

feedback control law of the form of eq. (12.59). This is achieved by mechanizing the following equations:

$$Z_m\delta_m + Z_L\delta_L = -Z_\alpha\alpha \tag{12.60}$$

$$M_m\delta_m + M_L\delta_L = -M_\alpha\alpha$$

i.e.:

$$\begin{bmatrix} \delta_m \\ \delta_L \end{bmatrix} = \begin{bmatrix} Z_m & Z_L \\ M_m & M_L \end{bmatrix}^{-1} \begin{bmatrix} -Z_\alpha \\ -M_\alpha \end{bmatrix} \alpha \tag{12.61}$$

Use of this control law, eq. (12.61), results in:

$$\dot{\alpha} = q \qquad \dot{q} = M_q q \tag{12.62}$$

Its synthesis is represented in Figure 12.13.

For aircraft ECHO the equations of motion for flight condition 2 were given in eq. (12.41), from which it can be inferred that:

$$Z_\alpha = -0.018 \qquad Z_L = -0.734$$

$$M_\alpha = 0.007 \qquad M_m = -0.18$$

$$M_q = -0.45 \qquad M_L = +0.2$$

$$Z_m = -0.52$$

With the feedback control of Figure 12.12 being used, and with a pulsed

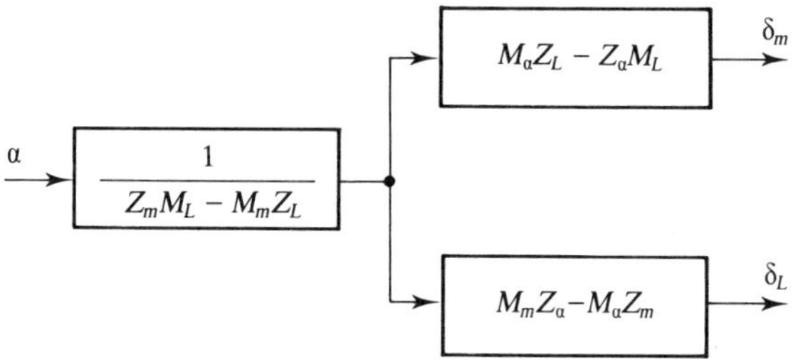

Figure 12.13 Controller/surface interconnect for constant θ.

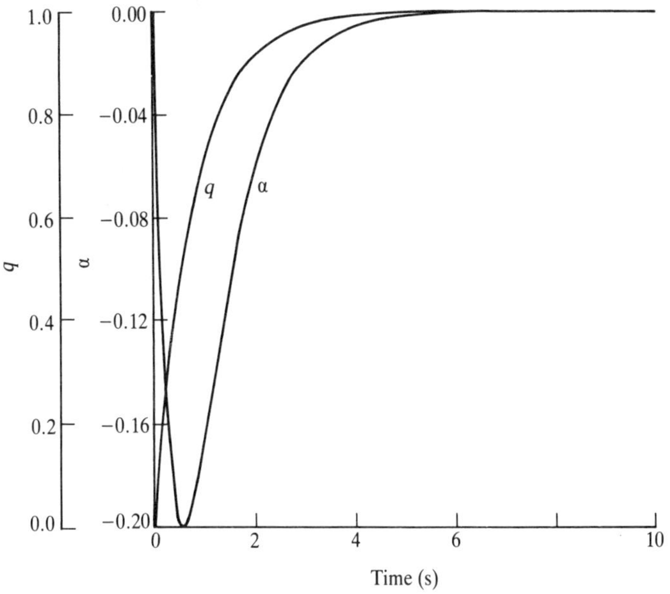

Figure 12.14 Response of angle of attack, α, and q to pitch rate command.

change of input command of $1° \, s^{-1}$ for 0.25 s the response shown in Figure 12.14 was obtained. Similar responses can be obtained for constant pitch attitude flight.

If it is necessary to arrange that any change in the aircraft's pitch attitude be independent of any change in its lift (i.e. the motion of the pitch rate and the angle of attack must be decoupled) then a more involved controller is required. The required result is that:

$$\begin{aligned} \dot{\alpha} &= Z_\alpha \alpha + Z_L \delta_{P_L} \\ \dot{q} &= M_q q + M_m \delta_{P_m} \end{aligned} \tag{12.63}$$

where δ_{P_L} is the pilot's direct lift command and δ_{P_m} is the pilot's moment command. Hence, if a feedback control law is to be used, then from eqs (12.52) and (12.63) it can be seen that it is necessary that:

$$\begin{aligned} q + Z_m \delta_m + Z_L \delta_L &= Z_L \delta_{P_L} \\ M_\alpha \alpha + M_m \delta_m + M_L \delta_L &= M_m \delta_{P_L} \end{aligned} \tag{12.64}$$

Thus:

$$\mathbf{x} \triangleq \begin{bmatrix} \alpha \\ q \end{bmatrix} = \begin{bmatrix} -\dfrac{M_m}{M_\alpha} & -\dfrac{M_L}{M_\alpha} \\ -Z_m & -Z_L \end{bmatrix} \begin{bmatrix} \delta_m \\ \delta_L \end{bmatrix} + \begin{bmatrix} \dfrac{M_m}{M_\alpha} & 0 \\ 0 & Z_L \end{bmatrix} \begin{bmatrix} \delta_{P_m} \\ \delta_{P_L} \end{bmatrix} \tag{12.65}$$

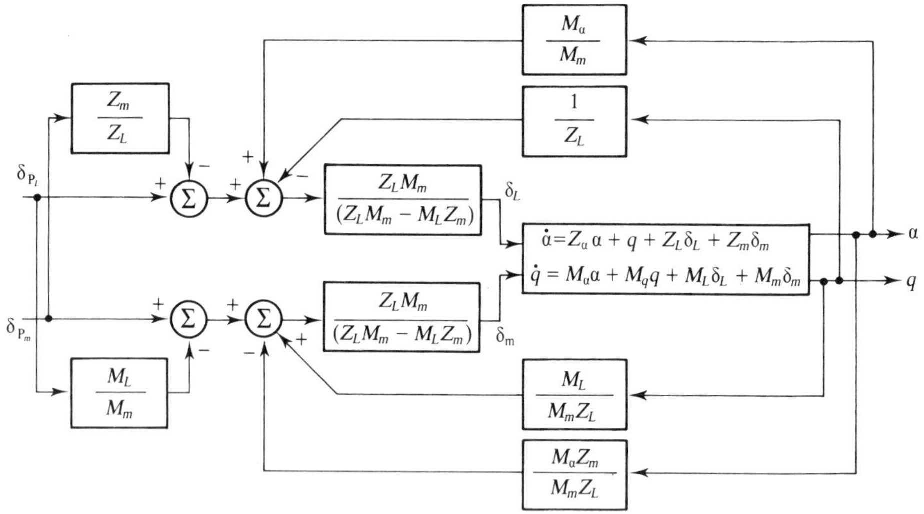

Figure 12.15 Decoupling controller/surface interconnect.

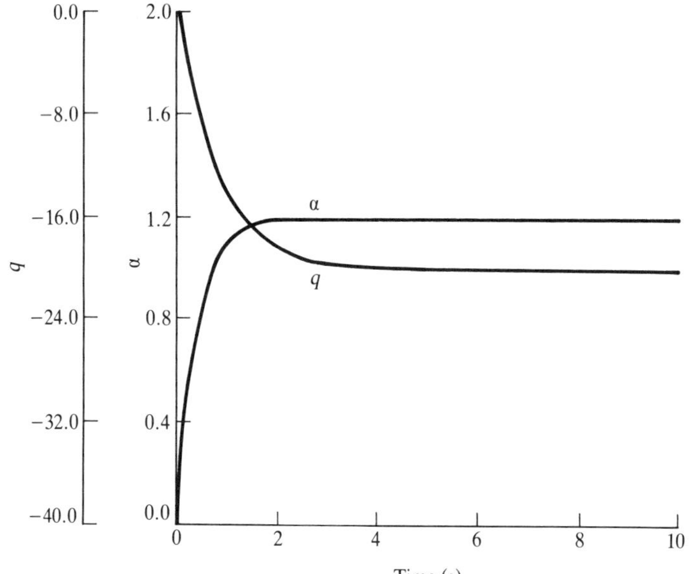

Figure 12.16 Step response for α and q.

Hence:

$$\begin{bmatrix} \delta_m \\ \delta_L \end{bmatrix} = \begin{bmatrix} -\dfrac{M_m}{M_\alpha} & -\dfrac{M_L}{M_\alpha} \\ -Z_m & -Z_L \end{bmatrix}^{-1} \begin{bmatrix} \alpha \\ q \end{bmatrix} - \begin{bmatrix} -\dfrac{M_m}{M_\alpha} & \dfrac{M_L}{M_\alpha} \\ -Z_m & -Z_L \end{bmatrix}^{-1} \begin{bmatrix} \dfrac{M_m}{M_\alpha} & 0 \\ 0 & Z_L \end{bmatrix} \begin{bmatrix} \delta_{P_m} \\ \delta_{P_L} \end{bmatrix} \tag{12.66}$$

$$\therefore \delta_m = -\frac{Z_L M_\alpha}{\Delta}\alpha + \frac{M_L}{\Delta}q + \frac{Z_L M_m}{\Delta}\delta_{P_m} - \frac{Z_L M_L}{\Delta}\delta_{P_L} \tag{12.67}$$

$$\delta_L = -\frac{Z_m M_\alpha}{\Delta}\alpha - \frac{M_m}{\Delta}q + \frac{Z_m M_m}{\Delta}\delta_{P_m} + \frac{M_m Z_L}{\Delta}\delta_{P_L} \tag{12.68}$$

where:

$$\Delta = (M_m Z_L - Z_m Z_L) \tag{12.69}$$

A synthesis of the control law eq. (12.66) is shown in Figure 12.15. The dynamic response of this system for ECHO-2, to a unit step command being applied to both δ_{P_m} and δ_{P_L} simultaneously, is shown in Figure 12.16.

12.7.3 Lateral Control System

The equations of lateral motion governing sideslip, rolling and yawing motion for a CCV, represented in Figure 12.17, can be written as:

$$\begin{bmatrix} \dot{\beta} \\ \dot{p} \\ \dot{r} \end{bmatrix} = \begin{bmatrix} Y_v & 0 & -1 \\ L'_\beta & L'_p & L'_r \\ N'_\beta & N'_p & N'_r \end{bmatrix} \begin{bmatrix} \beta \\ p \\ r \end{bmatrix} + \begin{bmatrix} Y^*_{\delta_{dw}} & Y^*_{\delta_{vf}} & Y^*_{\delta_{sfg}} \\ L'_{\delta_{dw}} & L'_{\delta_{vf}} & L'_{\delta_{sfg}} \\ N'_{\delta_{dw}} & N'_{\delta_{vf}} & N'_{\delta_{sfg}} \end{bmatrix} \begin{bmatrix} \delta_{dw} \\ \delta_{vf} \\ \delta_{sfg} \end{bmatrix} \tag{12.70}$$

If it is required to provide the aircraft with a control system for constant heading operation, with wings level and with sideslip angle constant, then the interconnect to the control surfaces should be governed by the following equations:

$$\begin{aligned} Y^*_{\delta_{dw}}\delta_{dw} + Y^*_{\delta_{vf}}\delta_{vf} + Y^*_{\delta_{sfg}}\delta_{sfg} &= -Y_v\beta_{comm} \\ L'_{\delta_{dw}}\delta_{dw} + L'_{\delta_{vf}}\delta_{vf} + L'_{\delta_{sfg}}\delta_{sfg} &= -L'_\beta\beta_{comm} \\ N'_{\delta_{dw}}\delta_{dw} + N'_{\delta_{vf}}\delta_{vf} + N'_{\delta_{sfg}}\delta_{sfg} &= -N'_\beta\beta_{comm} \end{aligned} \tag{12.71}$$

When zero sideslip is wanted, with wings level and yawing motion in operation, the input from the pilot's controller is r_{comm} and the equations become:

$$Y^*_{\delta_{dw}}\delta_{dw} + Y^*_{\delta_{vf}}\delta_{vf} + Y^*_{\delta_{sfg}}\delta_{sfg} = -r_{comm}$$

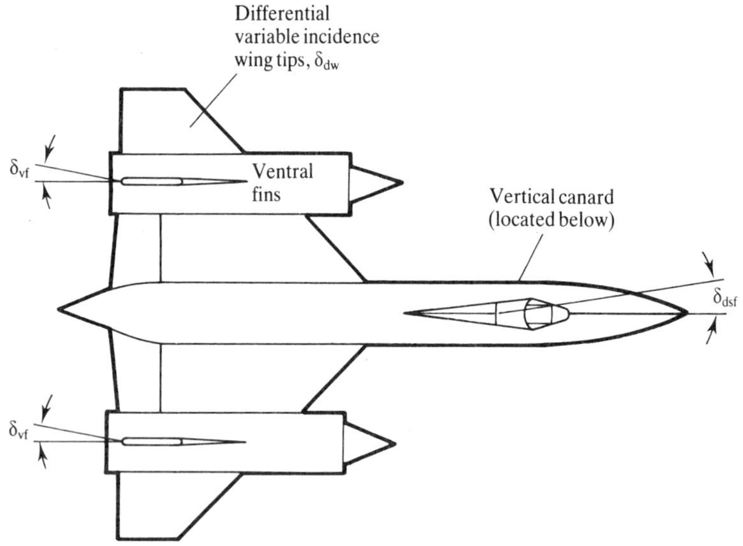

Figure 12.17 Control configured vehicle.

$$L'_{\delta_{dw}}\delta_{dw} + L'_{\delta_{vf}}\delta_{vf} + L'_{\delta_{sfg}}\delta_{sfg} = -L'_r r_{comm} \qquad (12.72)$$
$$N'_{\delta_{dw}}\delta_{dw} + N'_{\delta_{vf}}\delta_{vf} + N'_{\delta_{sfg}}\delta_{sfg} = -N'_r r_{comm}$$

If, however, it is required that the lateral/directional motion be decoupled, then three separate inputs and feedback paths are required:

$$-r + Y^*_{\delta_{dw}}\delta_{dw} + Y^*_{\delta_{vf}}\delta_{vf} + Y^*_{\delta_{sfg}}\delta_{sfg} = Y^*_{\delta_{sfg}}\delta_{sf}$$
$$L'_\beta\beta + L'_r r + L'_{\delta_{dw}}\delta_{dw} + L'_{\delta_{vf}}\delta_{vf} + L'_{\delta_{sfg}}\delta_{sfg} = L'_{\delta_{dw}}\delta_{rm} \qquad (12.73)$$
$$N'_\beta\beta + N'_p + N'_{\delta_{dw}}\delta_{dw} + N'_{\delta_{vf}}\delta_{vf} + N'_{\delta_{sfg}}\delta_{sfg} = N'_{\delta_{vf}}\delta_{ym}$$

where δ_{sf} is commanded direct sideforce, δ_{rm} commanded roll moment, and δ_{ym} commanded yaw moment.

For a future projects aircraft, coded OMEGA, which has differentially acting wing tips, a ventral fin, and a vertical canard to generate the sideforce, the equations of motion which obtain at FL 60 and at Mach 3 are given by:

$$\begin{bmatrix} \dot\beta \\ \dot p \\ \dot r \end{bmatrix} = \begin{bmatrix} -0.163 & 0 & -1.0 \\ 16.6 & -1.08 & -0.13 \\ 15.7 & -0.02 & -0.25 \end{bmatrix} \begin{bmatrix} \beta \\ p \\ r \end{bmatrix} + \begin{bmatrix} -0.0054 & 0.05 & -0.025 \\ 42.3 & 6.88 & 0.08 \\ 1.08 & -11.7 & -1.25 \end{bmatrix} \begin{bmatrix} \delta_{dw} \\ \delta_{vf} \\ \delta_{sfg} \end{bmatrix} \qquad (12.74)$$

Using the control law of eq. (12.73) for unit step commands in δ_{sf}, δ_{rm} and δ_{ym} results in the dynamic response shown in Figure 12.19 when eq. (12.73) can be expressed as:

$$\begin{bmatrix} \delta_{dw} \\ \delta_{vf} \\ \delta_{sfg} \end{bmatrix} = \begin{bmatrix} 0.0126 & 0.985 & -0.135 \\ -0.087 & 0.094 & 0.814 \\ 0.823 & -0.025 & 1.66 \end{bmatrix} \begin{bmatrix} \delta_{sf} \\ \delta_{rm} \\ \delta_{ym} \end{bmatrix} - \begin{bmatrix} -0.568 & 0.0002 & -0.5 \\ 1.05 & -0.0014 & 3.47 \\ 2.24 & -0.003 & -32.91 \end{bmatrix} \begin{bmatrix} \beta \\ p \\ r \end{bmatrix} \tag{12.75}$$

A block diagram of the closed loop lateral positioning control system is given in Figure 12.18. It is evident from Figure 12.19 that the lateral/directional motion is truly decoupled: Figure 12.20 shows the response of the aircraft to step deflections of the control surfaces, without input command scaling or motion variable feedback.

12.8 CONCLUSIONS

In this chapter the important topic of active control technology is introduced by discussing some of the features of six ACT functions: MLC, GLA, RSS, RC, FMC and FR. This brief qualitative treatment is followed by an account of the development of gust alleviation from the earliest days of aviation up to its application on the B-1 bomber used by the USAF. A detailed consideration of a load alleviation system developed for the B-52E bomber aircraft is then presented before the problem of load alleviation is treated as a special problem in optimal linear control. One feature of controlling flexible aircraft is proper location of the sensors upon which the control law depends for its feedback signals: the sensor

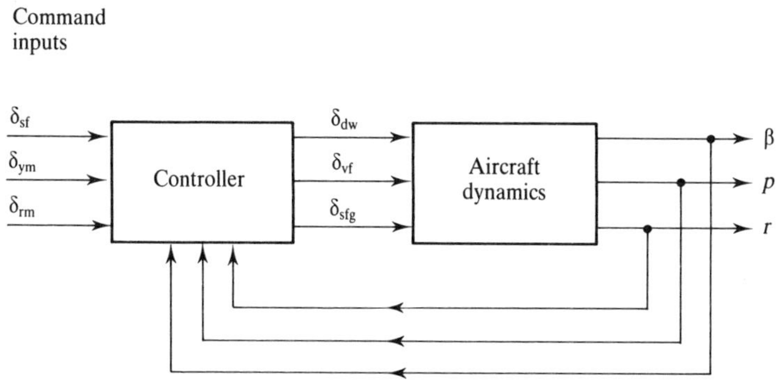

Figure 12.18 Lateral position control system.

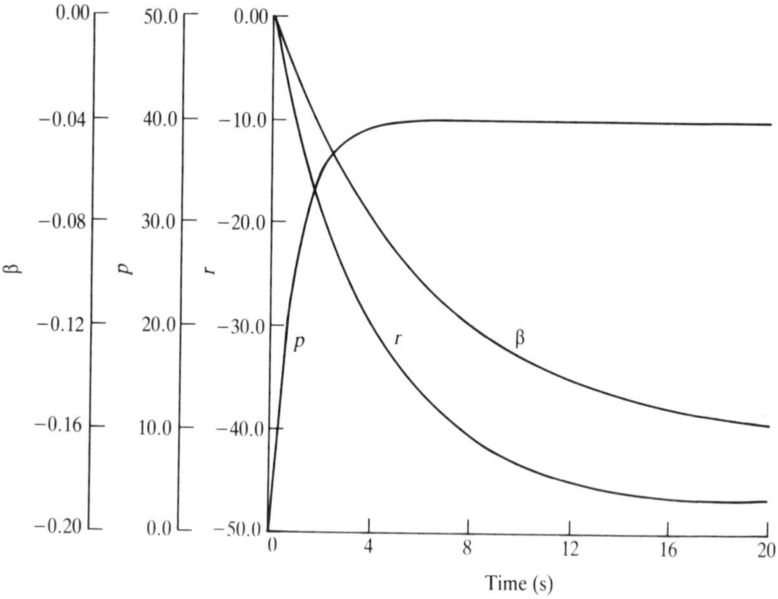

Figure 12.19 Step response of lateral position system.

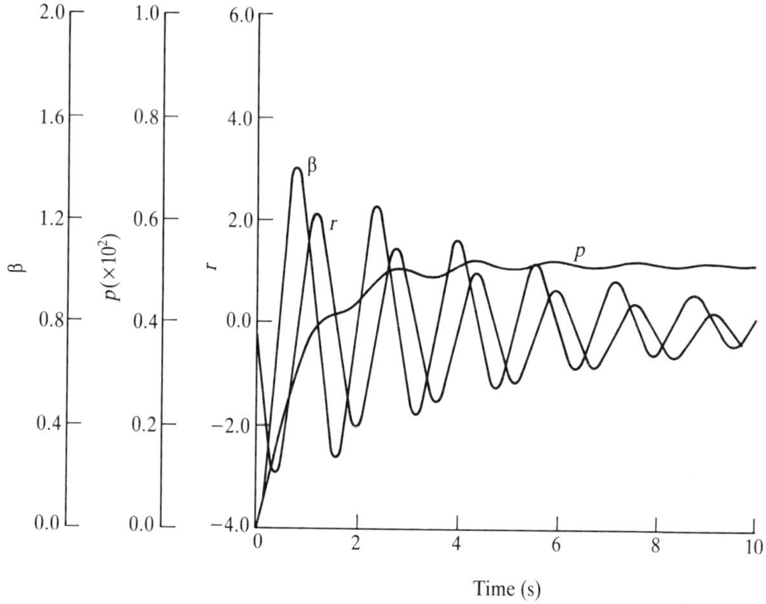

Figure 12.20 Step response of aircraft.

signals are invariably contaminated with components caused by the flexing of the structure which the control system is trying to reduce. A method of using blended signals from several identical sensors at different locations to obtain a 'bending mode free' feedback signal was presented, before showing how the alleviation problem could also be treated as a model-following problem. To illustrate the performance and structure of an RC system for a fighter aircraft, an optimal control problem was once more solved, but on this occasion the performance index was chosen to reflect a ride discomfort (RD) index. Finally, longitudinal and lateral aircraft positioning control systems which used auxiliary control surfaces to achieve the looked-for decoupling of the corresponding aircraft motion are treated.

12.9 EXERCISES

12.1 A pitch-pointing control system is fitted to an advanced fighter aircraft to provide it with improved air-to-air combat performance. Such a pitch pointing mode is characterized by the pitch attitude being decoupled from the flight path angle, i.e. both motion variables, γ and θ, can be controlled independently. For such an aircraft a suitable model is defined by the equations:

$$\dot{\mathbf{x}} = A\mathbf{x} + B\mathbf{u} \qquad \mathbf{y} = C\mathbf{x}$$

where:

$$\mathbf{x}' = [\theta \; q \; \alpha \; \delta_E \; \delta_F]$$

$$\mathbf{u}' = [\delta_{E_c} \; \delta_{F_c}]$$

$$\mathbf{y}' = [\theta \; \gamma]$$

α, q, θ and γ have their usual meanings; δ_E and δ_F represent the deflections of the elevator and flaperon respectively. δ_{E_c} and δ_{F_c} are the corresponding command inputs. The appropriate matrices, A and B, are:

$$A = \begin{bmatrix} 0 & 1 & 0 & 0 & 0 \\ 0 & -0.87 & 43.3 & -17.3 & -1.58 \\ 0.004 & 1.0 & -1.34 & 0.17 & 0.025 \\ 0 & 0 & 0 & -10.0 & 0 \\ 0 & 0 & 0 & 0 & -10.0 \end{bmatrix} \qquad B = \begin{bmatrix} 0 & 0 \\ 0 & 0 \\ 0 & 0 \\ 10.0 & 0 \\ 0 & 10.0 \end{bmatrix}$$

(a) Determine the corresponding output matrix, C.
(b) Find a control scheme which will result in it being possible to change θ without disturbing γ, and vice versa.
(c) Sketch a block diagram to show how your control scheme can be implemented.

12.2 A 'superaugmented' aircraft is one with active control and a considerable degree of stability augmentation. Without augmentation, these aircraft are assumed to be unstable; any pitch stability which they do possess is provided by the action of the flight control system. An example of such an aircraft with its c.g. at 50 per cent m.a.c. has the following matrices:

$$A = \begin{bmatrix} -0.014 & 0.18 & 0.0002 & -0.072 & -0.037 & 0 \\ -0.015 & -0.75 & 1 & 0.0013 & -0.063 & 0 \\ 0.001 & 0.08 & -0.87 & 0 & -3.4 & 0 \\ 0 & 0 & 1 & 0 & 0 & 0 \\ 0 & 0 & 0 & 0 & -20 & 10.72 \\ 0 & 0 & 0 & 0 & 0 & -50 \end{bmatrix}$$

$$B = \begin{bmatrix} 0 \\ 0 \\ 0 \\ 0 \\ 0 \\ 50.0 \end{bmatrix}$$

$$C = \begin{bmatrix} 0.0065 & 0.32 & -0.034 & 0 & -0.1 & 0 \\ 1.0 & 0 & 0 & 0 & 0 & 0 \\ 0.014 & 0.18 & -0.56 & -0.037 & 0 & 0 \\ 0 & -135.8 & 0 & 135.8 & 0 & 0 \\ 0 & 0 & 1.0 & 0 & 0 & 0 \end{bmatrix}$$

The state vector is defined as:

$$\mathbf{x}' = [u \;\; \alpha \;\; q \;\; \theta \;\; \delta_E \;\; \delta_F]$$

the control vector as:

$$\mathbf{u} = [\delta_{E_c}]$$

and the output vector as:

$$\mathbf{y}' = [n_z \;\; u \;\; \alpha \;\; \dot{h} \;\; q]$$

Design a stabilizing control law which will minimize the r.m.s. value of the normal load factor to any commanded change in the rate of change of height.

12.3 The fighter aircraft BRAVO is statically stable only at flight condition 2. Design a pitch rate SAS which will provide satisfactory performance at this flight condition and also at flight condition 4 without any change in the parameters or the structure of the controller. What advantages does relaxing the static stability of this aircraft bring?

12.4 Design a lateral ride control system for the B-52E such that the r.m.s. value of the side acceleration at the pilot's stations is minimized in response to a side gust velocity of intensity 3 m s^{-1}. Use the mathematical model defined by the matrices

A_1, B_1, C_{1_A} and D_{1_A} given in eqs (12.9), (12.10), (12.16) and (12.17) respectively.

12.5 A rate gyro placed at a point A on a B-52E measures the yaw rate and also components of the lateral bending displacement rates, $\dot{\gamma}_1$ and $\dot{\gamma}_3$. The output voltage from this rate gyro is:

$$v_A = 0.47r + 0.39\dot{\gamma}_1 + 0.22\dot{\gamma}_3$$

Two more identical gyros are located at different points B and C. Their output voltages are found to be:

$$v_B = 0.34r + 0.12\dot{\gamma}_1 + 0.27\dot{\gamma}_3$$

$$v_C = 0.11r + 0.46\dot{\gamma}_1 - 0.32\dot{\gamma}_3$$

Derive an expression for $\dot{\gamma}_1$ and $\dot{\gamma}_3$ in terms of the output voltages from the rate gyros and the corresponding blending gains.

12.6 Design a model-following control system to achieve gust load alleviation for the B-52E. The output matrix is restricted to the rigid body motion and the first and third lateral bending modes. The model matrix is defined as:

$$T = \text{diag}[-2.0 \; -10.0 \; -3.0 \; -10.0 \; -1.0 \; -6.0 \; -7.5]$$

12.7 For the aircraft OMEGA, defined by eq. (12.72), show that the lateral positioning control law given as eq. (12.73) is correct.

12.8 Find a control law to achieve longitudinal positioning of the aircraft ECHO if its static stability is neutral. Determine the response in pitch rate and angle of attack to a pulsed change of input command of $1° \, s^{-1}$ for 0.25 s. Compare your responses with those shown in Figure 12.14. Has the relaxed static stability been beneficial?

12.10 NOTE

1. The aircraft's c.g. is taken as being located at 21.88 m from the nose tip.

12.11 REFERENCES

ATTWOOD, J.L., R.H. CANNON, J.M. JOHNSON and G.M. ANDREW. 1961. Gust alleviation system. US Patent 2, 985, 409.

BURRIS, P.M. and M.A. BENDER. 1969. Aircraft load alleviation and mode stabilization (LAMS) – B52 system analysis, synthesis and design. AFFDL-TR-68-161. WPAFB, Dayton, Ohio.

HUNSAKER, J.C. and E.B. WILSON. 1915. Report on behavior of aeroplanes in gust turbulence. NACA TM-1 (MIT). October.

OSTGAARD, M.A. and F.R. SWORTZEL. 1977. CCVs: active control technology creating new military aircraft design potential. *Astrophys and Aero.* 15: 42–57.

ROUGHTON, D.J. 1978. Active control technology. *Inst. M.C. Colloquium, London.* March.

STOCKDALE, C.R. and R.D. POYNEER. 1973. Control configured vehicle – ride control system.

AFFDL-TR-73-83. WPAFB, Dayton, Ohio.
TAYLOR, G.I. 1937. Statistical theory of turbulence. *J. Aero. Sci.* 4: 311–5.
VON KARMAN, T. 1937. Fundamentals of the statistical theory of turbulence. *J. Aero. Sci.* 4: 131–8.

13

Helicopter Flight Control Systems

13.1 INTRODUCTION

Helicopters are a type of aircraft known as rotorcraft, for they produce the lift needed to sustain flight by means of a rotating wing, the rotor. Because rotors are powered directly, helicopters can fly at zero forward speed: they can hover. They can also fly backwards, of course. At present, there are two main kinds of helicopter: those which use a single main rotor and a small tail rotor,[1] and those which have two main rotors in tandem. These helicopter types are illustrated in Figure 13.1.

In the single main rotor type, the rotor produces vertical thrust. By inclining this lift vector a helicopter can be accelerated in both the fore and aft, and the lateral directions. This main rotor is usually shaft-driven and, as a result, its torque has to be countered, usually by a small tail rotor mounted at the end of the tail boom. Yaw control is achieved by varying the thrust developed by this tail rotor.

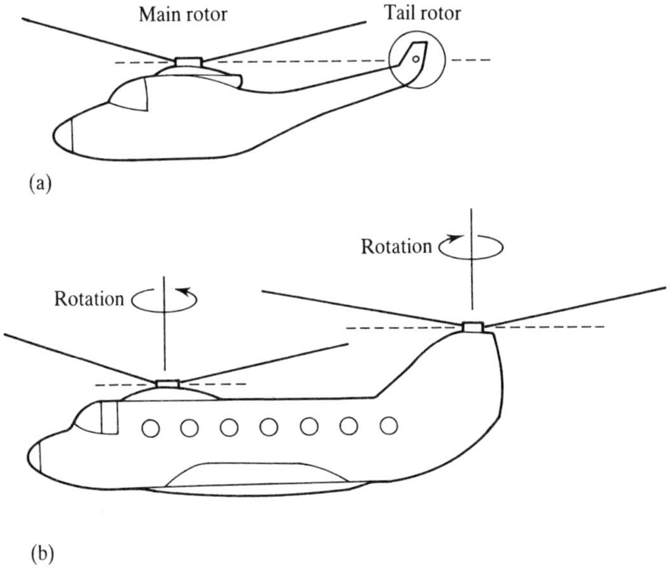

Figure 13.1 Most common helicopter types. (a) Single main rotor. (b) Tandem rotors.

In the USA and UK the main rotor rotates counterclockwise (viewed from above); in France, they use clockwise rotation. This has some significance in relation to the use of the tail rotor. To approach some point at which to hover, the pilot of a helicopter must make his aircraft flare to stop. Since it is customary for helicopter pilots to sit in the right-hand seat in the cockpit, the external view can be restricted in this flare manoeuvre, and, often, a sidewards flare is executed, which requires the pilot to apply more pressure to the left pedal in order to sideslip to the right, but this increased left pedal deflection demands a greater trimming moment from the tail rotor which has to be achieved by an increase in the thrust of that rotor. Pilots flying French helicopters do not have so great a problem in carrying out this manoeuvre.

The two rotors of the tandem helicopters are normally arranged to be at the top and the front and rear of the fuselage. These rotors rotate in opposite directions, thereby ensuring that the torque is self-balancing. There is normally a significant overlap between the rotor discs, however, the hub of the rear rotor being raised above the hub of the rotor at the front. The resulting aerodynamic interference causes a loss of power, but the amount lost, being about 8–10 per cent, is almost the same as that lost in driving a single tail rotor.

Every rotor has blades of high aspect ratio which are very flexible. These rotors are either articulated, in which case they use hinges at the root of the blades to allow free motion of the blades in directions normal to, and in the plane of, the rotor disc. A schematic representation of an articulated rotor hub is shown in Figure 13.2. At the blade hinge, the bending moment is zero; no moment is transmitted, therefore, through the root of the blade to the fuselage of the helicopter. Recent designs have eliminated hinges: these are referred to as hingeless, or rigid, rotors.

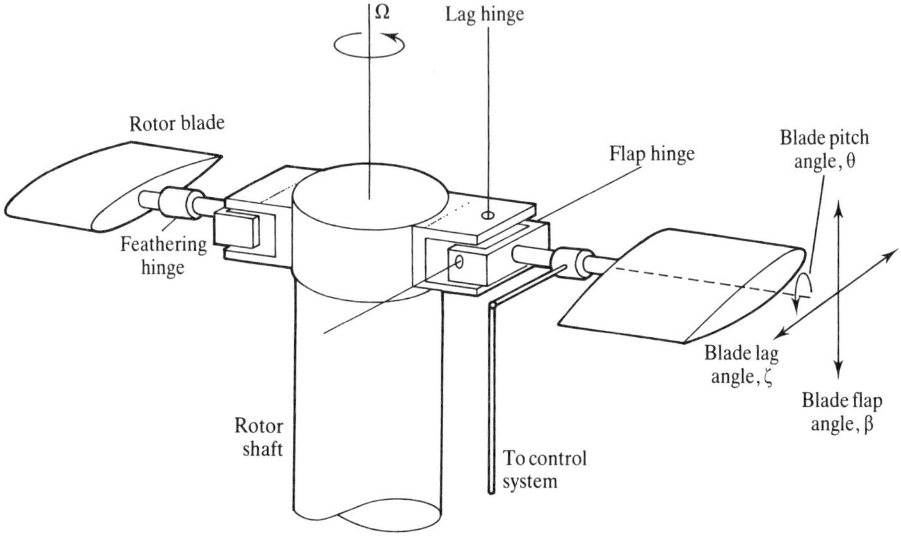

Figure 13.2 Rotor hub of an articulated rotor.

The out-of-plane motion of the blade, perpendicular to its radial direction, is referred to as its *flapping* motion. Motion about the vertical hinge causes the blade to deflect in the plane of the disc and such motion is referred to as *lagging* motion. In hingeless rotors, flapping and lagging motion are defined as the out-of-phase and the in-phase bending, respectively.

To control a rotor means that the pitch angles of its blades can be altered to cause a change in the blade's angle of attack, thereby controlling the corresponding aerodynamic forces. On a hinged blade, the pitch bearing is usually outboard of both the flapping and lagging hinges, but on a hingeless rotor the bearing may be found either in- or outboard of the major bending moment at the blade root.

With any type of rotor there will be an azimuthal variation of lift as the rotor rotates. Such variation affects the degree of flapping motion and, consequently, the direction of the average thrust vector of the rotor. A cyclic variation of lift can be effected, therefore, by changing a rotor blade's pitch as the blade is being rotated. This altering of blade pitch is termed the *cyclic pitch control*; when it causes a pitching moment to be applied to the helicopter it is called the *longitudinal cyclic*, usually denoted by δ_B. If the applied moment is about the roll axis, the control is called the *lateral cyclic*, denoted by δ_A. Yaw is controlled by changing, by the same amount, the pitch angle of all the blades of the tail rotor; such a collective deflection of the blades of the tail rotor is denoted by δ_T. When the pitch angles of all the blades of the main rotor are changed by an identical amount at every point in azimuth, a change is caused in the total lift being provided by the rotor. This type of control is called *collective pitch control*, denoted by δ_{θ_0}. Direct control of translational motion is by means of the collective control, since it is the means by which the direction of the thrust vector can be controlled.

The importance of the collective to helicopter flight cannot be overemphasized: it is a direct lift control which allows the helicopter's vertical motion to be controlled quickly and precisely. Since there is considerable energy stored when the rotor rotates (as a result of its angular momentum) only small changes in the collective setting are needed to change vertical motion without any accompanying exchange of height for airspeed. Moreover, for small collective inputs, the ability of the helicopter's engine (or engines) to change speed is not of great concern. However, this simple means of controlling height makes difficult the control of a helicopter's horizontal speed: to slow down, it is necessary to pitch a helicopter nose-up. Thus, a pilot achieves deceleration by means of pitch attitude, while maintaining his helicopter's height with the collective, which requires of the pilot greater control co-ordination. It is characteristic of helicopters during the approach to hover, and at hover, that any changes in the vehicle's speed require some adjustment of the collective which, in turn, causes a change in the helicopter's yawing motion, thereby resulting in the development of signficant sideslip. These coupled motions subsequently result (in the absence of immediate and effective pilot action) in the helicopter rolling and pitching. This complex dynamic response is of particular concern when considering a helicopter's approach on the glide slope, for it can lead to deviation from the desired flight path.

With tandem rotors, matters are different. If both rotors are tilted, a change is caused in both the forward force and the pitching moment. If differential collective pitch between the rotors is used, it is possible only to produce pitching motion; yaw control is provided by tilting the rotors in opposite directions. If the c.g. of the helicopter is not located exactly midway between the rotors, then use of the lateral cycle will inevitably produce a yawing moment.

If such a tandem helicopter is rolled towards starboard (to the right), yawing motion towards port (to the left) will be induced. This characteristic is opposite, unfortunately, to that needed to produce a co-ordinated turn.

The helicopter gives rise to a number of very distinctive AFCS problems, including the following: it is unstable; its control is effected through its major lift generator; it is capable of hovering motion; the pilot has to directly control its lift force, as well as controlling the motion about its three axes; and its speed range is narrow, the speeds involved not being very high (the upper limit is about 240 knots, i.e. $120\,\mathrm{m\ s^{-1}}$).

Only the problems involving stability and control of the helicopter are dealt with in this book, and then only briefly. However, for helicopters, more acutely than for fixed wing aircraft, the control and stability characteristics depend very heavily upon the vehicle's distinctive flight dynamics and aerodynamics.

The reader should consult Johnson (1980), Mil *et al.* (1966, 1967) and Nikolsky (1951), which are outstanding books giving excellent and comprehensive coverage. Bramwell (1976), Gessow and Myers (1952), Lefort and Menthe (1963), McCormick (1967) and Payne (1959) provide further information as useful background material, although there are a number of errors present in Payne (1959) so it must be read carefully.

13.2 EQUATIONS OF MOTION

13.2.1 Introduction

Any study of the dynamic response of a helicopter is complicated because each blade of the rotor has its own degrees of freedom, which are in addition to those of the fuselage. Yet, for small perburbations in the helicopter's motion, a knowledge of the motion of each blade is not required: only the rotor's motion as a physical entity needs to be considered. It is usual to assume that the rotor speed, Ω, is constant. Because such analyses are invariably carried out in a body-fixed axes system (see Figure 13.3) and it is assumed that all perturbations are small, the inertia terms can be linearized and the lateral and longitudinal motions may be considered as being essentially uncoupled. It should be

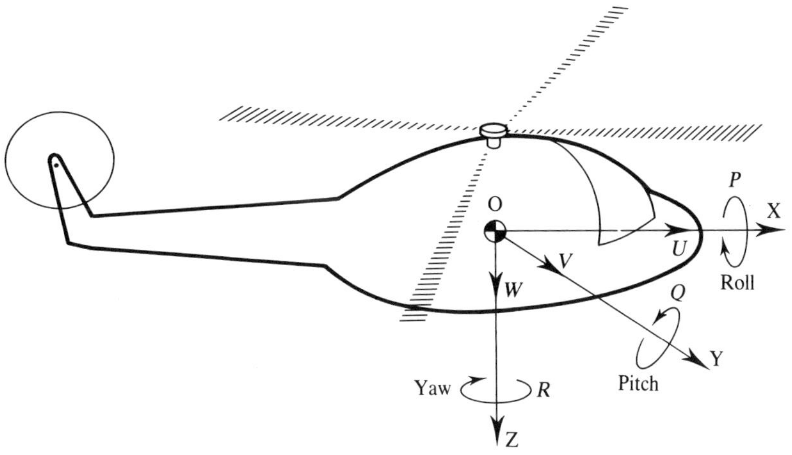

Figure 13.3 Helicopter axis system.

remembered, however, that because of the rotation of the rotors, a helicopter does not have lateral symmetry (except for coaxial or side-by-side rotor configurations). There is, consequently, considerable coupling of lateral and longitudinal motions.

For example, consider the roll coupling which can result from yawing motion. However the pedals in the cockpit are moved, a rolling acceleration is experienced because the tail rotor is generally above the roll axis. This can be easily seen from an examination of the equations governing rolling and yawing motion:

$$L = I_{xx}\ddot{\phi} - I_{xz}\ddot{\psi} \tag{13.1}$$

$$N = I_{zz}\ddot{\psi} - I_{xz}\ddot{\phi} \tag{13.2}$$

For a helicopter, if T_{tr} represents the thrust produced by the tail rotor, h represents the height of the hub of the tail rotor above the helicopter's c.g. and l is the distance aft of the c.g. at which the tail rotor is located, then:

$$L = hT_{tr} \tag{13.3}$$

$$N = -\, lT_{tr} \tag{13.4}$$

It is simple to show that the ratio of rolling to yawing acceleration can be expressed as:

$$\frac{\ddot{\phi}}{\ddot{\psi}} = \frac{hI_{zz} - lI_{xz}}{hI_{xz} - lI_{xx}} \tag{13.5}$$

Since $I_{xz} < I_{xx}$ in general, then:

$$\frac{\ddot{\phi}}{\ddot{\psi}} \simeq -\frac{h}{l}\frac{I_{zz}}{I_{xx}} + \frac{I_{xz}}{I_{xx}} \tag{13.6}$$

I_{xz}/I_{xx} can take a value in the range 0.1–0.25.

For more on equations of motion, readers should refer to Johnson (1980), Nikolsky (1951), Mil *et al.* (1966, 1977), Gessow and Myers (1952), Lefort and Menthe (1963) and Bramwell (1976).

13.2.2 Longitudinal Motion

In wind axes[2] the linearized equations of motion are:

$$m\dot{u} = -mg\theta_F\cos\gamma + \Delta X \tag{13.7}$$

$$m\dot{w} = mV\dot{\theta}_F - mg\theta_F\sin\gamma + \Delta Z \tag{13.8}$$

$$I_{yy}\ddot{\theta}_F = \Delta M \tag{13.9}$$

where ΔX and ΔZ are increments in the aerodynamic forces arising from disturbed flight, ΔM the corresponding increment in pitching moment, γ the angle of climb, and θ_F the pitch attitude of the fuselage. Because it is assumed that the perturbations in u, w and θ_F are small, the increments in the forces and the moment can be written as the first terms of a Taylor series expansion, i.e.:

$$\Delta X = \frac{\partial X}{\partial u}u + \frac{\partial X}{\partial w}w + \frac{\partial X}{\partial q}q + \frac{\partial X}{\partial \delta_B}\delta_B + \frac{\partial X}{\partial \delta_{\theta_0}}\delta_{\theta_0} \tag{13.10}$$

where δ_B is the cyclic pitch control term, and δ_{θ_0} the collective pitch control term. The coefficients $\partial X/\partial u$, $\partial X/\partial w$ etc. (or in the shorthand X_u, X_w, etc.) are the stability derivatives. Thus:

$$m\dot{u} = X_u u + X_w w + X_q q + mg\theta_F\cos\gamma + X_{\delta_B}\delta_B + X_{\delta_{\theta_0}}\delta_{\theta_0} \tag{13.11}$$

$$m\dot{w} = Z_u u + Z_w w + Z_q q + mV\dot{\theta}_F - mg\theta_F\sin\gamma + Z_{\delta_B}\delta_B + Z_{\delta_{\theta_0}}\delta_{\theta_0} \tag{13.12}$$

$$I_{yy}\ddot{\theta}_F = M_u u + M_w w + M_q q + M_{\dot{w}}\dot{w} + M_{\delta_B}\delta_B + M_{\delta_{\theta_0}}\delta_{\theta_0} \tag{13.13}$$

The term $M_{\dot{w}}\dot{w}$ is usually included to account for the effect of downwash upon any tailplane which may be fitted.

Because lift is generated by the rotating blades whose tilt angles are considered as the control inputs, it proves to be helpful to employ a non-dimensional form of those equations. Let the radius of the rotor blades be denoted by R. The tip speed of any blade is therefore given by ΩR. The blade area is $s\pi R^2$ where the solidity factor, s, of the rotor is given by:

$$s = bc/\pi R \tag{13.14}$$

where b represents the number of blades used in the rotor and c represents the chord of these blades (assuming, of course, that they are all identical).

Let:

$$\hat{u} = u/\Omega R \tag{13.15}$$

$$\hat{w} = w/\Omega R \tag{13.16}$$

$$\hat{q} = q/\Omega \tag{13.17}$$

Let there also be defined as non-dimensional time, τ:

$$\tau = t/\hat{t} \tag{13.18}$$

where:

$$\hat{t} = \frac{m}{\rho s A_{\text{ref}} \Omega R} \tag{13.19}$$

The reference area, A_{ref}, is given by:

$$A_{\text{ref}} \triangleq \pi R^2 \tag{13.20}$$

Hence:

$$\hat{t} = m/\rho bc\Omega R^2 = m/\rho s \pi R^3 \Omega \tag{13.21}$$

Note that:

$$\hat{q} \neq \mathrm{d}\theta_{\mathrm{F}}/\mathrm{d}\tau \tag{13.22}$$

but:

$$\hat{q} = \Omega\hat{t}(\mathrm{d}\theta_{\mathrm{F}}/\mathrm{d}\tau) \tag{13.23}$$

A relative density parameter, μ^*, is defined for longitudinal motion as:

$$\mu^* = \Omega\hat{t} = m/\rho s A_{\text{ref}} R \tag{13.24}$$

Therefore:

$$\hat{q} = \mu^*(\mathrm{d}\theta_{\mathrm{F}}/\mathrm{d}\tau) \tag{13.25}$$

The non-dimensional moment of inertia is defined as:

$$i_{yy} = I_{yy}/mR^2 \tag{13.26}$$

and the non-dimensional stability derivatives are defined as:

$$x_u = X_u/\rho s A_{\text{ref}} \Omega R \tag{13.27}$$

$$x_w = X_w/\rho s A_{\text{ref}} \Omega R \tag{13.28}$$

$$x'_q = X_q/\rho s A_{\text{ref}} \Omega R^2 \tag{13.29}$$

(The significance of the prime is explained after eq. (13.45).)

$$z_u = Z_u/\rho s A_{\text{ref}} \Omega R \tag{13.30}$$

$$z_w = Z_w/\rho s A_{\text{ref}} \Omega R \tag{13.31}$$

$$z'_q = Z_q/\rho s A_{\text{ref}}\Omega R^2 \tag{13.32}$$

$$m'_u = M_u/\rho s A_{\text{ref}}\Omega R^2 \tag{13.33}$$

$$m'_w = M_w/\rho s A_{\text{ref}}\Omega R^2 \tag{13.34}$$

$$m'_{\dot{w}} = M_{\dot{w}}/\rho s A_{\text{ref}}\Omega R^2 \tag{13.35}$$

$$m'_q = M_q/\rho s A_{\text{ref}}\Omega R^3 \tag{13.36}$$

$$x_{\delta_B} = X_{\delta_B}/\rho s A_{\text{ref}}\Omega^2 R^2 \tag{13.37}$$

$$z_{\delta_B} = Z_{\delta_B}/\rho s A_{\text{ref}}\Omega^2 R^2 \tag{13.38}$$

$$m'_{\delta_B} = M_{\delta_B}/\rho s A_{\text{ref}}\Omega^2 R^3 \tag{13.39}$$

$$x_{\delta_{\theta_0}} = X_{\delta_{\theta_0}}/\rho s A_{\text{ref}}\Omega^2 R^2 \tag{13.40}$$

$$z_{\delta_{\theta_0}} = Z_{\delta_{\theta_0}}/\rho s A_{\text{ref}}\Omega^2 R^2 \tag{13.41}$$

$$m'_{\delta_{\theta_0}} = M_{\delta_{\theta_0}}/\rho s A_{\text{ref}}\Omega^2 R^3 \tag{13.42}$$

Hence, if eqs (13.11) and (13.12) are divided by $\rho s A_{\text{ref}}\Omega^2 R^2$, and eq. (13.13) by $\rho s A_{\text{ref}}\Omega^2 R^3$, the following equations are obtained:

$$\frac{d\hat{u}}{d\tau} = x_u\hat{u} + x_w\hat{w} + \frac{x'_q}{\mu^*}\frac{d\hat{\theta}_F}{d\tau} - mg\hat{\theta}_F\cos\gamma + x_{\delta_B}\delta_B + x_{\delta_{\theta_0}}\delta_{\theta_0} \tag{13.43}$$

$$\frac{d\hat{w}}{d\tau} = z_u\hat{u} + z_w\hat{w} + \left(V + \frac{z'_q}{\mu}\right)\frac{d\hat{\theta}_F}{d\tau} - mg\theta_F\sin\gamma + z_{\delta_B}\delta_B + z_{\delta_{\theta_0}}\delta_{\theta_0} \tag{13.44}$$

$$\frac{d^2\hat{\theta}_F}{d\tau_2} = \frac{\mu^*}{i_{yy}}m'_u\hat{u} + \frac{\mu^*}{i_{yy}}m'_{\hat{w}}\hat{w} + \frac{\mu^*}{i_{yy}}m'_{\dot{w}}\hat{w}\frac{d\hat{w}}{d\tau} + \frac{m'_q}{i_{yy}}\frac{d\hat{\theta}_F}{d\tau}$$

$$+ \frac{\mu^*}{i_{yy}}m'_{\delta_B}\delta_B + \frac{\mu^*}{i_{yy}}m'_{\delta_{\theta_0}}\delta_{\theta_0} \tag{13.45}$$

This non-dimensional form of the equations of motion (eqs (13.43)–(13.45)) is due to Bryant and Gates (1930); it is, however, a cumbersome notation. The prime has been used here to indicate that the form being developed is not the final one. For notational convenience it is proposed to write:

$$\mu^* m'_u/i_{yy} = m_u \tag{13.46}$$

or

$$x'_q/\mu^* = x_q \tag{13.47}$$

Similarly, the circumflex will be dispensed with from hereon. Thus:

$$\frac{du}{d\tau} = x_u u + x_w w + x_q\frac{d\theta_F}{d\tau} - mg\theta_F\cos\gamma + x_{\delta_B}\delta_B + x_{\delta_{\theta_0}}\delta_{\theta_0} \tag{13.48}$$

$$\frac{dw}{d\tau} = z_u u + z_w w + (V + z_q)\frac{d\theta_F}{d\tau} - mg\theta_F\sin\gamma + z_{\delta_B}\delta_B + z_{\delta_{\theta_0}}\delta_{\theta_0} \tag{13.49}$$

$$\frac{dq}{d\tau} = m_u u + m_w w + m_{\dot{w}} \dot{w} + m_q q + m_{\delta_B} \delta_B + m_{\delta_{\theta_0}} \delta_{\theta_0} \tag{13.50}$$

$$d\theta_F/d\tau = q \tag{13.51}$$

13.2.3 Lateral Motion

To control lateral motion the following inputs are used: the deflection angle of the lateral cyclic, δ_{A_1} and the collective pitch angle of the tail rotor, δ_T. The corresponding equations of motion are:

$$m\dot{v} = Y_v v + Y_p p - mVr + Y_r r + mg\phi \cos\gamma + mg\psi_F \sin\gamma + Y_{\delta_A} \delta_A + Y_{\delta_T} \delta_T \tag{13.52}$$

$$I_{xx}\dot{p} - I_{xz}\dot{r} = L_v v + L_p p + L_r r + L_{\delta_A} \delta_A + L_{\delta_T} \delta_T \tag{13.53}$$

$$-I_{xz}\dot{p} + I_{zz}\dot{r} = N_v v + N_p p + N_r r + N_{\delta_A} \delta_A + N_{\delta_T} \delta_T \tag{13.54}$$

I_{xx}, I_{zz} and I_{xz} are the moments of inertia. The derivatives Y_p and Y_r are usually negligible in helicopter studies. Using the same procedure to non-dimensionalize these equations as that employed with the longitudinal motion produces:

$$i_{xx} = I_{xx}/mR^2 \tag{13.55}$$

$$i_{zz} = I_{zz}/mR^2 \tag{13.56}$$

$$i_{xz} = I_{xz}/mR^2 \tag{13.57}$$

$$\frac{dv}{d\tau} = y_v v + mg\phi \cos\gamma - \frac{V d\psi_F}{d\tau} + mg\psi_F \sin\gamma + y_{\delta_A} \delta_A + y_{\delta_T} \delta_T \tag{13.58}$$

$$\frac{dp}{d\tau} = l_v v + l_p p + l_r r + \frac{i_{xz}}{i_{xx}} \dot{r} + l_{\delta_A} \delta_A + l_{\delta_T} \delta_T \tag{13.59}$$

$$\frac{dr}{d\tau} = n_v v + n_p p + n_r r + \frac{i_{xz}}{i_{zz}} \dot{p} + n_{\delta_A} \delta_A + n_{\delta_T} \delta_T \tag{13.60}$$

13.2.4 Canonical Form

If the following are chosen as state vectors:

$$\mathbf{x}'_{long} \triangleq [u \;\; w \;\; q \;\; \theta_F] \tag{13.61}$$

$$\mathbf{x}'_{lat} \triangleq [v \;\; p \;\; r \;\; \phi \;\; \psi_F] \tag{13.62}$$

and the following as control vectors:

$$\mathbf{u}'_{long} \triangleq [\delta_B \;\; \delta_{\theta_0}] \tag{13.63}$$

$$\mathbf{u}'_{lat} \triangleq [\delta_A \;\; \delta_T] \tag{13.64}$$

then the equations of motion can be represented in a canonical form, namely:

$$\dot{\mathbf{x}} = A\mathbf{x} + B\mathbf{u} \tag{13.65}$$

i.e.:

$$\dot{\mathbf{x}}_{\text{long}} = A_{\text{long}}\mathbf{x}_{\text{long}} + B_{\text{long}}\mathbf{u}_{\text{long}} \tag{13.66}$$

$$\dot{\mathbf{x}}_{\text{lat}} = A_{\text{lat}}\mathbf{x}_{\text{lat}} + B_{\text{lat}}\mathbf{u}_{\text{lat}} \tag{13.67}$$

where:

$$A_{\text{long}} = \begin{bmatrix} x_u & x_w & x_q & -mg\cos\gamma \\ z_u & z_w & (V + z_q) & -mg\sin\gamma \\ \tilde{m}_u & \tilde{m}_w & \tilde{m}_q & 0 \\ 0 & 0 & 1 & 0 \end{bmatrix} \tag{13.68}$$

$$B_{\text{long}} = \begin{bmatrix} x_{\delta_B} & x_{\delta_{\theta_0}} \\ z_{\delta_B} & z_{\delta_{\theta_0}} \\ \tilde{m}_{\delta_B} & \tilde{m}_{\delta_{\theta_0}} \\ 0 & 0 \end{bmatrix} \tag{13.69}$$

in which

$$\tilde{m}_u = (m_u + m_{\dot{w}} z_u) \tag{13.70}$$

$$\tilde{m}_w = (m_w + m_{\dot{w}} z_w) \tag{13.71}$$

$$\tilde{m}_q = (m_q + m_{\dot{w}}(V + z_q)) \tag{13.72}$$

$$\tilde{m}_{\delta_B} = (m_{\delta_B} + m_{\dot{w}} z_{\delta_B}) \tag{13.73}$$

$$\tilde{m}_{\delta_{\theta_0}} = (m_{\delta_{\theta_0}} + m_{\dot{w}} z_{\delta_{\theta_0}}) \tag{13.74}$$

and where:

$$A_{\text{lat}} = \begin{bmatrix} y_v & 0 & -V + mg & 0 \\ \tilde{l}_v & \tilde{l}_p & \tilde{l}_r & 0 & 0 \\ \tilde{n}_v & \tilde{n}_p & \tilde{n}_r & 0 & 0 \\ 0 & 1 & 0 & 0 & 0 \\ 0 & 0 & 1 & 0 & 0 \end{bmatrix} \tag{13.75}$$

$$B_{\text{lat}} = \begin{bmatrix} y_{\delta_A} & y_{\delta_T} \\ \tilde{l}_{\delta_A} & \tilde{l}_{\delta_T} \\ \tilde{n}_{\delta_A} & \tilde{n}_{\delta_T} \\ 0 & 0 \\ 0 & 0 \end{bmatrix} \tag{13.76}$$

and in which, for example:

$$\tilde{l}_p = \left(l_p + \frac{i_{xz}}{i_{xx}} n_p \right) \Big/ \left(1 - \frac{i_{xz}^2}{i_{xx} i_{zz}} \right) \tag{13.77}$$

$$\tilde{n}_p = \left(n_p + \frac{i_{xz}}{i_{zz}} l_p \right) \Big/ \left(1 - \frac{i_{xz}^2}{i_{xx} i_{zz}} \right) \tag{13.78}$$

The other stability derivatives, $\tilde{l}_v$, $\tilde{l}_r$, $\tilde{n}_v$ and $\tilde{n}_r$, can be derived in similar fashion.

13.3 STATIC STABILITY

13.3.1 Introduction

Static stability is of cardinal importance in the study of helicopter motion since the several equlibrium modes so much affect each other. For example, any disruption of directional equilibrium will lead to a change in the thrust delivered from the tail rotor, resulting in a corresponding change of the moment of this force (relative to the longitudinal axis, OX) which causes a disruption in the transverse equilibrium of the helicopter. But how does any disruption of directional equilibrium occur in the first place? Suppose the helicopter rotates about the transverse axis, OY, i.e. its longitudinal equilibrium is disrupted. The angle of attack of the main rotor will then change; such a change causes a change in thrust and, consequently, a change in the reactive moment of the main rotor. That change disrupts the directional equilibrium.

The practical significance of this interplay between the balancing forces means that a helicopter pilot must constantly try to restore the disrupted equilibrium so that controlling (i.e. flying) a helicopter is more complicated and therefore more difficult than flying a fixed wing aircraft. That is why the simple question: 'Do helicopters possess static stability?' requires the examination of a number of factors before an answer can be attempted. Three factors are involved: (1) the static stability properties, if any, of the main rotor; (2) the static stability properties, if any, of the fuselage, and (3) the effect of the tail rotor and any tailplane on any static stability properties.

Further discussion of static stability can be found in Johnson (1980) and Mil *et al.* (1966).

13.3.2 Static Stability of the Main Rotor

Speed

In Figure 13.4 it is assumed that the helicopter is flying straight and level at a speed V. Subsequently, the speed is increased by a small amount, ΔV. The flapping motion of the blades therefore increases (see Section 4.9 of Chapter 4).

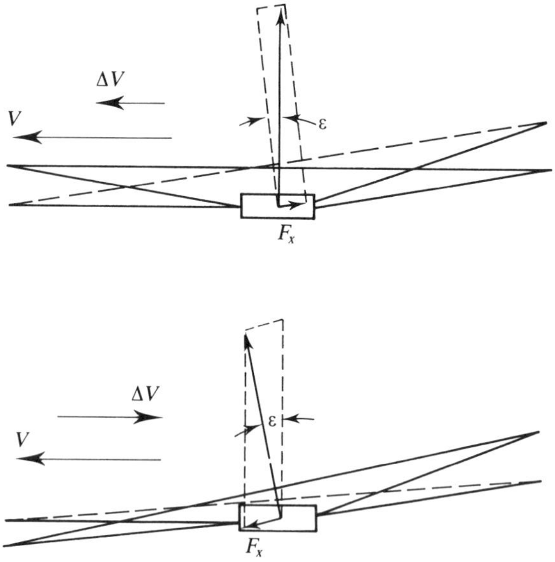

Figure 13.4 Static stability of main rotor with speed.

As a result, the axis of the cone of the main rotor is deflected aft, from its previous position, by an angle denoted by ε. (This movement is represented in Figure 13.4 by the dashed line.) Such a tilt of the coning axis leads to the development of a force F_x which is in an opposite sense to the direction of flight. As a result of this force, the velocity of the main rotor falls, and hence the helicopter reduces its forward speed.

If it had been assumed that, when the helicopter was flying straight and level, the speed has been reduced by an amount ΔV, the cone axis would then have been deflected forward, and the force, F_x, would have developed in the same sense as the direction of flight, thereby causing an increase in the forward speed.

It can be concluded that with respect to changes in speed, the main rotor is statically stable.

Angle of Attack

In Figure 13.5 the helicopter is once more assumed to be flying straight and level with its main rotor at an angle of attack of α_{MR_A}. The thrust delivered by the main rotor passed through the helicopter's c.g. and hence any moment of the thrust must be zero. Under the influence of a vertical air current, say, the helicopter lowers its nose and, therefore, the angle of attack of the main rotor is reduced by an amount $\Delta\alpha_A$. (See the dashed line in Figure 13.5.) The vector of thrust is now deflected forward.

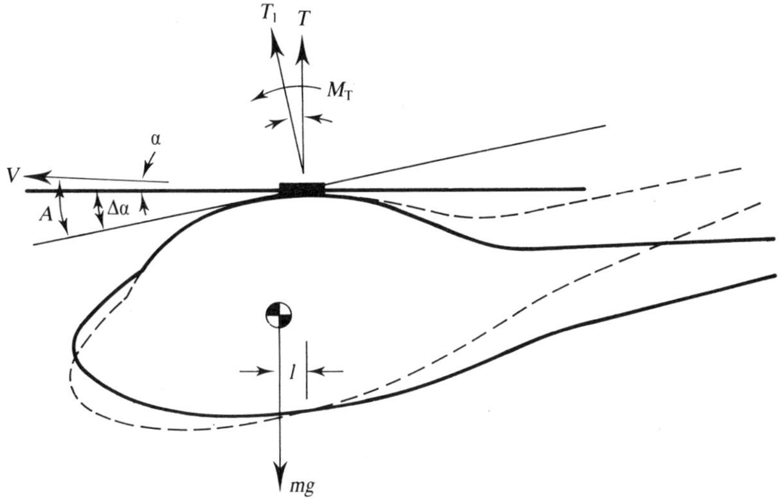

Figure 13.5 Static stability of main rotor with angle of attack.

A moment, M_T, given in eq. (13.72), is established which causes the value of the angle of attack of the main rotor to decrease:

$$M_T = Tl$$

This moment is destabilizing.

If the angle of attack of the main rotor is increased, however, the thrust vector will tilt aftwards and a nose-up moment, M_T, will be established causing the angle of attack of the main rotor to increase further.

The main rotor is statically unstable, therefore, with respect to fuselage angle of attack. Provided that no translation occurs, a helicopter in hovering motion has neutral stability with respect to any change in attitude.

Fuselage Stability

The greatest influence upon the static stability of a helicopter is that of the rotor; the contribution of the fuselage to static stability is not negligible, however. For a single rotor helicopter, for example, the fuselage is statically unstable in all three axes of motion. A small tailplane is sometimes installed at the aft end of the fuselage to improve the static stability of longitudinal motion in straight and level flight. Its influence is practically nil at low speeds and at hover. However, the degree of instability in longitudinal motion can be reduced from the value at hover by increasing forward speed and by reducing the angle of attack until, at negative angles of attack, the fuselage plus tailplane possesses some static stability. This principle can be seen by referring to Figure 13.6.

The longitudinal static stability is denoted by M_α. Curve 2 represents the change in M_α with forward speed for a helicopter with an articulated rotor. The same characteristic is represented in curves 1 and 3 for a helicopter with a hinge-

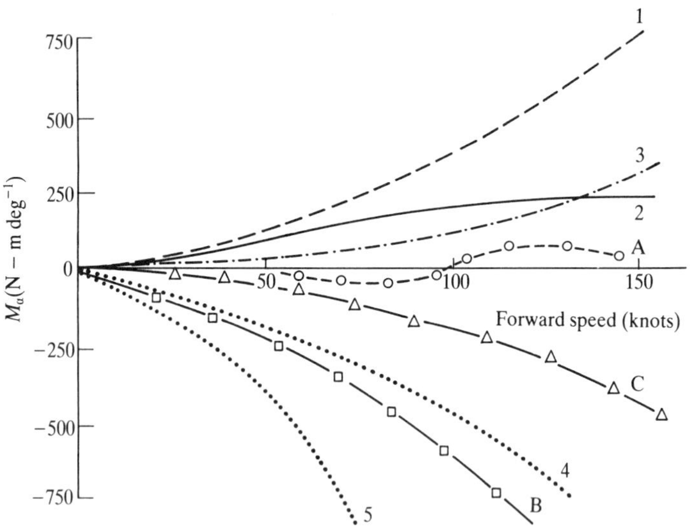

Figure 13.6 Fuselage stability characteristics.

less rotor and for the fuselage only of a helicopter, respectively. Note that in each of these curves dM_α/dV is positive. The changes in static stability with forward speed corresponding to a tailplane is shown as curve 4; curve 5 represents the same characteristic for another tailplane, the same as that corresponding to curve 4, but with twice its area. Note that for these curves dM_α/dV is negative. The effect of having a helicopter with a hingeless rotor, the fuselage of curve 3 and the tailplane of curve 4, is shown in curve A. Curve B represents the results of combining curves 2, 3 and 4 and curve C is the result of the combination 1, 3 and 5. It is obvious that providing adequate static stability throughout the speed range of a helicopter is particularly difficult.

If a helicopter is fitted with a tail rotor it has a profound effect on the fuselage's static stability for, if the directional equilibrium is disrupted and the helicopter turns to the right, [3] say, the angle of attack of the blade elements of the tail rotor will increase and, consequently, the thrust from the tail rotor increases by some amount, ΔT. Therefore, the moment of this thrust must also increase thereby restoring equilibrium. In this manner the tail rotor gives the fuselage directional static stability.

If the hub of the main rotor has offset horizontal (lagging) hinges (see Figure 13.2), the hinge moments associated with that offset have a considerable effect on both longitudinal and transverse static stability of that helicopter. The greater the offset of the hinge and the rotational speed of the rotor, the greater is the static stability possessed by the helicopter. These same factors also contribute to the increase in damping moment contributed by the main rotor.

13.4 DYNAMIC STABILITY

Since the flying qualities of a helicopter are markedly different in forward flight and in hovering motion, these two flight regimes are dealt with separately. The subject of dynamic stability is further discussed in Johnson (1980), Nikolsky (1951) and Mil *et al.* (1967).

13.4.1 Longitudinal Motion

Stick-fixed, forward flight

The pilot's stick being assumed fixed, there are no control inputs, δ_B, δ_{θ_0}, δ_A or δ_T: the dynamic stability properties are determined solely from the coefficient matrix.

For straight and level flight,

$$\gamma \triangleq 0 \tag{13.79}$$

$$V \geqslant z_q \tag{13.80}$$

Hence, the corresponding coefficient matrix, A^*_{long}, can be expressed as:

$$A^*_{\text{long}} = \begin{bmatrix} x_u & x_w & x_q & -mg \\ z_u & z_w & V & 0 \\ \tilde{m}_u & \tilde{m}_w & \tilde{m}_q & 0 \\ 0 & 0 & 1 & 0 \end{bmatrix} \tag{13.81}$$

and it corresponding characteristic polynomial can be found by evaluating: $|\lambda I - A^*_{\text{long}}|$, i.e.:

$$|\lambda I - A^*_{\text{long}}| = a_4\lambda^4 + a_3\lambda^3 + a_2\lambda^2 + a_1\lambda + a_0 \tag{13.82}$$

where:

$$a_4 \triangleq 1.0 \tag{13.83}$$

$$a_3 \triangleq -x_u - z_w - m_q - Vm_w \tag{13.84}$$

$$a_2 = \mathrm{x_u}(z_w + m_q) + V(x_u m_{\dot{w}} - m_w) + \mathrm{m_q}(\mathrm{x_u} + \mathrm{z_w}) \tag{13.85}$$

$$a_1 = mg(m_u + m_{\dot{w}} z_u) + V(x_u m_w - x_w m_u) - m_q(x_u z_w - x_w z_u) \tag{13.86}$$

$$a_0 = mg(z_u m_w - z_w m_u) \tag{13.87}$$

For complete dynamic stability it is necessary that every real root, or every real part of any complex root, shall be negative. With the wide availability of computers it is now a simple matter to assess helicopter stability: simply read in the coefficient matrix, use an eigenvalue routine to determine the eigenvalues of the coefficient matrix, and check the real eigenvalues and the real parts of the complex eigenvalues to determine if they are negative. Otherwise polynomial routines or the algebraic checks of Routh and Hurwitz (see Chapter 7) should be used.

Hovering Motion

When a helicopter hovers, V is zero and, usually, x_w, x_q, m_m and $m_{\dot{w}}$ are negligible, i.e the equations of motion given by eqs (13.48)–(13.52) now become:

$$\dot{u} = x_u u - mg\theta_F + x_{\delta_B}\delta_B + x_{\delta_{\theta_0}}\delta_{\theta_0} \tag{13.88}$$

$$\dot{w} = z_u u + z_w w + z_{\delta_B}\delta_B + z_{\delta_{\theta_0}}\delta_{\theta_0} \tag{13.89}$$

$$\dot{q} = m_u u + m_q q + m_{\delta_B}\delta_B + m_{\delta_{\theta_0}}\delta_{\theta_0} \tag{13.90}$$

Hence, the characteristic polynomial can be shown to be:

$$\Delta_{\text{hover}} = \lambda^3 - (x_u + m_q)\lambda^2 + x_u m_q \lambda + mgm_u \tag{13.91}$$

which is usually factored into the form:

$$\Delta_{\text{hover}} = (\lambda + p_1)(\lambda^2 + 2\zeta\omega\lambda + \omega^2) \tag{13.92}$$

The factor $(\lambda + p_1)$ corresponds to a stable, subsidence mode, whereas the quadratic factor corresponds to an unstable, oscillatory mode since ζ invariably lies in the range 0 to $-$ 1.0. Consequently, the longitudinal dynamics of a helicopter at hover separate into two distinct motions: vertical and longitudinal. It is easy to show (from eqs (13.88)–(13.90) that:

$$\frac{w(s)}{\delta_{\theta_0}(s)} = \frac{z_{\delta_{\theta_0}}}{(s - z_w)} = \frac{sh(s)}{\delta_{\theta_0}(s)} \tag{13.93}$$

i.e. the vertical motion of a helicopter at hover is described by a first order linear differential equation, with a time constant given by:

$$T_v = -1/z_w \tag{13.94}$$

The time-to-half amplitude is typically about 2 s since the value of z_w typically lies within the range $-$ 0.01 to $-$ 0.02.

In many ways, this simplified representation of the vertical motion in response to collective input is misleading. The vertical damping, z_w, is not a simple aerodynamic term but is composed of contributions from the fuselage and from the inflow created by the rotor. In hovering motion, the inflow contribution is predominant. The value of z_w, however, which is speed dependent, does have a marked effect on the thrust-to-weight ratio required for helicopter flight. Furthermore, the value of vertical damping required for a particular height response is considerably affected by the response time of the engine(s) driving the rotor. Of considerable importance to any control in helicopters is the nature of the engine response. In terms of system design and analysis it is imperative to have a reasonable mathematical representation of the dynamics of the engine and the transmission system. Unfortunately, such reasonable and simple models are not easily found in the open literature: representation by a low order linear model is frequently misleading. Since no adequate engine/transmission model was available to the author, it has been decided to omit such dynamic effects from the analyses presented in this chapter, but the reader who finds himself concerned with the practicality of helicopter flight control systems is reminded that such dynamics ought never to be ignored in practice.

The instability of the longitudinal dynamics is as a result of the coupling of the motion via the pitching moments which come about as a result of the change in longitudinal velocity, i.e. M_u (the so-called speed stability), and the longitudinal component of the gravititational force. For static stability, the requirement is that the constant term of the characteristic polynomial shall be positive, i.e.

$$mgm_u > 0 \tag{13.95}$$

The inequality (13.95) can be satisfied with a positive value of m_u. The oscillation associated with the longitudinal dynamics is only mildly unstable with a typical period of 10–20 s. Time-to-double amplitude, t_d, is about 3–4 s. Both the period and the time-to-double amplitude are sufficiently long for the motion to be controllable by a pilot.

Although the hub moments available in helicopters with hingeless rotors, or articulated rotors with offset hinges, are very much greater than in other types, thereby greatly increasing the capability of the rotor to produce moments about the helicopter's c.g., the character of the helicopter's dynamics are not radically altered, although there is a real improvement in the controllability. However, for hingeless rotors, the flap frequency is large enough to influence the dynamics. The moment derivatives, M_u, M_w, M_q, $M_{\delta_{\theta_0}}$, and M_{δ_B}, may be doubled (approximately) by using flap hinge offset; for a hingeless rotor, M_u and $M_{\delta_{\theta_0}}$ are increased by as much as three or four times.[4] The pitch damping derivative, M_q, is increased even more which results in an increase in the value of the real root, p_1, of the vertical mode; it also increases somewhat the period and time-to-double amplitude of the oscillatory mode. Because a helicopter with a hingeless rotor has such large pitch damping (and consequently a less unstable oscillatory mode) than a corresponding helicopter with an articulated rotor, and because it also has greater control power, the task of controlling such a helicopter is easier.

In summary, for a hovering helicopter, the longitudinal dynamics are described by a stable, subsidence mode (a large negative real root due to pitch damping) and a mildly unstable, oscillatory mode (due to the speed stability M_u). A pilot will have good control over the angular acceleration of the helicopter, but poor direct control over translation. Because of the low damping, in hover the control sensitivity is high. This combination of high sensitivity and only indirect control of translational velocity makes a hovering helicopter prone to pilot-induced oscillations (p.i.o.) thereby increasing the difficulty of the pilot's task.

To aggravate matters, the lateral and longitudinal motions are not decoupled, as supposed, and, for many types of helicopter, a longitudinal cyclic input can result in large corresponding lateral motion. Furthermore, because of the speed stability of its rotor, a helicopter is susceptible to gusts whenever it is hovering and, as result, its position relative to the ground drifts considerably: this makes the task of station-keeping, for which helicopters are universally employed, particularly taxing.

Forward Flight (with a Tailplane)

In forward flight the unstable, oscillatory mode is made worse with an increase of speed. However, the addition of a tailplane can provide sufficient extra damping to result in the oscillatory mode being stabilized.

The longitudinal dynamic stability of a helicopter with a hingeless rotor is particularly bad at high speed and is generally inferior to that of a comparable helicopter which has an articulated rotor, with flapping hinges of small offset. Of course, its control power is generally increased and, therefore, a suitable SAS may be used to recover the required degree of stability. From Figure 13.7 it can be seen that, for a helicopter with an articulated rotor, the period of the unstable oscillatory mode increases with forward speed, and becomes stable at about 85 knots. This value of speed is influenced by the size of tailplane used. In Figure 13.7(b) it will be seen that for a hingeless rotor, the period does not change much with forward speed; if anything, there is a tendency to a much greater degree of instability at high speed, as a result of the large and unfavourable value of M_{α} (see Figure 13.6). This tendency can be somewhat abated by increasing the area of the tailplane, which can be inferred from Figure 13.7(b).

13.4.2 Lateral Motion

Stick-fixed

Assume straight and level flight, i.e.:

$$\gamma \triangleq 0 \tag{13.96}$$

then the coefficient matrix, A_{lat}, can be re-expressed as:

$$A^*_{\text{lat}} = \begin{bmatrix} y_v & 0 & -V+mg & 0 \\ \tilde{l}_v & \tilde{l}_p & \tilde{l}_r & 0 & 0 \\ \tilde{n}_v & \tilde{n}_p & \tilde{n}_r & 0 & 0 \\ 0 & 1 & 0 & 0 & 0 \\ 0 & 0 & 1 & 0 & 0 \end{bmatrix} \tag{13.97}$$

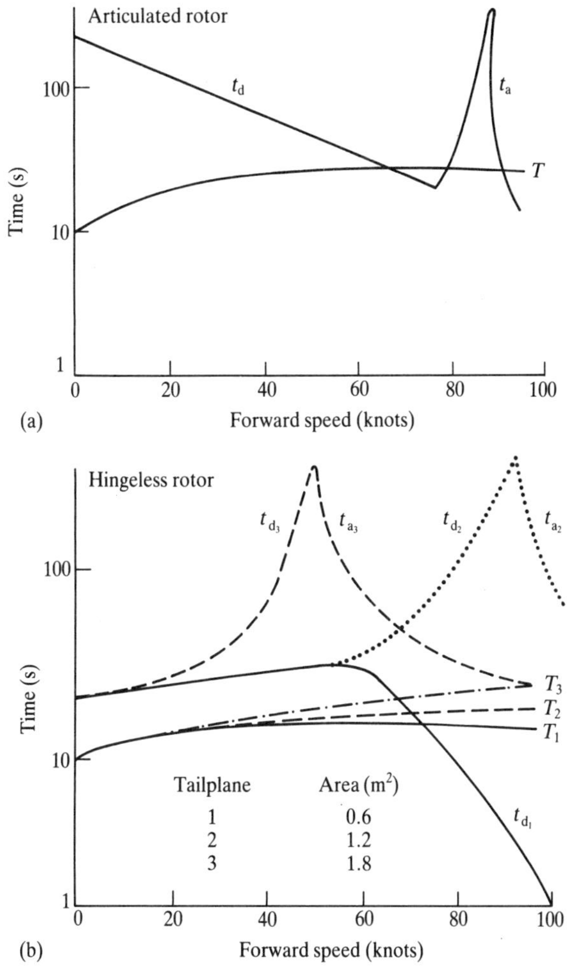

Figure 13.7 Forward flight stability parameters. (a) Articulated rotor. (b) Hingeless rotor.

The characteristic polynomial is given by $|\lambda I - A^*_{\text{lat}}|$ which can be expanded to:

$$\Delta_{\text{lat}} = \lambda(b_4\lambda^4 + b_3\lambda^3 + b_2\lambda^2 + b_1\lambda + b_0) \tag{13.98}$$

where:

$$b_4 = 1 - (i_{xz}^2/i_{xx}i_{zz}) \tag{13.99}$$

$$b_3 = -y_v(1 - (i_{xz}^2/i_{xx}i_{zz})) - l_p - n_r - (i_{xz}/i_{zz})l_r + (i_{xz}/i_{xx})n_p \tag{13.100}$$

$$b_2 = y_v(l_p + n_r + (i_{xz}/i_{zz})l_r + (i_{xz}/i_{xx})n_p) + l_p n_r - l_r n_p + l_v V(i_{xz}/i_{zz}) + n_v V \tag{13.101}$$

$$b_1 = y_v(l_p n_r - l_r n_p) + l_v(n_p V - mg) - n_v l_p V \tag{13.102}$$

$$b_0 = l_v n_r mg - mg - n_v l_r mg = mg(l_v n_r - n_v l_r) \tag{13.103}$$

The single λ term implies that $\lambda = 0$ is a solution of the characteristic equation, and, consequently, a helicopter has neutral stability in heading.

Hovering Motion

In hovering motion the forward speed is zero. When longitudinal motion in hover is considered it is found that a number of stability derivatives are either zero, or negligible, which leads to a substantial simplification of the equations of motion. However, such simplifications do not occur in lateral motion studies, because the yawing (r) and rolling (p) motions are coupled by virtue of the stability derivatives, l_r and n_p, which have significant values owing to the tail rotor. If, however, it is assumed that the shaft of the tail rotor is on the roll axis, then l_r can be considered negligible. Then the characteristic polynomial becomes:

$$(\lambda - n_r)(\lambda^3 - [y_v + l_p]\lambda^2 + y_v l_p \lambda - l_v mg) \tag{13.104}$$

The root ($\lambda = n_r$) means that the yawing motion is stable (since n_r is invariably negative) and independent of sideways and rolling motion. The cubic can be factored into:

$$(\lambda + p_2)(\lambda^2 - 2\zeta_1\omega_1\lambda + \omega_1^2) \tag{13.105}$$

The first factor corresponds to a stable rolling, subsidence mode; the quadratic represents an unstable, oscillatory mode. Typically, for the rolling subsidence mode, t_a is less than 0.5 s; the period of the oscillation is about 15–20 s, whereas the time-to-double amplitude is about 20–30 s. The time constant of the yawing mode is about 5 s.

Forward Flight

The quartic of eq. (13.98) has been solved for a range of values of the advance ratio, μ, and the values of the real and imaginary parts of the corresponding eigenvalues have been displayed as a root locus diagram in Figure 13.8. It is evident from this figure that as the forward speed of the helicopter increases the complex roots become stable. There is now a spiral mode, a rolling subsidence mode (still rapid) and a stable oscillatory mode corresponding to dutch roll oscillation, i.e.:

$$\dot{\psi}_F = -\dot{\beta} = -v/\mu \tag{13.106}$$

Hence, this helicopter will 'weathercock' with very little translation sideways.

If a hingeless rotor is employed it can increase the hub moment by about a factor of five, in relation to an articulated rotor with a hinge offset by 4 per cent. Such an increase in hub moment increases the stability derivatives, l_p and l_v, but not the stability derivative, n_v. The quartic then becomes:

$$(\lambda + n_r)(\lambda + p_2)(\lambda^2 + \omega_1^2) \tag{13.107}$$

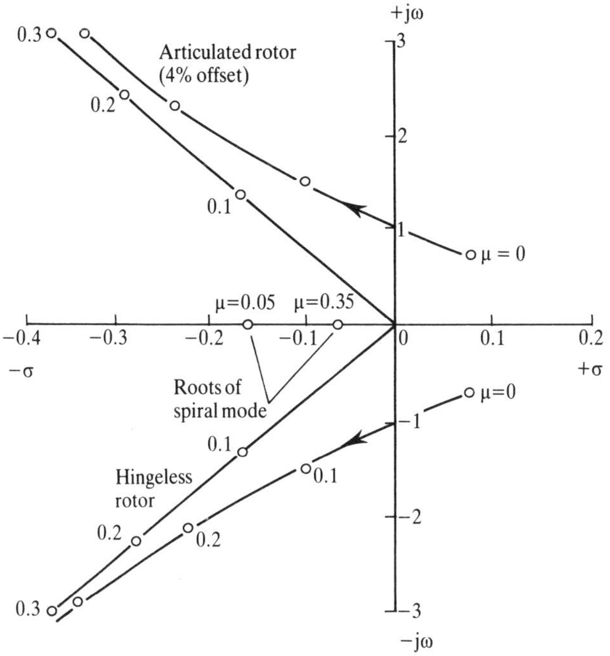

Figure 13.8 Root locus diagram.

The root of the rolling subsidence mode, p_2, has typically a value of about 10.0–15.0; t_a reduces. The oscillatory mode, which was unstable, is now neutrally stable, with a period of about 15–20 s.

13.5 STABILITY AUGMENTATION SYSTEMS

From earlier chapters it can be learned how the application of feedback control of the proper kind can result in an unstable system becoming stable. For helicopter longitudinal dynamics the most common feedback control laws are:

$$\delta_B = K_1\theta_F - K_2 q \tag{13.108}$$

or

$$\delta_B + \tau\dot{\delta}_B = K_2 q \tag{13.109}$$

How such feedback control laws are implemented can depend on whether passive or active methods are to be used.

There are a few passive techniques in current use; the best known is the stabilizer bar to be found on some Bell helicopters. (See, for example, the illustration of the Bell 212 in Jane's *All the World's Aircraft (1983–1984)*.)

13.5.1 Stabilizing Bar

This simple mechanical device is essentially a gyroscope: it is a bar pivoted to the rotor shaft and has a viscous damper provided. The bar is linked to the rotor blades so that if the bar is caused to tilt relative to the shaft a change in the pitch of the rotor blade will be caused (see Figure 13.9).

The angular displacement of the bar is denoted by δ. The equation motion of the bar is given by:

$$\ddot{\delta} + 2K\Omega\dot{\delta} + \Omega^2\delta = -2\Omega q \sin\phi + \dot{q}\cos\phi \quad (13.110)$$

where q is the angular pitching velocity of the rotor hub, and ϕ the azimuthal angle of the blade, i.e. the angle between the blade span and the rear centre-line of the helicopter. In practice the term $\dot{q}\cos\phi$ is negligible, hence:

$$\ddot{\delta} + 2K\Omega\dot{\delta} + \Omega^2\delta = -2\Omega q \sin\phi \quad (13.111)$$

Suppose the pitch angle, θ, of the rotor blade is arranged to be proportional to the bar displacement, i.e.:

$$\theta = k\delta \quad (13.112)$$

If the constant, k, is selected to be 1.0 then a tilt of the bar of 1° will produce a change of pitch of 1° of the rotor blade. The bar does not affect the collective pitch of the rotor. Therefore, although the pitch angle of the rotor can be defined as:

$$\theta = \theta_0 - \delta_A \cos\phi - \delta_B \sin\phi \quad (13.113)$$

where δ_A represents the amplitude of the lateral cyclic deflection, and δ_B the amplitude of the longitudinal cyclic deflection. θ can be written as:

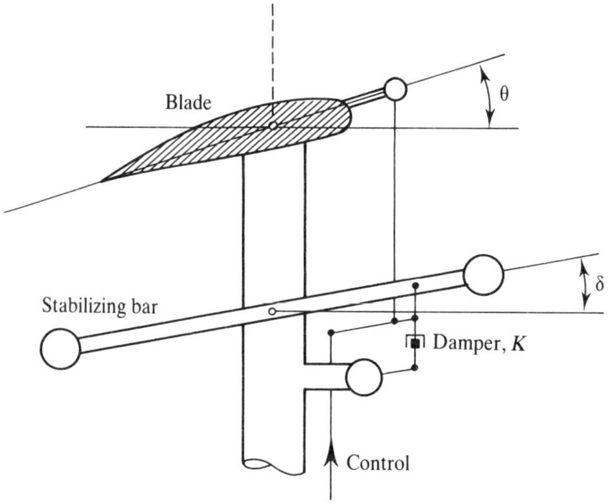

Figure 13.9 Schematic representation of Bell stabilizing bar.

$$\theta = k\delta = -\delta_A \cos\phi - \delta_B \sin\phi \qquad (13.114)$$

If eq. (13.114) is substituted in eq. (13.111), and if the coefficients of the resulting $\sin\phi$ and $\cos\phi$ terms are equated then the following equations result:

$$\delta''_A + 2K\Omega\delta'_A + 2\delta'_B + 2K\Omega\delta_B = 2k\Omega q \qquad (13.115)$$

$$2\delta'_A + 2K\Omega\delta''_B - 2K\Omega\delta'_B = 0 \qquad (13.116)$$

The prime denotes $d/d\phi$.

The characteristic equation of these simultaneous differential equations is a cubic which can be factored into a first order and quadratic term. The quadratic factor corresponds to a high frequency, nutation mode which is of little practical use. The first order factor can be shown (with a little manipulation) to be:

$$(d\delta_B/d\phi) + K\delta_B = k\Omega q \qquad (13.117)$$

which is of the form of eq. (13.109). Thus, any change in the rotor's speed, or the pitch rate of the rotor hub, will cause a change in the longitudinal cyclic deflection which tends to oppose the causative change. Note that the settling time of the response of the system represented by eq. (13.117) depends upon K, the damper coefficient. Flight tests of this stabilizing bar have shown that it provides a lagged feedback control and has been observed to increase the stability derivative, M_q, by an effective factor of 3.

Other examples of passive stabilizing devices are the Hiller bar and the gyro bar which is a feature of the Lockheed rigid rotor. The Hiller bar has a close resemblance to the Bell stabilizing bar except that damping is provided aerodynamically by means of small aerofoils mounted on the bar, rather than by using a viscous damper. Unlike the Bell stabilizer, a Hiller pilot controls the bar directly. Both the Bell and the Hiller bars are best suited to a two-bladed see-saw rotor. The Lockheed rigid rotor is a three-bladed rotor.

The most serious disadvantage of stabilizer bars, apart from mechanical complexity, is that they add to the total drag of the rotor.

13.5.2 AFCSs for Helicopters

SAS

In helicopters, the basis instability is such that the AFCS has to provide both restoring and damping moments. The control laws in general use tend to be either eq. (13.108) or (13.109). However, only limited control authority can ever be allowed, since control is through the rotor which provides the helicopter's sustaining lift and forward propulsion. 'Hands-off' operation of any helicopter, even with the use of an AFCS, is possible only for a few minutes; consequently, the pilot's stick system is very important in helicopter flight. A representative block diagram of such a stick feel system is shown in Figure 13.10. Note the presence of an input signal, F_{trim}, provided from the trim actuator, which reduces

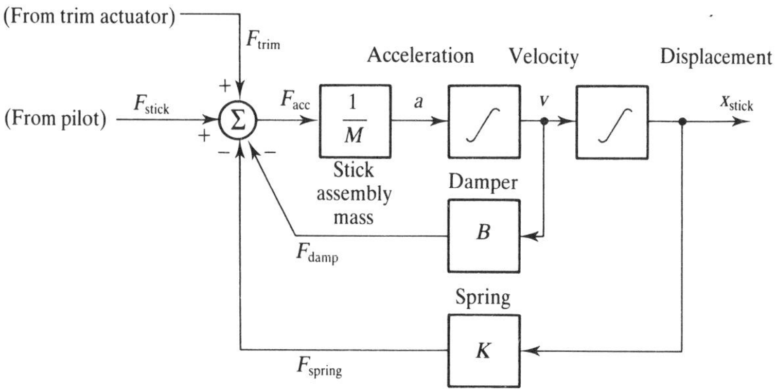

Figure 13.10 Block diagram of a stick feel system.

to zero the force required to be produced by a pilot for a constant manoeuvre demand. The feedback spring can be preloaded, and its stiffness can be altered as a function of speed to provide constant feel characteristics. The speed range of a helicopter is not very great, however, and such variability of the feedback spring force is often dispensed with. It should be appreciated, nevertheless, that the dynamics of the stick feel system act as a pre-filter, in the manner outlined in Section 10.8 of Chapter 10.

The simple SAS represented by Figure 13.11 is robust and requires no electrical trim signal for varying c.g. margins, because there will be no input to the servomechanism when there is no rate of change of displacement from the datum. The system is an excellent regulator which maintains its helicopter at the datum to which it has been trimmed. Although the block diagram shows a 'leaky integrator' path in parallel with the output from the rate gyroscope, the effect of these parallel paths is identical to that of a phase-lag network. The feedback control law is:

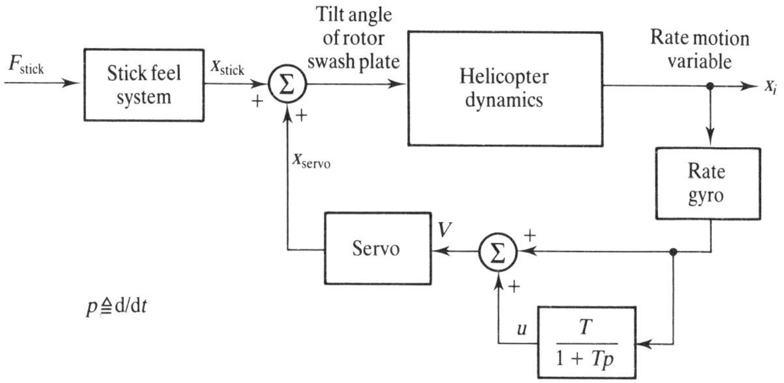

Figure 13.11 Block diagram of an SAS.

$$V(s) = K_q \left(1 + \frac{T}{1 + Ts}\right) q(s) \qquad (13.118)^5$$

Hence:

$$\frac{V(s)}{q(s)} = K_q K \frac{(1 + T_1 s)}{(1 + Ts)} \qquad (13.119)$$

when:

$$K = 1 + T \qquad (13.120)$$

$$T_1 = T/(1 + T) \qquad (13.121)$$

In response to a disturbance, the 'leaky integrator' path produces a signal proportional to the angle through which the helicopter has been displaced from its equilibrium value at the time of the disturbance. The control action applied through the swash plate tends to reduce this angular disturbance to zero. If the helicopter does not respond to this corrective control action, or it is held in this new attitude by the pilot, the quasi-integrated signal, u, decays to zero in about $5\,T$ seconds, and the new angular position is considered as the equilibrium.

ASE

ASE is an attitude control system, represented in Figure 13.12. The rate signal required for the inner loop SAS is obtained by differentiating the output signal from the attitude gyroscope, the use of which implies a real attitude datum. Since a helicopter has to be flown at any speed or attitude, this datum must be variable. The input from the c.g. trim system centres the gyro for any given flight condition. However, since the attitude control system tends to hold the datum and therefore opposes even manoeuvre demands, a signal from the stick system is used to 'break off' the gyro signal produced as a result of a manoeuvre. When the stick is trimmed to some new datum position, this signal establishes a new datum for the gyro. When the ASE is being used to control bank angle, the resulting characteristic is unusual. If the stick is held over to maintain some desired bank angle, it is *not* centred once the angle has been reached; in any emergency, release of the stick re-establishes straight and level flight. An ASE can hold attitude indefinitely. Although it is more complicated than a SAS it performs the same function. However, it does offer the means for providing automatic trim, automatic flight control and, of course, of changing the control characteristics. On helicopters the failure of SAS functions must not be critical, hence it is rare to provide redundant channels.

CSAS

When a helicopter has poor handling qualities, the performance of a specified mission without an AFCS can lead to levels of workload for the pilot which are unacceptably high, particularly if he is required continuously to monitor such

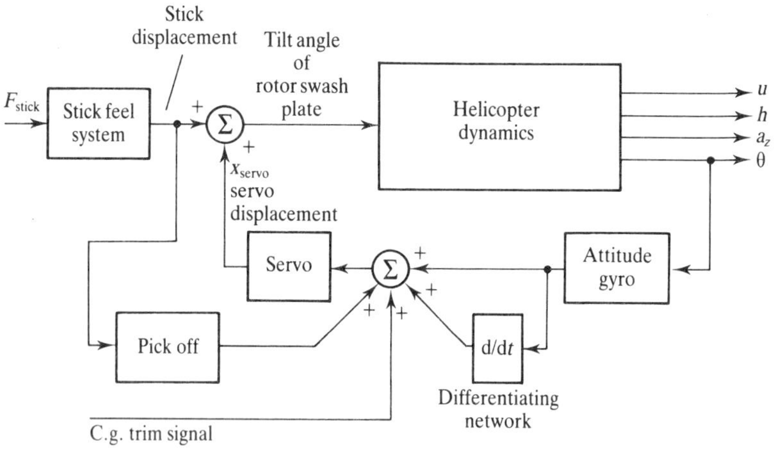

Figure 13.12 Block diagram of pitch attitude control system.

quantities as rotor speed and control loads during certain manoeuvres to ensure that the flight is being carried out within the limits of safe operation. A CSAS is usually provided in such cases. It is similar to the ASE but involves the use of a Kalman filter, requiring input signals from the gyroscopes, an accelerometer and the inertial navigation system (INS) velocity sensor. The resulting estimated signal is compared with a reference value generated by a set of model dynamics (see Figure 13.13). A signal proportional to any error between these values is filtered and then added to the feedback signals from the attitude and rate gyros. Decoupling signals from other axes are added at the same point. Such an AFCS is larger and more complicated than any discussed earlier and its use is confined to large helicopters, often twin rotor types. Since the forces are correspondingly larger, a booster servo is usually added to amplify the stick displacement.

Station-keeping System

This AFCS is used to enable a helicopter to maintain its position fixed in space – to keep its station – for quite long periods of time. (See Hall and Bryson (1973) for further discussion of this system.) Obviously, the situation requires that the flight is carried out at hover, or near hover, i.e. with forward speeds not greater than 1 m s^{-1}. For a Sikorsky S-61 helicopter, in which the blade dynamics are also taken into account, the state and control vectors are defined as:

$$\mathbf{x}' = [\theta_R \ \phi_R \ q_R \ p_R \ \theta_F \ \phi_F \ q_F \ p_F \ u \ v] \tag{13.122}$$

$$\mathbf{u} = \begin{bmatrix} \delta_A \\ \delta_B \end{bmatrix} \tag{13.123}$$

where θ_R denotes the pitch tilt angle of the rotor, ϕ_R the roll tilt angle of the rotor, q_R the rate of pitch tilt angle, p_R the rate of roll tilt angle, θ_F the pitch

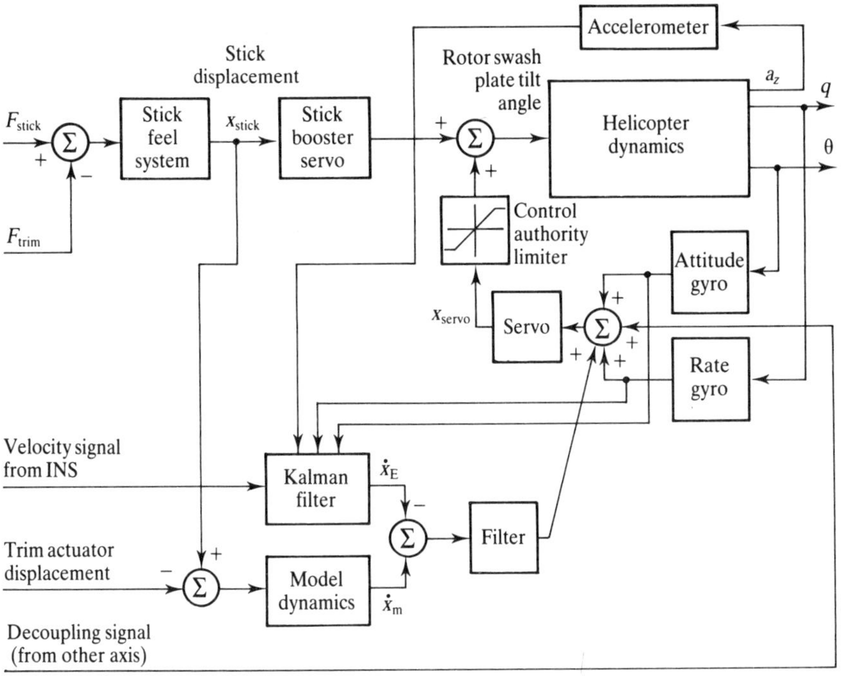

Figure 13.13 Block diagram of CSAS.

attitude of fuselage, ϕ_F the roll angle of fuselage, q_F the pitch rate of fuselage, p_F the roll rate of fuselage, u the velocity along the x-axis of the fuselage, v the velocity along the y-axis of the fuselage, δ_A the pitch angle of longitudinal cyclic, and δ_B the pitch angle of lateral cyclic.

The corresponding coefficient matrix, A, and driving matrix, B, are:

Rotor dynamics

$$A = \left[\begin{array}{ccccc|c}
0 & 0 & 1 & 0 & 0 & \\
0 & 0 & 0 & 1 & 0 & \text{Rigid body (fuselage)} \\
-41.3 & -600.0 & -30.3 & -42.6 & 0 & \text{coupling effects (shown on page 478)} \\
600.0 & -54.3 & 41.4 & -27.3 & 0 & \\
\hline
0 & 0 & 0 & 0 & 0 & \\
0 & 0 & 0 & 0 & 0 & \\
5.0 & -0.92 & -0.04 & 0.004 & 0 & \text{Rigid body (fuselage)} \\
3.5 & 18.4 & -0.01 & -0.17 & 0 & \text{dynamics (shown on page 478)} \\
-15.0 & 21.6 & 1.0 & -0.05 & -32.2 & \\
22.0 & 15.0 & -0.05 & -1.0 & 0 &
\end{array}\right]$$

Rotor coupling effects

$$\begin{array}{c:ccccc}
 & \multicolumn{5}{c}{\text{Rigid body (fuselage) coupling effects}} \\
 & 0 & 0 & 0 & 0 & 0 \\
\text{Rotor dynamics} & 0 & 0 & 0 & 0 & 0 \\
\text{(shown on page 477)} & 0 & -30.4 & -50.6 & 0.14 & -0.26 \\
 & 0 & 50.2 & -30.3 & -0.28 & -0.12 \\
\hdashline
 & 0 & 1 & 0 & 0 & 0 \\
 & 0 & 0 & 1 & 0 & 0 \\
\text{Rotor coupling} & 0 & -0.05 & 0.03 & 0.001 & -0.002 \\
\text{effects (shown on} & 0 & -0.1 & -0.2 & -0.0008 & -0.06 \\
\text{page 477)} & 0 & 4.37 & 1.44 & -0.017 & 0.007 \\
 & 32.2 & 1.4 & -4.4 & -0.007 & -0.017 \\
 & \multicolumn{5}{c}{\text{Rigid body (fuselage) dynamics}}
\end{array}$$

$$B = \begin{bmatrix} 0 & 0 \\ 0 & 0 \\ -600 & -1.5 \\ 5.5 & 600 \\ 0 & 0 \\ 0 & 0 \\ -0.94 & 1.32 \\ -5.0 & -3.5 \\ 21.8 & -16.8 \\ -16.8 & -21.8 \end{bmatrix}$$

It is obvious from an inspection of A that there are profound coupling effects involved because of the inclusion of the rotor dynamics, which arise from the blade flapping motion. If it is assumed that the rotor disc can be tilted instantaneously the appropriate model becomes:

$$\dot{\mathbf{x}} = A_1\mathbf{x}_1 + B_1\mathbf{u}_1 \tag{13.124}$$

where:

$$\mathbf{x}_1 \triangleq [\theta_F \ \phi_F \ q_F \ p_F \ u \ v]' \tag{13.125}$$

$$\mathbf{u}_1 \triangleq \begin{bmatrix} -\phi_R \\ \theta_R \end{bmatrix} \tag{13.126}$$

where ϕ_R is the lateral tilt of the rotor disc and θ_R is the longitudinal tilt.

The corresponding matrices are:

$$A_1 = \begin{bmatrix} 0 & 0 & 1 & 0 & 0 & 0 \\ 0 & 0 & 0 & 1 & 0 & 0 \\ 0 & 0 & -0.042 & 0.32 & 0.003 & 0.001 \\ 0 & 0 & -1.23 & -1.6 & 0.004 & -0.012 \\ -32.2 & 0 & 4.7 & -1.0 & -0.02 & -0.005 \\ 0 & 32.2 & -1.0 & -4.7 & 0.005 & -0.02 \end{bmatrix}$$

$$B_1 = \begin{bmatrix} 0 & 0 \\ 0 & 0 \\ -0.3 & 6.3 \\ -23 & -1.1 \\ 1.0 & -32.2 \\ -32.2 & 1.0 \end{bmatrix}$$

The eigenvalues corresponding to these two models are shown in Table 13.1. The response of the basic helicopter, with and without rotor dynamics, is shown in Figure 13.14. The responses shown are the pitch and roll attitude of the fuselage and the change in forward and side velocities, corresponding to an impulse control input, in the longitudinal cyclic. Similar impulse responses can also be found for the lateral cyclic. It should be noted from Table 13.1 and Figure 13.14 that when it is assumed that the rotor disc tilts instantaneously (i.e. that the rotor dynamics can be ignored) one of the rigid body modes of the fuselage is more lightly damped and slower.

A feedback control law can easily be found using the LQP method outlined in Section 8.3 of Chapter 8. For the modes including the rotor dynamics, a choice of state weighting matrix of:

$$Q = \text{diag}[0\ 0\ 0\ 0\ 1.0\ 1.0\ 0\ 0\ 0.04\ 0.04] \tag{13.127}$$

Table 13.1 Eigenvalues of uncontrolled helicopter with/without rotor dynamics

With rotor dynamics		*Without rotor dynamics*	
$\lambda\{A\} =$	$0.1145 \pm j0.3686$	$\lambda\{A_1\} =$	$0.102 \pm j0.348$
	$0.1976 \pm j0.9268$		$0.0331 \pm j0.484$
	-0.8317		-1.03
	-1.928		-1.2995
	$-13.392 \pm j5.6146$		
	$-14.4822 \pm j37.1315$		

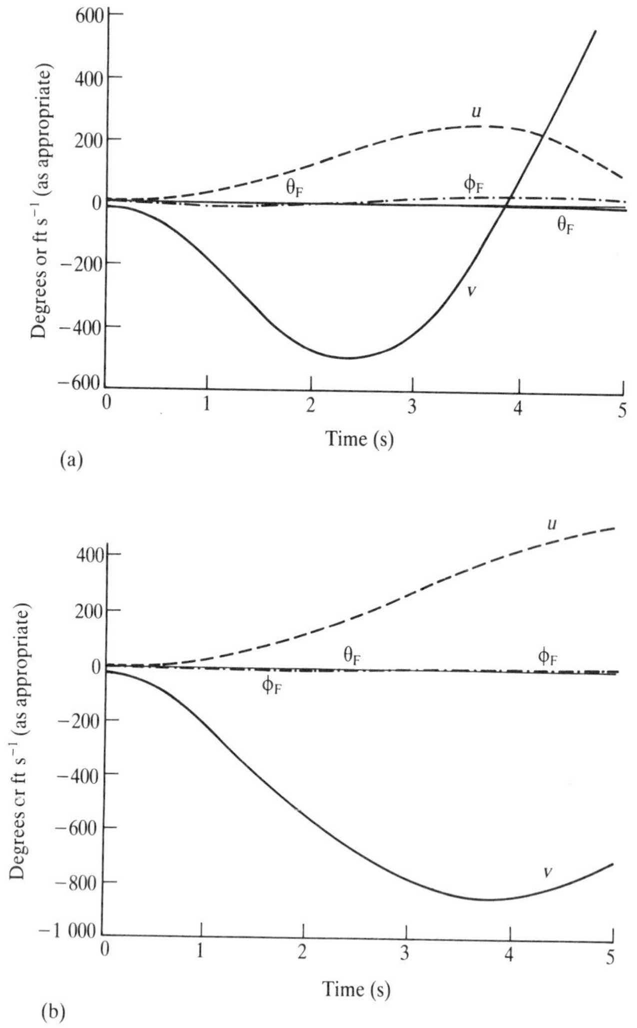

Figure 13.14 Response of uncontrolled helicopter. (a) With rotor dynamics. (b) Without rotor dynamics.

placing emphasis on the dynamic behaviour of the pitch and roll angles of the fuselage and, to a much lesser extent, the changes in forward and side velocity, and a control weighting matrix of:

$$G = \text{diag}[1.0 \;\; 1.0] \tag{13.128}$$

to penalize excessive controlled deflections of the longitudinal and lateral cyclic, results in an optimal gain matrix, K, which is found to be:

$$K = \begin{bmatrix} 0.1866 & -1.137 & -0.0126 & -0.0129 & 2.776 & 3.4074 & 2.0337 \\ -0.3016 & -0.0151 & -0.1973 & & & & \\ -1.0884 & 1.254 & 0.0106 & 0.0267 & -7.2072 & 1.7091 & -2.912 \\ 0.1079 & 0.1912 & -0.0241 & & & & \end{bmatrix} \quad (13.129)$$

The eigenvalues corresponding to the closed loop optimal system are given in Table 13.2.

Table 13.2 Eigenvalues of optimal closed loop system

With rotor dynamics	*Without rotor dynamics*
$\lambda\{A_{\text{closed loop}}\} = -1.2973 \pm j2.31$	$\lambda\{A_{1_{\text{closed loop}}}\} = -0.6206 \pm j2.2816$
$-2.2378 \pm j3.787$	$-1.7294 \pm j3.8915$
-1.9525	-7.2387
-14.1864	-8.1667
$-12.3237 \pm j7.7384$	
$-14.5858 \pm j37.2012$	

Another optimal feedback control law may be obtained in a like manner for the helicopter with instantaneous tilting of the rotor disc. The choice of weighting factors on the state and control variables were identical to those used earlier, i.e.

$$Q_1 = \text{diag}[1.0 \;\; 1.0 \;\; 0 \;\; 0 \;\; 0.04 \;\; 0.04] \quad (13.130)$$

$$G = \text{diag}[1.0 \;\; 1.0] \quad (13.131)$$

The resulting optimal gain matrix was found to be:

$$K_1 = \begin{bmatrix} -0.094 & -2.37 & 0.088 & -0.16 & 0.016 & -0.2 \\ 2.8532 & -0.324 & 0.2582 & 0.0092 & -0.1985 & -0.016 \end{bmatrix} \quad (13.132)$$

The corresponding closed loop eigenvalues are also given in Table 13.2. The responses of the pitch and roll attitudes of the helicopter fuselage, and the changes in the forward and side velocities, to a unit impulse, in first the longitudinal cyclic and then the lateral cyclic, are shown in Figure 13.15 for the helicopter with/without rotor dynamics. It should be noted from these responses how effectively the controlled helicopter keeps its station: compare particularly the responses of the translational velocities with those which arose in the uncontrolled case.

Further discussion on stability augmentation systems can be found in Johnson (1980) and Mil *et al.* (1966, 1967).

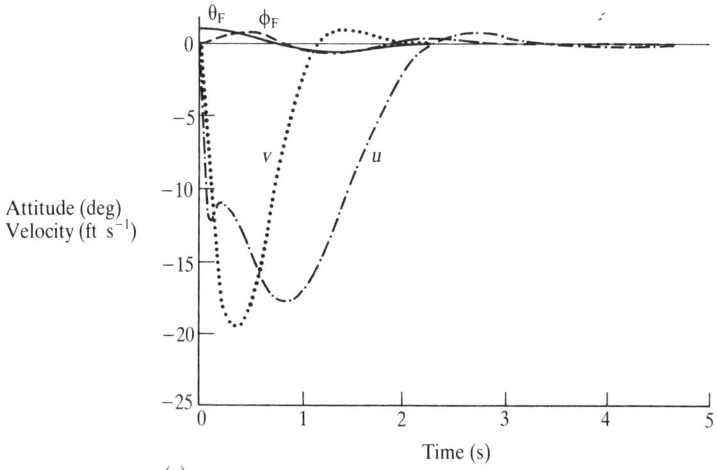

(a)

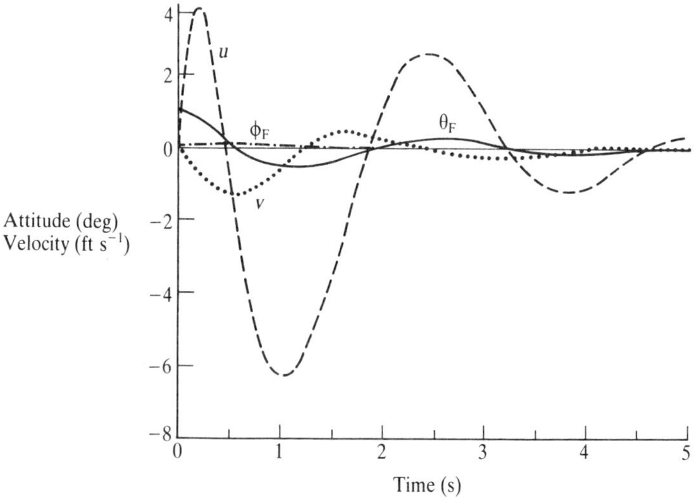

(b)

Figure 13.15 Optimal control response of helicopter. (a) With rotor dynamics. (b) Without rotor dynamics.

13.6 CONCLUSIONS

This chapter opens with a brief introduction to the helicopter and its rotor systems. Some distinctive features of helicopter flight which give rise to particular control problems were indicated before proceeding to a development of appropriate equations of small perturbation motion for both longitudinal and lateral motion. Next, the particular qualities of static stability which obtain in helicopters are dealt with, before turning to the special problems of dynamic stability for which the most effective means of cure is provision of effective SASs. The objectives of such SASs are discussed before a description and analysis of a rotor stabilizing bar, a very common helicopter SAS, are presented. Active SAS and CSASs are then discussed before dealing finally with optimal control of a station-keeping helicopter. A special feature of this analysis is the impact which the inclusion of the dynamics of the main rotor in the equations of motion can make to the response obtained from the controlled helicopter.

13.7 EXERCISES

13.1 The state vector of the Black Hawk helicopter (UH-60) can be defined as:

$$\mathbf{x}' = [u\ w\ q\ \theta\ v\ p\ r\ \phi]$$

and the control vector as:

$$\mathbf{u}' = [\delta_B\ \delta_A\ \delta_T\ \delta_{\theta_0}\ i_{ht}]$$

where i_{ht} represents the change in incidence of the horizontal tail. The corresponding matrices A and B are:

$$A = \begin{bmatrix} -0.015 & 0.02 & 1.35 & -32.2 & -0.009 & -1.61 & -0.35 & 0 \\ -0.005 & -0.28 & U_0 & 0 & -0.01 & -0.17 & 2.08 & 0 \\ 0.0005 & 0.002 & -0.52 & 0 & 0.009 & 0.294 & -0.07 & 0 \\ 0 & 1 & 0 & 0 & 0 & 0 & 0 & 0 \\ 0.017 & 0.004 & -1.42 & 0 & -0.05 & -1.61 & 0.45 & g/U_0 \\ 0.04 & 0.002 & -1.7 & 0 & -0.03 & -3.35 & 0.21 & 0 \\ 0.002 & -0.001 & -0.42 & 0 & 0.008 & -0.19 & -0.29 & 0 \\ 0 & 0 & 0 & 0 & 0 & 1 & 0 & 0 \end{bmatrix}$$

$$B = \begin{bmatrix} 1.7 & 0.05 & 1.13 & 1.1 & -0.001 \\ 0.11 & 0.004 & 0.68 & -8.6 & 0.002 \\ -0.33 & -0.005 & 0.04 & -0.018 & 0 \\ 0 & 0 & 0 & 0 & 0 \\ -0.09 & 0.97 & -1.72 & 0.23 & 0 \\ -0.06 & 1.31 & -0.93 & -0.06 & 0 \\ -0.002 & 0.03 & 0.72 & 0.07 & 0 \\ 0 & 0 & 0 & 0 & 0 \end{bmatrix}$$

$g = 32.2\ \text{ft s}^{-2}$
$U_0 = 1.0\ \text{ft s}^{-1}$ or $150\ \text{ft s}^{-1}$

(a) Find the eigenvalues of the helicopter at forward speed:

(i) 1 ft s^{-1}
(ii) 150 ft s^{-1}

Comment on the stability of the helicopter at each of these flight conditions, and compare.

(b) Find the following transfer functions for the hovering condition:

(i) $\dfrac{w(s)}{\delta_{\theta_0}(s)}$ (iii) $\dfrac{\theta(s)}{i_{ht}(s)}$ (v) $\dfrac{r(s)}{\delta_T(s)}$

(ii) $\dfrac{p(s)}{\delta_A(s)}$ (iv) $\dfrac{q(s)}{\delta_B(s)}$

(c) Find the transfer functions at $U_0 = 150$ ft s^{-1} relating:

(i) normal acceleration at the c.g. to a deflection of the longitudinal cyclic control;
(ii) lateral acceleration at the c.g. to a deflection of lateral cyclic control;

(d) What is the peak normal acceleration to a unit step deflection of the longitudinal cyclic, and how long does it take after the application of the step function to attain the peak?

(e) Is the acceleration response concave downwards within 2.0 s of the application of the control?

13.2 A helicopter, which is perturbed by a wind gust, is to be maintained at zero ground speed by means of controlling its motion about the pitch axis. If the deflection angle of the rotor swash plate is denoted by η and a feedback control law, $\eta = K_\theta\theta + K_u u + K_q q$ is used, find values of K_θ, K_q, and K_u which will optimize the helicopter's hovering flight, in the sense that its use minimizes the ISE where u is taken to be the error, since u represents any small variation in horizontal speed from the derived ground speed of 0.0. The helicopter being used is a Sikorsky S-58 and the appropriate, but approximate, equations of motion are given by:

$$\dot{u} = 0.0004u - 32.2\theta \qquad \ddot{\theta} = 0.003u - 0.6\dot{\theta} - 6.0\eta$$

13.3 The Iroquois (UH-1H) helicopter has its state vector defined as:

$$\mathbf{x}' = [u \ w \ q \ \theta \ v \ p \ \phi \ r]$$

and its control vector as:

$$\mathbf{u}' = [\delta_B \ \delta_{\theta_0} \ \delta_A \ \delta_T]$$

The appropriate matrices A and B for the hovering case, i.e. $U_0 \triangleq 0$ m s^{-1}, are:

$$A = \begin{bmatrix} -0.07 & -0.017 & 16.62 & -18.4 & 0.001 & -1.0 & 0.02 & -0.07 \\ 0.04 & -0.65 & 0.14 & -1.39 & -0.04 & 0.07 & -0.33 & -0.03 \\ 0.01 & 0.007 & -2.72 & -2.22 & 0.0002 & 0.15 & -0.001 & -0.04 \\ 0 & 0 & 1 & 0 & 0 & 0 & 0 & 0 \\ -0.007 & -0.006 & -0.97 & 0.005 & -0.14 & -6.91 & 22.3 & 3.76 \\ -0.0006 & 0.003 & -0.81 & 0.001 & -0.014 & -4.56 & -6.26 & 0.63 \\ 0 & 0 & 0 & 0 & 0 & 1 & 0 & 0 \\ 0.007 & 0.015 & -0.55 & 0.0001 & 0.014 & -1.03 & -0.92 & -3.68 \end{bmatrix}$$

$$B = \begin{bmatrix} -2.2 & 0.54 & 0 & 0.0001 \\ -0.01 & -12.1 & -314.45 & 0 \\ 0.36 & -0.003 & -0.001 & 0.008 \\ 0 & 0 & 0 & 0 \\ -0.034 & -0.17 & 1.81 & -1.0 \\ 0.093 & -0.098 & 1.09 & -0.25 \\ 0 & 0 & 0 & 0 \\ 0.25 & 0.04 & 0.04 & 0.73 \end{bmatrix}$$

$g = 9.81\,\text{m s}^{-2}$
$U_0 = 0.0\,\text{m s}^{-1}$

(a) Find the eigenvalues of the uncontrolled helicopter.
(b) Determine, by any appropriate means, a state feedback control law which will completely stabilize the helicopter.
(c) Does the controlled helicopter have acceptable flying qualities?

13.4 (a) Show that, for hovering motion, the vertical velocity of a helicopter can be expressed as a simple, first order differential equation:

$$\dot{w} - Z_w w = Z_{\delta_{\theta_0}} \delta_{\theta_0} - Z_w w_g$$

(b) How significant was your assumption in part (a) that the rotor speed was constant?
(c) If the rotor speed is not fixed, design a height control system to allow the helicopter to hover without the pilot's attention.
(d) If w_g is represented by a $(1 - \cos)$ gust (see Chapter 5), what would be the corresponding height change if $Z_w = -0.015$? The scale length of the gust is 10.0 m.

13.5 A helicopter has the capability of making a landing by means of maintained autorotation in which the lift force being generated by the rotor is maintained, even though there is a loss of power due to engine failure, and the helicopter descends at a steady rate. (Warning: even for forward flight, this autorotation descent rate is quite large, so autorotational descents are used only in emergencies.)

Assume that the collective pitch is unchanged. The equation of motion for the vertical acceleration of a helicopter is given by:

$$(W/g)\ddot{h} = W - T$$

where h is the height of the helicopter above the ground, W is the gross weight and T the thrust developed by the rotor. The equation of motion for the rotor speed is:

$$NI_b\dot{\Omega} = -Q$$

NI_b is the total moment of inertia of the rotor, Ω is the rotor speed, and Q the decelerating torque on the rotor.

If Q_0 and Ω_0 represent the torque needed in level flight and the initial rotor speed, respectively, show that:

(a) The descent velocity (sinking speed) of the helicopter can be expressed as:

$$\dot{h} = gt^2/(t + \tau)$$

where the time constant $\tau \triangleq NI_b\Omega_0/Q_0$

(b) The rotor speed becomes:

$$\Omega = \Omega_0\tau/(t + \tau)$$

(c) If $NI_b = 3\,000\,\text{kg m}^2$, $Q_0 = 7\,500\,\text{N-m}$, and $\Omega_0 = 36\,\text{rad s}^{-1}$, sketch the response of h and Ω with time.

(d) If the aircraft is at a height of 100 ft when autorotation begins, calculate the aircraft's sinking rate and its rotor speed at the moment of ground contact.

13.6 A helicopter at near hover flight condition, with constant rotor speed, has the following state equation:

$$\dot{\mathbf{x}} = A\mathbf{x} + B\mathbf{u}$$

where:

$$\mathbf{x}' \triangleq [\theta_R\ \phi_R\ p_R\ q_R\ \theta_F\ \phi_F\ p_F\ q_F\ u\ v]$$

$$\mathbf{u}' \triangleq \begin{bmatrix} \delta_B \\ \delta_A \end{bmatrix}$$

θ_R denotes the pitch tilt angle of the rotor, ϕ_R the roll tilt angle of the rotor, p_R the rate of roll tilt angle of the rotor, q_R the rate of pitch tilt angle of the rotor, θ_F the pitch attitude of the fuselage, ϕ_F the roll attitude of the fuselage, p_F the roll rate of the fuselage, q_F the pitch rate attitude of the fuselage, u a small change in the velocity of the c.g. along the X-axis of the fuselage, v a small change in the velocity of the c.g. along the Y-axis of the fuselage, δ_B the longitudinal cyclic pitch, and δ_A the lateral cyclic pitch. The corresponding matrices A and B are shown below.

$$
A = \left[\begin{array}{ccccc|ccccc}
\multicolumn{5}{c|}{\text{Rotor dynamics}} & \multicolumn{5}{c}{\text{Rigid body (fuselage) coupling effects}} \\
0 & 0 & 1 & 0 & 0 & 0 & 0 & 0 & 0 & 0 \\
0 & 0 & 0 & 1 & 0 & 0 & 0 & 0 & 0 & 0 \\
-41.3 & -600.0 & -30.3 & -42.6 & 0 & 0 & -30.4 & -50.6 & 0.14 & -0.26 \\
600.0 & -54.3 & 41.4 & -27.3 & 0 & 0 & 50.2 & -30.3 & -0.28 & -0.12 \\
\hline
0 & 0 & 0 & 0 & 0 & 0 & 1 & 0 & 0 & 0 \\
0 & 0 & 0 & 0 & 0 & 0 & 0 & 1 & 0 & 0 \\
5.0 & -0.92 & -0.04 & 0.004 & 0 & 0 & -0.05 & 0.03 & 0.001 & -0.002 \\
3.5 & 18.4 & -0.01 & -0.17 & 0 & 0 & -0.1 & -0.2 & -0.0008 & -0.06 \\
-15.0 & 21.6 & 1.0 & -0.05 & -32.2 & 0 & 4.37 & 1.44 & -0.017 & 0.007 \\
22.0 & 15.0 & -0.05 & -1.0 & 0 & 32.2 & 1.4 & -4.4 & -0.007 & -0.017 \\
\multicolumn{5}{c|}{\text{Rotor coupling effects}} & \multicolumn{5}{c}{\text{Rigid body (fuselage) dynamics}}
\end{array}\right]
\qquad
B = \begin{bmatrix}
0 & 0 \\
0 & 0 \\
-600 & -1.5 \\
5.5 & 600 \\
0 & 0 \\
0 & 0 \\
-0.94 & 1.32 \\
-5.0 & -3.5 \\
21.8 & -16.8 \\
-16.8 & -21.8
\end{bmatrix}
$$

Note that the rotor dynamics have been incorporated in the aircraft equations of motion. When the helicopter is represented simply as a rigid body, with the rotor dynamics being represented as a solid disc, the state vector is then defined as:

$$\mathbf{x}_1' = [\theta_F \ \phi_F \ p_F \ q_F \ u \ v]$$

and the control vector becomes:

$$\mathbf{u}' = [-\ \phi_R \ \theta_R]$$

where ϕ_R denotes the lateral tilt angle of the rotor disc, and θ_R denotes the longitudinal tilt angle of the rotor disc. The corresponding matrices are A_1 and B_1:

$$A_1 = \begin{bmatrix} 0 & 0 & 1 & 0 & 0 & 0 \\ 0 & 0 & 0 & 1 & 0 & 0 \\ 0 & 0 & -0.042 & 0.32 & 0.003 & 0.001 \\ 0 & 0 & -1.23 & -1.6 & 0.004 & -0.012 \\ -32.2 & 0 & 4.7 & -1.0 & -0.02 & -0.005 \\ 0 & 32.2 & -1.0 & -4.7 & 0.005 & -0.02 \end{bmatrix}$$

$$B_1 = \begin{bmatrix} 0 & 0 \\ 0 & 0 \\ -0.3 & 6.3 \\ -23 & -1.1 \\ 1.0 & -32.2 \\ -32.2 & 1.0 \end{bmatrix}$$

(a) Evaluate the eigenvalues for the helicopter with blade flapping motion and then with the solid rotor disc.
(b) What is significant about the eigenvalues obtained for the two cases?
(c) For the following weighting matrices, Q_1 and G_1, find an optimal feedback control law for the helicopter without blade flapping motion:

$$Q_1 = \text{diag}[10.0 \ 2.0 \ 2.0 \ 5.0 \ 1.0 \ 10.0]$$

$$G_1 = \text{diag}[2.0 \ 5.0]$$

(d) Using the feedback control law obtained in part (c), determine the pitch rate response to an initial value of the fuselage pitch rate of $-\ 3° \ s^{-1}$ of the solid rotor disc helicopter.
(e) Find the same response for the helicopter with blade flapping motion, still using the control law found in part (c). Compare the response with that of part (d) and comment upon any significant differences.
(f) Using weighting matrices Q and G

$$Q = \text{diag}[4.0 \ 2.0 \ 2.0 \ 4.0 \ 20.0 \ 2.0 \ 2.0 \ 5.0 \ 1 \ 10]$$

$$G = \text{diag}[5.0 \ 2.0]$$

determine a feedback control law for the helicopter with state vector, x.

(g) Use the control law found in part (f) to determine the pitch rate response to an initial value of the fuselage pitch rate of $-3° \, s^{-1}$. Compare the response with that determined in parts (d) and (e). Comment upon these results.

13.7 A small experimental helicopter, with a single main rotor and a NOTAR system, is flying at a near hover condition i.e. $U_0 = 0.3 \, m \, s^{-1}$. In the course of the flight the NOTAR system ceases to operate causing the stability derivatives L'_r, N'_v and N'_p to have values of almost zero. The stability derivatives of the helicopter in this flight condition are:

$$
\begin{array}{ll}
Y_v = -0.14 & Y_{\delta_R} = 1.3 \\
L'_p = -0.28 & N'_p = 0.0012 \\
L'_v = -0.01 & N'_v = 0.00005 \\
L'_r = 0.0007 & N'_r = -0.72 \\
L'_{\delta_B} = 0.73 & N'_{\delta_B} = -0.05 \\
L'_{\delta_R} = -0.14 & N'_{\delta_R} = -0.48
\end{array}
$$

(a) If an impulse of 0.035 rad-s is applied to the lateral cyclic, what is the resulting steady state value of the helicopter's yaw angle?

(b) How long does it take the helicopter to reach its new heading?

(c) Is the helicopter stable? Can it be maintained in its near hover state with the NOTAR system failure? Could you design an AFCS to permit automatic hovering without using the NOTAR system?

13.8 NOTES

1. Some newer types of helicopter are called NOTARs (no tail rotors), yet even though the method of generating the countering moment has been changed in these types, the same function as the tail rotor performance is maintained.
2. That is OX parallel to the flight path, OZ pointing vertically downwards, and OY pointing starboard.
3. This assumes that the direction of rotation of the main rotor is counter-clockwise (viewed from above), the usual direction for USA and UK manufactured helicopters.
4. These comparisons are made in relation to an articulated rotor of the same type, but with no flap hinge offset.
5. This supposes that x_i is q, the pitch rate. The same system operates on p, the roll rate, provided that a properly oriented rate gyroscope is fitted.

13.9 REFERENCES

BRAMWELL, A.R.S. 1976. *Helicopter Dynamics*. London: Arnold.

GESSOW, A.E. and G.C. MYERS. 1952. *Aerodynamics of the Helicopter*. Ungar.

HALL, W.E. and A.E. BRYSON. 1973. Inclusion of rotor dynamics in control design for helicopters. *J. Air* 10(4): 200–206.

JOHNSON, W. 1980. *Helicopter Theory*. Princeton University Press.

LEFORT, P. and R. MENTHE. 1963. *L'Helicoptre-Theorie et Practique*. Editions Chiron.

McCORMICK, B.W. 1967. *Aerodynamics of V/STOL Flight*. New York: Academic Press.

MIL, M.L. *et al.* 1966. *Helicopter Calculation and Design Vol. 1. Aerodynamics*. NASA TTF-494.

MIL, M.L. *et al.* 1967. *Helicopter Calculation and Design. Vol. 2. Vibration and Dynamic Stability*. NASA TTF-519.

NIKOLSKY, A.A. 1951. *Helicopter Analysis*. New York: Wiley.

PAYNE, P.R. 1959. *Helicopter Dynamics and Aerodynamics*. London: Pitman.

14

Digital Control Systems

14.1 INTRODUCTION

In the preceding chapters it is assumed that any AFCS being considered had a feedback control law which was synthesized as a continuous function of time. Most current and new types of AFCS now depend (and all future types of AFCS will depend) upon digital synthesis of the control law, that is to say, that the AFCS is now, or is going to be, digital. The objectives of this chapter are, therefore:

1. To introduce several essential concepts of digital control.
2. To discuss a few effective methods of designing suitable digital controllers for AFCS.
3. To note the effects upon the dynamic performance of an AFCS of using such a means of control.

The distinguishing feature of digital control is that some of the signals within the system cannot be known at every instant of time, but are known only at particular instants. For example, imagine that a switch is being used to control some electrical signal $x(t)$, in the way shown in Figure 14.1. If that switch be closed at some instant of time, say t_1, its output will be as shown in Figure 14.2(b). ($x(t)$ is shown in Figure 14.2(a) for comparison.) If the switch remains closed for only a brief period, Δt, and is then opened once again, the output signal will be as represented in Figure 14.2(c). If some longer period of time, T, passes, and then the switch is once again rapidly closed and opened, the resulting output is as represented in Figure 14.2(d). If it is arranged to rapidly close and open the switch in a regular cycle, of period T, the output which results has the form represented in Figure 14.3. Whenever the duration of switch closure is extremely brief, the period $\Delta t \rightarrow 0$; the output from the switch (as it periodically closes and opens) can be represented in the manner shown in Figure 14.4. This signal has been denoted as y^*, and it is said to be the sampled version of the input signal, $x(t)$. The discrete signal, y^*, is known accurately only at the sampling intervals $(kt_1 + T)$, where $k = 0, 1, 2, \ldots$. When the sampling period, T, is constant, the sampling is uniform; much of the work in this chapter assumes uniform sampling.

When $\Delta t \rightarrow 0$ and the switch is closed periodically every T seconds, the switch is referred to as a *sampler* (or sampling device) and can be represented as

Figure 14.1 Sampling switch.

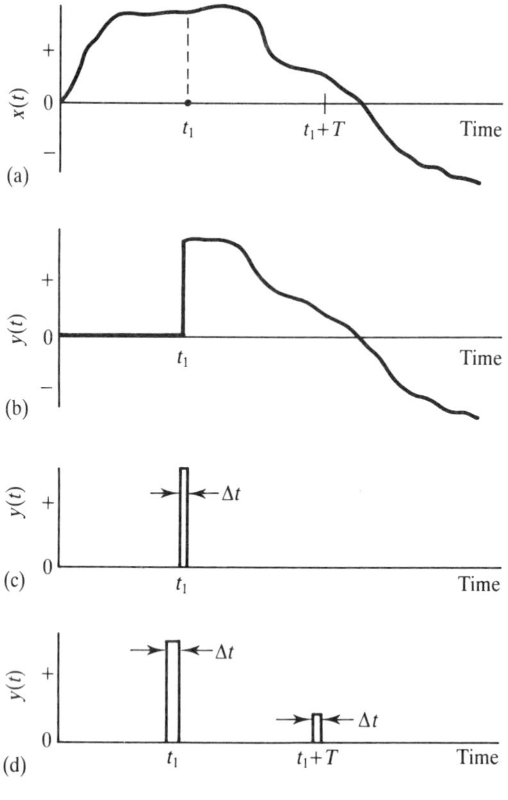

Figure 14.2 Switch output signals.

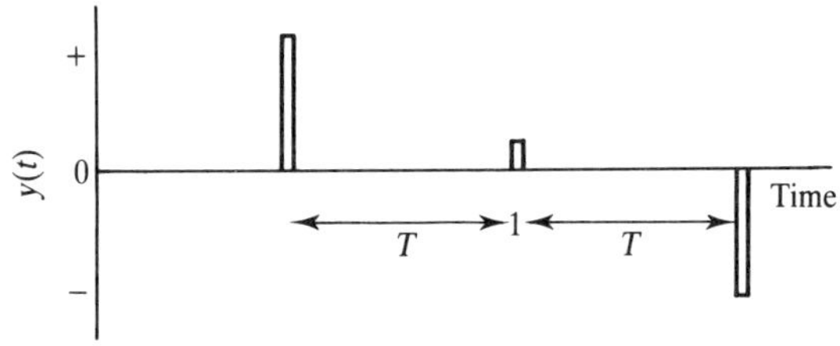

Figure 14.3 Periodically sampled signal.

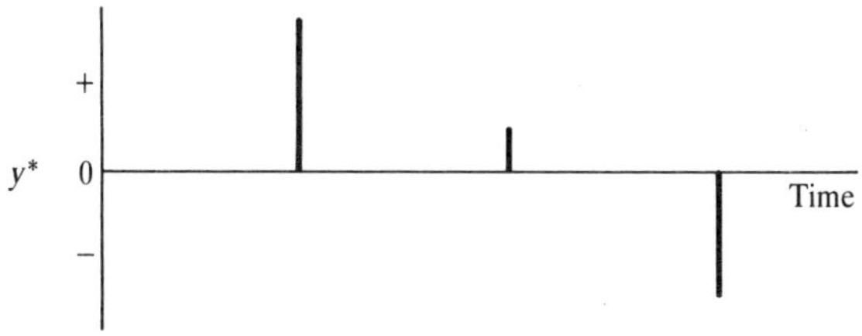

Figure 14.4 Sampled signal.

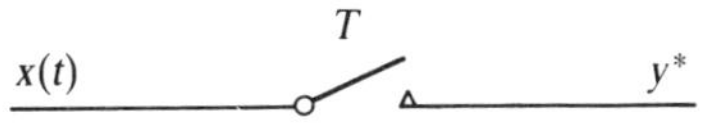

Figure 14.5 Idealized sampler.

in Figure 14.5. A sampler, then, is a device for transforming a continuous into a discrete signal. Whenever the amplitude of a discrete signal is quantized, that signal is regarded as being digital.[1]

14.2 A SIMPLE DISCRETE CONTROL SYSTEM

A simple system, in which the variables are continuous, is represented by Figure 14.6. The system is merely an integrator whose output is also used as a negative feedback signal. The transfer function of this simple system can easily be shown to be:

$$Y(s)/R(s) = K/(s + K) \tag{14.1}$$

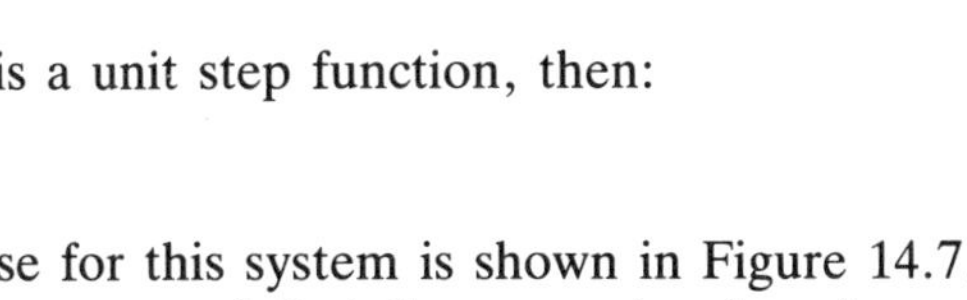

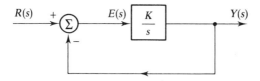

Figure 14.6 Simple first order system.

If the input, $r(t)$, is a unit step function, then:

$$y(t) = 1 - e^{-kt} \tag{14.2}$$

The output response for this system is shown in Figure 14.7.

Now if it is supposed that the error signal, e, is sampled in the manner shown in Figure 14.8, the output signal, y, will change at a constant rate, being proportional to the error during the sampling period T. Let the error signal at an

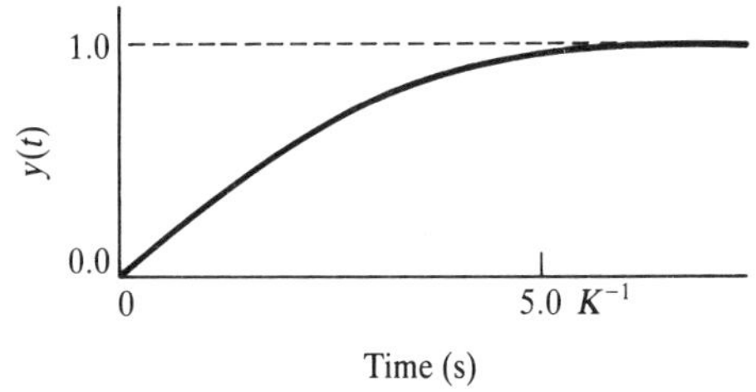

Figure 14.7 Step response of simple first order system.

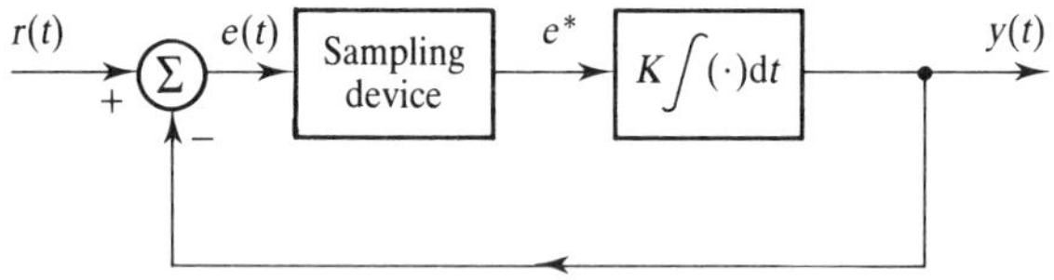

Figure 14.8 Sampled first order system.

instant kT be denoted by e_k. The rate of change of the output signal can then be expressed as:

$$dy/dt = Ke_k \tag{14.3}$$

For any arbitrary input, $r(t)$, the situation may be represented by Figure 14.9, from which it can be deduced that:

$$y_{k+1} - y_k = KTe_k = KT(r_k - y_k) \tag{14.4}$$

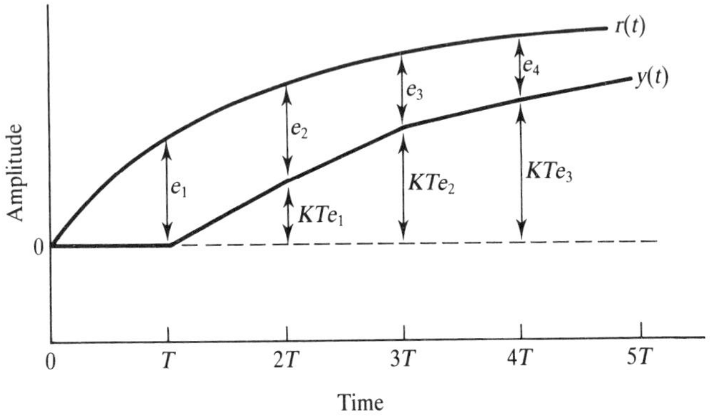

Figure 14.9 Error signals at sampling instants.

Let:

$$\lambda \triangleq KT \tag{14.5}$$

(sometimes referred to as the specific control step), then:

$$y_{k+1} + (\lambda - 1)y_k = \lambda r_k \tag{14.6}$$

If only the transient motion is considered, i.e. $r(t)$ is assumed to be zero, then:

$$y_{k+1} = (1 - \lambda)y_k \tag{14.7}$$

i.e.:

$$y_k = (1 - \lambda)^{k-1}y_1 \tag{14.8}$$

The output response is heavily dependent upon the particular value of λ. For example, suppose both λ and y_1 are unity. Then y_2, y_3, y_4, etc. are all zero. If λ is 0.5, then for $y_1 = 1.0$, the output sequence becomes: $y_2 = 0.5$, $y_3 = 0.25$, $y_4 = 0.125$, $y_5 = 0.0625$, etc.

If λ is increased to 1.5 the output sequence becomes: $y_2 = -0.5$, $y_3 = 0.25$, $y_4 = -0.125$, $y_5 = 0.0625$, $y_6 = -0.03126$, etc.

When λ is increased to 2.0, however, the output sequence alternates between -1.0 and 1.0.

The responses corresponding to these sequences are shown in Figure 14.10, having been obtained from a digital simulation of the system shown in Figure 14.8.

The dynamic situation can be summarized thus:

If $0 < \lambda < 1$, $y(t)$ tends to zero *without oscillation*.
If $\lambda = 1$, $y(t)$ reaches zero in a *single sampling interval*.
If $1 < \lambda < 2$, $y(t)$ tends to zero *with oscillation* (at a frequency equal to sampling rate, $1/T$).
If $\lambda < 0$, $y(t)$ is *unstable*.
If $\lambda > 2.0$, $y(t)$ is *oscillatory* and *unstable*.

If the input $r(t)$ is constant and non-zero, then, in the steady state:

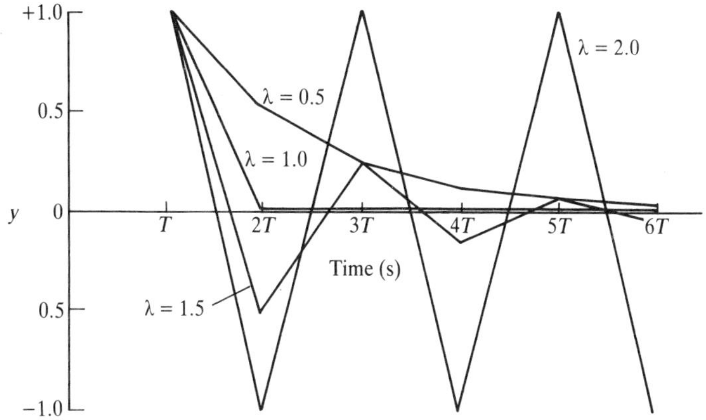

Figure 14.10 Responses of sampled first order system.

$$y_{k+1} = r \tag{14.9}$$

It should be noted that, whereas the continuous system of Figure 14.6 can never oscillate and can never be unstable (unless K is negative), the digital version may oscillate and can even be unstable merely as a consequence of the value chosen for the sampling period, T, in relation to K. Such an oscillatory response is referred to as a 'hidden oscillation' since it occurs solely as a result of having used digital control with a particular value of sampling rate. The condition should be avoided in every digital AFCS by a proper choice of T.

Example 14.1

Find a discrete equation which will represent the transfer function of a phase advance network:

$$G(s) = U(s)/E(s) = (1 + \tau s)/(1 + \alpha\tau s) \qquad 0 \leq \alpha \leq 1$$

The corresponding differential equation is given by: $e - \tau\dot{e} = u + \alpha\tau\dot{u}$.

Let e_{n-1}, u_{n-1}, e_n and u_n be the value of the continuous signal at the $(n-1)$th and nth sampling instants respectively. Now:

$$\dot{e} \triangleq (e_n - e_{n-1})/T \qquad \dot{u} \triangleq (u_n - u_{n-1})/T$$

T is the sampling period. Then:

$$u_n = e_n + \frac{(e_n - e_{n-1})}{T}\tau - \frac{\alpha\tau}{T}(u_n - u_{n-1})$$

i.e.:

$$u_n\left(1 + \frac{\alpha\tau}{T}\right) = e_n\left(1 + \frac{\tau}{T}\right) - \frac{\tau}{T}e_{n-1} + \frac{\alpha\tau}{T}u_{n-1}$$

$$\therefore \qquad u_n = e_n\frac{\left(1 + \frac{\tau}{T}\right)}{\left(1 + \frac{\alpha\tau}{T}\right)} - \frac{\frac{\tau}{T}}{\left(1 + \frac{\alpha\tau}{T}\right)}e_{n-1} + \frac{\alpha\tau}{T\left(1 + \frac{\alpha\tau}{T}\right)}u_{n-1}$$

$$= c_1 e_n + c_2 e_{n-1} + c_3 u_{n-1}$$

where:

$$c_1 = (T + \tau)/(T + \alpha\tau) < 1.0$$

$$c_2 = -\tau/(T + \alpha\tau) < 1.0$$

$$c_3 = \alpha\tau/(T + \alpha\tau) < 1.0$$

An inappropriate choice of T can cause another undesirable feature in the dynamic performance of AFCSs: aliasing. Consider the signal, $x(t)$, shown in Figure 14.11(a). If it is sampled once per cycle, and is then reconstructed, the

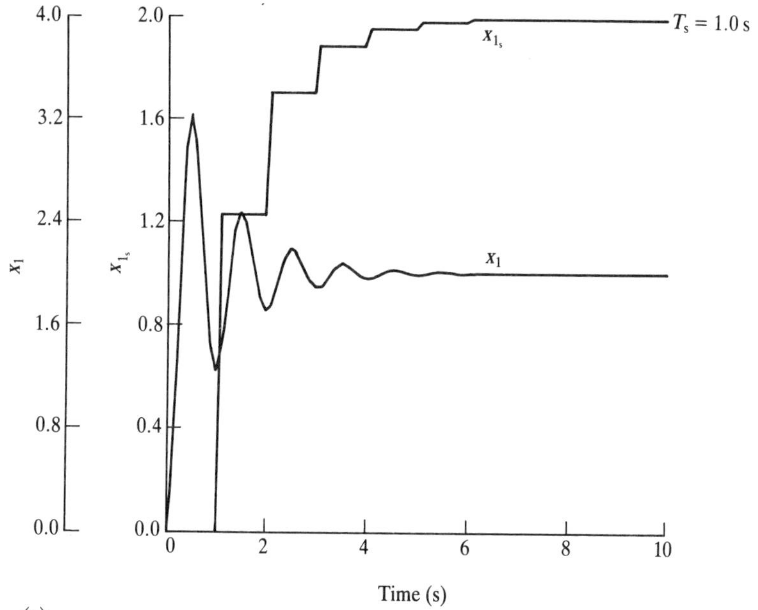

(a)

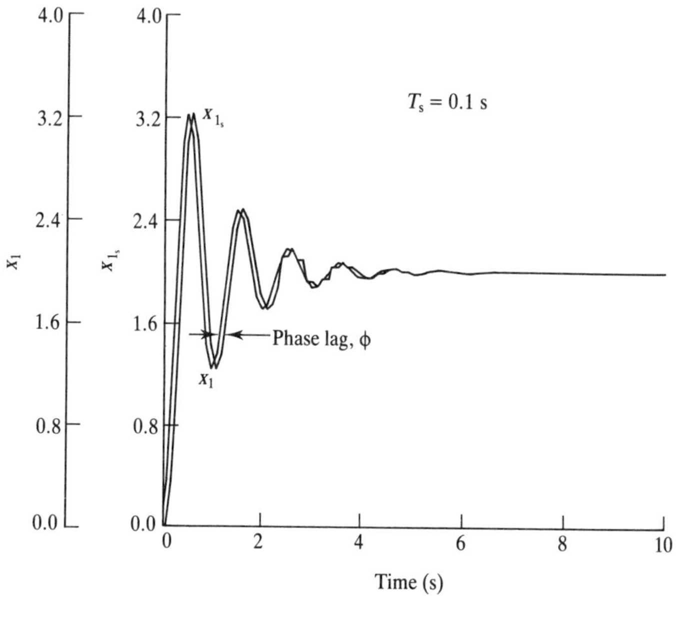

(b)

Figure 14.11 Signal sampled: (a) once per cycle, (b) ten times per cycle,

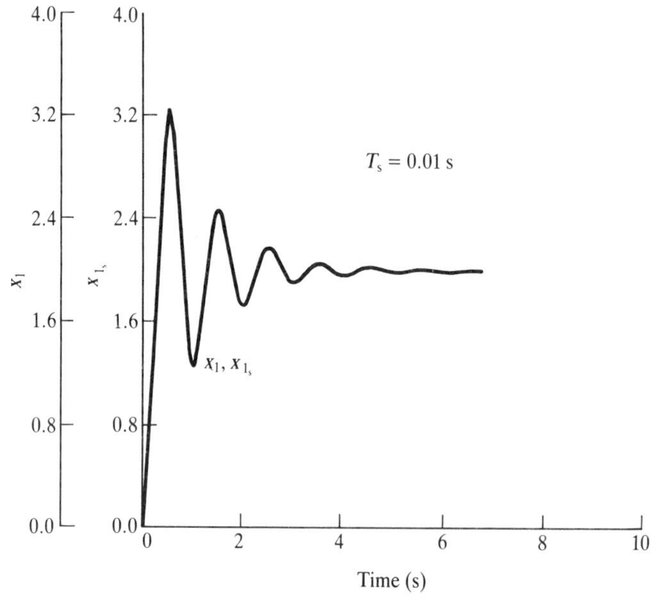

(c) one hundred times per cycle.

result will be as represented by the response x_{1_s}. The reconstructed signal can be seen to be nothing like the original, continuous signal. If, next, the sampling rate is increased to ten times per cycle, and the sampled signal is reconstructed, it is apparent from Figure 14.11(b) that the reconstructed signal is still different from $x(t)$, for a significant phase lag, ϕ, is observable. In Figure 14.11(c) the result of sampling at one hundred times per cycle and again reconstructing is shown with more acceptable responses. The lowest limit for the sampling rate is known, from Shannon's theorem, to be twice per cycle (see Berman and Gran, 1974). However, this lower limit often results in unacceptable reconstruction.

The essential problem with uniform sampling is that it is impossible to distinguish between two periodic signals when the sum of (or the difference between) their fundamental frequencies equals $2\pi k/T$ where $k = 1, 2, \ldots$. Therefore, the only range of frequency in which uniform sampling can be effective is $0 < \omega_N \leq \pi/T$, where π/T is the folding (or Nyquist) frequency. In a number of books on control theory it is proposed that the sampling period should be chosen to be one-tenth the value given by π/ω_N. Such a proposal is made to avoid problems with aliasing, but it has been found with digital AFCSs that in practice larger values of T can be used with impunity (Katz and Powell, 1973). Using a sampling period with a value one-third that of the folding value provides a conservative margin of safety. To mitigate the effects of any occurrence of aliasing in AFCSs it is customary to insert before the sampler in the system an 'anti-aliasing' filter (sometimes called a guard filter) to eliminate any components of the signal at frequencies higher than the folding frequency.

The sampling device represented in Figure 14.8 differs in operation from that shown in Figure 14.5; the difference can be seen from a study of Figure 14.9. The signal e^* remains at a constant value after the switch opens having been closed briefly; when the switch closes once again e^* takes on a new amplitude, and then maintains that new value when the switch opens. The value of e is said to have been 'held': the sampler of Figure 14.5 has been followed by a 'hold' circuit.

14.3 A DATA HOLD ELEMENT

In any practical, discrete control system with a single sampler, the sampler is followed by a data hold; if the output from that data hold depends only upon the value of the sampled function at the beginning of the sampling interval, it is referred to as zero order hold (ZOH). A data hold which depends upon two prior samples is called a first order hold, and so on. In practice, the use of data hold elements of order higher than first is unusual, since higher order holds introduce into AFCSs undesirable phase lag effects which tend to result in poorer dynamic response.

The impulse response of ZOH element (for a unit impulse input) is defined as:

$$h(t) = U_{-1}(t) - U_{-1}(t - \tau) \tag{14.10}$$

where $U_{-1}(\;)$ denotes a unit step function.

An alternative definition of the dynamic characteristic of a ZOH element is:

$$y(\tau) = y(nT) \qquad nT \leq \tau < (n+1)T \tag{14.11}$$

The transfer function is obtained by taking the Laplace transform of $h(t)$ in this manner:

$$\mathcal{L}\{h(t)\} \triangleq G(s) = (1/s) - (\mathrm{e}^{-s\tau}/s)$$

i.e.

$$G(s) = (1/s)(1 - \mathrm{e}^{-s\tau}) \tag{14.12}$$

A ZOH element, which has as its input the sampled signal represented by Figure 14.3, has an output signal as represented in Figure 14.12.

14.4 THE z-TRANSFORM

Suppose that:

$$z = \mathrm{e}^{sT} \tag{14.13}$$

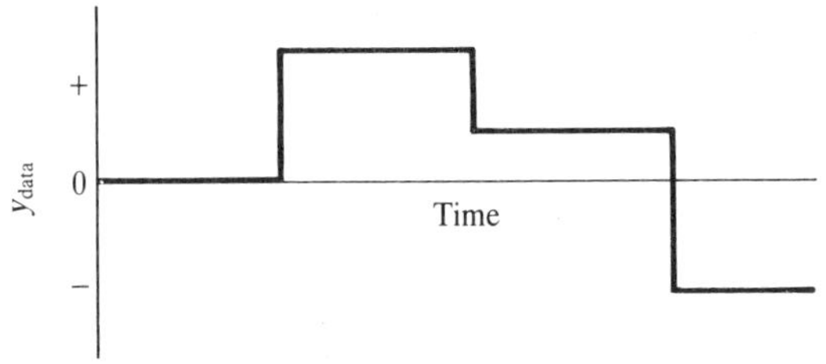

Figure 14.12 Output of zero order hold.

then z^{-1} represents a pure time delay of T seconds.

Any sampled signal, f^*, can be represented by the sequence:

$$f^* = f(0)\delta(t) + f(T)\delta(t - T) + f(2T)\delta(t - 2T) \tag{14.14}$$

where $\delta(\ )$ represents a Dirac impulse function.

By taking Laplace transforms:

$$F^*(s) = \sum_{k=0}^{\infty} f(kT)e^{-skT} = \sum_{0}^{\infty} f(kT)z^{-k} \triangleq F(z) \tag{14.15}$$

Now consider a function of time, $f(t)$, where:

$$f(t) \triangleq e^{-at}$$

then:

$$f^* \Leftrightarrow F(z) = \sum_{k=0}^{\infty} e^{-akT}z^{-k} = 1 + e^{-aT}z^{-1} + e^{-2aT}z^{-2} + \ldots \tag{14.16}$$

i.e.:

$$F(z) = 1 + \frac{e^{-aT}}{z} + \frac{e^{-2aT}}{z^2} + \ldots$$

$$= \frac{1}{1 - (e^{-aT}/z)} = \frac{z}{z - e^{-aT}} \tag{14.17}$$

If:

$$a = R + jQ \tag{14.18}$$

then:

$$f^* = \left[e^{-(R + jQ)t}\right]^* = \frac{z}{z - e^{-RT}e^{-jQT}} \tag{14.19}$$

or:

$$\left(e^{-Rt}\cos Qt - je^{-Rt}\sin Qt\right) = \frac{z}{z - e^{-RT}(\cos QT - j\sin QT)} \tag{14.20}$$

$$\left[\mathrm{e}^{-(R\,+\,\mathrm{j}Q)t}\right]^* \Leftrightarrow \frac{z\{(z - \mathrm{e}^{-RT}\cos QT) - \mathrm{j}\mathrm{e}^{-RT}\sin QT\}}{(z - \mathrm{e}^{-RT}\cos QT)^2 + (\mathrm{e}^{-RT}\sin QT)^2} \tag{14.21}$$

$$\left[\mathrm{e}^{-RT}\cos QT\right]^* \Leftrightarrow \frac{z(z - \mathrm{e}^{-RT}\cos QT)}{(z - \mathrm{e}^{-RT}\cos \mathbf{QT})^2 + (\mathrm{e}^{-RT}\sin QT)^2} \tag{14.22}$$

$$\left[\mathrm{e}^{-Rt}\sin Qt\right]^* \Leftrightarrow \frac{z\mathrm{e}^{-RT}\sin QT}{z^2 - 2\mathrm{e}^{-RT}\cos QT + \mathrm{e}^{-2RT}} \tag{14.23}$$

When $R = 0$, then:

$$[\cos Qt]^* \Leftrightarrow \frac{z(z - \cos QT)}{z^2 - 2\cos QTz + 1} \tag{14.24}$$

$$[\sin Qt]^* \Leftrightarrow \frac{z\sin QT}{z^2 - 2\cos QTz + 1} \tag{14.25}$$

If $a = 0$, however, then:

$$\left\{\mathrm{e}^{-at}\Big|_{a\to 0}\right\}^* = \left\{U_{-1}(t)\right\}^* \Leftrightarrow \frac{z}{(z-1)} \tag{14.26}$$

The z-transform of $tf(t)$ can be found in the following way:

$$\{tf(t)\}^* = \{kTf(kT)\} \Leftrightarrow \sum_{k=0}^{\infty} (kT)f(kT)z^{-k}$$

$$\Leftrightarrow -zT\sum_{k=0}^{\infty} f(kT)[-(k)z^{(-k-1)}] \tag{14.27}$$

The term in the square brackets in eq. (14.27) is the derivative of z^{-k} with respect to z. Hence:

$$\{tf(t)\}^* \Leftrightarrow -zT\frac{\mathrm{d}}{\mathrm{d}z}\left\{\sum_{k=0}^{\infty} f(kT)z^{-k}\right\}$$

$$\Leftrightarrow -zT\frac{\mathrm{d}F(z)}{\mathrm{d}z} \tag{14.28}$$

Consequently, if:

$$f(t) \triangleq \mathrm{e}^{-at} \tag{14.29}$$

then:

$$\{t\mathrm{e}^{-at}\}^* \Leftrightarrow -zT\frac{\mathrm{d}}{\mathrm{d}z}\left(\frac{z}{z - \mathrm{e}^{-aT}}\right)$$

$$\Leftrightarrow -zT(z - \mathrm{e}^{-aT} - z)/(z - \mathrm{e}^{-aT})^2$$

$$\Leftrightarrow zT\mathrm{e}^{-aT}/(z - \mathrm{e}^{-aT})^2 \tag{14.30}$$

If $a = 0$, the z-transform of a ramp function t ($\triangleq U_{-2}(t)$) can be obtained, namely:

Table 14.1 *z*-transforms pairs

$F(s)$	$f(t)$	$F(z)$
1.0	$U_0(t)$	1.0
$\frac{1}{s}$	$U_{-1}(t)$	$\frac{z}{z-1}$
$\frac{1}{s_2}$	$U_{-2}(t)$	$\frac{zT}{(z-1)^2}$
$\frac{1}{(s+a)}$	e^{-at}	$\frac{z}{(z-e^{-aT})}$
$\frac{1}{(s+a)^2}$	$t\,e^{-at}$	$\frac{zT\,e^{-aT}}{(z-e^{-aT})^2}$
$\frac{s}{(s+Q)^2}$	$\cos Qt$	$\frac{z(z-\cos QT)}{z^2-2\cos QT\,z+1}$
$\frac{Q}{(s+Q)^2}$	$\sin Qt$	$\frac{z\sin QT}{z^2-2\cos QT\,z+1}$
$\frac{(s+R)}{(s+R)^2+Q^2}$	$e^{-Rt}\cos Qt$	$\frac{z(z-e^{-RT}\cos QT)}{z^2-2e^{-RT}\cos QT\,z+e^{-2RT}}$
$\frac{Q}{(s+R)^2+Q^2}$	$e^{-Rt}\sin Qt$	$\frac{z\,e^{-RT}\sin QT}{z^2-2e^{-RT}\cos QT\,z+e^{-2RT}}$
$-\frac{d}{ds}F(s)$	$tf(t)$	$-zT\frac{dF(z)}{dz}$

$$\{t\}^* \Leftrightarrow zT/(z-1)^2 \tag{14.31}$$

All the results obtained in this section have been tabulated in Table 14.1.

Example 14.2

In Example 8.4 a full state feedback control law was determined for aircraft BRAVO-4. Relevant details are repeated here.

$$\dot{\mathbf{x}} = A\mathbf{x} + B\mathbf{u}$$

where:

$$\mathbf{x}' = [u \;\; w \;\; q \;\; \theta]$$

$$\mathbf{u} \triangleq \delta_E$$

$$A = \begin{bmatrix} -0.0007 & 0.012 & 0 & -9.81 \\ -0.128 & -0.54 & 1 & 0 \\ 0.064 & 0.96 & -0.98 & 0 \\ 0 & 0 & 1 & 0 \end{bmatrix}$$

$$B' = [0 \ -0.036 \ -12.61 \ 0]$$

$$\mathbf{u}^{o} = K\mathbf{x}$$

$$K = [4.75 \ -0.387 \ -3.225 \ -5.35]$$

Find the corresponding transfer functions relating pitch rate to elevator deflection in terms of: (a) the Laplace transform, and (b) the z-transform.

Find the transfer functions for the closed loop system if the commanded input is pitch rate.

$$y(s)/u(s) \triangleq C[sI - A]^{-1}B$$

$z \triangleq e^{sT}$ where T is the sampling period. For the uncontrolled aircraft it is easily shown that:

$$\frac{q(s)}{\delta_E(s)} = \frac{12.63s^3 - 6.863s^2 - 0.024s}{s^4 + 1.52s^3 - 0.43s^2 + 0.63s - 0.866}$$

$$= \frac{-12.63s(s + 0.54)(s + 0.0036)}{(s + 1.99)(s - 0.664)(s^2 + 0.18s + 0.65)}$$

For any z-transform transfer function the choice of sampling period is significant. For this problem two values, $T = 1.0s$ and $T_1 = 0.1s$, will be used.

For $T = 1.0s$ it can be shown that:[2]

$$\left.\frac{q(z)}{\delta_E(z)}\right|_{T = 1.0s} = \frac{-9.05z^3 + 23.328z^2 - 20z + 5.72}{z^4 - 3.34z^3 - 3.73z^2 - 2.06z + 0.22}$$

$$= \frac{-9.05(z - 1.0)(z - 0.79 + j0.094)(z - 0.79 - j0.094)}{(z - 0.135)(z - 1.942)(z - 0.634 + j0.66)(z - 0.634 - j0.66)}$$

For $T = 0.1s$ the z-transform transfer function becomes:

$$\left.\frac{q(z)}{\delta_E(z)}\right|_{T = 0.1} = \frac{-1.2z^3 + 3.55z^2 - 3.48z + 1.14}{z^4 - 3.86z^3 + 5.59z^2 - 3.58z + 0.86}$$

$$= \frac{-1.2(z - 0.915)(z - 0.9995)(z - 1.0)}{(z - 0.82)(z - 1.07)(z - 0.988 + j0.08)(z - 0.998 - j0.08)}$$

When the commanded input is pitch rate, the input to the closed loop system, $\mathbf{u}_c$, is defined as:

$$\mathbf{u}_c \triangleq [0 \ 0 \ 1 \ 0]'q_c = B_c q_c$$

and the transfer function $q(s)/q_c(s)$ is given by:

$$q(a)/q_c(s) = C[sI - A_c]^{-1}B_c$$

where $A_c = (A + B \times K)$. It can be shown that:

$$\frac{q(s)}{q_c(s)} = \frac{s^3 + 0.55s^2 + 0.002s}{s^4 + 42.21s^3 + 94.29s^2 + 96.59s + 37.49}$$

$$= \frac{s(s + 0.552)(s + 0.003)}{(s + 39.9)(s + 0.77)(s^2 + 1.53s + 1.21)}$$

For $T = 1.0$ s the z-transform transfer function of the controlled aircraft is:

$$\left.\frac{q(z)}{q_c(z)}\right|_{T = 1.0} = \frac{-0.001z^3 - 0.0035z^2 + 0.007z - 0.0026}{z^4 - 1.115z^3 - 0.518z^2 - 0.1z}$$

$$= \frac{-0.001(z - 0.54)(z - 1.0)(z + 5.6)}{z(z - 0.461)(z^2 + 0.653z + 0.217)}$$

For $T = 0.1$ s the transfer function becomes:

$$\left.\frac{q(z)}{q_c(z)}\right|_{T = 0.1} = \frac{0.021z^3 - 0.063z^2 + 0.062z - 0.02}{z^4 - 2.79z^3 + 2.62z_2 - 0.842z + 0.015}$$

$$= \frac{0.021(z - 0.946)(z - 1.0))(z - 1.004)}{(z - 0.019)(z - 0.926)(z^2 + 1.84z + 0.86)}$$

Note the differences in the forms of the Laplace and z-transform versions of the transfer function for the same aircraft, and also the differences which arise in the z-transform version of a transfer function with a change in sampling period.

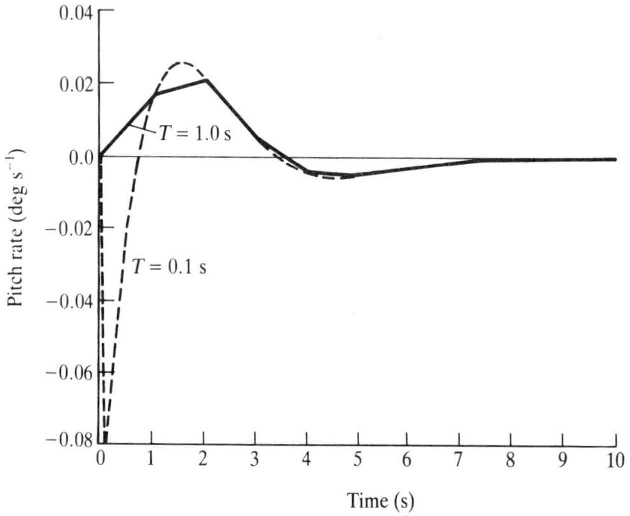

Figure 14.13 Pitch rate response for BRAVO-4 for two sampling rates.

The response of the controlled aircraft using its discrete AFCS, for sampling periods $T = 1.0s$ and $T = 0.1s$, are shown in Figure 14.13. It is worth pointing out here that, for identical choices of sampling period, the response obtained by using a digital simulation language (ACSL) to solve the equation $\dot{\mathbf{x}} = A\mathbf{x} + B\mathbf{u}$ for $U \triangleq 0$ and $\mathbf{x}(0) = [0\ 1\ 0\ 0]'$ is identical to that shown in Figure 14.13. These responses represent the response of pitch rate to an initial vertical velocity of 1 m s^{-1}. Although the responses appear somewhat oscillatory, it should be noted that the amplitudes are very small. It should be observed too that the choice of $T = 1.0s$ for the sampling period has caused the pitch rate response to differ from the response obtained from the continuous system, particularly at the time when the pitching acceleration is at its most rapid. When the value of the pitching acceleration is low the responses more nearly correspond.

14.5 BILINEAR TRANSFORMATIONS

One of the most useful methods of approximating differentiation by means of a difference equation, and one which is particularly effective with linear systems, is the Tustin transform method. The z-transform has been defined as:

$$z \triangleq e^{sT} \tag{14.32}$$

thus:

$$s = (1/T)\log_e z \tag{14.33}$$

Now:

$$\log_e z = 2\left\{w + \frac{w^3}{3} + \frac{w^5}{5} + \dots\right\} \tag{14.34}$$

in which:

$$w = \frac{1 - z^{-1}}{1 + z^{-1}} = \frac{z - 1}{z + 1} \tag{14.35}$$

i.e.:

$$z \triangleq \frac{w + 1}{1 - w} \tag{14.35a}$$

If the series of eq. (14.34) is truncated after the first term, then:

$$s_{\mathrm{T}} = \frac{2}{T}\frac{(1 - z^{-1})}{(1 + z^{-1})} = \frac{2}{T}\frac{(z - 1)}{(z + 1)} \tag{14.36}$$

This is known as the Tustin transform, or the w'-transform. Both w and w' are bilinear transforms.

As the value of the sampling period, T, approaches zero, w tends to zero:

$$w\Big|_{\lim\limits_{T\to 0}} = \lim_{T\to 0}\left\{\frac{z-1}{z+1}\right\} = \lim_{T\to 0}\left\{\frac{e^{sT}-1}{e^{sT}+1}\right\}$$

$$= \lim_{T\to 0}\left\{\frac{sT+(sT)^2/2!+\ldots}{2+sT+(sT)^2/2!}\right\} \to 0 \tag{14.37}$$

On the other hand, w' tends to s, i.e.

$$w' = \frac{2}{T}w = \frac{2}{T}\left\{\frac{sT+(sT)^2/2!+\ldots}{2+sT+(sT)^2/2!+\ldots}\right\}$$

$$\therefore \qquad w'\Big|_{\lim\limits_{T\to 0}} \to s\,.\,. \tag{14.38}$$

Now:

$$z = \frac{Tw'+2}{2-Tw'} \tag{14.39}$$

Also:

$$w' = \frac{2}{T}\left\{\frac{(z-1)}{(z+1)}\right\} = \frac{2}{T}\left\{\frac{e^{sT}-1}{e^{sT}+1}\right\}\left\{\frac{e^{-sT/2}}{e^{-sT/2}}\right\}$$

$$= \frac{2}{T}\left\{\frac{e^{sT/2}-e^{-sT/2}}{e^{sT/2}+e^{-sT/2}}\right\} = \frac{2}{T}\tan\text{h}\left(\frac{sT}{2}\right) \tag{14.40}$$

The imaginary axis of the s-plane is defined by $s = j\omega$. Hence:

$$w' \triangleq \mu + j\nu = \frac{2}{T}\tan\text{h}\left(\frac{j\omega T}{2}\right) = \frac{j2}{T}\tan\left(\frac{\omega T}{2}\right) \tag{14.41}$$

or:

$$\nu = \frac{2}{T}\tan\left(\frac{\omega T}{2}\right) \tag{14.42}$$

Thus, the imaginary axis of the s-plane is mapped onto the imaginary axis of the w′-plane. When $\omega T/2$ has a small value then:

$$\nu = \lambda \tag{14.43}$$

The real axis of the s-plane is defined by $s = \sigma$. Hence,

$$w' = \frac{2}{T}\tan\text{h}\left(\frac{\sigma T}{2}\right) \triangleq \mu \tag{14.44}$$

If:

$$\sigma T/2 \triangleq x \tag{14.45}$$

then:

$$\tanh x = \frac{x + \dfrac{x^2}{3!} + \ldots}{1 + \dfrac{x^2}{2!} + \ldots} \tag{14.46}$$

when:

$$\begin{aligned} & x^2 \ll 2 \\ & \mu = \sigma \end{aligned} \tag{14.47}$$

Consequently, whenever the approximations are valid:

$$w' = \mu + j\nu = \sigma + j\omega \triangleq s \tag{14.48}$$

Note that $(w')^{-1}$ is analogous to s^{-1} in that it represents a trapezoidal integration operator. The scaling factor, $2/T$, is highly important, since its presence means that a mathematical representation in the w' domain will result in an exact model of the sampling and data hold operations, irrespective of the sampling period which is used. A table of w'-transforms, in terms of z, for $T = 0.1s$, is given in Table 14.2.

Example 14.3

A continuous system has a transfer function $G(s)$, given by:

$$G(s) = \frac{5}{s^2 + 2s + 5}$$

Table 14.2 w'-transform table for $T = 0.1$ s

$$z = \frac{w'T + 2}{-w'T + 2}$$

For $T = 0.1$ s

$$z = \frac{0.1\,w' + 2}{-0.1\,w' + 2}$$

$$z^2 = \frac{0.01\,w'^2 + 0.4\,w' + 4}{0.01\,w'^2 - 0.4\,w' + 4}$$

$$z^3 = \frac{0.001\,w'^3 + 0.06\,w'^2 + 1.2\,w' + 8}{-0.001\,w'^3 + 0.06\,w'^2 - 1.2\,w' + 8}$$

$$z^4 = \frac{0.0001\,w'^4 + 0.008\,w'^3 + 0.24\,w'^2 + 3.2\,w' + 16}{0.0001\,w'^4 - 0.008\,w'^3 + 0.24\,w'^2 - 3.2\,w' + 16}$$

It is required to know the z-transform transfer function, with a sampling period of $T = 0.1s$.

Now $\mathscr{L}^{-1}([G(s)]) \triangleq g(t) = 2.5\mathrm{e}^{-t}\sin 2t$. From Table 14.1 it can be seen that:

$$G(z) = \frac{0.45z}{z^2 - 1.775z + 0.82}$$

However, if the truncated eq. (14.36) is substituted, the transfer function $G(z)$, becomes:

$$G(z) = \frac{0.011(z+1)^2}{(z^2 - 1.775z + 0.82)}$$

Substituting for z and z^2 from Table 14.2 yields:

$$G(w') = \frac{-0.0087(w' - 20.736)}{0.0359w'^2 + 0.0724w' + 0.1816}$$

$$= \frac{5.025(1 - 0.048w')}{(w' + 2.017w' + 5.06)}$$

When the approximation $w' = s$ is used:

$$G(w') = \frac{5}{w'^2 + 2w' + 5}$$

which is very close to the value already obtained for $G(w')$ by means of substituting for z, z^2, etc. Thus, direct substitution of w' for s to obtain the bilinear transform version of the transfer function is permissible and reasonably accurate.

14.6 DISCRETE STATE EQUATION

For any state equation of the form:

$$\dot{\mathbf{x}} = A\mathbf{x} + B\mathbf{u} \tag{14.49}$$

it is shown in Bellman (1960) and d'Azzo and Houpis (1975), for example, that a discrete state equation can be represented by the recursive algebraic equation:

$$\mathbf{x}_{k+1} = \Phi\mathbf{x}_k + \Delta\mathbf{u}_k \tag{14.50}$$

where eq. (14.50) represents:

$$\mathbf{x}([k+1]T) = \Phi(T)\mathbf{x}(kT) + \Delta(T)\mathbf{u}(kT) \tag{14.51}$$

$$\Phi(T) \triangleq \mathrm{e}^{AT} \tag{14.52}$$

$$\Delta(T) \triangleq \int_0^T \Phi(T)B\mathbf{u}(\lambda)\mathrm{d}\lambda \tag{14.53}$$

The output equation for such a discrete equation is given by:

$$\mathbf{y}_k = C\mathbf{x}_k + D\mathbf{u}_k \tag{14.54}$$

Of course, when these equations are employed, the values of the state, output and control variables can be known only at the sampling intervals, kT.

Example 14.4

For aircraft BRAVO-4 of Example 14.2 with sampling periods $T = 1.0s$ and $T = 0.1s$, it can be shown that:

$$\Phi(1.0) = \begin{bmatrix} 0.95 & -1.12 & -3.85 & -9.66 \\ -0.09 & 0.877 & 0.69 & 0.48 \\ 0.006 & 0.52 & 0.564 & -0.101 \\ 0.01 & 0.315 & 0.717 & 0.95 \end{bmatrix}$$

$$\Delta'(1.0) = [17.02 \ -4.67 \ -9.05 \ -4.95]$$

$$\Phi(0.1) = \begin{bmatrix} 1.0 & -0.0003 & -0.048 & -0.98 \\ -0.012 & 0.95 & 0.093 & 0.006 \\ 0.006 & 0.089 & 0.91 & -0.003 \\ 0.0003 & 0.0046 & 0.095 & 1.0 \end{bmatrix}$$

$$\Delta'(0.1) = [0.02 \ -0.064 \ -1.2 \ -0.06]$$

For the controlled aircraft (using the control law given in Example 14.2) the corresponding matrices are:

$$\Phi_c(1.0) = \begin{bmatrix} 0.6 & 0.214 & -0.09 & -4.0 \\ -0.04 & 0.56 & 0.001 & -0.46 \\ -0.002 & 0.02 & -0.013 & -0.027 \\ 0.06 & -0.025 & -0.001 & -0.027 \end{bmatrix}$$

$$\Delta_c'(1.0) = [-0.06 \ 0.007 \ -0.001 \ 0.01]$$

$$\Phi_c(0.1) = \begin{bmatrix} 1.0 & 0.004 & -0.017 & -0.93 \\ -0.002 & 0.94 & 0.018 & -0.12 \\ 0.13 & -0.08 & -0.002 & -1.56 \\ 0.01 & -0.007 & 0.02 & 0.88 \end{bmatrix}$$

$$\Delta_c'(0.1) = [-0.0007 \ 0.0015 \ 0.02 \ 0.002]$$

14.7 STABILITY OF DIGITAL SYSTEMS

14.7.1 The Unit Circle Method

It is shown in Sections 14.4 and 14.5 how the input/output characteristics of a discrete system could be represented either by means of a z-transform function or by the use of an appropriate bilinear transform, such as the w' or the Tustin. As an alternative to these representations, the state equation methods of Section 14.6 could be used.

A digital control system can become unstable not only because of an inappropriate choice of system parameters, such as gains or time constants, but also because of an inappropriate choice of sampling period. There are a few analytical methods for determining the limiting conditions for stability which can help a designer to choose the values of the parameters of his system.

On the s-plane, for example, the boundary for stability is the imaginary axis, i.e. $s = j\omega$ (see Section 7.3.4). On the z-plane, the boundary for stability is a circle, of radius unity. Since $z \triangleq e^{j\omega T}$, z is a complex number of unit modulus and with a phase angle of ωT. Thus, the z-plane illustrates the periodic nature of e^{sT}, because z has the same value whenever its angle, ωT, has increased by 2π radians. It is usual, when checking for stability on the s-plane, to examine the right halfplane to discover if any system poles are located there, in which event the system will be unstable. To check for stability in the z-plane, it is necessary to determine if any system poles lie *outside* the unit circle. Figure 14.14 shows the regions of stability for both the s- and z-planes. The location of the poles for the transfer functions for the uncontrolled and controlled aircraft, BRAVO-4, dealt with in Example 14.2 are shown in Figure 14.15(a); the corresponding poles of

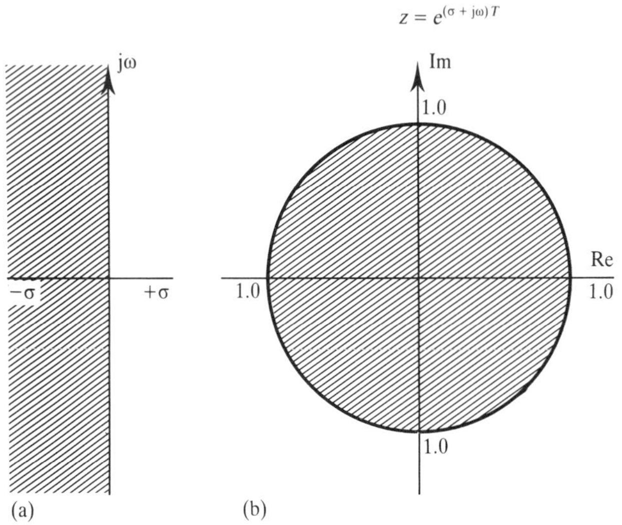

Shaded regions represent regions of stability

Figure 14.14 Regions of stability. (a) s-plane. (b) z-plane.

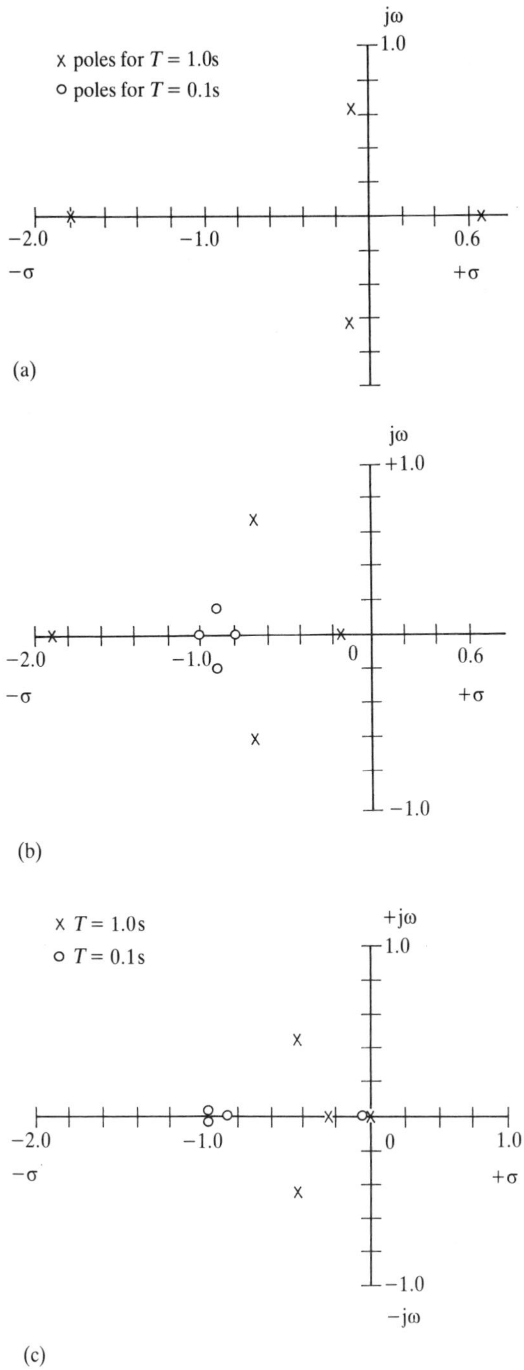

Figure 14.15 (a) s-plane of uncontrolled aircraft. (b) z-plane of uncontrolled aircraft. (c) z-plane of controlled aircraft.

the z-transform functions for $T = 1.0$ and $T = 1.0$ and $T = 0.1$ are shown in Figure 14.14 for the uncontrolled aircraft, and in Figure 14.15(c) for the controlled aircraft. Note that the uncontrolled aircraft is unstable whatever form of representation is used, and whatever value of sampling period is chosen. For the controlled aircraft, the system is stable for both forms of representation, and for each value of sampling period.

Note that when $T = 0.1s$ the poles tend towards the boundary of the unit circle. This phenomenon is common with digital control systems: as the sampling period gets small, the poles and zeros in the z-plane tend to cluster on the unit circle boundary which can cause considerable numerical difficulty in analytical studies.

Thus, for a digital system to be stable, it is necessary and sufficient for the poles of the z-transform function of the closed loop system to lie within the unit circle. Obviously, the closed loop digital system is stable, even if a pole lies in the right halfplane, provided that it lies within the unit circle. The nature of the response of the digital system depends upon the location of its poles and zeros on the z-plane; it is important to remember, therefore, that a different z-plane diagram is needed for each different value of sampling period being considered.

The nature of the dynamic response corresponding to the locations on the z-plane of the z-transform functions in summarized in Table 14.3 (Houpis and Lamont, 1982).

14.7.2 Jury's Stability Criterion

The characteristic equation of the z-transform function of the closed loop digital control system can be expressed as:

$$a_n z^n + a_{n-1} z^{n-1} + a_{n-2} z^{n-2} + \ldots + a_2 z^2 + a_1 z + a_0 = 0 \qquad (14.55)$$

Jury's criterion states that if the l.h.s. of eq. (14.55) is positive for a unity value of z, *and* is positive for $z = -1$ when n is even, and is negative for $z = -1$ when n is odd, then all the roots of the characteristic equation (14.55) will lie within the unit circle of the z-plane and, consequently, the system will be stable. (See Ragazinni and Franklin (1958) for further discussion.)

Table 14.3 Summary of system response for corresponding pole locations in z-plane

z-plane location	*Resulting system response*
Outside unit circle	Unstable
Inside unit circle	
Real pole	
Right half of unit circle	Decaying output sequence
Left half of unit circle	Alternating output sequence – diminishing amplitude
Complex conjugate poles	Damped oscillatory output sequence

Example 14.5

Consider the z-transform transfer functions derived in Example 14.2. Determine if the aircraft system is stable.

For $T = 1.0s$:

$$\left.\frac{q(z)}{\delta_E(z)}\right|_{z=1} = \frac{-9.05 + 23.33 - 20 + 5.72}{1 - 3.34 + 3.73 - 2.06 + 0.219} \simeq 0.0$$

$$\left.\frac{q(z)}{\delta_E(z)}\right|_{z=-1} = \frac{9.05 + 23.33 + 20 + 5.72}{1 + 3.34 + 3.73 + 2.06 + 0.22} = \frac{58.1}{10.35}$$

Hence, only one stability condition is satisfied: the second; the aircraft is unstable.

For the controlled aircraft, when $T = 0.1s$:

$$\left.\frac{q(z)}{q_c(z)}\right|_{z=1} = \frac{-0.0214}{0} \times 0 \simeq 0$$

Note how difficult it is to determine stability by this method when the sampling time is small: numerical round-off can result in an incorrect view being taken of the system's stability. When the l.h.s. of the characteristic equation is in polynomial form, and is not easily factorizable, Jury's criterion can be used; but, in general, the third method is more effective.

14.7.3 The Routh–Hurwitz Criterion of Stability

If an appropriate bilinear transformation is used, the region of the z-plane outside the unit circle can be mapped into the right half of an auxiliary plane, and the region inside the unit circle can be mapped into the left half of this new plane. It is then possible to determine if the roots of the characteristic equation, in terms of the z-transform, lie in the left half of this plane by using the well known Routh–Hurwitz criterion.

From eq. (14.35):

$$w \triangleq \frac{z - 1}{z + 1} \tag{14.35}$$

i.e.:

$$z \triangleq \frac{w + 1}{1 - w} \tag{14.35a}$$

For simplicity, suppose that there is a closed loop z-transform function given by:

$$\frac{C(z)}{R(z)} = \frac{0.09(z + 0.72)}{z^2 - 1.2z + 0.32} \tag{14.56}$$

The characteristic equation is:

$$z^2 - 1.2z + 0.32 = 0 \tag{14.57}$$

Substituting for w yields:

$$\left(\frac{w + 1}{1 - w}\right)^2 - 1.2\left(\frac{w + 1}{1 - w}\right) + 0.32 = 0 \tag{14.58}$$

i.e.:

$$2.52w^2 + 1.36w + 0.12 = 0 \tag{14.59}$$

Applying the Routh–Hurwitz criterion to this equation will show that the system is stable.

If Jury's criterion is applied to the same z-transform functions then, for n even:

$$(z^2 - 1.2z + 32)\Big|_{z = 1} = 0.12$$

$$(z^2 - 1.2z + 0.32)\Big|_{z = -1} = 2.52$$

which confirms that the system is stable.

The right-half criterion may be used, of course, if the w'-transform is used, since $w' \to s$. Thus, if the characteristic polynomial, $1 + G(s)H(s)$, is known, the stability of the digital system can be established by substituting w' for s. The technique is shown in the next example.

Example 14.6

Take the characteristic equation for BRAVO-4 (see Example 14.2) for $T = 0.1$ s, for (1) the uncontrolled aircraft, and (2) the aircraft with feedback control applied. Determine by means of the w'-transform and the Routh–Hurwitz criterion if the aircraft is dynamically stable.

$$\frac{q(s)}{\delta_E(s)} = \frac{-12.63s^3 - 6.863s^2 - 0.024s}{s^4 + 1.52s^3 - 0.43s^2 + 0.63s - 0.866}$$

$$\therefore \quad \frac{q(w')}{\delta_E(w')} = \frac{-12.63w'^3 - 6.863w'^2 - 0.024w'}{w'^4 + 1.52w'^3 - 0.43w'^2 + 0.63w' - 0.866}$$

Routh's array is then:

1	− 0.43	− 0.866
+ 1.52	0.63	
− 0.8445	− 0.866	− 0.929
− 0.866		

There is one change of sign in the leftmost column: a root with a positive real part exists and the aircraft is unstable.

$$\frac{q(s)}{q_c(s)} = \frac{s^3 + 0.55s^2 + 0.002s}{s^4 + 42.21s^3 + 94.29s^2 + 96.59s + 37.49}$$

$$\therefore \quad \frac{q(w')}{q_c(w')} = \frac{w'^3 + 0.55w'^2 + 0.002w'}{w'^4 + 42.21w'^3 + 94.29w'^2 + 96.59w' + 37.49}$$

The corresponding Routh's array is:

1	94.29	37.49
42.21	96.59	
92	37.49	
79.39	×	
37.49		

No sign change has occurred in the leftmost column: the controlled aircraft is stable.

14.8 OPTIMAL DISCRETE CONTROL

Suppose the aircraft dynamics can be represented by a state transition equation:

$$\mathbf{x}_{k+1} = \Phi\mathbf{x}_k + \Delta\mathbf{u}_k \tag{14.60}$$

An optimal discrete control law can be obtained by minimizing a quadratic performance index, such as:

$$J = \tfrac{1}{2}\sum_{k=0}^{N-1}\left\{\mathbf{x}_k' Q x_k + \mathbf{u}_k G u_k\right\} + \tfrac{1}{2}\mathbf{x}_N' S \mathbf{x}_N \tag{14.61}$$

where N represents the final sampling period.

The control law can be shown to be:

$$\mathbf{u}_k^{o} = -G^{-1}\Delta'[P_{k+1}^{-1} + \Delta G^{-1}\Delta']^{-1}\Phi\mathbf{x}_k = K_k\mathbf{x}_k \tag{14.62}$$

where:

$$\begin{aligned} P_k &= Q + \Phi' P_{k+1}[I + \Delta G^{-1}\Delta' P_{k+1}]^{-1}\Phi \\ &= Q + \Phi'[P_{k+1}^{-1} + \Delta G^{-1}\Delta']^{-1}\Phi \end{aligned} \tag{14.63}$$

$$P_N \triangleq S \tag{14.64}$$

(See Franklin and Powell (1980) and Kwakernaak and Sivan (1972) for further explanation.) Equation (14.63) is the matrix Riccati difference equation which is solved iteratively, and backwards in time, from P_N to P_0.

From a computational view, there are some advantages in using what is called the Joseph stabilized version (Joseph and Tou, 1982) of the solution to the same problem, i.e.:

$$\mathbf{u}_k^{\text{o}} = -K_k\mathbf{x}_k \text{ (as before)} \tag{14.65}$$

But:

$$K_k = +(\Delta' F_{k+1}\Delta + G)^{-1}\Delta' F_{k+1}\Phi \tag{14.66}$$

$$F_k = (\Phi - \Delta K_{\text{R}})' F_{k+1}(\Phi - \Delta K_k) + K_k' G K_k + Q \tag{14.67}$$

Example 14.7

For the aircraft used in Example 14.2, find the discrete optimal control law for a sampling period of (1) $T = 1.0s$, and (2) $T = 0.1s$. The weighting matrices of Example 8.4 should be used, namely:

$$Q = \text{diag}[1 \ \ 10 \ \ 10 \ \ 1]$$

$$G = [5.0]$$

Compare the controlled responses of the aircraft for the two sampling periods, and also for a discrete representation of the aircraft using continuous feedback control.

By solving eqs (14.59) and (14.60), for the Φ and Δ matrices evaluated in Example 14.4, and the weighting matrices Q and G, the resulting feedback control laws are:

$$K\Big|_{T=1.0} = [0.0061 \ \ -0.0649 \ \ -0.1184 \ \ -0.145]$$

$$K\Big|_{T=0.1} = [0.1056 \ \ -0.1417 \ \ -0.7639 \ \ -1.3054]$$

The corresponding digital responses of the pitch rate of BRAVO-4 for these control laws are shown in Figure 14.16. These digital responses were obtained from solving:

$$\mathbf{x}_{k+1}\Big|_{T=1.0} = (\Phi + \Delta \times K_1)\mathbf{x}_k$$

$$\mathbf{x}_{K+1}\Big|_{T=0.1} = (\Phi_1 + \Delta_1 \times K_{0.1})\mathbf{x}_k$$

Also shown in Figure 14.15 are the same pitch rate responses, but obtained from the digital version of the continuous feedback controlled aircraft, i.e.:

$$\dot{\mathbf{x}}_{\text{c}} = (A + B \times K)\mathbf{x}_{\text{c}}$$

where:

$$K = [-0.475 \ \ 0.387 \ \ 3.225 \ \ 5.35]$$

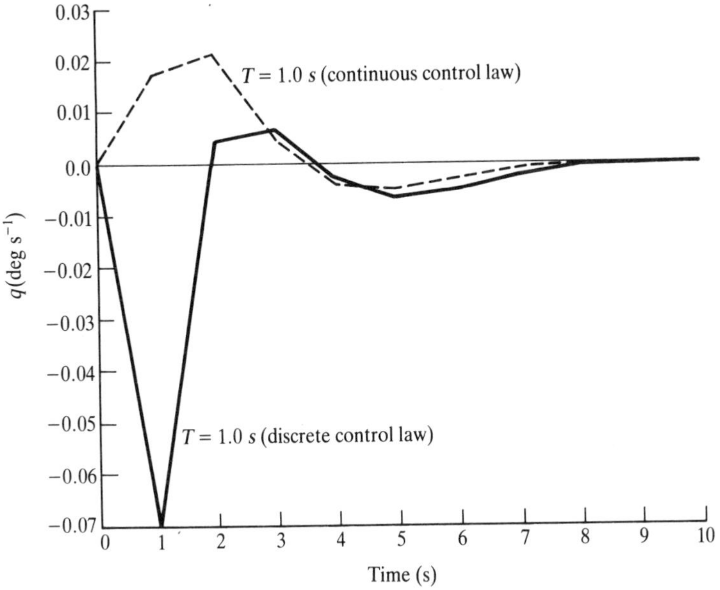

(a)

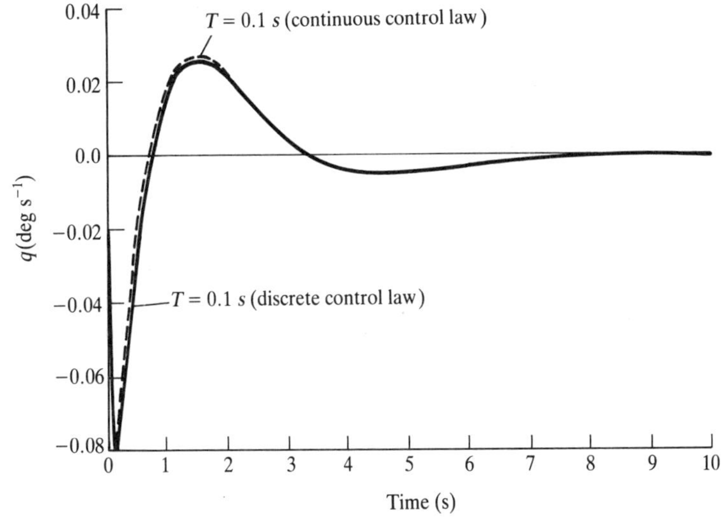

(b)

Figure 14.16 Pitch rate response for BRAVO-4 for two digital control laws. (a) $T = 1.0$ s. (b) $T = 0.1$ s.

(from Example 14.2) from which:

$$\mathbf{x}_{c_{k+1}}\Big|_{T=1.0} = \Phi_{c_{1.0}}\mathbf{x}_{c_k}$$

or:

$$\mathbf{x}_{c_{k+1}}\Big|_{T=0.1} = \Phi_{c_{0.1}}\mathbf{x}_{c_k}$$

The transition matrices $\Phi_{c1.0}$ and $\Phi_{c0.1}$ were calculated in Example 14.4.

Note from Figure 14.16(a) that neither of the optimal control laws is particularly effective, although both stabilize the unstable uncontrolled aircraft. The response corresponding to the discrete control law ($\mathbf{u}_k = K_{1.0}\mathbf{x}_k$) is a better approximation to the continuous optimal response than that obtained from first applying the continuous feedback control law to the continuous aircraft state equation and then digitizing the resulting closed loop system. However, when the sampling period T is reduced to $0.1s$ there is very close correspondence between the responses. The resulting digital response is very close to that obtained from the continuous control, which can be seen from inspection of Figure 8.3. The peak overshoot, evident in Figure 14.14 at approximately 0.15 s, does not correspond with the time of occurrence of the peak obtained in Figure 8.3, although the peak amplitudes are close.

14.9 USE OF DIGITAL COMPUTERS IN AFCSs

14.9.1 Phase Lag Caused by Sampling

It should be evident from the preceding section that, if the sampling period is short, the amplitude of the response is not greatly affected by the sampling operation. But, of course, the process of sampling is effectively the introduction of a time delay, with an attendant phase shift of ωT: the mean phase shift is $\omega T/2$.

If a digital computer is involved, it needs some time to perform the corresponding numerical calculations; let that processing time be T_c. The effective delay due to computer operation is, therefore:

$$T' = T_c + (T/2) \tag{14.68}$$

The effects on the operation of the AFCS of the phase lag corresponding to this effective time delay is destabilizing. If the crossover frequency of the open loop of the AFCS is ω_c, say, then to account for the delay an additional phase lag of $\omega_c T'$ must be added at ω_c. For example, if the crossover frequency, ω_c, of the AFCS is $5\,\text{rad s}^{-1}$ and the sampling period is 0.01 s, with a mean processing time of $5\,\text{m s}^{-1}$, the phase lag introduced by the computer is $5(0.005 + (0.001/2) = 0.05\,\text{rad} \simeq 3°$. Such a phase lag would need to be overcome in a lightly damped loop. This result implies that fast computing times and high sampling rates must be used for digital AFCSs.

14.9.2 Effect of Word Size

Algorithms for synthesizing a digital control law for an AFCS can be implemented either by using special-purpose digital components or, more commonly, by using special software on a general-purpose digital computer. In either case the values and the coefficients of the digital sequences have to be stored as binary numbers in finite length registers. Consequently, the length of the digital word is finite and affects the performance of the algorithm. If the digital computer being used is a machine using an 8-bit word, say, it would require two, or even three, words to represent a floating point number, and virtually all the data associated with the algorithm would have to be stored in the computer in integer format. With such machines the performance limitations are so severe that it would probably be necessary to avoid floating point operations. For AFCSs this is hardly possible since it would mean very severe quantization performance requirements being imposed upon both the sensor signals and the signal conversion equipment.

If data are stored in integer format, the amount of core storage available is at once reduced. For example, in a processor using a 16-bit word, two words are needed to store a floating point number. Manipulation of such floating point data is slower, because two memory cycles are required to retrieve a floating point number from memory, whereas only a single cycle is required for an integer.

Even when the data are adequately represented by words of finite length, processing usually results in numbers which will need extra bits if they are to be accurately represented. For example, a data sample represented by a word of x bits is to be multiplied by some coefficient also represented by a word of x bits: the resulting product is a word of length $2x$ bits. With a recursive form of a control algorithm, if the results of arithmetic operations are quantized, the number of bits required for representation increases rapidly, since after the first operation $2x$ bits are needed; after the second, $3x$ bits are required; after the fourth, the requirement is for $5x$ bits, and so on. Obviously, the results of such arithmetic operations have to be truncated (rounded), but such a procedure has the dynamic effect of having introduced into the control algorithm a non-linearity which can manifest itself physically in the form of a limit cycle.

In the digital implementation of an AFCS control law the basic arithmetic operations are multiplication by a constant (a coefficient) and addition. For fixed point arithmetic, the result of every multiplication has to be truncated, but for the results of any addition this does not have to be done. However, because the word length of an addition can exceed the length of the register, the same considerations of dynamic range as those which arise when quantizing samples of an analogue signal also apply: wide dynamic range and small quantization error are mutually exclusive requirements.

14.10 CONCLUSIONS

In this chapter the nature of sampling and data holding are introduced, and a brief discussion of some features of the analysis of such discrete systems is undertaken to illustrate some of the dynamic effects which are specific to digital systems. Quantization, aliasing and hidden oscillations are discussed in relation to the important parameter, sampling rate. Transformation methods, such as the z-transform and w'-transform, are introduced to provide a means of analysing simple systems and to provide a basis for discussion of the special stability problems relating to digital control. Discrete state equations representation is also presented and subsequently used in the development of optimal discrete control laws. The direct equivalence of an optimal discrete feedback control law controlling a continuous plant, like an aircraft, and a discretized version of a continuous optimal control law applied to the same continuous plant, is demonstrated before closing the chapter with a short discussion of the effect of digital word size on the dynamic performance of an AFCS.

14.11 EXERCISES

14.1 Write down the equations representing the short period motion of BRAVO-4. Assume that the dynamics of the elevator actuator are negligible but that the elevator is moved through a digital actuator with unity gain, and a sampling period of 0.2s. Determine the response of the aircraft's angle of attack for 2.0 s. Determine the response of the aircraft's angle of attack for 2.0 s following the application of a 1° step command to the elevator actuator.

14.2 Determine the state transition matrix for the longitudinal dynamics of FOXTROT-4 for sampling periods 0.01, 0.1 and 1.0 s respectively.

14.3 Determine the eigenvalues of the three transition matrices found in Exercise 14.2. Are these eigenvalues significant in terms of the stability of the aircraft's motion? Explain your answers.

14.4 Find the z-transform function corresponding to the transfer function $a_{z_{cg}}(s)/\delta_E(s)$ for FOXTROT-4 for a sampling period of 0.1 s. By means of any appropriate stability check, determine if the discrete representation of the aircraft's motion is stable. Are your findings here comparable with the answer found in Exercise 14.3?

14.5 For FOXTROT-4 use a bilinear transformation to find a discrete transfer function, relating normal acceleration at the aircraft's c.g. to its elevator deflection, which can be used to plot a corresponding root locus. The sampling period is 0.01 s. Would the discrete transfer function found still be useful if the sampling period was increased to 0.1 s?

14.6 For the solution to part (a) of Exercise 10.3 determine the response $\beta(t)$ to a unit step command of yaw rate if there is inserted between the pilot's control and the rudder an ideal sampler and a ZOH with a period of 0.1 s.

14.7 (a) Consider Example 8.7. For the same flight control system, but with the addition of a sampler and a ZOH, find the discrete state equation:

$$\mathbf{x}_{k+1} = \Phi \mathbf{x}_k + \Delta \mathbf{u}_k$$

for a sampling period of 0.1 s.

(b) Using the weighting matrices given in Exercise 8.7 determine the discrete optimal control, $\mathbf{u}_k^o$, for the given sampling period.

(c) Compare the response of the optimal discrete flight control system to an initial angle of attack of 1°, for a period of 10.0 s, with that obtained from implementing the continuous optimal control law found in answer to Exercise 8.7, but with a sampler and ZOH inserted in the forward path and using a sampling period of 0.1 s.

14.8 In Example 10.2 it was shown how the closed loop roll control system for CHARLIE-2 could be represented by the differential equation:

$$0.153 \frac{d\phi}{dt} + \phi = 4.41 \phi_{comm}$$

If a sampler was inserted in the forward loop of that continuous roll angle control system, and a sampling period of 0.05 s was employed, write down the corresponding difference equation. Thence obtain an appropriate z-transform representation. Evaluate ϕ_k at each sampling interval in response to a unit step command, ϕ_{comm}. Compare the response with that obtained from the continuous system.

14.9 The lateral dynamics of the B-52, including structural flexibility effects, are described by the state equation $\dot{\mathbf{x}}_1 = A_1\mathbf{x}_1 + B_1\mathbf{u}_1$ where the state vector, $\mathbf{x}_1$, and the control vector, $\mathbf{u}_1$, are defined in eqs (12.5) and (12.6) and A_1 and B_1 are defined in eqs (12.9) and (12.10) respectively. These are shown in Figure 12.3.

(a) Find the eigenvalues of the aircraft. Is the aircraft stable?

(b) Determine the discrete state equation for this aircraft. Find the eigenvalues of the corresponding transition matrix, Φ, for sampling intervals of 0.2 s and 0.01 s respectively. Thence determine if the discrete representation of this aircraft is stable.

(c) Explain why you think the use of z-transforms to obtain a discrete transfer model may be inappropriate in this example.

(d) Do you think that in aircraft problems like this aliasing could be a problem for discrete control? Give reasons for your answer.

14.12 NOTES

1. This property implies that if a signal is to be processed using digital hardware, then that signal must have its amplitude quantized.
2. Most easily by using some computer package such as TOTAL, CTRL-C or MATRIX_x.

14.13 REFERENCES

BELLMAN, R. 1960. *Introduction to Matrix Analysis.* New York: McGraw-Hill, pp. 230–231.

BERMAN, H. and R. GRAN. 1974. Design principles for digital autopilot synthesis. *J. Air.* 11(7): 414–22.

d'AZZO, J.J. and C.H. HOUPIS. 1975. *Linear Control Systems Analysis and Design.* New York: McGraw-Hill.

FRANKLIN, G.F. and J.D. POWELL. 1980. *Digital Control of Dynamic Systems.* Reading, Mass.: Addison Wesley.

HOUPIS, C.H. and G.B. LAMONT. 1982. *Digital Control Systems.* New York: McGraw-Hill.

JOSEPH, P.D. and TOU, J.T. 1982. Modern synthesis of computer control systems. *Trans IEEE. Appl. Ind. 82* 63: 61–65.

KATZ, P. and J.D. POWELL. 1973. Sample rate selection for aircraft digital control. *JAIAA* 13(8).

KWAKERNAAK, H. and R. SIVAN. 1972. *Linear Optimal Control Systems.* New York: Wiley.

RAGAZINNI, J.R. and G.F. FRANKLIN. 1958. *Sampled Data Control Systems.* New York: McGraw-Hill.

15

Adaptive Flight Control Systems

15.1 INTRODUCTION

Those flying and handling qualities which are generally considered to be necessary for an aircraft to be flight-worthy and safe are dealt with in Chapter 6. But even without a knowledge of that material it can be readily appreciated, from Appendix B and Chapters 2 and 3, that the flying qualities of any aircraft will change widely with its flight conditions, so that it is quite usual for an aircraft to have acceptable flying qualities at many points in its flight envelopes, yet to possess unacceptable qualities at other points in that envelope. However, even when the complete ranges of dynamic pressure and acceleration are considered for a variety of flight missions, it will be found that the need for an AFCS to possess other than gain-scheduling as a means of ensuring that its dynamic performance remains acceptable is seldom justified (Gregory, 1959). But there are four flight missions where such gain-scheduled AFCSs cannot easily provide acceptable performance:

1. When an aircraft is at considerable height and is rapidly climbing or diving.
2. When an aircraft is performing rapid manoeuvres involving large angles of attack.
3. When an aircraft has just released a significant quantity of external stores.
4. When an ICBM, or some booster stage, is climbing rapidly through the earth's atmosphere.

In cases 1 and 4, the vehicle experiences in such flights a considerable variation of both speed and atmospheric density, that is, the vehicle undergoes a great change of dynamic pressure. In case 2 the large changes of angle of attack cause corresponding changes in many of the stability derivatives and, consequently, in the aircraft's dynamic response. In case 3 there can be a very considerable change in an aircraft's mass with the release of external stores. Such mass changes cause changes in the stability derivatives. There is a considerable change in the vehicle's mass in case 4 too, as a result of the very rapid expenditure of fuel.

To provide an illustration of the kinds of change which can occur in these situations, the short period flying qualities of the aircraft FOXTROT are considered. How the short period frequency, ω_{sp}, and the damping ratio, ζ_{sp}, vary

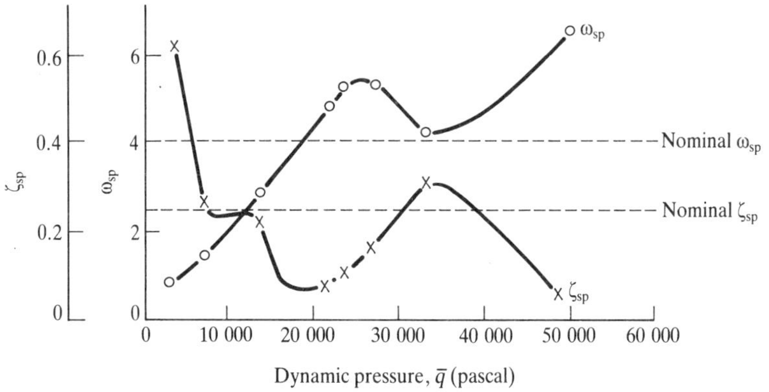

Figure 15.1 Variation of ω_{sp} and ζ_{sp} with dynamic pressure.

with dynamic pressure, $\bar{q}$, is shown in Figure 15.1. For the same aircraft, the trajectory (or, more exactly, the height/Mach number profile) for the shortest time-to-climb, from sea level to 20 000 m, with the least energy being used, is shown in Figure 15.2. This graph was based on Bryson *et al.* (1969) and represents case 1 above. Such a work is concerned with optimizing flight trajectories and it ignores the effects of the aircraft's flying qualities, although it assumes that a pilot can execute the resulting optimal profile. Yet it can be seen from Figure 15.3, which is based upon the data of Figures 15.1 and 15.2, by how much the principal parameters governing the flying qualities of aircraft FOXTROT would change as the least time-to-climb profile was flown.

For the four missions listed above a different kind of AFCS is needed – a self-adaptive AFCS. Such a flight control system is 'one which has the capability of changing its parameters through an internal process of measurement,

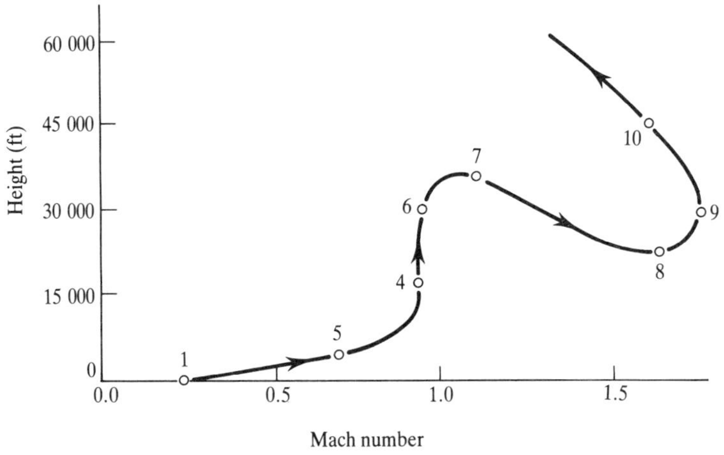

Figure 15.2 Optimal time-to-climb trajectory for FOXTROT aircraft.

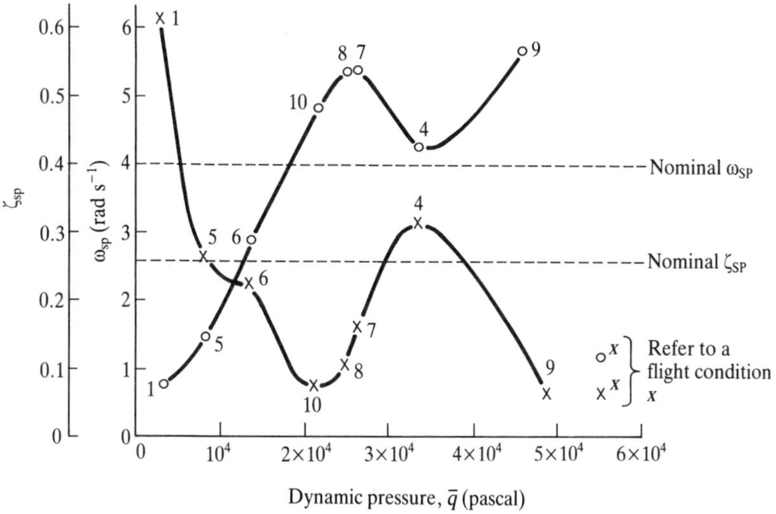

Figure 15.3 Variation of ω_{sp} and ζ_{sp} with $\bar{q}$ for optimal time-to-climb.

evaluation, and adjustment, to adapt to a changing environment, either external or internal, to the vehicle under control' (Gregory, 1959).[1]

According to C. S. Draper, a distinguished professor who was head of the Department of Aeronautics, and also of the Instrumentation Laboratories, of MIT in the 1960s, the idea of an adaptive system was first used in 1939 in fire control systems for anti-aircraft guns. From what is known now of the almost complete ineffectiveness of such anti-aircraft gunnery in the early years of the Second World War, it cannot be regarded as a successful application. It would seem more satisfactory, therefore, to regard self-adaptive control as having originated from work carried out at the Flight Control Laboratories of the USAF, at Wright-Patterson Air Force Base, at Dayton, in 1955. That work is comprehensively reported in Gregory (1959).

From the published work it can be inferred that two of the types of adaptive AFCS being worked on at that time are the only types which have been used successfully in flight operations. Indeed, the type which was regarded as the least attractive, from early theoretical considerations, has been successfully developed for use in the tactical strike aircraft, the F-111, used by the USAF. The two types of adaptive flight control system, the model reference and the parameter-adaptive, are the subjects of this chapter.

15.2 MODEL REFERENCE SYSTEMS

Control system performance models have long been popular in the field of automatic control. The idea of using a feedback element to ensure that the loop gain was always sufficiently high to guarantee rapid, though stable, dynamic

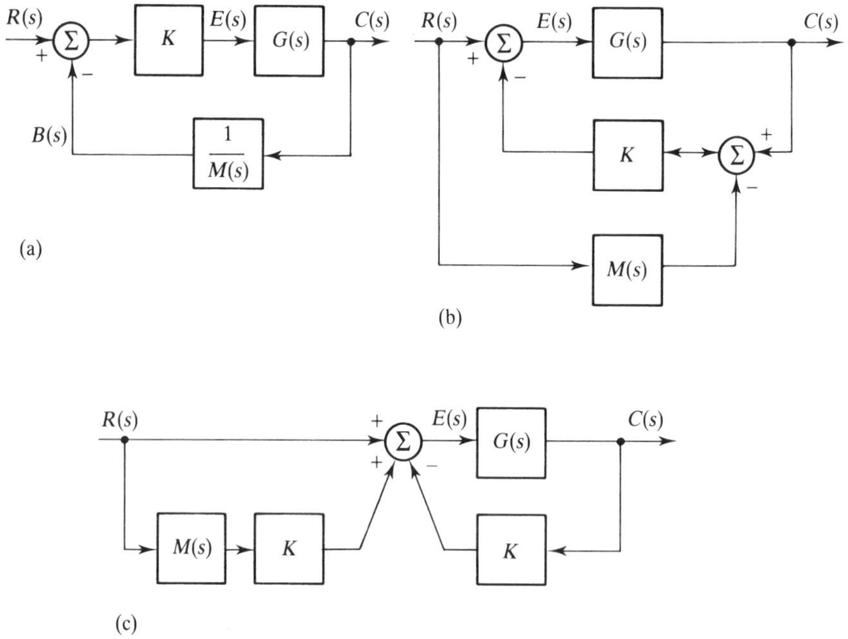

Figure 15.4 Model systems.

response, and to provide insensitivity to both external disturbances and internal parameter variations, has always been dominant. That the feedback element should be one whose dynamics were those of some model system was an idea first tried in 1955 (Lang and Ham, 1955). Figure 15.4(a) shows the proposed scheme. Because it is intended that the transfer function of the closed loop system should be close to that of the model, the transfer function of the feedback element is chosen to be the inverse of $M(s)$. From Figure 15.4(a) it can be seen that:

$$C(s)/R(s) = M(s)KG(s)/(M(s) + KG(s)) \tag{15.1}$$

If it can be arranged that:

$$KG(s) \gg M(s) \tag{15.2}$$

then:

$$C(s)/R(s) \Rightarrow M(s) \tag{15.3}$$

However, the required inverse function, $M^{-1}(s)$, can easily be physically unrealizable. For example, if:

$$M(s) \triangleq \omega_m^2/(s^2 + 2\zeta_m\omega_m s + \omega_m^2) \tag{15.4}$$

then $M^{-1}(s)$ would not be physically realizable. Moreover, to ensure that the inequality (15.2) is maintained throughout the flight envelope is no easier than the basic flight control problem.

An improvement is to use the model ahead of the feedback loop, in the manner shown in Figure 15.4(b). For the purpose of analysis, the block diagram may be redrawn as shown in Figure 15.4(c). It can then be easily shown that:

$$C(s)/R(s) = G(s)(1 + KM(s))/(1 + KG(s)) \tag{15.5}$$

and arranging that:

$$KG(s) \gg 1 \qquad (15.6)^2$$

If:

$$KM(s) \gg 1 \qquad (15.7)^3$$

then:

$$C(s)/R(s) \Rightarrow M(s) \tag{15.8}$$

Neither method is adequate, however, being merely passive schemes involving pre-filtering and high loop gain to achieve invariance of the closed loop response when the system is subjected to changes in the values of its parameters.

15.3 THE MIT SCHEME

This scheme is a model reference adaptive AFCS and was first developed in 1962 in the Instrumentation Laboratory of MIT by Whitaker (1962). A block diagram is presented in Figure 15.5. The specified dynamic response of the closed loop system is characterized by the reference model which has been arranged to be forced with the same command signal as that driving the basic flight control

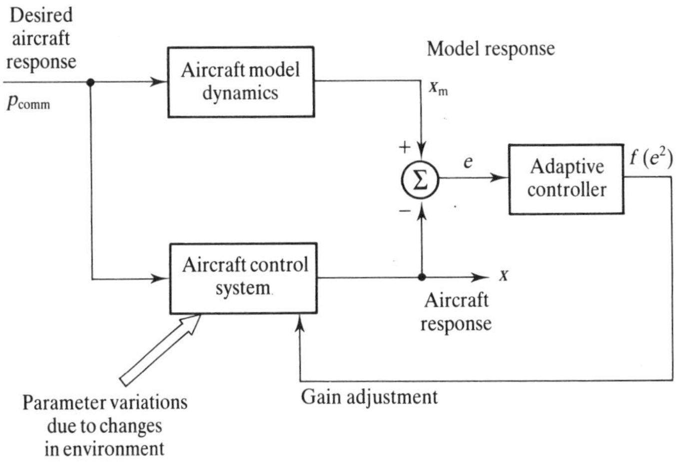

Figure 15.5 Block diagram of model reference adaptive system.

system. The output from the model is directly compared with that of the flight control system and, if these outputs do not correspond, an error signal is formed. A number of parameters of the flight control systems, which are considered to be the best to control, are adjusted so that the integral of the error squared is minimized.

At a desired operating point, the slope of this integral, taken as a function of the adjustable parameters, K_j, must be zero, i.e.:

$$\frac{\partial^m}{\partial K_1, \partial K_2, \ldots, \partial K_m} \int_0^\infty e^2 \mathrm{d}t = 0$$

Provided that the limits of the integral are independent of K_j (and that the integral of the partial derivatives of the function exists), the partial differentiation can be carried out under the integral sign, i.e.:

$$\begin{aligned} F &= \frac{\partial}{\partial K_n} \int_0^\infty e^2 \mathrm{d}t = \int_0^\infty \frac{\partial e^2}{\partial K_n} \mathrm{d}t \\ &= 2 \int_0^\infty \left(\frac{\partial e}{\partial K_n} \right) e \, \mathrm{d}t = \int_0^\infty w(t) e \, \mathrm{d}t \end{aligned} \tag{15.9}$$

F is then the integral of the error, weighted by another function, w, such that F indicates the condition of the system.

Equation (15.9) can be re-expressed as:

$$\dot{F} = K_{\text{adapt}} \mathbf{e} \partial \mathbf{e} / \partial \mathbf{F} \tag{15.10}$$

where the vector $\partial \mathbf{e}/\partial \mathbf{F}$ represents the sensitivity derivatives of the error with respect to the adjustable parameters; these sensitivity derivatives may be generated as the output signals from a linear system which has as its drive inputs the input and output signals of the aircraft system. The constant, K_{adapt}, determines the rate at which the adaptive action takes place.

The MIT rule is based upon the notion that any changes which occur in those parameters making up the elements of $\mathbf{F}$ are slow in relation to the changes taking place in the aircraft's motion variables. To reduce the ISE it is logical to change the parameters of the system in a direction which is the negative gradient of e^2, i.e.:

$$\mathbf{F} = -K_{\text{adapt}} \int \mathbf{e}(\lambda) \frac{\partial \mathbf{e}(\lambda)}{\partial \mathbf{F}} \mathrm{d}\lambda \tag{15.11}$$

From eq. (15.11) it is evident that the adaptive process consists of three distinct components:

1. A linear system using as its input the input and output signals obtained from the aircraft itself to construct the sensitivity derivatives, $\partial \mathbf{e}/\partial \mathbf{F}$.
2. A multiplier to produce the product $\mathbf{e}(\partial \mathbf{e}/\partial \mathbf{F})$.
3. An integrator.

This structure is commonplace in adaptive schemes. Provided that K_{adapt} is small (thereby reinforcing the earlier assumption that any changes in the system's parameters are slow compared to those taking place in the motion variables) any adaptive system based on the MIT rule will work reasonably well, but it may possibly become unstable. Since the permissible value of K_{adapt} depends upon the amplitude of the forcing signal, p_{comm}, the stability analysis of any model reference adaptive system based upon the MIT rule is invariably difficult, and the limits of stable operation of such systems are normally fixed by means of extensive simulation studies.

15.4 EXAMPLE SYSTEM

If a pitch damper system of the type dealt with in Section 9.4 is considered, the idea is to continuously adjust the gain, K_c, to maintain the values of the damping ratio and the natural frequency of the closed loop system at 0.25 and 4.0 rad s^{-1} respectively (see Figure 15.3), irrespective of flight condition. Because the height and speed of the aircraft are different for each flight condition the parameters ζ_{sp} and ω_{sp} change as illustrated in Figure 15.3. Note that both the aircraft gain, K_A, and its time constant, T_A, also change, but, for the purpose of illustrating how the MIT rule is used, they are assumed here to be constant for every flight case. Using the aircraft FOXTROT as an example, the transfer function of the pitch rate SAS is given by:

$$q(s)/p_{comm}(s) = K(1 + sT_A)/(s^2 + \zeta_c\omega_c s + \omega_c^2) \qquad (15.12)$$

where K represents the gain, ζ_c represents the damping ratio, and ω_c the natural frequency of the closed loop aircraft SAS. What is required for every flight condition is that the SAS should behave as though it were a model system defined by:

$$q_m(s)/p_{comm}(s) = 16(1 + sT_A)/(s^2 + 2s + 16) \qquad (15.13)$$

Referring to Figure 15.6, it can be deduced that K_{mod} has been taken as unity, that the zero for the model dynamics is identical to that of the SAS, and that both the damping ratio and the natural frequency correspond to the nominal values given on Figure 15.3.

Application of the MIT rules provides:

$$\dot{K}_c = K_1 e(\partial e/\partial K_c) \qquad (15.14)$$

$$e \triangleq q_m - q \qquad (15.15)$$

Given eq. (15.15), it can be shown that:

$$\frac{\partial e}{\partial K_c} = \frac{-(1 + sT_A)}{(s^2 + 2\zeta_c\omega_c s + \omega_c^2)} p_{comm}(s) = -aq(s) \qquad (15.16)$$

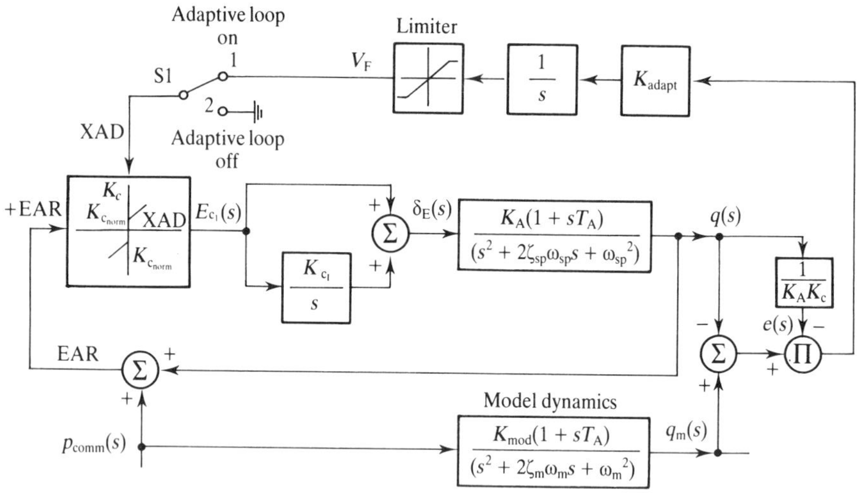

Figure 15.6 Block diagram of MIT rule model reference system for FOXTROT aircraft.

where:

$$a = 1/K \tag{15.17}$$

Therefore, from eqs (15.14) and (15.16):

$$\dot{K}_c = -K_{adapt}eq \tag{15.18}$$

Figure 15.6 represents this adaptive control scheme. From results obtained from a digital simulation, it will be seen that, for example, for flight condition 3, the aircraft has a short period damping ratio of 0.224 and a frequency of 2.85 rad s^{-1}, and for a rate gyro sensitivity of 1.0 V deg^{-1} s^{-1} and a controller gain, K_c, of 0.283 the nominal values of closed loop damping ratio and frequency are obtained, namely $\zeta_c = 0.25$ and $\omega_c = 4.0$ rad s^{-1}. As a result of the action of the adaptive loop it can be seen from the aircraft's dynamic response, shown in Figure 15.7, how the dynamic response of the aircraft SAS is forced to correspond to that of the model. The effectiveness of the adaptive control can be appreciated from the results shown in Table 15.1, from which it is evident how closely, throughout the full climbing mission of the aircraft FOXTROT, the adaptive system has maintained both the closed loop systems's damping ratio and its natural frequency at their nominal values. However, the reader is reminded that these results were obtained from a deliberately simplified system, for illustrative purposes only, and which was relatively benign to simulate. The changes in the aircraft characteristic were introduced in a fixed fashion and so it did not change continuously, as it would if the aircraft followed the optimal climb profile of Figure 15.3. Consequently, the overriding practical concern of flight control engineers with the relationship between system stability and the rate of adaptation has not been fully addressed. For any practical design this would be a central concern.

Table 15.1 Flying qualities of basic aircraft and aircraft with adaptive control

Flight condition	*Dynamic pressure* (kN m^{-2})	*Basic aircraft* K_A	T_A	ζ_{SP}	ω_{SP}	*With adaptive control acting* ζ_{SP}	ω_{SP}
1	4.675	− 4.79	0.5	0.32	1.51	0.61	7.2
5	6.033	− 6.02	0.2	0.16	1.91	0.62	7.32
6	13.55	− 16.3	0.55	0.19	3.53	0.65	7.48
10	20.876	− 13.9	0.23	0.065	4.26	0.62	7.48
8	23.413	− 18.4	0.39	0.08	5.39	0.60	7.36
7	24.08	− 23.3	0.62	0.125	5.78	0.61	7.26
4	32.415	− 33.5	1.09	0.29	4.54	0.63	7.4
9	41.61	− 22.2	0.37	0.1	4.73	0.63	7.3

15.5 A LYAPUNOV SCHEME

A number of different examples of adaptive flight controls appear in Gupta (1986) in which it will be seen, in a paper by Parks (1966), how the use of Lyapunov theory can improve the stability of the MIT rule adaptive control scheme. From Figure 15.8 it can be seen how the adaptive scheme based upon Lyapunov theory requires the addition of a rate term which provides the adaptive loop with the necessary damping.

Suppose that the aircraft system is defined by a state equation driven by a single command input, p_{comm}, i.e.:

$$\dot{\mathbf{x}} = A\mathbf{x} + BK_cK_Ap_{comm} \tag{15.19}$$

$$y = C\mathbf{x} \tag{15.20}$$

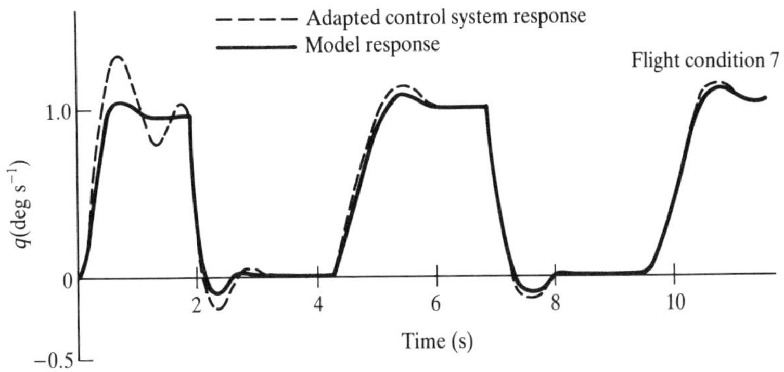

Figure 15.7 Dynamic response of MIT adaptive system for FOXTROT aircraft.

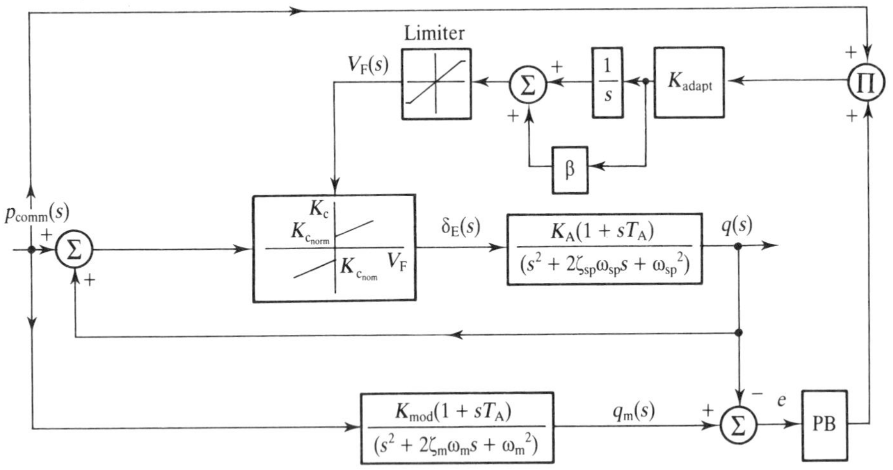

Figure 15.8 Block diagram of Lyapunov rule model reference system.

If it is assumed, for the purposes of this development, that only the aircraft gain, K_A, changes with height and speed, and that the model dynamics are characterized by:

$$\dot{\mathbf{x}}_m = A\mathbf{x}_m + BK_{mod}P_{comm} \tag{15.21}$$

$$\mathbf{y}_m = C\mathbf{x}_m \tag{15.22}$$

then, when the difference between the model's output and that of the aircraft system is defined as:

$$\mathbf{e} = \mathbf{y}_m - \mathbf{y} \tag{15.23}$$

where it is implied that as t tends to infinity, **e** will tend to zero, the response of the aircraft system will exactly correspond with that of the model. If:

$$\mathbf{e}_1 \triangleq C\mathbf{e} \tag{15.24}$$

it can easily be shown that:

$$\begin{aligned} \dot{\mathbf{e}} &= A\mathbf{e}_1 + BCK_{mod} - K_cK_Ap_{comm} \\ &= A\mathbf{e}_1 + BK_{adapt}p_{comm} \end{aligned} \tag{15.25}$$

Now a Lyapunov function, V, is chosen such that:

$$V \triangleq \mathbf{e}_1'P\mathbf{e}_1 + \lambda(K_{adapt} + \beta K_A v)^2 \tag{15.26}$$

where:

$$v = K_{adapt}\mathbf{e}_1'PBp_{comm} \tag{15.27}$$

$$K_{adapt} = K_{mod} - K_AK_v \tag{15.28}$$

Hence:

$$\dot{V} = \mathbf{e}_1'(A'P + PA)\mathbf{e}_1 + 2\mathbf{e}_1'PBK_{\text{adapt}}p_{\text{comm}} + 2\lambda(K_{\text{adapt}} + \beta K_A v)(\dot{K}_{\text{adapt}} + \beta K_A \dot{v}) \tag{15.29}$$

Choosing as the adaptive rule (called the Lyapunov rule, for convenience):

$$\dot{K}_{\text{adapt}} \equiv K_A \dot{K}_c = -K_A v - \beta K_A \dot{v}$$

$$\therefore \quad \dot{K}_c = v + \beta \dot{v} \tag{15.30}$$

then:

$$\dot{V} = -\mathbf{e}_1' Q \mathbf{e}_1 - 2\beta\lambda K_A^2 v^2 \tag{15.31}$$

where:

$$-Q = A'P + PA \tag{15.32}$$

P and Q are p.d. matrices which satisfy eq. (15.32); the equation, referred to as the Lyapunov equation, is a degenerate Riccati equation of the type dealt with in Section 8.4 of Chapter 8.

Hence, the Lyapunov adaptive rule is given by eqs (15.30) and (15.27), namely:

$$\dot{K}_c = v + \beta \dot{v} \tag{15.30}$$

where:

$$v = K_{\text{adapt}} \mathbf{e}_1' PB p_{\text{comm}} \tag{15.27}$$

15.6 PARAMETER ADAPTATION SCHEME

It was shown in eqs (15.1)–(15.3) that if the loop gain of a feedback system can be made sufficiently high, the closed loop response is the inverse of the feedback model response.

A system based upon a parameter adaptation scheme is shown in block diagram form in Figure 15.9. The desired model parameters, $\omega_m = 4.0 \text{ rad s}^{-1}$ and $\zeta = 0.3$, appear in the numerator of the feedback model. The adaptive loop maintains the loop gain of the aircraft system at its highest value for closed loop stability by monitoring the gain of the closed loop frequency response when the aircraft system is subjected to an 'adaptive' mode oscillatory input of 20 rad s^{-1}. The gain is adjusted so that the damping ratio is 0.3. The adaptive oscillation is usually imperceptible to a pilot. This system is described in Mallery and Neebe (1966).

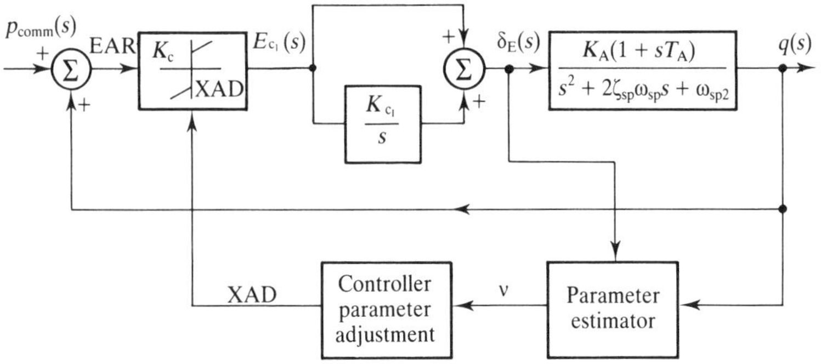

Figure 15.9 Block diagram of parameter adaptive control system.

15.7 CONCLUSIONS

This final chapter treats very briefly the topic of adaptive flight control systems. Although the discussion is based upon deterministic adaptive schemes such as the MIT and Lyapunov rules, the reader should consider the application of such modern techniques as rule-based control, fuzzy logic and expert systems to the problem of providing acceptable flight control for aircraft whose parameters vary considerably throughout their flight envelopes. Such newer methods are the topics of current extensive research and cannot properly be included in an introductory textbook.

15.8 NOTES

1. It has often been suggested at conferences that to define adaptive control is to invite an argument. The author, having no wish to quarrel with his readers, humbly suggests, therefore, that the definition given here is adequately descriptive for the purposes of an introductory textbook.
2. A customary feedback system requirement.
3. A simpler condition than eq. (15.6), since $M(s)$ is fixed and does not change with flight condition.

15.9 REFERENCES

BRYSON, A.E., M.N. DESAI and W.C. HOFFMAN. 1969. Energy state approximation in performance optimization of supersonic aircraft. *J. Air.* 6: 481–8.

GREGORY, P.C. (ed.). 1959. *Proceedings of the Self-adaptive Flight Control Systems Symposium.* WADC TR 59–49, WPAFB, Dayton, Ohio.

GUPTA, M.M. (ed.). 1986. *Adaptive Methods for Control System Design.* New York: IEEE Press.

LANG, G. and J.M. HAM. 1955. Conditional feedback systems – a new approach to feedback control. *Trans AIEE* 74(2): 152–61.

MALLERY, C.G. and F.C. NEEBE. 1966. Flight test of general electric self-adaptive control. *J. Air.* 3(5).

PARKS, P.C. 1966. Lyapunov redesign of model reference adaptive control systems. *Trans IEEE.* AC-11(7): 362–7.

WHITAKER, P.H. 1962. Design capabilities of model reference adaptive systems. *Proc. Nat. Electron. Conf.* 18: 241–9.

Appendix A

Actuators and Sensors

A.1 INTRODUCTION

There are too many kinds of actuator and sensor in use on aircraft to be able successfully to present a complete discussion here of their mathematical representations. Good accounts can be found in Collette (1970) and Ahrendt and Savant (1960). Although the USA is investigating the possibilities of there being an 'all-electric' airplane by 1999, most current transport and military aircraft use hydraulically-powered actuators, with a few employing some electrical actuators. General aviation aircraft mostly use electrical actuators, although a not insignificant number, at the upper end of the weight range, use hydraulic actuators. Similarly, the majority of aircraft fitted with AFCSs use inertial sensors, such as gyroscopes and accelerometers, which involve electrical motors or force actuators, although an increasing number of transport aircraft use laser gyroscopes for sensing angular rates and attitudes.

In this appendix mathematical models are presented for hydraulic and electrical actuators, and then for two degrees of freedom and single degree of freedom gyroscopes, concluding with that for a force balance accelerometer, the derived transfer function being representative of all that type of sensor.

A.2 ACTUATOR USE IN AFCSs

For any control surface there is a hinge moment given by:

$$M_{\mathrm{h}} = \bar{q}\bar{c}SC_{\mathrm{h}} \tag{A.1}$$

where $\bar{q}$ represents the dynamic pressure, $1/2\rho V^2$, $\bar{c}$ the mean aerodynamic chord of the surface, S the effective surface area of the control surface, and C_{h} the hinge moment coefficient.

If the control surface was connected directly to the pilot's controller via a linkage system, the force which the pilot would be required to provide is given by:

$$F_{\mathrm{stick}} = K_{\mathrm{G}}M_{\mathrm{h}} \tag{A.2}$$

where K_{G} represents the 'gearing' of the linkage system.

It is evident from eq. (A.1) that the hinge moment is a function of dynamic pressure. Moreover, C_{h} also changes with height and speed. As a result, in modern aircraft, it is simply impossible for a pilot to provide the stick force required to move the control surface directly for anything but the shortest period of time. The mechanical advantage which can be obtained from control rod linkages, or cables and pulleys, is limited, and, consequently, hyrdaulic or electrical actuators must be used to provide the large force assistance required.

Hydraulic actuators are superior to electrical actuators in terms of the power/weight ratio they achieve, although the reader is cautioned that direct comparison is often difficult because it is never easy to decide upon whether the hydraulic or electrical power supply is fitted wholly for the benefit of the primary flight control systems. Rules-of-thumb which assist in first, gross assessments are that for a transport aircraft fleet the operational cost of each kilogram is about \$120 per aircraft per year. And for hydraulic actuators, power/weight ratios of approximately 350 W kg^{-1} can be achieved. Hydraulic actuators can typically produce forces of the order of 20 000 N, although greater forces can be provided. Above all, the choice of hydraulic actuator is inevitably made because of their reliability which, for commercial aircraft, should be less than 10^{-7} per flying hour.

The mathematical models of actuators used in the analysis or design of AFCSs are usually linear in the first instance. Thus, the actuator has no threshold, deadzone, or saturation effects; it will also provide the rate of change of output variable which the command input demands. In practice, these non-linear effects are present and, in particular, the performance of actuators is limited in practice by the limited rate of change of output they can provide. The piston of an actuator can never move at a speed greater than the corresponding flow rate (which occurs when the value is wide open) can provide.

A.3 ACTUATORS

A.3.1 Hydraulic

Valve and Piston

All hydraulic actuators work on the same principle (see Green, 1985). Special oil under pressure (typically at 21 MPa, i.e. 3 000 lbf in^{-2} although modern miniaturized system are being developed which work at 56 MPa, or 8 000 lbf in^{-2}) is admitted by a control valve into a chamber where a piston is free to move under the action of the high pressure fluid. A schematic representation of the system is shown in Figure A.1. The displacement of the pilot valve is denoted by x_i and that of the piston is denoted by x_0. The flow of the hydraulic fluid is controlled by the valve which is really an orifice whose area is varied by the displacement of the spool (see Figure A.2). The relationship of the exposed area, A, to the displacement, x_i, can be shown to be:

$$A = \frac{1}{4} d^2 \cos^{-1}\left(\frac{d - 2x_i}{d}\right) - \frac{1}{2}\left(d - 2x_i\right) \sqrt{(x_i d - x_i^2)} \qquad \text{(A.3)}$$

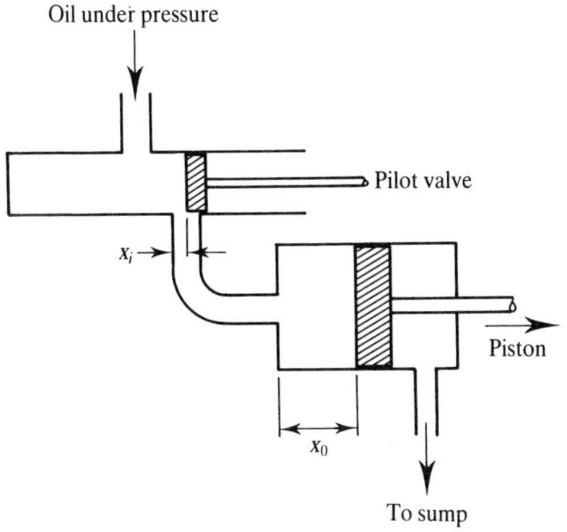

Figure A.1 Valve and piston.

where d is the diameter of the orifice. If $x_i > d/2$ the exposed area becomes:

$$A = \frac{1}{4} d^2 \cos^{-1}\left(\frac{d - 2x_i}{d}\right) + \frac{1}{2}\left(2x_i - d\right)\sqrt{(x_i d - x_i^2)} \tag{A.4}$$

A graph showing how A varies with x_i is shown in Figure A.3, from which it can be inferred that the exposed area is (approximately) a linear function of the displacement, x_i. Therefore, a reasonable approximation is that:

$$A = bx_i \tag{A.5}$$

where b is a constant representing the slope of the curve shown in Figure A.3.

As a result of a unit area of valve opening, the quantity of oil flowing per second into the chamber is a constant, λ, and, hence, the volume of oil flowing through the orifice each second is given by:

$$q = \lambda A = \lambda b x_i = Q_0 x_i \tag{A.6}$$

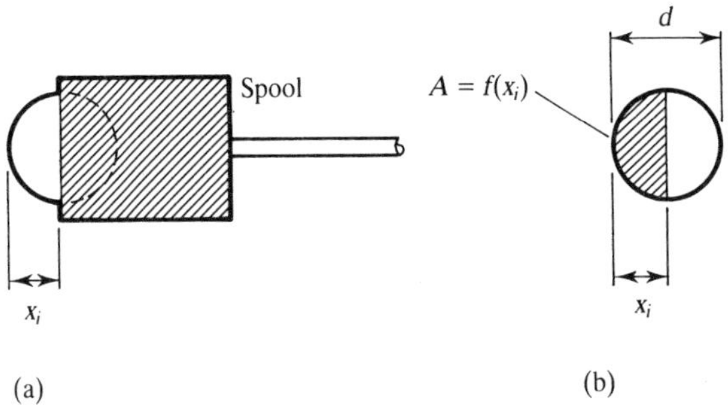

Figure A.2 Spool valve and orifice area.

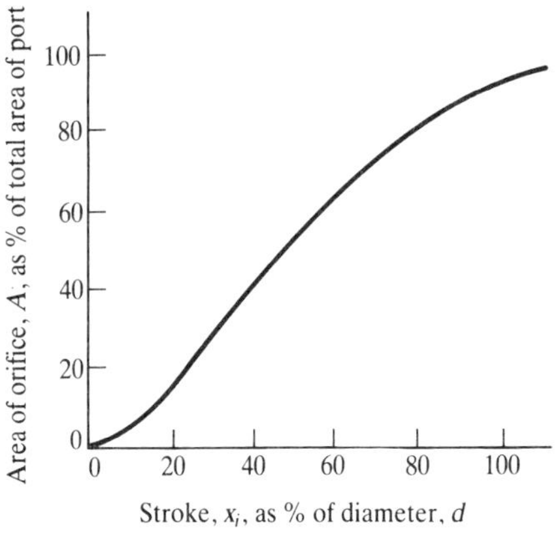

Figure A.3 Graph of area vs. stroke.

where Q_0 is a constant representing the flow gradient of the valve at zero pressure.

The piston has a surface area, S, and, consequently, the volume which must be swept by the piston to accommodate the inflow of high pressure oil is Sx_0; the rate of change of volume caused by the piston's motion must equal (if there is no leakage) the rate of flow of the high pressure oil, i.e.:

$$Q_0 x_i = S\dot{x}_0 \tag{A.7}$$

i.e.:

$$\dot{x}_0/x_i = Q_0/S = K \tag{A.8}$$

The corresponding transfer function is represented in Figure A.4.

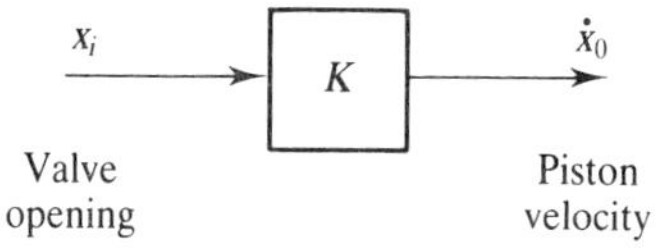

Figure A.4 Block diagram of valve and piston transfer function.

Obviously, the arrangement of Figure A.1 has little value for AFCS applications since a small valve opening will cause the piston to move at a constant velocity until it reaches the end stop. Moreover, there is no way to move the piston in the opposite direction, nor does the piston do any work.

A double acting pilot valve is needed to ensure that the piston can move in either direction. Usually, in AFCS, pistons are linked directly or through a mechanism to a control surface which, for the purposes of a linear mathematical model, can be represented by a lumped mass and viscous friction. The real situation is not always well modelled by such a linear presentation.

Double-acting pilot valve and piston

In treating the arrangement shown in Figure A.5, allowance for leakage and compressibility effects has also been made.

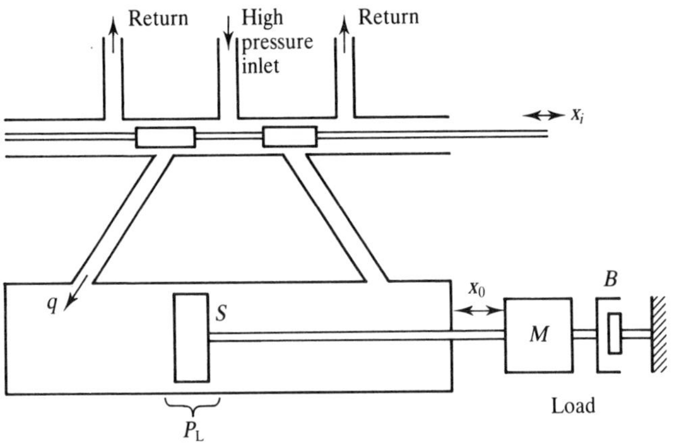

Figure A.5 Valve and piston with mechanical load.

For a given valve displacement there is a corresponding flow of hydraulic oil given by the relationship:

$$q = Q_0 x_i \tag{A.6}$$

The valve performance is typically represented by a series of curves such as are shown in Figure A.6 but to evaluate Q_0 it is often more convenient to replot the flow characteristic in the manner shown in Figure A.7. To move the mechanical load requires that the piston should produce a force, F, given by:

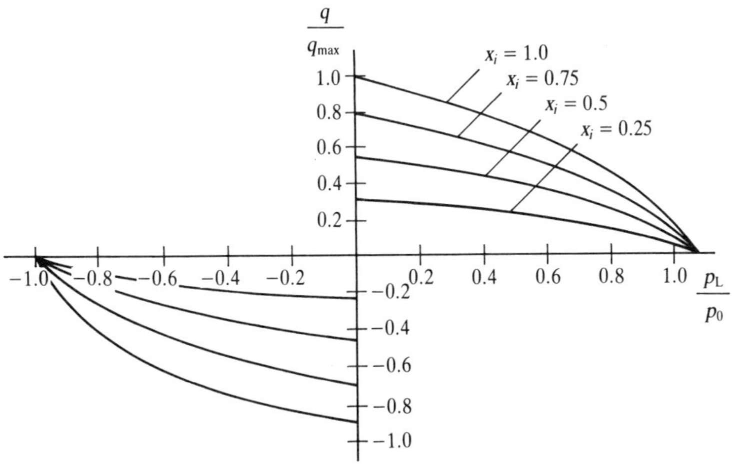

Figure A.6 Valve characteristics.

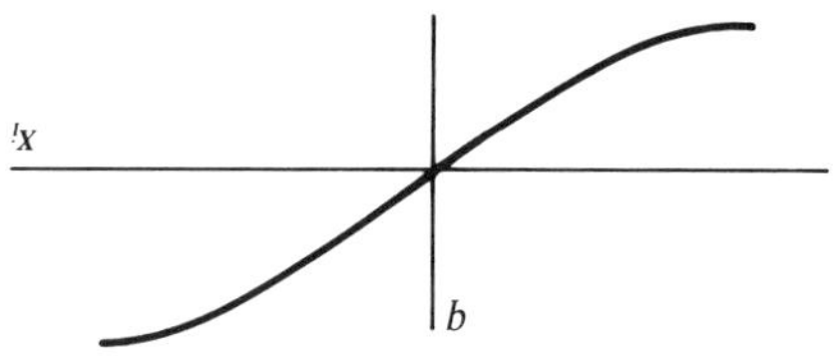

Figure A.7 Valve flow/input curve.

$$F = \frac{M\mathrm{d}^2x_0}{\mathrm{d}t^2} + \frac{B\mathrm{d}x_0}{\mathrm{d}t} \tag{A.9}$$

That force must be obtained from the hydraulic pressure across the piston, P_L, acting on the surface area, S, i.e.:

$$F = P_L S \tag{A.10}$$

However, when allowance is made for leakage and compressibility effects, the result is that the full oil flow from the valve is not available to move the piston in its chamber. Leakage flow rate, q_L, is assumed to be proportional to PL, i.e.:

$$q_L = K_L P_L \tag{A.11}$$

and the flow rate, q_c, caused by compressibility is given by:

$$q_c = (V/B_m)\dot{P}_L \tag{A.12}$$

where V represents the volume of hydraulic oil trapped in the piston chamber, and B_m denotes the bulk modulus of the hydraulic oil. Thus:

$$q = q_F + q_c + q_L \tag{A.13}$$

i.e.:

$$q = S\dot{x}_0 + (V/B_m)\dot{P}_L + K_L P_L = Q_0 x_i \tag{A.14}$$

Hence, it can be shown that:

$$\frac{\dot{x}_0}{x_i} = \frac{Q_0}{\frac{VM}{B_m S}p^2 + \left(\frac{K_L M}{S} + \frac{VB}{B_m S}\right)p + \left(\frac{S^2 + K_L B}{S}\right)} \tag{A.15}$$

where $p \triangleq \mathrm{d}/\mathrm{d}t$.

In actuators intended for use in typical AFCSs, the volume of oil trapped is small (of the order of $0.0002\ \mathrm{m}^3$), whereas the hydraulic oil commonly used has a bulk modulus, B_m, of the order of $40\ \mathrm{N\ m}^{-3}$. Consequently, the transfer function of eq. (A.15) can be approximated to:

$$\frac{\dot{x}_0}{x_i} = \frac{\frac{Q_0 S}{(K_L B + S^2)}}{1 + \frac{(K_L M B_m + VB)}{B_m(K_L B + S^2)}p} = \frac{K}{1 + Tp} \tag{A.16}$$

Table A.1 Parameters of hydraulic actuator

$V = 0.000132\ \text{m}^3$
$S = 0.0013\ \text{m}^2$
$B_\text{m} = 36.275\ \text{N m}^{-2}$
$K_\text{L} = 5160\ \text{m}^5\ \text{N} - \text{s}^{-1}$
$Q_0 = 38.82\ \text{m}^2\ \text{s}^{-1}$
$B = 0.86\ \text{N m}^{-1}\ \text{s}^{-1}$
$M = 1.43 \times 10^{-3}\ \text{kg}$

As an example, consider the small hydraulic actuator which has the parameters given in Table A.1. Note that the mass of the surface is very small. The transfer function which corresponds to these parameters is given in eq. (A.14).

$$\frac{\dot{x}_0}{x_i} = \frac{K\omega_\text{n}^2}{p^2 + 2\zeta\omega_\text{n}p + \omega_\text{n}^2} \tag{A.17}$$

where:

$$K = 125 \qquad \omega_\text{n} = 500\ \text{rad s}^{-1} \qquad \zeta = 0.45 \tag{A.18}$$

Actuator with Mechanical Feedback Link

Both the valve and piston arrangements just discussed allow the piston to move at a constant velocity, for a given valve displacement, until it reaches the end stop. To prevent this, and to ensure a positional correspondence between the output and input displacements, it is normal practice to connect a mechanical feedback link between the piston and the spool valve, in the manner shown in the diagram of Figure A.8. The valve is now displaced by means of the linkage which is pivoted about point, W. From a mathematical point of view the displacement x_0 and W are the same point: they are named separately here merely for ease of explanation. Should the input x_i be displaced to the right, the point Z will move to the right; since the mass of the spool valve is considerably less than that of the piston and load combined, point W can be considered, for the moment, to be stationary. With this displacement of the spool valve high pressure fluid is permitted to flow through orifice G to the left-hand side of the piston. At the same time, the right-hand side of the actuator is opened to the sump via orifice H. The difference in pressure across the piston causes it to move to the right, thus following the input. As W moves right it causes the linkage to move about point X, as a pivot, which causes Z to be moved to the left, thereby closing the valve and hence causing the motion of the piston to cease, with the piston in its new position, x_0. The displacement of the spool valve from its equilibrium mid position depends on the lengths l_1 and l_2 of the lever, which is the mechanical feedback link. The total displacement, z, of the spool valve can be shown (from simple geometry) to be:

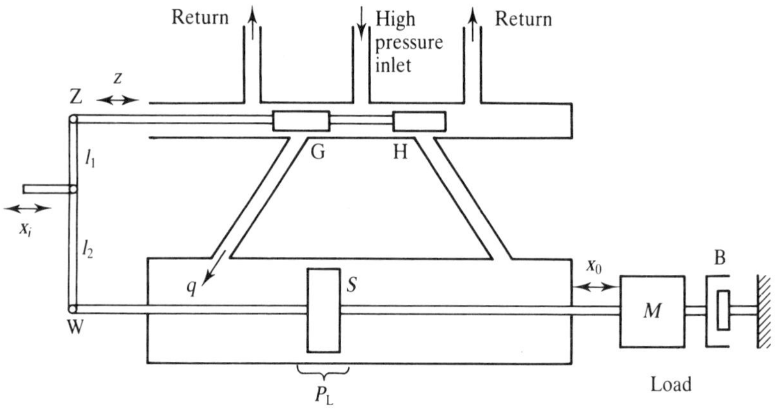

Figure A.8 Hydraulic actuator with mechanical feedback.

$$z = \frac{(l_1 + l_2)}{l_2} x_i \; \frac{l_1}{l_2} x_0 \tag{A.19}$$

From the previous subsection:

$$\frac{\dot{x}_0}{z} = \frac{K\omega_n^2}{p^2 + 2\zeta\omega_n p + \omega_n^2} \tag{A.17}$$

A block diagram representing eqs (A.17) and (A.19) is shown in Figure A.9 from which it can be deduced that:

$$\begin{aligned}\frac{x_0}{x_i} &= \frac{(l_1 + l_2)}{l_2} \frac{K\omega_n^2}{\{p(p^2 + 2\zeta\omega_n p + \omega_n^2) + K(l_1/l_2)\omega_n^2\}} \\ &= \frac{K(l_1 + l_2)\omega_n^2}{p^3 l_2 + 2\zeta\omega_n l_2 p^2 + \omega_n^2 l_2 p + K l_1 \omega_n^2}\end{aligned} \tag{A.20}$$

In the steady state:

$$x_0 = \frac{(l_1 + l_2)}{l_1} x_1 \tag{A.21}$$

In many AFCS applications, the input displacement, x_i, is produced by a solenoid driven by an electronic amplifier, the actuator then being regarded as an electrohydraulic actuator. If thc solenoid has the transfer funtion:

$$\frac{x_i}{V_{in}} = \frac{K_s}{1 + T_s p} \tag{A.22}$$

then the complete transfer function of the electrohydraulic actuator is given by:

$$\frac{x_0}{V_{in}} = \frac{K_s K \omega_n^2 (l_1 + l_2)}{(1 + T_s p)(p^3 l_2 + 2\zeta\omega_n l_2 p^2 + \omega_n^2 l_2 p + K l_1 \omega_n^2)} \tag{A.23}$$

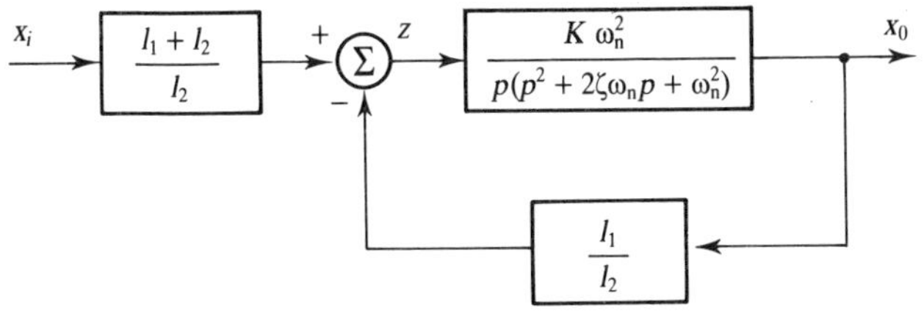

Figure A.9 Block diagram of actuator of Figure A.8.

Generally, however, the time constant of the solenoid is negligible (or is made so), so that a fourth order transfer function is rarely used in AFCS work. If the parameters of the actuator are such that the approximate transfer function given in eq. (A.16) is valid, the resulting transfer function of the system of Figure A.9 can be expressed as:

$$\frac{x_0}{x_i} = \frac{K}{\left(p(1 + Tp) + \frac{Kl_1}{l_2}\right)} \frac{(l_2 + l_1)}{l_2}$$

$$= \frac{K(l_2 + l_1)}{l_2 Tp^2 + l_2 p + Kl_1} \tag{A.24}$$

However, if the time constant can be made negligible, the actuator transfer function can be approximated to:

$$\frac{x_0}{x_i} = \frac{(l_2 + l_1)}{l_1} \frac{1}{\left(1 + \frac{l_2}{Kl_1} \mathrm{p}\right)} = \frac{\hat{K}}{1 + p\hat{T}} \tag{A.25}$$

which is the form used as a first approximation when considering the SAS, the attitude control, and the path control systems described in Chapters 9–11 respectively. When the actuator is an electrohydraulic one, the mechanical feedback link is frequently replaced by a position transducer such as a potentiometer, or LVDT. The block diagram of such an arrangement is given in Figure A.10, but if the approximations made earlier about volume and bulk modulus of the hydraulic oil, and the time constant of the solenoid, are once more invoked, it is easy to show that the corresponding transfer function is given by:

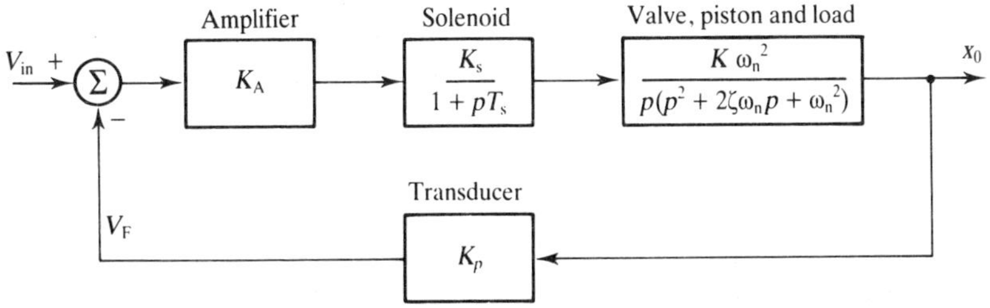

Figure A.10 Block diagram of electrohydraulic actuator.

$$\frac{x_0}{V_{\text{in}}} = \frac{K_A K_s K}{p(1 + Tp) + K_A K_s K K_p}$$

$$= \frac{\alpha\omega_E^2}{p^2 + 2\zeta_E\omega_E p + \omega_E^2} \qquad \text{(A.26)}$$

where:

$$\alpha = 1/K_p \qquad \text{(A.27)}$$

$$\omega_E = \left(\frac{K_A K_s K K_p}{T}\right)^{1/2} \qquad \text{(A.28)}$$

$$\zeta_E = 1/2(TK_A K_s K K_p)^{-1/2} \qquad \text{(A.29)}$$

By appropriate choice of K_A and K_p it is possible to arrange that the damping of the actuator is high enough for it to be approximately represented by a first order transfer function of the type given in eq. (A.25).

A.3.2 Electrical Actuators

Although in many applications hydraulic actuators are superior to electrical actuators, there are applications where the relative simplicity of electrical drive is preferred. With the advent of rare earth magnetic materials, the power/weight ratio of electrical motors is becoming more favourable, and the promise of superconductive materials at reasonable temperatures makes it necessary to keep open the option of using electrical actuators in future AFCSs. Modern electrical actuators, using four permanent magnet (PM) motors in a single package, are capable of providing a force of 85 000 N at a piston velocity of 0.2 m s^{-1} for a stroke of 0.4 m but such motors require large d.c. voltages (about 270 V). One difficulty with such actuators is heat dissipation. Although such modern electrical actuators provide better acceleration than the normal wound-rotor electrical actuators, the improvement in power/weight ratio (120 W kg^{-1}) does not yet match the figures which can be achieved by using an hydraulic actuator.

A PM Electrical Actuator

A schematic of a PM electrical motor driving a mechanical load is shown in Figure A.11. From that diagram the following mathematical model can be constructed. The armature current, i_A, is related to the applied voltage, V_{in}, by the equation:

$$V_{\text{in}} - E_B = i_A R_A + L_A \frac{di_A}{dt} \qquad \text{(A.30)}$$

where E_B is the back e.m.f.

Since the magnetic field, Φ, is constant, being provided by the PM, the motor torque, Q, is directly controlled by the armature current:

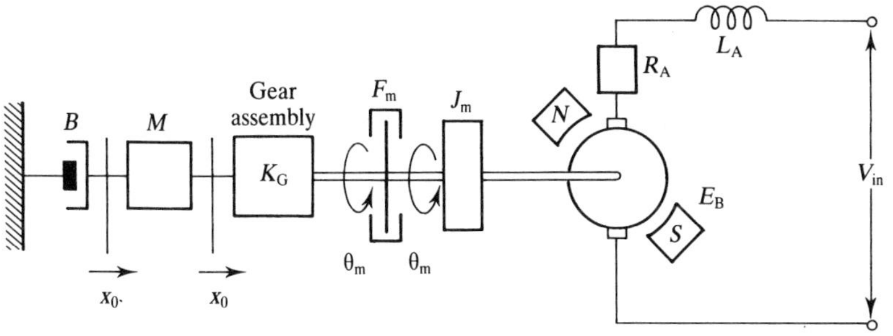

Figure A.11 Schematic of PM electrical actuator.

$$Q = k\Phi i_A = K_T i_A \tag{A.31}$$

This torque accelerates the armature, overcoming the motor friction, and drives the load via the gear assembly which typically is a ball screw assembly to convert the motor's rotary motion into a linear displacement. Thus:

$$Q = Q_A + Q_F + Q_u \tag{A.32}$$

where:

$$Q_A \triangleq J_m \frac{d^2\theta_m}{dt^2} \tag{A.33}$$

$$Q_F \triangleq F_m \frac{d\theta_m}{dt} \tag{A.34}$$

$$F_L = K_G Q_u = M \frac{d^2 x_0}{dt^2} + B \frac{dx_0}{dt} \tag{A.35}$$

Once the armature of the motor turns, the current-carrying conductors will move in a magnetic field and, consequently, an e.m.f. is induced in the armature winding. This relationship is defined by the equation:

$$E_B = K_B \frac{d\theta_m}{dt} \tag{A.36}$$

Also:

$$K_G x_0 = \theta_m \tag{A.37}$$

A block diagram representing the actuator is shown in Figure A.12. Substituting eqs (A.33)–(A.35) and (A.37) into eq. (A.32) results in:

$$\begin{aligned} Q &= J_m \frac{d^2\theta_m}{dt^2} + F_m \frac{d\theta_m}{dt} + \frac{M}{K_G^2}\frac{d^2\theta_m}{dt^2} + \frac{B}{K_G^2}\frac{d\theta_m}{dt} \\ &= \left(J_m + \frac{M}{K_G^2}\right)\frac{d^2\theta_m}{dt^2} + \left(F_m + \frac{B}{K_G^2}\right)\frac{d\theta_m}{dt} \end{aligned}$$

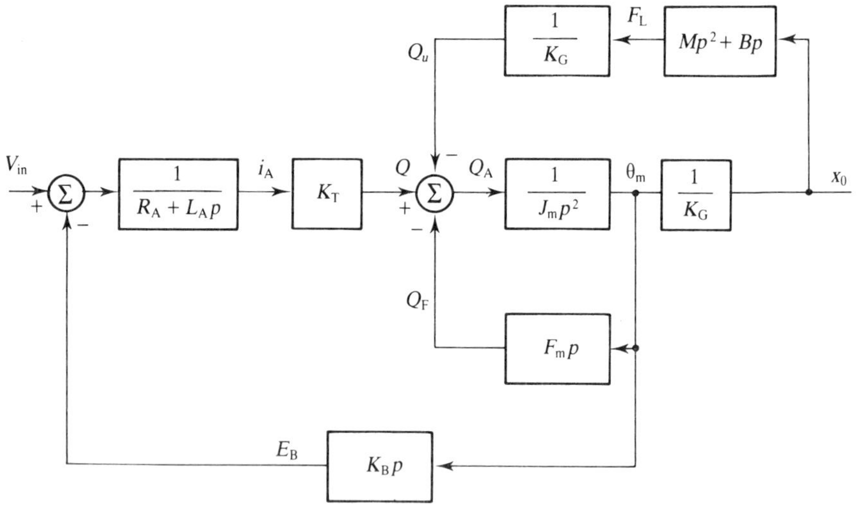

Figure A.12 Block diagram of electrical motor.

$$= J'p^2\theta_m + F'p\theta_m = (J'p + F)p\theta_m \tag{A.38}$$

$$\therefore \quad \frac{p\theta_m}{V_{in}} = \frac{K_T}{(R_A + L_A p)(J'p + F) + K_T K_B} \tag{A.39}$$

If, as is usual in AFCS work, $L_A/R_A \rightarrow 0$, then:

$$\frac{\dot{\theta}_m}{V_{in}} = \frac{K_T/R_A}{J'p + F + \dfrac{K_T K_B}{R_A}} \tag{A.40}$$

Assuming $K_T K_B/R_A \gg F$ then:

$$\frac{\dot{\theta}_m}{V_{in}} = \frac{1/K_B}{1 + \dfrac{J'R_A}{K_T K_B}p} = \frac{\hat{K}}{1 + p\hat{T}} \tag{A.41}$$

and:

$$\frac{\dot{x}_0}{V_{in}} = \frac{1/K_B K_G}{(1 + pT)} = \frac{\bar{K}}{(1 + pT)} \tag{A.42}$$

A.4 SENSORS

A.4.1 Introduction

Sensors are used in AFCSs to provide the essential feedback signals that the AFCS requires. Although many motion variables are involved, only a few are used for measurement to provide these feedback signals: angular rates and attitudes are the chief variables and are invariably measured by means of gyroscopes. Linear acceleration and angle of attack, or sideslip angle, are also required occasionally. This brief treatment will present a short resumé of linear mathematical models which are appropriate for the following sensors: rate gyroscopes, displacement gyroscopes, accelerometers, and pressure ratio angle of attack sensors.

A.4.2 Gyroscopes

A gyroscope (gyro) is usually an inertial instrument in which a rotor is spun at high speed so that the gyroscope has a large angular momentum, a vector of which tends to maintain its inertial orientation. It senses the magnitude and direction of any disturbing torque. Figure A.13 shows the three orthogonal axes of a gyroscope, and its input and output. If a disturbing torque is applied along either of the two axes orthogonal to the spin axis, a precession motion results which tends to align the spin axis with the direction of the applied torque. Although it is a property not often used in AFCSs, the gyro law is reversible in as much as any input motion will result in an output torque.

The gyroscope law is derived from Newton's laws of motion, namely that the rate of change with respect to an inertial reference frame of the angular momentum of a body about its centre of mass is equal to the torque being applied:

$$Q = \dot{\mathbf{H}}_{\mathrm{I}} \tag{A.43}$$

The subscript I indicates 'with respect to an inertial reference frame'. If the Earth is taken as a moving reference frame then:

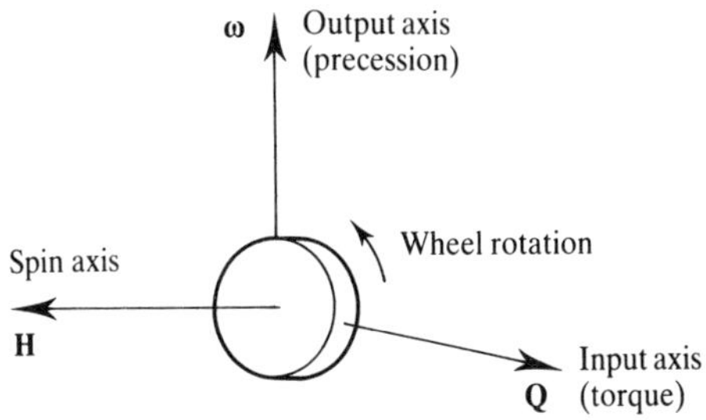

Figure A.13 Axes of gyroscope.

$$\dot{\mathbf{H}}_{\mathrm{I}} = \dot{\mathbf{H}}_{\mathrm{E}} + \boldsymbol{\omega}_{\mathrm{IE}} \times \mathbf{H} \tag{A.44}$$

The gyroscope is itself mounted on a base in an aircraft which is moving with respect to the Earth, thus:

$$\dot{\mathbf{H}}_{\mathrm{E}} = \dot{\mathbf{H}}_{\mathrm{B}} + \boldsymbol{\omega}_{\mathrm{EB}} \times \mathbf{H} \tag{A.45}$$

However, the case of the gyroscope can be mounted on a platform so that it can rotate relative to the base. Then:

$$\dot{\mathbf{H}}_{\mathrm{B}} = \dot{\mathbf{H}}_{\mathrm{c}} + \boldsymbol{\omega}_{\mathrm{BC}} \times \mathbf{H} \tag{A.46}$$

Finally, the inner gimbal (see Figure A.14) can rotate relative to the case. Hence:

$$\dot{\mathbf{H}}_{\mathrm{c}} = \dot{\mathbf{H}}_{\mathrm{g}} + \boldsymbol{\omega}_{\mathrm{CG}} \times \mathbf{H} \tag{A.47}$$

Substituting eqs (A.44)–(A.47) in eq. (A.43) yields:

$$\mathbf{Q} = \dot{\mathbf{H}}_{\mathrm{g}} + (\boldsymbol{\omega}_{\mathrm{CG}} + \boldsymbol{\omega}_{\mathrm{BC}} + \boldsymbol{\omega}_{\mathrm{EB}} + \boldsymbol{\omega}_{\mathrm{IE}}) \times \mathbf{H} \tag{A.48}$$

But:

$$(\boldsymbol{\omega}_{\mathrm{CG}} + \boldsymbol{\omega}_{\mathrm{BC}} + \boldsymbol{\omega}_{\mathrm{EB}} + \boldsymbol{\omega}_{\mathrm{IE}}) \triangleq \boldsymbol{\omega}_{\mathrm{IG}} \tag{A.49}$$

$$\therefore \quad Q = \dot{\mathbf{H}}_{\mathrm{G}} + \boldsymbol{\omega}_{\mathrm{IG}} \times \mathbf{H} \tag{A.50}$$

By proper construction of the gyroscope, and by maintaining the spin velocity of the rotor constant, $\dot{\mathbf{H}}_{\mathrm{G}}$ can be made to be zero, so that the law of the gyro can be written as:

$$Q = \boldsymbol{\omega}_{\mathrm{IG}} \times \mathbf{H} \tag{A.51}$$

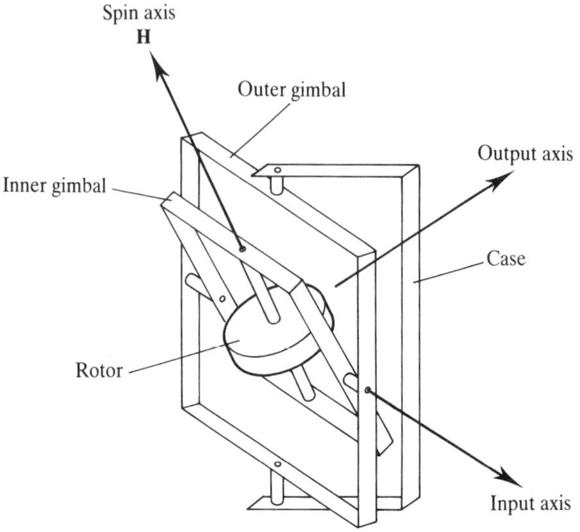

Figure A.14 Two degrees of freedom gyroscope.

i.e. if a torque Q is applied to the gyroscope, the inner gimbal will precess with respect to the inertial reference frame with a velocity, ω, such that eq. (A.51) is satisfied.

A.4.3 Rate Gyroscopes

Figure A.15 represents a rate gyro with the elastic restraint being provided by a torsional spring, K, fixed to the inner gimbal. A viscous damper, F, is added to provide some damping.

$$Q = \omega_{IG} \times H = J_{out}\ddot{\theta}_G + F\dot{\theta}_G + K\theta_G \tag{A.52}$$

where J_{out} is the moment of inertia of the gimbal and rotor about the output axis. Therefore:

$$\theta_G(s)\left\{s^2 + \frac{Fs}{J_{out}} + \frac{K}{J_{out}}\right\} = \frac{H}{J_{out}}\,\omega_{IG}(s) \tag{A.53}$$

Thus, the transfer function for a rate gyro relating the output (the gimbal angle, θ_G) to an angular velocity input, ω_{IG}, can be shown to be:

$$\frac{\theta_G(s)}{\omega_{IG}(s)} = \frac{\dfrac{H}{J_{out}}}{s^2 + \dfrac{F}{J_{out}}s + \dfrac{K}{J_{out}}} = \frac{\alpha\omega_G^2}{(s^2 + 2\zeta_G\omega_G s + \omega_G^2)} \tag{A.54}$$

where:

$$\omega_G = (K/J_{out})^{1/2} \tag{A.55}$$

$$\zeta_G = 1/2\,F(J_{out}/K)^{1/2} \tag{A.56}$$

$$\alpha = H/K \tag{A.57}$$

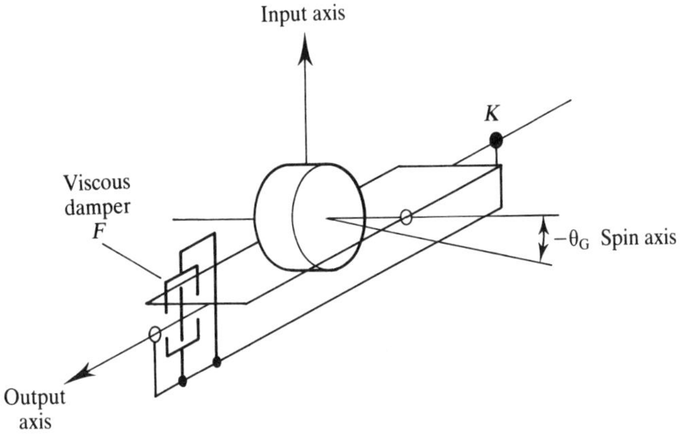

Figure A.15 Rate gyroscope schematic.

The constant, α, is referred to as the gyro sensitivity; it has the unit of seconds. Common values for ζ_G are $0.7 \leq \zeta < 1.0$, and the value of the natural frequency, ω_G, lies in the range 200–500 rad s^{-1}. Such large values of natural frequency and damping usually mean that the dynamics associated with the rate gyro may be neglected in AFCS work.

Thus, the output from the rate gyro is proportional to the angular velocity of the case about its input axis with respect to inertial space. The motion of the gimbal is generally converted into an electrical signal by connecting the gimbal to a position transducer such as a potentiometer, or E-type pick-off, for example.

A.4.4 Displacement Gyroscopes

By removing the elastic restraint from the rate gyro, the resulting configuration is referred to as an integrating gyro, i.e. a displacement gyro. The equation of motion can be obtained from eq. (A.52) by setting $K = 0$, i.e.:

$$Q = \omega_{IG} \times \mathbf{H} = J_{out}\ddot{\theta}_G + F\dot{\theta}_g \tag{A.58}$$

$$\therefore \quad \frac{\theta_G(s)}{\omega_{IG}(s)} = \frac{H}{s(J_{out}s + F)} = \frac{H/F}{s(1 + sT)} \tag{A.59}$$

where:

$$T = J_{out}/F \tag{A.60}$$

Typical values of T lie in the range 0.002 to 0.01 s. For AFCS work, the dynamics of the integrating gyro can be neglected, being much more rapid than the motion of the aircraft. Thus:

$$\frac{\theta_G(s)}{\omega_{IG}(s)} = \frac{H/F}{s} \tag{A.61}$$

Usually the gimbal angle is 'sensed' by a position transducer, thereby providing the gyro with an output signal in electrical form.

The displacement gyroscope is inevitably used in a negative feedback servomechanism loop.

A.5 ACCELEROMETERS

Almost every accelerometer is based upon the following principle of operation: the motion of a restrained mass is measured when it is subjected to an acceleration. Spring-mass types can be found, but these depend upon the accuracy of the spring and the inevitable non-linearities and hysteresis associated with the spring result in output errors. Thus, it is usual to employ servo or force-balance types; a schematic of one such type is shown in Figure A.16. The mass, M, can

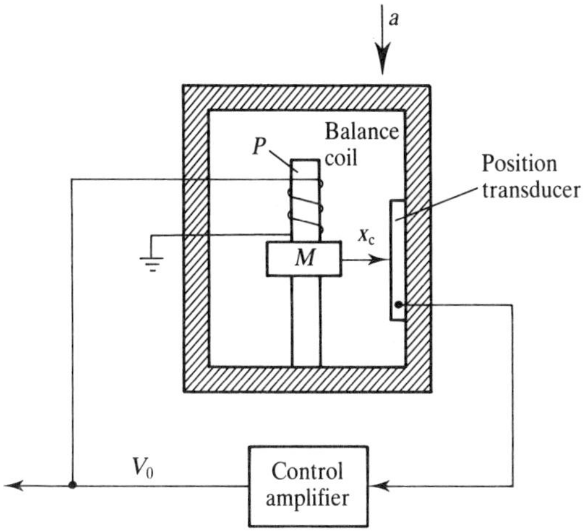

Figure A.16 Force-balance accelerometer.

move along the rod, P, as a result of acceleration, a. The motion of M is measured by means of the position transducer, the output voltage from which is the input to the control amplifier which applies a voltage, V_0, to the balance coil which produces a magnetic force to restore the displaced mass to its original equilibrium position. The instrument is a force-balance system and the voltage needed to provide the current in the coil to produce the force is a direct measurement of the applied acceleration. A block diagram of the system is shown in Figure A.17. It is usually arranged that the inductance of the balance coil is negligible, so that the transfer function relating the output voltage, V_0, to the applied acceleration can be shown to be:

$$\frac{V_0(s)}{a(s)} = \frac{MK_pG_A(s)}{Ms^2 + \dfrac{K_pK_cG_A(s)}{R_A}} \tag{A.62}$$

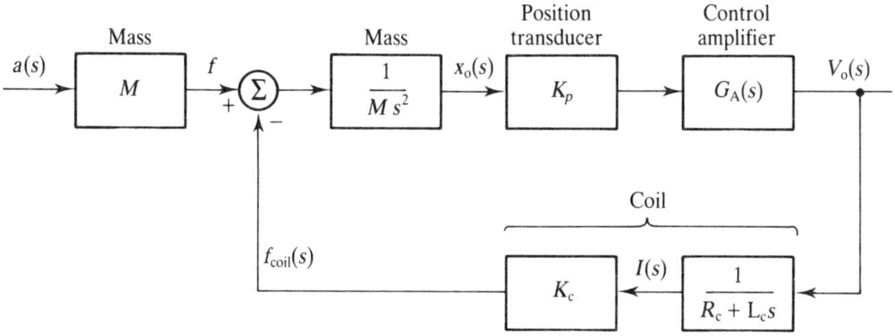

Figure A.17 Block diagram of Figure A.16.

It is evident from inspection of (A.62) that some stability has to be provided by the control amplifier and, consequently, it has a transfer function of the form:

$$G_A(s) = K_A \frac{(1 + sT_1)}{(1 + sT_2)} \qquad T_1 \gg T_2 \tag{A.63}$$

$$\therefore \quad \frac{V_0(s)}{a(s)} = \frac{MK_pK_A(1 + sT_1)}{MT_2s^3 + Ms^2 + \frac{T_1K_pK_AK_c}{R}s + \frac{K_pK_AK_c}{R_A}} \tag{A.64}$$

Usually T_2 is negligible, therefore:

$$\frac{V_0(s)}{a(s)} = \frac{MK_pK_A(1 + sT_1)}{Ms^2 + \frac{T_1K_pK_AK_c}{R_A}s + \frac{K_pK_AK_c}{R_A}} = \frac{\alpha\omega_A^2(1 + sT_1)}{s^2 + 2\zeta_A\omega_As + \omega_A^2} \tag{A.65}$$

where:

$$\omega_A = (K_pK_AK_c/R_AM)^{1/2} \tag{A.66}$$

$$\zeta_A = 1/2\,T_1(K_pK_AK_c/MR_A)^{1/2} \tag{A.67}$$

$$\alpha = R_AM/K_c \tag{A.68}$$

A.6 ANGLE OF ATTACK SENSOR

There are a number of methods of sensing angle of attack, but essentially only two types are in general use. In low speed flight, the moving vane type is preferred. It is a small vane protruding into the airstream, close to the body of the aircraft. The vane can rotate over a limited angular range. It is mounted on the shaft of a position transducer which provides an electrical signal proportional to the angle of attack. The use of this type in AFCS work is restricted since its accuracy is much affected by local flow conditions. The other method employs a stationary pressure-ratio sensing probe, a sketch of which is shown in Figure A.18. The angle of attack is usually obtained from the pressures measured at two (often more) suitable positioned orifices, i.e.:

$$\alpha = K\frac{(P_1 - P_2)}{(P_T - P_s)}\phi(M)f(\beta) \tag{A.69}$$

where K is a constant, M is the Mach number of the moving air, β is the sideslip angle, $(P_T - P_s)$ is a measure of the dynamic pressure $\bar{q}$, and ϕ and F are non-linear functions, in general. Both dynamic pressure and Mach number change slowly compared to changes in the angle of attack, which is governed by the short

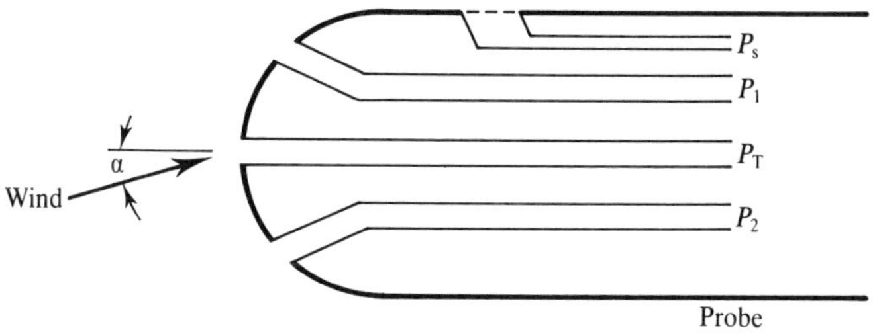

Figure A.18 Pressure-ratio angle of attack sensor.

period motion of the aircraft. The sideslip effect cannot be easily ignored.

With the pressures from the probe being fed to bellows via pneumatic lines, the motion of the bellows, which results from volume changes caused by the changes in pressure, is used to drive position transducers to provide an electrical output signal. There is, however, an unavoidable time delay involved in pneumatic line transmission, and there is also a time lag associated with any bellows transducer.

Thus, the transfer function of the angle of attack sensor becomes:

$$\frac{V_0(s)}{\alpha(s)} = \frac{Ke^{-s\tau}}{(1 + sT_L)(1 + sT_B)} \tag{A.70}$$

where τ represents the transport time delay, T_L the time constant of the interconnecting pneumatic lines, and T_B the time constant of the bellows.

A.7 REFERENCES

AHRENDT, W.R. and C.J. SAVANT. 1960. *Servomechanism Practice.* New York: McGraw-Hill.

COLLETTE, J.G.R. 1970. Sensor and actuator dynamics. In A.L. Greensite, *Analysis and Design of Space Vehicle Flight Control Systems*, Vol. II, Chapter 3. New York: Spartan Books.

GREEN, W.L. 1985. *Aircraft Hydraulic Systems.* Chichester: Wiley.

Appendix B

Stability Derivatives for Several Representative Modern Aircraft

B.1 NOMENCLATURE

Some stability data for seven aircraft are presented here. These aircraft are generic types and are referred to as follows:

ALPHA	a four-engined, executive jet aircraft
BRAVO	a twin-engined, jet fighter aircraft
CHARLIE	a very large, four-engined, passenger jet aircraft
DELTA	a very large, four-engined, cargo jet aircraft
ECHO	a single-engined, CCV, jet fighter aircraft
FOXTROT	a twin-engined, jet fighter/bomber aircraft
GOLF	a twin-piston engined, general aviation aircraft

When referring to an aircraft and its particular flight condition, the aircraft name is given first followed by a number corresponding to the flight condition. For example, FOXTROT-3 means flight condition 3 for the aircraft, FOXTROT.

B.2 AIRCRAFT DATA

B.2.1 ALPHA – A four-engined, executive jet aircraft

General Parameters

Wing area (m^2)	50.4
Aspect ratio:	5.325
Chord, $\bar{c}$ (m):	3.33
Total related thrust (kN):	59.2
C.g.:	$0.25\bar{c}$
Pilot's location (m) (relative to c.g.)	
l_{x_p}:	6.77
l_{z_p}:	– 0.73

Weight (kg):	*Approach*	*All other flight conditions*
	10 635	17 000
Inertias (kg m^2)		
I_{xx}:	57 000	162 000
I_{yy}:	171 500	185 000
I_{zz}:	218 500	330 000
I_{xz}:	7 500	6 900

Flight Conditions

Parameter	*Flight condition* 1	2	3	4
Height (m)	S.L.	6 100	6 100	12 200
Mach no.	0.2	0.35	0.75	0.8
U_0 (m s^{-1})	67.7	110.6	237.1	236.0
$\bar{q}$ (N m^2)	2 844.0	4 000	18 338	8 475
α_0 (degrees)	+ 6.5	+ 9.9	+ 2.6	+ 4.2
γ_0 (degrees)	0	0	0	0

Stability Derivatives

Longitudinal Motion

Stability derivative	*Flight condition* 1	2	3	4
X_u	-0.0166	-0.00324	-0.0157	-0.211×10^{-5}
X_w	0.108	0.00102	-0.0005	-0.0043
X_{δ_E}	0.6	0.8	1.02	0.774
X_{δ_T}	0.92×10^{-4}	5.73×10^{-5}	5.73×10^{-5}	5.73×10^{-5}
Z_u	-0.175	-0.08	-0.02	-0.035
Z_w	-1.01	-0.565	-1.33	-0.665
Z_{δ_E}	-5.24	-4.57	-22.4	-10.55
M_u	0.0043	0.0033	-0.0015	-0.014
M_w	-0.033	-0.022	-0.051	-0.025
$M_{\dot{w}}$	-0.003	-0.0015	-0.002	-0.001
M_q	-0.546	-0.439	-1.09	-0.506
M_{δ_E}	-2.26	-2.95	-14.5	-6.78
M_{δ_T}	-0.65×10^{-5}	-0.6×10^{-5}	-0.6×10^{-5}	-0.6×10^{-5}

Lateral Motion

Stability derivative	Flight condition 1	2	3	4
Y_v	-0.014	-0.076	-0.167	-0.078
$Y^*_{\delta_R}$	0.034	0.018	0.037	0.016
L'_β	-4.05	-3.23	-4.93	-2.27
L'_p	-1.85	-0.58	-1.34	-0.64
L'_r	0.52	0.17	0.09	0.06
L'_{δ_A}	2.21	1.1	5.83	2.64
L'_{δ_R}	1.11	0.57	2.43	1.21
N'_β	1.34	1.21	5.63	2.66
N'_p	-0.25	-0.12	-0.14	-0.07
N'_r	-0.19	-0.125	-0.25	-0.12
N'_{δ_A}	-0.006	-0.08	-0.06	-0.072
N'_{δ_R}	-0.64	-0.62	-2.66	-1.16

B.2.2 BRAVO – A twin-engined, jet fighter aircraft

General Parameters

Wing area (m^2):	56.5	
Aspect ratio:	3.0	
Chord, $\bar{c}$ (m):	4.86	
Total related thrust (kN):	210 (no reheat)	
C.g.:	$0.255\,\bar{c}$ or $0.311\,\bar{c}$	
Pilot's location (m) (relative to c.g.)		
l_{x_p}:	8.2	
l_{z_p}:	-1.3	
Weight (kg):	*Approach*	*All other flight conditions*
	15×10^3	16×10^3
Inertias (kg m^2):		
I_{xx}:	35 250	38 000
I_{yy}:	176 250	255 000
I_{zz}:	210 000	285 000
I_{xz}:	3 000	4 000

Flight Conditions

Parameter	*Flight condition* 1	2	3	4
Height (m)	S.L.	6 100	6 100	9 150
Mach no.	0.4	0.6	0.6	0.8
U_0 ($\mathrm{m\,s^{-1}}$)	136	190	190	240
$\bar{q}$ ($\mathrm{N\,m^{-2}}$)	11 348	11 760	11 760	10 700
α_0 (degrees)	+ 3.5	+ 8.5	+ 8.5	+ 2.5
γ_0 (degrees)	0	0	0	0
c.g.	0.311	0.255	0.311	0.311

Stability Derivatives

Longitudinal Motion only

Stability derivative	*Flight condition* 1	2	3	4
X_u	− 0.017	− 0.011	− 0.012	− 0.007
X_α	0.026	0.018	0.017	0.012
Z_u	− 0.143	− 0.113	− 0.113	− 0.128
Z_α	− 1.02	− 0.72	− 0.72	− 0.54
Z_q	− 0.0076	− 0.0044	− 0.0044	− 0.0027
Z_{δ_E}	− 0.064	− 0.047	− 0.047	− 0.036
M_u	0	0	0	0
M_α	1.4	− 2.7	1.09	0.69
$M_{\dot{\alpha}}$	− 0.66	− 0.61	− 0.54	− 0.51
M_q	− 0.53	− 0.64	− 0.57	− 0.48
M_{δ_E}	− 11.56	− 13.04	− 12.25	− 12.63

B.2.3 CHARLIE – A very large, four-engined, passenger jet aircraft

General Parameters

Wing area ($\mathrm{m^2}$):	510
Aspect ratio:	7.0
Chord, $\bar{c}$ (m):	8.3
Total related thrust (kN):	900
C.g.:	0.25 $\bar{c}$

Pilot's location (m)
(relative to c.g.)

l_{x_p}:	26.2	
l_{z_p}:	− 3.05	
Weight (kg):	*Approach* 250 000	*All other flight conditions* 290 000
Inertias (kg m^2):		
I_{xx}:	18.6×10^6	24.6×10^6
I_{yy}:	41.35×10^6	45×10^6
I_{zz}:	58×10^6	67.5×10^6
I_{xz}:	1.2×10^6	1.32×10^6

Flight Conditions

Parameter	*Flight condition* 1	2	3	4
Height (m)	S.L.	6 100	6 100	12 200
Mach no.	0.198	0.5	0.8	0.8
U_0 (m s^{-1})	67	158	250	250
$\bar{q}$ (N m^{-2})	2 810	8 667	24 420	9 911
α_0 (degrees)	8.5	6.8	0	4.6
γ_0 (degrees)	0	0	0	0

Stability Derivatives

Longitudinal Motion

Stability derivative	*Flight condition* 1	2	3	4
X_u	− 0.021	0.003	− 0.0002	0.0002
X_w	0.122	0.078	0.026	0.039
X_{δ_E}	0.292	0.616	0.0	0.44
$X_{\delta_{th}}$	3.88×10^{-6}	3.434×10^{-6}	3.434×10^{-6}	3.434×10^{-6}
Z_u	− 0.2	− 0.07	− 0.09	− 0.07
Z_w	− 0.512	− 0.433	− 0.624	− 0.317
Z_q	− 1.9	− 1.95	− 3.04	− 1.57
Z_{δ_E}	− 1.96	− 5.15	− 8.05	− 5.46
$Z_{\delta_{th}}$	-1.69×10^{-7}	-1.5×10^{-7}	-1.5×10^{-7}	-1.5×10^{-7}
M_u	0.000036	0.00008	− 0.00007	0.00006
M_w	− 0.006	− 0.006	− 0.005	− 0.003
$M_{\dot{w}}$	− 0.0008	− 0.0004	− 0.0007	− 0.0004

Longitudinal Motion Cont'd

Stability derivative	*Flight condition* 1	2	3	4
M_q	− 0.357	− 0.421	− 0.668	− 0.339
M_{δ_E}	− 0.378	− 1.09	− 2.08	− 1.16
$M_{\delta_{th}}$	0.7×10^{-7}	0.67×10^{-7}	0.67×10^{-7}	0.67×10^{-7}

Lateral Motion

Stability derivative	*Flight condition* 1	2	3	4
Y_v	− 0.089	− 0.082	− 0.12	− 0.056
$Y^*_{\delta_R}$	0.015	0.014	0.014	0.012
L'_β	− 1.33	− 2.05	− 4.12	− 1.05
L'_p	− 0.98	− 0.65	− 0.98	− 0.47
L'_r	+ 0.33	+ 0.38	+ 0.29	+ 0.39
L'_{δ_A}	0.23	0.13	0.31	0.14
L'_{δ_R}	0.06	0.15	0.18	0.15
N'_β	0.17	0.42	1.62	0.6
N'_p	− 0.17	− 0.07	− 0.016	− 0.032
N'_r	− 0.217	− 0.14	− 0.232	− 0.115
N'_{δ_A}	0.026	0.018	0.013	0.008
N'_{δ_R}	− 0.15	− 0.39	− 0.92	− 0.48

B.2.4 DELTA – A very large, four-engined, cargo jet aircraft

General Parameters

Wing area (m^2)	576	
Aspect ratio:	7.75	
Chord, $\bar{c}$ (m):	9.17	
Total related thrust (kN):	730	
C.g.:	$0.3\bar{c}$	
Pilot's location (m) (relative to c.g.)		
l_{x_p}:	25.0	
l_{z_p}:	+ 2.5	
Weight (kg):	*Approach* 264 000	*All other flight conditions* 300 000

Inertias (kg m^2)

I_{xx}:	2.6×10^7	3.77×10^7
I_{yy}:	4.25×10^7	4.31×10^7
I_{zz}:	6.37×10^7	7.62×10^7
I_{xz}:	3.4×10^6	3.35×10^6

Flight Conditions

Parameter	*Flight condition*			
	1	*2*	*3*	*4*
Height (m)	S.L.	6 100	6 100	12 200
Mach no.	0.22	0.6	0.8	0.875
U_0 (m s^{-1})	75	190	253	260
$\bar{q}$ (N m^2)	3 460	11 730	20 900	10 100
α_0 (degrees)	+ 2.7	+ 2.2	+ 0.1	+ 4.9
γ_0 (degrees)	0	0	0	0

Stability Derivatives

Longitudinal Motion

Stability derivative	*Flight condition*			
	1	*2*	*3*	*4*
X_u	− 0.02	− 0.003	− 0.02	− 0.03
X_w	0.1	0.04	0.02	0.0
X_{δ_E}	0.14	0.26	0.32	0.45
$X_{\delta_{th}}$	0.17×10^{-4}	0.15×10^{-4}	0.15×10^{-4}	0.15×10^{-4}
Z_u	− 0.23	− 0.08	− 0.01	0.17
Z_w	− 0.634	− 0.618	− 0.925	− 0.387
Z_{δ_E}	− 2.9	− 6.83	− 9.51	− 5.18
$Z_{\delta_{th}}$	0.06×10^{-5}	0.05×10^{-5}	0.05×10^{-5}	0.05×10^{-5}
M_u	-2.55×10^{-5}	3.28×10^{-4}	14.21×10^{-4}	54.79×10^{-4}
M_w	− 0.005	− 0.007	− 0.0011	− 0.006
$M_{\dot{w}}$	− 0.003	− 0.001	− 0.001	− 0.0005
M_q	− 0.61	− 0.77	− 1.02	− 0.55
M_{δ_E}	− 0.64	− 1.25	− 1.51	− 0.92
$M_{\delta_{th}}$	1.44×10^{-5}	1.42×10^{-5}	1.42×10^{-5}	1.42×10^{-5}

Lateral Motion

Stability derivative	*Flight condition* 1	2	3	4
Y_v	-0.078	-0.11	-0.15	-0.07
$Y^*_{\delta_A}$	-0.0001	-0.29×10^{-4}	-0.38×10^{-4}	-0.18×10^{-4}
$Y^*_{\delta_R}$	0.0065	0.0055	0.006	0.002
L'_β	-0.635	-1.33	-2.38	0.333
L'_p	-1.09	-1.0	-1.42	-0.63
L'_r	0.613	0.28	0.30	0.26
L'_{δ_A}	0.46	0.43	0.37	0.36
L'_{δ_R}	0.1	0.187	0.29	0.107
N'_β	0.11	0.432	0.885	0.386
N'_p	-0.16	-0.09	-0.09	-0.07
N'_r	-0.23	-0.2	-0.25	-0.009
N'_{δ_A}	0.05	0.03	0.09	0.04
N'_{δ_R}	-0.21	-0.52	-0.83	-0.34

B.2.5 ECHO – A single-engined, CCV, jet fighter aircraft

General Parameters

Wing area (m^2):	26
Aspect ratio:	3.0
Chord, $\bar{c}$ (m):	3.33
Total related thrust (kN):	11
C.g.:	$0.35\,\bar{c}$
Pilot's location (m) (relative to c.g.)	
l_{x_p}:	3.9
l_{z_p}:	-0.326
Weight (kg):	84.52
Inertias ($kg\,m^2$):	
I_{xx}:	11×10^3
I_{yy}:	6.38×10^4
I_{zz}:	7.24×10^4
I_{xz}:	4.7×10^4

Flight Conditions

Parameter	*Flight condition* 1	2	3	4
Height (m)	S.L.	4 600	9 100	15 250
Mach no.	0.6	0.8	0.95	1.7
U_0 (m s^{-1})	207	258	288	502
$\bar{q}$ (N m^{-2})	26 245	25 860	17 362	23 400
α_0 (degrees)	+ 1.92	+ 2.17	+ 4.25	+ 1.6
γ_0 (degrees)	0	0	0	0

Stability Derivatives

Longitudinal Motion only

Stability derivative	*Flight condition* 1	2	3	4
Z_α	− 0.0272	− 0.023	− 0.016	− 0.008
$Z_{\dot{\alpha}}$	− 0.484	− 0.295	− 0.288	0.19
Z_q	− 2.605	− 1.866	− 1.5	− 0.46
Z_{δ_E}	− 0.721	− 0.67	− 0.4	− 0.4
Z_{δ_F}	− 0.925	− 0.95	− 0.612	0.0
M_α	0.0055	0.0005	− 0.0002	− 0.0018
$M_{\dot{\alpha}}$	− 0.136	− 0.348	− 0.318	0.726
M_q	− 1.013	− 0.952	− 0.913	− 1.014
M_{δ_E}	− 0.364	− 0.362	− 0.251	− 0.66
M_{δ_F}	− 0.034	− 0.056	− 0.084	0.0

B.2.6 FOXTROT – A twin-engined, jet fighter/bomber aircraft

General Parameters

Wing area (m^2):	49.24
Aspect ratio:	4.0
Chord, $\bar{c}$ (m):	4.88
Total related thrust (kN):	160
C.g.:	0.29 $\bar{c}$
Pilot's location (m) (relative to c.g.)	
l_{x_p}:	5.32
l_{z_p}:	− 1.0

	Approach	*All other flight conditions*
Weight (kg):	148	173
Inertias (kg m^2):		
I_{xx}:	32 100	33 900
I_{yy}:	16 000	166 000
I_{zz}:	181 400	190 000
I_{xz}:	2 100	3 000

Flight Conditions

Parameter	*Flight condition*			
	1	*2*	*3*	*4*
Height (m)	S.L.	10 650	10 650	13 700
Mach no.	0.206	0.9	1.2	2.15
U_0 (m s^{-1})	70	265	350	650
$\bar{q}$ (N m^{-2})	2 997	13 550	24 090	48 070
α_0 (degrees)	11.7	2.6	1.6	1.4
γ_0 (degrees)	0	0	0	0

Stability Derivatives

Longitudinal Motion

Stability derivative	*Flight condition*			
	1	*2*	*3*	*4*
X_u	− 0.042	− 0.009	− 0.0135	0.016
X_w	0.14	0.016	0.006	0.004
Z_u	− 0.177	− 0.088	0.0125	− 0.001
Z_w	− 0.452	− 0.547	− 0.727	− 0.494
Z_q	− 0.76	− 0.88	− 1.25	− 0.39
M_u	0.0024	− 0.008	0.009	0.07
M_w	− 0.006	− 0.03	− 0.08	− 0.07
$M_{\dot{w}}$	− 0.002	− 0.001	− 0.001	− 0.001
M_q	− 0.317	− 0.487	− 0.745	− 0.41
$X_{\delta_{th}}$	0.00007	0.00006	0.00006	0.00006
$Z_{\delta_{th}}$	− 0.0006	− 0.00005	− 0.00005	− 0.00005
$M_{\delta_{th}}$	− 0.00005	− 0.000003	− 0.000003	− 0.000003
X_{δ_E}	1.83	0.69	0.77	0.62
Z_{δ_E}	− 2.03	− 15.12	− 27.55	− 25.45
M_{δ_E}	− 1.46	− 11.4	− 20.7	− 16.1

Lateral Motion

Stability derivative	*Flight condition* 1	2	3	4
Y_{β}	– 21.1	– 80.6	– 176.0	– 277.0
L'_{β}	– 10.4	– 18.3	– 14.1	– 8.67
L'_p	– 1.43	– 1.24	– 1.38	– 1.08
L'_r	0.929	0.395	0.318	0.22
N'_{β}	1.44	4.97	12.3	8.37
N'_p	– 0.026	– 0.0504	– 0.038	0.015
N'_r	– 0.215	– 0.238	– 0.4	– 0.275
$Y^*_{\delta_A}$	– 0.004	– 0.0007	– 0.0009	– 0.0005
$Y^*_{\delta_R}$	0.0053	0.0043	0.004	0.0026
L'_{δ_A}	2.74	9.0	10.9	5.35
L'_{δ_R}	0.7	1.95	3.0	2.6
N'_{δ_A}	0.42	0.2	0.67	0.36
N'_{δ_R}	– 0.67	– 2.6	– 3.2	– 1.86

B.2.7 GOLF – A twin-piston engined, general aviation aircraft

General Parameters

Wing area (m^2)	21.0	
Aspect ratio:	8.2	
Chord, $\bar{c}$ (m):	1.77	
Total related thrust (kN):	48.5	
C.g.:	$0.25\bar{c}$	
Pilot's location (m) (relative to c.g.)		
l_{x_p}:	1.0	
l_{z_p}:	– 0.3	
Weight (kg):	*Approach* 20	*All other flight conditions* 27.75
Inertias ($kg\,m^2$)		
I_{xx}:	13 470	20 420
I_{yy}:	20 450	27 560
I_{zz}:	27 200	46 000
I_{xz}:	2 150	5 870

Flight Conditions

Parameter	*Flight condition* 1	2	3	4
Height (m)	S.L.	S.L.	1 600	6 500
Mach no.	0.143	0.19	0.207	0.345
U_0 (m s^{-1})	50.0	65	70	105
$\bar{q}$ (N m^2)	1 530	2 590	1 960	3 440
α_0 (degrees)	—	—	—	—
γ_0 (degrees)	—	—	—	—

Stability Derivatives

Longitudinal Motion

Stability derivative	*Flight condition* 1	2	3	4
X_u	− 0.053	− 0.023	− 0.021	− 0.018
X_α	21.01	12.8	12.57	18.34
Z_u	− 0.002	− 0.001	− 0.001	− 0.005
Z_α	− 1.05	− 1.333	− 1.241	− 1.234
Z_q	− 0.024	− 0.025	− 0.021	− 0.012
M_u	0.016	0.0076	0.005	0.003
M_α	− 12.3	− 21.26	− 23.46	− 38.43
M_q	− 6.22	− 8.15	− 7.58	− 7.2
X_{δ_E}	− 0.046	− 0.061	− 0.055	− 0.052
X_{δ_F}	− 0.017	− 0.08	− 0.074	− 0.074
Z_{δ_F}	− 0.96	− 1.811	− 1.811	− 2.83
Z_{δ_E}	− 1.04	− 2.24	− 2.2	− 3.1
M_{δ_E}	− 13.55	− 23.4	− 23.5	− 34.85
M_{δ_F}	1.0	1.414	1.29	1.55

Lateral Motion

Stability derivative	Flight condition 1	2	3	4
Y_v	− 0.145	− 0.188	− 0.174	− 0.184
Y_p	0.087	0.087	0.09	0.05
L'_β	− 2.18	− 3.71	− 3.71	− 5.33
L'_p	− 2.01	− 2.63	− 2.43	− 2.33
L'_r	0.303	0.39	0.36	0.31
N'_β	2.182	3.71	3.71	6.33
N'_p	− 0.222	− 0.29	− 0.27	− 0.17
N'_r	− 0.27	− 0.35	− 0.325	− 0.314
$Y^*_{\delta_R}$	0.038	0.049	0.049	0.045
L'_{δ_A}	1.541	2.63	2.62	4.16
L'_{δ_R}	0.6	1.02	1.02	1.6
N'_{δ_A}	− 0.036	− 0.036	− 0.061	− 0.044
N'_{δ_R}	− 1.25	− 1.25	− 2.1	− 3.33

Appendix C

Mathematical Models of Human Pilots

C.1 INTRODUCTION

Notwithstanding the extent to which flight control is being made automatic, it remains essential for the designers of flight control systems to remember that a human pilot acts as the 'outer loop' of a complete flight control system. As AFCSs have been improved and developed, the need to represent human pilots by appropriate mathematical models has become more pressing, although the need for such representation has been recognized for a considerable time. It has been the cause of a great amount of research which is recorded in a most extensive literature. Chief among the workers researching in this field have been McRuer, Krendel and Graham, and it is their work (see the various references at the end of this appendix) which provides the basis for those models dealt with briefly below. More extensive models exist, such as Paper Pilot (Dillow, 1971), but they are beyond the scope of an introductory textbook such as this.

There are several reasons for using a mathematical model in studies relating to the performance of closed loop flight control systems being operated by a human pilot; the include the following:

1. The prediction of what may be possible from some given arrangement.
2. The evolution and, perhaps, development of critical flight or simulator experiments.
3. The interpretation of flight tests or simulator results.
4. The determination of the limitations of validity of any experimental results.

From examining the nature of a pilot's behaviour when flying it becomes clear that he normally demonstrates those characteristics commonly described as adaptive and multimodal. Even when carrying out familiar tasks, the pilot is also capable of learning. This knowledge suggests that the construction of any appropriate mathematical model may incorporate some of the following features:

1. The differential equations involved should be invariant , or time-varying.
2. The model may be multi- or single-variable.
3. The equations may be linear or non-linear.
4. The data may be continuous or sampled.

The model should represent adequately the pilot's actions when carrying out a pursuit task or controlling the aircraft using a compensatory display. From extensive experiments on human operators it has been learned that one appropriate form of model was a describing function which represents the linear response of the operator whose actual response can only be accurately described by non-linear equations. But these describing functions represent very good approximations for most pilot actions. The validity of the describing function model does depend upon the addition of a remnant term, but, for simplicity, only the linear models represented by describing functions are used here. A remnant term can be considered to be a bias term to ensure that the describing function corresponds to the appropriate operating point. One example of how such a term can be included in the model is given in paragraph 4 below.

C.2 CLASSICAL MODELS

1. The pilot's response is denoted by v_p; his command is taken as p_{comm}. Basically, the model assumes that the response is linear and proportional to the command, with some prediction, but with a pure time delay caused by the finite reaction time of the pilot. The model is represented in Figure C.1 from which it can be deduced that

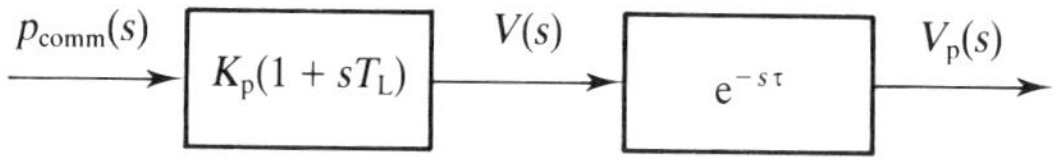

Figure C.1 Block diagram of pilot model – lead term and pure time delay.

$$\frac{V_p(s)}{p_{comm}(s)} = K_p(1 + sT_L)e^{-s\tau} \quad \text{(C.1)}$$

The transfer function representing the pure time delay, namely:

$$V_p(s)/V(s) = e^{-s\tau} \quad \text{(C.2)}$$

is a transcendental function and can only be completely represented by an infinite series. Consequently, a suitable approximation is needed. One of the most accepted is the first order Padé approximation:

$$V_p(s)/V(s) = -(s - 2/\tau)/(s + 2/\tau) \quad \text{(C.3)}$$

i.e.:

$$\dot{v}_p + \frac{2}{\tau} v_p = -\dot{v} + \frac{2}{\tau} v \quad \text{(C.4)}$$

Let:

$$\dot{x}_1 = \dot{v}_p + \dot{v} \quad \text{(C.5)}$$

then:

$$\dot{x}_1 = \dot{v}_p + \dot{v} = \frac{2}{\tau} v - \frac{2}{\tau} v_p$$
$$= \frac{4}{\tau} v - \frac{2}{\tau} x_1 \qquad \text{(C.6)}$$

However,

$$v = K_p T_L \dot{p}_{comm} + K_p p_{comm} \qquad \text{(C.7)}$$

$$\therefore \quad \dot{x}_1 = \frac{4K_p T_L}{\tau} p_{comm} + \frac{4K_p}{\tau} p_{comm} - \frac{2}{\tau} x_1 \qquad \text{(C.8)}$$

$$v_p = x_1 - K_p p_{comm} - K_p T_L \dot{p}_{comm} \qquad \text{(C.9)}$$

2. Refer to Figure C.2.

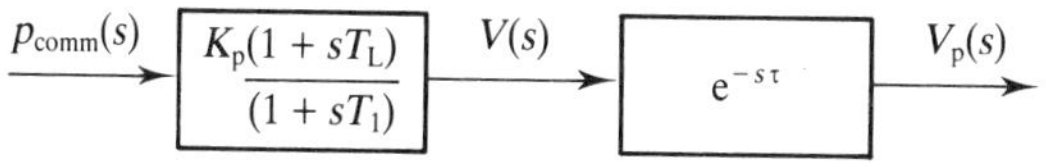

Figure C.2 Block diagram of pilot model – phase advance and pure time delay.

$$\frac{V_p(s)}{p_{comm}(s)} = K_p \frac{(1 + sT_L)}{(1 + sT_1)} e^{-s\tau} = \frac{V(s)}{p_{comm}(s)} \cdot \frac{V_p(s)}{V(s)} \qquad \text{(C.10)}$$

$$\therefore \quad \dot{v} = -\frac{1}{T_1} v + \frac{K_p}{T_1} p_{comm} + \frac{K_p T_L}{T_1} \dot{p}_{comm} \qquad \text{(C.11)}$$

Using the first order Padé approximation of eq. (C.3) and choosing the state variables for this model to be:

$$x_1 = v_p + v \qquad \text{(C.12)}$$

$$x_2 = v \qquad \text{(C.13)}$$

the following equations are obtained:

$$\begin{bmatrix} \dot{x}_1 \\ \dot{x}_2 \end{bmatrix} + \begin{bmatrix} 0 \\ -\frac{K_p T_L}{T_1} \end{bmatrix} \dot{p}_{comm} = \begin{bmatrix} -\frac{2}{\tau} & \frac{4}{\tau} \\ 0 & -\frac{1}{T_1} \end{bmatrix} \begin{bmatrix} x_1 \\ x_2 \end{bmatrix} + \begin{bmatrix} 0 \\ \frac{K_p}{T_1} \end{bmatrix} p_{comm} \qquad \text{(C.14)}$$

$$v_p = [1 \quad -1] \begin{bmatrix} x_1 \\ x_2 \end{bmatrix} \qquad \text{(C.15)}$$

3. Refer to Figure C.3.

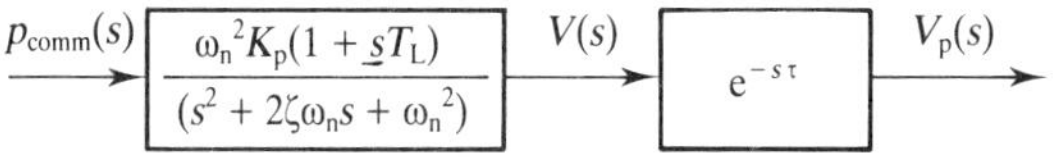

Figure C.3 Block diagram of pilot model – lead term, pure time delay and neuromuscular lag.

$$\frac{V_p(s)}{p_{comm}(s)} = \frac{\omega_n^2 K_p(1 + sT_L)e^{-s\tau}}{(s^2 + 2\zeta s\omega_n + \omega_n^2)} = \frac{V_p(s)}{V(s)}\frac{V(s)}{p_{comm}(s)} \tag{C.16}$$

The term:

$$\omega_n^2/(s^2 + 2\zeta\omega_n s + \omega_n^2)$$

represents the addition of a neuromuscular lag to the model. The transfer function $V(s)/p_{comm}(s)$ can easily be represented by the following state equation:

$$\begin{bmatrix} \dot{x}_1 \\ \dot{x}_2 \end{bmatrix} = \begin{bmatrix} 0 & 1 \\ -\omega_n^2 & -2\zeta\omega_n \end{bmatrix} \begin{bmatrix} x_1 \\ x_2 \end{bmatrix} + \begin{bmatrix} 0 \\ 1 \end{bmatrix} p_{comm} \tag{C.17}$$

$$v = \omega_n^2 K_p[1 \quad T_L] \begin{bmatrix} x_1 \\ x_2 \end{bmatrix} \tag{C.18}$$

Finally, if we define x_3 as $v + v_p$, and use the Padé approximation of (C.3) then:

$$\begin{bmatrix} \dot{x}_1 \\ \dot{x}_2 \\ \dot{x}_3 \end{bmatrix} = \begin{bmatrix} 0 & 1 & 0 \\ -\omega_n^2 & -2\zeta\omega_n & 0 \\ \left(\frac{4}{\tau} K_p\omega_n^2\right) & \left(\frac{4}{\tau} K_p T_L \omega_n^2\right) & \left(\frac{-2}{\tau}\right) \end{bmatrix} \begin{bmatrix} x_1 \\ x_2 \\ x_3 \end{bmatrix} + \begin{bmatrix} 0 \\ 1 \\ 0 \end{bmatrix} p_{comm} \tag{C.19}$$

$$v_p = [-K_p\omega_n^2 \quad -K_p T_L \omega_n^2 \quad 1]\mathbf{x} \tag{C.20}$$

4. Refer to Figure C.4. Using a more comprehensive model relating to hovering motion in which a remnant term and phase advance compensation are added, the following equations are obtained:

$$e_1 = -\frac{1}{T_1} e_1 - \frac{K_{p_1}}{T_1} p_{comm} - \frac{K_p T_{L_1}}{T_1} p_{comm} \tag{C.21}$$

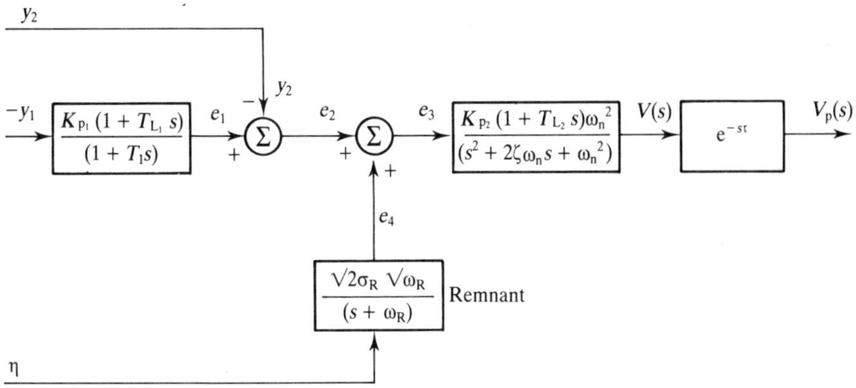

Figure C.4 Block diagram of pilot model – phase advance, pure time delay, lead term neuromuscular lag and remnant term.

$$e_2 = e_1 - y \tag{C.22}$$

$$e_3 = e_2 + e_4 \tag{C.23}$$

$$\dot{e}_4 = -\omega_R e_4 + \sigma_R \sqrt{(2\omega_R)} n \tag{C.24}$$

Also:

$$\begin{bmatrix} \dot{x}_3 \\ \dot{x}_4 \end{bmatrix} = \begin{bmatrix} 0 & 1 \\ -\omega_n^2 & -2\zeta\omega_n \end{bmatrix} \begin{bmatrix} x_3 \\ x_4 \end{bmatrix} + \begin{bmatrix} 0 \\ 1 \end{bmatrix} e_3 \tag{C.25}$$

$$V = [\omega_n^2 K_{p_2} \quad \omega_2^2 K_{p_2} T_{L_2}] \begin{bmatrix} x_3 \\ x_4 \end{bmatrix} \tag{C.26}$$

Now let:

$$x_1 = e_1 \qquad x_2 = e_4 \qquad x_5 = v + v_p \tag{C.27}$$

then the following state equation can be obtained:

$$\dot{\mathbf{x}} + E\dot{\mathbf{z}} = A\mathbf{x} + Bz + Mn \tag{C.28}$$

$$v_p = C\mathbf{x} \tag{C.29}$$

where:

$$\mathbf{x}' = [x_1 \; x_2 \; x_3 \; x_4 \; x_5] \tag{C.30}$$

$$\mathbf{z}' = [p_{\text{comm}} \; y] \tag{C.31}$$

$$E = \begin{bmatrix} \frac{K_{p_1} T_{L_1}}{T_1} & 0 \\ 0 & 0 \\ 0 & 0 \\ 0 & 0 \\ 0 & 0 \end{bmatrix} \tag{C.32}$$

$$A = \begin{bmatrix} \frac{-1}{T_1} & 0 & -\omega_R\ 0 & 0 & 0 & 00 \\ 0 & -\omega_R & 0 & 0 & 0 \\ 0 & 0 & 0 & 1 & 0 \\ 1 & 1 & -\omega_n^2 & -2\zeta\omega_n & 0 \\ 0 & 0 & \left(\frac{4}{\tau} K_{p_2}\omega_n^2\right) & \left(\frac{4}{\tau} K_{p_2} T_{L_2}\omega_n^2\right) & \frac{-2}{\tau} \end{bmatrix} \tag{C.33}$$

$$B = \begin{bmatrix} \frac{-K_{p_1}}{T_1} & 0 \\ 0 & 0 \\ 0 & 0 \\ 0 & -1 \\ 0 & 0 \end{bmatrix} \tag{C.34}$$

$$M = \begin{bmatrix} 0 \\ \sigma_R \sqrt{(2\omega_R)} \\ 0 \\ 0 \\ 0 \end{bmatrix} \tag{C.35}$$

$$C = [0 \quad 0 \quad -K_{p_2} \quad \omega_n^2 \quad -K_{p_2} T_{L_2} \omega_n^2 \quad 1] \tag{C.36}$$

C.3 REFERENCES

DILLOW, J.D. 1971. 'Super Pilot' – a revised version of Paper Pilot. AFFDL/FGC-TM-71-9, WPAFB, Dayton, Ohio.

KRENDEL, E.S. and D.T. McRUER. 1960. A servomechanisms approach to skills development. *J. Frank. Inst.* 269 (1): 24–42.

McRUER, D.T. and D. GRAHAM. 1964. Pilot vehicle control system analysis. *Progress in Astronautics and Aeronautics,* Vol. 13, Guidance and Control II. New York: Academic Press, pp. 603–21.

McRUER, D.T., D. GRAHAM and E.S. KRENDEL. 1967. Manual control of single loop systems. *J. Frank. Inst.* 283 (182): 1–29, 145–68.

McRUER, D.T. and E.S. KRENDEL. 1974. Mathematical models of human pilot behaviour. *Agardograph* no. 188.

McRUER, D.T., R.E. MAGDALENO and G.P. MOORE. 1968. A neuro-muscular actuation system model. *Trans IEEE.* MMS-9(3): 61–71.

Index